B.
an
R
54

DUE F

27

Habituation, Sensitization, and Behavior

BEHAVIORAL BIOLOGY

AN INTERNATIONAL SERIES

Series editors

James L. McGaugh

Department of Psychobiology
University of California
Irvine, California

John C. Fentress

Department of Psychology
Dalhousie University
Halifax, Canada

Joseph P. Hegmann

Department of Zoology
The University of Iowa
Iowa City, Iowa

Habituation, Sensitization, and Behavior

Edited by

HARMAN V. S. PEEKE

Department of Psychiatry
University of California
San Francisco, California

LEWIS PETRINOVICH

Department of Psychology
University of California
Riverside, California

1984

ACADEMIC PRESS, INC.

(Harcourt Brace Jovanovich, Publishers)

Orlando   San Diego   San Francisco   New York   London
Toronto   Montreal   Sydney   Tokyo   São Paulo

ACADEMIC PRESS, INC.
Orlando, Florida 32887

United Kingdom Edition published by
ACADEMIC PRESS, INC. (LONDON) LTD.
24/28 Oval Road, London NW1 7DX

Library of Congress Cataloging in Publication Data

Main entry under title:

Habituation, sensitization, and behavior.

  (Behavioral biology)
  Includes bibliographies and index.
    1. Habituation (Neuropsychology)--Addresses, essays,
lectures. I. Peeke, Harman V. S. (Harman Van Slyke),
Date   . II. Petrinovich, Lewis F. III. Series:
Behavioral biology (New York, N.Y. : 1978)
QP374.H325 1983   599'.051   83-7161
ISBN 0-12-549860-8

PRINTED IN THE UNITED STATES OF AMERICA

84 85 86 87   9 8 7 6 5 4 3 2 1

Contents

PART I
Theory and Methods

3. A Theory of the Mechanism of Habituation: The Assignment of Responses to Stimuli
Michel Treisman

4. Memory and Habituation
Jesse W. Whitlow, Jr. and Allan R. Wagner

5. An Evaluation of Statistical Strategies to Analyze Repeated-Measures Data
Lewis Petrinovich and Keith F. Widaman

PART II
Basic Processes

6. An Introduction to Cellular Approaches Used in the Analysis of Habituation and Sensitization in *Aplysia*

   Thomas J. Carew

7. Habituation of Central Nervous System Evoked Potentials: Intrinsic Habituation Examined in Neocortex, Allocortex, and Mesencephalon

   T. J. Teyler, N. Chiaia, P. DiScenna, and R. A. Roemer

8. Intrinsic and Extrinsic Mechanisms of Habituation and Sensitization: Implications for the Design and Analysis of Experiments

   Michael Davis and Sandra E. File

12. Evolutionary Determination of Response Likelihood and Habituation

Michel Treisman

Contributors

Numbers in parentheses indicate the pages on which the authors' contributions begin.

Thomas J. Carew (205), *Department of Psychology, Yale University, New Haven, Connecticut 06520*

N. Chiaia (251), *Neurobiology Program, Northeastern Ohio Universities College of Medicine, Rootstown, Ohio 44272*

Michael Davis (287), *Department of Psychiatry, Yale University, New Haven, Connecticut 06508*

P. DiScenna (251), *Neurobiology Program, Northeastern Ohio Universities College of Medicine, Rootstown, Ohio 44272*

Sandra E. File (287), *Department of Pharmacology, School of Pharmacy, University of London, London, England*

Harman V. S. Peeke (1, 393), *Department of Psychiatry, University of California, San Francisco, California 94143*

Lewis Petrinovich (1, 17, 155), *Department of Psychology, University of California, Riverside, California 92521*

Richard A. Roemer* (251, 325), *Health Sciences Center, Temple University Medical School, Philadelphia, Pennsylvania 19129*

Charles Shagass (325), *Health Sciences Center, Temple University, Philadelphia, Pennsylvania 19129*

Michael D. Shalter (349), *Clinical Research and Development, Wyeth Laboratories, Philadelphia, Pennsylvania 19101*

Timothy J. Teyler (251, 325), *Neurobiology Program, Northeastern Ohio Universities College of Medicine, Rootstown, Ohio 44272*

Michel Treisman (57, 423), *Department of Experimental Psychology, University of Oxford, Oxford OX1 3UD, England*

*Present address: Philadelphia Psychiatric Center, Philadelphia, Pennsylvania 19131.

Allan R. Wagner (103), *Department of Psychology, Yale University, New Haven, Connecticut 06520*

Jesse W. Whitlow, Jr. (103), *Psychology Department, Rutgers University, Camden, New Jersey 08102*

Keith F. Widaman (155), *Department of Psychology, University of California, Riverside, California 92521*

Preface

In 1973 two edited volumes* surveyed the research and theory pertaining to habituation. Now, more than 10 years later, we have brought together another volume once again surveying the current status of research on habituation. Whereas the earlier volumes had a descriptive and taxonomic organization, the present one is more conceptual in focus. Important advances have been made toward understanding the mechanisms underlying, and the significance of, the phenomena traditionally associated with habituation processes; the current volume attempts to represent some of these. One important change that has come about is the realization that the term *habituation* is not appropriate to describe behavior, but should be reserved to refer to an underlying theoretical process. This realization was brought about by an awareness of the powerful role of *sensitization* processes required to understand changes in response levels as a function of repeated stimulation. The chapters in this volume reflect this change in terminological focus: habituation and sensitization are used to refer to underlying theoretical processes, and behavior changes are described at the response level. The chapters in this volume were chosen to represent perspectives ranging from those of the basic neurosciences, to behavioral analyses, to evolutionary considerations. The emphasis has been to understand the phenomena of habituation and sensitization at a level that contributes to understanding molar behavior in intact organisms. This broad perspective was taken in the hope that consideration of the different chapters will lead to the development of some integrative theoretical principles regarding the nature and integration of habituation and sensitization.

The contributors were chosen to represent active research programs seeking to develop new theoretical viewpoints. Each contributor was given a relatively free hand in selecting the specific material to be included. The editors suggested the

*Peeke, H. V. S., and Herz, M. J. (Eds.), *Habituation: Behavioral Studies* (2 vols.). New York: Academic Press, 1973.

approach they thought appropriate at the outset, and the authors improved on these suggestions considerably in the realization of the chapters. In most instances there was opportunity for some interchange between authors and editors that we believe improved the final product. We enjoyed interacting with the authors and hope that they, too, found the interactions pleasant and useful.

CHAPTER 1

Approaches, Constructs, and Terminology for the Study of Response Change in the Intact Organism

Harman V. S. Peeke

Department of Psychiatry
University of California
San Francisco, California

Lewis Petrinovich

Department of Psychology
University of California
Riverside, California

I. Introduction

We intend the chapters in this volume to further the understanding of behavior in intact organisms. Even though some of the preparations discussed are at the level of model systems, the general intent is to consider these molecular models within a general explanatory structure suitable to increase understanding at the molar level.

Many of the important theoretical advances in habituation have been made by investigators whose primary research was molecular. Thompson and his associates advanced one of the major theories of habituation, primarily based on research with spinal cats. Although the research was molecular, the theoretical concerns were not. Thompson, Groves, Teyler, and Roemer (1973) made it clear that "hypothetical processes can be

1

characterized and differentiated, which makes feasible identification and analysis of the neuronal mechanisms underlying habituation and sensitization in the intact, behaving central nervous system [p. 269]." Their intent was to provide strong evidence to validate the use of the spinal flexion reflex as a model system for the study of habituation.

Another research program centered on a molecular level of analysis has been that of Kandel and associates. Kandel (1976) insisted that his interest was not to understand invertebrate neural systems per se, but to develop a comparative understanding of behavior modification. For example, Kandel (1976) wrote, "Since in the end we are concerned with identifying biological principles applicable to human behavior, the invertebrate is simply a convenient, but necessary, substitute for people [p. 29]."

The chapters in this volume share the interest expressed by Thompson *et al.* and Kandel that theory and research on habituation and sensitization should occur at the molar, functional level. Although molecular preparations—or, as with Treisman (Chapter 3), formal game theoretic analyses—are sometimes employed, the aim is to understand the functioning of intact organisms adapting to the demands of the environment.

II. Level of Constructs

Problems and controversies have arisen in the literature concerned with habituation and sensitization because of a confusion regarding the level of constructs under discussion. The same words have been used to refer to quite different constructs, and the shifting of construct levels has resulted in fruitless debates.

A. Proximate and Ultimate Explanations

The difference between proximate and ultimate factors in the causation of behavior has bedeviled those who seek to understand and explain behavior. Considerable confusion has occurred in scientific discussions about the causation of behavior, especially in discussions between psychologists (and other social scientists) and biologists—a result of a blurring of the proximate and ultimate distinction. Biological explanations can be made in terms of proximate causes—internal motivational and physiological states elicited by external or internal stimuli, ecological events, or social factors. At this level, behavior is explained in terms of mediating mechanisms—processes that immediately influence an organism's activities.

Ultimate explanations of behavior are at the evolutionary level and refer to the genotype acquired through natural selection over evolutionary time. At this level, adaptive value is of primary importance, and the currency is fitness as indexed by reproductive success.

For example, we might ask why birds of a given species migrate southward in the late summer. An explanation could be offered at the proximate level: they migrate because the days become shorter. This results in an alteration of hormonal activity, which induces a restlessness that finally results in migration. We might even go further and analyze the endocrine events and the nature of the neurosecretory systems involved. If these events are tied together many would consider migration to be explained; and it would be explained at the proximate level.

But the ultimate level has not been considered. An explanation at this level would take the following form: with shortening of days, those birds survive who become restless with the shortening of days and then migrate southward; those who did not would starve or die during the winter. Those who do migrate south are able to locate feeding grounds and remain there until the days begin to lengthen in the spring. Those who return occupy an ecological niche to which they are competitively adapted. This niche is sufficient to support courtship and mating and to allow them to reproduce and successfully rear young who continue the genetic tradition.

Further study would consider the preadaptations that made this migratory behavior possible; the selection pressures that drive the system would also be examined. The explanations' adequacy could be evaluated by comparing the ecological system of sedentary and migratory species to establish the generality of the explanatory mechanisms. If a relationship could be established between such things as weather, food supply, migration, and reproductive success, then the causes of migration would be considered to be explained at the ultimate level. It should be emphasized that a complete explanation of migration (or any other phenomenon) requires the understanding of causation at both levels. Understanding the processes at one level might well provide insights regarding the probable processes operating at the other.

Proximate causes, then, relate to the functions and parts of an organism considered from the level of functional morphology down to that of biochemistry. Ultimate causes involve questions of why an organism is the way it is. Proximate causes are concerned with decoding the genetic program of a given individual. Ultimate causes are concerned with the changes of the genetic programs through time and with the reasons for these changes. The two levels of explanation demand different methods of approach: to obtain an understanding of proximate factors, the experiment is the ideal—as it is for the physicist and chemist. The aim is to isolate the phenomenon from the complexities of the organism—to develop a simplified version of the phenomenon, one amenable to systematic manipulation. To understand ultimate factors, the comparative method is the method of choice. This involves careful and detailed descriptive studies at a qualitative level, and the examination of patterns of similarities and differences with other studies of the same or different species in similar or different habitats. The questions often involved are such as: Why are some avian species sedentary and some migratory? Why do two sexes occur in most species of organisms? Why are some fauna of some areas rich in species and those of others poor? Why do some members of a species nest colonially in some areas and nest as dispersed pairs in others? No biological problem is solved satisfactorally until proximate *and* ultimate causation have been dealt with. Studying the origin of genetic programs and their change through evolutionary time is as important as the biology of the proximate translation of the genetic causes.

Confusion has arisen in discussing habituation, because some investigators focus on habituation at the level of proximate mechanisms and seek to explain events at the level of mediating processes. Others are concerned with changes in responsiveness to environmental events and how these events contribute to adaptations and survival. The focus of these inquiries occurs at the ultimate level. But we have seen that neither level is *the* level, and the results obtained at each should be used to develop a complete causal picture of the nature and function of changes in responsiveness.

B. Inferential and Behavioral Constructs

The terms *habituation* and *sensitization* have been used in two senses for many years. In one sense they refer to inferential, hypothetical processes invoked to explain behavioral changes. Used in this sense, the terms are not capable of being directly measured; they must be translated operationally in terms of stimulus and response. This in itself causes no difficulty, because all theoretical constructs in science must be used in this way.

A problem arises, however, when the two terms describe behavioral outcomes. Thus, we find discussions of the habituation of a response, for example, followed by speculations regarding the underlying theoretical processes. Labeling the behavioral description and the explanatory mechanism with the same term causes a great deal of confusion.

One way to avoid the problem would be to use habituation to refer to the observed change in behavior and to develop a new term when discussing theoretical issues. The difficulty with this solution is that habituation has been used, historically, to designate inquiry into a process and to a body of theory. Restricting the use of the term at this time would probably confuse rather than clarify attempts to describe and explain the phenomena.

Thompson *et al.* (1973) expressed concern with this issue and suggested the use of the term *response habituation* for the operational specification and *habituation* for the theoretical construct. The problem involved in adopting this suggestion is that both terms use the word *habituation,* and this leaves the door open for confusion to anyone not explicitly attuned to the terminological issues.

A preferable solution would restrict the use of the term *habituation* to refer to theoretical processes and never use it as a behavioral description. Behavioral descriptions should be made in terms of observables such as response decrement, increase in latency, or reorganization of the pattern of behavior. Strict adherence should help to avoid the many ambiguities that have characterized discussions of habituation. All of the points made above also apply to the concept of *sensitization.*

III. Operations and Terminology: Sources of Confusion

Numerous examples of confusing the terms *stimulus specificity, stimulus generalization,* and *dishabituation* occur in the literature. It is important to clarify the meaning of each of these terms, for no other reason than to allow reasonable communication between investigators. Precision in terminology can also sharpen the contrast among theories that predict different dishabituation functions, but that predict similar degrees of stimulus specificity (see Graham, 1973).

Stimulus specificity and stimulus generalization can be viewed as two sides of a single coin. After a series of identical stimuli are presented and response levels are recorded, a new stimulus—differing on some stimulus dimension—is presented. The change in the level of response would indicate the similarity of the new stimulus to the previous stimulus. A very different new stimulus should elicit a large response; a response similar to the original should elicit a response similar to that occurring at the previous level. It is precisely the stimulus-specific nature of the waning of response that rules out sensory adaptation and fatigue as explanations of response decrement to an iterative stimulus and provides one operational specification for habituation.

Another way of viewing stimulus specificity and stimulus generalization was suggested by Wyers, Peeke, and Herz (1973). They point out that stimulus generalization of habituation can be determined only when a second habituation series is done using a new stimulus. Comparing the rates of habituation between the original and the new stimulus will demonstrate the amount of generalization, with faster habituation in the second series indicating generalization and similar rates between the two series indicating lack of generalization. From the point of view offered by Wyers *et al.*, stimulus specificity can be demonstrated by the response to a single novel stimulus; but generalization requires comparing the habituation rates of the original stimulus and the new one.

Unfortunately, all too often the response to the novel stimulus itself is referred to as *dishabituation*. This is incorrect. Dishabituation refers to the response to the next iterative stimulus in the series after a novel stimulus. Dishabituation is the effect on the repetitive stimulus caused by some extraneous stimulus. For example, if a series of ten 500-Hz tones is presented in a sequence, followed by a single 1000-Hz tone and then another 500-Hz tone, we can judge stimulus specificity by the response to the 1000-Hz tone. But, dishabituation caused by the 1000-Hz tone would be detected in response to the final 500-Hz tone. The distinction between stimulus specificity and dishabituation is particularly important in light of the theoretical interpretation of dishabituation in the model presented by Thompson and colleagues (e.g., Groves & Thompson, 1973).

The distinction between recovery and retention is as confused as the distinction between stimulus specificity and dishabituation. Wyers *et al.* (1973) clearly specify the difference. After an iterative series, a rest period can be interpolated before a second series of the same stimuli. This interpolated rest period may vary from minutes to weeks. The response to the first stimulus of the second series, when compared to the initial response of the first series, is the measure of recovery during the rest interval. The amount of retention can best be assessed by comparing the rate of waning of the response between the first and second series. Complete recovery may well occur, but significant retention may also result when the curves for the first and second series are compared. In statistical terms, the intercepts for the two series might be identical, but the slopes may differ.

IV. Associative and Nonassociative Learning: Short- and Long-Term Effects of Experience

Habituation has usually been thought of as a short-term change in response. Indeed, an early review of habituation research appeared in a volume titled *Short-Term Changes in Neural Activity and Behavior* (Hinde, 1970). The title is unfortunate because the distinction between short- and long-term effects has been used, at least implicitly, to distinguish habituation (short term) from other forms of learning (long term). Long-term effects of habituation (lasting days or weeks) have been demonstrated in several studies (see Peeke, Chapter 11, this volume). Real underlying differences (see Kling & Stevenson, 1970) might occur, but the differences might well be apparent, resulting from different preparations.

Most of the support for the view that habituation and extinction reflect two processes rather than variations on one process has been based on studies of long-term effects of extinction, on the one hand, and short-term decrements in habituation on the other. We believe that, other than the operational specifications of the paradigms, little difference occurs between habituation and extinction and, thus, between associative and nonassociative learning. Both associative and nonassociative learning are the products of experience; both can be permanent, or at least of long duration; and both can be context specific: change produced by experience in one environment does not transfer well to another, particularly when highly prepared behaviors with functional significance are studied. Viewing habituation as one form of learning among others [as Fantino and Logan (1979) do] and concentrating on the functional significance of the phenomena in question rather than the operations used to distinguish among them may be most profitable.

V. The Field and the Laboratory

There have been several discussions of the relative merits of laboratory and naturalistic methods in the study of behavior (e.g., Miller, 1977; Petrinovich, 1979). Each method has inherent advantages and disadvantages, and each is ill and well suited for certain purposes. We hope that discussing these methods will make it easier to direct the choice of method suitable to the type of question being asked.

A. Naturalistic Methods

Field observation has always occupied a prominent position in biology: the major concepts of evolutionary and population biology, for example, were developed by naturalists who followed in the Darwinian tradition. The initial focus is usually on the construction of a life history of the species under consideration. The essential questions concern reproductive behavior, ecological factors supporting and influencing behavior, intra- and interspecific social interactions, and the like.

These initial descriptions concern the location of activities important to the life cycle: for example, what aspects of the ecology seem to influence behavior, and what aspects of the ecology are available to support different behavioral patterns? Such descriptions lead to the consideration of ecological resources and their fluctuations. In addition, life-history descriptions are influenced strongly by a consideration of other organisms that influence response patterns, both inter- and intraspecific. It is important to know the prevalence and the types of interspecific predators the species must deal with, the prevalence and the types of animals the species preys upon, those the species must compete with for resources, and the nature of symbiotic relationships, such as the use of common alarm signals, with other species. At the intraspecific level such phenomena as the nature of social groupings, spacing mechanisms, feeding strategies, and population dispersal should be described in careful detail.

Field study is primarily inductive at the outset, and many of the rules good field workers set for themselves are safeguards against a deductive bias that might distort basic observations. For example, records are taken immediately upon the occurrence of a behavior and not at a later time when selective distortions could influence the memory for the events.

Advantages

One paramount advantage of field observation is that behavior occurs naturally in its typical context with a minimal intrusion on the part of the observer. The behavioral sequences noted in the field are not influenced by the fact that the animals were reared or are being kept in artificial circumstances of captivity. The effect of ecological variables can be observed because the behavior is recorded in their presence. Those variables that influence behavior do so in natural combinations and exert their influences at naturally occurring levels; the correlational texture of the environment is preserved. Clearly, such observations, if done adequately, provide an ideal base for framing hypotheses. The heuristic value of careful and intensive naturalistic observation can scarcely be overestimated.

Most behavioral scientists now realize that ethology has contributed rich and valuable insights to our understanding of behavior because ethograms were carefully constructed before formal theoretical phases of behavioral analysis were begun.

Disadvantages

Many observational studies have been flawed by the tendency to rely on what is little more than a series of anecdotes representing a biased selection of behavior. The sampling procedures often used do not produce a representative sampling of behavior, but rather concentrate on occurrences of a given type. Conclusions drawn on the basis of field data must be carefully examined to ensure that a subjective bias has not been allowed to influence the observations.

After reliable field data have been collected, it often is quite voluminous, and we must face the problems of reducing it to a manageable form for description and interpretation. The risk is great at this point that the richness and complexity of the behavioral systems and the subtle patterns of interaction of the factors that influence them will be lost in the act of summarization.

B. Laboratory Methods

The laboratory permits the experimenter to control variables systematically. If the experimenter suspects that a set of variables $(A, B, C, \ldots, N)$ bear a functional relationship to some other variable of interest (Y), then the laboratory is ideal if we wish to manipulate each in turn while holding all others constant. Thus, the proposition $Y = f(A)$ can be evaluated with $B, C, \ldots, N$ held constant, either through randomization of subjects or by experimentally controlling them at some constant value. In this way a set of equations $Y = f(A); Y = f(B); Y = f(C); \ldots ; Y = f(N)$ can be developed for each variable in turn with the others held constant.

When studying animals, living conditions, diet (or deprivation of nutrients), stimuli, or physiological systems can be standardized. We can work with strains of animals with known genetic backgrounds, breed animals in standard conditions and with the mating under control of the experimenter, and rear the young in controlled environments. Such subjects can then be tested under a wide range of controlled conditions. We can systematically manipulate stimuli to be presented to the various groups and to establish comparable or systematically varying response requirements of subjects. In short, it is possible to standardize and control variables so that the research is easily replicated.

Advantages

The advantages of laboratory experimentation are inherent in the pre-ceeding characterization. Because objectivity is a major requirement for science, laboratory procedures are a major step toward that end. The application of good laboratory procedures will be reliable: the experiments can be repeated by the same investigator (to establish intraobserver reliability) and by other investigators (to establish interobserver reliability).

If we have a strong deductive theory, we can arrange stimulus combinations orthogonally and arrange combinations of particularly interesting stimuli within the theoretical framework. Response requirements can be manipulated as demanded by theory.

The ability to control subjects and variables in this manner makes the laboratory an ideal arena for investigating the *possibility* that a variable can control a behavior. If we are interested in isolating the physiological processes underlying behavior or want to understand how physical stimulation is mediated, transformed, and transmitted to result in a response, then the control afforded by the laboratory is essential.

Disadvantages

The very strength of laboratory method also constitutes its major disadvantage. Eliminating the effect of extraneous variables, so that the variable of interest can achieve its strongest expression, makes it difficult either to use the method to investigate the probability that a given variable controls behavior outside the laboratory or to establish its relative importance. Variables tend to interact in a complex manner, so it is not possible to move from single statements of the $Y = f(A)$ variety to a general statement $Y = f(A, B, C, \ldots, N)$ in which the relative weights of each variable are stated.

Establishing the relative importance of variables in the laboratory is difficult for several reasons. One difficulty is that the variables are artificially tied together by the very act of designing an experiment. This tying and untying of variables is accomplished by decisions regarding which stimuli and which responses will be studied and how and in what magnitudes the variables will be combined to form experimental groups; by decisions concerning which variables to hold at constant levels and decisions regarding the structure of the test environment.

It is difficult to know whether the stimulus values chosen are those that are biologically significant to the organism. If the values chosen are not of biological significance, then some of the independent variables may lack the strength that others have by nature of those others being within a more biologically salient range. It might also be difficult to understand the impact of independent variables on the organism's response systems if only one or two arbitrarily chosen responses are studied. These responses might not reflect net behavioral outcomes, because they could represent either more or less labile aspects of the total response systems of interest; and the outcome would be biased accordingly.

C. Field Experimentation

A hybrid method not yet extensively used is available. This method circumvents many of the disadvantages of naturalistic and laboratory methods while retaining the advantages of both. The field experimental method begins with naturalistic observation, because the intent is to perform experiments in natural settings. If this enterprise is to be successful, then we must study the life history of the organism to gain an understanding of the species and the nature of the environment. When this has been accomplished, we can obtain a representative sample of subjects and of situations in which they behave. We can then manipulate variables in an ecologically meaningful context while making as little intrusion as possible. Stimuli are introduced and environmental manipulations are done in such a manner that other background variables are not disturbed. The manipulated variable is thereby embedded in the normal context of the natural environment. A classic field experimental test of ideas derived from field observation can be found in studies done by Tinbergen (e.g., Tinbergen, Broekhuysen, Feekes, Houghton, Kruuk, & Szulc, 1963), who noted the functional significance of egg-shell removal by gulls.

In the field experiment, the subject's behavior is not constrained, and it is possible to record a large number of responses at the same time. This allows the investigator to understand a particular response of interest within the context of the entire behavioral repertoire of the organism. Using current data acquisition technology, behavior can be recorded in "real time," preserving the timing of events and permitting an analysis at any desired level of precision.

Advantages

With this method we do not suffer the problems attendant upon the artificiality of the laboratory experiment. The animals are engaged in their natural activities in natural settings. All extraneous stimuli play their usual role, and the subjects' responses are not constrained. This allows us to assess the effect of a stimulus, with extraneous variables enjoying full play. The significance of this natural covariance cannot be overemphasized. Only if ecological variables are assessed within the context of an experimental manipulation can they be included in general behavioral theory.

Disadvantages

One of the major disadvantages of field experimentation is that certain combinations of variables might not occur in nature with sufficient frequency. If these combinations of variables are critical as a test of theory, then arranging conditions for the appropriate test might not be possible. We could argue that if the frequency of the event is so low, it could not be of much importance. This argument is not convincing for two reasons. The first is that a rare event might be one of the most important in the life of an organism or in the perpetuation of a species—the response to a rare event could make the difference between survival and death or between successful and unsuccessful reproduction. The second is that the investigation might focus on testing general laws applying to all organisms rather than understanding the particular species in question. In this case separating the species-specific from the species-general might not be possible.

Experimental mortality produces problems as well. In the laboratory, subjects are housed in captivity under conditions gauged to guarantee the health of animals. In the field, animals are subject to normal pressures

TABLE 1

Summary of the Strengths and Weaknesses of the Three Methods[a]

Characteristic	Field observation	Laboratory experiment	Field experiment
Natural covariance of			
Stimuli	+	−	=
Extraneous variables	+	−	+
Responses	+	−	+
Control of			
Subjects	=	+	=
Situations	+	−	+
Extraneous variables	+	+	+
Power to test theory	−	+	=
Normal living conditions	+	−	+
Understanding mediation	−	+	−
Understanding variable interactions	=	−	+
Experimental mortality	−	+	−

[a] +, Strong; =, adequate; −, weak.

that lead to mortality; they might wander away from the study site or be replaced by another animal and be forced to leave. This could produce a strain on the experimenter's time and energy budget.

Comparison of the Three Methods

Table 1 compares the strengths and weaknesses of the three methods in terms of some of the characteristics used to describe research paradigms. The characterization is derived from the preceding discussion and is meant only as a quick and rough evaluation to highlight similarities and differences.

VI. Summary

This introductory chapter has examined several persistent problems in terminology, construct levels, and methodology. The biases of the editors are evident, but the biases stem from extensive experience in habituation research and a longer experience with psychobiological approaches to the study and behavior of intact organisms. We have emphasized these problems because they seem to have been ones that have impeded progress in the study of habituation. We hope that a clear perspective regarding these issues will enable research and theory on habituation and sensitivity to maintain a steady rate of progress.

We have grouped the chapters in this volume into three sections. The first concerns broad theoretical issues. The second concentrates on structural and physiological levels of analysis. The third section examines molar functional issues involving the adaptation of organisms to their environment. A brief introduction by the editors precedes each section.

References

Fantino, E., & Logan, C. A. *The experimental analysis of behavior.* San Francisco: Freeman, 1979.

Graham, F. K. Habituation and dishabituation of responses innervated by the autonomic nervous system. In H. V. S. Peeke & M. J. Herz (Eds.), *Habituation* (Vol. 1). *Behavioral Studies,* New York: Academic Press, 1973. Pp. 163–218.

Groves, P. M., & Thompson, R. F. Dual-process theory of habituation: Neural mechanisms. In H. V. S. Peeke & M. J. Herz (Eds.), *Habituation* (Vol. 2). *Physiological substrates,* New York: Academic Press, 1973. Pp. 175–206.

Hinde, R. A. Behavioral habituation. In G. Horn & R. A. Hinde (Eds.), *Short-term changes in neural activity and behavior.* London & New York: Cambridge University Press, 1970.

Kandel, E. R. *Cellular basis of behavior: An introduction to behavioral neurobiology.* San Francisco: Freeman, 1976.

Kling, J. W., & Stevenson, J. G. Habituation and extinction. In G. Horn & R. A. Hinde (Eds.), *Short-term changes in neural activity and behaviour.* London & New York: Cambridge University Press, 1970.

Miller, D. B. Roles of naturalistic observation in comparative psychology. *American Psychologist,* 1977, *32,* 211–219.

Petrinovich, L. Probabilistic functionalism: A conception of research method. *American Psychologist,* 1979, *34,* 373–390.

Tinbergen, N., Broekhuysen, F., Feekes, F., Houghton, C. W., Kruuk, H., & Szulc, E. Egg shell removal by the Black-headed Gull (*Larus ridibundus*): A behaviour component of camouflage. *Behaviour,* 1963, *19,* 74–117.

Thompson, R. F., Groves, P. M., Teyler, T. J., & Roemer, R. H. A dual-process theory of habituation: Theory and behavior. In H. V. S. Peeke & M. J. Herz (Eds.), *Habituation* (Vol. 1). *Behavioral studies,* New York: Academic Press, 1973. Pp. 239–272.

Wyers, E. J., Peeke, H. V. S., & Herz, M. J. Habituation and related phenomena in invertebrates. In H. V. S. Peeke & M. J. Herz (Eds.), *Habituation* (Vol. 1). *Behavioral Studies,* New York: Academic Press, 1973. Pp. 1–58.

PART I

Theory and Methods

The chapters in Part I deal with historical, theoretical, and methodological issues. Petrinovich (Chapter 2), Treisman (Chapter 3), and Whitlow and Wagner (Chapter 4) suggest general theories to account for habituation, sensitization, and related phenomena. Each theoretical view stems from quite different conceptual bases.

The theory outlined by Petrinovich develops the dual-process model of Thompson and associates. The conceptual base comes from Thompson's neurophysiological constructs blended with evolutionary and ethological concerns. Petrinovich begins by examining the history of the habituation literature in several fields and argues that the concept of habituation has been initially conceived as purely inhibitory. As the development of the concept progressed in each of the research areas examined, it became necessary to devote increased attention to sensitization. Research since provided evidence for long-term effects as well as stimulus-specific and stimulus-general effects. A two-factor dual-process theory is developed based on a series of field experiments with birds. The dual processes are habituation and sensitization, and the two factors are relative stimulus specificity and relative permanence.

Whereas the theory developed by Petrinovich is at the functional level that makes no assumptions concerning the underlying processing mechanisms, Treisman's theory is a process-oriented model. The theory is based on data from studies at the levels of physiology, evolution, and behavior. The model contains three types of systems: a perceptual system, a primary-comparator system, and a response system. The model is essentially a decision theory, and the primary-comparator system contains the decision point that considers input from the perceptual system and processes information for transfer to the response system.

The model leads to a series of equations that quite successfully reproduce a number of observed features of behavior: habituation curves and the effects of stimulus intensity and massing of trials; sensitization; dishabituation; spontaneous recovery; decomposition of response sequences; behavioral contrast; and the law of initial value. The model is developed with sufficient specificity that it could be tested both at the neural level and at the functional level.

Whitlow and Wagner's model takes a memory-oriented approach to habituation and integrates the data on behavioral habituation. They describe a memory system, the basic unit being a memory node. The principles of action of these nodes are described, and these principles account for sensitivity to contextual changes, response facilitation, stimulus specificity, dishabituation, and such phenomena as overshadowing and serial position effects. The authors argue that the theory establishes the merits of a memory-oriented approach. They further insist that this approach is superior to reflex-oriented approaches because it views habituation within a context that considers the association history of the organism. The emphasis on memory and information processing should make the model of special interest to those who believe that habituation serves biologically important functions.

Evaluating the relative merits of these three models is impossible: each is cast at a different conceptual level, and each refers essentially to different bodies of data. It would be a useful exercise to analyze literature to which all can be brought to bear, to develop a set of experimental tests that would yield information relevant to each of them, to derive predictions from each, and refine each where it seems to be inadequate. Thus might we obtain a single, more adequate theory with broader generality in levels of response variables and covering a broader range of phenomena than any one of the extant models.

The last chapter is methodological. Petrinovich and Widaman (Chapter 5) have simulated data that have the characteristics of those often encountered in habituation experiments. The issues are not specific to habituation studies, but are general to any experiment involving repeated measurements. The simulated data are examined using two group-level analyses (repeated measures analysis of variance and group regression analysis) and one individual-level analysis (individual regression). The latter method seems the most preferable in terms of power when assumptions for the first two methods are violated, and it is as satisfactory when such assumptions are met. The individual regression method has an additional advantage: we can probe the pattern of individual differences in the data, thereby detecting any subsets of individuals within the set being considered as well as understanding the probable causal factors producing aberrant "outliers."

Petrinovich and Widaman also investigate the problem of evaluating the effect of a single probe trial following an initial series of trials. The same analytic procedures used with the simulated data are applied to real data. The implications of the mode of statistical analysis in scientific theory construction are discussed in terms of the needs for scientific justification as compared to those of heuristic value.

CHAPTER 2

A Two-Factor Dual-Process Theory of Habituation and Sensitization

Lewis Petrinovich

Department of Psychology
University of California
Riverside, California

I. Introduction

Habituation has been discussed for several decades by experimental psychologists, ethologists, learning theorists, and physiologists. In this chapter I shall outline some of the salient points in the development of the concept of habituation. Two points seem to emerge: at the outset the conceptualizations concentrate on response inhibition; and as experimentation and theorizing progress, an excitation component begins to assume more and more importance.

I shall then outline the two-factor habituation theory developed by Thompson and collaborators, because it represents the beginning of cur-

HABITUATION, SENSITIZATION,
AND BEHAVIOR

rent conceptual models. The important research on *Aplysia* begun in Kandel's laboratory will not be discussed here, because Carew has reviewed it at length in this volume (Chapter 6). Kandel's research leads to some extensions of Thompson's theory, especially in the recognition of long-term habituation effects and the importance of sensitization in producing dishabituation. I shall discuss the results of my research program, which studied the habituation of the responses of birds to playback of song. This research began with a concern for the role of habituation in producing response decrements in a field setting. As the research progressed it became apparent that many of the effects observed were caused by a pronounced sensitization component; and this realization has led to the formulation of a two-factor dual-process theory. The theory originally was stated qualitatively but has now been cast in a more quantitative form. The interpretive and heuristic value of the theory will be evaluated in the last section.

II. Historical Developments

A. Experimental Psychology

Some of the earliest research on habituation was done by experimental psychologists interested in the adaptation of visual after-nystagmus to repeated bodily rotation. For example, Dodge (1923) exposed subjects to 19 bodily rotations per day for 6 days and found that after-nystagmus decreased across trials and days. R. C. Davis (1934) studied day-to-day changes in the amplitude of galvanic skin responses (GSRs) to repetitions of noise and the onset of music and found similar results. The level of response showed partial recovery after 6 days; almost complete recovery occurred after 33 days. Seward and Seward (1934) reported habituation of the amplitude of GSR and respiratory patterns to the general testing situation, as well as habituation to the specific stimuli used. They also found a restoration of GSR by a novel stimulus.

Coombs (1938) reported that the GSR adapted rapidly on the first few presentations of auditory stimuli and continued to adapt more slowly for a period of time. Adaptation to a successive series—each series consisting of a new stimulus—proceeded more and more rapidly, indicating that a transfer of adaptation occurred. Coombs also found that the repetition of five stimuli at 15-second intervals resulted in more rapid adaptation than did repetition at a 30-second interval for the five stimuli.

Porter (1938) studied cross-modality adaptation of the GSR. Subjects were adapted to one stimulus (a buzzer) and then were presented with a series of flashing lights. Porter reported some stimulus-specific adaptation and some generalization to the light stimulus.

Duffy and Lacey (1946) studied palmar conductance when tones were presented and subjects were instructed to indicate whenever they heard the sound. A decrease occurred in conductance within and across days, a slight recovery on the initial presentation of a trial within a day, and a small spontaneous recovery across days.

The research by these experimental psychologists suggested that response decrements occurred as a function of continued presentation of stimuli and that these decrements were specific to the stimuli presented and general to the overall situation. There also seemed to be evidence for a short-term, within-days effect and a long-term, across-days effect. There was little discussion regarding any sensitization components that might occur with these preparations. The emphasis was almost entirely on adaptation.

This rather active research field was prominently mentioned in Woodworth's two editions of his classic compendium *Experimental Psychology* (1938, 1954) but were not included in the other leading textbooks: Stevens's *Handbook of Experimental Psychology* (1951), Osgood's *Method and Theory in Experimental Psychology* (1953), or Underwood's *Experimental Psychology* (1966). This absence may have resulted from the distrust existing at that time (because of problems with instrumentation and measurement) regarding the reliability and meaning of the labile GSR as a dependent variable. Theory in experimental psychology also seemed to have moved from a consideration of molar sensory processes to a concern with learning, perceptual processes, and concept formation.

B. Learning Theory

Hilgard and Marquis (1940), in their classic review of the experimental and theoretical literature on learning, discussed habituation under the heading of "adaptation of conditioned responses." They believed that to obtain such adaptation, the repeated elicitation of a response was essential. They cited studies by Sherrington (1906) on spinal cats and by Prosser and Hunter (1936), who studied the rapid habituation of startle responses of rats. Hilgard and Marquis (1940, pp. 105–108) abstracted five principles to summarize the literature:

1. Adaptation is cumulative. The greater the number of repetitions the greater the decrement. There is sub-zero adaptation as shown by a longer time for spontaneous recovery if the repetitions continue beyond the point where responses cease.

2. Adaptation is a function of the rate of elicitation of the response.
3. Adaptation is not permanent. The amount of recovery is a function of the interval between training and testing. Following recovery, readaptation is faster and the spontaneous recovery that occurs is not complete.
4. Adaptation may be generalized: it is not restricted to the particular response but is reflected in other responses as well, and also within and across sensory modalities.
5. Stimulation that produces an adapted response may inhibit another response.

These five principles appear in Thompson and Spencer's (1966) statement of the dual-process theory.

The concern with habituation seemed to disappear from the literature on learning. Kimble's (1961) revision of Hilgard and Marquis's work had no entry concerning habituation or adaptation. Hilgard's *Theories of Learning* (1948) mentioned only Humphrey's classic book (1933) and indicated that habituation might be the simplest instance of learning. No entries on habituation occurred in Hilgard's (1956) second edition, and in the third edition (1966) Humphrey is again cited—as are Thorpe (1956) and Sokolov (1963). Hilgard (1956) suggested that "some learning is involved in habituation, but is again a marginal case [p. 5]." In the fourth edition (Hilgard & Bower, 1975) habituation is discussed in a chapter devoted to the neurophysiology of learning, with emphasis placed on Thompson's research with spinal cats and Kandel's work with *Aplysia* (see Carew, Chapter 6). Again, there is almost no discussion of any sensitization component in any of the research considered by these authors (except for Hilgard and Bower's treatment of Kandel's research).

One of the most intensive efforts to build a hypothetico-deductive theory of learning was undertaken by C. L. Hull (1943). The general point to be emphasized here is that the initial views of the learning theorists included only inhibitory components when discussing the processes involved in habituation paradigms and, as theory and research became more precise, the importance of sensitization effects became more and more evident. I shall recast Hull's theory in the language of habituation theory to illustrate that, in Hull's initial formulations, the primary consideration was with inhibitory variables and, as the research program continued, it became essential to consider excitatory variables in more detail. (The progress of habituation theory, in general, has followed much the same course.) Hull's earliest versions of the theory considered several inhibitory variables, but in his later revisions (e.g., 1952) data led him to include some sensitization variables as well. Inhibitory variables in Hull's

1943 system include reactive inhibition (I_R) which is a short-term, stimulus-specific, and stimulus-general tendency to not respond that develops with repeated trials. Another inhibitory variable is conditioned inhibition ($_SI_R$), a permanent, learned variable that remains after the I_R has dissipated. Hull also included a generalized $_SI_R$ variable that would transfer to other stimuli as a function of their similarity to the original stimulus. These two variables provide a long-term, stimulus-specific and long-term, stimulus-general component, respectively.

In the 1943 version one could construe effective reaction potential ($_SE_R$) to be a long-term, stimulus-specific sensitization variable. If the level of $_SE_R$ exceeded that of the inhibitory variables the response would occur. The theory underwent a series of major revisions to account for anomalous results, and by 1952 two more variables were added to account for excitatory effects that had not been anticipated in the earlier versions of the theory. One was stimulus intensity dynamism (V), which was added to account for the fact that strong stimuli evoke stronger responses than do weak ones. This variable had a generalization aspect as well. The addition of V and its generalization aspect provided a short-term, stimulus-specific variable and a short-term, stimulus-general variable, respectively. Finally, incentive motivation (K) was added to account for the fact that a general increase in response strength occurred immediately following an increase in the quality or quantity of an incentive object. This added a long-term, stimulus-general variable.

The manner in which these components interact to produce behavior is not relevant here, nor is the adequacy of the overall theory. The precise nature of the components and their interaction is much more complex in Hull's system. I included this brief treatment to emphasize that it became necessary to include sensitization components of the types I shall discuss later.

C. Ethology

Ethologists have taken an active interest in habituation, and much of the behavioral research on habituation has been done by those working within this tradition. Thorpe, in the second edition of his *Learning and Instinct in Animals* (1963), reviewed the extensive habituation research done with animals from different phyla and offered what has become the standard ethological definition of habituation: "the relatively permanent waning of a response as a result of repeated stimulation which is not followed by any kind of reinforcement. It is specific to the stimulus, and relatively enduring, and . . . [is] distinct from fatigue and sensory adaptation [p. 61]." Thorpe considered habituation to be a primitive form of learning; learning not to respond to stimuli that tend to have no significance in the life of the animal. Habituation describes a tendency to drop out, rather than incorporating new responses or complicating those already present. As we shall see, this latter statement is probably inadequate. On the basis of his review Thorpe argued that habituation is most evident in nature in relation to those more generalized and elementary stimuli that put the animal in the mood for flight. Habituation is universal to mild and generalized warning stimuli and can occur in exceptional cases based on inborn responses to specific predators, such as the fright response of birds to classes of stimuli associated with predators.

Another classic treatment of habituation is Hartshorne's (1956) paper on the "monotony threshold" in singing birds. Hartshorne's presented evidence that song repertoires and song patterns of singing birds are constructed to avoid persistent repetition that would produce habituation in potential recipients of the song.

Hinde (1954a, 1954b, 1960) studied habituation of mobbing behavior in the Chaffinch (*Fringilla coelebs*). The mobbing was elicited by a wide range of stimulus objects: among them were live owls, stuffed owls, and a toy dog. Hinde found that the mobbing response waned gradually if the stimulus was presented continuously and that, 24 hours after stimulus presentation, the response recovered but not to the initial level. The results indicated that some stimulus specificity occurred because a greater reduction usually resulted if a second stimulus that was the same as the first stimulus was presented. But some reduction still occurred when a different type of stimulus was presented. This, then, indicates the presence of stimulus-specific *and* stimulus-general effects. The latter Hinde referred to as related to the "circumstances of the experiment."

When an almost complete response decrement produced by a 30-minute exposure to a test stimulus occurred, the level of recovery of response was about 55% of the initial level following a 30-minute rest interval. In fact, lowered levels of response were found to be "virtually permanent." Thus, there seems to be both short-term effects that dissipate during a rest interval and long-term effects that persist. In discussing the research, Hinde (1970) wrote, "Evidence that more than one process may be involved in the waning of responsiveness comes also from the fact that different aspects of the response may wane, or recover from waning at different rates [p. 300]."

In one phase of these experiments Hinde used two types of stimuli, a stuffed owl (O) and a toy dog (D) in all possible combinations: D-D, O-O, O-D, and D-O. Hinde found O to be a stronger stimulus than D. The results were complex but supported Hinde's conclusion (1970) that there is "considerable evidence that the decremental processes concealed less powerful but nonetheless influential incremental ones [p. 303]."

Hinde has, therefore, provided evidence for both decremental and incremental effects and suggested that they can be relatively stimulus-specific or stimulus-general. In addition, there is evidence that both decremental and incremental effects can be relatively short-lived or relatively permanent and that their growth and decay occur at different rates.

A series of experiments in the ethological tradition has been reported by Peeke and associates. Peeke (1969) studied the course of habituation in three-spined stickleback (*Gasterosteus aculeatus* L.) and found a decrease in response levels within a day and some spontaneous recovery across days, followed by a decrease to a lower level at the end of each day. Thompson, Groves, Teyler, and Roemer (1973) reported a reanalysis of these data using a 1-minute time block instead of the 3 minutes used by Peeke. They demonstrated that, at the beginning of each day, an increment in response level occurred followed by a subsequent decrement. The incremental process had been obscured by analyzing the data using time blocks that were too large.

Peeke, Herz, and Gallagher (1971) studied habituation of aggressive responses using convict cichlids (*Cichlosoma nigrofasciatum*). The fish were separated by a glass partition, but they were able to see each other and would bite at each other through the partition. The results of this experiment led the authors to suggest that habituation enables adjacent territorial fish to inhibit their mutual aggressive tendencies, "thus allowing them to pursue and respond to other stimuli necessary to . . . survival [p. 53]."

Peeke and Veno (1973) reported that habituation to a conspecific three-spined stickleback occurred as a result of exposure to a stimulus and was independent of whether a response was made. Peeke, Avis, and Peeke (1979) separated two underlying components—habituation and sensitization—that influenced response levels in convict cichlids; Peeke (1982) experimentally separated these two components in research with three-spined stickleback. In the latter study, habituation seemed to be stimulus specific, but sensitization did not.

Evidence for both long-term and short-term habituation were found in three-spined stickleback (Peeke, Figler & Blankenship, 1979), and sensitization was found to be a major factor in regulating the aggressive responses and feeding behavior in three-spined stickleback (Peeke, 1983).

This series of studies provided evidence that habituation is important in regulating the territorial behavior in fishes; that there are habituation and sensitization components; and that the habituation component was stimulus specific, but the sensitization component, under the conditions of their experiment, was not. There also seem to be long- and short-term habituation effects, and the habituation effects do not seem to be response dependent. Finally, later analytic studies provided evidence for the major importance of sensitization in regulating the course of behavior.

D. Dual-Process Theory

A highly significant advance in habituation theory took place when Thompson and Spencer (1966) outlined a dual-process theory based on their research with spinal cat. More recent versions of this theory outline several characteristics of habituation and sensitization (Thompson et al., 1973). The dual-process theory invokes two inferential processes—habituation and sensitization—to predict the course of response changes. It is assumed that every stimulus has two properties: (a) it elicits a response through stimulus–response (S–R) sensory-motor pathways and (b) it influences the state of the organism.

Repetition of an effective stimulus results in an inferred decremental process in the S–R pathway. This is the habituation component. There are five assumptions regarding habituation:

1. Habituation develops exponentially and reaches an asymptotic level.
2. The rate of development and degree of relative habituation is directly related to stimulus frequency and inversely related to stimulus intensity. Frequency has a strong effect, and intensity has a weak effect.
3. Upon cessation of stimulation, habituation decays spontaneously.
4. A repeated series of habituation trials and spontaneous recovery periods results in progressively more habituation.
5. Response habituation exhibits generalization to a test stimulus.

Presentation of an effective stimulus results in an inferred incremental process in a state of excitation or tendency to respond. This is the sensitization component. There are eight assumptions regarding sensitization:

1. Sensitization occurs in state systems but not in S–R pathways.
2. During habituation training, sensitization first grows and then decays.
3. The amount and duration of sensitization are directly related to stimulus intensity. At high intensities, sensitization is directly related to stimulus intensity. At high intensities, sensitization is directly re-

lated to stimulus frequency. At low intensities there may be no sensitization.

4. Sensitization decays spontaneously.
5. Repeated presentations of a sensitization stimulus result in progressively less sensitization.
6. Response sensitization will exhibit generalization.
7. Dishabituation is an instance of sensitization.
8. Temporal conditioning of sensitization may occur.

Finally, it is assumed that habituation and sensitization occur and develop independently of one another but interact to yield the final response output function.

Although the model was developed with decorticate, spinal-cat hindlimb responses, it has been useful to describe the changes in rat startle responses to repeated stimulus presentations (e.g., M. Davis & Wagner, 1969; Thompson *et al.*, 1973). Thompson and his collaborators have directed most of their attention toward understanding the underlying physiological mechanisms involved in these functional specifications.

Most of the important characteristics of habituation and sensitization have been demonstrated for the rat startle response (see Groves, Wilson, & Miller, 1976) using short-term (within-sessions) habituation. It has been suggested by Hinde (1970), M. Davis (1970), Groves *et al.* (1976), Wagner (1976), and Peeke, Avis, and Peeke (1979) that two habituation processes might exist: a short-term process that persists for minutes or hours and a long-term process that lasts for hours or days.

Sokolov (1963) proposed a similar model to understand responses to external stimulation in humans. Sokolov assumed that the cerebral cortex produces a model of the properties of external stimulation. A succeeding stimulus is compared with this model, and this comparison produces signals of match or mismatch. An orienting reflex (OR) appears whenever sensory input does not coincide with the neuronal model, and the OR amplifies activity in nonspecific paths. A matching signal blocks stimulus-produced impulses arriving over nonspecific paths and leads to habituation of the OR. This model invokes specific sensory-motor effects and arousal, or state effects (as suggested in the Thompson model). Sokolov also argued for the existence of a nonspecific defensive reflex evoked by stimulus intensity and not by stimulus change. This defensive reflex habituates slowly, or it can be intensified by repetitive stimulation. Close examination suggests that the model is basically a special instance of the more general Thompson model; the differences being the idea of a defensive reflex, specification of the complex neural circuitry that might be involved with humans, and an emphasis on the importance of sensitization as an independent process.

III. Habituation of White-crowned Sparrows (*Zonotrichia leucophrys nuttalli*) to Playback of Territorial Song

A. The Experimental Program

The research program described in this section is a step toward realizing a Brunswikian approach to the study of behavior (Brunswik, 1952; Petrinovich, 1979). Substantial progress has been made toward developing a theoretical framework by directing careful attention to the natural history of the species being studied. This has led to some understanding of behavior of the bird species within the natural ecology of breeding pairs (Petrinovich & Patterson, 1982b, in press). The field experiments described here implement the Brunswikian approach by involving a minimum of stimulus manipulation, no selection of responses for observation and measurement, and little experimenter intrusion into the setting. Thus, the natural correlational texture between variables is preserved to a great extent, behavioral changes that occur can be evaluated within the context of the total behavioral repertoire of the animals, and background variables are present in their representative density.

The experimental manipulations were chosen because they involve a behavior system that many animal behaviorists believe to be of general importance in intraspecific social adaptations: changes in the responsiveness to the territorial song of conspecifics. Pairs of breeding birds were played songs of a territorial male, and their rates of responding were recorded. Habituation theory provides the substantive theoretical focus for the research. Habituation was chosen for study because it has been demonstrated that it is an important process regulating the social behavior of birds (e.g., Falls & Brooks, 1975; Falls & McNicholl, 1979) and of fishes (e.g., Peeke & Peeke, 1972) and because of the extensive body of literature and theory at both the neurophysiological and the behavioral levels (see Peeke, Chapter 11). The emphasis in this presentation will be on the contribution of each of the specific experiments to the habituation model.

These experiments were all done in the field with pairs of breeding White-crowned Sparrows. This sedentary subspecies is territorial. The male patrols the boundaries of the territory (which on the average is a little over 1000 m^2) from about March through July. Typically, one male sings, and the other males fly about and respond to the songs, all staying within their respective territorial boundaries. Early in the season frequent territorial conflicts occur, and these are marked by physical encounters between males. By the time the breeding season starts, territorial conflicts are reduced to bouts of singing and countersinging between neighboring males.

In early April, the female builds a nest, the pair copulates, and the female lays a clutch of about three eggs, one per day. The young hatch after about 13 days, and the nestlings are fed insects. When the young fledge they stay in the region of the nest for 20–30 days, with the male assuming an increasing responsibility to feed the young during the latter part of the period. A few days after the brood fledges, the female begins a new nest; the whole cycle starts again and continues until sometime in July or until the pair have two broods. At that time, feeding flocks of juveniles and adults forage through the territories, and the territories begin breaking down. The young suffer heavy predation from land and aerial predators, with only about 30% of the eggs resulting in a fledgling (Petrinovich & Patterson, in press).

Each male usually has one song about 2 seconds long, and the song is repeated with an 11-second intersong interval (ISI) during a bout of singing. There are pronounced regional dialect groups (Baptista, 1975) whose songs comprise similar elements combined in different orders.

When a song is played in a territory, the male and female appear almost immediately. They respond by flying about and often perform aggressive displays such as rapid wing flutters and trills. The female, under some circumstances, will emit rapid metallic sounding "chinks," and the male will begin to sing.

Most of the behaviors that could be observed by two experimenters were recorded with the aid of a 20-pen event recorder. One O recorded the male behaviors: full songs, partial songs, intersong interval, flights, chinks, trills, flutters, attacks on other birds, and the distance from the speaker, here reported as 0, <2, and >8 m. The other O recorded the number of countersongs by neighboring birds and the behaviors of female: the flights, chinks, trills, flutters, and time in view (the females do not ordinarily sing).

In all experiments the nest of the breeding pair was located, the territory mapped, and subjects banded for identification. A given pair was subjected to playback of the song of a territorial male of the same dialect group.

B. Experimental Results

1. Experiment 1

In the first experiment (Petrinovich & Patterson, 1979), the playback was presented to the pairs in trial blocks. Each trial block was constructed as follows: ten 2-second songs with a fixed 11-second intersong interval, an 11-minute silent period, another 10 songs as before, and a 5-minute silent period. Each trial, then, contained 20 songs—a song about every 30 seconds on the average. The initial playback series consisted of 8 trials (160 songs over an 80-minute period). The pattern for this group is illustrated as Group 1-S in Fig. 1. This initial series was followed by an additional set of playback trials. Some pairs had no delay interval, some a 60-minute delay, others had a 300-minute delay, and still others a 2880-minute delay. The second playback series consisted of another eight trial blocks followed by a generalization stimulus—another song from the same dialect group.

The results indicated that the reproductive condition of the female was a major variable influencing response level and rate of change: The response patterns for males and females were determined to a large extent by whether the female was incubating eggs, brooding nestlings, or feeding fledglings. [Peeke and Peeke (1982) have found that the stage of the reproductive cycle is an important variable influencing the course of habituation and sensitization in convict cichlids.] It was found that, for the first eight trial blocks, the behavior levels and their changes for the different behaviors were quite complex and could be interpreted meaningfully only in the context of ongoing behavior during the different stages of the reproductive cycle. The changes made sense in terms of the behaviors appropriate in the context of environmental demands.

The male whose female is brooding eggs behaves in a manner similar to a paired territorial male prior to the nesting season. He sings and flies about a great deal and engages in what appear to be aggressive responses at the outset (trills and flutters). The females brooding eggs have no young to warn and issue practically no fright chinks.

The female with nestlings is in view very little, and when she is flies about but emits few chinks, trills, or flutters. In short, she is cryptic; if she was in the nest bush when the playback began, she stayed there quietly, if she was out of the nest bush foraging, she remained concealed—away

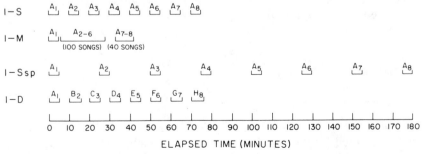

Fig. 1. Summary of experimental conditions. A–H, Songs; 1–8, trials.

from the nest. The male flies about and sings somewhat in general is quite unresponsive at this stage of the reproductive cycle.

The female with fledglings is in view most of the time and issues a large number of chinks. The fledglings tend to cease moving and emitting begging calls when either the male or female chinks, thus enhancing the concealment of the young. The female also flutters and trills at a high rate. The male sings and flies more than he does in the other two conditions. He initially flutters but stops as the trials progress. At this stage he is taking a more active role in feeding the young and often stops responding to the playback to forage for insects to feed the young during the later playback trials. Thus, a response decrement did result from the repeated playback of recorded song for some responses, but not for others.

Those pairs that had no delay between the first 8 trial blocks and the second 8 trial blocks can be considered to have received 16 continuous trials. It was anticipated that doubling the number of trials would result in a greater number of response decrements, because the amount of habituation is considered to increase as a function of the number of stimulus presentations (Thompson *et al.*, 1973). But it was found that the number of response decrements observed with the 16 trial blocks was no greater than it was with 8 trial blocks. In fact, for some variables such as male flights, the response rate increased as the last eight trials progressed, suggesting that the additional trials produced more sensitization than they did habituation.

Following the delay interval all pairs received eight more playback trials. No further response decrements occurred during the eight trials following the delay interval: apparently, any decrement that was going to appear was complete by the end of the first eight trials.

No spontaneous recovery following any of the delay intervals occurred for any response. This lack of spontaneous recovery could be the result of an accumulation of sensitization that masked the habituation occurring during the predelay period. Following the delay interval the less permanent sensitization had dissipated, and the relatively more permanent habituation manifested itself. By this argument, the net result would be that the response levels would either be the same (if some of the habituation also dissipated) or lower (if little of the habituation had dissipated) than the levels preceding the delay.

2. Experiment 2

Because the increase in the number of trials beyond the first eight did not result in an increase in response decrements, the second study in this series (Patterson & Petrinovich, 1979) was done. One purpose of this study was to mass the rate of stimulus presentations to produce an increased number of response decrements. This was done by presenting the songs at a more rapid rate: In the first study, 160 songs were presented over a period of 4784 seconds, or a song every 30 seconds on average. In this second study 230, songs were presented over a period of 3476 seconds or a song every 15 seconds on average. In this study a 60-second silent period followed the first series of songs, and this silent period was followed by an additional 100 songs. The pattern for this group is illustrated as Group 1-M in Fig. 1.

When response decrements for the same number of presentations were considered for these first two studies, there were fewer response decrements for Group 1-M compared to Group 1-S. When the total initial period is considered, the response decrement was the same for Group 1-M (230 songs, 11.5 trials) as for Group 1-S (160 songs, 8 trials). It was concluded that massing resulted in fewer response decrements. The model developed by M. Davis (1970) led us to expect that massing would result in more response decrements; but Kandel's results were similar to ours (see Carew, Chapter 6).

Again, response levels had no systematic tendency to recover spontaneously over the 60-minute delay interval. It was also found that no recovery occurred when some birds were tested as long as 5 to 15 days later; in fact, there were more decreases in response level than there were increases.

Although these results were not the same as those reported by Thompson et al. (1973), they can be interpreted quite nicely with the two-process model of habituation. It is assumed that the observed response output is a function of two opposed processes, habituation and sensitization. The habituation is more permanent than the sensitization, and habituation accumulates more gradually. In the experiments using the distributed procedure, increasing the number of trials to 16 (instead of the usual 8) did not result in a greater number of decrements. This could have been caused by an increase in general sensitization, which offset the increase in habituation. Massing the trials did not result in as many decrements as found with the distributed presentation until the number of trials was increased. This could indicate that sensitization increased more with massed presentation because it did not have time to dissipate between trials. But habituation would be constant for the two types of presentation, and the response decrement would be less with the massed presentation.

3. Experiment 3

These considerations led to yet another study (Petrinovich & Patterson, 1981) that tested these assumptions. An attempt was made to indepen-

2. A Theory of Habituation and Sensitization

dently manipulate habituation processes (See Fig. 1). For one group [1-day–same-song (1-S)] the usual eight trial blocks (160 songs) were used with the species-typical 11-second intersong interval and a 5-min. interval between trial blocks. For a second group [1 day–same-song–massed (1-M)], the time between trial blocks was decreased to allow more sensitization to accumulate. For a third group [1 day–same song–spaced (1-S$_{sp}$)], the typical intersong interval was used for the 20 songs of each trial block. But the time between trial blocks was increased to 20 minutes to allow sensitization to decay more and, thereby, to decrease the amount that accumulated. For a fourth group [1-day–different-song (1-D)], a different song was used for each trial block (the rate of presentation was the same as for Group 1-S) to decrease the amount of stimulus specific habituation that accumulated. It was assumed that sensitization should accumulate as before if it were less stimulus specific.

No differences occurred in the number of response decrements for the different groups; few decrements were obtained. But there were a large number of significant intercept differences. Group 1-D (which was played a different song on each trial) was generally more responsive than Group 1-S (which was played the same song on each trial). It was suggested that this heightened responsiveness was caused by an accumulation of general sensitization not counteracted by any substantial amount of stimulus-specific habituation. When the trials were massed (Group 1-M) the patterns of response were interpreted to indicate that there was an accumulation of stimulus-general and stimulus-specific sensitization that overwhelmed the accumulated habituation. The result of this accumulation was a large number of responses that seemed to typify states of fear and aggression—chinks, trills, and flutters. Spacing the trials (Group 1-S$_{sp}$) resulted in low-level responding that could be the result of a decrease in short-term sensitization. In the absence of sensitization, habituation might be expected to manifest itself to a fuller extent.

This study suggested that the different levels of response were primarily the result of effects on underlying sensitization processes. Considering the studies in this series, careful attention must be paid to the nature of presumed habituation processes *and* counteracting sensitization components. Therefore, an additional experiment was done to test the properties of the model developed to account for the results of the first studies (Petrinovich & Patterson, 1982a). This two-factor dual-process theory, incorporates dual inferential processes of habituation and sensitization. Each process is assumed to vary along dimensions of relative permanence and relative stimulus specificity. The way these presumed effects interact with one another to produce observed patterns of behavior was the central theoretical concern.

4. Experiment 4

Habituation and sensitization processes were manipulated by varying the patterning and type of stimulus presentation. Four different groups were tested: Two groups had all eight trial blocks conducted on one day (1-day groups) and two had one trial block on each of 8 days (8-day groups). This was done to separate short-term, within-session effects from long-term, across-session effects. One of the groups tested on one day was presented with same song on each of the eight trial blocks [1-day–same-song group (1-S)], and the other was presented with a different song on each of eight trial blocks [1-day–different-song group (1-D)]. The same procedure was followed with those tested over an 8-day period (Group 8-S, the same song over 8 days; and Group 8-D, a different song presented on each of 8 days). The use of different songs on each trial allows the separation of stimulus-specific effects from stimulus-general effects.

Results indicated that the 1-day groups were more responsive throughout the experiment than the 8-day groups, and that the groups who were played a different song on each trial (Groups 1-D and 8-D) were more responsive throughout than those played the same song on each trial (Groups 1-S and 8-S). In general, more response decrements occurred for the 8-day groups, with few occurring for the 1-day groups. Group 8-S had the greatest number of significant response decrements.

IV. Two-Factor Dual-Process Theory

The proposed model will now be outlined in some detail to provide a clearer picture of the relationships between results and the model. As indicated earlier dual processes, habituation, and sensitization are each influenced by two factors, stimulus specificity and relative permanence. It should be emphasized strongly that these two factors vary along continuous scales in terms of their relative strength. The presentation that follows will be phrased in terms of polar positions for ease of presentation only, and the model should not be construed to represent discrete cells in a contingency table.

The eight polar positions are as follows:

1. Short-term (ST) stimulus-specific habituation. This is not caused by motor fatigue or sensory adaptation, and its strength has to be indexed using test probes with novel stimuli to separate those short-term effects from the effects caused by short-term habituation. If there is an increment

in responsiveness to a novel stimulus, as compared to the habituated stimulus, this will permit an inference regarding the extent to which the observed effects are the result of habituation and the extent they result from motor fatigue or sensory adaptation.

2. ST stimulus-general habituation that is a phasic adaptation to the test situation. Again, this is not the same as motor fatigue or sensory adaptation and can be indexed by the application of novel test probes. These two components dissipate each day.

3. Long-term (LT) stimulus-specific habituation that is similar to the conception of habituation developed by Thompson *et al.* (1973).

4. LT stimulus-general habituation similar to the adaptation effects that occur for a variety of species of animals in laboratory and field. This component would not dissipate each day, and its presence can be detected by applying a novel probe stimulus.

5. ST stimulus-specific sensitization. This component dissipates each day.

6. ST stimulus-general sensitization similar to Sokolov's (1963) nonspecific orienting reflex.

7. LT stimulus-specific sensitization as proposed by Thompson *et al.* (1973). Shalter (1978a) found evidence for this process in his studies of the mobbing response of the Pied Flycatcher (*Ficedula hypoleuca*).

8. LT stimulus-general sensitization that could be related to arousal and orienting responses. This component is similar to the sensitization effect discussed by Kandel (1979).

Petrinovich and Patterson (1982a) presented a qualitative description of the presumed processes as the processes would affect response levels and their change. The dual processes of habituation and sensitization have been broken down further into the two proposed factors of permanence and stimulus specificity. A table was included to clarify the processes as applied to the groups of the last experiment (Table 2, Petrinovich & Patterson, 1982a). A revised and more explicit version of this qualitative description is contained in Table 1 of this chapter.

Group 1-S would be affected by ST stimulus-specific and stimulus-general habituation and sensitization. Because all testing is done on one day the subjects in this group would not be influenced by long-term effects. Thus, there are entries in the ST stimulus-specific and ST stimulus-general cells. This means that, throughout the course of testing, all effects would be produced only by the two processes. Group 1-D would be affected by ST stimulus-general habituation and sensitization effects but would not be affected by long-term effects or by stimulus-specific effects, because the song is changed on each trial. Group 8-S would be affected by

TABLE 1

A Characterization of Habituation and Sensitization Effects Influencing Each Group

| | Habituation | | | | | | | Sensitization | | | | | | |
| | Short-term | | Long-term | | | | Short-term | | Long-term | | | |
Group	Stimulus-specific	Stimulus-general	Stimulus-specific	Stimulus-general			Stimulus-specific	Stimulus-general	Stimulus-specific	Stimulus-general	
1-S	Weak	Weak	XX	XX			Moderate	Strong	XX	XX	
1-D	XX[a]	Weak	XX	XX			XX	Strong	XX	XX	
8-S	Weak	Weak	Moderate	Moderate			Weak	Weak	Strong	Strong	
8-D	XX	Moderate	XX	Moderate			XX	Weak	XX	Strong	

[a] XX, Indicates that the effect would not be present for the group.

ST stimulus-specific and ST stimulus-general habituation and sensitization effects present on the trial of the last day only. This group would be affected by LT stimulus-specific and stimulus-general habituation and sensitization. Group 8-D would be affected by ST stimulus-general habituation and sensitization effects on the trial of the last day and by LT stimulus-general habituation and sensitization.

The relative strength of each process is suggested in Table 1. These relative strengths are completely post hoc, but they are presented to illustrate how the general view might be useful in organizing data of the type obtained in habituation experiments.

The results were interpreted to mean that, for Group 1-S, ST stimulus-specific and stimulus-general sensitization accumulated and overrode the accumulated effects of the ST stimulus-specific and stimulus-general habituations. Assumptions regarding relative strengths are indicated by the cell entries in Table 1: ST stimulus-specific and stimulus-general habituation effects are presumed to be relatively weak; the ST stimulus-specific and stimulus-general sensitization effects are presumed to be stronger.

Group 1-D would be affected by strong ST stimulus-general sensitization that overrides weak ST stimulus-general habituation effects.

Group 8-S would be affected by ST stimulus-specific and stimulus-general affects from the last trial and by LT stimulus-specific and stimulus-general habituation and sensitization. This group had fewer response decrements than did Group 8-S, so this could mean that the ST habituation effects are weak, and the LT effects are of moderate strength. Long-term sensitization effects are relatively strong.

Group 8-D would be affected by moderate ST and LT stimulus-general habituation, by weak ST stimulus-general sensitization, and strong LT stimulus-general sensitization. When Petrinovich and Patterson (1979) presented the same song on one day, it was found that doubling the number of trials presented at the same rate did not increase the number of behaviors that showed a significant response decrement. Patterson and Petrinovich (1979) found that massing trials within a single day did not result in more response decrements for different behaviors. This supports the assumption that ST sensitization effects override ST habituation effects. In these two studies it was also found that response levels tended to be lower 1 hour after the stimulus trials. This could indicate that strong ST sensitization dissipated quickly and allowed the relatively weak habituation effect to manifest itself.

The various processes proposed here have been proposed by several investigators. Hinde (1970), for example, suggested that repetition of a stimulus had decremental and incremental effects, and Peeke, Avis, and Peeke (1979) isolated each type of effect operationally. Hinde (1970) suggested that there were stimulus-specific and stimulus-general habituation processes as well as short-term and long-term processes. Kandel (1979), Groves *et al.* (1976), Wagner (1976), and M. Davis (1970) found evidence for short-term and long-term habituation processes.

Processes of sensitization have not received the attention devoted to those of habituation. Peeke (1982) considered stimulus-general sensitization to be important and presented evidence for ST and LT sensitization effects that often mask habituation (Patterson & Petrinovich, 1979). I have also found evidence for strong long-term sensitization effects (Petrinovich & Patterson, 1982a).

V. Revised Model

The qualitative description of the preceding findings helped conceptualize the results of Petrinovich and Patterson (1982a) and received some support from results of other experiments in the series (Patterson & Petrinovich, 1979; Petrinovich & Patterson, 1979, 1981). The qualitative characterization had a low heuristic value because the strength estimates were based on assumptions neither clearly conceptualized nor sufficiently explicit.

To overcome these limitations a more explicit and quantitative model has been developed. This model avoids the previous qualitative assumptions regarding the relative strength of the processes. The relative strengths of the various components are based on some simple and explicit assumptions. The same basic processes already discussed are used.

A. Assumptions

The model assumes the following:

1. Two basic processes—habituation and sensitization—interact to influence the behavior patterns and levels.
2. Each process is influenced by two factors: relative stimulus specificity and relative permanence.
3. Within a single testing period, only short-term effects are active.
4. Short-term effects are transferred as long-term effects after a period of time. (The length of this time has not been determined empirically. In our research, short-term effects are considered to

be effective when testing is concentrated on one day, and long-term effects are brought into play when testing is conducted on different days.)

5. The two processes are affected by stimulus-specific and stimulus-general effects. Stimulus-specific effects apply only to the test stimulus; stimulus-general effects are active whenever the testing procedures are used in a particular context. (The nature and breadth of generalization gradients for these effects have not been investigated in this research.)
6. Each effective component increases two units per trial.
7. All short-term habituation accumulated each day becomes long term; habituation is permanent.
8. One unit of each two units of short-term sensitization decays each day and the remaining unit becomes long term; sensitization is less permanent.
9. The maximum short-term habituation that can be effective is 20 units. The amount of habituation that can be accumulated on any one day is limited.
10. Short-term habituation continues to be stored as long-term habituation on the following day until the short-term value reaches 20.
11. Long-term habituation continues to accumulate beyond 20 units to some as yet unspecified maximum.
12. The maximum sensitization that can be effective on any day is 25 units. There is an excitability limit.
13. Any value over 25 sensitization units does not become long-term.

The preceding assumptions can be translated by reference to Table 2. This table contains a trial-by-trial tabulation of the strength of the different habituation and sensitization components. For all groups the first two columns of the data field for habituation and sensitization contain a 2, indicating that two units of short-term (ST) components are present (Assumption 1). The next two columns for each contain zeros, indicating that there are no accumulated long-term (LT) processes as yet. For the one-day groups the accumulated LT columns all contain zeros because all of the trials are conducted on one day, and there are only ST effects (Assumption 3). The summation columns (ΣH and ΣS) contain the value present immediately after the end of a given trial. Each group has a value of 4 for habituation and sensitization on Trial 1. The last column contains the value ($\Sigma S - \Sigma H$) for each trial. This value represents the relative amount of accumulated sensitization and habituation and is used to predict the response level (Assumption 1).

TABLE 2

Tabulation of the Strength of Habituation and Sensitization Components for Each Group across Trials

| Group | Trial | Habituation | | | | ΣH | Sensitization | | | | ΣS | $\Sigma S - \Sigma H$ |
| | | Short-term | | Long-term | | | Short-term | | Long-term | | | |
		Stimulus-specific	Stimulus-general	Stimulus-specific	Stimulus-general		Stimulus-specific	Stimulus-general	Stimulus-specific	Stimulus-general		
1-S	1	2	2	0	0	4	2	2	0	0	4	0
	2	2	2	0	0	8	2	2	0	0	8	0
	3	2	2	0	0	12	2	2	0	0	12	0
	4	2	2	0	0	16	2	2	0	0	16	0
	5	2	2	0	0	20	2	2	0	0	20	0
	6	2	2	0	0	20	2	2	0	0	24	+4
	7	2	2	0	0	20	2	2	0	0	25	+5
	8	2	2	0	0	20	2	2	0	0	25	+5
1-D	1	2	2	0	0	4	2	2	0	0	4	0
	2	2	2	0	0	6	2	2	0	0	6	0
	3	2	2	0	0	8	2	2	0	0	8	0
	4	2	2	0	0	10	2	2	0	0	10	0

38

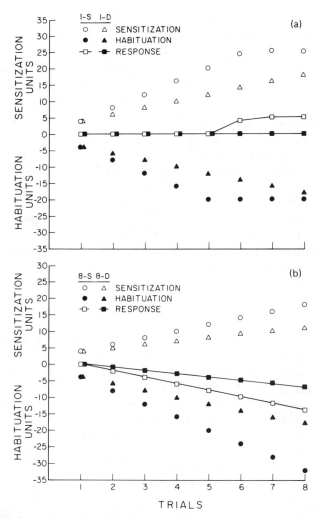

Fig. 2. (a) Theoretical values of habituation and sensitization and predicted response levels for Groups 1-S and 1-D. (b) Habituation and sensitization values for Groups 8-S and 8-D.

and reaches a ΣS value of -14 by Trial 8 (Figure 2b). These figures lead to a prediction of a linear decrease in response.

4. Group 8-D

Group 8-D accumulates only ST stimulus-specific units, because a different song is used for each trial. Therefore, two stimulus-general habituation units are added at Trial 2 and at each succeeding trial, reaching a ΣH

value of 18 at Trial 8. Only stimulus-general sensitization units accumulate, and this occurs at the rate of -1 unit per trial to a Trial-8 ΣS value of -7. The $(\Sigma S - \Sigma H)$ value is -1 for Trial 2 and increases by -1 at each trial to a value of -7 for Trial 8 (Fig. 2b). These figures lead to a prediction of a linear decrease in response roughly half that expected for Group 8-S.

C. Prediction of Response Level

The curves generated above (Table 2 and Fig. 2) can be used to predict the relative response level of each group. The $(\Sigma S - \Sigma H)$ value for each trial is summed and divided by the number of trials to obtain a mean response level for the group. The values for Group 1-S are $0 + 0 + 0 + 0 + 0 + 4 + 5 + 5 = 14$, giving a mean value of $+1.75$. The values for Group 8-S are $0 + (-2) + (-4) + (-6) + (-8) + (-10) + (-12) + (-14) = -56$, for a mean value of -7.0. The mean value obtained for Group 1-D is 0, and that for Group 8-D is -3.38.

D. Results

The present characterization of the experimental results will be somewhat coarse for several reasons. A large number of behaviors are recorded in these experiments. The characterization of the outcomes for four different groups is, therefore, quite complex and difficult to comprehend. And some of the variables are usually highly correlated: for example, trills and flutters for males and females, and full songs and ISI for males. This reduces the meaningfulness of the "box-score" approach used here to index relative response levels and their change.

I am now attempting to reduce the behavioral variables to a set of uncorrelated factors and to use scores on these factors to represent the response levels and change for each subject. Preliminary analysis suggests that the behavior may fall into several meaningful groupings, such as aggressive behaviors (partial songs, female flutters), male responsiveness (full song, flight, flutters), and female responsiveness (flights, chinks, time in view). Behaviors with such different adaptive significance might require different parameters to characterize the function forms.

Following the development of a factorially pure scoring system, the behavior of each pair should be considered individually. The patterns of individual differences between pairs could well fall into systems of lawful regularities reflecting the different behavioral organization the subjects use to cope with environmental demands. The necessity to approach data at the idiographic level of analysis is argued in Chapter 5 of this volume.

At the present time all data for all of the habituation experiments I have conducted are being subjected to an idiographic analysis. But the analyses in this chapter will be at the group level and will be presented only to illustrate the elements of the model.

Another coarse index characterizes the response levels of each group. The response levels for the males reported in Petrinovich and Patterson (1982a) have been ranked across groups (Figs. 3–6). For example, for male flights the level for Group 1-D (Fig. 4) was significantly higher than for all others and was assigned a rank of 1; the levels for Groups 1-S and 8-D were not significantly different from one another (Figs. 3 & 6), and each was assigned a rank of 2.5. Group 8-S (Fig. 5), which was significantly lower than the two preceding groups, was assigned a rank of 4. The rank value assigned is in parentheses above the upper graph denoting

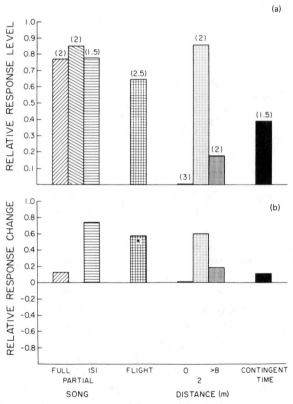

Fig. 3. Relative response level (a) and response change (b) for each variable for which the intercept differences, slopes, or interaction is significant for Group 8-S (males; 1 day–same song). ISI, Intersong interval; *, significant change, $p < .05$.

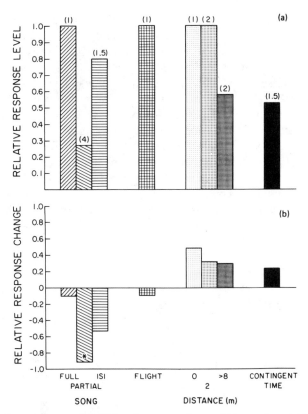

Fig. 4. Relative response level (a) and response change (b) for each variable for which the intercept differences, slopes, or interaction is significant for Group 1-D (males; 1 day–different song). ISI, Intersong interval; *, significant change $p < .05$.

response level in each of the figures. Each behavior was ranked in this manner, and the ranks were summed for each group. The sum of the ranks (ΣR) for each group was as follows: 1-S = 16.5, 1-D = 14, 8-S = 28.5, and 8-D = 21. Table 3 contains the predicted ΣR and the obtained ΣR for all groups, with a low ΣR indicating a low level of response. A Friedman nonparametric matched-sample test was calculated (Marascuilo & McSweeney, 1977), and a significant difference occurred between the groups over all variables ($\chi^2 = 9.11$; $df = 3$; $p < .05$).

Inspecting Table 3 indicates that the predicted levels of response correspond quite well to the obtained levels in their relative values. The only variation from expectation was that the level for Group 1-S should have been higher than that for 1-D, and the obtained level for 1-D was higher

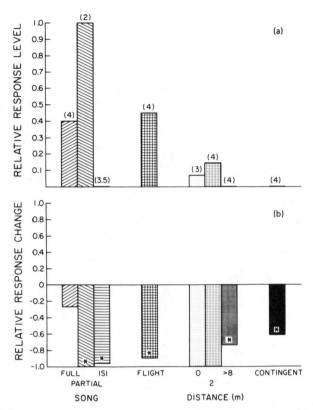

Fig. 5. Relative response level (a) and response change (b) for each variable for which the intercept differences, slopes, or interaction is significant for Group 8-S (males; 8 days–same song). ISI, Intersong interval; *, significant change, $p < .05$.

than for 1-S. This is not devastating, because of the slight predicted difference ($+1.75$) between the two. The major predictions were well supported: the 1-day groups were considerably higher than the 8-day groups, and the different-song groups were higher than the same-song groups.

The relative amount of habituation was indexed by tabulating the number of significant changes in level. These changes are indicated in the lower portion of Figs. 3–6. The predicted values for response change were taken from the Trial-8 ($\Sigma S - \Sigma H$) value as calculated in Table 2 for each group. These sums were then ranked in order of magnitude. The number of behaviors for which a significant change was observed is listed in the column headed Observed (Table 3) and these numbers were also ranked. The order of response changes was predicted completely. Al-

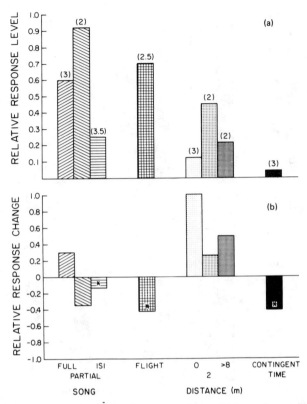

Fig. 6. Relative response level (a) and response change (b) for each variable for which the intercept differences, slopes, or interaction is significant for Group 8-D (males; 8 days–different song). ISI, Intersong interval, *, significant change, $p < .05$.

TABLE 3

Predicted and Observed Response Levels and Changes for Each Group

Group	Response level				Response change			
	Predicted	Rank	Observed	Rank	Predicted	Rank	Observed	Rank
1-S	+1.75	1	16.5	2	+5	4	+1	4
1-D	0.00	2	14.0	1	0	3	−1	3
8-S	−7.04	4	28.5	4	−14	1	−5	1
8-D	−3.38	3	21.0	3	−7	2	−3	2

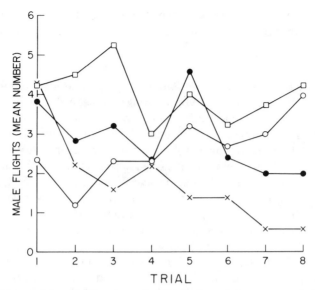

Fig. 7. Mean number of flights by male White-crowned Sparrows to playback of recorded song (means are expressed over the 10 noncontingent songs that began each trial block). ○, 1 day–same song $(n = 6)$; □, 1 day–different song $(n = 4)$; x, 8 days–same song $(n = 5)$; ●, 8 days–different song $(n = 5)$.

though the "box-score" procedure is not satisfactory, it does lend support to the presumed model.

I have selected one of the variables, male flights, for a more detailed examination. Based on the calculations from Table 2, it was predicted that the level for Group 1-D would remain constant and, as expected, no significant change occurred (Fig. 7). It was predicted that Group 1-S would show a large decrease relative to Group 8-D (Table 2), as illustrated in Figs. 3, 6, and 7. It was predicted that Group 8-S and Group 8-D would decrease in level and that the decrease would be greater for Group S (Table 2). Inspecting Figs. 5, 6, and 7 indicates that this expectation was supported. For this one variable, at least, the obtained changes conformed quite nicely to the predicted changes.

E. Further Tests of the Model

The model, as it now stands, can be evaluated further using data collected in other studies. In qualitative terms, as described earlier, Patterson and Petrinovich (1979) found that massing the rate at which trials

were presented resulted in few response decrements. This supports the
assumption that ST sensitization effects override ST habituation effects.

1. Experiment 3

The study by Petrinovich and Patterson (1981) that involved manipulation of the distribution and type of song has been described. It is not
reasonable to assign unit values to the various manipulations, because
effects of different spacings between trials cannot be determined without
studies to determine the form of such parametric manipulations. A coarse
index of a change in level was developed for each behavior by subtracting
the initial score from the final score and dividing that by the final level.
These scores were then ranked across all groups (ΣR: 1-S = 25.5, 1-M =
33, 1-S_{sp} = 16, 1-D = 25.5). A low sum of ranks indicates a low response
decrement. These ranks were analyzed using the Friedman test, and a
significant difference occurred between groups ($\chi^2 = 8.73$, $df = 3$, $p <$
.05). As expected, Group S_{sp} had the smallest decrement: Presentation of
the same song at the greatest spacing resulted in less sensitization, because the decay rate of ST sensitization occurs more quickly within a day.
The greatest response decrement occurred for Group 1-M: presentation of
the same song at the most rapid rate allowed more ST sensitization to
accumulate, because less ST sensitization dissipated between each trial.
The decrements of the other two groups (1-S and 1-D) were intermediate
between these two groups.

2. Generalization across Days

An unexpected prediction was derived using some additional data from
the Petrinovich and Patterson (1982a) study. Following presentation of
the eight trials to each of the 8-day groups, yet another trial was conducted on the ninth day. For the 8-S and 8-D Groups, a different song was
used than was used during the first eight days. Thus, the 8-S Group was
played a different song for the first time, and the 8-D Group received a
song different from any used previously. (Groups 1-S and 1-D could not
be included in this comparison, because they were not tested subsequent
to the original day.)

Using the model, it was predicted that the response level of Group 8-S
should increase on the ninth trial and that of Group 8-D should show a
slight drop. Table 4 contains the calculations for this prediction. The first
row for each group is a repeat of the Trial-8 row from Table 2. For Trial 9,
ST habituation is assumed to increase as before: two units of specific and
two of general habituation are produced. But for Group 8-S, LT habituation drops: the 14 units of LT stimulus-specific habituation are lost be-

TABLE 4

Predicted Values for Groups 8-S and 8-D When a New Song Is Presented on Day 9

| | Habituation | | | | | Sensitization | | | | | |
| | Short-term | | Long-term | | | Short-term | | Long-term | | | |
Trial	Stimulus-specific	Stimulus-general	Stimulus-specific	Stimulus-general	ΣH	Stimulus-specific	Stimulus-general	Stimulus-specific	Stimulus-general	ΣS	$\Sigma S - \Sigma H$
Group 8-S											
8	2	2	14	14	32	2	2	7	7	18	−14
9	2	2	0	14	18	2	2	0	8	12	−8
Group 8-D											
8	2	2	0	14	18	2	2	0	7	11	−7
9	2	2	0	16	20	2	2	0	8	12	−8

cause the song is different, and the LT stimulus-general habituation remains. At Trial 9, the accumulated habituation value is 20. The ST sensitization also increases by four, but only the one stimulus-general unit is added to Trial 9. The accumulated sensitization value is 12, and the ($\Sigma S - \Sigma H$) value is -8. The difference between this and the Trial 8 value of -14 leads to the prediction of an increase in response level on Trial 9. Group 8-D would accumulate units as before, and response levels should continue to decline as before: ($\Sigma S - \Sigma H$) changes from -7 to -8.

The median value was determined for Trials 8 and 9 for males of Groups 8-S and 8-D for those behaviors that were other than zero for at least one of the groups. These variables were full and partial songs, ISI, flights, distance >8 m from the speaker, and contingent time (following an initial fixed playback of the songs, the time required to emit 10 songs, each of which was answered with a playback by the experimenter). The absolute difference between Trials 8 and 9 was determined for each group. The group with the largest difference in the positive direction was ranked 1, and the other was ranked 2. A Friedman test was run and $\chi^2 = 12.2$, $df = 1$, and $p < .001$. The significant value indicates that Group 8-S increased in level (on all variables) more than did Group 8-D (which increased on only one variable). This unexpected prediction from the model was thus supported.

The model, as developed here, assumes a linear function for the initial trials. Peeke (Chapter 11, this volume) has argued that, for many species and preparations, the curve is at first positive in slope and then becomes negative. There would be no problem to accommodate a curvilinear function with this model, as I have already discussed. This could be done by modifying the rates of increment for sensitization during the early trials. A linear function was used for the early trials because there seemed to be little tendency for an initial curvilinearity in these data. The nature of the appropriate constants will have to be determined for any given preparation through some parametric exploration.

I also should point out that the model could be used with experiments in which response changes to a constant exposure of a stimulus are recorded. Instead of analyzing the data in terms of trials, the data could be analyzed in terms of time—with time bins (of any size) being used in place of trials.

F. Conclusions

The theory proposed here is post hoc—as is any theory—and it is quite complex. The complexity does not seem to be inappropriate, because the underlying reality influencing behavioral patterns and levels is complex. I believe that the theory is now specific enough to bear on the results of a large number of habituation studies. The theory is stated at a level of specificity that should make it possible to evaluate it further and to determine if it has sufficient heuristic value to develop a progressive research program (Lakatos, 1970).

Many have argued that habituation is a basic process found at all phylogenetic levels. But this need not imply that all habituation has the same properties. The relative strengths of the different components should vary with different species according to the dictates of the ecological pressures to which they have had to adapt. Some of the processes outlined might be of minor importance, or even absent, for some species and in some circumstances. For example, it might be expected that long-term, stimulus-specific sensitization would be of minor importance in organisms with simple nervous systems, but would be of major importance in species with complexly structured and interacting neural systems. The ideas developed here are stated broadly enough to include phenomena from the simplest level of behavior to such phenomena as associative learning.

There is no commitment or speculation regarding any underlying mechanisms in the views proposed here. The development is at the level of hypothetical process at a functional level of analysis. The intent is to provide a language that is useful in describing and explaining behavioral operations. This language might help to eliminate some of the ambiguity caused by a confusion between theoretical processes (e.g., habituation) and observed behavioral outcomes (e.g., response decrement). The term *habituation* often refers to a decrease in response level, and *sensitization* often refers to an increase—rather than identifying two different inferential processes. I have used the processes to refer to underlying functional dynamics that can be invoked to explain patterns and levels of responsiveness. This issue is discussed in more detail in Chapter 1 (this volume).

The adequacy of my conceptualizations will be determined by their value in stimulating research that makes it possible to understand the relative strengths and manner of interaction of the various components. The next steps in developing the research program will be determining time constants for growth and decay functions of the different components under constant experimental conditions and investigating the extent of generalization effects. This can probably be done best in a laboratory rather than in a field setting because of the time required to run a series of field experiments. Although the initial research used birds as subjects, it would be desirable to use a different class of subjects—those exhibiting many of the characteristics of habituation observed with birds. These considerations would make the three-spined stickleback a good choice for a subject species (see Chapter 11 and the numerous references to the research of Peeke and his collaborators).

A strong advantage of field experimentation will be lost in this endeavor: Much less stimulus specificity will be built into field experiments, because of ever-changing background factors. Shalter (1978a, 1978b) has demonstrated that these factors are important and are not represented in the usual laboratory situation. But, the advantages of efficiency and economy would seem to outweigh the disadvantages. When some of the precise characteristics of various elements have been identified, it should be possible to return to a species in a field setting to test crucial aspects of theory; and the important ecological factors influencing the process of natural selection could have their sway.

I have attempted to highlight some of the major trends in habituation research and theory. One of the major themes has been that the initial research focus has been on habituation, and that, as procedures become more refined, the importance of sensitization processes become more apparent. Little research has been directed toward understanding the nature of sensitization or the manner it interacts with habituation to produce behavioral outcomes. It appears that as research programs become more analytic, the dual processes of habituation and sensitization have short-term and long-term aspects and that they tend to vary in stimulus specificity. The two-factor dual-process theory I have proposed takes cognizance of these trends and attempts to organize systematically the principles found in the literature.

References

Baptista, L. F. Song dialects and demes in sedentary populations of the White-crowned Sparrow (*Zonotrichia leucophrys nuttali*). *University of California, Berkeley, Publications in Zoology*, 1975, *105*, 1–52

Brunswik, E. The conceptual framework of psychology. In *International encyclopedia of unified science* (Vol. 1). Chicago: University of Chicago Press, 1952.

Coombs, C. H. Adaptation of the Galvanic response to auditory stimuli. *Journal of Experimental Psychology*, 1938, *22*, 244–268.

Davis, M. Effects of interstimulus interval length and variability on startle-response habituation in the rat. *Journal of Comparative and Physiological Psychology*, 1970, *72*, 177–192.

Davis, M., & Wagner, A. R. Habituation of the startle response under incremental sequence of stimulus intensities. *Journal of Comparative and Physiological Psychology*, 1969, *67*, 486–492.

Davis, R. C. Modification of the Galvanic reflex by daily repetition of a stimulus. *Journal of Experimental Psychology*, 1934, *17*, 504–535.

Dodge, R. Habituation to rotation. *Journal of Experimental Psychology*, 1923, *6*, 1–35.

Duffy, E., & Lacey, O. L. Adaptation in energy mobilization changes in general level of palmar skin inductance. *Journal of Experimental Psychology*, 1946, *36*, 437–452.

Falls, J. B., & Brooks, R. J. Individual recognition by song in White-throated Sparrows. II. Effects of location. *Canadian Journal of Zoology*, 1975, *53*, 1412–1420.

Falls, J. B., & McNicholl, M. K. Neighbor–stranger discrimination by song in male Blue Grouse. *Canadian Journal of Zoology*, 1979, *57*, 457–462.

Groves, P. M., Wilson, C. J., & Miller, S. W. Habituation of the acoustic startle response: A neural systems analysis of habituation in the intact animal. In A. H. Riesen & R. F. Thompson (Eds.). *Advances in psychobiology: Vol. 3*. New York: Wiley. Pp. 327–379.

Hartshorne, C. The monotony threshold in singing birds. *Auk*, 1956, *73*, 176–192.

Hilgard, E. R. *Theories of learning*. New York: Appleton-Century-Crofts, 1948.

Hilgard, E. R. *Theories of learning* (2nd ed.). New York: Appleton-Century-Crofts, 1956.

Hilgard, E. R., & Bower, G. H. *Theories of learning* (3rd ed.). New York: Appleton-Century-Crofts, 1966.

Hilgard, E. R., & Bower, G. H. *Theories of learning* (4th ed.). New York: Appleton-Century, 1975.

Hilgard, E. R., & Marquis, D. G. *Conditioning and learning*. New York: Appleton-Century-Crofts, 1940.

Hinde, R. A. Factors governing the changes in strength of a partially inborn response, as shown by the mobbing behaviour of the Chaffinch (*Fringilla coelebs*). I. The nature of the response and an examination of its course. *Proceedings of the Royal Society of London, Series B*, 1954, *142*, 306–331. (a)

Hinde, R. A. Factors governing the changes in strength of a partially inborn response, as shown by the mobbing behaviour of the Chaffinch (*Fringilla coelebs*). II. The waning of the response. *Proceedings of the Royal Society of London, Series B*, 1954, *142*, 331–358. (b)

Hinde, R. A. Factors governing the changes in strength of a partially inborn response, as shown by the mobbing behaviour of the Chaffinch (*Fringilla coelebs*). III. The interaction of short-term and long-term incremental and decremental effects. *Proceedings of the Royal Society of London, Series B*, 1961, *153*, 398–420.

Hinde, R. A. Behavioural habituation. In G. Horne & R. A. Hinde (Eds.), *Short-term changes in neural activity and behaviour*. London & New York: Cambridge University Press, 1970, Pp. 3–40.

Hull, C. L. *Principles of behavior*. New York: Appleton-Century-Crofts, 1943.

Hull, C. L. *A behavior system*. New Haven, Conn.: Yale University Press, 1952.

Humphrey, G. *The nature of learning*. London: Kegan Paul, Trench, Trubner, 1933.

Kandel, E. R. *Behavioral biology of Aplysia*. San Francisco: Freeman, 1979.

Kimble, G. A. *Hilgard and Marquis' conditioning and learning* (2nd ed.). New York: Appleton, 1961.

Lakatos, I. Falsification and the methodology of scientific research programmes. In I. Lakatos & A. Musgrave (Eds.), *Criticism and the growth of knowledge*. London & New York: Cambridge University Press, 1970. Pp. 91–196.

Marascuilo, L. A., & McSweeney, M. *Nonparametric and distribution-free methods for the social sciences*. Monterey, Calif.: Brooks/Cole, 1977.

Osgood, C. E. *Method and theory in experimental psychology*. London & New York: Oxford University Press, 1953.

Patterson, T., & Petrinovich, L. Field studies of habituation. II. Effect of massed presentation. *Journal of Comparative and Physiological Psychology*, 1979, *93*, 351–359.

Peeke, H. V. S. Habituation of conspecific aggression in the three-spined stickleback (*Gasterosteus aculeatus* L.). *Behaviour*, 1969, *35*, 137–156.

Peeke, H. V. S. Stimulus- and motivation-specific sensitization and the redirection of aggression in the three-spined stickleback (*Gasterosteus aculeatus* L.). *Journal of Comparative and Physiological Psychology,* 1982, *96,* 816–822.

Peeke, H. V. S. Habituation, sensitization and redirection of aggression and feeding behavior in the three-spined stickleback (*Gasterosteus aculeatus* L.). *Journal of Comparative Psychology,* 1983, *97,* 43–51.

Peeke, H. V. S., Avis, H. H., & Peeke, S. Motivational variables and the sensitization and habituation of aggression in the convict cichlid (*Cichlasoma nigrofasciatum*). *Zeitschrift für Tierpsychologie,* 1979, *51,* 363–379.

Peeke, H. V. S., Figler, M. H., & Blankenship, N. Retention and recovery of habituated territorial aggressive behavior in the three-spined stickleback (*Gasterosteus aculeatus* L.): The roles of time and nest reconstruction. *Behaviour,* 1979, *69,* 171–182.

Peeke, H. V. S., Herz, M. J., & Gallagher, J. E. Changes in aggressive interaction in adjacently territorial convict cichlids (*Cichlasoma nigrofasciatus*): A study of habituation. *Behaviour,* 1971, *40,* 43–54.

Peeke, H. V. S., & Peeke, S. C. Habituation, reinstatement and recovery of predatory responses in two species of teleosts, *Carassius auratus* and *Macropodus opercularis.* *Animal Behaviour,* 1972, *20,* 268–273.

Peeke, H. V. S., & Peeke, S. Parental factors in the sensitisation and habituation of territorial aggression in the convict cichlid (*Cichlasoma nigrofasciatum*). *Journal of Comparative and Physiological Psychology* 1982, *96,* 955–966.

Peeke, H. V. S., & Veno, A. Stimulus specificity of habituated aggression in the stickleback (*Gasterosteus aculeatus*). *Behavioral Biology,* 1973, *8,* 427–432.

Petrinovich, L. Probabilistic functionalism: A conception of research method. *American Psychologist,* 1979, *34,* 373–390.

Petrinovich, L. Field studies of habituation. VI. Dishabituation. *Journal of Comparative Psychology,* in press.

Petrinovich, L., & Patterson, T. L. Field studies of habituation. I. Effect of reproductive condition, number of trials, and different delay intervals on responses of the White-crowned Sparrow. *Journal of Comparative and Physiological Psychology,* 1979, *93,* 337–350.

Petrinovich, L., & Patterson, T. L. Field studies of habituation. IV. Sensitization as a function of the distribution and novelty of song playback to White-crowned Sparrows. *Journal of Comparative and Physiological Psychology,* 1981, *95,* 805–812.

Petrinovich, L., & Patterson, T. L. Field studies of habituation. V. Evidence for a two-factor, dual-process system. *Journal of Comparative and Physiological Psychology,* 1982, *96,* 284–296. (a)

Petrinovich, L., & Patterson, T. L. The White-crowned Sparrow: Stability, recruitment, and population structure in the Nuttall subspecies (1975–1980). *Auk,* 1982, *99,* 1–14. (b)

Petrinovich, L., & Patterson, T. L. The White-crowned Sparrow: Ecology and reproductive success (1975–1980). *Auk,* in press.

Porter, J. M., Jr. Adaptation of the galvanic skin response. *Journal of Experimental Psychology,* 1938, *23,* 553–557.

Prosser, C. L., & Hunter, W. S. The extinction of startle responses and spinal reflexes in the white rat. *American Journal of Psychology,* 1936, *117,* 609–618.

Seward, J. P., & Seward, G. H. The effect of repetition on reactions to electric shock: With special reference to the menstrual cycle. *Archives of Psychology, New York,* 1934, *168,* 1–103.

Shalter, M. D. Location of passerine seet and mobbing calls by Goshawks and Pygmy Owls. *Zeitschrift für Tierpsychologie,* 1978, *46,* 260–267. (a)

Shalter, M. D. Mobbing in the pied flycatcher. Effect of experiencing a live owl on responses to a stuffed facsimile. *Zeitschrift für Tierpsychologie,* 1978, *47,* 173–179. (b)

Sherrington, C. S. *The integrative action of the nervous system.* New Haven, Conn.: Yale University Press, 1906.

Sokolov, E. N. *Perception and the conditioned reflex.* Oxford: Pergamon, 1963.

Stevens, S. S. (Ed.). *Handbook of experimental psychology.* New York: Wiley, 1951.

Thompson, R. F., Groves, P. M., Teyler, T. J., & Roemer, R. H. A dual-process theory of habituation: Theory and behavior. In H. V. S. Peeke & M. J. Herz (Eds.), *Habituation* (Vol. 1). New York: Academic Press, 1973. Pp. 239–271.

Thompson, R. F., & Spencer, W. A. Habituation: A model phenomenon for the study of neuronal substrates of behavior. *Psychological Review,* 1966, *173,* 16–43.

Thorpe, W. H. *Learning and instinct in animals.* London: Methuen, 1956.

Thorpe, W. H. *Learning and instinct in animals* (2nd ed.). London: Methuen, 1963.

Underwood, B. J. *Experimental psychology* (2nd ed.). Appleton-Century-Crofts, 1966.

Wagner, A. R. Priming in STM: An information-processing mechanism for self-generated or retrieval-generated depression in performance. In T. J. Tighe & R. N. Leaton (Eds.) *Habituation.* Hillsdale, N. J.: Lawrence Erlbaum Associates, 1976. Pp. 95–128.

Woodworth, R. S. *Experimental psychology.* New York: Holt, Rinehart & Winston, 1938.

Woodworth, R. S., & Schlosberg, H. *Experimental psychology* (2nd ed.). New York: Holt, Rinehart & Winston, 1954.

CHAPTER 3

A Theory of the Mechanism of Habituation: The Assignment of Responses to Stimuli

Michel Treisman

Department of Experimental Psychology
University of Oxford
Oxford, England

I. Introduction

The conditions determining natural selection of behavior can account for major features of habituation (see Chapter 12). But the appreciation that waning in the response to an invariant signal may be understood as the mode of reaction that has been most strongly favored by selection still leaves us with the problem of identifying the nature of the mechanisms that produce this behavior. The physiological basis of habituation is not

This chapter was written while in receipt of support from the Medical Research Council of Great Britain.

57

HABITUATION, SENSITIZATION,
AND BEHAVIOR

necessarily the same in different species or even for different responses (Sharpless & Jasper, 1956). Common evolutionary pressures may ensure behavioral convergence, but this may be achieved through different physiological mechanisms. But even so, there are so many features, even minor ones, of habituation in different species that are so similar that it is tempting to suspect that, at least in animals with complex nervous systems, similar principles of biological design are involved. This chapter puts forward a model for a basic component of systems determining responses. The model is described at an abstract level and could be embodied in nervous systems of differing structures. It will be argued that the way this component responds to repeated stimuli may explain some major and minor features of habituation, and may also account for certain other observations on performance not usually considered under the rubric of habituation.

The main features of habituation have been frequently listed and described (e.g., Hinde, 1970; Humphrey, 1933; Petrinovich, 1973; Thompson & Spencer, 1966; Thorpe, 1963; Wyers, Peeke, & Herz, 1973). Among properties that must be encompassed by any explanation are the relatively permanent reductions in frequency and magnitude of response that form the primary observation, spontaneous recovery, dishabituation, sensitization, the pattern of disappearance of the components of a response sequence, the intrusion of novel responses, habituation below zero, stimulus specificity, the increased speed of rehabituation, and the effect of the interval between trials.

A number of attempts have been made to account for habituation by proposing neural models (Gray, 1975; Groves & Thompson, 1973; Horn, 1967; Pakula & Sokolov, 1973; Sokolov, 1960, 1963). These models are elaborations of the idea of a reflex arc linking stimulus and response. Such models may attribute the cessation of responses to depression of conduction at a synapse or to inhibitory processes. And the models add special assumptions to account for features that are thought surprising, such as dishabituation in response to reduction in the intensity of a regular stimulus or even its omission. These models will not be discussed here [see Gray (1975) for a review].

Let us consider the problem of coordinating effectors in an evolutionary perspective. Most response systems have undergone changes in their application in the course of evolution. Muscles that control respiration evolved in creatures that had no lungs, and those that control the ossicles of the middle ear were once concerned with mastication. Mechanisms that originally evolved to produce independent and unrelated responses may have been brought by evolution into opposition to one another. In the living animal, relations between response systems may change from one time to another. Muscles that are antagonists in walking may act as synergists to maintain a stationary posture. Effectors may require coordination for one response but not for another. Approaching or retreating from a novel stimulus may require an opposite use of locomotors but similar adjustments of the autonomic system. Thus we may regard the organism as in part composed of a republic of primary effectors (von Uexküll, 1934/1957), which must be coordinated in different ways for different purposes (Treisman, 1984).

In part, we may attribute those effectors active at a given time to selection by the stimulus input, but this is obviously an insufficient account. The same stimuli may evoke approach or avoidance—eating at one stage of a meal and withdrawal at a later stage. Thus under the right conditions, these stimuli may activate opposite effectors. In trying to understand these complex relations, the analogy of the reflex arc may be unhelpful and even misleading. I suggest instead that we need to consider separately the perceptual system possessed by a given species, the effectors that may be activated by it, and the decision mechanisms that must choose between potential responses. These general distinctions supply a basis for analyzing the different physiological embodiments that may be employed by different species.

Two main points emerge from these distinctions. The first is that any discrimination a perceptual system can make, it can use to select or modify a response. The nature of the limits on such discriminations is a problem properly assigned to the study of perception. If we group together a particular discrimination (such as detection of a decrease in the intensity of a stimulus) and a performance modification (such as an increase in response magnitude) and consider this combination to be a single and unique phenomenon that can only be explained by a correspondingly elaborated reflex arc, this is likely to be more confusing than helpful.

The second point is that to explain the phenomena of habituation we need to understand the nature of the coordinative system or decision mechanism that arbitrates between opposing response tendencies. Even if the observed responses appear to lie along a single continuum, as from bradycardia to tachycardia, the actual response made may arise as a compromise between the outputs of different competing and opposed effectors. For the present analysis I shall consider only the simplest possible arrangement, in which two tendencies are in opposition, and a choice must be made between them by a decision unit. A theory of such a system will be put forward, and predictions will be derived from it.

II. The Primary-Comparator Model

Hering's (1905/1964) concept of opponent-color processes has proved an enormously productive insight and provides an antecedent for the present model. Applied to color vision, this theory envisages that the relative activation of opposite receptors, such as green- and red-sensitive cones, determines a graded output on a dimension representing variation between green and red. There is evidence that such mechanisms exist in the afferent visual system, but we have no detailed understanding of how they work (Boynton, 1979; Hurvich & Jameson, 1974; Judd, 1951). Another important antecedent is Sherrington's (1906/1947) concept that reflexes express the action of different afferent arcs in competition for a final common path, a pioneering insight whose implications have not yet been adequately developed. Clynes' (1961, 1969) concept of "rein control" of physiological functions—that is, control by two separate channels, one sensitive to the rate of change of an independent variable in one direction and the other to its change in the opposite direction—is also relevant.

The basic principles of the theory to be presented are, first, that the components of the system determining behavior are best regarded not primarily as pathways or connections but as decision points; and the functioning of these decision points is biassed by past experience and current influences. Second, such points are not connected one-to-one (except in the most extreme cases), but more diffusely; and many features of behavior may arise from processes that tend to reduce this diffuseness, making the connections more specialized and sharply defined. Third, a behavioral system may consist of many such decision points connected in a variety of ways. In the present treatment, however, it will usually be sufficient to consider the single decision point that may be decisive in determining a selection between particular alternative responses. This decision point will be referred to as a primary-comparator system *PC*. The organism is assumed to embody many such systems, corresponding to pairs of alternatives it must habitually choose between.

The primary-comparator model of response selection is concerned with three types of systems and their relations: the perceptual system, the primary-comparator systems—which are responsible for selecting responses—and the response system—which produces them. We do not need to discuss the last system here. The structure of a primary-comparator system and its relations to other components of the model are illustrated in Fig. 1. The assumptions that prescribe the workings of this model follow. (See the Appendix to this chapter for a glossary of symbols.)

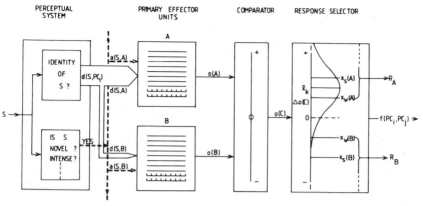

Fig. 1. Primary-comparator model: a schematic diagram of the stages underlying the production of a response to a stimulus S. This model comprises three systems: the perceptual system, the primary-comparator system, and the response-organization system, of which the first two are illustrated in the figure. The perceptual system is shown on the left and the primary-comparator system (two primary units, comparator, and response selector) on the right. The identification subsystem of the perceptual system (shown as the box asking "Identity of S?") produces outputs dependent on the identity of S, $d(S,A)$ and $d(S,B)$. In the present case the first is larger and excites primary-effector unit A (PU_A) more strongly then PU_B, as indicated by the broad arrow to PU_A and the narrow arrow to PU_B. If S is novel or intense or has certain other such properties, the activation subsystem (the box asking "Is S novel? . . .") directs activation signals $a(S,A)$ and $a(S,B)$ (the dashed lines) to the primary units (PU_A and PU_B), where they reduce the level of excitation. The primary-effector units A and B send outputs $o(A)$ and $o(B)$ to the comparator. This computes their algebraic sum $o(C)$ and relays this output to the response-selector system. The latter looks for any rapid change in $o(C)$, $\Delta o(C)$, and compares it with response criteria to select a response. The varying magnitude of $\Delta o(C)$ is represented as a normal distribution on the decision axis x, as noise will cause it to change from time to time under nominally constant conditions. The expected value of $\Delta o(C)$ on trial k is shown as $\bar{x}_k$, and criteria are shown $[x_s(A), x_w(A), x_w(B), x_s(B)]$ that allow the selection of weak or strong A or B responses. A given primary-comparator system PC_i may also transmit a function of $\Delta o(C)$ as a forward message $f(PC_i, PC_j)$ to primary-comparator system j or a similar positive feedback message to itself.

A. Perceptual System

Assumption 1. The perceptual system analyzes the input from stimulus S. For our purpose, perception can be regarded as the assignment to an input of values on certain sensory and perceptual dimensions of importance to the species. These dimensions fall into two groups. The first group relates to the identification of the stimulus; for example, such dimensions may specify its color, shape, or position. The second group records certain features of special importance to the animal, such as high intensity or deviations from past experience. In Fig. 1 we represent these types of analyses for convenience as separate components of the perceptual system; these components will be referred to as the identification and activation subsystems. The outputs from these two subsystems constitute the inputs to the primary effector units. (The figure should not be taken to imply that they necessarily function in parallel.)

Assumption 2. The identification subsystem (which is shown in Fig. 1 as a box enclosing the question "Identity of S?") gives rise to an output to the next stage, which will be referred to as an identity message. The message is labeled $d(S,PC_i)$, indicating that it is a discriminatory message elicited by stimulus S and directed to the primary-comparator system that is appropriate to that stimulus, PC_i. S is biologically appropriate to PC_i if PC_i controls responses that should be excited or suppressed when S occurs. S may cause more or less strong identity messages to be sent to a range of primary-comparator systems to which it is more or less appropriate.

Assumption 3. The activation subsystem is represented by a box asking, "Is S novel? Intense? . . ." If the answer is positive, it gives rise to an activation message $a(S,PC_i)$.

A number of different features of a stimulus may cause the activation perceptual subsystem to emit activation messages. These features will usually include

1. *Unexpectedness or unfamiliarity of the stimulus*. An activation message of this sort $[a_u(S,PC_i)]$ is produced if novel information is extracted from the stimulus. It will be large in magnitude when the stimulus is highly unexpected and will be less if the stimulus has become familiar. Its magnitude is a function of the improbability of the stimulus. If a new stimulus is presented repeatedly, the activation produced may not decline immediately: when the stimulus is first experienced, it was not expected and so the animal may not be well positioned to extract information from it. On the next trial the animal may be better prepared and so may gain further novel information. Thus $a_u(S,PC_i)$ may be maintained or may increase in size over the first few trials; but eventually it will decline to zero as all aspects of the stimulus become familiar. If at any time there is a perceptible change in the stimulus, however, its effective novelty will increase, and $a_u(S,PC_i)$ will become larger again.

2. *A stimulus of high intensity* will produce a similar activation message $a_i(S,PC_i)$ on each presentation of that intensity.

3. *Relevance for priming*. A stimulus S may give rise to an identity message directed to the primary-comparator system PC_i and related PCs that control responses that S should excite or suppress. For example, S

may be the sight of prey and PC_i may control hunting. But S may also be relevant to the readiness for action of a system PC_r, although the responses controlled by PC_r are not immediately excited by S. Thus PC_r might control consummatory eating responses. Then the activation subsystem may also direct a priming activation message $a_p(S,PC_r)$ to the system PC_r. Such a message may bias PC_r if the internal tuning of PC_r to $a_p(S,PC_r)$ is sharp ("tuning" is defined later). That is, the message will produce greater activation of one of the primary effector units in PC_r than of the other.

4. *Instructional relevance.* Depending on the species, yet other perceptual or cognitive mechanisms may cause activating messages to be produced. In the human an instruction to attend to the stimulus might have this effect. Activation in the present sense would be one of the mechanisms underlying the phenomena usually grouped together as "attention."

B. Primary-Comparator System

Assumption 4.   A PC is the decision mechanism determining choice between a particular pair of responses. It consists of two primary effector units (shown in Fig. 1 as PU_A and PU_B), a comparator, and a response selector. It accepts inputs from the perceptual system or from higher order PCs and transmits directive outputs to the system responsible for response organization, to lower-order PCs, or as feedback to its own PUs.

Assumption 5.   A PU mediates between perception and later components of the decision stage; it receives inputs from the perceptual system or higher-order PCs and initiates an output that may result in the selection of a corresponding response. Two PUs, PU_A and PU_B, are illustrated in Fig. 1. An output message from PU_A,$o(A)$ will bias the decision toward evoking the response R_A. An output message from PU_B will tend to evoke the opposed response R_B.

Assumption 6.   A primary-comparator system is tuned to a range of perceptual inputs. That is, it may receive and respond to messages generated by more than one stimulus. The PC is narrowly tuned for identity inputs: it may respond best to a given size, shape, and color of object; and its response will fall off sharply as these features depart from the required values. If PC_i is best tuned to stimulus S_m, then the identity message $d(S_m,PC_i)$ will be significantly greater than those PC_i receives from similar stimuli, such as $d(S_{m+1},PC_i)$. Conversely, the identity outputs generated by a given stimulus are directed preferentially to one or a few PCs, but lesser outputs may also be transmitted to other PCs. The major identity message evoked by S_m may be $d(S_m, PC_i)$, but lesser messages $d(S_m, PC_j)$, etc. may also be emitted.

These relations constitute the external tuning of the PC to perceptual system messages. This must be distinguished from the relative response of the two PUs in a PC to a given perceptual message, which will be referred to as the internal tuning of that PC. If the internal tuning to a perceptual message is sharp, then $d(S_m, PU_{Ai}) \gg d(S_m, PU_{Bi})$, for example. But if the PUs are broadly tuned, each will be similarly affected by a given identity message; and if they are equally tuned to S_m, then $d(S_m, PC_{Ai}) = d(S_m, PC_{Bi})$.

Assumption 7. PCs also receive activation messages and are usually broadly tuned to them externally and internally. That is, they accept activation messages of similar strength from a wide range of stimuli. Conversely, a given stimulus may transmit similar activation messages to a wide range of PCs: $a(S_m, PC_i) \simeq a(S_m, PC_j)$. . . . The internal tuning of PCs to activation messages is also usually broad, that is, $a(S_m, PU_{Ai}) \simeq a(S_m, PU_{Bi})$.

Assumption 8. The identity message from a source S to a receiver PC or to one of its primary effector units (say PU_A) $d(S, PC)$ or $d(S, A)$ may be written for brevity as d_{PC} or d_A when the source is known. Similarly, the activation messages $a(S, PC)$ and $a(S, A)$ may be written a_{PC} or a_A. We assume that when a message d_{PC} divides between PU_A and PU_B it does so by duplication: $d_A = d_{PC}$ and $d_B \leq d_{PC}$, or the reverse. Then the strength of the stimulus is represented by the magnitude of d_{PC}, and the breadth of the internal tuning may be measured by the ratio $\min(d_A, d_B)/\max(d_A, d_B)$. A low value will indicate narrow tuning.

In Fig. 1 the internal tuning to the identification message from S is sharp. This is represented by a broad arrow to PU_A for $d(S, A)$ and a narrow arrow to PU_B for $d(S, B)$. The ratio $d(S, B)/d(S, A)$ would be low. The activation messages to the two primary units are represented by dashed lines of the same width: $a(S, B)/a(S, A) = 1$, indicating very broad internal tuning of PC_i to the activation message from S.

An identity message directed to PC_i may cause it to produce an output. An activation message will alter its responsiveness to identity messages.

Assumption 9. The performance of a primary unit is determined by its internal level of activity. This may be more or less stable at a fixed value, but may be reset to a different value. This "level of activity" could be realized by a number of mechanisms. In the simplest and perhaps the most likely embodiment, a primary unit would correspond to a single neuron with a maintained spontaneous firing rate that could be reset at different levels. A quantitative account of the model may be developed however, in a simple way if we suppose the primary unit to consist of a bundle of n nerve fibers, some of which are active and some quiescent. Then the magnitude of an identity message d represents a probability of causing excitation of a randomly selected fiber in the primary unit; thus an identity message will excite a proportion d of the previously silent fibers. In Fig. 1 PU_A is strongly tuned to S and PU_B weakly tuned to S. Presentation of S excites a proportion $d(S,A)$ of the currently inactive fibers in PU_A, and a proportion $d(S,B)$ in PU_B, with $d(S,A) > d(S,B)$.

An activation message produces its effect by terminating firing in a proportion a of previously active fibers. Thus $0 \le a,d \le 1$.

Assumption 10. If stimulus S generates activation and identity messages directed to primary unit X, then $a(S,X)$ will act on PU_X before the arrival of $d(S,X)$.

Assumption 11. When the primary unit is in its resting state, a proportion e_0 of the fibers are excited at any time. This will be referred to as the preset noise level. This resting level of excitation reflects the resultant effect of various sources of noise that may affect all or some of the primary units. Because the preset noise level is an important determinant of the magnitude of response to an input, its value cannot be left wholly to random factors. We assume that its sources include mechanisms designed to maintain their contribution to the PU's excitation at a preferred level. Thus e_0 is a parameter of a PU, as is the number of fibers n.

In Fig. 1, $n_A = n_B = n = 10$, and $e_0(A) = e_0(B) = 0.2$; 2 of the 10 fibers are shown to be active in each unit.

Modulation of the preset noise level e_0 and activation provide two ways of modifying the responsiveness of a primary unit. The former produces mainly long-term effects and the latter short-term effects.

Assumption 12. Excitation of a fiber constitutes a memory mechanism: it preserves the impact of a previous input. The fibers excited by an input will vary in their responses. Some are made active for a short time and revert to inactivity, but others become stably excited—that is, they continue in this state for a significant period. Thus a proportion e of the fibers that are inactive prior to the arrival of the identity message becomes stably excited, with $0 \le e \le d \le 1$ (d is the proportion of inactive fibers initially excited by the identity message). If the interstimulus intervals (ISIs) are short, e will be high; if they are long, e will be low; if they are sufficiently long, e will be zero. The effect of fibers still active after previous excitations summates with the preset noise level e_0 to give what will be referred to as the total residual noise.

Assumption 13. The relation between e and the ISI has been presented as given. A number of mechanisms could be suggested that would generate this relation, but we do not wish to tie the model to any of these.

However, one possible mechanism will be noted here as an auxiliary assumption. We suppose that when a fiber is stimulated and becomes active, the subsequent period comprises two stages. If it is restimulated in the first, or "blocking," stage, this will prevent the fiber converting to a state of stable excitation. If it is restimulated in the second, or "critical," stage, this may cause the fiber to convert to a state of stable excitation in which it will continue firing indefinitely, with some probability of returning to the inactive state at any moment.

Fibers vary in their properties. For simplicity we assume two classes. "Short-duration" or transient fibers respond to a single stimulus by firing for a brief period only—the blocking stage and the critical stage are short—and if a fiber is restimulated in the critical interval and converts to the stable state, the momentary probability of reverting to inactivity is high and so stable firing may not last long. "Long-duration" or sustained fibers maintain the initial response to a single stimulus for a longer period—the blocking and critical stages are longer—and if the fiber converts to the stable state the momentary probability of reverting to inactivity is low and so it will continue firing stably for a longer time.

On this assumption, of the fibers stimulated on one trial, a proportion will be restimulated while in their critical periods by the stimulus presented on the next trial. These fibers will become stably excited and this will determine e. If ISIs are short, a second stimulus will find many fibers still active from the preceding stimulus, and so the number that may be restimulated in the critical period will be high, giving a high value of e. These will be largely short-duration fibers, since many long-duration fibers will be in their initial blocking stages, and restimulation will not cause them to become stably excited. If ISIs are long, a second stimulus will find fewer fibers still active, but these will be largely long-duration fibers in their critical periods. So e will be low and the fibers recruited to stability largely long-duration fibers.

Because each identity message randomly selects the PU fibers it excites, for constant stimulus intensity and constant ISI e will tend to be constant. An exception is the first trial; the first stimulus is unlikely to find fibers in their critical periods.

These assumptions will have the following consequence. If a series of stimuli is presented rapidly, the level of residual firing during the series may be large. But if the series is then interrupted for a period, because a high proportion of the residual firing is contributed by short-duration fibers, it will drop off rapidly during the interruption. But if the initial stimuli were presented at long ISIs, the residual activity will be caused by long-duration fibers with greater expected durations of stability—and so more of the residual activity will be maintained across an intermission.

Assumption 14. The output from a primary unit at any time is constituted by the summed firing of all its fibers. The outputs from the two primary units in a primary comparator system, $o(A)$ and $o(B)$ in Fig. 1, are delivered continually to a comparator that assigns them opposite signs and records their algebraic sum. This sum constitutes its own output $o(C)$.

Assumption 15. Responses may be determined in two ways:

1. *Level-sensitive determination.* The level of the output $o(C)$ may continually determine the level of a correlated variable, such as blood pressure or heart rate. A measure of this variable constitutes the response, and it will directly reflect any gradual or sudden change in $o(C)$.

2. *Rate-sensitive determination.* In this case a response is determined by any sufficiently large and sudden change in $o(C)$, but not by drift in its resting level. The output from the comparator is transmitted to the response selector. This records any change in the magnitude of $o(C)$ during a short critical period t_c, and if this rate of change is sufficient, the direction of this change will determine a corresponding response.

Let stimulus S be administered on trial k. Prior to the receipt of the identity inputs $d(S,A)$ and $d(S,B)$ by the primary units, the output from the comparator has the background level $o_{k,0}(C)$. When the stimulus transmits identity messages to the primary units, their outputs are altered, and consequently the output of the comparator changes to a final value for the trial $o_k(C)$. The shift in comparator output may be represented as

$$x_k = \Delta o_k(C) = o_k(C) - o_{k,0}(C). \tag{1}$$

This shift is recorded by the response selector as the value x_k, a value on a decision axis x. Because of noise arising from various sources in the system, the value of x_k will vary for trials under nominally constant conditions. For this reason the effect of the stimulus is represented in the figure by a probability density distribution, taken to be normal, with mean $\bar{x}_k$. The effect of x_k will depend on whether responses are continuous or discrete. Thus the magnitude of x_k may determine the amplitude of a continuously variable rate-sensitive response evoked by S; for example, the extent of an approach toward (for $x_k > 0$) or retreat away from (for $x_k < 0$) the stimulus. For discrete responses, x_k may be compared with criteria that allow a choice between a small number of responses. For example, there may be two possible responses, R_A and R_B. If x_k is greater than a criterion $x(A)$, the response R_A may be produced. If $x_k < x(B)$, the response R_B is produced. If $x(B) \le x_k < x(A)$, no response ensues.

Figure 1 illustrates the case in which the response in each direction may occur at two strengths: for example, strong (R_{As}) and weak (R_{Aw}) responses; and there are two criteria for each direction of response to allow a choice between the two response strengths. If $x_k \geq x_s(A)$, the response is R_{As}; if $x_w(A) \leq x_k < x_s(A)$, the response is R_{Aw}; if $x_w(B) \leq x_k < x_w(A)$, no response is made, and so on.

Note that a single stimulus may simultaneously produce both level- and rate-sensitive responses: continuous variations correlated with $o(C)$ and continuous or discrete responses determined by $\Delta o(C)$.

Assumption 16. Primary-comparator System i may transmit a forward message $f(PC_i, PC_j)$ to another such system, PC_j. The magnitude of the forward message to a primary unit in PC_j, say A_j, is given by

$$f(PC_i, A_j) = k_{fA}|\Delta o(C)|, \tag{2}$$

where k_{fA} is a scaling factor. This factor is necessary to ensure that $0 \leq f(PC_i, A_j) \leq 1$, because any input message to a PU may be regarded as a probability of effecting a change in a fiber. A similar expression applies for PU_{Bj}. Forward messages are processed by PCs in the same way as identity messages.

The tuning of PC_j to the forward message from PC_i depends on the sign of $\Delta o(C)$. If this is positive, $f(PC_i, A_j)$ is greater than $f(PC_i, B_j)$. If $\Delta o(C)$ is negative, this relation is reversed. The sign of $\Delta o(C)$ may also determine whether, for example, the forward message goes to PC_j or PC_k.

These assumptions allow a set of responses to be emitted in sequence, controlled, for example, by PC_i and then PC_j, the magnitude of each successive response depending on that of the original identity inputs $d(S, A_i)$ and $d(S, B_i)$. This is sufficient for a ballistic sequence. But for some behaviors it will be inappropriate for a later response in the sequence to occur in the absence of a specific releasing stimulus. To cover this we add the assumption that such a stimulus gates the transmission of the forward message at that stage. (These assumptions may be compared with the system put forward by Deutsch in 1960.)

These assumptions tell us that if a hypothetical spider receives strong evidence—a highly active vibration—that prey has landed in its web, not only its initial orientation movement but also its subsequent run toward the prey will be forceful, even though the stimulus releasing the latter (which might be evidence that one radius is vibrating discriminably more actively than its neighbors) might be weak (because of widespread radiation of the vibration).

An alternative mechanism for behavior in which each response has its own releasing stimulus is that the forward message might take the form of an activation-priming input from one PC to the next, $a_p(PC_i, PC_j)$. This would suppress noise in PC_j and thus potentiate its response when it receives an identity message from its own releasing stimulus. This alternative is not explored here.

Assumption 17. Under some circumstances the response that ought to follow R_A is a repetition of R_A. That is, a repeated action of the PC that produced R_A is required. Successful behavior may require that a transient stimulus initiate a maintained course of action, as when a predator pursues prey although the latter is only intermittently visible through the undergrowth. This need is met by converting the forward message into a positive feedback message, $f_b(PC_i,PC_i)$. For certain PCs under defined conditions, cessation of an input from S will be followed by the substitution of the alternative input $f_b(PC_i,PC_i)$.

The initial feedback input is scaled to be equal in magnitude to the last value of $d(S,PC_i)$ received from the perceptual system. This sets the values of k_{fA} and k_{fB}. This initial feedback will act on PC_i to produce a new output $\Delta o(C)$; this in turn determines a new feedback input, given by Eq. (2) with $j = i$ and the same scaling factor and so a cycle of comparator outputs and feedback inputs will continue until the successive values of $\Delta o(C)$ become negligible.

Primary-comparator systems control behavior ranging from individual acts to choices between major sequences, such as hunting for food rather than seeking water. When the behavior is simple, that is, the required continuation of it is predictable, the feedback can be directed primarily to the corresponding PU. An example is the phenomenon of after-discharge in the flexion reflex of the spinal dog: this reflex may reach its maximum amplitude after the stimulus has ended, and it may continue for more than 5 seconds following the stimulus, the after-discharge often showing a marked clonus (Sherrington, 1906/1947). Whatever the neural mechanisms that produce this after-discharge, they have the effect that the flexion continues to be produced as though an internally generated input has been substituted for the input initially provided by the stimulus. The clonus is consistent with a feedback mechanism.

When behavior is complex it may be far more difficult to predict what response sequence should follow when the stimulus input ceases. Continuing the response requires an element of choice. Feedback may replace the missing stimulus, but the feedback does not contain independent information about the current state of the world, and so it would be arbitrary to distribute the feedback between PU_A and PU_B according to a fixed rule, for example, in the same proportions as the original identity message. The alternative is to let PC_i be broadly tuned to its own positive feedback: $f_b(PC_i,A_i) = f_b(PC_j,B_i)$. Whether this results in repetition of R_A or substitution of R_B will then be determined by biases imposed on PC_i by its own previous activity and other mechanisms recently or currently active. Under some conditions (e.g., when the prey normally flees in a straight line even if it is invisible for part of the time) it may be best to follow R_A (pursuit) with R_A (further pursuit). Under others (e.g., when the prey is inclined to zigzag or double back) it may be better to substitute R_B (casting around). When prey is encountered and lost from sight, either response may be of some value: persistence in seeking prey by whatever method is more likely to be advantageous at this time than a switch to some different motivational system. The mechanism ensuring the required persistence is the positive feedback message.

These assumptions ensure that a feedback message may maintain the effect of an input stimulus after it has ceased. It may also sometimes be desirable to use feedback to augment the effect of a stimulus that is present. This will ensure that a weak or sporadic stimulus, yet one indicating a valuable goal not easily found by searching, is adequately exploited when encountered. One example might be the consumption of salt (and one consequence, the "salted-peanuts phenomenon"); another example, in some species, might be indications of the presence of a sexual partner.

Assumption 18. Thus far, we have mainly described the properties of a single PC system. A natural extension is to suppose that such systems are organized in hierarchies or networks. Thus the sight of a possible predator may cause PC_i to select the high-order output "respond to possible danger" rather than "continue feeding." This output may be the input to PC_j, which chooses flight rather than freezing. If PC_j selects flight, its output may go to further PCs that determine choices of direction, extent of movement, and so on.

Assumption 19. Some PCs may be affected by nonperceptual sources, such as hormones or other blood constituents. Consider PC_f, which chooses between a commitment to food-seeking (mediated by PU_F), or a null output(PU_N), which effectively allows other drives to dominate behavior. If changes in the constitution of the blood following fasting can reduce e_0 in PU_F, thus activating it, and so producing a relatively long-term increase in a bias toward food-seeking and increasing the responsiveness of PC_f to even minor food stimuli, then PC_f will constitute a mechanism of "drive" or "motivation."

Note that the present model does not require drive to be centralized in a single primary location. Metabolic consequences of food deprivation may produce a high-level commitment to the behaviors involved in food-seeking by increasing the responsiveness of PC_f. But they can also reduce e_0 in peripheral PUs concerned with narrowly defined actions that may be involved in food acquisition. For example, a fall in blood nutrients might act directly on the *PC*, which may produce a snapping movement in response to stimulation of the lips, increasing the likelihood of that response. Thus "drive" may be thought of as a change in state distributed in various patterns among different *PC*s concerned with a behavioral system. For a more extended discussion of this point, see Treisman (1984).

C. A Summary of the Primary-Comparator Model

There is a long-established bias to think of the nervous system as consisting primarily of one-to-one connections, and to suppose that simple behavior is mediated by precise connections of this sort. Habituation has then to be explained by special processes occurring at synapses in such paths or in elaborated versions of these pathways. But an organism prewired with just one output for each input would be suitable for a single, invariant environment only. It would have difficulty in adjusting to changes requiring new relations between inputs and outputs and would do poorly in the real world.

In contrast to this, a striking feature of nervous organization is the richness of branching of axons and dendrites—the many synaptic connections that a nerve cell may make. The present account is based on this feature. It assumes that neural connectivity is normally rich and diffuse, one-to-one connections being a rare specialization, and attempts to model an organization with diffuse connectivity, affording many-to-many connections. This offers potentialities for matching outputs to inputs in novel or changing ways, as required to adapt to a variable environment. But it carries the cost that mechanisms are required that can choose between the options and realize them. Although there may be direct or indirect connections that would mediate the behavior required in a particular situation, often these will not be active or will be dominated by other connections mediating different behaviors. Thus mechanisms are required that can use the ongoing flux of information that the organism receives to modify its behavior in the desired direction. This encompasses many problems, of which habituation is perhaps the simplest: the reduction in amplitude and probability of a given behavior, often to allow the substitution of an alternative in its place.

Simple S–R connections have not provided an adequate account of the present problems, and cognitive descriptions of learning are too remote from the behavioral detail. The required mechanisms that can operate on diffuse connections to vary behavior have been conceived in the present model as decision mechanisms that use the balance of evidence accumulating over time—from sensory inputs and other mechanisms—to select between dichotomized alternative courses of action. The nervous system is viewed here not as a network of simple connections but as a network of local decision elements, switching messages along alternative paths— their choices determined by the weight of long- and short-term biasing factors.

These are the basic ideas employed in the present model. But at this abstract level it is difficult to derive consequences that can either support or refute the interpretation. Therefore, the model has been fleshed out with particular assumptions, which are arbitrary in detail and may well prove wrong, but which provide a necessary starting point from which to analyze, test, and improve the model.

These detailed features of the model have been listed in the previous section. They describe a single decision mechanism (or *PC*), choosing between two alternative courses of action in response to a sensory input. The model starts by examining the type of information the perceptual system must extract from a stimulus. This falls into two classes. Certain aspects of stimuli are best taken as general warnings to indicate that action, of whatever sort, may be required in the near future. In the model, the activation subsystem monitors incoming stimuli for such evidence. If the stimulus is unfamiliar, intense, or has certain other features that may be species-specific, this perceptual subsystem will direct activation messages to a more or less wide range of *PC*s that may shortly be subject to inputs from the environment that will require them to actively reach a decision and initiate a course of action. These messages do not themselves elicit outputs from the *PC*s; they ensure that if the latter receive appropriate, specific information, they can respond more quickly and strongly.

The second class of information consists of aspects of stimuli that are relevant to the choice between particular courses of action. Identification of the stimulus will cause messages to be sent to a limited range of *PC*s, from which it may evoke responses.

A *PC* decides between two courses of action. It is based on two *PU*s, each of which accumulates information favoring a corresponding response. The weight of information at any time is represented by the state of the *PU*. A relevant stimulus will usually send an input to each *PU*. This reflects the fact that most stimuli can evoke more than one response and often opposed responses. We may approach warmth, or cold, or an item of food, or a possible predator, or we may avoid them. Because of long-term biases or recent events, the identity message to one *PU* may be greater than the message to the other: a big disparity is described as sharp tuning. Each *PU* "votes" for its choice by sending an output [$o(A)$ and $o(B)$] to a comparator that takes their algebraic sum and compares it with the balance existing before the identity messages arrived. For discrete responses, the comparator transmits the magnitude and direction of the shift in this balance $\Delta o(C)$ to a response selector where it determines the selection of a response and its magnitude. Alternatively, $\Delta o(C)$ may determine the level of a continuous variable directly.

This is the basic functioning of the *PC*. Additional features of the network have also been considered. In particular, *PC*s can be linked in series, providing a capacity to produce a sequence of behavioral acts; and their output can be fed back to their own *PU*s to ensure a maintained response to an intermittent stimulus or a continued response after a transient stimulus.

The model has been described at a fairly abstract "black-box" level. Each of the mechanisms envisaged could be analyzed into more detailed components. The most detailed model has been presented for the *PU*s, to provide a basis for quantitative predictions. It is possible that in different species, or at different loci in a single nervous system, different neural mechanisms may function as *PU*s. Only one possibility has been explored in detail here, however: a model in which the *PU* consists of a number of hypothetical neurons or fibers that may be active or inactive and whose summed activity constitutes the *PU* output.

To avoid confusion in describing the functioning of this system, it is necessary to distinguish between the language we apply at two levels: to the *PU*s as a whole, on the one hand, and to their components, the hypothetical nerve fibers, on the other. If we describe the *PU* as being "activated," we mean that a relevant stimulus will evoke a bigger output from it. But at the level of components, we say that fibers are "stimulated," and this may succeed in "exciting" them; or "inhibited," which may block or terminate their activity. The relation between these two levels is not simple. "Activation" of the *PU* is accomplished by suppressing or terminating activity in its fibers; the magnitude of the output evoked by an identity message is determined by the number of inactive fibers it succeeds in exciting. Because the comparator compares the states before and after the arrival of the identity message, prior suppression of firing makes a larger number of silent fibers available for the identity message to excite, and thus allows it to have a greater effect. Thus, "activation" of the *PU* is produced by a reduction in the level of activity of its constituent fibers.

III. Applications of the Model

Equations describing the model's functioning will now be derived. These will then be applied to habituation and some related behavioral phenomena.

A. The Course of Habituation

We first consider a series of trials on each of which the stimulus S is presented, and this generates an identity message $d(S,PC_i)$ but no activation message. The stimulus provides an input $d(S,A)$ to PU_A and an input $d(S,B)$ to PU_B. For brevity, I shall write d_A for $d(S,A)$ in the following equations.

The preset background level of activity in PU_A is given by $e_0(A)$. In deriving equations we take e_A and e_B to be constant over trials. If Assumption 13 holds, this can be considered as an approximation. Then on Trial 1, the initial output from PU_A prior to the receipt of $d(S,A)$ is

$$o_{1,0}(A) = e_0 n_A,$$

where n_A is the number of fibers in PU_A. When the identity message arrives, the level of activity will increase to

$$o_1(A) = [e_0 + (1 - e_0)d_A]n_A = [1 - (1 - d_A)(1 - e_0)]n_A.$$

A proportion e_A of the newly excited fibers becomes stably active. Then the initial level of activity on Trial 2 will be given by substituting e_A for d_A:

$$o_{2,0}(A) = [1 - (1 - e_A)(1 - e_0)]n_A,$$

and the excitation following the second stimulus presentation will increase this to

$$o_2(A) = [1 - (1 - d_A)(1 - e_A)(1 - e_0)]n_A.$$

In general, on trial k,

$$o_{k,0}(A) = [1 - (1 - e_A)^{k-1}(1 - e_0)]n_A, \tag{3}$$

and

$$o_k(A) = [1 - (1 - d_A)(1 - e_A)^{k-1}(1 - e_0)]n_A. \tag{4}$$

Similar expressions apply to PU_B. Then the comparator output will be

$$o_{k,0}(C) = o_{k,0}(A) - o_{k,0}(B) \tag{5a}$$

at the onset of trial k, and it will rise to

$$o_k(C) = o_k(A) - o_k(B) \tag{5b}$$

following the identity message. The change in comparator output recorded by the response selector will be

$$x_k = \Delta o_k(C) = o_k(C) - o_{k,0}(C).$$

These equations apply to a simple case without activation messages. But if, for example, the stimulus is unfamiliar or intense, then activation may occur. Activation messages reduce the residual noise level prior to the arrival of the identity message, and so allow a larger response to it. Following each trial, the mechanisms maintaining the preset level of background activity restore their effect to the proportion e_0 (cf. Assumption 11).

If activation occurs, the form of the equations describing the course of habituation will depend on the distribution of activation over trials. Let us abbreviate the activation (of unfamiliarity) message $a_{u,k}(S,PC)$ from S to the PC on trial k to a_k and consider the effect of nonzero activation messages on the first two trials. For $k = 1,2$, the probability that a randomly selected active fiber will be rendered inactive will be $a_k > 0$. This will reduce $o_{k,0}(A)$ and $o_{k,0}(B)$, so that PU_A and PU_B contain more silent fibers capable of being excited by $d(S,A)$ and $d(S,B)$. Thus, on the first trial the initial level of activity in A, following the arrival of $a(S,A)$, but prior to the receipt of $d(S,A)$, is

$$o_{1,0}(A) = (1 - a_1)e_0 n_A$$

and

$$o_1(A) = \{(1 - a_1)e_0 + d_A[1 - (1 - a_1)e_0]\}n_A$$
$$= \{1 - (1 - d_A)[1 - (1 - a_1)e_0]\}n_A.$$

By the onset of the next trial the preset background contribution will be restored to e_0. The second presentation of S first generates an activation message that reduces the total residual activity in the proportion a_2, giving

$$o_{2,0}(A) = (1 - a_2)\{1 - (1 - e_A)[1 - (1 - a_1)e_0] + a_1 e_0\}n_A,$$

and the identity message then gives

$$o_2(A) = \{1 - (1 - d_A)[1 - (1 - a_2)[1 - (1 - e_A)[1 - (1 - a_1)e_0] + a_1 e_0]]\}n_A.$$

In general, if

$$o_{k,0}(A) = X_k n_A, \tag{6}$$

then

$$o_k(A) = [d_A + (1 - d_A)X_k]n_A \tag{7}$$

and

$$o_{k+1,0}(A) = (1 - a_{k+1})[e_A + (1 - e_A)X_k + a_k e_0]n_A = X_{k+1}n_A. \tag{8}$$

Some calculations based on these equations are shown in Fig. 2. Because many different response measures have been used in studies of habituation, $\Delta o(C)$ is plotted, and not the distribution of probability over

Michel Treisman

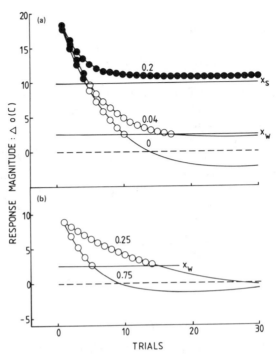

Fig. 2. Primary-comparator model: habituation. Calculations of $\Delta o(C)$ based on Eqs.(3)–(8) are shown: (a) for different values of a_i (with $d_A = 0.4$; $d_B = 0.2$; $e/d = 0.25$; $e_0 = 0.1$); (b) for different values of e/d (with $d_A = 0.2$; $d_B = 0.1$; $e_0 = 0.1$; $a_i = 0$).

strong, weak, and zero responses that would be given by the response selector illustrated in Fig. 1. The stimuli are assumed to send larger identity messages to PU_A and smaller messages to PU_B, and positive values of $\Delta o(C)$ determine A responses. The parameters for each PU are otherwise the same. $\Delta o(C)$ is plotted against trial number for the parameters shown in each panel. The number of fibers in each primary unit was taken to be 100. The criterion for strong responses (x_s) was arbitrarily set at 10 and x_w at 2.5. Strong responses (R_{As}) are represented by filled circles, weak responses (R_{Aw}) by empty circles. Figure 2a represents responses to a strong stimulus, Fig. 2b the responses to a weak stimulus. Each curve shows some degree of habituation: as residual activity builds up, response magnitude declines. Initial strong responses are replaced by weak responses, and eventually response ceases. Figure 2a shows the effects of "activation of intensity" messages. The parameters for each curve are the same, except that the intensity of the stimulus is assumed to be sufficient to produce an activation message on every trial for the upper two curves: $a_i(S,PC)$ is 0.2 or 0.04. The same activation message goes to each *PU*. The higher level of suppression of residual activity produced by the larger activation messages arrests habituation, and the lower level retards it. Thus the model produces the failure of habituation that is known to occur with very strong stimuli (Thompson & Spencer, 1966).

Figure 2b shows habituation to a weak stimulus for two levels of e/d. (There is no activation in this case.) Massed stimulus presentations often give more rapid habituation. On the present model, short intervals between trials will give higher values of e/d. The more rapid habituation produced by the higher value of e/d illustrates the advantage of massed presentations. We may also note that $\Delta o(C)$ may fall to zero and below, returning eventually to zero.

More intense stimuli usually produce slower habituation [but see Davis and Wagner (1968)]. In the model, this effect of intensity depends on the magnitude of the activation message that an intense stimulus may generate.

It is generally found that shorter ISIs produce greater habituation than do long ones (Hinde, 1970; Thompson & Spencer, 1966). This is to be expected on the present model, because the residual noise level will be greater with short intervals, which will give a higher value of e/d (Assumption 12). The consequent more rapid habituation is shown in Fig. 2b.

Davis (1970) presented a loud tone 1000 times to rats at intervals of either 2 or 16 seconds. With the short interval the probability of a startle response decreased more than with the long one, as we would expect. Davis also made, however, an interesting additional observation. When members of both groups were subsequently given identical tests, either 1 minute or 24 hours after the habituation session, greater residual habituation was shown by the 16-second group than by the 2-second group. This result can be explained by Assumption 13: the 2-second group would recruit proportionately more short-duration fibers that show less-persistent stability, and fewer long-duration fibers, than the 16-second group. The first group should therefore retain less residual excitation after an interval.

Patterson and Petrinovich (1979) played recorded male song to White-crowned Sparrows using massed or spaced presentation, and observed less response decrement with massed presentation. But it may be that massed singing by an intruder in a bird's territory signals a greater threat to the resident than does more occasional song; if so, massing would here be confounded with an effective increase in stimulus intensity. This is supported by Petrinovich and Patterson's (1981) observation that birds receiving massed presentations did not approach the speaker as closely as the birds in other groups did, and they performed more trills and flutters.

The authors noted that "These two behaviors are usually emitted when two males are having a territorial encounter, and they frequently precede a physical encounter [p. 809]."

B. Sensitization

On the first few trials of a series, we may see an increase rather than a decrease in the magnitude of response (Hinde, 1970; Thompson & Spencer, 1966). This has been described as sensitization (Thompson & Spencer, 1966). If the stimulus is unexpected or unfamiliar, then, on the present account, the first few presentations may generate activation messages whose effect is to reduce the residual noise level. The magnitude a_u of these messages may increase initially if a previously unprepared animal improves its observing responses. Figure 3 shows habituation curves calculated from Eqs.(5)–(8) for representative parameters. For the dashed lines, a_u is always zero. For the continuous lines, it takes the values 0.4, 0.8, and 0.4 on the first three trials; it is zero thereafter. The figure demonstrates that, with appropriate parameters, the model is capable of showing sensitization: an initial rise in the curve followed by a subsequent fall of increased steepness. The effect is greater when the preset background noise level is larger.

C. Spontaneous Recovery

If a sequence of trials is interrupted, the signal presentation loses its familiarity. When S is again presented, it is less familiar and may be unexpected. The perceptual system therefore generates an activation of unfamiliarity message which acts on the PC to reduce the residual noise level. This will increase the magnitude of the response, and this will constitute spontaneous recovery.

In the curves shown in Fig. 4, $a_u = 0.4$ on the first trial in every case, and it also takes this value on the third, sixth, tenth, or fourteenth trial in successive panels; on other trials it is zero. These curves model sequences in which there has been a delay between the fifth and sixth trials, or between the ninth and tenth trials, etc. The resulting rise in a_u causes the spontaneous recovery of response seen.

Without the interruption, responses cease to occur on the seventh trial for the parameters in the figure. Thus the stimulus interruptions and resumptions on both the tenth and fourteenth trials were given to a previously unresponding animal. A greater response is evoked on the tenth

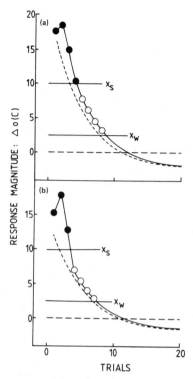

Fig. 3. Primary-comparator model: sensitization. Curves for habituation to a familiar stimulus $(a_u = 0$ throughout; ---) are compared with those for an initially unfamiliar stimulus $(a_u = 0.4, 0.8$ and 0.4 on the first three trials; ——). (a) Curves for $e_0 = .02$ (with $d_A = .03$; $d_B = 0.1$; $e/d = 0.5$). (b) Curves for $e_0 = .04$ (with $d_A = 0.3$; $d_B = 0.1$; $e/d = 0.5$).

than on the fourteenth trial; this illustrates the phenomenon of "habituation beyond zero" (Thompson & Spencer, 1966).

Another experimental observation that can also be seen in the curves in Fig. 4 is that rehabituation proceeds with greater speed from the level of response reached at the peak of spontaneous recovery than did original habituation from that level.

A second feature of the model (not included in the simulation illustrated in Fig. 4) that may also contribute to spontaneous recovery is that an interpolated period of rest will allow some of the fibers subject to residual firing to revert to the inactive state. If the interval is long enough, the initial position will be restored. If the interruption is shorter, the probability that a fiber is active will fall to an intermediate level. The effect will be equivalent to resetting the trial number to a smaller value. But this effect alone would not account for the speedier course of rehabituation.

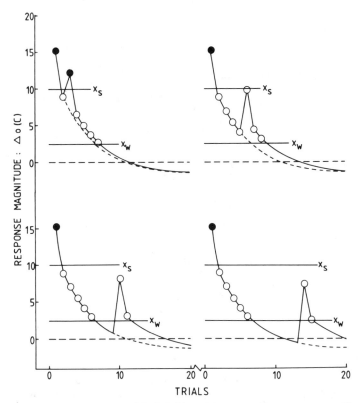

Fig. 4. Primary-comparator model: dishabituation or spontaneous recovery. The effect of activation produced by the unexpectedness or unfamiliarity of the signal when it resumes after an interruption (spontaneous recovery) or when an unexpected extraneous event occurs (dishabituation) is shown; the graphs represent either process. In successive panels the extraneous event or resumption of the signal sequence after a temporary interruption occurs on Trials 3 $(a_3 = 0.4)$, 6 $(a_6 = 0.4)$, 10 $(a_{10} = 0.4)$, or 14 $(a_{14} = 0.4)$ (with $d_A = 0.3$, $d_B = 0.1$, $e/d = 0.5$, and $e_0 = 0.4$). a_u is also equal to 0.4 on Trial 1; on other trials it is always zero. In the absence of any departure from the norm, habituation follows the dashed curve.

D. Dishabituation

This phenomenon receives an explanation similar to that for spontaneous recovery. Dishabituation is observed when the stimulus, or the timing of its presentation, is modified, or an extraneous stimulus that is unfamiliar or unexpected intrudes or is added. Any of these events may generate an activation message. Even though the extraneous stimulus does not direct an identity message to PC_i (the PC governing the A and B responses with which we are concerned), the activation messages it produces may affect PC_i, because activation messages are distributed widely and PCs are broadly tuned for such messages. Thus a change in S or an extraneous occurrence will cause a reduction in residual activity in PC_i and a consequent increase in response magnitude. Figure 4 can also be read as simulating the dishabituating effect of such an event presented at various stages of habituation. An increase or a decrease in the intensity of S should be equally effective in causing the perceptual system to produce dishabituation, because each will be a perceptible change and each will be equally unexpected.

Figure 4 simulates the presentation of an extraneous stimulus on a single trial for different habituation runs. In simulation in which an additional event occurs on several trials during an habituation sequence [a_u was raised (from zero) to the same nonzero value on each of those trials], the successive dishabituation peaks tend to decrease, which illustrates "habituation of dishabituation." If the same additional event occurred each time, then a_u should itself decline on successive presentations, which would further increase this effect.

E. Response Priming

Stimuli do not normally occur in wholly random and unrelated sequences in the real world, and this is reflected in the phenomenology of behavior. In particular, a stimulus presentation may alter the probability of a response other than the response it normally evokes (R_A) or the response with which R_A is paired (R_B) in its PC (PC_i). One example is the scratch reflex in the spinal dog, as described by Sherrington (1906/1947). He noted that a stimulus moving over a receptive field is likely to excite a sequence of allied reflexes, but that these are linked by more than the coincidence of the successive presence of the stimulus: the threshold of each succeeding reflex is lowered by the preceding excitation. The effect is short-lived. Sherrington suggested that it was to avoid this effect that the flea evolved its hop.

A more recent example of response priming is reported by Ewert and Ingle (1971). If a frog (*Rana pipiens*) is exposed to a series of dummy prey stimuli presented about 100° to the left of midline, its tendency to snap at that position will habituate. If it is tested during the later stages of the habituation sequence by the simultaneous presentation of two dummy stimuli, one 100° to the left of the midline and one 100° to the right, it will snap at the one on the right. This demonstrates habituation (see the discussion to follow on response potentiation). But, if it is tested by presenting the dummy stimuli with one at 30° to the left of the midline and the other 30° to the right, it snaps at the prey in the 30°-left position nearly 80% of the time (Ewert & Ingle, 1971). Although the frog has not experienced either of these test stimuli before, the left-going response has been primed. The consequence in the natural state is that if a stimulus appears laterally, and the frog snaps at it and misses, it will in the process of doing this turn toward it, and the missed prey will now be nearer the midline, in a position the frog is now primed to respond to.

Findings of this kind may be explained by the assumption (3) that the perceptual system may direct special priming activation messages $a_p(S, PC_j)$ to one or more appropriate PCs, other than the systems receiving identity messages from S. In the present example, appearance of prey to one side would cause the perceptual system to generate activation-priming messages to those PCs that would organize response to near-midline prey on the same side: these messages tend to reduce the noise levels in the primary units controlling the snapping response. Thus, if the prey is originally presented on the left side and subsequently two near-midline prey stimuli are presented, one on the left and one on the right, the PC systems determining the prey-catching response to stimuli on the left will give larger outputs than those responding on the right. Then, at the higher-level PC that arbitrates between simultaneous competing outputs directed to the two sides, the left response will usually dominate.

The assumption that the message $a_p(S, PC_j)$ comes from the perceptual system, and is not a forward output from PC_i itself, is supported by the observation that even when the prey-catching response to the lateral stimulus is habituated, the priming is still seen (i.e., it is not itself also habituated). This assumption is also supported by observations of Russo, Reiter, and Ison (1975). These authors noted that a brief electric shock that evoked a reflexive jump in naive rats also inhibited the startle response to a burst of white noise presented 96 msec later. When the direct response to the electric shock was habituated, this did not reduce the effectiveness of that shock in suppressing the acoustic startle response. It seems that the message a_p (shock, $PC_{startle}$), which mainly primed the primary unit opposing the acoustic startle response, was not diminished when the reflex jump was habituated.

A further example of response priming is provided by Kimble and Ray's (1965) observation that repeatedly stimulating the identical spot on a frog's back with a bristle led to decreased numbers of wiping responses, but stimulating the frog only in the same general area resulted in increasing numbers of responses. This effect differs from Sherrington's (1906/ 1947) description of the priming of the spinal scratch reflex in that the latter effect is short-lived, lasting a few seconds, whereas Kimble and

Ray's (1965) observations were made over 12 successive days. Although the PC activated by stimulation from an individual spot may habituate, it seems that activation messages go to neighboring PCs and increase their readiness to respond. This would be adaptive in relation to stimulation caused, for example, by a moving insect.

F. Decomposition of Response

If a stimulus that evokes a series of responses in fixed order is repeatedly presented, the components of the response sequence may drop out at different rates during the course of habituation. The terminal responses are more vulnerable to such habituation, and initial components are retained longer (Hinde, 1970). For example, the spider *Uloborus* responds to a vibrating stimulus applied to its web by first opening its legs, then turning toward the vibrating radius, then running to the center of vibration. During habituation, it is the final run that is the first part of the response sequence to disappear; then the orienting turn goes; and finally the initial leg movements become extinct (Szlep, 1964).

Assumption 16 provides an account of these relations. A sequence of responses may be organized by a sequence of PCs, the output $\Delta o(C)$ from one determining not only its own response but also a forward message to the next PC, as described by Eq.(2). Figure 5 shows calculations for a sequence of two responses R_{Ai} and R_{Aj} produced in that order by PC_i and PC_j. When PC_i receives an identity message from S, it evokes the response R_{Ai} and also directs forward messages $k_{fA}|\Delta o(C)|$ and $k_{fB}|\Delta o(C)|$ to the primary units A_j and B_j of PC_j.

For the simulation in Fig. 5, $d(S,A_i) = 0.3$ and $d(S,B_i) = 0.1$. On trial g these inputs evoke an output $\Delta o_g(C)$ from the comparator in PC_i, which determines the response R_{Ai} or R_{Bi}. It also determines forward messages to PC_j. If $\Delta o_g(C) > 0$, then these are $k_{fA}|\Delta o_g(C)|$ to primary unit A_j of PC_j and $k_{fB}|\Delta o_g(C)|$ to primary unit B_j. For the calculations, k_{fA} was given the value $0.3/|\Delta o_1(C)|$, and k_{fB} the value $0.1/|\Delta o_1(C)|$. The effect of this is that on the first trial the inputs to the primary-effector units of PC_i and PC_j are identical in magnitude. On subsequent trials the same values of k_{fA} and k_{fB} apply [for $\Delta o(C_i) > 0$] but $\Delta o(C_i)$ may change as a consequence of internal changes in PC_i. If $\Delta o_g(C_i) < 0$, the internal tuning of PC_j reverses its direction: that is, the scaling factors become $k_{fA} = 0.1/|\Delta o_1(C_i)|$ and $k_{fB} = 0.3/|\Delta o_1(C_i)|$.

Because increase in residual noise in both systems will now contribute to waning of the second response, R_{Aj} weakens more rapidly and drops out sooner than R_{Ai} during the course of habituation. Similar effects may

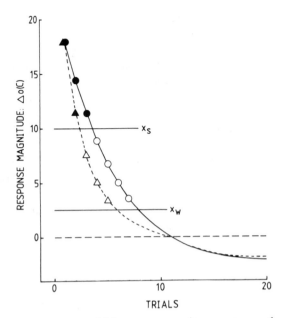

Fig. 5. Primary-comparator model for a sequence of two responses, the first governed by PC_i, the second by PC_j. ○——○, R_{A_j}; △---△, R_{A_j}. On each trial a function of the output from the first comparator, $\Delta o(C_i)$, serves as input to the second unit, PC_j. It is directed to the primary-effector units A_j and B_j in the same proportions as the original identity inputs to the primary units of PC_i, if $\Delta o(C_i)$ is positive. When $\Delta o(C_i) < 0$, the relative sizes of the forward messages to PC_j are reversed. The parameters are: $e/d = 0.5$; $e_0 = 0.1$; $a_u = 0$; for PC_i: $d_A = 0.3$, $d_B = 0.1$. When $\Delta o_g(C_i) > 0$ on trial g the forward message to PU_{A_j} is $[0.3/|\Delta o_1(C_i)|]|\Delta o_g(C_i)|$; to B_j it is $[0.1/|\Delta o_1(C_i)|]|\Delta o_g(C_i)|$. For $\Delta o_g(C_i) < 0$, $f(PC_i, A_j) = [0.1/|\Delta o_1(C_i)|]|\Delta o_g(C_i)|$, and $f(PC_i, B_j) = [0.3/|\Delta o_1(C_i)|]|\Delta o_g(C_i)|$.

be expected if the chain extends to further responses. Thus our model can also account for the order of decomposition of response.

G. Behavioral Contrast

There are three cases of the phenomenon that may be referred to as *behavioral contrast*. In each case, presentation of S_A—the stimulus which normally favors R_A—induces a bias in favor of R_B.

1. Response Reversal

When *response reversal* occurs, habituation may not only proceed to a state in which the original response no longer occurs, but continued presentation of the stimulus may cause another response to be evoked in-

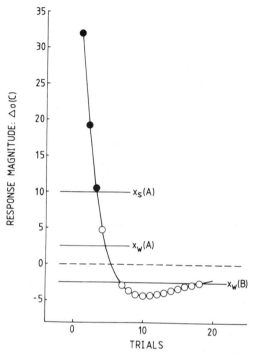

Fig. 6. Primary-comparator model: response reversal. For the parameters (d_A = 0.6, d_B = 0.2, e/d = 0.5, e_0 = 0.2, and a = 0), habituation results in a reversal of response, the disappearance of response A being followed by the appearance of response B for a temporary period.

stead—even though there is no change in the stimulus. For example, Sherrington (1906/1947) noted that if, in the spinal dog, a flexion reflex of high intensity is maintained by very prolonged excitation, it is frequently broken at irregular intervals by sudden extension movements. Another example is provided by the application of a vibrating stimulus to a radius of the web of *Uloborus*. Normally the spider orients toward the vibrating radius and then runs toward the center of vibration. But after a sufficient period of habituation, it may substitute for this orientation response a turn in the direction directly opposite to the vibrating radius (Szlep, 1964). Similarly, Sokolov (1963) noted that repeated shocks, which initially caused vasodilatation of blood vessels in the head, eventually caused cephalic vasoconstriction.

With appropriate parameters, the present model generates such effects. This is illustrated in Fig. 6, in which habituation of R_A results in a reversal of $\Delta o(C)$ sufficient to generate several weak B responses before final habituation to zero.

2. Response Potentiation

In the second type of behavioral contrast, *response potentiation,* a stimulus S_A is repeatedly presented. Then habituation of the response to S_A is interrupted, and S_B, the stimulus normally evoking R_B, is interpolated. Following this, habituation to S_A is resumed, and it is found that the response R_A is strengthened.

Sherrington (1906/1947) was perhaps the first seriously to discuss this effect, which he called "successive induction." If a spinal dog is suspended so that its limbs hang freely, they assume a state of reflex extension. If one foot is momentarily stimulated so as to induce a brief flexion reflex, this is followed by a resumption of active extension, but to a degree more marked than before flexion. A similar effect can be shown using the crossed-extension reflex in the spinal dog. In this reflex, stimulation of the skin of one hind leg causes extension at the ankle, knee, and hip of the opposite leg. If this reflex is elicited from one limb at regular intervals, say once a minute, the movements recur in a very similar fashion. If, during one of the intervals, a strong prolonged flexor reflex is induced in the limb showing the regular extensions, the crossed-extension reflex in this limb subsequently shows an increased amplitude, an effect that may endure for 4 or 5 minutes (Sherrington, 1906/1947). Sherrington draws an analogy with visual contrast. Another example, of interest because the contrast is between states in which the response is either present or absent, is provided by the "mark-time" reflex. In this reflex, an alternating stepping movement of the hindlimbs occurs when the spinal dog is held with its limbs hanging down. If the skin of the tail is stimulated, the movement stops. When this stimulus ends, the movement resumes more vigorously and at a frequency up to 30% greater. Sherrington (1906/1947) explained this as a "rebound to superactivity."

Wolda (1961) described response potentiation evoked by an opposed response in the waterbug *Notonecta glauca*. If a vibrating stimulus is applied to the surface of the water, the bug makes a prey-catching approach. In one experiment the animal was habituated to such stimuli presented on the left; there followed a 5-minute pause, then a further series of stimuli was presented on the left. In one condition the 5-minute pause was uninterrupted; in a second condition, the initial 4 minutes of the pause were followed by the presentation of stimuli on the right for 1 minute. When the stimuli on the left resumed, the response made to them was considerably greater in the second condition than after the rest period only. This was not simply dishabituation: no beneficial effect was produced if the interpolated stimuli were presented in front of the animal rather than in the symmetrical position.

The effect of interpolating stimuli of the opposite type is shown in Fig. 7. The stimulus normally evoking response A is presented on Trials 1–9, producing habituation. On Trials 10–15 the stimulus for R_B is presented, and from Trial 16 the calculation reverts to the stimulus for R_A. The parameters are shown in the figure. At each change, a_u takes the value 0.4, otherwise it is zero. The effect of spontaneous recovery alone (with no presentations on Trials 10–15 and $a_u = 0.4$ on Trial 16) is shown by the dashed curve. There is an increase in the number and magnitude of R_A responses following the interpolation of opposed stimuli, as compared with spontaneous recovery alone.

3. Response Rebound

In the third case, *response rebound,* the stimulus S_A evokes the response R_A. When S_A ceases, the response R_B is produced spontaneously in the absence of any stimulus.

A striking example is provided by the effect of an electric shock on heart rate in the curarized dog. During presentation of the shock the heart rate increases to a peak from which there is then some decline. After cessation of the shock it falls below the resting level to a minimum, and then returns to normal. Both the initial rise and the rebound bradycardia increase with the intensity of the stimulus (Church, LoLordo, Overmier, Solomon, & Turner, 1966).

Solomon and Corbit (1974) and Solomon (1980) apply the terms *affective* or *hedonic contrast* to a number of such alternations between opposed classes of behavior or opposite changes in the value of physiological variables. Thus they note that morphine addicts may experience euphoria, followed by a subsequent craving. If a duckling is offered a mother surrogate, it grows excited and may approach the surrogate; when the stimulus is removed, the duckling utters distress calls (Solomon, 1980; Starr, 1978). A similar rebound effect is described by Domjan, Gillan, and Gemberling (1980). They exposed rats to an odor paired with an injection of lithium chloride to produce an aversive association. Subsequently they tested the effect of that odor on drinking. Conditioned rats that were exposed to the odor for 30 minutes with a palatable fluid available during that period drank less than did controls. But if the 30-minute exposure to the odor had ended, and the fluid was first presented 5 minutes later, conditioned rats drank more than controls in the subsequent 2-hour period.

It may be appropriate to use terms such as "hedonic" or "affective" of states about which human subjects can provide introspective reports, but it can be questioned whether such terms should be applied to animals

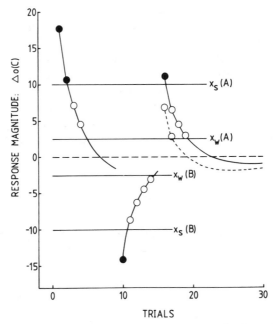

Fig. 7. Primary-comparator model: response potentiation. The figure shows the effect on habituation of an interruption during which stimuli are presented that normally excite the opposite response (with $e/d = 0.5$; $e_0 = 0.2$). One stimulus S_A is presented on Trials 1–9 and 16–30 ($d_A = 0.4$; $d_B = 0.2$). On Trials 10–15 an opposed stimulus S_B is presented such that the strengths of $d(S,A)$ and $d(S,B)$ are reversed ($d_A = 0.2$; $d_B = 0.4$). On Trials 1, 10, and 16, $a_u = 0.4$; on the other trials $a_u = 0$. The dashed line shows the effect of spontaneous recovery alone following an interposed interval in which neither stimulus has been presented ($a_u = 0.4$ on the first trial after the notional interval).

solely on a basis of cross-species intuition. Here the terms *response* or *motivational rebound* will be preferred.

Solomon and Corbit (1974) note several characteristic features of the phenomenon. First, the direct effect (e.g., shock-induced tachycardia) may show an initial peak from which it descends to a plateau; when the stimulus ceases, the effect rebounds to an opposite peak from which it returns to the normal level. Further, if the exposure is frequently repeated, the primary response declines in magnitude and the secondary state becomes more marked. With repeated shocks the dog shows less tachycardia. But when the stimulus is removed the heart rate falls to a greater extent, and the bradycardia persists for a longer time. When the imprinting stimulus is repeatedly presented to the duckling, its initial excitement is less; but when the stimulus is removed, distress-calling is more prolonged.

Solomon and Corbit (1974) explained these observations by a theory in which affective responses are produced by two opponent processes with different temporal characteristics, linked by a single negative-feedback loop. The primary process evokes the secondary process, and this acts to restore hedonic equilibrium by suppressing the effects of the primary process.

It is of interest that behavioral rebound may show an advantage for massed presentation which is reminiscent of the similar advantage of massing usually found for habituation. Starr (1978) observed that if ducklings are given twelve 30-second exposures to a stuffed female Mallard duck, with 5-minute intervals between each exposure, the amount of distress calling each time the stimulus is removed does not increase. But if the interval between presentations is 1 minute, the amount of distress calling following each exposure increases to a high asymptote. A similar high level of calling is shown if the 12 half-minute exposures are replaced by a single 6-minute exposure.

Can behavioral rebound be explained by an extension of the present model? We have noted that many stimuli, such as shock, or the mother, may signal a state of the world in which it is best for the animal to respond consistently over a period of time, whether or not the stimulus persists. When caught by a predator the prey must attempt to escape and it must do so in a persistent fashion; if a mouse does momentarily wriggle out of the claws of a cat, it should not then relax but must secure its safety by running away. If the mother disappears, the duckling should not turn to some other pursuit: it must summon her. In such cases the stimulus is an intermittent indicator of the state of the world, but what it indicates is important and continues to be relevant even though the stimulus may disappear from view. Therefore, the systems governing the behavior of an animal must be capable of holding course even when the stimulus is absent. This does not imply that the behavior must continue unchanged when the stimulus ceases; but any change should be to a relevant, alternative mode of behavior.

This need for persistence applies to major sequences of behavior, such as chasing or searching for prey; and to quite minor ones, such as scratching an itch to dislodge what may be a parasite. The feature of the model that meets these requirements is given by Assumption 17. This postulates that when the sensory input ceases, a *PC* may maintain its activation by positive feedback. To examine the implications of this assumption, sequences were simulated in which *S* was presented for five successive trials; there was then a pause during which five cycles of positive feedback occurred, and this series was then repeated. The magnitude of the feedback is based on the greater of the identity inputs to the two primary

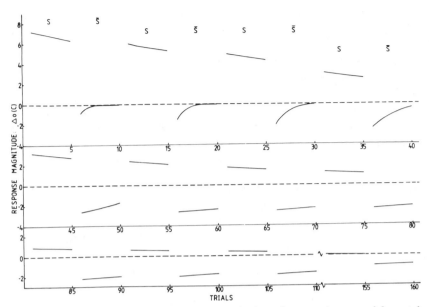

Fig. 8. Primary-comparator model: behavioral rebound. Successive sets of five trials represent either five successive presentations of the stimulus (they are then labeled S) or a pause during which five feedback events occur (labeled $\bar{S}$), as described in the text. (With $d_A = 0.1$, $d_B = 0.02$, $e/d = 0.25$, $e_0 = 0.1$, and $a_u = 0$.)

units, $\max(d_A, d_B)$. The feedback messages to PU_A and PU_B are assumed to be identical (see Assumption 17) and are determined by $\Delta o(C)$ and a constant k_b. At the commencement of each pause k_B is given the value $k_b = \max(d_A, d_B)/|\Delta o_x(C)|$, where x is the final trial preceding the pause. Then the next five feedback inputs are given by

$$f_{b,t}(PC_i, PC_i) = \min[k_b|\Delta o_{t-1}(C)|, \max(d_A, d_B)], \tag{9}$$

where t is the trial number. The scaling factor k_b ensures that the initial feedback at the start of the pause is equal to the larger of the stimulus inputs d_A and d_B. Subsequent feedback messages are given by $k_b|\Delta o_t(C)|$ provided that they do not exceed the larger of d_A and d_B. If they do, the feedback input is reset to the latter value.

Figure 8 shows in alternation successive series of five presentations of a stimulus and a pause during which five feedback events occur for the parameter values given in the figure. The experimental findings lead us to expect that each period of stimulus presentation should produce a peak effect that declines during the presentation, and successive such periods should show habituation, down to a near-zero or zero effect. In each pause we expect to see a rebound to an initial opposite peak followed by a decline of the effect toward the resting level. As the alternations continue, the rebound should become larger and more persistent.

All these effects are shown by the simulation. Evidently it can reproduce the main features of motivational contrast, as described by Soloman and Corbit (1974). There is also an eventual slow habituation of the rebound effect. The detail of the simulation can be made to vary considerably by varying the parameter values; for example, if the stimulus values are made sufficiently large, the rebound effect habituates from the beginning.

H. The Law of Initial Value

The *law of initial value* refers to a finding that has not usually been considered in relation to habituation but that perhaps deserves to be. The basic observation has been made on a number of physiological and psychophysiological variables such as blood pressure. If the initial value of the variable is measured, and a stimulus is then administered or a manipulation performed whose characteristic action is to raise the magnitude of the variable, then the higher the initial level of the variable when the stimulus is given, the smaller the response will be. Furthermore, if the initial value is sufficiently high the response may not occur or paradoxical reversed responses may even be obtained (Lacey & Lacey, 1962; Wilder, 1957, 1962).

To study habituation, we examine the effects produced by a stimulus when it follows a regular series of controlled presentations of the same stimulus. In contrast, the law of initial value is a generalization that refers to the effects produced by a stimulus when there is no control and little knowledge of preceding events that may have biased the mechanisms responsible for the response. However, we do have a measure of the net effect of these unknown prior events or influences in the form of the initial value of the variable.

A variable such as blood pressure may be described as level-sensitive (Assumption 15). That is, its level directly reflects $o(C)$. We may record its level prior to the kth stimulus as an estimate of $o_{k,0}(C)$, and the value subsequent to that stimulus then gives $o_k(C)$. To study habituation of the blood-pressure response, we take the latter as the difference between these two values. The *PC* model would ascribe variation in this measure to changes in residual noise in the primary units—one *PU* determining a rise in blood pressure, the other a fall—of a *PC*. If this model is on the right lines, the law of initial value should follow from the characteristics of such a *PC* system. Under the circumstances in which the law has usually

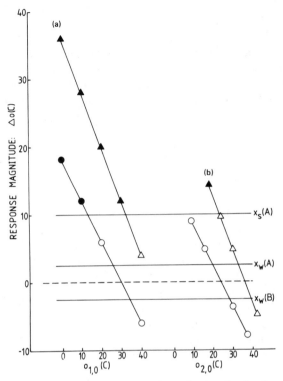

Fig. 9. Primary-comparator model: the law of initial value. For five levels of the preset noise level in A, $e_0(A) = 0.1, 0.2, 0.3, 0.4,$ and 0.5, with $e_0(B) = 0.1$ in each case, the corresponding values of $o_{k,0}(C)$ have been found for two successive stimulus presentations $(k = 1,2)$. The corresponding response magnitudes $\Delta o(C)$ are plotted against the initial values in each case: (a) first response; (b) second response. Results are shown for two stimuli, differing in intensity and tuning as indicated by the parameters ($\bigcirc$: $d_A = 0.6$, $d_B = 0.4$; $\triangle$: $d_A = 0.8$, $d_B = 0.4$; $e/d = 0.5$).

been observed, the causes of such levels of residual noise as there may be are unknown, although there is a measure of their resultant effect $o_{k,0}(C)$. In the case of blood pressure this might express the residual effects of recent traumatic or relaxing events, life stress, or constitutional physiological imbalances, which determine a greater preset noise level in one primary unit than in the other. If we assume that such imbalances may occur, does the present model generate the law?

Figure 9 shows the magnitude of the first and second responses to a stimulus, for 5 cases of imbalance in the residual noise in the two primary-effector units. These correspond to $e_0(A) = 0.1, 0.2, \ldots 0.5$ with $e_0(B) = 0.1$ in each case. We may suppose that a positive value of $\Delta o(C)$

corresponds to a rise in blood pressure from the initial level. As the preset noise level for A, $e_0(A)$ increases from 0.1 to 0.5 both $o_{1,0}(C)$ and $o_{2,0}(C)$ (the initial levels of comparator output on the first and second trials) increase from 0 to 40. As the initial level (the resting level of blood pressure) increases, the magnitude of the response in the corresponding direction (the increase in blood pressure) evoked by the stimulus decreases. This decrease takes the response magnitude through a zone in which it is negligible and ultimately produces "paradoxical" reversed responses. The figure illustrates this for two stimuli, differing in strength and internal tuning. On Trial 1 the law is determined by the asymmetry in preset noise levels in PU_A and PU_B and on the second (and later) trials by the asymmetry in total residual noise. It seems that the present model can account for the law of initial value.

IV. Discussion

An account has been presented that envisages a rich structure of diffuse connections linking sensory inputs by direct and indirect paths to a variety of mechanisms responsible for responses. To control the level of activity and choose between paths in this network, decision mechanisms are necessary; and a general model for such a mechanism, the primary-comparator system has been presented. Each PC contains two primary effector units. These produce outputs favoring (ultimately) two alternative responses. The immediate processing of these outputs by a comparator balances them against each other. The net comparator output may determine some (level-sensitive) response variables directly. Or the rate of change of this output may direct the selection of a (rate-sensitive) response. A distinction is made between two types of sensory information that may be extracted from the stimulus by the perceptual system: information that may direct the preparation of PCs for possible future inputs to them (activation), and (identity) information which is transmitted to specific PCs and is directly effective in eliciting outputs from them. The processing of these two types of information by the PU was modeled in greater detail, and equations were derived describing the resultant behavior of the system as a whole.

These equations have been used to simulate a number of behavioral situations. Calculations have been performed for arbitrary parameter values, to examine whether the model could in principle reproduce known features of behavior. In this it has been quite successful. It reproduces habituation curves and shows appropriate effects of stimulus intensity and massing of trials. Sensitization was successfully modeled, as was dishabituation and spontaneous recovery, including features such as more rapid rehabituation and habituation of dishabituation. The order of decomposition of response sequences was reproduced, as was behavioral contrast, classified here into three types: response reversal, response potentiation, and response rebound. Finally, a connection was shown with the phenomena underlying the law of initial value, and this law was also successfully reproduced.

The model is more complex than traditional approaches to habituation, which assume a "fatigue process" at a synapse, possessing whatever properties are needed to give a habituation curve. But it is intended to explain and integrate a wider range of data and to provide a framework for understanding simple behavior in general. In some respects, the model is quite economical. For example, we have seen that an identity message to the PC may initiate a rate-sensitive response by provoking a sufficiently rapid change in the comparator output $\Delta o(C)$. But we know that activation messages also alter the levels of activity of the PUs and so may also produce changes in $o(C)$; and therefore it may seem that extra wiring or additional assumptions are necessary to prevent such changes producing spurious responses. In fact this is not a problem. Because PCs are broadly tuned to activation messages, arrival of $a_A \simeq a_B$ at the PUs will produce similar proportionate changes in the level of excitation in each PU. Provided the preceding noise levels in the two PUs are not too different, this will have a minimal effect on the balance between them represented by the algebraic sum $o(C)$. Thus changes in $o(C)$ produced in this way will usually be small. Only if there are considerable differences in residual noise in opposing PUs, or the activation messages are very large, should changes in $o(C)$ be produced sufficiently large to initiate responses in the absence of appropriate identity information. This possible effect of high activation may explain the "unmotivated" behavior (such as agitated pacing about or grooming) that may be precipitated by a violent stimulus for which there is no immediate response, whether this is an electric shock in a laboratory cage or a letter with bad news.

The present model is unlikely to be correct in detail, and the detail is unlikely to be the same in species ranging from protozoa to man (Humphrey, 1933). Nevertheless, the simple principle of nervous organization developed here does appear to give a first-order account of the most frequent features of habituation. These have been observed in an enormous range of species and therefore should reflect not only major evolutionary pressures (Treisman, Chapter 12 in this volume), but also common principles of behavior organization. Thus the model may prove of heuristic value.

The specification of detailed neural circuits has been avoided. The mechanisms by which the general principles are realized may differ between species and for different purposes in the same animal. The comparator might operate by lateral inhibition in one case, but not in another. The primary units have been envisaged as collections of active or inactive fibers, but this is a matter of convenience: they could take other forms, such as single neurons capable of maintaining various levels of resting activity. At this stage it may be more helpful to pursue general similarities. The model respects the importance of distinguishing between hypothetical processes at the neural level, such as synaptic inhibition, and at the functional level that applies to the generation of components of behavior. For example, in the present model responses may be reduced in magnitude or prevented from occurring ("inhibition" at the behavioral level) by a rise in preset noise or total residual activity, which may correspond to increased "excitation" at the neural-fiber level. The occurrence of responses is facilitated (i.e., "activation" is produced) by activation messages which, at the neural level, operate by inhibiting neural fibers. Habituation may result in disappearance of a response ("inhibition" at the behavioral level) or substitution or strengthening of an alternative response ("excitation" at the behavioral level). Both effects simply correspond to a change in the sign of $\Delta o(C)$, which produces, in the case of behavioral inhibition, a preponderant effect of a PU giving a null output; or in the case of response substitution, of a PU that determines a paired alternative response.

Recent work on invertebrates such as the sea snail *Aplysia* has thrown light on the biophysical mechanisms underlying habituation of elementary responses in such species, notably the gill-withdrawal reflex in *Aplysia* (Kandel, 1979). It has been found that habituation of this reflex is effected through a reduction in synaptic transmission at synapses connecting sensory and motor neurons. This is brought about by a short- or long-term suppression of calcium channels responsible for the calcium current into the presynaptic terminal. Sensitization is brought about by a serotonergic system that depresses the outward potassium current, thus restoring the inward calcium current. We do not know what mechanisms maintain the properties of a presynaptic terminal over time, so it is not possible to speculate whether there may be any parallel between this system as a whole and the PC model; perhaps we should not expect to find one at this level. But these results do establish the existence of mechanisms capable of modifying the responsiveness or level of activity of individual fibers for long periods of time—a finding in the spirit of the assumptions that underlie the present model.

The present approach looks at all responses, except possibly the simplest, as being partly determined by a decision-making device that may be biased by various sources, the most important being its own previous activity, and with parameters that may be adjusted for particular purposes (so that it may habituate rapidly in one case, not at all in another). This may seem to conflict with the traditional view of the reflex arc as a unique pathway connecting stimulus and response as well as the generalizations of this view intended to explain more complex learning. But I believe that on a careful reading, Sherrington's (1906/1947) seminal views on reflexes are consistent with this approach.

The PC concept may apply to further problems. The major area that invites consideration is conditioning, but this is too large a subject to discuss here. Another application may be to the variability of behavior between individuals. A threat may cause flight in one animal, freezing in another. Anger may turn one man white, another red. Fear may make the heart race or may cause it to stand still. The present analysis suggests that such variations may arise from asymmetries in preset or residual noise levels in those PCs determining such behaviors, and that such asymmetries (and other parameters) may vary from one person to another. We usually observe the rate-sensitive responses determined by $\Delta o(C)$. If we could find ways in each case to measure the prior levels $o_{k,0}(C)$, the apparent variability and unpredictability of natural behavior might be reduced. The question of the causes of these asymmetries in residual noise might then offer itself for research.

Differences in the noise levels of paired PUs may favor particular response alternatives on a short-term or long-term basis. They provide a means whereby the organism can preset a given response strategy and ensure its rapid execution should the need arise. Thus a short-term bias in favor of R_A ["preparedness" in a reaction-time task (Bertelson & Tisseyre, 1968; Holender & Bertelson, 1975; Thomas, 1974)] might be produced by an activation message tuned to PU_A, a long-term bias by a permanently raised value for the preset noise $e_0(B)$. In such cases a sudden high-intensity stimulus (or even a minor irrelevant stimulus if the imbalance in activation is large) may lead to performance of the prepared response—even though this stimulus normally sends a minor identity message to PC_i and the internal tuning of PC_i for this stimulus is broad. Such suggestions might explain phenomena such as the anticipation of a simple reaction time, the premature start of a sprinter listening for the starting gun, or even a defensive reply to a neutral comment.

These suggestions may seem to venture into the field of personality, and it is possible that the model may have something to say here (although there is no space to discuss this). It is sufficient to note at this point that a person with generally small values of e_0, but large values of d and e/d, would show large responses to small stimuli; and these would habituate rapidly. With e_0 large and d and e/d small, responses would have high thresholds and small amplitudes but would be more resistant to habituation. The former combination may suggest features of an "impulsive extravert," a person with the latter combination of parameters might be described as persistent and an introvert. Thus at least one interindividual distinction might be derivable from characteristic differences in the parameters of the model.

Appendix: Glossary of Symbols

a_k	Activation message on trial k
a_{PC}	$a(S,PC)$
a_X	$a(S,PU_X)$
$a(S,PC_i)$	An activation message; this is emitted by the activation perceptual subsystem when it detects a critical feature, such as novelty, in the stimulus S and is directed to the primary-comparator system i
$a(S,X)$ or $a(S,PU_X)$	An activation message directed to primary effector unit X in a primary-comparator system; a is the probability of terminating activity in a randomly selected fiber
$a_i(S,PC_i)$	An intensity activation message to PC_i elicited by the high intensity of stimulus S
$a_p(S,PC_r)$	A priming activation message directed to PC_r in response to a stimulus S whose identification message goes elsewhere
$a_u(S,PC_i)$	An unfamiliarity activation message to PC_i elicited by unfamiliarity of the stimulus S
d_{PC}	$d(S,PC)$
d_X	$d(S,PU_X)$
$d(S,PC_i)$	Identity message evoked from the identification perceptual subsystem by the stimulus S and directed to primary-comparator system i
$d(S,X)$ or $d(S,PU_X)$	An identity message directed to primary effector unit X in a primary-comparator system; d is the probability of exciting a randomly selected fiber
e	Proportion of the previously inactive fibers stably excited by an identity message to a primary effector unit
e_0	Preset noise level: the proportion of the fibers in a primary unit maintained in a state of excitation by mechanisms independent of the current and recent stimulus input

$e_0(X)$	Preset noise level in PU_X
$f_{b,t}(PC_i,PC_i)$	Feedback message generated by PC_i on trial t
$f_{b,t}(PC_i,X_i)$	Component of the feedback message generated by PC_i that is directed to PU_{Xi} on trial t
$f(PC_i,PC_j)$	Feed-forward message from PC_i to PC_j
$f(PC_i,X_j)$	Feed-forward message from PC_i to PU_X of PC_j
k_b	A scaling constant ensuring that the initial feedback message produces an effect equivalent to that of the previous stimulus
k_{fX}	Scaling factor for the feed-forward message from PC_i to PU_X of PC_j
n	Number of nerve fibers in a primary unit
n_X	Number of nerve fibers in PU_X
$o(C)$	Output from the comparator; given by the algebraic sum of the inputs to it from the two PUs
$o(X)$	Output from primary effector unit X to the comparator
$o_k(C)$	Output from the comparator on trial k, subsequent to the receipt of the identity messages from stimulus S on that trial
$o_{k,0}(C)$	Output from the comparator on trial k, prior to the receipt of identity messages from stimulus S on that trial
$\Delta o_k(C)$	Shift in $o(C)$ on trial k as a result of the receipt of identity messages from the stimulus on that trial
PC	A primary-comparator system; this consists of two opposed primary effector units, a comparator, and a response selector
PU	A primary effector unit; this receives activation and identity messages from the perceptual system or higher-order PCs and transmits an output o to the comparator
PU_X	Primary effector unit X
PU_{Xi}	Primary effector unit X in primary-comparator system i
R_X	Response X
R_{Xi}	Response X of PC_i
R_{Xs}	Response X, strong form
R_{Xw}	Response X, weak form
S	A stimulus
t_c	A critical period during which a sufficient change in $o(C)$ must occur for the response selector to initiate a response
x	Response selector decision axis
x_k	Effect produced on the response selector decision axis by $\Delta o_k(C)$ on trial k

$\bar{x}_k$ Expectation of the effect produced by $\Delta o_k(C)$ on the response selector decision axis on trial k

$x(X)$ A criterion which must be exceeded to give R_X

$x_s(X)$ A criterion which must be exceeded to give the strong form of R_X

$x_w(X)$ A criterion which must be exceeded to give the weak form of R_X

References

Bertelson, P., & Tisseyre, F. The time-course of preparation with regular and irregular foreperiods. *Quarterly Journal of Experimental Psychology,* 1968, *20,* 297–300.

Boynton, R. M. *Human color vision.* New York: Holt, Rinehart & Winston, 1979.

Church, R. M., LoLordo, V. M., Overmier, J. B., Solomon, R. L., & Turner, L. H. Cardiac responses to shock in curarized dogs: Effects of shock intensity and duration, warning signal, and prior experience with shock. *Journal of Comparative and Physiological Psychology,* 1966, *62,* 1–7.

Clynes, M. Unidirectional rate sensitivity: A biocybernetic law of reflex and humoral systems as physiologic channels of control and communication. *Annals of the New York Academy of Sciences,* 1961, *92,* 946–969.

Clynes, M. Cybernetic implications of rein control in perceptual and conceptual organization. *Annals of the New York Academy of Sciences,* 1969, *156,* 629–670.

Davis, M. Effects of interstimulus interval length and variability on startle-response habituation in the rat. *Journal of Comparative and Physiological Psychology,* 1970, *72,* 177–192.

Davis, M., & Wagner, A. R. Startle responsiveness after habituation to different intensities of tone. *Psychonomic Science,* 1968, *12,* 337–338.

Deutsch, J. A. *The structural basis of behavior.* London & New York: Cambridge University Press, 1960.

Domjan, M., Gillan, D. J., & Gemberling, G. A. Aftereffects of lithium-conditioned stimuli on consummatory behavior in the presence or absence of the drug. *Journal of Experimental Psychology; Animal Behavior Processes,* 1980, *6,* 49–64.

Ewert, J.-P., & Ingle, D. Excitatory effects following habituation of prey-catching activity in frogs and toads. *Journal of Comparative and Physiological Psychology,* 1971, *77,* 369–374.

Gray, J. A. *Elements of a two-process theory of learning.* New York: Academic Press, 1975.

Groves, P. M., & Thompson, R. F. A dual-process theory of habituation: Neural mechanisms. In H. V. S. Peeke & M. J. Herz (Eds.), *Habituation* (Vol. 2) New York: Academic Press, 1973. Pp. 175–205.

Hering, E. *Outlines of a theory of the light sense* (L. M. Hurvich & D. Jameson, trans.) Cambridge, Mass.: Harvard University Press, 1964. (Originally published, 1905.)

Hinde, R. A. Behavioural habituation. In G. Horn & R. A. Hinde (Eds.), *Short-term changes in neural activity and behaviour.* London & New York: Cambridge University Press, 1970. Pp. 3–40.

Holender, D., & Bertelson, P. Selective preparation and time uncertainty. *Acta Psychologica,* 1975, *39,* 193–203.

Horn, G. Neuronal mechanisms of habituation. *Nature (London),* 1967, *215,* 707–711.

Humphrey, G. *The nature of learning.* London: Kegan Paul, Trench, Trubner, 1933.

Hurvich, L. M., & Jameson, D. Opponent processes as a model of neural organization. *American Psychologist,* 1974, *29,* 88–102.

Judd, D. B. Basic correlates of the visual stimulus. In S. S. Stevens (Ed.), *Handbook of experimental psychology.* New York: Wiley, 1951. Pp. 811–867.

Kandel, E. R. Small systems of neurons. *Scientific American,* 1979, *241,* 60–70.

Kimble, D. P., & Ray, R. S. Reflex habituation and potentiation in *Rana pipiens. Animal Behaviour,* 1965, *13,* 530–533.

Lacey, J. I., & Lacey, B. C. The law of initial value in the longitudinal study of autonomic constitution: Reproducibility of autonomic responses and response patterns over a four-year interval. *Annals of the New York Academy of Sciences,* 1962, *98,* 1257–1290.

Pakula, A., & Sokolov, E. N. Habituation in Gastropoda: Behavioral, interneuronal and endoneuronal aspects. In H. V. S. Peeke & M. J. Herz (Eds.), *Habituation* (Vol. 2). New York: Academic Press, 1973. Pp. 35–107.

Patterson, T. L., & Petrinovich, L. Field studies of habituation. II. Effect of massed stimulus presentation. *Journal of Comparative and Physiological Psychology,* 1979, *93,* 351–359.

Petrinovich, L. A species-meaningful analysis of habituation. In H. V. S. Peeke & M. J. Herz (Eds.), *Habituation* (Vol. 1). New York: Academic Press, 1973.

Petrinovich, L., & Patterson, T. L. Field studies of habituation. IV. Sensitization as a function of the distribution and novelty of song playback to White-crowned Sparrows. *Journal of Comparative and Physiological Psychology,* 1981, *95,* 805–812.

Russo, J. M., Reiter, L. A., & Ison, J. R. Repetitive exposure does not attenuate the sensory impact of the habituated stimulus. *Journal of Comparative and Physiological Psychology,* 1975, *88,* 665–669.

Sharpless, S., & Jasper, H. Habituation of the arousal reaction. *Brain,* 1956, *79,* 655–681.

Sherrington, C. *The integrative action of the nervous system* (2nd ed.). New Haven, Conn.: Yale University Press, 1947. (Originally published, 1906.)

Sokolov, Y. N. Neuronal models and the orienting reflex. In M. A. B. Brazier (Ed.), *The central nervous system and behavior.* New York: Josiah Macy, Jr. Foundation, 1960. Pp. 187–276.

Sokolov, Y. N. *Perception and the conditioned reflex.* Oxford: Pergamon, 1963.

Solomon, R. L. The opponent-process theory of acquired motivation: The costs of pleasure and the benefits of pain. *American Psychologist,* 1980, *35,* 691–712.

Solomon, R. L., & Corbit, J. D. An opponent-process theory of motivation. I. Temporal dynamics of affect. *Psychological Review,* 1974, *81,* 119–145.

Starr, M. D. An opponent-process theory of motivation. VI. Time and intensity variables in the development of separation-induced distress calling in ducklings. *Journal of Experimental Psychology; Animal Behavior Processes,* 1978, *4,* 338–355.

Szlep, R. Change in the response of spiders to repeated web vibrations. *Behaviour,* 1964, *23,* 203–239.

Thomas, E. A. C. The selectivity of preparation. *Psychological Review,* 1974, *81,* 442–464.

Thompson, R. F., & Spencer, W. A. Habituation: A model phenomenon for the study of neuronal substrates of behavior. *Psychological Review,* 1966, *73,* 16–43.

Thorpe, W. H. *Learning and instinct in animals* (2nd ed.). London: Methuen, 1963.

Treisman, M. A theory of response selection. 1984. Manuscript submitted for publication.

von Uexküll, J. Streifzüge durch die Umwelten von Tieren und Menschen. Berlin: Springer, 1934. Transl. C. Schiller. A stroll through the worlds of animals and men. In C. Schiller (ed.) *Instinctive behavior.* London: Methuen, 1957.

Wilder, J. The law of initial value in neurology and psychiatry. *Journal of Nervous and Mental Disease,* 1957, *125,* 73–86.

Wilder, J. Basimetric approach (law of initial value) to biological rhythms. *Annals of the New York Academy of Sciences,* 1962, *98,* 1211–1220.

Wolda, H. Response decrement in the prey catching activity of *Notonecta glauca* L. (Hemiptera). *Archives Neerlandaises de Zoologie,* 1961, *14,* 61–89.

Wyers, E. J., Peeke, H. V. S., & Herz, M. J. Behavioral habituation in invertebrates. In H. V. S. Peeke & M. J. Herz (Eds.) *Habituation* (Vol. 1). New York: Academic Press, 1973.

CHAPTER 4

Memory and Habituation

Jesse W. Whitlow, Jr.

Psychology Department
Rutgers University
Camden, New Jersey

Allan R. Wagner

Department of Psychology
Yale University
New Haven, Connecticut

Preparation of this chapter and portions of the research reported were supported by National Science Foundation Grant BNS 80-23399. Preparation of the chapter was also supported by a grant from the Rutgers University Research Council.

I. Introduction

Charles Sherrington's (1906) analysis of "reflex fatigue" in spinal dogs established the foundations for a perspective on habituation that has proven durable and fruitful. Sherrington's analysis was centered on the conceptual framework of the reflex arc, consisting of a receptor surface and sensory neuron, a chain of interneurons, and a final common path of motoneurons and effectors. Overt behavior is seen as the product of activation of a reflex pathway, and the ultimate account of behavior changes is seen as the identification of the locus and nature of changes in the pattern of neural activity permitted by the reflex arc. The power of Sherrington's approach is readily apparent in the modern literature by the vigorous research programs of Kandel (e.g., 1976), Thompson (e.g., Thompson & Glanzman, 1976), Krasne (e.g., 1976), and others, which have produced fundamental insights into the synaptic mechanisms that may be associated with the changes in reflex excitability following repeated stimulation.

An alternate perspective on the phenomena of habituation is that of molar behavior theories such as those of Sokolov (1963), Konorski (1967), and Wagner (1976). Such theories may address "simple" reflexes and may sometimes involve assertions about possible neuronal processes, but they may be best understood as applicable to stimulus–response tendencies of unspecified physiological origin and as *abstract* formulations in which supposed concrete mechanisms serve only to capture the *functional* regularities assumed to hold in the plasticity of these tendencies. Thus, for example, Sokolov (1963) emphasized the operation of a "comparator," evaluating the relationship between the stimulus and a "neuronal model" of past stimulation, but Horn (1970) has illustrated how the functional properties of Sokolov's theory could be mimicked by intrinsic changes in various neural networks. Pfautz and Wagner (1976) similarly indicated how certain assumptions involving the functioning of a comparator could be stated as well in terms of a system involving recurrent inhibition of input channels.

There are several potential advantages of molar, functional theories. One is that certain phenomena may exhibit consistent regularities from instance to instance in spite of important differences in the underlying molecular processes. This is a familiar argument. In the case of habituation it is certainly possible that nature has solved the problem of allowing inattention to repetitive stimuli in various ways, just as it has solved the problem of respiration in various ways, but with functional properties of the solution being similar at an abstract level precisely because the problem has been similar (see, e.g., Simon, 1969).

The advantages we would emphasize are more prosaic. Behavioral theories may help us to identify and organize the essential phenomena that must be accounted for and to be cognizant of the potential relationship of these phenomena to other behavior tendencies, in performance and learning, outside the circumscribed domain of "reflex fatigue." This chapter is an attempt to illustrate such a theory. Our approach is to view habituation from the vantage of a quantitative model that precisely states a functional description of the *standard operating procedures* of a memory system, hence the model has the acronym SOP. This model assumes that habituation reflects the processing dynamics of a memory system that has transient *and* durable components, each component making separate—though interrelated—contributions to performance. A more detailed specification of the model necessary for developing substantive implications of this proposal is presented in the next section of the chapter; but two general comments regarding the approach to habituation taken in the present chapter are in order.

First, there is no necessary conflict between a behavior-theory approach and the Sherringtonian approach mentioned previously. Indeed, they may complement each other. What they would both displace is a more superficial, descriptive appreciation of habituation. Thompson and Spencer (1966), for example, attempted to identify the essential phenomena of habituation by an empirical cataloging of the available findings (based largely on simple reflexes). They pointed to nine parametric variations that had such characteristic effects that the constellation of effects might be said to "define" habituation. As influential as this cataloging has been, analytical studies motivated by the Sherringtonian approach and the behavior theory approach make it clear that some of the generalizations involved can be quite misleading. For example, Thompson and Spencer (1966) maintained that habituation is more pronounced the shorter the interval between successive stimuli. We now know from both a neurophysiological and a behavior-theory perspective that one must make a distinction between relatively transient and more permanent effects in habituation experiments and that, in fact, habituation as measured on a remote test is more pronounced with distributed as compared to massed stimulation (e.g., Carew, Pinsker, & Kandel, 1972; Davis, 1970).

Second, many of the assumptions embodied in SOP can be identified as part of a core set of assumptions about the characteristics of memory that are widely shared among various theorists (see, e.g., Wagner, 1981). To the extent these shared assumptions provide a conceptual framework within which methods of empirical analysis and interpretations of data can be developed that are distinctive relative to other molar theories of behavior, it may be useful, following Estes's (1973) distinction regarding conditioning experiments, to identify our approach as offering a *memory-oriented* rather than a *response-oriented* view of habituation. According to Estes, in the response-oriented view, learning consists of the acquisition of a response, and, with the judicious selection of a performance measure, one can monitor the course of learning directly by recording changes in the dependent measure. But in a memory-oriented view the organism acquires memories of event sequences as a result of experience, and these memories may be expressed in a variety of measures of performance. In consequence, measures of learning are necessarily indirect, and selection of a dependent measure can be guided only by the reliability of the measure and the utility of the data it provides.

As documented in subsequent sections of this chapter, the choice of a memory-oriented perspective influences the selection of strategies and tactics of research as well as the language used to interpret the resulting observations; and two general consequences of adopting the viewpoint of SOP are worth noting at the outset. One is the recognition that other measures besides those assessing reflex elicitation by an unconditioned stimulus (US) may be useful as indicators of the effects of iterated stimulus presentation. Thus we describe studies in which the development of a conditioned response (CR) to a conditioned stimulus (CS) that signals the US also serves as an index of memory, for example, in addition to studies that use the more traditional measure of a change in the ability of the US to elicit an unconditioned response (UR). The other consequence is to allow the possibility that habituation mechanisms may not necessarily depress the response tendencies controlled by an iterated stimulus. This possibility is considered in Section VII in terms of some work that suggests a common mechanism may be responsible for certain instances of response facilitation as well as of response depression.

In outline, the chapter has the following plan. The next section describes the particular theoretical assumptions of SOP. Following sections apply SOP to the analysis of phenomena pertaining to five theoretically significant issues regarding habituation:

1. Analysis of transient changes in responsiveness
2. Associative basis of durable response decrements
3. Effects of concurrent stimulation on habituation
4. Effects of stimulus intensity and interstimulus interval
5. Common basis for response facilitation and response depression

The final section provides an overview of our approach to habituation and suggests one way a molar, behavior-theory perspective may complement the Sherringtonian view.

II. SOP: A Theory of Automatic Memory Processing

The theory we shall outline has been formulated to address equally phenomena of habituation and associative learning as observed in investigations of infrahuman organisms. It stands in line of development as an extension and elaboration of a set of speculations on the variability in "rehearsal" of expected-versus-surprising events (e.g., Wagner, Rudy, & Whitlow, 1973) and how this might be more generally understood in terms of the consequences of "priming" of short-term memory (e.g., Wagner, 1976, 1978, 1979; Whitlow, 1975, 1976), to account for the essential regularities of Pavlovian conditioning subsumed in the equations of the Rescorla–Wagner model (Rescorla & Wagner, 1972; Wagner & Rescorla, 1972).

Here we cannot summarize the considerable evidence that has shaped the formation, but can only point to the sources already mentioned. Neither can we present the theory in the full detail that would be necessary to appreciate its application to the variety of phenomena of associative learning that it is intended to cover. For such, the reader may consult Wagner (1981) for an overview and Donegan and Wagner (in press) and Mazur and Wagner (in press) for more specific treatments. Here it is necessary to restrict ourselves to describing the gist of the theory as it relates to phenomena of habituation, only briefly hinting at the manner it has been formalized in a quantitative fashion as has been required for certain applications.

A. General Propositions

SOP has a number of unique characteristics that follow from the particular, stochastic manner in which it has been formalized. But the essence of the theory can be largely appreciated by seeing how it embodies rather conventional assumptions from an information-processing perspective.

1. System Overview

The learner is conceptualized as a communication system involving an initial stimulus-encoding device (sensory register) and a final decoder (response generator), the two joined by components that include a knowledge structure (memory system) for representing past experience. In many situations theoretical issues will revolve around the variable operation of the sensory register and response generator or upon the manner in which the several components, including the memory system, are subject to flexible routines under the attention of an executive monitor. But in approaching phenomena of infrahuman habituation and associative learning, involving conventional, well-characterized responses to simple, obtrusive stimuli, some gross simplifications are countenanced. That is, the subject's performance and learning is taken to rather directly mirror the momentary states of the memory system, which are in turn presumed to be dictated by obligatory stimulus-encoding and automatic operating characteristics. By design, SOP attempts to comment (only) on the "standard operating procedures" of the memory system.

2. The Memory System as a Graph Structure

In agreement with numerous theorists (e.g., J. R. Anderson & Bower, 1973; Konorski, 1967; Shiffrin & Schneider, 1977) the memory system is conceptualized as a network of representational units, or memory nodes, interconnected by directional associative links. We assume that any effective stimulus, through coding in the sensory register, will "activate" (see next section) a corresponding memory node. This representational process itself is not presumed to be dependent on learning (see, e.g., J. R. Anderson & Bower, 1973). What is dependent on prior experience are the linkages between the separate nodes, and hence the likelihood that activation of one node will "spread" from one to another. And what otherwise can reflect past experience is whether some node or nodes remain active as a perseverative result of prior stimulation.

3. Activity State Distinctions

Different spaces of the memory structure are distinguished by whether or not the nodes involved are currently "active" or currently "inactive." It is common to say that whereas all of the nodes and their linkages constitute "long-term store" (LTS), those currently active are in "working memory" (e.g., Norman, 1968) or some similar manner of distinguishing the active from dormant areas of the memory system (J. R. Anderson & Bower, 1973; W. James, 1890).

It is central to SOP to further distinguish between two states of nodal activity beyond inactivity. We were led to this view (e.g., Wagner, 1976; Whitlow, 1976) by Atkinson and Shiffrin's (1968) distinction between the totality of active units in "short-term store" (STS) and the smaller subset that may be presumed to be enjoying a special degree of processing in a "rehearsal buffer." But it has been proposed in a variety of theories. Thus, for example, Konorski (1967) distinguished between the totality of active units in "transient memory" and the smaller subset that is "the object of attention." And Bower (1975) similarly distinguished between those active units in "working memory" and those in "focal STS." Because there has been such different and sometimes inconsistent terminology employed by different theorists to capture relatively similar ideas, SOP distinguishes as neutrally as possible among a state of inactivity (I) and two states of activity, a primary state (A1) and a secondary state (A2).

In fact, the stated designations are meant to suggest an assumed sequence. When a memory node is in the I state, it is assumed that activation by its corresponding stimulus will be to the A1 state from which activation will "decay" to the A2 state and then back to I. This description of state transitions is intended to correspond to the commonly voiced notion that stimulus presentation is likely to produce an initial representation in a focal, short-term buffer, from which it will drift to more marginal working memory, before returning to rest in LTS (e.g., Bower, 1975).

It may broaden the intuitive appreciation of the basic conceptualization thus far to see that it shares certain formal similarities with Solomon and Corbit's (1974) opponent-process theory of affective dynamics. In this theory it is assumed that any (strong) stimulus will produce a primary affective process α, the time course of which closely follows stimulus onset and termination. The α process is, moreover, assumed to arouse a secondary, or slave, process β, which (a) is more sluggish to recruit and dissipate and (b) generally functions to oppose the α process. The presumed result is that stimulus presentation and removal will be followed by a characteristic sequence of isolated α process, eventually being suppressed and replaced by the β process, before the system returns to inactivity. At an abstract level there is an interesting correspondence of this reasoning to our notion that memorial processing of a stimulus observes the usual sequence A1 $\rightarrow$ A2 $\rightarrow$ I. An important difference, among others, is that SOP does not necessarily assume that A2 activity is the functional "opposite" of A1 activity. But because A2 activity may be in opposition to A1 activity in *some* influences, Wagner (1981) has noted that SOP could stand for a "sometimes opponent-process" theory.

4. Qualifications in Nodal Dynamics

If a node is (a) inactive and (b) stimulated by the environmental event it represents, it will be provoked to the activity sequence A1 $\rightarrow$ A2 $\rightarrow$ I. The activity sequence is assumed to be altered in theoretically significant ways if either of the two conditions is not met.

As previously mentioned, there is assumed to be "spread of activation" over the linkages that connect the separate nodes, and it is in this manner that one stimulus (e.g., a Pavlovian CS) can presumably acquire the ability to activate the node of another stimulus (e.g., a US) and thus provoke a conditioned response. But SOP assumes that associative activation of a node does not produce A1 activity of that node. In discussions of human memory there is a long tradition of acknowledging that events recalled from memory are less vivid or salient than are those provoked by immediate experience (e.g., W. James, 1890). There is a comparable appreciation in discussions of animal conditioning that the conditioned response may not mimic the unconditioned response (e.g., Zener, 1937). One way to approach these observations is to deny that a CS can provoke the full complement of activation in a US node as can the US itself. It is assumed in SOP that associative activation provokes an inactive node directly to the *A2 state*. The distinctive proposal of SOP is that the associative activation of a node is not like a "weaker" form of the activation resulting from direct exposure to the stimulus the node represents, but a "decayed" (i.e., A2) form of such activation with all of the properties assigned to that state. In sympathy with such a notion, Schull (1979) has proposed that associative learning between a CS and US embues the CS with the tendency to elicit the β process normally attendant on the US, but not the α process.

The other qualification is that activation of a node by some stimulus occurs only to the degree that the node is in the I state. To the degree that the node is already in A1, stimulation is presumed to have no further effect. This has been a core assumption of the background theories (e.g., Wagner, 1976, 1978) and is the model's way of recognizing that "expected" events are less likely to be processed than are "surprising" events (e.g., Bobrow & Norman, 1975; Bower, 1975; Kamin, 1968). If a stimulus is presented when its node is already in the A1 state, the additional presentation is simply redundant with respect to indices of processing. But, the important case is when its node is in the *A2 state*. Then the stimulus will be ineffective in occasioning the A1 activity that it otherwise would. Although the A2 state does not literally "oppose" the A1 state, it can preclude it.

It should be obvious how the latter restriction prepares us to deal with certain phenomena of habituation: there should be a period of time after a node has been activated by presentation of its corresponding stimulus [so-called self-generated priming (Wagner, 1976)], during which additional presentation of that stimulus will be less capable of placing the node in a state of primary activation. And there should be occasions in which the prior activation of a node by associated stimuli [so-called associatively generated priming (Wagner, 1976)] can produce the same decrement in stimulus processing.

5. Rules for Response Generation and Associative Learning

The model does not attempt an explanation of the qualitative mapping of nodal activity into observed behavior by the response generator. But SOP does make one fundamental allowance: that the two states of activity A1 and A2 can have separable influences on any response measure. The transfer functions $w_{1,j}$ and $w_{2,j}$, relating A1 and A2 activity, respectively, to any response R_j are accepted as empirically determined, with no a priori restriction on either the relative magnitudes or algebraic signs of w_1 and w_2. One reason for this openness is that there are many instances in Pavlovian conditioning in which the CR, presumably mediated by associatively generated A2 activity of a US node, is similar to the prominent UR to the US (e.g., Mackintosh, 1974) and other instances in which the CR is opposite or "compensatory" to the UR (e.g., Siegel, 1975). What should consistently be the case is that the CR will mimic a secondary component of the UR, that is, the response to the delayed (A2) consequence of the US.

The model is explicit about the conditions that modify the linkages between stimulus nodes. In brief, it is assumed that excitatory learning occurs to increase the possibility for spread of activation between two nodes whenever the two nodes are concurrently in the A1 state. This is a rephrasing of the familiar notion (e.g., Atkinson & Shiffrin, 1968) that associative learning depends on the separate stimuli being represented in STS. SOP assumes that inhibitory learning also occurs to decrease the possibility for spread of activation between two nodes, as a specific result of the concurrent activity of the nodes involved. In this case, however, it is assumed that the directional inhibitory link from one node to another occurs whenever the former node is in the A1 state while the latter node is in the A2 state. In the present chapter we are not able to develop the implications of these rules (see Mazur & Wagner, in press) except to draw attention to several instances in which excitatory Pavlovian conditioning is diminished, just as a UR may be diminished, by "habituation" manipulations that reduce the A1 activity of one or more of the stimulus nodes involved.

6. Capacity Limitations

One of the most common assumptions of theories of the general type of SOP is that there are limitations on the portion of the memory system that can be active at any one time, with more severe limitations on focal STS than on more marginal working memory (e.g., Bower, 1975; Konorski, 1967). SOP makes use of these notions in various ways. First, it is assumed that competition for the limited concurrent activity is what is responsible for any nodal "decay" from A1 to A2 and from A2 to I. Second, it is assumed that because of the differential capacity limitations of A1 and A2, decay from A1 to A2 will be faster than the decay from A2 to I. And, finally, it is assumed that while any experimental context contains intrinsic sources of competing stimulation to assure the aforementioned decay, explicit additions of experimental "distractors" will accelerate the rates of decay.

B. Formalization

These notions can be followed to many implications without further specification. Indeed, most of the relevant data presented in the following sections can be related to the theory at this level. There are many cases, however, where the determinacy of the prediction would be in doubt without further theoretical commitments. For this reason we will briefly indicate the manner the essential reasoning has been formalized in SOP.

Let us assume that a representational node is not the most primitive component of the memory system but is, rather, composed of a large but finite number of informational elements. It could be assumed that subsets of the elements correspond to separable aspects of the represented event, so that generalization phenomena might be approached in terms of overlapping nodal elements in the spirit of stimulus-sampling theory (Estes, 1950). But we shall assume that a node is "unitized" [to use a term of Shiffrin and Schneider (1977)] in the sense that experimental events that would affect the activity state of one element will have equal probabilistic effects on all elements of the node that are in the same state. From this reasoning one can transform the preceding notions about the discrete activity-state transitions of a node into a continuous process in which different proportions of nodal elements may be activated by different experimental stimuli and in which there is a characteristic and well-defined course of subsequent "decay" with different proportions of elements in A1, A2, and I in successive moments in time. And one can state the rules for response generation and associative learning in terms of the proportion of elements in the several states to arrive at more determinant characterization of the predicted products of conceivable experimental episodes.

Figure 1a depicts an individual representational node. The connected circles I, A1, and A2 indicate the several states of activation in which individual elements may reside, and they can be conceived as each containing some specifiable proportion of the total nodal elements. Such proportions are presumed to change only as a result of the stated transi-

(a)   (b)

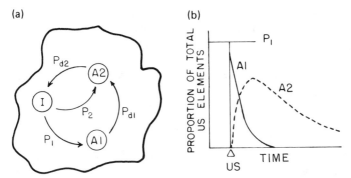

Fig. 1. (a) State transition diagram of the transitions among a state of inactivity (I), primary activation (A1), and secondary activation (A2) for elements of the memory node. (b) Time course of activation processes in a memory node following a single brief presentation of a US. From Wagner (1981).

tions indicated by the connecting arrows and with the magnitudes specified by the adjoining p values. The latter refer to the transitional probabilities for individual elements in any moment (defined as an arbitrarily small unit of time), which will depend upon the nodal environment at the moment.

Suppose that the stimulus that the node represents (its US) is presented. SOP assumes that for each moment the US is presented, there is a consistent probability p_1 that any element of the node that is in the I state will transfer to the A1 state, with the value of p_1 being an increasing function of stimulus intensity. This is the only assumed direct effect of the US upon its node. Once an element is in the A1 state, however, it is assumed that it may decay to the A2 state in any moment, according to the probability p_{d1} and from the A2 state may correspondingly decay back to the I state with probability p_{d2}. The values of p_{d1} and p_{d2} will depend on the experimental context, having nonnegligible values as a result of extraexperimental sources of competition for nodal activity and increasing with identifiable experimental "distractors" (see Wagner, 1981, for more specific dependencies). The differential state limitations require that p_{d1} be greater than p_{d2}.

Figure 1b illustrates some characteristic products of these assumptions in simulation. It describes the activity course over time of a node that is initially completely inactive and is then activated by a punctate "US." In the moment of the US, p_1 of the elements are activated to the A1 state. In successive moments, p_{d1} of the elements that remain in A1 will decay to A2, so that the course of A1 activation observes a simple exponential function. The dashed function depicts the proportion of elements in the

A2 state as they enter this state from A1 and decay with the probability p_{d2} back to I. The characteristic course involves a complex but specifiable (see Wagner, 1981) buildup and then dissipation of secondary activation.

If the same "US" node in Fig. 1a were associatively activated (i.e., received input by the activation of a CS node with which it had excitatory linkages), the picture of nodal activity would be quite different from that in Fig. 1b. In moments of CS nodal activity, p_2 of the US node would be assumed to have nonzero value, increasing as a product of the proportion of CS elements in the A1 state and a measure of the associative linkage (see Wagner, 1981). The result is a singular increase in proportion of elements in the A2 state, followed by eventual decay back to I according to p_{d2}.

For the moment we shall not pursue further the quantitative rules of SOP. What should be apparent is that with this stochastic approach it is possible to arrive at an explicit characterization of the assumed processes. In the sections that follow we call on such characterizations as necessary.

III. Analysis of Transient Response Depression

Persisting nodal activation provides a mechanism for producing transient changes in responsiveness to a stimulus following an initial presentation of that event. The present section focuses on the implications of this mechanism for the analysis of the refractorylike diminution frequently observed to the second of two successive presentations of a stimulus.

The procedure of arranging stimulus repetitions as pairs, in which S_1, an initial presentation, is followed after a relatively short interval by a second probe presentation S_2, offers a fairly direct method for assessing the dynamics of activation. According to SOP, an S_1 presentation would initiate the sequence of events depicted earlier in Fig. 1. Some number of the elements in the nodal representation of the stimulus would enter the A1 state, from which they would gradually change to the A2 state. There would be an initial rise followed by a gradual decrease in the number of elements in A2, with the eventual return of all elements to the I state. To the degree that elements have not returned to I, an S_2 repetition of the stimulus will transfer fewer elements to A1. The behavioral consequences of this circumstance will depend in part on the particular index of processing examined; but three characteristics of the effects of S_1 on the processing of S_2 should be invariant across behavioral indices: the effects should be (a) stimulus-specific (i.e., restricted to a reapplication of the same nominal stimulus), (b) transient, dissipating as the interval between S_1 and S_2 increases, and (c) susceptible to disruption by the occurrence of "distractor" stimuli intervening between the S_1 and S_2 presentations.

These considerations lead to a simple set of guidelines for the experimental analysis of the basis for transient performance changes to S_2, which we illustrate in the remainder of this section, using a variety of indices of memory activation that differ according to whether the index involves the elicitation of a UR or of a CR and whether the experimental manipulation involves a US or a CS.

A. Decrements in UR Magnitude

In general, according to SOP, the magnitude of the UR to the second of two successive presentations of a US may be expected to exhibit a complex dependency on the S_1–S_2 interval, the intensity of S_2, and the particular response system studied. For example, extremely short intervals between S_1 and S_2 will prevent any significant decay of activated elements from an A1 to an A2 state, hence there will be temporal summation of the elements activated to A1 by the first and second presentation, resulting in a larger response to S_2 than to S_1. Response facilitation with rapidly occurring US presentations has in fact been reported (e.g., Pfautz, 1980), but there has been little analysis of the basis for such facilitation in relation to the tenets of SOP.

A different situation arises at intermediate intervals, when activation initiated by the S_1 presentation has decayed from A1 to A2 but not yet back to I. In this case, the magnitude of the UR to a second US will depend on the number of elements that remain in A2, the number newly activated to A1, and the relative contribution of A1 and A2 to the response. Discussion of the full range of possibilities is deferred to Section VII, however, after the application of SOP to the more typical phenomena of habituation is clear. For this purpose, it is convenient to suppose that there is no contribution of A2 to the UR (i.e., that w_2 equals 0). In this case there is expected to be a decrement in the response to S_2 whenever elements remain in A2 and cannot be provoked to A1.

Transient decrements in the magnitude of the UR to the second of two successively presented USs have been frequently demonstrated (e.g., Davis, 1970), but it is important from a memory-oriented view that such decrements be specific to a re-presentation of the initial US. The presentation of Stimulus A, prior to a presentation of Stimulus B, should not activate the node for B (unless A and B nodes are associatively connected), but decrements could be observed to B from factors other than the persisting activation of memory. Some transient decrements, such as prepulse inhibition (e.g., Hoffman & Ison, 1980), are known to be nonspecific. Hence whether or not a decrement is stimulus-specific must be determined empirically.

The stimulus specificity of a transient response decrement was evaluated in a study by Whitlow (1975, Exp. 1) of habituation of auditory-evoked vasoconstriction in rabbits. Subjects were tested over two daily sessions, each about 2 hours long, with each test trial consisting of presentations of two tonal stimuli as an S_1–S_2 pair. The sequence of presentations of S_1 and S_2 was designed so that on half the trials S_1 and S_2 were both tones of the same frequency, and on half the trials they were tones of different frequencies. The interval between S_1 and S_2 was 30, 60, or 150 seconds (these intervals occurring equally often in a balanced schedule) and each S_1–S_2 pair was followed by a 150-second intertrial interval.

The data of interest are depicted in Fig. 2, which shows average evoked vasoconstriction at 5-second intervals for S_1 and S_2 at each interstimulus interval (ISI). Data are shown separately for trials in which S_1 and S_2 were the same frequency and trials in which they were different. The major result was a transient depression of responding to S_2 that was specific to trials in which S_1 and S_2 were of the same frequency. Thus, at a 30-second interval (Fig. 2a), there was substantially less responding to S_2 on trials in which S_2 was the same as S_1 than on trials in which S_1 and S_2 were different; at a 60-second interval (Fig. 2b) the separation between the trial types was less; and at a 150-second interval (Fig. 2c) the two trial types produced essentially identical responses.

A traditional interpretive concern has been whether to attribute transient response decrements to effector fatigue or sensory adaptation. The stimulus specificity of the effect shown in Fig. 2 argues against interpreting it in terms of effector fatigue (or nonspecific state changes) that should be insensitive to the identity of the repeated stimulus. But the data could reflect some kind of sensory adaptation, whereby the sensitivity of receptors for a specific tonal frequency is temporarily diminished as a result of the presentation of that frequency, but sensitivity for other tones is unaffected.

Distinguishing sensory adaptation from habituation at the level of molar behavior analysis has often been done in terms of recovery rates, the assumption being that decrements caused by sensory adaptation recover relatively quickly, whereas those caused by habituation recover more slowly. Unfortunately, some "sensory" effects, such as the McCullough effect (e.g., McCullough, 1965), are extremely persistent. From a memory-oriented perspective, the distinction between sensory adaptation and

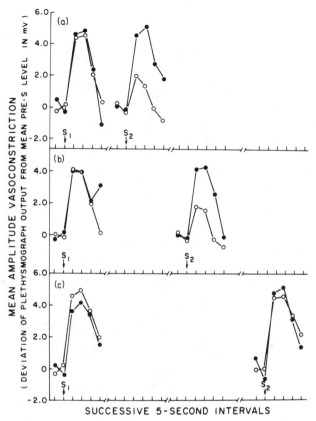

Fig. 2. Averaged auditory-evoked response to successive tones S_1 and S_2 when the tones were of the same (○) and of different (●) frequencies. (a) 30-Second separation between S_1 and S_2. (b) 60-Second separation between S_1 and S_2. (c) 150-Second separation between S_1 and S_2. From Whitlow (1975). Copyright 1975 by the American Psychological Association. Reproduced by permission.

habituation can be more sharply drawn by determining whether or not a transient decrement like that depicted in Fig. 2 can be disrupted by presentation of "distractor" stimuli in the S_1–S_2 interval. Such stimuli should act to accelerate the rate of loss of activation initiated by S_1, thereby restoring more elements to the I state prior to the occurrence of S_2. Consequently, there will be more elements available for activation to A1 by the S_2 presentation. The reversibility of a transient decrement by presentation of interpolated distractors is not a characteristic assumed of sensory adaptation.

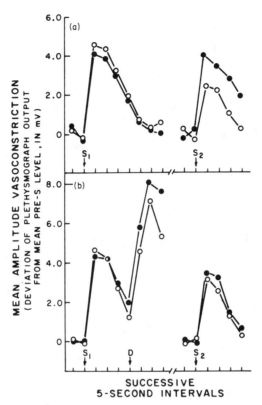

Fig. 3. Averaged auditory-evoked responses to successive tones S_1 and S_2 presented at a 60-second interval when the tones were of the same (O) or of different (●) frequencies. (a) Data from trials in which no stimuli were scheduled in the S_1–S_2 interval. (b) Data for trials in which a distractor stimulus occurred 20 seconds after S_1 at the point marked D on the abscissa. From Whitlow (1975). Copyright 1975 by the American Psychological Association. Reproduced by permission.

Whitlow (1975, Exp. 2) assessed the effects of presenting distractor stimuli in the interval between S_1 and S_2 in a second study conducted along the same general lines as the first, with the exceptions that (a) all S_1–S_2 pairs were 60 seconds apart and (b) on half of the same and half of the different trials, a distractor stimulus consisting of a sequential compound of a 1-second flashing light and a 1-second electrotactile stimulus was presented 20 seconds after S_1.

The main results are shown in Fig. 3. On trials without a distractor stimulus (Fig. 3a), there was a selective response depression on same trials relative to different trials, as had been found in the prior study at a 60-second interval. On trials in which a distractor stimulus occurred 20 seconds after S_1, however, there was essentially no difference in respond-ing to S_2 on same and different trials (Fig. 3b). These results appear to rule out an interpretation of the stimulus-specific decrement in terms of sen-sory adaptation, and suggest that the distractor stimulus abbreviated the duration over which a representation of S_1 remained active in memory.

The data in Fig. 3 also illustrate what Krasne (1976) has termed "true dishabituation." That is, the depressed response otherwise observed with respect to a stimulus repetition was restored selectively, without similar increments in responsivity to other events. This selective increase can be contrasted with the more general increase in responsiveness to stimula-tion—whether or not the response tendencies to the stimuli have been depressed by repeated presentations—characteristic of "sensitization" (e.g., Thompson & Spencer, 1966). True dishabituation, Krasne (1976) suggested, is most readily understood in terms of the operation of a mem-ory system. We agree.

B. Conditioning Decrements Following US Preexposure

SOP anticipates a reduction in the ability of a US to support the devel-opment of conditioned responses that parallels the modulation of UR magnitude described in the preceding section. The formation of excitatory associative connections is assumed to depend on the degree to which both the CS node and the US node are concurrently in the A1 state. Hence, if the US node is less activated to A1, as will presumably happen when the activation initiated by a prior US presentation persists in A2, there will be less opportunity for excitatory connections to develop with the CS.

In the most detailed studies to date of the transient effects of an initial US presentation on the conditioning promoted by a subsequent CS–US episode, William Terry (1976) has demonstrated a depression in acquisi-tion of the conditioned eye-blink response of rabbits that parallels the decrements in UR magnitude in the Whitlow (1975) studies. In each of a series of studies, Terry scheduled conditioning trials with presentations of a 100-msec, 4.5-mA shock US delivered through two stainless steel su-tures in the skin surrounding the eye, the US being preceded by and coterminating with an 1100-msec CS. The measure of conditioned perfor-mance was closure of the eyelid detected during the first 1000 msec of the CS on test trials with the CS alone.

In an initial study, Terry (1976, Exp. 1) found that an isolated presenta-tion of the US 4 seconds earlier than each CS–US sequence resulted in impaired acquisition of conditioned-responding to the CS. That is, an S_1

presentation of the US depressed performance generated by an S_2 presentation of the same US, with the measure of performance being the acquisition of conditioned responding to the CS with which S_2 was paired.

As in the case of the habituation paradigm, this depression could be indicative of memory for the initial S_1 presentation at the time of S_2, but it could also be the product of sensory adaptation. Additionally, in this paradigm the initial US may overshadow or mask the CS, making the latter less effective in acquiring a CR. Terry clarified the interpretive possibilities with analytic techniques of the kind suggested by SOP. Thus, to the degree CR acquisition is impaired as a result of persisting activation of the US node—on the occasion of the CS–US pairing—it should be critical for the pretrial and conditioning USs to be the same stimulus. Alternately, the occurrence of any strong stimulus prior to a CS–US episode should equally depress conditioning if the underlying mechanism of depression were a masking of the CS. In addition, a stimulus–specific depression caused by persisting nodal activation should be reversible by presentation of distractors in the S_1–S_2 interval, whereas such reversibility would not appear if the mechanism were sensory adaptation.

The results of Terry's analysis are illustrated in a study (Terry, 1976, Exp. 3) that evaluated an interpretation of the effects of S_1 in terms of sensory adaptation and also provided negative evidence for nonspecific interference interpretations. Four groups of rabbits were trained with pairings of a CS and a US on each of eight daily conditioning episodes. Group N simply received the CS–US pairing with no pretrial stimulation. Group US received an S_1 presentation of the US 7 seconds prior to each CS–US pairing. This group was expected to show impaired conditioning relative to Group N. Group US + D also received an S_1 presentation of the US 7 seconds before each CS–US pairing, but in addition this group received a distractor (D) stimulus 2 seconds after S_1. The distractor, a 1-second sequence of clicks and vibrotactile stimulation that occurred in a unique pattern on each presentation, was chosen to be a salient stimulus that would effectively deactivate the US node. Hence this group would not be expected to show a conditioning decrement if such decrement depended on persisting activation of the US node at the time of the CS–US pairing. To control for any nonspecific effects of the distractor, Group D received the distractor stimulus 5 seconds before the CS–US pairing but did not receive prior S_1 presentation of the US.

Figure 4 depicts performance of all four groups both during the daily training trials and on special test trials in which the priming US was omitted. The data show clearly that what mattered in producing a conditioning decrement was not whether *something* may have persisted in active memory at the time of CS–US pairing, but whether the *US* was in

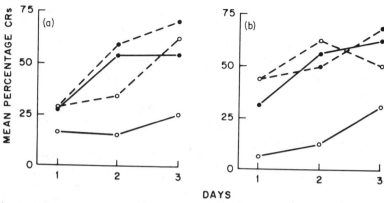

Fig. 4. Mean percentage conditioned-responding in four groups receiving either no stimulus (N, ●——●), a US (US, ○——○), a US followed by a distractor (US + D, ○——○), or a distractor (D, ●——●) alone, preceding each CS–US conditioning trial. (a) Training trials. (b) Test trials. From Terry (1976). Copyright 1976 by the American Psychological Association. Reproduced by permission.

active memory. Only Group US exhibited impaired acquisition of responding relative to Group N. Neither Group US + D, which received the pretrial US followed by a distractor, nor Group D, which received the distractor alone prior to the CS–US pairing, was detectably different from Group N. Thus it would appear that neither a general-interference (e.g., masking) nor a sensory-adaptation mechanism can account for the conditioning decrement observed as a result of preexposure to the US proximal to CS–US pairing. These data are also of interest in showing a selective effect of a dishabituator on a recently presented stimulus, akin to the selective effect reported by Whitlow (1975). Although the distractor stimulus facilitated the acquisition of responding in Group US + D, as compared to Group US, it did not have a similar facilitating effect when presented alone in Group D as compared to Group N. Thus there was no indication of a sensitizing effect of the distractor.

C. Conditioning Decrements Following CS Preexposure

There is nothing in the preceding account of transient performance decrements that requires an exclusive focus on US manipulations. In SOP the pertinent mechanism of persisting nodal activation is indifferent to the experimental designation of stimuli as CSs and USs. Thus SOP anticipates finding observations similar to those just described when the same manipulations are employed with CSs (i.e., an S_1 presentation of a CS should interfere with the conditioning produced by a shortly following CS–US episode).[1] The formation of excitatory associations is assumed to depend on A1 activation in both the CS and the US nodes, so a loss in the number of elements placed in the A1 state on a conditioning trial will be detrimental whether such loss occurs in the US node or in the CS node. Thus studies like those of Terry (1976), but with CS–CS–US sequences rather than his US–CS–US sequences, would be expected to produce a similar pattern of decreased associability of the CS with the US. The decrement should be specific to prior presentations of the same CS as is paired with the US and be disruptable by distractor stimuli interpolated between the initial and conditioning presentations of the CS.

Investigations of eyelid conditioning involving CS preexposure exactly parallel to the studies of Terry are not currently available, but experiments on flavor-aversion learning in rats have reported data that appear supportive of SOP's predictions concerning the effects of CS preexposure. This work is the more interesting, because it was initially interpreted in a quite different fashion. Kalat and Rozin (1973) made the initial observation that, in a taste-aversion learning paradigm, a single presentation of a flavor CS 4 hours prior to a pairing of the CS with a toxin US attenuated conditioning in relationship to that which was otherwise seen to result from the flavor–toxin pairing. They interpreted this effect in terms of a "learned-safety" mechanism, arguing that when initial consumption of the novel flavor was not followed by toxic effects, the rat learned that the novel flavor was "safe." This learning that the taste was "safe" presumably worked against establishing an aversion to the taste when it was paired with the toxin 4 hours later.

Best and Gemberling (1977) have argued, however, that these data are better interpreted as the result of a transient memory for the initial CS interfering with CS processing at the time of the CS–US pairing. They have reported several observations in support of this idea. The most decisive for distinguishing between the learned-safety and the memory interpretations was that as the interval between the CS preexposure and the CS–US pairing was increased—so that the CS preexposure was more remote in time from the CS–US episode—the amount of conditioning systematically *increased*. This would be expected in SOP, because the effects of the initial CS should diminish as greater opportunity is provided

---

[1] Actually, SOP anticipates that there will be a facilitation of conditioning to S_2 under a special set of circumstances (see Wagner, 1981). Thus with very short intervals between the S_1 and S_2 presentations of brief or weak CSs, there may be a summation effect that places more CS elements in an A1 state than would result from a single presentation. Available data, in fact, point toward this added complexity (e.g., Best & Gemberling, 1977).

for activation to decay. The results are precisely opposite those expected from a learned-safety view, in that increasing the intervals between preexposure and conditioning should provide greater opportunity for the subject to learn that the flavor is safe and thereby produce even more robust interference with conditioning.

The transient decrement observed by Kalat and Rozin and by Best and Gemberling following a single CS preexposure presentation must be distinguished from a relatively durable depression of conditioning attendant on more extensive CS preexposure experience, described, for instance, by Domjan (1972). The latter decrement appears to reflect not the persistence of nodal activation but the development of associative linkages, a circumstance that will be developed in Section IV. It may be noted, however, that Westbrook, Bond, and Feyer (1981) recently have presented evidence that under some conditions there is a relatively durable as well as a more transient decrement following even a single CS preexposure in an odor-aversion learning task. The possibility that durable decrements may sometimes arise from single CS preexposures is also suggested by observations reported by Best, Gemberling, and Johnson (1979).

D. Modulation of CR Elicitation

Interestingly, SOP anticipates that under certain conditions one should observe a transient decrement in the elicitation of a CR to the second of a pair of CS presentations that closely resembles in its functional characteristics the transient decrements in UR magnitude reported by Whitlow (1975). Theoretical analysis of the modulation of CR elicitation becomes complicated as SOP allows there to be a response facilitation as well as a response depression, the former arising from a summation of associatively generated activation at the US node. The additional complexity caused by summation effects are most likely to arise when the S_1 and S_2 presentations involve different CSs, and we may obtain a convenient simplification of analysis by restricting our attention to the interference predicted to occur when S_1 and S_2 involve the same CS, because the essential logic here closely resembles that presented with respect to Whitlow's (1975) studies. [A more complete treatment of the modulation of CR elicitation and the manner of allowing both summative and interfering effects of stimulus presentation can be found in sources such as Pfautz and Wagner (1976).]

Thus, presentation of a CS will render a shortly following presentation of the same CS less capable of inducing A1 activation, which decrement will be reflected in a diminution of the CR to the second, S_2, presentation relative to that seen in absence of an S_1 presentation. Pfautz and Wagner (1976) evaluated this possibility in a study using rabbit eyelid conditioning. Subjects were trained with several CSs, then administered test trials in which a given CS was preceded at 2.5, 5, or 10 seconds by presentation of either the same or a different CS or was preceded by no recent stimulation. Relative to the no-stimulation condition, prior presentations of the same CS produced a transient depression, which was not observed with presentations of a different CS. (Indeed, the latter produced a transient facilitation of performance to the target CS.)

Following up on these results, Primavera and Wagner (cited in Wagner, 1978) asked whether a distractor event would disrupt the selective decrement observed to the second of two successive presentations of the same CS. The logic of this study followed that of the studies by Whitlow (1975) and Terry (1976), using distractor manipulations. Primavera and Wagner used a conditioned emotional response (CER) paradigm with rats, first pairing a 30-second tone CS with a foot-shock US, then in a later session evaluating conditioned responding by the degree to which the CS suppressed drinking during a 180-second presentation of the CS. This test presentation of the CS was immediately preceded by one of four conditions, represented by different groups of subjects. Group N received no prior stimulation, Group CS received an initial 30-second presentation of the CS 300 seconds prior to the test presentation; Group CS + D received the same 30-second initial CS followed 30 seconds later by a distractor stimulus; and Group D received only the distractor event 240 seconds prior to the test presentation. The distractor event was the multimodal complex of stimulation produced by opening the door of the isolation unit enclosing each experimental chamber for 30 seconds.

The results of this study closely parallel the effects of interpolated distractor stimuli on performance decrements with respect to USs. Relative to performance in the absence of prior stimulation, as shown by Group N, conditioned responding to the test CS in Group CS was attenuated by an S_1 presentation of a 30-second CS. There was no similar attenuation in Group D, which received only a 30-second distractor stimulus, indicating that the decrement was not the result of simply preceding the test presentation by some event, nor was there any intensification of suppression, indicating that the distractor was not a sensitizing stimulus. The most important observation was that interpolating a distractor event in the interval between the initial CS and the test CS in Group CS + D effectively eliminated the performance decrement that was seen in Group CS. Thus the transient depression produced by an S_1 presentation could be selectively disrupted.

Following the same reasoning previously applied to the case of USs, these results rule out interpretations of the effects of S_1 in terms of simple sensory or motor effects. In addition, as Wagner (1978) has noted, these results address the possibility that the transient decrements seen in connection with a (nonreinforced) CS presentation should be attributed to extinction. Finding that an interpolated distractor restores the effectiveness of the target CS provides little encouragement for an emphasis on extinction effects. Taken together, the studies by Pfautz and Wagner (1976) and by Primavera and Wagner (Wagner, 1978) point to the persistence of activation in memory as an interpretation of the effects of an initial CS on the response elicited by a subsequent, target CS.

E. Summary

The procedure of scheduling an S_1 presentation of a stimulus prior to a target S_2 presentation of the same stimulus produces remarkably similar effects whether one examines refractory-like decrements in UR magnitude (short-term habituation), transient effects of US or CS preexposure on conditioning, or induction-like phenomena in CR elicitation. As is especially clear in the case of short-term habituation and US preexposure effects, initial presentation of a stimulus often produces a performance depression that is stimulus-specific and susceptible to disruption by interpolated distractor stimuli. These characteristics define a form of transient depression readily understood in terms of a memory-oriented analysis such as that of SOP.

IV. Associative Basis of Durable Response Decrements

In the framework of SOP, the basis for relatively durable changes in responsiveness is to be sought in the development of associative connections between representations of an iterated stimulus and other stimuli also present in the experimental situation. This view offers an important counterpoint to the position, which can be traced to Sherrington, that habituation is a nonassociative, adaptation-like process.

The basic idea of SOP is that stimuli concurrently presented with a target US may acquire a retrieval-cue function (i.e., can act like a CS to place elements of the node for the target US in the A2 state). This associatively generated activation leaves fewer US elements in the I state, so that presentation of the US will be less able to excite the node to A1. Thus the degree of responsiveness to a target stimulus during a test session remote in time from an initial training session will depend on the integrity of the mechanism for associative activation of the target's node. This formulation leads to two distinctive predictions. To the degree that associatively generated activation is based on associations involving the experimental context, for example, one would anticipate finding, first, that relatively durable changes in responsiveness are *context-specific,* varying with the similarity between the context present in training and that present in testing; and second, that such changes are subject to *extinction,* decreasing with exposure to the training context alone in the period between training and testing. Such contextual manipulations should be ineffective, however, if the underlying mechanism of the response decrements were an adaptationlike process.

There is now a fairly substantial body of data concerned with performance depression that is consistent with SOP, and we shall briefly review some of these studies. As with the analysis of transient response decrements, we shall point to the similarity of outcome among studies that differ with respect to whether the dependent measure involved the elicitation of a UR or the acquisition of a CR, and in the latter case whether the habituated stimulus was a US or a CS.

A. Decrements in the UR

1. Context Specificity

Several reports in the ethological literature have suggested that declines in UR magnitude with repeated US presentations are context-specific. Both Peeke and Veno (1973) and Shalter (1975), for instance, reported that retention of a response decrement resulting from iterated stimulation depends in part on presenting the test stimuli in the same location as the training stimuli. When the location was changed, the response "recovered." Unfortunately, changing the location at which a target event is presented within an otherwise unchanged situation is open to the question of whether the location of an event should be considered as the context of the event or as an attribute of the event itself. Perhaps the "recovered" response was simply the response to a different stimulus.

More definitive examples of context specificity come from the work of Siegel and associates (e.g., Siegel, 1975, 1977; Siegel, Hinson, & Krank, 1978) on habituation of the analgesia induced by morphine injections in rats. An initial injection of morphine has a strong analgesic effect, as indicated, for example, by the fact that morphine-injected rats placed on a hot plate are slower to lick their paws than are nondrugged rats. Across repeated injections, however, the analgesic effect wanes, and rats with a history of morphine injections are sometimes as quick to respond as are nondrugged rats. Such waning of responsiveness, or morphine tolerance, has often been interpreted as evidence for some kind of nonassociative, adaptationlike mechanism, through which the effectiveness of the drug US is reduced simply as a function of the frequency and dosage level of drug experience.

Siegel and associates have argued, however, that tolerance is best interpreted as a product of associative learning involving the context of drug exposure and the presentation of the drug. Testing for tolerance in a context different from that present during the initial drug exposure should therefore produce little evidence of habituation to the drug. And in a variety of studies these investigators have shown that the habituation is context-specific. For example, Siegel (1975) administered three morphine injections to rats and then assessed the analgesic effects of morphine on a fourth injection. For the initial series of morphine administration, one group was injected in the context in which the subsequent analgesia testing took place, whereas a second group was injected in the home cages. On the analgesia test following the fourth injection, Siegel found evidence of habituation (i.e., tolerance) only in the group that received injections in the test context. The group that had received injections in a different context (i.e., the home cages) showed no evidence of a reduced analgesic effect of the drug, relative to control subjects without a history of morphine injections. Such context specificity of habituation to the analgesic effects of morphine has been routinely replicated (e.g., Siegel *et al.*, 1978) and context-specific habituation has been extended to other response measures and other drugs (Siegel, 1979).

2. *Extinction of Habituation*

Perhaps the most striking prediction of SOP's memory-oriented analysis is that durable response decrements can be extinguished by reexposing the subject to the context in which prior presentations of a target US occurred but in the absence of further USs. The theoretical result of such a manipulation should be that contextual cues should lose their ability to activate the memory node for the US, and thus no longer deplete the number of elements in the I state available for primary activation upon presentation of the US.[2]

[2] This description ignores the mechanics of extinction in SOP. It should be appreciated that when a CS activates a US node to the A2 state, there is the circumstance of A1 activity of the CS node and A2 activity of the US node that we have noted (Section II) is assumed to produce inhibition. In the model, extinction involves such formation of inhibitory connections rather than a loss of excitatory connections, and the behavioral loss of an acquired response tendency is complete when the strength of inhibition matches the strength of excitation.

Siegel (1977) has reported data in line with this prediction for habituation of morphine analgesia. Using the latency of paw retraction to pressure as a dependent measure with rats, Siegel found a decline in the analgesic effects of morphine over a series of injections. He then gave some subjects a series of daily exposures to the test context in the absence of any further drug administration, a manipulation that, according to SOP, should extinguish the contextual associations. In a subsequent test, Siegel found more analgesia (less evidence of habituation) in animals that received this extinction manipulation than in other animals given an equivalent duration retention interval spent in the home cages. Thus tolerance did not simply dissipate over time, as would be expected of an adaptationlike process. Instead, whether or not there was a loss of tolerance over time depended on where the time was spent. Specifically, there was a loss of tolerance (i.e., dishabituation) only when the retention interval involved reexposure to the training context.

Extinction of habituation has also been shown for evoked peripheral vasoconstriction in rabbits in a study we did in collaboration with Penn Pfautz (Wagner, 1976). The study was further informative in showing that the extinction manipulation did not act by producing a general change in responsivity. Two groups of rabbits each were given an initial 2-hour training session during which a 1-second tone stimulus was presented 32 times, with a 150-second interval between successive presentations. For half the subjects in each group, the tone was 530 Hz, and for the remainder it was 4000 Hz. The following day, subjects in the control group were left in their home cages, and subjects in an extinction group were returned to the experimental apparatus, connected to the recording equipment, and given a session identical to the first except that no tones were presented. On the third and final day, all subjects received a retention test session in which the tone used in initial training was again presented for 32 trials at 150-second intervals. Following these trials there were two presentations of the alternate frequency tone.

Figure 5 summarizes the relevant data. Figure 5a depicts average evoked vasoconstriction to the first two tone presentations of the initial training session; Fig. 5b shows the response to the first two presentations of the same tone (A) on the retention test. Both groups exhibited diminished responding on the retention test relative to initial training, but the decrement was much more profound for the control subjects than for subjects that received an intervening extinction session of exposure to the context alone. The difference in response level shown in Fig. 5b did not appear to be the result of nonspecific state changes (e.g., sensitization) arising from the extinction manipulation: as depicted in Fig. 5c the two groups showed nearly identical responses to the nonhabituated tone (B).

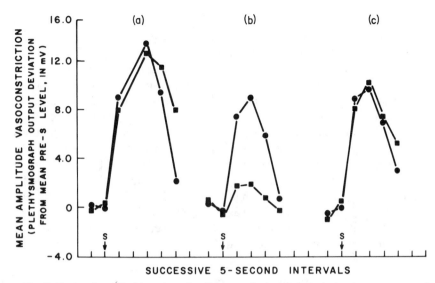

Fig. 5. Extinction of habituation of auditory-evoked vasoconstriction in two groups of rabbits. (a) Mean evoked response to the first two presentations of a to-be-habituated tone (A) of the initial session. (b) Response to the first two presentations of the same tone on a posthabituation retention test. (c) Response to the first two presentations of a novel tone (B). Between habituation and testing, one group (●, extinguished) was returned to the experimental context with no further tone presentations, whereas the other group (■, control) remained in their home cages over the retention interval. From Wagner (1976).

B. Conditioning Decrements Following US Preexposure

Following the same logic outlined for transient changes in responsiveness, SOP anticipates that a history of US preexposure should produce a durable retardation of conditioning—when the preexposed US is subsequently paired with a CS—as well as a durable change in UR magnitude. Relatively durable conditioning decrements following US preexposure have been widely reported (see Randich & Lolordo, 1979 for a review) and, consistent with the predictions of SOP, substantial evidence implicates an associative process in this effect.

1. Context Specificity

The context specificity of the decremental effects of US preexposure on subsequent conditioning have been documented for preparations ranging from flavor-aversion learning in rats (e.g., Batson & Best, 1979; Willner, 1978), to autoshaping in pigeons (e.g., Tomie, 1976), and eyelid conditioning in rabbits (e.g., Hinson, 1982). A study by Hinson (1982, Exp. 1) will

illustrate the basic finding. Over the course of a 10-day preexposure period, Hinson gave 200 presentations of a 100-msec, 5-mA shock US to the
paraorbital region of the eye to each of two groups of rabbits. The US
preexposure phase was followed by 8 days of conditioning in which the
US was paired with a tonal CS. For one group of subjects, preexposure
took place in the same experimental environment used during conditioning, whereas for a second group, preexposure took place in a context
different from that used during conditioning. As compared to a third
group of subjects that received no US preexposure prior to conditioning,
US preexposure reduced the average total frequency of CRs by about
50% when the preexposure context was the same as the conditioning
context. But US preexposure had no significant effect on conditioning
when the preexposure context was different from that used in conditioning. The decremental effects of preexposure were specific to the context
in which the preexposure occurred.

2. Extinction of US Preexposure Effects

Studies parallel to those showing context specificity for US preexposure effects on conditioning have also shown that such effects can be
extinguished by sessions in which the context is presented in the absence
of the US (e.g., Batson & Best, 1979; Hinson, 1982; Tomie, 1976; Willner,
1978). For example, in a second study using the same stimulus parameters
as in the study just described, Hinson (1982, Exp. 3) gave 200 US preexposure trials to each of two groups of rabbits ($n = 12$/group). Following
preexposure, subjects in one group were left in their home cages for the
next 5 days, whereas subjects in the other group were returned on each of
these days to the experimental context and placed in the apparatus, but
did not receive any further US presentations. Finally, both of these
groups, as well as two other groups that had not received any US preexposures but had either been placed in the apparatus on each of 5 days or
spent the time in their home cages, received an 8-day conditioning period
in which the US was paired with a tonal CS. Comparing the two groups
given US preexposure, subjects given subsequent extinction sessions
showed significantly more conditioned-responding in the final phase of the
experiment than those left in the home cages. Hinson's extinction treatment did not eradicate all trace of the effects of preexposure, as assessed
by comparison with the performance of the nonpreexposed groups. This
may indicate the contribution of mechanisms in addition to the associative
retrieval mechanism postulated in SOP. Alternately, it may have been the
case that extinction of the contextual associations was not complete after
five sessions.

C. Conditioning Decrements Following CS Preexposure

SOP does not attach special significance to the designation of stimuli as CSs or USs (cf. Section III,C). Hence, repeated presentations of a CS should also promote the development of associative connections involving contextual stimuli. If contextual stimuli can associatively activate a CS node to the A2 state, there will be a reduction in the number of elements in the CS node available for activation to A1 upon presentation of the CS. Such a process would diminish the opportunity for CS and US nodes to be jointly active in an A1 state when the CS and a US are presented in a conditioning episode, so that the development of CRs would be retarded.

It is a well-established phenomenon, termed "latent inhibition" (see, e.g., Lubow, 1973, for a review), that a history of CS preexposure leads to impaired acquisition of CRs during subsequent Pavlovian conditioning. Latent inhibition is generally assumed to involve an acquired deficit in the ability of the CS to initiate processing. The interesting possibility raised by SOP is that latent inhibition may have an associative basis and depend on contextual manipulations.

1. Context Specificity

The context specificity of latent inhibition is not as extensively documented as is the context specificity of US preexposure effects. But a number of studies have shown that the effect of CS preexposure is reduced if the environment at the time of CS–US pairing differs from that present at the time of preexposure (e.g., D. C. Anderson, O'Farrell, Formica, & Caponegri, 1969; Westbrook *et al.*, 1981). For example, Westbrook *et al.* (1981, Exp. 4) have reported that context specificity exists for a relatively durable effect of CS preexposure in an odor-aversion learning task. A 12 minute exposure to an odor 24 hours before pairing the odor with a toxin US attenuated the aversion to the odor normally produced by such a pairing. Westbrook *et al.*, however, found that the attenuation of conditioning was much less evident if the preexposure context (defined by the flavor of a drinking solution) was different from the conditioning context, than if it was the same.

2. Extinction

Wagner (1978) has summarized two studies of the extinction of latent inhibition, one in rabbit eyelid conditioning, and the other in CER conditioning conducted by Wagner, Pfautz and Donegan. In the basic comparisons of interest, subjects were placed in the conditioning context and repeatedly exposed to the stimulus to be used as a CS (100 stimuli/day for 1 or 2 days in the eyelid conditioning study, 4 stimuli/day for 6 days in the CER study). Half the subjects thus preexposed were then returned to the experimental context for the same number of extinction sessions—during which no stimulation was administered—and the remaining subjects were simply left in their home cages. Finally, all subjects were given CS–US pairings in the conditioning chambers. In both studies, the groups receiving the "extinction" session between CS preexposure and CS–US pairings showed reliably more conditioned-responding than groups left in the home cages.

Evidence for extinction of latent inhibition has also been reported in flavor-aversion learning in rats. Westbrook *et al.* (1981) reported that the relatively durable CS preexposure effect they observed with a single protracted preexposure presentation of an odor CS was attenuated when extinction of contextual cues was interposed between CS preexposure and the pairing of the CS with a toxin.

V. Concurrent Stimulation and Habituation

The selective disruption of transient response decrements achieved by presenting distractor stimuli between the training (S_1) and test (S_2) stimuli in an S_1–S_2 pair plays a key role in arguing that the decrements involved reflect persisting activation of memory. Distractor stimuli have such effects, according to SOP, because of the capacity limitations of the memory system. The present section will describe three additional findings relevant to the claim that capacity limitations play a significant role in habituation. The first indicates that habituation is subject to overshadowing, the second that poststimulation distractors also disrupt the habituation observed on a remote test, and the third indicates that habituation is influenced by the serial position of the target event in a stimulus sequence.

A. Overshadowing Effects

A classic pointer to the kind of capacity limitation assumed in SOP is what Pavlov (1927) termed *overshadowing:* when two stimuli are presented as a simultaneous compound CS, there is less evidence of conditioning to one of the stimulus elements than if that element had been paired singly with the US. Such an element is said to be *overshadowed* by the CS with which it is in compound. Now, in fact, according to SOP there are several reasons why this can occur in different circumstances (see Mazur & Wagner, in press). But the most obvious reason is that the activation of the elements in any stimulus node will be diminished by the concurrent presentation of other stimuli.

J. H. James and Wagner (1980) have reported an overshadowing-like phenomenon in habituation in two experiments. They used a lick-suppression paradigm, in which stimuli were presented to thirsty rats while they were licking to obtain water; stimulus effectiveness was assessed by the degree to which licking was disrupted by the stimulus. Typically, the initial presentation of a novel stimulus disrupts licking, but with repeated stimulus presentations, the amount of suppression decreases. This paradigm has the characteristic that substantial habituation can be detected after a single stimulus exposure (e.g., Leaton, 1974).

In their first study, J. H. James and Wagner (1980, Exp. 2) compared the performance of three groups of rats. After several sessions of lick training, subjects received an habituation session during which there was a single, 30-second presentation of either an 1800-Hz, 86-db tone (Group T), the illumination of a 6-W, shielded bulb (Group L) or both the tone and the light in a simultaneous compound (Group TL). Subsequently, subjects received four sessions of testing, with one presentation of either the tone or the light in each session in counterbalanced order.

For the stimulus preexposed in the single stimulus groups, that is, the tone in Group T and the light in Group L, there was a substantial and reliable reduction in lick suppression produced during the test session as compared to that seen on the initial (habituation) presentation. Moreover, this decrement was specific to the preexposed stimulus. The degree of lick suppression to the nonpreexposed stimulus, that is, the light in Group T and the tone in Group L, was not reliably different from the average levels otherwise observed during the habituation session.

The data of most interest concern the degree of lick suppression to the tone and the light in Group TL. If habituation did not involve a capacity limitation, this group, which was preexposed to both the tone and the light, might have been expected in testing to exhibit the same (reduced) suppression to the tone as seen in Group T and to the light as seen in Group L. The results provided clear evidence to the contrary, pointing to the presence of capacity limitations. For example, suppression to the light in Group TL was not reliably different from suppression to the light in Group T, suggesting that the simultaneous presence of a tone effectively precluded habituation to the light. This overshadowing of habituation did not appear to be caused by some difficulty in registering simultaneous inputs, because J. H. James and Wagner (1980, Exp. 4) found in a second experiment that overshadowing also occurred with a sequential compound in which sequential pulses of tone and light were alternated.

B. Effects of Poststimulus Distractors

Information-processing approaches to memory commonly assume that long-term storage of information depends on the nature and extent of active processing received by the relevant events. Correspondingly, in SOP it is assumed that excitatory associative links develop between two nodes as a function of the degree to which both nodes are jointly active in the A1 state. As a result, poststimulation manipulations that may be presumed to alter the time course of activation should also affect the associative basis for more durable habituation.

In the previously mentioned vasomotor study by Whitlow (1975), a distractor interposed between S_1 and S_2 was presumed to have curtailed the persisting nodal activity of S_1, as evidenced by enhanced responding to the same S_2. It would thus be expected that such a distractor would also interfere with the formation of associations between S_1 and the context and therefore impair the development of a durable response decrement.

To test this prediction, we conducted a study (cited in Wagner, 1976) using stimulus events and ISIs comparable to those used by Whitlow (1975). Rabbits were tested in a single, 2.5-hour session segregated by 15-minute intervals into pretest, training, and posttest periods. During the pretest period, each of two tonal stimuli was presented three times at 150-second intervals with different counterbalanced orders determining the schedule of presentations. The training period consisted of 32 habituation trials—16 with each stimulus—again at 150-second intervals. Trials with one stimulus (A) were consistently followed 20 seconds later by the presentation of the visual-electrotactile dishabituator used by Whitlow; trials with the other stimulus (B) were never followed by the distractor. The designations of tonal frequencies as A and B were balanced over subjects, and the schedule of presentations of A and B was determined by different counterbalanced orders to equate the frequency with which each stimulus was *preceded* by the distractor. Finally, in the posttest period, subjects again received three presentations of each stimulus in the absence of any distractor presentations, just as in the pretest.

Figure 6 displays the main results in the form of average evoked vasoconstriction waveforms to each stimulus. Prior to training (Fig. 6a), both stimuli evoked substantial and equivalent levels of vasoconstriction. Fol-

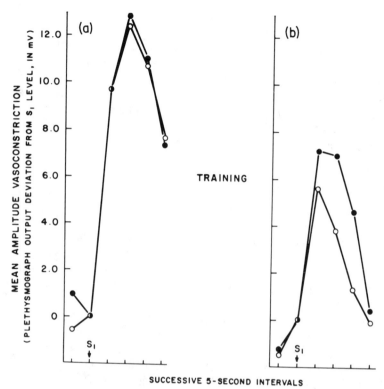

Fig. 6. Mean auditory-evoked response to each of two tones is shown for the first two presentations of each during (a) a pretest session prior to habituation training and (b) for the first two presentations in a posthabituation retention test. During the intervening habituation training, one tone (●) was consistently followed by a dishabituator, whereas the other tone (○) was never followed by a dishabituator. From Wagner (1976).

lowing training (Fig. 6b), there was a depression of response levels to each stimulus, but this depression was less pronounced for Stimulus A—which had been consistently followed by the distractor event during the training trials—than for Stimulus B, which was never followed by the distractor. That is, there was less evidence of habituation to Stimulus A than to Stimulus B—the result expected if the distractor event curtailed the formation of associations between the context and the target event.

C. Serial-Position Effects

One of the most widely documented (e.g., Bower, 1971; Crowder, 1976) products of the presumed capacity limitations in human memory is the fact that memory for an item presented in a list depends on its serial position in the list. There have been various theoretical rationalizations (e.g., Bower, 1971; Feigenbaum & Simon, 1962) of how capacity limitations may shape the specific outcome. But empirically the most common effects are superior performance for items at the beginning of a list (primacy effect) or at the end of the list (recency effect), with the presence of both primacy and recency effects giving rise to the familiar bowed serial-position curve. The capacity limitations assumed in SOP lead one to anticipate that habituation would also be influenced by the serial position of a to-be-habituated event in a stimulus "list."

1. Immediate Retention Tasks

Whitlow (1975) examined the degree to which the transient response decrement to 1-second tonal stimuli in the rabbit vasoconstriction paradigm was influenced by the serial position of the tones in a "list" of five stimuli. Subjects received 36 trials in each of two 3-hour sessions. Each trial consisted of a list of five 1-second stimuli presented at 5-second intervals, which was then followed 40 seconds later by a single probe stimulus. One of the list stimuli was a tone (S_1) of either 530 or 4000 Hz, which occurred in the first, third, or fifth position in the list, with the tonal frequency and its list position varying irregularly from trial to trial. The remaining stimuli in each list were drawn from nonauditory modalities, and different lists were constructed by rearrangements of the order in which these stimuli occurred. The probe stimulus (S_2) was also a tone, being the same frequency as S_1 on half the trials that S_1 occurred in each of the three list positions and the alternate frequency on the remaining trials.

The main result of this study is displayed in Fig. 7a, where performance is expressed in terms of the magnitude of the decrement detected at S_2 that is specific to a repetition of the same stimulus as S_1. This measure was derived by subtracting the response to S_2 on same trials from the response on different trials, and can be interpreted as a direct measure of stimulus-specific habituation (i.e., higher levels of performance on this measure correspond to greater amounts of habituation). Figure 7a depicts the amount of habituation detected at S_2 as a function of the position of S_1 in the immediately preceding list. It shows a pronounced recency effect; the amount of habituation detectable with the S_2 probe was greatest for the last list position and least for the first list position. The difference between the first and last serial positions was associated with an S_1–S_2 interval difference of 60 versus 40 seconds and a difference in the number of interpolated distractor events of 4 versus 0, respectively. Hence, these data complement the previously reported findings on transient response

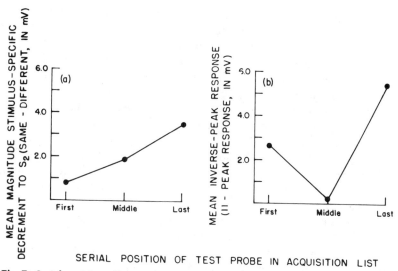

SERIAL POSITION OF TEST PROBE IN ACQUISITION LIST

Fig. 7. Serial-position effects in habituation. (a) Average amount of stimulus-specific response decrement to a tone as a function of its position in an immediately prior list of stimuli. (Adapted from Whitlow, 1975. Copyright 1975 by the American Psychological Association. Reproduced by permission.) (b) Magnitude of the peak response to an electrotactile stimulus on a remote test, following a series of exposures to a stimulus list, where the serial position of the target US varied across different subjects. From Wagner and Pfautz (1978). Copyright 1978 by the Psychonomic Society. Reproduced by permission.)

decrements (Section III,A) in showing that as the S_1–S_2 interval is lengthened and the number of interpolated distractors increases, there is a reduction of short-term habituation. What was noticeably absent in this study was any indication of a primacy effect.

2. Remote Retention Tasks

A markedly different picture emerges from a study by Wagner and Pfautz (1978) using the same experimental preparation, but designed to bring out the effect of serial position on more permanent response depression. In this study a constant list was presented on either 8 or 16 occasions during a training period, and habituation was assessed on a temporally remote test given 15 minutes after the series of list exposures. The lists were similar in construction to those used by Whitlow (1975) but were either 5 or 9 items long. The target event was an electrotactile stimulus to the paraorbital region of the eye and occurred in either the first, middle, or last position in the list for different groups of subjects.

Figure 7b summarizes the major result of this study. The figure depicts the average peak response during the test period to the electrotactile stimulus as a function of its serial position in the list presented during training. [The scale on the ordinate has been inverted (the higher the measure the greater the habituation) to permit direct comparison with Whitlow's data in Fig. 7a.] As can be seen, Wagner and Pfautz found a recency effect (as did Whitlow), but they also found a primacy effect, the combination giving rise to the bowed serial-position curve found so often in human verbal training.

It is quite sensible that the serial-position effects observed by Pfautz and Wagner were different from those observed by Whitlow. For the Whitlow investigation, a study list was presented once, and the subject was quickly interrogated about its memory for one of the items. Assuming that test performance was primarily, if not exclusively, determined by the persistent activation initiated by the item during study, it should have been favored by relative recency and lack of subsequent distracting events. For the Pfautz and Wagner investigation, 15 minutes intervened between the last exposure to the list and the test. Assuming that test performance was then primarily determined by the degree of association between the contextual cues at the time of test and the target item, it is reasonable that such associations would be better for those items at the beginning and end of the list than for those in the middle of the list. For an item in the middle of the list, the relevant context to which associations may have formed would more likely involve other members of the list in which it was embedded.

Numerous other suggestions have been made in investigations of human memory (e.g., Glanzer & Cunitz, 1966; Watkins, 1979) about why serial-position effects may be different on immediate-versus-remote tests. What is remarkable is that serial-position effects occur equally in studies of simple habituation and that their differential form, depending on the specifics of training and testing, present the same theoretical challenge.

VI. Effects of Stimulus Intensity and Interstimulus Interval

We noted in Section I that adopting a theoretical approach to habituation may lead one to emphasize somewhat different distinctions than those that present themselves in an empirical listing. The preceding sections have underscored this point by offering a different set of observations regarding habituation than those identified as the parametric characteristics of habituation by Thompson and Spencer (1966). A particular concern of SOP is the need for distinguishing between relatively transient and more durable forms of response depression; and Section VI applies this distinction to studies on the effects of stimulus intensity and ISI on habituation. According to Thompson and Spencer (1966), greater habituation is produced the weaker is the intensity of the stimulus and the more closely spaced in time are stimulus presentations, whereas SOP anticipates exactly the opposite conclusion concerning the more durable form of habituation.

A. Effects of Stimulus Intensity

As previously noted (Section II), SOP assumes that the more intense a stimulus, the greater the proportion of nodal elements that will initially be placed in A1. This will be reflected in a UR of greater magnitude for relatively intense as compared to less-intense USs. Additionally, by placing a greater number of elements in A1, the former will provide a better opportunity for the development of durable (context-specific) habituation. In consequence of the assumptions made regarding the activation sequence, however, it also follows that the more intense the US, the more protracted will be the period before the US node will have reverted to the I state and therefore again be capable of full activation to A1.

Evidence consistent with this reasoning can be found in studies of habituation of the acoustic-startle response of the rat. Ison and Krauter (1974), for instance, observed a more prolonged refractory period for the startle response following a relatively intense S_1 of 125 db than following a relatively weak S_1 of 95 db. These data suggest that a stimulus of 125 db produces more activation than one of 95 db; and that over a series of spaced presentations the former intensity would provide more opportunity for associative learning—hence durable evidence of habituation—than would the latter intensity. This is essentially the result reported by Davis and Wagner (1968), who found that responsiveness to various intensities of tone in a remote test of startle habituation was more depressed after 300 presentations (at 20-second intervals) of a 120-db US than after a similar presentation schedule of a 95-db US.

B. Effects of Interstimulus Interval

Manipulations of the ISI lead to a set of relationships empirically more complex than are the effects described for stimulus intensity. The nature of the effects of ISI is nicely illustrated in the work of Davis (1970) on habituation of the acoustic-startle response in the rat.

Davis compared two groups of rats in their responsiveness to a 50-msec, 120-db tone of 4000 Hz during pretest, training, and posttest periods. During both the pretest and the posttest periods, both groups of subjects received 300 tone exposures at intervals of 2, 4, 8, and 16 seconds, the intervals being scheduled in an irregular order that balanced the frequency with which a given duration interval on trial n was followed on trial $n + 1$ by itself and every other duration. The two groups differed only in that in the training period, during which subjects received 1000 tone exposures, the interval between stimuli was a constant 16 seconds in one group and 2 seconds in the other group.

Figure 8 summarizes the results obtained when the posttest period began 1 minute following habituation training. The important findings are that (a) during both pretest and posttest periods, the frequency of startle responses increased as the interval between trial n and trial $n + 1$ increased from 2 to 16 seconds, i.e., there was a refractory period; (b) this effect of ISI was also observed during the training period, as responsiveness was consistently lower in the group receiving tones every 2 seconds than in the group receiving tones every 16 seconds; and (c) there was a striking reversal of the effects of ISI on the overall level of responsiveness from the training period to the posttest period, such that subjects in the 16-second group were less responsive at all intervals in the posttest than were subjects in the 2-second group.

Davis's results can be interpreted in terms of SOP as follows: the increase in responding seen on trial $n + 1$ of pretraining and testing as the interval between trial n and trial $n + 1$ increases from 2 to 16 seconds is a reflection of the increasing number of nodal elements that had been allowed to decay back to the inactive state. Similarly, during training, there was more responding in the 16-second group than in the 2-second group because of the relatively greater number of elements that had been allowed to return to I in the former case. The response attenuation in the 2-second group, however, is coupled with less opportunity for the formation of associations between contextual events and the target US, for at least two reasons. One reason is simply that there is less time between trials n and $n + 1$ for the joint activation in A1 of representations of the context and the target. This is essentially a "retroactive" influence, similar to that discussed in relation to the effect of poststimulation distractors on durable habituation. A second reason concerns the proactive influence of trial n on trial $n + 1$, with regard to which there will be a greater carryover of nodal activation in the 2-second case than in the 16-second case. Hence, on trial $n + 1$ there will be a reduced amount of primary activation to A1 in the 2-second case with an attendant reduction in the occasions for association formation, as was assumed in the case of higher-

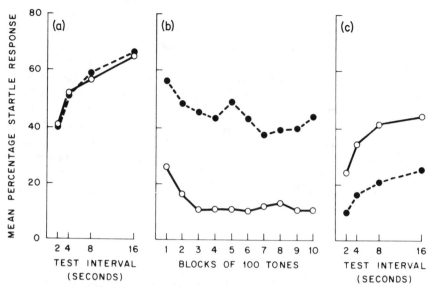

Fig. 8. Mean percentage startle response for two groups of rats, both of which were tested at each of four ISIs. (a) Prehabituation test period. (b) Intervening habituation training. (c) 1-Minute posthabituation test period. The groups differed with respect to whether intervening habituation training was conducted at a constant 2-second (O) or 16-second (●) ISI. From Davis (1970). Copyright 1970 by the American Psychological Association. Reproduced by permission.

versus-lower stimulus intensity. The overall level of responsiveness in the post-test period presumably reflects the strength of associative learning acquired during training. Hence the overall reduced opportunity for association formation in the 2-second group as compared to the 16-second group was expressed in a higher level of responsiveness.

VII. Conditioned Modulation of the Unconditioned Response

In relating SOP to the available data we have employed a theoretical simplification. That is, in considering the effect of some recent instance of the same stimulus or the effect of some associated context on the processing of a target stimulus, we have generally been content to emphasize how an A2 process initiated in advance of the target can reduce the A1 activity it produces and hence the vigor of the UR or the associative learning that it occasions. In effect we have acted as though the degree of A2 activity at the time of the target stimulus would itself have no effect on the measured "UR" or upon the acquisition of a CR. While we are relatively comfortable that this simplification for expository purposes did not produce any mischief in the cases we have addressed, it *is* a gross simplification of the workings of SOP. As pointed out in the description of the model in Section II, we assume that A2 activity of the US can lead to inhibitory associative learning and can either add to or detract from the UR provoked by A1 activation, depending on the transfer function w_2. In this closing section it is appropriate that we acknowledge how the full possibilities encompassed by SOP may be important to our understanding of habituation in some situations. This is forcefully illustrated in the studies of Nelson Donegan (1981) on the "conditioned modulation of the UR" in Pavlovian conditioning.

A. Experimental Findings

Over a series of CS–US conditioning trials, one may observe that the UR to the US decreases or "habituates." Kimble and Ost (1961) were the first to point out that the diminution of the UR in this case may be a "conditioned diminution," depending on the US being signaled by an associated CS. Indeed, following observance of a diminished UR on CS–US trials, the response was observed to be of full magnitude on test trials with the US alone, and the decrement on CS–US trials was abolished by CS-alone extinction trials (Kimble & Ost, 1961; Kimmel, 1966).

The basis for such conditioned diminution of the UR should be obvious from SOP. The phenomena could, in fact, be viewed as the prototypical example of associatively generated, context-specific habituation: to the degree that a CS is capable of activating a US node to an A2 state, it can reduce the A1 activation and, hence, the UR that can be provoked by the US in its presence.

But in such instances of Pavlovian conditioning, it is equally obvious that the derivation is not that simple. The A2 activity of the US node assumed to be elicited by the CS is also presumed to be what is responsible for producing any CR. And the CR may variously mimic the UR or be antagonistic to the UR in different instances (e.g., Pavlov, 1927; Siegel, 1975; Wagner, Thomas, & Norton, 1967) in ways that influence the response that is measured post-US as the so-called UR. In the case of the original data of Kimble and Ost (1961) in eyelid conditioning, the CS— when recorded—mimics the UR, so that the observed response decrement post-US may have underestimated the degree of conditioned diminution of the UR per se. In other instances (e.g., Siegel, 1975), the CR may be antagonistic to the UR, so that the observed response decrement post-US may equally overestimate the degree of conditioned diminution of the UR. Furthermore, when the CR mimics the UR it is theoretically possible that behavior tendencies controlled by the CS could be sufficient to counteract the conditioned diminution of the UR. Indeed, Hupka, Kwaterski, and Moore (1970) reported a conditioned *facilitation* of the post-US response measure in nictitating membrane conditioning with the rabbit.

Donegan (1981) evaluated the quantitative applicability of SOP to this situation. Rabbits were given Pavlovian discrimination training with an auditory and a visual stimulus designated as CS^+ or CS^- in counterbalanced fashion, the former CS consistently reinforced with a 5-mA, paraorbital shock US; the latter CS consistently nonreinforced. Two response measures were taken, the eye-blink response and gross body movement. The significance of the two measures was that one, the eye blink, could be expected to be elicited as a CR to CS^+ alone, whereas the other—the gross-movement response—was known not to be elicited as a CR to CS^+ alone. Thus, from the above reasoning about the potential contribution of the CR to the so-called UR, measured post-US, one might anticipate more substantial evidence of conditioned diminution of the "UR" in the case of the gross body movement than in the case of the eye-blink measure when the two were recorded concurrently. Evaluation of conditioned modulation of the UR was accomplished in test sessions in which the US was presented either alone, preceded by CS^+, or preceded by CS^-. The inclusion of the CS^-–US tests was to allow assurance that any difference in the post-US response in the CS^+–US versus US-alone test could not be attributed to nonspecific stimulus effects but was dependent on the associative relationship between CS^+ and the US.

The more theoretically challenging assessment in the Donegan (1981) study requires somewhat greater amplification of the quantitative assumptions of SOP. It is assumed that the response observed post-US will be determined by the relationship

$$R_j = f_j(w_{1,j}p_{A1} + w_{2,j}p_{A2}). \tag{1}$$

That is, the response will be a function of the weighted proportion of elements in the A1 state plus the weighted proportion of elements in the A2 state. In the case of a US-alone trial it can be assumed that, prior to US application, all of the US nodal elements are in the I state and that the immediate effects of the US will be to provoke p_1 of the elements to the A1 state so that the immediate response will be

$$R_j = f_j(w_{1,j}p_1). \tag{2}$$

In the case of a CS^+–US trial, it must be assumed that prior to US application some of the nodal elements of the US are in the A2 state and that the immediate effect of the US will be to provoke p_1 of the elements remaining in the I state to the A1 state so that the immediate response will be

$$R_j = f_j[w_{1,j}p_1(1 - p_{A2}) + w_{2,j}(p_{A2})], \tag{3}$$

which can be rewritten as

$$R_j = f_j[w_{1,j}p_1 - p_{A2}(w_{1,j}p_1 - w_{2,j})]. \tag{4}$$

Thus it should be appreciated that the expected response will be comparatively less on CS^+–US trials [Eq.(4)] than on US-alone trials [Eq.(2)] when the subtractive term in Eq.(4), $p_{A2}(w_{1,j}p_1 - w_{2,j})$, is positive, but the expected response will be comparatively greater on CS^+–US trials when the term is negative. Furthermore, we can see that the latter term will be positive (predicting a conditioned diminution) when $p_1 > w_{2,j}/w_{1,j}$. Correspondingly, we can see that the latter term will be negative (predicting a conditioned facilitation) when $p_1 < w_{2,j}/w_{1,j}$. The quantity p_{A2}, determined by the degree of conditioning to CS^+, will simply amplify the consequences of these relationships.

The value of $w_{2,j}$ and, hence, the ratio of $w_{2,j}/w_{1,j}$ could be presumed to be more positive in the case of the eyeblink measure in which $w_{2,j}p_{A2}$ presumably led to observable CRs that mimicked the UR, than in the case of the gross-movement measure in which $w_{2,j}p_{A2}$ apparently led to no observable CRs. Thus, as already observed from less quantitative reasoning, conditioned diminution should have been less likely with the former response than with the latter. But the quantitative relationships also make clear that the modulation of the "UR" will also depend on the parameter p_1, which is determined by the intensity of the US. As US intensity is increased, it should be more likely that $p_1 > w_{2,j}/w_{1,j}$ in either response measure. Indeed, one can anticipate that with the same response measure (hence, the same $w_{2,j}/w_{1,j}$) one might observe *either* a conditioned diminution or a conditioned facilitation depending on the intensity of the US (i.e., p_1) in testing.

It was this reasoning that Donegan (1981) evaluated by including post-conditioning test trials with CS^+–US, CS^-–US, and the US-alone when the US intensity was either 1-, 2-, or 5 mA. Figure 9 summarizes the peak post-US eye-blink and gross-movement responses observed for trials involving US intensities of 5 mA (Fig. 9a,b) and 1 mA (Fig. 9c,d). We ignore data for trials with the 2-mA US, because they predictably fell between these extremes. The data for the gross-movement response (Fig. 9b,d)

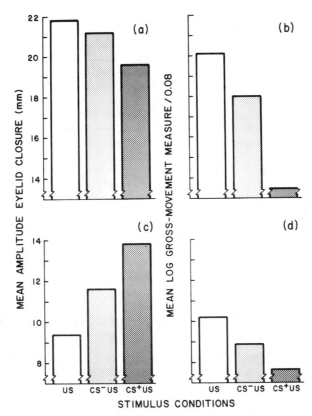

Fig. 9. Mean amplitude of eyelid-closure and gross-movement responses. (a) Eye-blink response to 5-mA target US. (b) Gross-movement response to 5-mA target US. (c) Eye-blink response to 1-mA target US. (d) Gross-movement response to 1-mA target US. The US was presented (paraorbitally) either in isolation (US), preceded by a conditioned inhibitor (CS⁻ US), or preceded by a conditioned excitor (CS⁺ US). From Wagner (1981).

have been scaled to simplify comparison with the data for the eye blink (Fig. 9a,c).

The major pattern of the data is quite clear. With the 5-mA US, which presumably produced a large p_1 value, a smaller amplitude of response occurred on CS⁺–US trials than on US-alone (or CS⁻–US) trials according to either measure (i.e., conditioned diminution of the UR was consistently observed). With the 1-mA US, which presumably produced a smaller p_1 value, there was less evidence of conditioned diminution of the UR in the gross-movement measure and a reversal of the effect in the eye-blink measure. In the eye-blink measure there was a conditioned facilitation of the UR with greater response amplitude on CS^+–US trials than on US-alone (or CS^-–US) trials.

Conditioned modulation of the UR appears to be determined by the specific response measure and US intensity in the interactive fashion predicted by SOP. Using a variety of estimation procedures, Donegan and Wagner (in press) could carry the theoretical assessment of the Donegan data further to calculate that as US intensity was increased from 1 to 5 mA, p_1 increased from .41 to .92, and that w_2 was positive in the case of both measures but was 3.3 times greater in the case of the eye-blink response than in the case of the gross-movement response. At this level of specification much more detailed tests of the model become possible. To mention a simple implication, the positive w_2 of the movement response indicates that, with a more sensitive recording device than employed by Donegan (1981), anticipatory gross-movement CRs that mimic the UR should be detectable.

B. Implications

In acknowledging that the A2 activation that is associatively generated by a CS may have performance effects manifest in the observed "UR" to the US, SOP points to the possibility of greater complexity in the analysis of habituation than we have entertained in the present chapter. At the moment, however, an adequate empirical foundation to guide theoretical developments in this direction is lacking, with the available evidence merely suggesting the need for greater attention to this issue.

Thus Siegel (1975) has reported evidence of a contextual CR that is compensatory (i.e., antagonistic to the UR) in rats, given a history of morphine injections. Recording the latency for a subject to lick its paw after being placed on a hot plate, Siegel found that the context elicited a hypersensitivity. Rats that had experienced morphine injections in the context were *quicker* to respond on the hot plate in the presence of contextual stimulation alone—after receiving a placebo injection—than were control subjects that had not received any drug injections. Obviously, conditioned compensatory CRs to contextual cues may contribute to some of what we have taken as simple evidence of less A1 in the analysis of durable, context-specific habituation (cf. Section IV).

Outside the domain of pharmacological manipulation like that employed by Siegel (1975), it is less clear that contextual stimuli will provoke phasic CRs that would influence the response measure in conventional studies of habituation. Thus, while there is substantial evidence (e.g., Baker, Mercier, Gabel, & Baker, 1981; Blanchard & Blanchard, 1969) for the acquisition of CRs to contextual stimulation, the available data are limited because it all involves relatively diffuse changes in response tendencies (i.e., tonic CRs). There is no comparable evidence for contextual elicitation of the more discrete, phasic responses, such as defensive reflexes, that are often studied in habituation paradigms. But the lack of evidence here may indicate that relatively static cues are not well suited to initiate phasic responses. This possibility is suggested by the phenomenon of *pseudoconditioning,* in which it is observed that following repeated presentations of an isolated US, a discrete but neutral stimulus presented in the same context in which the US was administered will elicit a "CR-like" response (e.g., Grethier, 1938; Kimble, 1961). Pseudoconditioning appears to be mediated by contextual associations (Sheafor, 1975), and the neutral stimulus simply acts as a "trigger" to activate a phasic output. But perhaps a US can also "trigger" a phasic contextual CR that could modulate the observed "UR." Thus we are left to wonder how the potential contribution of contextual CRs complicates the findings when context manipulation has had no overall influence on habituation (e.g., Baker *et al.,* 1981; Marlin & Miller, 1981).

VIII. Conclusion

The preceding sections have identified as theoretically significant a number of functional relationships that extend considerably beyond the nine parametric characteristics of habituation listed by Thompson and Spencer (1966) in their influential review. The observations reviewed here present a picture of habituation in the intact organism as being a more complex process than one of a nonassociative, adaptation-like change in the efficacy of an iterated stimulus. We have been encouraged to approach habituation from the memory-oriented view embodied in SOP because such a view appears to offer a relatively straightforward account of such phenomena as (a) a transient, stimulus-specific response depression that can be selectively disrupted by poststimulation distractors, (b) a durable response depression that is context-specific and subject to extinction, (c) the sensitivity of habituation to the presence of concurrent stimulation as revealed in the effects of overshadowing, poststimulation distractors, and serial position, (d) the manner stimulus intensity and interstimulus interval (ISI) affect transient and durable changes in responsiveness, and (e) the facilitative as well as depressive effects of conditioned modulators on the magnitude of a UR.

We have been additionally attracted to the approach embodied in SOP because (a) it has provided us with a set of theoretical guidelines to frame the experimental analysis of habituation in productive ways and (b) it accounts for habituation in terms of the same set of theoretical constructs found to have considerable explanatory power with respect to more traditional learning tasks such as Pavlovian conditioning.

It is important, however, to recognize that the particular formalism of SOP is not the only means to approach a theoretical treatment of the set of observations we have described. We have already noted, for example, that some striking parallels exist between the characteristics assumed of the A1 and A2 states in SOP and those of the α and β processes in the opponent-process theory of affective dynamics (e.g., Schull, 1979; Solomon & Corbit, 1974). Likewise, one can develop more neurophysiological sounding schemes in which A1 and A2 states correspond to successive stages in a neural activation sequence but with a recurrent inhibitory loop from the analogue of A2 to the analogue of A1. What is important is not the manner of formalism but that the formalism be adequate to deal with the functional regularities we have described in terms of SOP.

There may, of course, be some advantage in one or another manner of theoretical expression in suggesting useful avenues of empirical analysis. It appears to us, for example, that SOP has been helpful in directing our attention to a concern that the amount of habituation obtained with any schedule of presentations of a target event cannot be predicted without reference to those stimuli that are coepisodic with the target event. Habituation in the intact organism takes place against the background of a rich and varied assortment of other events. And we have argued, in a variety of ways, that these events are intimately involved in habituation. Thus such events may act as poststimulation distractors to disrupt habituation or as concurrent competitors for activation that overshadow habituation. Concurrent events may also form associative connections with the memory node for a target event and thereby determine the degree of long-term retention.

This attention to *extrinsic* influences on habituation contrasts with a view that habituation arises solely from changes that are *intrinsic* to a reflex pathway, which has often marked the consideration of habituation at the more molecular level of neurophysiological analysis. In the latter case, there is clear evidence that in a simple reflex pathway isolated from its neural context there are intrinsic mechanisms of response depression (e.g., Kandel, 1976). And such evidence has been taken to support the assumption that stimulation outside the reflex pathway has an influence only on performance, not on habituation (e.g., Krasne, 1976). For example, in Groves and Thompson's (1970) dual-process theory, extraneous stimuli may produce sensitization, which is assumed to be a process separate from habituation. Because the performance associated with a particular event is assumed to result from the summed outputs of habituation and sensitization processes, performance will be influenced by concurrently presented stimuli; but the habituation process itself is assumed to depend only on the to-be-habituated event.

It would seem unreasonable to suggest that intrinsic mechanisms of response depression are not operative in the intact organism. But it is worth noting, for instance, that the synapses in the crayfish tail-flip preparation, which have been shown to exhibit intrinsic depression, are "protected" from depression during the normal activity of the animal (Wine & Krasne, 1972). A critical issue appears to be one of determining the relative contributions of intrinsic and extrinsic sources of response modulation as one varies the preparation studied and the parameters of stimulation—a view expressed by other investigators as well (e.g., Baker *et al.,* 1981). In addressing this issue, a memory-oriented, molar behavioral approach appears to offer an important complement to the more molecular concerns of the Sherringtonian tradition.

References

Anderson, D. C., O'Farrell, T., Formica, R., & Caponegri, V. Preconditioning CS exposure: Variation in the place of conditioning and presentation. *Psychonomic Science,* 1969, *15,* 54–55.

Anderson, J. R., & Bower, G. H. *Human associative memory.* Washington, D.C.: Winston, 1973.

Atkinson, R. C., & Shiffrin, R. M. Human memory: A proposed system and its control processes. In K. W. Spence & J. T. Spence (Eds.), *The psychology of learning and motivation* (Vol. 2). New York: Academic Press, 1968, Pp. 89–195.

Baker, A. G., Mercier, P., Gabel, J., & Baker, P. Contextual conditioning and the US preexposure effect in conditioned fear. *Journal of Experimental Psychology, Animal Behavior Processes,* 1981, *7,* 109–128.

Batson, J. D., & Best, P. J. Drug-exposure effects in flavor-aversion learning: Associative interference by conditioned environmental stimuli. *Journal of Experimental Psychology, Animal Behavior Processes,* 1979, *5,* 273–283.

Best, M. R., & Gemberling, G. A. The role of short-term processes in the CS preexposure effect and the delay of reinforcement gradient in long-delay taste-aversion learning. *Journal of Experimental Psychology, Animal Behavior Processes,* 1977, *3,* 253–263.

Best, M. R., Gemberling, G. A., & Johnson, P. E. Disrupting the conditioned stimulus preexposure effect in flavor aversion learning: Effects of interoceptive distractor manipulations. *Journal of Experimental Psychology, Animal Behavior Processes,* 1979, *5,* 321–334.

Blanchard, R. J., & Blanchard, C. D. Crouching as an index of fear. *Journal of Comparative and Physiological Psychology,* 1969, *67,* 370–375.

Bobrow, D. G. & Norman, D. A. Some principles of memory schemata. In D. G. Bobrow & A. M. Collins (Eds.), *Representation and understanding: Studies in cognitive science.* New York: Academic Press, 1975.

Bower, G. H. Adaptation-level coding of stimuli and serial-position effects. In M. H. Apley (Ed.), *Adaptation-level theory*. New York: Academic Press, 1971. Pp. 175–201.

Bower, G. H. Cognitive psychology: An introduction. In W. K. Estes (Ed.), *Handbook of learning and cognitive processes* (Vol. 1). Hillsdale, N.J.: Lawrence Erlbaum Associates, 1975. Pp. 25–80.

Carew, T. J., Pinsker, H. M., & Kandel, E. R. Long-term habituation of a defensive withdrawal reflex in *Aplysia*. *Science*, 1972, *175*, 451–454.

Crowder, R. *Principles of learning and memory*. Hillsdale, N.J.: Lawrence Erlbaum Associates, 1976.

Davis, M. Effects of interstimulus interval length and variability on startle response habituation in the rat. *Journal of Comparative and Physiological Psychology*, 1970, *72*, 177–192.

Davis, M. & Wagner, A. R. Startle responsiveness after habituation to different intensities of tone. *Psychonomic Science*, 1968, *12*, 337–338.

Domjan, M. CS preexposure in taste-aversion learning: Effects of deprivation and preexposure duration. *Learning and Motivation*, 1972, *3*, 389–402.

Donegan, N. H. Priming-produced facilitation or diminution of responding to a Pavlovian unconditioned stimulus. *Journal of Experimental Psychology, Animal Behavior Processes*, 1981, *7*, 295–312.

Donegan, N. H., & Wagner, A. R. Conditioned diminution and facilitation of the UR: A sometimes opponent process interpretation. In I. Gormezano, W. F. Prokasy & R. F. Thompson (Eds.), *Classical conditioning* (Vol. 3). Hillsdale, N.J.: Lawrence Erlbaum Associates, in press.

Estes, W. K. Toward a statistical theory of learning. *Psychological Review*, 1950, *57*, 94–107.

Estes, W. K. Memory and conditioning. In F. J. McGuigan & D. B. Lumsden (Eds.), *Contemporary approaches to conditioning and learning*. New York: Wiley, 1973. Pp. 265–286.

Feigenbaum, E. A., & Simon, H. A. A theory of the serial position effect. *British Journal of Psychology*, 1962, *53*, 307–320.

Glanzer, M., & Cunitz, A. R. (1966) Two storage mechanisms in free recall. *Journal of Verbal Learning and Verbal Behavior*, 1966, *5*, 351–360.

Grethier, W. F. Pseudo-conditioning without paired stimulation encountered in attempted backward conditioning. *Journal of Comparative Psychology*, 1938, *25*, 91–96.

Groves, P. M., & Thompson, R. F. Habituation: A dual-process theory. *Psychological Review*, 1970, *77*, 419–450.

Hinson, R. E. The effects of UCS preexposure on excitatory and inhibitory rabbit eyelid conditioning: An associative effect of conditioned contextual stimuli. *Journal of Experimental Psychology, Animal Behavior Processes*, 1982, *8*, 49–61.

Hoffman, H. S., & Ison, J. R. Reflex modification in the domain of startle. I. Some empirical findings and their implications for how the nervous system processes sensory input. *Psychological Review*, 1980, *87*, 175–189.

Horn, G. Changes in neuronal activity and their relationship to behavior. In G. Horn & R. A. Hinde (Eds.), *Short-term changes in neural activity and behavior*. London & New York: Cambridge University Press, 1970. Pp. 567–606.

Hupka, R. B., Kwaterski, S. E., & Moore, J. W. Conditioned diminution of the UCR: Differences between the human eyeblink and the rabbit nictitating membrane response. *Journal of Experimental Psychology*, 1970, *83*, 45–51.

Ison, J. R., & Krauter, E. E. Reflex-inhibiting stimuli and the refractory period of the acoustic startle reflex in the rat. *Journal of Comparative and Physiological Psychology*, 1974, *86*, 420–425.

James, J. H., & Wagner, A. R. One-trial overshadowing: Evidence of distributive process-ing. *Journal of Experimental Psychology, Animal Behavior Processes,* 1980, *6,* 188–205.

James, W. *Principles of psychology.* New York: Holt, 1890.

Kalat, J. W., & Rozin, P. "Learned safety" as a mechanism in long-delay taste-aversion learning in rats. *Journal of Comparative and Physiological Psychology,* 1973, *83,* 198–207.

Kamin, L. J. "Attention-like" processes in classical conditioning. In M. R. Jones (Ed.), *Miami symposium on the prediction of behavior, 1967: Aversive stimulation.* Coral Gables, Fla.: University of Miami Press, 1968. Pp. 9–31.

Kandel, E. R. *Cellular basis of behavior.* San Francisco: Freeman, 1976.

Kimble, G. A. *Hilgard and Marquis' conditioning and learning.* New York: Appleton, 1961.

Kimble, G. A., & Ost, J. W. P. A conditioned inhibitory process in eyelid conditioning. *Journal of Experimental Psychology,* 1961, *61,* 150–156.

Kimmel, H. D. Inhibition of the unconditioned response in classical conditioning. *Psychological Review,* 1966, *73,* 232–240.

Konorski, J. *Integrative activity of the brain: An interdisciplinary approach.* Chicago: University of Chicago Press, 1967.

Krasne, F. B. Invertebrate systems as a means of gaining insight into the nature of learning and memory. In M. R. Rosenzweig & E. L. Bennett (Eds.), *Neural mechanisms in learning and memory.* Cambridge, Mass.: MIT Press, 1976. Pp. 401–429.

Leaton, R. N. Long-term retention of the habituation of lick suppression in rats. *Journal of Comparative and Physiological Psychology,* 1974, *87,* 1157–1164.

Lubow, R. E. Latent inhibition. *Psychological Bulletin,* 1973, *79,* 398–407.

Mackintosh, N. J. *The psychology of animal learning.* New York: Academic Press, 1974.

Marlin, N. A., & Miller, R. R. Associations to contextual stimuli as a determinant of long-term habituation. *Journal of Experimental Psychology, Animal Behavior Processes,* 1981, *7,* 313–333.

Mazur, J. E., & Wagner, A. R. An episodic model of associative learning. In M. Commons, R. J. Herrnstein, & A. R. Wagner (Eds.), *Quantitative analysis of behavior: Acquisition* (Vol. 3). Cambridge, Mass.: Ballinger, in press.

McCullough, C. Color adaptation of edge detectors in the human visual system. *Science,* 1965, *149,* 1115–1116.

Norman, D. A. Toward a theory of memory and attention. *Psychological Review,* 1968, *75,* 522–536.

Pavlov, I. P. *Conditioned reflexes* (G. V. Anrep, trans.). London & New York: Oxford University Press, 1927.

Peeke, H. V., & Veno, G. Stimulus specificity of habituated aggression in three-spined sticklebacks (*Gasterosteus aculeatus*). *Behavioral Biology,* 1973, *8,* 427–432.

Pfautz, P. L. *Unconditioned facilitation and diminution of the unconditioned response.* Unpublished doctoral dissertation, Yale University, 1980.

Pfautz, P. L., & Wagner, A. R. Transient variations in responding to Pavlovian conditioned stimuli have implications for the mechanism of "priming." *Animal Learning and Behavior,* 1976, *4,* 107–112.

Randich, A., & Lolordo, V. Associative and nonassociative theories of the UCS pre-expo-sure phenomenon: Implications for Pavlovian conditioning. *Psychological Bulletin,* 1979, *86,* 523–548.

Rescorla, R. A., & Wagner, A. R. A theory of Pavlovian conditioning: Variations in the effectiveness of reinforcement and nonreinforcement. In A. H. Black & W. F. Prokasy (Eds.), *Classical conditioning. II: Current research and theory.* New York: Academic Press, 1972. Pp. 64–99.

Schull, J. A conditioned opponent theory of Pavlovian conditioning and habituation. In G. H. Bower (Ed.), *The psychology of learning and motivation* (Vol. 13). New York: Academic Press, 1979. Pp. 57–90.

Shalter, M. D. Lack of spatial generalization in habituation tests of fowl. *Journal of Comparative and Physiological Psychology*, 1975, *89*, 258–262.

Sheafor, P. J. "Pseudoconditioned" jaw movements of the rabbit reflect associations conditioned to contextual background cues. *Journal of Experimental Psychology, Animal Behavior Processes*, 1975, *1*, 245–260.

Sherrington, C. S. *The integrative action of the nervous system*. New Haven, Conn.: Yale University Press, 1906.

Shiffrin, R. M., & Schneider, W. Controlled and automatic processing. II. Perceptual learning, automatic attending, and a general theory. *Psychological Review*, 1977, *84*, 127–190.

Siegel, S. Evidence from rats that morphine tolerance is a learned response. *Journal of Comparative and Physiological Psychology*, 1975, *89*, 498–506.

Siegel, S. Morphine tolerance as an associative process. *Journal of Experimental Psychology, Animal Behavior Processes*, 1977, *3*, 1–13.

Siegel, S. The role of conditioning in drug tolerance and addiction. In J. D. Keehn (Ed.), *Psychopathology in animals: Research and treatment implications*. New York: Academic Press, 1979. Pp. 143–168.

Siegel, S., Hinson, R., & Krank, M. D. The role of predrug signals in morphine analgesic tolerance: Support for a Pavlovian conditioning model of tolerance. *Journal of Experimental Psychology, Animal Behavior Processes*, 1978, *4*, 188–196.

Simon, H. A. *The sciences of the artificial*. Cambridge, Mass.: MIT Press, 1969.

Sokolov, E. N. *Perception and the conditioned reflex*. Oxford: Pergamon, 1963.

Solomon, R. S., & Corbit, J. P. An opponent-process theory of motivation. *Psychological Review*, 1974, *81*, 119–145.

Terry, W. S. The effects of priming US representation in short-term memory on Pavlovian conditioning. *Journal of Experimental Psychology, Animal Behavior Processes*, 1976, *2*, 354–370.

Thompson, R. F., & Glanzman, D. L. Neural and behavioral mechanisms of habituation and sensitization. In T. J. Tighe & R. N. Leaton (Eds.), *Habituation: Perspectives from child development, animal behavior and neurophysiology*. Hillsdale, N.J.: Lawrence Erlbaum Associates, 1976. Pp. 49–93.

Thompson, R. F., & Spencer, W. A. Habituation: A model phenomenon for the study of the neuronal substrates of behavior. *Psychological Review*, 1966, *73*, 16–43.

Tomie, A. Interference with autoshaping by prior context conditioning. *Journal of Experimental Psychology, Animal Behavior Processes*, 1976, *2*, 323–334.

Wagner, A. R. Priming in STM: An information-processing mechanism for self-generated or retrieval-generated depression of performance. In T. J. Tighe & R. N. Leaton (Eds.), *Habituation: Perspectives from child development, animal behavior, and neurophysiology*. Hillsdale, N.J.: Lawrence Erlbaum Associates, 1976, Pp. 95–128.

Wagner, A. R. Expectancies and the priming of STM. In S. H. Hulse, H. Fowler, & W. K. Honig (Eds.), *Cognitive processes in animal behavior*. Hillsdale, N.J.: Lawrence Erlbaum Associates, 1978. Pp. 177–209.

Wagner, A. R. Habituation and memory. In A. Dickinson & R. A. Boakes (Eds.), *Mechanisms of learning and motivation: A memorial volume for Jerzy Konorski*. Hillsdale, N.J.: Lawrence Erlbaum Associates, 1979. Pp. 53–82.

Wagner, A. R. SOP: A model of automatic memory processing in animal behavior. In N. E. Spear & R. R. Miller (Eds.), *Information processing in animals: Memory mechanisms*. Hillsdale, N.J.: Lawrence Erlbaum Associates, 1981. Pp. 5–47.

Wagner, A. R., & Pfautz, P. F. A bowed serial-position function in habituation of sequential stimuli. *Animal Learning and Behavior,* 1978, *6,* 395–400.

Wagner, A. R., & Rescorla, R. A. Inhibition in Pavlovian conditioning: Application of a theory. In R. A. Boakes & M. S. Halliday (Eds.), *Inhibition and learning.* New York: Academic Press, 1972. Pp. 301–335.

Wagner, A. R., Rudy, J. W., & Whitlow, J. W. Rehearsal in animal conditioning. *Journal of Experimental Psychology,* 1973, *97,* 407–426. (Monograph)

Wagner, A. R., Thomas, E., & Norton, T. Conditioning with electrical stimulation of motor cortex: Evidence of a possible source of motivation. *Journal of Comparative and Physiological Psychology,* 1967, *64,* 191–199.

Watkins, M. J. Engrams as cuegrams and forgetting as cue overload: A cueing approach to the structure of memory. In C. R. Puff (Ed.), *Memory organization and structure.* New York: Academic Press, 1979.

Westbrook, R. F., Bond, N. W., & Feyer, A. Short- and long-term decrements in toxicosis induced, odor aversion learning: The role of duration of exposure. *Journal of Experimental Psychology, Animal Behavior Processes,* 1981, *7,* 362–381.

Whitlow, J. W., Jr. Short-term memory in habituation and dishabituation. *Journal of Experimental Psychology, Animal Behavior Processes,* 1975, *1,* 189–206.

Whitlow, J. W., Jr. Dynamics of episodic processing in Pavlovian conditioning. In D. Medin, W. Roberts, & R. Davis (Eds.), *Processes of animal memory.* Hillsdale, N.J.: Lawrence Erlbaum Associates, 1976. Pp. 203–227.

Willner, J. A. Blocking of a taste aversion by prior pairings of exteroceptive stimuli with illness. *Learning and Motivation,* 1978, *9,* 125–140.

Wine, J. J., & Krasne, F. B. The organization of escape behavior in the crayfish. *Journal of Experimental Biology,* 1972, *56,* 1–18.

Zener, K. The significance of behavior accompanying salivary secretion for theories of the conditioned response. *American Journal of Psychology,* 1937, *50,* 384–403.

CHAPTER 5

An Evaluation of Statistical Strategies to Analyze Repeated-Measures Data

Lewis Petrinovich
Keith F. Widaman

Department of Psychology
University of California
Riverside, California

HABITUATION, SENSITIZATION,
AND BEHAVIOR

I. Introduction

The characteristics of several different statistical approaches to the analysis of data often obtained in habituation experiments are investigated in this chapter. The chapter should be understandable to anyone who has a rudimentary knowledge of inferential statistics and the linear-regression model. From time to time, however, some points are discussed that require somewhat more statistical sophistication to be understood or that provide detailed information regarding the construction of data for the present chapter. These sections are included because they concern issues that are important in terms of the underlying statistical models and are important to statisticians and specialists in measurement. These sections are set in smaller type and can be skipped with no loss of continuity in the argument.

We begin with a general discussion of the statistical procedures used to detect response changes over a series of trials. This discussion is followed by a consideration of the problems involved in testing the effects of a single probe stimulus that follows a series of trials.

To evaluate the different statistical methods, we have taken two approaches. The first is to define four sets of artificial data, each containing two groups of 10 subjects each. Assuming that a linear function of trials represents the data from each subject, ideal data sets were constructed by determining the equation for a straight line for each subject, and from these ideal sets, simulated sets of data were obtained that had a component of random error added to each data point. The data obtained from this computer simulation were analyzed using each of the statistical procedures we are evaluating. Following this, the same analytic procedures were applied to a set of real data from a field experiment on habituation. The limitations and advantages of the different approaches are discussed, and a series of recommendations are offered. Finally, some general points are outlined to illustrate the importance of methodological decisions to theory construction in science.

Little systematic attention has been given to statistical procedures used to analyze data obtained in the typical habituation experiment. A data set from an habituation experiment usually consists of several blocks of trials based on the responses of one or more groups of subjects. At the end of the trial blocks, there are often additional trials to investigate the effects of presenting a novel (generalization) stimulus—as well as a repetition of the original stimulus—to test for dishabituation. Sometimes another set of habituation trials are presented on one or more later occasions. The statistical procedures discussed here are those most appropriate for use with these types of data. It should be noted, however, that these procedures are appropriate for any set of data that involves repeated measures on the same subjects.

II. Statistical Procedures Used to Detect Response Changes

There are at least four distinct approaches to analysis of data from the typical habituation experiment. The first three approaches, widely used in the literature, share the characteristic that the analyses are performed at the group level, with individual information used only in the error term against which group trends are compared. The fourth approach, fitting regression parameters to data from each individual, allows the evaluation of the degree of habituation exhibited by each subject as well as that exhibited by groups of subjects as aggregates.

A. Tests Comparing Final to Initial Levels of Response

The first and most common procedure used in habituation studies is to determine an initial level of response, present the test stimulus a number of times, determine the final level of response, subtract the final level from the initial level, and then test that difference for statistical significance. Because it is recognized that behavior on any one trial may be subject to undesired random fluctuations, data are often blocked; and the value of initial and final levels are based on a number of individual stimulus presentations. The scores for the members of a group are combined, a mean or a median is determined, and a p level for the obtained difference is obtained using a parametric t test for correlated means, or a nonparametric Wilcoxon matched-pairs test. Illustrations of these procedures can be found in Hinde (1954a, 1954b, 1961), who often used the t test in his classic studies of the mobbing behavior of Chaffinch (*Fringilla coelebs*), and Peeke, Wyers, and Herz, (1969) who utilized the Wilcoxon test in their study of aggressive responses of the three-spined stickleback (*Gasterosteus aculeantus* L.).

Nothing is intrinsically wrong with these modes of analysis, but they are wasteful of the information that has been gathered. Through the use of only initial and final sets of trials, most of the data that have been gathered are discarded. In most field experiments a fair amount of data are collected on each subject, because of the difficulty of locating subjects and implementing experimental procedures. In the laboratory a large number of repeated trials often are gathered to observe the time course of response changes. Thus a large amount of information between the initial and final segments is eliminated when the typical methods of analysis are used. Additionally, the stability, from a sampling point of view, of the values used to represent the initial and final segments depends on an arbitrary choice of the amount of data used to characterize each segment.

Another serious problem is that the pattern of results for the individual subjects is lost. Data from the following distinctly different types of subjects might be combined: (a) subjects that started at baseline and remained there; (b) subjects that started rather higher and demonstrated the expected decrease in response level resulting from habituation; (c) subjects that started at a high level and showed no change in response level at all. Thus the interpretation of the data are confounded by any systematic trial × individual difference interactions that might exist. As has been pointed out elsewhere (Petrinovich, 1981) the curve describing the change for the group might not be representative of any individual subject in the group.

Some investigators have recognized the problem caused by different initial levels in response and have attempted to resolve it by using relative rather than absolute response differences. On the whole, this is not a satisfactory approach, because of statistical problems (see Cohen & Cohen, 1975, pp. 378ff). The problem is that a change score has a necessary dependence on the level of prescore. Subtracting the prescore from the postscore leaves some variance in the change score, wholly a result of the level of the prescore, distorting the relationship of the change score to other variables. The use of change scores will be given no further consideration in the computer simulations to follow.

B. Repeated-Measures Analysis of Variance

One commonly used method that includes data from all trials is the repeated measures analysis of variance (ANOVA), which may be calculated after data are classified into blocks of trials. If the F ratio for the trials effect is significant, then either a priori or a posteriori t tests are performed between the individual blocks to identify the nature of the significant effects in the data. The problems involved in making such multiple comparisons were investigated in Petrinovich and Hardyck (1969), and some useful guidelines were developed.

One major problem with this procedure involves size of the data blocks. If the data are broken into a small number of blocks, systematic differences in behavior levels across time might not be detected because of the coarseness of the blocking (see Thompson, Groves, Teyler, & Roemer, 1973, p. 245). Alternately, if the data are analyzed using a large number of small blocks, the greatly increased intertrial variability, resulting from sampling instability of trial-block means, may obscure major trends in the data. In addition, the extremely large number of degrees of freedom (df) produced by using a large number of small blocks for each subject may so deflate the estimates of the standard error that a large number of statistically significant differences result, each of which accounts for a very small amount of the total variance. In addition, patterns of individual differences are lost with this method: they are treated as error variance against which the main effects and interaction terms are evaluated. Illustrations of the use of repeated measures ANOVA procedures can be found in Peeke and Peeke (1982), who studied sensitization and habituation in convict cichlid (*Cichlasoma nigrofasciatum*), and in Megela and Teyler (1979), who studied changes in human evoked potentials.

C. Group Regression

Another method has been used that includes all of the data and avoids the problem attendant on collapsing the data into blocks. A regression equation across trials is calculated, and the slope coefficient is tested to determine whether the response level changes over trials. If there is more than one group, the slope coefficient for each group can be calculated and then tested to determine if the slopes of the response curves are parallel; if there are significant slope differences among groups, this means that there is an interaction between group membership and change over trials. If so, individual comparisons can be made to understand the interaction. If the slope coefficients for the different groups can be considered to be from the same population, the significance of the common slope coefficient can be tested to determine if response level changes significantly over trials, and the intercepts for the groups can be tested to determine whether response levels differ significantly. This method has two of the same problems present in the repeated measures ANOVA: there are a large number of df generated when considering subjects over trials, and this often results in significant differences that account for little of the total variance. In addition, the pattern of the individual differences is lost. This method has been used in a series of studies of the changes in levels of response by White-crowned Sparrows (*Zonotrichia leucophrys nuttalli*) to the playback of territorial song (e.g., Petrinovich & Patterson, 1979).

D. Individual Regression Analysis

To our knowledge this procedure has not yet been used to investigate habituation effects, but it has a great deal to recommend it. It has all the advantages of the group regression method and minimizes the disadvantages. Because the analysis is done using each subject as an individual case, it allows the investigator to probe individual differences.

The method is related to the multivariate ANOVA (MANOVA) approach used to analyze repeated-measures data. The latter approach involves transforming each subject's scores on the repeated trials into a mean contrast and orthogonal-trend contrasts. The mean contrast is used to test all between-subjects effects, and the orthogonal-trend contrasts are used to test within-subjects effects; the error term for each test of significance is based on individual differences on the particular contrast of interest. Using individual regression analysis, an intercept (rather than mean contrast) and linear slope (rather than all possible orthogonal-trend contrasts) are computed for each subject; but all tests of significance between groups are still compared against individual differences in the computed parameters.

To use the individual regression method, a regression equation is calculated for each subject. The intercept value for each subject can be tested to determine if it is significantly above zero, using the standard error of the intercept for that subject, and the slope can be tested to determine if it is significantly different from zero, using the standard error of the slope. After this is done for each individual subject the z values can be combined to obtain a representative value for the entire group, and the combined value can be tested for significance. If there are large individual differences between subjects this is seen at once. For example, if the slope for some subjects increases significantly and for some it decreases significantly, it is possible to determine whether this is related to intercept differences: those that are significantly above the zero intercept may have decreased significantly in response levels, and those that started at zero may have increased significantly. The question of individual differences is of paramount importance in habituation studies: if one wishes to study dishabituation, the subjects must have shown evidence of habituation. Through systematic probing of the data at the individual level it is possible to include in a test of dishabituation only those subjects that demonstrate the required behavioral characteristics. In addition, it is possible to discover unexpected relationships between variables, a consideration of special importance if the data were obtained in field settings in which many variables are uncontrolled and their values are registered actuarially by the experimenter. The general advantages of this idiographic approach to data analysis has been discussed at length by Hammond (e.g., 1980).

If individual behavior is highly unreliable, the individual regression approach would have little power; but this is true of all methods described. The solution to this problem would be to insist that each trial is based on a sample of behavior sufficient to ensure the reliability of the data, thus minimizing the standard errors against which parameters are evaluated for statistical significance.

III. Methods to Detect Stimulus Generalization, Dishabituation, and Spontaneous Recovery

One of the critical tests that must be made when invoking habituation as an explanation for an observed response decrement is to rule out sensory adaptation and motor fatigue. This is done by demonstrating that the decrements are specific to the original test stimulus. Usually, a probe stimulus is introduced after a number of presentations of the test stimulus. This probe stimulus usually reflects the same stimulus dimension as the original stimulus, the investigator being interested in testing the degree of generalization to this new stimulus. If complete generalization of the response occurs, it is possible to argue that the observed effects are general and could be more parsimoniously explained in terms of sensory adaptation and motor fatigue. If there is little generalization to a new stimulus, the habituation explanation is plausible. Another aspect of habituation theory is that a novel stimulus should produce dishabituation: the response level to the original stimulus to which the subject has been habituated should be higher than it was prior to the introduction of a novel stimulus.

One of the common features of habituation is considered to be spontaneous recovery (but, see Patterson & Petrinovich 1979; Petrinovich & Patterson, 1979), that is, it is assumed that a habituated response will recover after a period of time. The test for this is either a comparison of response level on the last trial of the initial habituation series with the level on the first trial after the recovery interval, or a comparison of the first trial level of the initial habituation series with the first trial level of the recovery series (Hinde, 1954b, used the latter method).

A. Single Probe Trials

The usual method to test for effects of an interpolated trial is to compare the response level on the last trial in the habituation series to the level on the generalization trial using a *t* test for correlated means or a Wilcoxon matched-pairs test. To test for dishabituation, the response level on the last habituation trial is compared to the response level on the next presentation of the original stimulus. The major problem with this procedure is that it ignores all data but the two values involved in the comparison. Any random variation in the level of the last habituation trial will have a profound influence, because it is used as the value against which the generalization and dishabituation trial values are compared. Another concern is that there must be a significant change in response level to reject the null hypothesis and, thereby, conclude that generalization of dishabituation had occurred. This requirement is reasonable only if it has been demonstrated that the response curve had reached an asymptote. If the curve is still decreasing, the probe-trial level might be at the same level as the preceding trial but would still indicate a significant degree of dishabituation or generalization. If the response level has not yet stabilized, a presentation of the original stimulus would not have produced the same level of response as on the preceding trial: it might be expected to be higher or lower, depending on the form of the curve. If this is the case, a probe value that is the same as the last presentation of the original stimulus might well represent a significant difference. This method of testing the significance of probe-trial values is usually employed when the data have been analyzed using only initial and final values, as already discussed, or after a repeated-measures ANOVA (e.g., Megela & Teyler, 1979).

B. Test Using the Group Regression Line

A more satisfactory approach to the problems involved in testing for generalization, dishabituation, and spontaneous recovery is to use the entire response curve to predict the expected level of the test trial. If the changing phase of the regression line is linear, the best-fit straight line can be obtained, and the line can be extrapolated beyond the last point to obtain the expected value of the test trial. The significance level of the observed difference can be estimated using the standard error of a group mean to establish a confidence interval. This provides a more sensitive test because it uses all of the prior data points to make the extrapolation and to establish the standard error. This extrapolation is less affected by random fluctuations that might influence any given trial. As already discussed, if the slope is pronounced a test value that is the same as the last habituation value could prove to be significantly different from the value predicted using the regression equation. Use of the regression equation provides a more rational procedure to test generalization to a novel stimulus, the dishabituating effect of a novel stimulus, and the effect of a time interval on response level.

It should be emphasized that this method will only be adequate if the regression is linear. This can be determined by visual inspection of the data and by examining the size of the standard error of the slope. If the standard error is small this demonstrates that the linear fit is good. If the relationship is curvilinear, then higher-order polynomials can be added to the equation and tested to determine whether they account for significant additional variance. If so, the best-fitting curvilinear line should be used to extrapolate beyond the final point.

If a second habituation series follows the initial one, another advantage of this method can be realized. One can test the initial level of the second series against the value expected based on the first series and also test for differences between the slopes of the first and second series, as we have already outlined.

The major shortcoming is that the method does not take into consideration the pattern of individual differences. As already suggested, this is especially important if one is interested in the generalization of habituation effects, in dishabituation, and in spontaneous recovery. These concepts have meaning only if the response level has shown a significant decrement; the tests are meaningful only with habituated responses. If some of the subjects have not habituated, the group curves might represent highly confounded results.

C. Test Using the Individual Regression Line

This procedure is similar to the group regression one except that the regression equation is developed for each individual subject, and the slope constant and standard error of a point are used to perform the significance test. Following this test, the standard scores obtained as test statistics can be combined to represent the group, and these standard scores can be analyzed using a one-way ANOVA to determine if there are significant differences across groups. Again, this method presumes a linear regression, as already discussed.

IV. Additional Problems

There are three problems that have not been considered in our discussion, but which will be considered in the computer simulations and analyses to follow. One problem is the effect of unequal variances between different groups to be compared. A second is the problem of unequal variances across trials: often the variance at the beginning of a series of trials is large, but with repeated trials the variance becomes smaller. Finally, there is the problem of baseline effects. If some subjects begin near a baseline response level, it is not possible for them to demonstrate any marked response decrement. But the standard error for the subjects in the group that essentially is at baseline will be very small, and almost any random change in response level might produce a significant test statistic for slope and intercept. The simulations to be discussed in the next section have been done with these problems taken into consideration.

V. Strategy of This Chapter

A. Simulations of an Initial Data Set for Two Groups

Artificial data sets were created with four major characteristics (the numerical description of these data sets is presented in Section VI,A, this chapter). The data generated were analyzed using three of the methods described in Section I: repeated-measures ANOVA, group regression, and individual regression.

1. Case I: Equal Variance within Groups and Equal Slope (Fig. 1a)

Each of the two groups had an equal variance that is constant across trials; each had the same linear slope, but the intercepts were different for the two.

2. Case II: Equal Variance within Groups and Different Slope (Fig. 1b)

The intercepts were different for the two groups, the variances were equal across trials, but the slopes for the two groups were unequal such that the final point for each of the subjects in one group was the same as it was for the subject with the same relative standing in the other group.

3. Case III: Different Unequal Variance within Groups across Trials and Different Slope (Fig. 1c)

The scores making up Group 1 had a higher intercept, and there was no overlap with the scores of Group 2 at the outset. There was a negative slope and a gradually decreasing variance across trials, with all scores converging on a point slightly above the highest score of Group 2. Group 2 has a lower intercept, an equal variance across trials, and a zero slope.

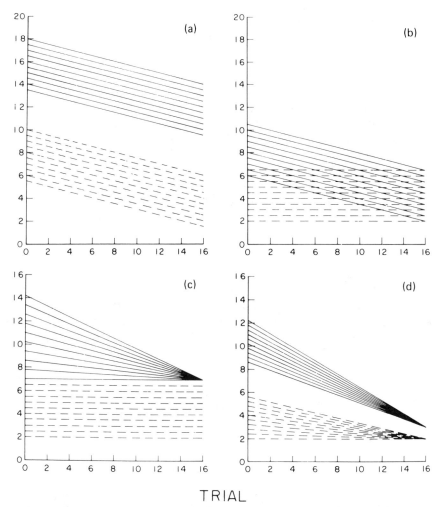

Fig. 1. Characteristics of simulated data sets. Group 1, ———; Group 2, ---. (a) Case I, equal variance within groups and equal slope. (b) Case II, equal variance within groups and different slope. (c) Case III, different unequal variance within groups across trials and different slope. (d) Case IV, similar unequal variance within groups across trials and different slope.

TRIAL

4. Case IV: Similar Unequal Variance within Groups across Trials and Different Slope (Fig. 1d)

The level of Group 1 was higher across all trials as compared to Group 2. The variance for both groups was large at the outset and decreased to a point at the end (with Group 1 higher than Group 2). The slope was highly negative for Group 1 and less so for Group 2.

B. Tests of a Single Data Point

A single data point was created for each subject, and this point represents a probe stimulus. Points were chosen that were either identical to the last point in the initial set, that were 2.0 within-subjects SD higher than the last point, or 2.0 within-subjects SD below the last point. The value of this point can be taken as the obtained value when a generalization stimulus is presented, when a test is made for dishabituation of the original stimulus, or after a time interval to test for spontaneous recovery.

C. Analyses of Real Data

Data from a study of habituation and dishabituation (Petrinovich, in press) to the playback of territorial song to 20 breeding pairs of White-crowned Sparrows have been analyzed by each of the three methods discussed in Section I (See Chapter 2 for a brief description of the playback procedure used: it is the same as that for the 1-day–same-song group described there.)

VI. Simulated Data

A. Generation of Simulated Data

Simulation Model

As already noted, four sets of simulated data, each containing two groups of subjects, were generated and then analyzed using the three methods of analysis discussed in the preceding section. The sets of simulated data were constructed to model a variety of patterns of results that commonly appear in the habituation literature. Each set of simulated data consisted of two groups of subjects, with 10 subjects per group and 16 habituation trials. The simulated data for each subject was constructed according to the following procedure:

Assuming that the general linear model is an adequate representation of the form of the response of subjects during a set of habituation trials, the ideal data for each subject was constructed according to the model

$$Y_{ij} = a_i + b_i(\text{Trial}),$$

where Y_{ij} is the ideal data point for subject i on trial j, a_i the intercept for individual i, and b_i the regression weight for subject i. We next detail the parameter values used to generate the ideal data for each set.

Simulated data were obtained from the ideal data by adding a component of random error to each data point. The error component e_{ij} had a mean of zero and standard deviation of σ_e. For the present simulations, σ_e was set to a value of 1.00, based on a set of preliminary simulation analyses that revealed trial-to-trial correlations in the range of .60–.80 after partialing-out group differences, a level of trial-to-trial correlation found in preliminary analyses of real data from a field experiment (Petrinovich, in press). Thus the full linear model according to which the simulation data were generated was

$$Y_{ij} = a_i + b_i(\text{Trial}) + e_{ij},$$

where the i subscript refers to individuals, the j subscript to trials, and remaining parameters are defined as before.

B. Generation of Probe (Test-Trial) Values

The single probe-trial value for each subject was estimated in one of three ways relative to the nth, or sixteenth trial: as a value 2.0 within-subjects SD above the nth-trial simulated value, as a value equal to the nth-trial simulated value, and as a value 2.0 within-subjects SD below the nth-trial simulated value.

C. Parameter Values for the Four Data Sets

The parameter values used in the four data sets were as follows.

1. Case I: Equal Variance within Groups and Equal Slope

Case I represents the situation in which subjects in each of two groups showed similar patterns of response decrement across trials, although the subjects in the two groups showed rather different initial levels of response which were preserved across the set of trials.

The intercept values for the subjects in Group 1 ranged from 13.5–18.0 by 0.5 steps; the intercept values for the subjects in Group 2 varied from 5.5–10.0 by 0.5 steps, and a slope of -0.25 was used for all subjects in both groups. The resulting pattern of ideal data is displayed in Fig. 1a. As can be seen in Fig. 1a and as summarized in Table 1, the mean intercept varied across groups, but the within-group standard deviations of both intercept and slope and the mean value of the slope constant were identical across groups. This resulted in equal variances of the ideal scores across trials, both within and between groups.

TABLE 1

Simulated and Recovered Means and Standard Deviations of the Intercept and Slope of the Two
Groups for Each of the Four Cases

		Group 1				Group 2			
		Mean		Standard deviation		Mean		Standard deviation	
Case	Parameter	Simu-lated	Recov-ered	Simu-lated	Recov-ered	Simu-lated	Recov-ered	Simu-lated	Recov-ered
I	Intercept	15.75	15.56	1.51	1.85	7.75	7.79	1.51	1.70
	Slope	−0.25	−0.23	0.00	0.06	−0.25	−0.24	0.00	0.06
II	Intercept	8.25	8.06	1.51	1.85	4.25	4.29	1.51	1.70
	Slope	−0.25	−0.23	0.00	0.06	0.00	0.01	0.00	0.06
III	Intercept	10.60	10.41	2.42	2.74	4.25	4.29	1.51	1.70
	Slope	−0.23	−0.20	0.15	0.18	0.00	0.01	0.00	0.06
IV	Intercept	10.40	10.21	1.21	1.56	3.80	3.84	1.21	1.42
	Slope	−0.46	−0.44	0.08	0.11	−0.11	−0.10	0.08	0.09

2. Case II: Equal Variance within Groups and Different Slope

The situation reflected by the Case-II data is that situation in which one group of subjects began responding at a higher level than the second group of subjects and then showed a steady drop in level of response until it was responding at the level of the second group, which had not changed its level of response.

The intercept values for subjects in Group 1 ranged from 6.0–10.5 in 0.5 steps; those for Group 2 varied from 2.0–6.5 in 0.5 steps. A regression slope of −0.25 was used for subjects in Group 1, and a slope of zero was used for subjects in Group 2. As shown in Fig. 1b and Table 1, both the mean intercept and the mean value of the slope constant differed across groups, although the within-group standard deviations of the two parameters did not differ. This resulted in equal within-group variances of the ideal scores across trials, although the total variance across trials changed systematically because of the difference in the mean slope constant between the two groups.

3. Case III: Different Unequal Variance within Groups across Trials and Different Slope

Case III corresponds to situations in which subjects in one group showed a response decrement to a common level, demonstrating an amount of decrement directly related to their initial level; subjects in the other group evidenced no response decrement.

The intercept values for subjects in Group 1 ranged from 7.0–14.20 in 0.80 steps, the regression slopes for Group-1 subjects varied from 0 to −0.45 in 0.05 steps, and there was a perfect negative correlation between ideal intercept and slope parameters for these subjects. The intercept values for subjects in Group 2 varied from 2.0–6.5 in 0.5 steps, and a uniform regression slope of zero was used for Group-2 subjects. The pattern of ideal data for Case III is presented in Fig. 1c and Table 1; the two groups differed in all four parameters, mean and standard deviation of intercept and mean and standard deviation of slope.

4. Case IV: Similar Unequal Variance within Groups across Trials and Different Slope

Case IV reflects situations in which subjects in each of two groups showed a decreased level of responding, but the group with the higher initial level of responding showed the greater decrement.

The intercept values for subjects in Group 1 ranged from 8.6–12.2 in 0.4 steps, and their slope values varied from −0.350 to −0.575 in steps of 0.025. For subjects in Group 2, intercept values ranged from 2.00–5.60 in steps of 0.4, and their slope values varied from 0–0.225 in steps of 0.025. As can be seen in Fig. 1d and Table 1, both the mean intercept and mean slope differed across groups, although the standard deviations of both parameters were comparable across groups.

D. Methods of Analysis of Simulated Data

Three methods of analysis were applied to the data generated for the four cases already described. These methods were the repeated-measures analysis of variance, group regression analysis, and individual regression analysis.

1. Repeated-Measures Analysis of Variance (ANOVA)

The repeated-measures ANOVA used with the simulated data was a one-factor between, one-factor within design, with group as the between-subjects factor and trial as the within. Because the simulated data were generated according to the general linear model, one would expect that the means across trials would trace a fairly linear trend; in such situations, the overall F tests of the trial main effect and the trial × group interaction are known to be unduly conservative (e.g., Hale, 1977). Because the repeated-measures ANOVA is currently the most widely accepted mode of analysis of habituation data, and because the effects tested by the linear trial main effect and linear trial × group interaction from the group regression approach are identical to the more powerful trend tests using the repeated-measures ANOVA, only the conservative overall tests of significance will be presented.

2. Group Regression Analysis

The group regression approach involves fitting a slope coefficient to represent the linear trial main effect, as well as coefficients for interaction vectors representing the linear trial × group interaction; these latter interaction vectors are formed by multiplying the vector representing trial times each of the $g - 1$ pseudovariates representing membership in the g groups. If the interaction vectors are nonsignificant, the interaction vectors may be deleted from the regression model. The intercept differences between groups may then be tested using the pseudovariates indexing group membership.

In a manner similar to the ANOVA approach, the variance explained by the group regression analysis may be divided into between-subjects and within-subjects portions (see Cohen & Cohen, 1975, pp. 403–425). The between-subjects portion of the variance corresponds to the between-subjects effects from the ANOVA approach, and is calculated on each subject's mean level of response across trials. The within-subjects portion of the variance—comprising the trial main effect and trial × group interaction—attempts to represent the within-subjects variance with economy of estimates. Thus one may often account for the significant aspects of within-subjects variation using only linear trends of the associated effects. Because the simulated data were generated to contain only linear trends, only the linear trends of the trial and trial × group effects were estimated and tested, leaving an error term that was a composite of nonlinear trends of the trial and trial × group effects, as well as the usual pooled within-group estimates of individual differences in trends across trials.

3. Individual Regression Analysis

The third method of analysis applied to the sets of simulated data is the individual regression analysis. Using this approach, intercept and slope parameters were estimated for each subject to model the behavior emitted by the subject on the 16 habituation trials. For each subject, the intercept and slope parameters can be tested for significance; such tests would reveal whether the subject demonstrated a significant level of behavior, and whether that level changed as a function of trials, respectively. In addition, the intercept and slope parameter estimates can be subjected to a t test or one-way ANOVA to assess group differences on the parameters. A significant group-effect using the intercept as a dependent variable would be analogous to a significant group-main-effect from the group regression analysis, because both would reflect significant differences in level of responding among the groups. A significant group-effect using the slope as a dependent variable would be similar to a significant group × trial interaction with the group regression approach, because each of these effects would reflect differences among groups in the change in level of behavior exhibited across trials. The mean slope across all groups is also testable using a one-sample t or F test; a mean slope significantly different from zero is analogous to a significant-trial main effect from the group regression analysis, since both represent significant changes in performance across trials for all subjects.

E. Analyses of Probe Trials

The value for the seventeenth trial was designated as the probe-trial value. Three simulated probe-trial values were generated for each simulated subject by the following procedure. One probe-trial value was equal to the simulated value for the sixteenth trial and was designated as the "same-as-sixteenth-trial" value for the subject. Another value was 2.0 within-subject standard deviations above a subject's 16th trial-simulated value and was designated the "above-sixteenth-trial" value. Another value was 2.0 within-subject standard deviations below a subject's 16th trial-simulated value and was designated the "below-sixteenth-trial" value. The predicted value was that for the seventeenth trial, using the group regression equations.

The statistical significance of the simulated, from the predicted, probe-trial values was then assessed in the following way. After the ANOVA, the mean for the sixteenth trial was compared against each of the three simulated probe-trial means using Dunn's test (Kirk, 1968), a reasonably conservative test of a priori hypotheses. The formula used was

$$d = \frac{w_1 \bar{X}_1 + w_2 \bar{X}_2}{\sqrt{MS_e(w_1^2/n_1 + w_2^2/n_2)}},$$

where the w_i are the weights used to combine the group means, the $\bar{X}_i$ the group means, the n_i the number of observations on which the means were based, and MS_e is the within-subjects-mean-square error term. The Dunn's test is computed in precisely the same manner as an a priori t ratio, so one may compare the d value against critical t values if one computes only one comparison test per ANOVA, or against the more conservative Dunn's test critical values if more than one comparison per ANOVA is performed. Following the group regression analysis, the significance of the simulated probe-trial mean from the probe-trial mean predicted by extrapolating the regression line to Trial 17 was tested using a t test, noting whether the simulated trial value was greater than the predicted value. The formula used (see Wonnacott & Wonnacott, 1981, p. 44) was

$$t_{(N-2)} = \frac{\text{Observed} - \text{Predicted}}{\sqrt{\sigma_{y \cdot x}^2 (1/N + x_0^2/\Sigma x_i^2)}},$$

where σ_y^2 is the residual variance of the dependent variable, N the number of observations on which the analysis is based, x_0 the score on the independent variable (in deviation score units) for which a test of the mean is desired, and the x_i are deviation scores on the independent variable for all observations in the original analysis. After the individual regression analyses, a similar t-test procedure as used for the group analyses was used again, except that the tests were run on the data of each subject, rather than at the group level. The formula used (Wonnacott & Wonnacott, 1981, p. 45) was identical to that above, except that the term in the denominator in parentheses is $(1 + 1/N + x_0^2/\Sigma x_i^2)$.

F. Results

1. Case I

The mean and standard deviation of both the intercept- and slope-parameter estimates for each group as recovered from the simulated data

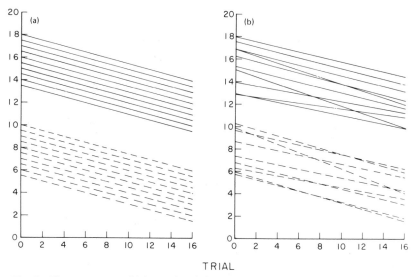

Fig. 2. Characteristics of (a) simulated data set and (b) recovered values for Case I.
Group 1, ——; Group 2, ---.

are presented in Table 1 and graphically presented in Fig. 2. The similarity
of the ideal (Fig. 2a) and simulated (Fig. 2b) parameter values attests to
the validity of the simulation. The individual regression analyses revealed
that all 10 subjects in each of the two groups had significant positive-
intercept and significant negative-slope estimates.

The results of analyses of the Case I simulated data are presented in
Table 2. Looking first at the ANOVA results, the three F ratios show
clearly that the two groups had a large mean difference in performance,
that subjects demonstrated a highly significant decline in performance
across trials, and that there was a nonsignificant group × trial interaction.
The results of the group regression analysis provided much the same
picture, with only the group and trial main effects significant. But it is
instructive to note that the F ratio for the trial effect from the group
regression analysis was much larger than that from the ANOVA, because
a very large portion of all of the variance associated with trial, as indicated in the ANOVA analysis (sum of squares $SS = 383.96$), was related
to only a single trend, the linear trend of trial ($SS = 368.07$). Because the
sums of squares for the linear trend are divided by only one degree of
freedom, the mean square for the linear-trial effect from the group regression (368.07) was much larger than the mean square for the overall trial
effect from the ANOVA (25.60); hence the considerably larger F ratio in

TABLE 2

Summary of Analyses of Simulated Data for Case I

Source	SS	df	MS	F	Variance explained
ANOVA					
Group	4955.4	1	4955.4	118.36***	.868
Subject	753.6	18	41.9	—	—
Trial	384.0	15	25.6	23.77***	.560
Trial × group	10.8	15	0.7	.67	.016
Trial × subject	290.8	270	1.1	—	—
Group regression					
Group	4955.4	1	4955.4	118.36***	.868
Subject	753.6	18	41.9	—	—
Trial	368.1	1	368.1	345.74***	.537
Trial × group	0.2	1	0.2	0.23	.000
Trial × subject	317.2	298	1.1	—	—
Individual regression					
Group	301.8	1	301.8	95.67***	.842
Subject	56.8	18	3.2	—	—
Trial	1.1	1	1.1	332.39***	.948
Trial × group	0.0	1	0.0	.22	.001
Trial × subject	0.1	18	0.0	—	—

*** $p < .001$.

the group regression analysis. Interestingly enough, though, the proportion of trial variance explained is almost the same for the two analyses.

The results of the individual regression analysis revealed levels of significance similar to those from the group regression analysis. The only notable difference between the group and individual regression analyses involved the tests of significance of the trial main effect and the trial × group interaction. The F ratios for these two effects were comparable across the two types of analysis, which is not surprising because the simulated trends in the data were linear, and the variance across trials was constant. But, in the group regression analysis, the trial main effect and the trial × group interaction were tested against an error term that was a composite of individual differences in all possible trends, as well as group differences in the quadratic and higher trends: thus the error term had 298 degrees of freedom. In the individual regression analysis, these two effects were evaluated against an error term composed only of individual differences in linear trend across trials, resulting in only 18 degrees of freedom for the error term. The latter error term may provide a less-

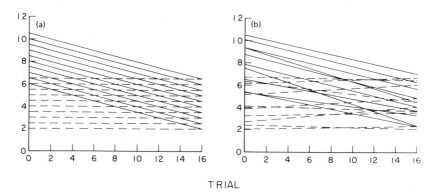

Fig. 3. Characteristics of (a) simulated data set and (b) recovered values for Case II. Group 1, ——; Group 2, ---.

powerful test of significance because of the decreased number of degrees of freedom, but it does represent the appropriate error term against which one should compare linear effects associated with trials. But the proportion of trial variance explained with the individual regression analysis jumped to .948. The individual regression analysis accounted for substantially more variance in all analyses on the trial and trial × group effects. This occurred because it accounted for substantial portions of each subject's data and any nonlinear effects were excluded from the analysis.

2. Case II

The group summary of the recovery of regression parameters from simulated data for Case II is given in Table 1, and graphically presented in Fig. 3. The results indicate a fairly close correspondence between the simulated (Fig. 3a) and recovered (Fig. 3b) estimates of parameters. All subjects in both groups had significant positive-intercept estimates; all 10 subjects in Group 1 had significant negative-slope estimates; and 9 of 10 subjects in Group 2 had nonsignificant slope estimates, the remaining Group-2 subject having a significant positive-slope estimate.

The results of the analyses of Case II simulated data are presented in Table 3. The significance tests from the ANOVA correctly mirror the patterns in the data, showing significant differences between groups in mean level of response, significant overall decrease in level of performance across trials, and a significant difference between groups in their change in level across trials. The results from the group regression showed a similar pattern of results. While the variance explained by the trial main effect and the trial × group interaction based on the group regression approach were slightly reduced from the parallel effects in the

TABLE 3

Summary of Analyses of Simulated Data for Case II

Source	SS	df	MS	F	Variance explained
Anova					
Group	243.70	1	243.70	5.82*	.244
Subject	753.61	18	41.87	—	—
Trial	94.70	15	6.31	5.86***	.192
Trial × group	106.88	15	7.13	6.62***	.217
Trial × subject	290.75	270	1.08	—	—
Group regression					
Group	243.70	1	243.70	5.82*	.244
Subject	753.61	18	41.87	—	—
Trial	78.81	1	78.81	74.03***	.160
Trial × group	96.28	1	96.28	90.44***	.196
Trial × subject	317.24	298	1.06	—	—
Individual regression					
Group	71.00	1	71.0	22.51***	.556
Subject	56.77	18	3.15	—	—
Trial	0.23	1	0.23	71.17***	.404
Trial × group	0.38	1	0.28	86.95***	.494
Trial × subject	0.60	18	0.003	—	—

* $p < .05$.
*** $p < .001$.

ANOVA, the F ratios for the effects were much larger in the group regression, because the variance of the effects was associated with only a single degree of freedom, the linear component of each effect.

The individual regression results once again appeared more similar to the results from the group regression than those from the ANOVA. Although the test of the intercept from the individual regression analysis appeared to be more powerful than the corresponding test from the group regression, the tests of the remaining two effects are quite comparable across types of analysis. As before, the most salient difference between the group and individual regression analyses was the degrees of freedom in the error term for the within-subjects effects. Again, the individual regression analysis accounted for a much greater proportion of the variance.

3. Case III

The results of the simulation for Case III are presented in Fig. 4 and Table 1. As before, the fit between the simulated (Fig. 4a) and recovered

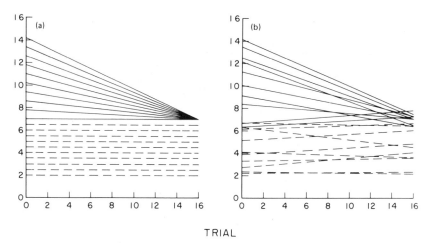

TRIAL

Fig. 4. Characteristics of (a) simulated data set and (b) recovered values for Case III. Group 1, ———; Group 2, – – –.

(Fig. 4b) estimates of the parameters of the general linear model underlying the response patterns supported the validity of the simulation procedures. All subjects in Groups 1 and 2 had significant positive-intercept estimates. In line with the ideal data for this case, 7 of the 10 subjects in Group 1 had significant negative-slope estimates, and the remaining three had nonsignificant estimates; 9 of 10 subjects in Group 2 had nonsignificant-slope estimates.

The results of the ANOVA and group regression complemented each other in much the same manner as with Cases I and II: the effects that revealed significance with one of the types of analysis also revealed significance for the other (Table 4). The F ratios for within-subjects effects from the group regression analysis were larger than the corresponding F ratios from the ANOVA, because the linear components of the within-subjects effects explained most of the variance.

In contrast to the patterns from the simulated data in Cases I and II, the results of the individual regression analysis were not very similar to those from the group regression. Although all three F ratios from both the group- and individual regression analyses were significant, those from the individual regression analysis were smaller than those from the group regression analysis: this occurred because of the obvious violation of an assumption underlying both the ANOVA and group regression analyses. The traditional assumption that must be met for the F test to be valid when using repeated-measures ANOVA is that of compound symmetry—that all trials have equal variances, and there are equal covariances among

TABLE 4

Summary of Analyses of Simulated Data for Case III

Source	SS	df	MS	F	Variance explained
ANOVA					
Group	1484.60	1	1484.60	44.87***	.714
Subject	595.57	18	33.09	—	—
Trial	77.46	15	5.16	3.70***	.143
Trial × group	87.71	15	5.85	4.19***	.162
Trial × subject	376.60	270	1.39	—	—
Group regression					
Group	1484.60	1	1484.60	44.87***	.714
Subject	595.57	18	33.09	—	—
Trial	61.56	1	61.56	45.52***	.114
Trial × group	77.12	1	77.12	57.01***	.142
Trial × subject	403.09	298	1.35	—	—
Individual regression					
Group	187.16	1	187.16	36.09***	.667
Subject	93.34	18	5.19	—	—
Trial	0.18	1	0.18	10.48**	.252
Trial × group	0.23	1	0.23	13.12**	.315
Trial × subject	0.31	18	0.02	—	—

** $p < .01$.
*** $p < .001$.

all trials (Kirk, 1968; Winer, 1971). Huynh and Mandeville (1979) have shown that a less-restrictive condition of the data, equality of treatment-difference variances, will ensure a valid F test. Neither of the preceding conditions was met for the present data, because the data for one group showed a greatly diminished variance as a function of trial, and data from the other group did not. The standard output from an ANOVA or group regression of the data, as shown in Table 4, would not indicate any problems with the validity of the significance tests. Once again, the individual regression analysis accounted for more than twice the amount of trial and trial × group variance than did the other two methods.

The problem surrounding determination of the validity of the significance test points up an advantage of the individual regression analysis. The within-group means and standard deviations of the slope- and intercept-parameter estimates, listed in Table 1, are a natural adjunct of the individual regression analysis, because the tests of significance are simple and straightforward. It is clear from Table 1 that Group 1 and Group 2 of Case III showed rather different standard deviations for both regression

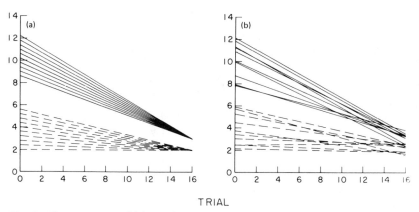

Fig. 5. Characteristics of (a) simulated data set and (b) recovered values for Case IV. Group 1, ———; Group 2, – – –.

parameters: for the intercept, the significance of the difference between variances was only marginal, $F(9,9) = 2.60$, $.05 < p < .10$, but the difference between the within-group variances in slope was highly significant, $F(9,9) = 9.74$, $p < .002$. Even when the degrees of freedom were modified to correct for the differences in within-group variances, however, the obtained mean differences between groups for both the intercept and slope parameters were still significant beyond the .001 level.

4. Case IV

The simulated and recovered results for Case IV data are presented in Fig. 5 and Table 1. As in each of the previous sets of simulated data, the recovered estimates (Fig. 5b) are rather close to the simulated values (Fig. 5a). Once again, all subjects in both groups had significant positive-intercept estimates. Following the pattern in the simulated data, all 10 subjects in Group 1 had significant negative slope estimates, but 5 of the 10 subjects in Group 2 had significant negative-slope estimates; the remaining 5 had nonsignificant estimates.

The results of the analyses of the Case IV data are given in Table 5. The ANOVA and group regression analyses provided similar pictures of the patterns extant in the data. Because over 90% of the variance of the trial main effect and the trial × group interaction were explained by the linear component of each, the F ratios differed greatly between the two types of analyses, but the explained variance differed little.

As with Case III, the individual regression analysis is dissimilar to the other two types of analysis, because the validity conditions for the re-

TABLE 5

Summary of Analyses of Stimulated Data for Case IV

Source	SS	df	MS	F	Variance explained
Anova					
Group	977.39	1	977.39	127.33***	.876
Subject	138.17	18	7.68	—	—
Trial	512.18	15	34.15	27.64***	.488
Trial × group	204.80	15	13.65	11.05***	.195
Trial × subject	333.55	270	1.24	—	—
Group regression					
Group	977.39	1	977.39	127.33***	.876
Subject	138.17	18	7.68	—	—
Trial	496.28	1	496.28	410.77***	.472
Trial × group	194.20	1	194.20	160.74***	.185
Trial × subject	360.04	298	1.21	—	—
Individual regression					
Group	202.77	1	202.77	90.88***	.835
Subject	40.16	18	2.23	—	—
Trial	1.46	1	1.46	142.42***	.659
Trial × group	0.57	1	0.57	55.73***	.259
Trial × subject	0.18	18	0.01	—	—

*** $p < .001$.

peated-measures F tests are once again not met with the present data. In contrast to Case III, the tests of significance reported in Table 5 for the individual regression analysis are valid as stated, because the differences in within-group variance for both the intercept and slope parameters are negligible. The individual regression analysis accounted for considerably more of the trial and trial × group variance.

5. Probe-Trial Analyses

As outlined previously, for each subject in each set of simulated data, three probe-trial values were generated. The above-sixteenth-trial value was 2.0 within-subject standard deviation units above each subject's simulated sixteenth trial score, the "equal" probe value was identical to each subject's sixteenth trial score, and the below-sixteenth-trial value was 2.0 within-subject standard deviation units below each subject's simulated sixteenth trial score.

a. Analysis of Variance. The results of the probe-trial analyses performed after the ANOVA are presented in Table 6. All of the Dunn's test values in the "above 16th trial" and the "below 16th trial" conditions were highly significant. Because the probe-trial values were generated relative to each subject's simulated sixteenth score, above-sixteenth-trial and below-sixteenth-trial values are identical—although opposite in sign—and the "equal" condition results in Dunn's test ratios of zero.

b. Group Regression. The group regression analyses resulted in tests of the significance of the probe-trial data that were approximately as powerful as those performed after the ANOVA (Table 6). Using the group regression equation, a predicted group mean for the probe trial was generated, assuming that the probe was the seventeenth trial. Because there was, in general, a decrease in the dependent variable as a function of trial, the predicted probe value was somewhat lower than the actual probe value in the "equal" condition. This tended to lead to positive, though nonsignificant, t values in the "equal" condition. In the above-sixteenth-trial condition, all eight t ratios were significant beyond the 0.1 level as were those in the below-sixteenth-trial condition.

c. Individual Regression. After the individual regression analyses, the probe-trial scores were compared to the predicted probe-trial score generated from each subject's regression equation. In Table 6, the results of the individual-level analyses are summarized. In Case I, 15 of 20 comparisons across the two groups led to a conclusion that the actual probe-trial value was significantly higher than the predicted probe value in the above-sixteenth-trial condition, a condition in which the actual probe value for each subject was generated to be above the subject's predicted probe value. Thus, in 15 of the 20 cases, the correct decision was made that the actual probe value was significantly above the predicted value, and the totally incorrect decision that the actual probe value was significantly *below* the predicted value was never made.

Turning to the "equal" condition for Case I, the significance tests revealed appropriate results, with none of the 20 tests showing a significant difference between observed and predicted probe values.

In the below-sixteenth-trial condition, in which the actual probe value was generated to fall rather lower than the predicted probe value for each subject, the correct determination that the actual probe was indeed lower was made in 11 of 20 comparisons across the two groups. It should also be noted that the totally incorrect decision, that the actual probe was significantly *above* the predicted, was never made.

The results from the remaining conditions—Cases II, III, and IV—

TABLE 6

Results of Analyses of Simulated Probe Data for the Three Methods of Analysis

| | | Probe-trial value | | |
Case	Group	Above 16th	Equal	Below 16th
ANOVA[a]				
I	1	6.44***	0.0	−6.44***
	2	6.28***	0.0	−6.28***
II	1	6.46***	0.0	−6.46***
	2	4.33***	0.0	−4.33***
III	1	6.09***	0.0	−6.09***
	2	3.84***	0.0	−3.84***
IV	1	9.47***	0.0	−9.42***
	2	4.64***	0.0	−4.64***
Group regression[b]				
I	1	6.53***	0.33	−5.87***
	2	6.51***	0.46	−5.59***
II	1	6.54***	0.34	−5.88***
	2	4.11***	−0.06	−4.23***
III	1	5.60***	−0.15	−6.14***
	2	4.16***	0.47	−3.23**
IV	1	9.85***	0.72	−8.40***
	2	4.64***	0.16	−4.31***
Individual regression[c]				
I	1	7 of 10+	0 of 10+	0 of 10+
		0 of 10−	0 of 10−	6 of 10−
	2	8 of 10+	0 of 10+	0 of 10+
		0 of 10−	0 of 10−	5 of 10−
II	1	7 of 10+	0 of 10+	0 of 10+
		0 of 10−	0 of 10−	5 of 10−
	2	3 of 10+	0 of 10+	0 of 10+
		0 of 10−	0 of 10−	2 of 10−
III	1	6 of 10+	0 of 10+	0 of 10+
		0 of 10−	0 of 10−	6 of 10−
	2	3 of 10+	0 of 10+	0 of 10+
		0 of 10−	0 of 10−	2 of 10−
IV	1	10 of 10+	0 of 10+	0 of 10+
		0 of 10−	0 of 10−	9 of 10−
	2	6 of 10+	0 of 10+	0 of 10+
		0 of 10−	0 of 10−	3 of 10−

[a] Tabled are the Dunn's test values for each group.
[b] Tabled are the *t*-ratio values for each group.
[c] Tabled values represent a summary of the 10 *t* ratios computed for each group.
** $p < .01$.
*** $p < .001$.

evidenced similar trends: when the probe-trial value was above the predicted probe value, significance tests tended to reveal this to be the case; when the probe trial was equal to the sixteenth trial and was thus only somewhat higher on the average than the predicted probe, nonsignificant test values were always found; and when the probe-trial value was rather lower than the predicted probe value, the significance test results tended to attest to this pattern.

The Group-2 results for Cases II, III, and IV were included to simulate control group results. Because slopes of the lines for the subjects in these groups were near zero, it might be expected that not many significant probe-trial effects would be detected. Indeed, for Cases II and III the "above 16th trial" values were significant only 3 of 10 times, and the "below 16th trial" value only 2 of 10; for Case IV there were 5 of 10 and 3 of 10, respectively.

VII. Real Data

A. Experimental Procedures

Three variables from an experiment in which song was played to pairs of breeding White-crowned Sparrows (*Zonotrichia leucophrys nuttallii*) were chosen to illustrate the use of the three analytic techniques with real data. In this experiment, 20 pairs of birds were subjected to playback of song of a territorial male of the same dialect group. During the portion of the experiment that will be considered here birds were presented with 100 2-second songs with a fixed 11-second intersong interval (ISI) on one day. The data were blocked into 10 trial units in the initial series, each trial consisting of 10 songs. Following this initial series the same song was presented 10 times 24 hours later: these 10 songs comprised one additional trial. This can be considered to be an initial habituation series of 10 trials followed by a single probe trial to test for spontaneous recovery. A large number of male and female behaviors were recorded (see Petrinovich & Patterson, 1979, for a complete description of experimental procedures) and three of these variables were chosen for analysis here. The first is number of full songs by the male, the second is number of partial songs by the male, and the third is number of seconds the female was in view during the playback series.

These three variables were chosen for analysis because preliminary examination of the data indicated that the patterns for individual subjects were quite different for each. For full songs there were some birds that

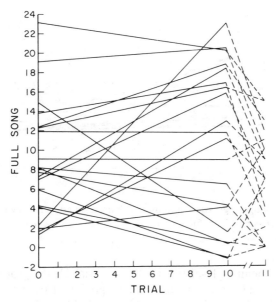

Fig. 6. Full songs: regression of number of full songs on 10 playback trials (———) for each of 20 subjects. The value for Trial 11 (– – –) is the observed number of full songs for each subject.

increased in number of full songs, some decreased, and some remained at a constant level (Fig. 6); the intercept levels were high for most birds. For partial songs about half of birds showed a decrease in the number of songs, and the other half showed no change; the intercept levels were high for about half of the birds and low for the other half (Fig. 7). For the number of seconds the females were in view there were increases, decreases, and no change in level; about half of the birds had high intercept levels, and about half had low levels (Fig. 8). These data were subjected to the same analyses as were the simulation data. In addition, some analyses of the patterns of response level and change for each individual subject were done to probe the texture of the individual differences more thoroughly.

B. Results

Analyses of these probe data were undertaken using the same three analytic approaches used with the simulated data. The ANOVA analysis

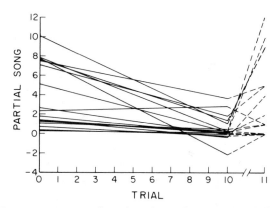

Fig. 7. Partial songs: regression of number of partial songs on 10 playback trials (——) for each of 20 subjects. The value for Trial 11 (– – –) is the observed number of partial songs for each subject.

compared the mean of Trial 10 with that of Trial 11, the group regression analysis compared the mean for Trial 11 predicted from the regression equation to the obtained mean, and the individual regression analysis compared the value predicted for Trial 11 with the obtained value for each subject. The analyses of probe-trial data, therefore, paralleled those for the simulated-data probe trials, with the addition of the *t* test for noninde-pendent means and the Wilcoxon matched-pair, signed-ranks nonpara-

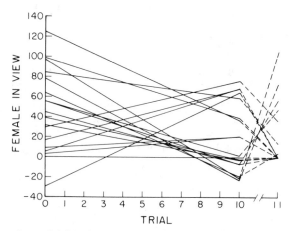

Fig. 8. Time (seconds) female is in view: regression of number of seconds on 10 playback trials (——) for each of 20 subjects. The value for Trial 11 (– – –) is the observed number of seconds for each subject.

TABLE 7

Analyses of Real Data: Male Full Songs

Source	SS	df	MS	F	η^2	R^2
ANOVA						
Group	412	3	137.0	0.34	.060	—
Subject	6420	16	401.2	—	—	—
Trial	248	9	27.6	1.75	.084	—
Trial × group	413	27	15.3	0.97	.140	—
Trial × subject	2280	144	15.8	—	—	—
Group regression						
Group	412	3	137.0	0.34	—	.060
Subject	6420	16	401.2	—	—	—
Trial	65	1	65.0	4.18*	—	.022
Trial × group	132	3	44.0	2.83*	—	.045
Trial × subject	2734	176	15.5	—	—	—
Individual regression						
Group	35	3	11.7	0.30	—	.053
Subject	625	16	39.1	—	—	—
Trial	1	1	1	1.17	—	.060
Trial × group	2	3	0.5	0.52	—	.122
Trial × subject	11	16	0.7	—	—	—

* $p < .05$.

metric test (Siegel, 1956) that are used frequently in the habituation literature.

1. Full Song

The results of the three analyses of full songs are shown in Table 7. [Tables 7, 9, and 10 contain entries for a group effect. These entries are not pertinent to this discussion. Four different groups were formed later in the experiment, and the purpose of analyzing the group effect (all had been treated alike for the data considered here) was to demonstrate that the groups were comparable prior to the experimental manipulations.] The only differences in results are that the trial and trial × group effects reached the .05 level of confidence with the group regression analysis; but these effects were not significant with either ANOVA or individual regression analyses. This occurred because the trial mean square (MS) was much larger with the group regression analysis (65) than it was with ANOVA (27.6), and the MS for error was similar for the two analyses. The differences in F ratios between the group and individual regression

TABLE 8

Individual Differences in Intercept and Slope Constants

		Slope			
	Intercept	+	−	NC[a]	Sum
Full Song	+	1	3	12	16
	0	3	0	1	4
	Sum	4	3	13	20
Male partial song	+	0	7	2	9
	0	0	0	11	11
	Sum	0	7	13	20
Time female is in view	+	0	4	5	9
	0	2	0	9	11
	Sum	2	4	14	20

[a] No change.

analyses for both trial and trial × group effects were the result, primarily, of the large difference in the number of degrees of freedom. These differences are probably not very meaningful, because estimates of effect sizes (R^2) are smaller with the group regression than with the other two methods. This point will be considered in more detail in the discussion. The Pearsonian correlation between values of the intercept constant and slope constant were not significant ($r = -.35$; $df = 18$; $p > .05$).

The advantages of the individual regression analysis are particularly apparent when results for individual subjects are examined more closely. For each subject, z scores for each parameter estimate were calculated; this was done for the intercept by dividing the intercept value by the standard error (SE) of the intercept for that subject, and the same was done for the slope by dividing the slope estimate by the SE of the slope. Each bird was categorized as having an intercept above zero if the z value was at least 1.96. Each bird was then categorized as having shown an increase or decrease in level if the z value for the slope was at least plus or minus 1.96, respectively. It was found that the intercept value was above zero for 16 birds and not above zero for 4. The slope was significantly positive for 4, negative for 3, and did not indicate any significant change for 13 (Table 8).

Because most cases showed no change in behavior as a function of trials, it is not possible to make strong comparative conclusions based only on the seven cases that showed either a significant positive or a nonsignificant slope. But, of the three cases with a negative slope all were

TABLE 9

Analyses of Real Data: Male Partial Songs

Source	SS	df	MS	F	η^2	R^2
ANOVA						
Group	69	3	23	0.43	.074	—
Subject	859	116	54	—	—	—
Trial	235	9	26	3.63***	.160	—
Trial × group	197	27	7	1.01	.134	—
Trial × subject	1041	144	7	—	—	—
Group regression						
Group	69	3	23	0.43	—	.074
Subject	859	16	54	—	—	—
Trial	210	1	210	30.29***	—	.143
Trial × group	37	3	12	1.81	—	.025
Trial × subject	1223	176	7	—	—	—
Individual regression						
Group	38	3	113	0.61	—	.103
Subject	333	16	21	—	—	—
Trial	3	1	3	12.83***	—	.412
Trial × group	0.4	3	0.1	0.76	—	.073
Trial × subject	3	16	0.2	—	—	—

** $p < .01$.
*** $p < .001$.

significantly above zero intercept and three of the four with a positive slope were not significantly above the zero intercept, the other case was significantly above zero.

2. Partial Song

Results of the analyses of partial song are shown in Table 9. All three analyses detected a trial effect. The striking difference in results is that the estimate of effect size was .412 using the individual regression analysis and only .160 and .143 using the other two methods. The Pearsonian correlation between the constant values for intercept and slope was $-.96$ ($df = 18$; $p < .001$).

When the pattern of individual differences is examined after the individual regression analysis there were seven birds that had a significantly negative slope. All seven of these birds had a significant intercept constant as well. Only 2 of the intercept constants were significant for the other 13 birds, and these two both had a negative slope, although the slopes were not statistically significant (Table 8). A χ^2 was calculated from

TABLE 10

Analyses of Real Data: Female Time in View

Source	SS	df	MS	F	η^2	R^2
ANOVA						
Group	1132	313	379	0.06	.011	—
Subject	101232	16	6327	—	—	—
Trial	18419	9	2047	1.45	.075	—
Trial × group	22752	27	843	0.60	.093	—
Trial × subject	204438	144	1413	—	—	—
Group regression						
Group	1137	3	379	0.06	—	—
Subject	101232	16	6327	—	—	—
Trial	5511	1	5511	4.20*	—	.023
Trial × group	7100	3	2367	1.80	—	.029
Trial × subject	231115	176	1313	—	—	—
Individual regression						
Group	2972	3	991	0.45	—	.078
Subject	35336	16	2208	—	—	—
Trial	67	1	67	0.23	—	.081
Trial × group	86	3	29	0.68	—	.104
Trial × subject	676	16	42	—	—	—

* $p < .05$.

the data in Table 8, omitting the empty "+ slope" column. The obtained value was highly significant: $\chi^2(1) = 9.66$, $p < .01$. For this variable there was a strong interaction between intercept level and pattern of change: birds that were not above zero did not have a significant slope across trials, and those above zero had a significantly negative slope.

3. Female in View

Results of the analyses of the number of seconds the female was in view are shown in Table 10. Only one effect was significant (the group-regression trial effect), and the estimates of effect size were all low. The Pearsonian correlation between intercept and slope was $-.86$ ($df = 18$; $p < .001$). The pattern of individual differences indicated that all four birds that had a significant negative slope also had a significant intercept value, and that the other five birds with a significant intercept value all had a nonsignificant slope. The intercept value was not significant for the remaining 11 birds: 2 of them had a significant positive slope, none a significant negative slope, and 9 a nonsignificant slope (Table 8). Again, there appears to be some systematic pattern when the individual differences are examined.

The analyses of these three variables suggest that it is not meaningful to combine the results of the members of a group that have received the same treatment to arrive at a generalization regarding response change. A sizable proportion of birds do not show any responsiveness to the treatment, and combining their data with that of the others can mask effects that are quite significant in terms of underlying habituation and sensitization processes. Combining data for group analyses can be particularly misleading if one is studying such things as dishabituation: if a bird has not shown any habituation, there cannot be any dishabituation. The individual regression approach permits one to detect and study only those birds that meet the behavioral requirements demanded by the theory under consideration.

The negative correlation between intercept and slope is to be expected during the course of later trials, because it is possible for organisms exhibiting higher original levels of response to show greater decreases in behavior as a function of trials. Too, if the level of behavior is to change, organisms that show rather low initial levels of response can change only in the direction of an increase in later trials if they are to change at all, and this will imply sensitization to the presented stimuli. These trends would produce a negative correlation between slope and intercept, and underscore the need to examine the different patterns of responding by the individual subjects in an experiment.

4. Probe Trial

The probe trial as presented here is a test for spontaneous recovery. The logic, however, would be the same for a test of generalization or dishabituation. Five different analyses were performed to determine if the data of Trial 11 represent a significant departure from that expected on the basis of the results of the first 10 trials (Table 11); the 5 analyses were t test for nonindependent means, Wilcoxon signed-ranks test, repeated measures ANOVA, group regression, and individual regression.

The results were similar for all analyses: there was significant decrease in number of full songs on Trial 11 compared to Trial 10, indicating not spontaneous recovery, but spontaneous decrement; there was a significant increase in number of partial songs, indicating spontaneous recovery; there were no significant differences in time the female was in view. For the t and Wilcoxon statistics, the values of the test statistics were higher when the value based on the regression equation was used to establish the Trial-10 value than when the actual scores on Trial 10 were

TABLE 11

Results of Analyses of Probe Trial for Real Data

	Scores from Trials 10 and 11		Prediction from regression equation		ANOVA[a]		Group regression	
	tp	p[b]	tp	p[b]	d	p	t	p
Full song	<.025	<.01	<.005	<.01	−2.86	<.01	−1.70	>.05
Partial song	<.05	<.01	<.005	<.01	3.09	<.01	1.82	<.10
Female in view	>.05	>.05	>.05	>.05	.99	>.05	0.00	>.05

[a] Dunn's test.
[b] Wilcoxon test.

used. This occurred because the predicted value is more reliable when generated using the regression equation. All of the first 10 trials are included, providing a larger and, hence, more stable behavior sample. Similarly, the values of the test statistic were lower using the group regression as compared to the ANOVA. This occurred because the confidence intervals for extrapolated values on the independent variable following the group regression analysis were quite large.

a. Full Song. Again, the advantages of the individual regression analysis are particularly apparent when the individual results are examined more closely. With the individual regression analysis, 13 of the 20 individual tests indicated that the Trial-11 value was lower than predicted. On closer inspection, the reality appeared to be quite systematic. The subjects could be classified into three types on the basis of the slope constant: those whose slope was significantly positive, those whose slope was significantly negative, and those that showed no significant slope. For full songs there were 4 subjects with a significant positive slope, 3 with a significant negative slope, and 13 that showed no significant slope. When these groupings were examined, all 4 of the subjects that had a significant positive slope were found to have Trial-11 values that were lower than the predicted value for Trial 11, and all 3 subjects with a significant negative slope were higher than predicted on Trial 11. Of the 13 subjects who did not show a significant linear change across trials, 4 were above the predicted value for Trial 11 and 9 were below the predicted value. The

TABLE 12

Analysis of Probe-Trial Results as Related to Slope for Real Data, Trial 11

		Slope			
	Observed − predicted	+	−	NS[a]	Sum
Full songs	+	0	3	4	7
	−	4	0	9	13
	Sum	4	3	13	20
Partial songs	+	2	4	6	12
	−	0	2	1	3
	NC[b]	0	1	4	5
	Sum	2	7	11	20
Female in view	+	1	3	4	8
	−	2	0	7	9
	NS[b]	0	0	3	3
	Sum	3	3	14	20

[a] No significant slope.
[b] No change.

relationship between slope and sign of predicted value was highly significant ($\chi^2 = 12.34$; $p < .01$; Table 12, Full songs).

Thus, there is a relationship between the change between Trials 10 and 11 and the initial pattern of responsiveness: those showing a significantly positive slope decreased on Trial 11, those showing a significant negative slope increased, and those showing no significant slope tended to decrease. This interpretation is supported by an r of -0.58 ($p < .01$) between slope and the t ratio between for observed and predicted values. When the t values for the difference between Trials 10 and 11 were compared, it was found that the mean t value for the 4 subjects that had a positive slope (-2.38) was significantly lower than for the 3 with a negative slope slope (0.83), or the 14 that showed no change (1.26), $F(1,17) = 12.34$, $p < .01$.

b. *Partial Song.* The Wilcoxon and ANOVA analyses both indicated there was a significant increase in the partial songs over the expected value ($p < .05$), and the group regression indicated a tendency in the same direction ($p < .10$). However, the individual-level analysis revealed that the apparently consistent increase in behavior emerges from a mixed pattern of differences. For 25% of the subjects, both predicted and observed Trial-11 values were identical (all bearing zero). For the remaining

15 subjects, 12 had a higher than expected value and 3 were lower than expected, but these values were not related to the slope ($r = +0.17$; $p > .05$).

c. *Female in View*. None of the group-level analyses detected any significant differences between Trials 10 and 11. Similarly, no patterns were evident with the individual-level analysis, there being approximately equal numbers showing increases higher than expected values and half lower than expected. These values were only weakly related to the slope ($r = -0.39$; $p < .10$).

VIII. Discussion

The aim of this chapter is to compare and contrast commonly used methods and to propose an alternate statistical method to analyze data from habituation experiments. The commonly used methods, ANOVA and group regression analyses, share the feature that group trends only are considered, with individual differences being relegated to error terms against which group trends are tested. Although ANOVA and group regression methods may accurately reflect and test group trends, these methods may seriously misrepresent data if the group trends are assumed to represent the pattern of responding of any individual subject. That the group trend may be of a totally different form than the trend from any individual subject has been amply documented (e.g., Estes, 1956; Petrinovich, 1981); this assumption is the fallacy to which the ANOVA and group regression methods of analysis are subject.

The method proposed here involves regression analyses of data from individual subjects and allows the modeling of each subject's patterns of responding. From individual regression analyses, one can determine whether subjects show similar patterns of response; if this is the case, a single model of the habituation process, with different parameters for individual subjects, may be plausible. But, if different subsets of subjects evidence different patterns of responding, some subjects perhaps showing increasing levels of response and others showing decreasing levels as a function of trials, a different situation obtains. One must either formulate a more complex model to account for the different patterns of response or develop two or more models, each of which represents the data from subsets of subjects. Although the latter state of affairs may not be most parsimonious it might represent the true state of affairs more accurately. It is possible to represent more accurately data from individual subjects using an idiographic approach: only the individual regression approach would indicate the need to proceed to increased levels of complexity. After obtaining model parameter estimates for each subject, one may still compute tests of significance for group trends that are analogous to those from ANOVA and group regression approaches. Thus, using the individual regression approach to analyze habituation data, one may test the same group hypotheses as with the other approaches, with the added benefit of determining whether the group trends represent the patterns of response exhibited by individual subjects.

A. Simulated Data

1. Sixteen-Trial Analyses

Four sets of simulated data were generated to embody individual and group trends often observed in habituation data. Data were generated according to the general linear model and contained only group, linear trial, and trial × group, along with random error components. Data were generated only with linear components for simplicity, to emphasize the similarities and differences among various methods of analysis, and because representation of nonlinear trends with regression models is a simple generalization from the linear case (Cohen & Cohen, 1975).

When the three methods of analysis were applied to the simulated data, ANOVA and group regression approaches provided similar results. Although ANOVA and group regression methods relegate individual differences to error terms and the variance explained by trial and trial × group terms were similar using the two methods of analysis, the F ratios for trial and trial × group effects were rather different. As already discussed, this difference was the result of the combination of significant linear trends of trial and trial × group effects with a large number of nonsignificant trends when ANOVA was used; linear effects were tested separately when group regression analysis was used.

Group- and individual-regression analyses resulted in very similar F ratios for Cases I and II, the cases for which the simulated data met the assumptions of repeated measures ANOVA. For Cases III and IV, in which the assumptions were not met, results for the group- and individual regression analyses diverged, with the latter method of analysis yielding more valid F ratios. Although tests of group trends after individual regression analyses were performed with an error term based on considerably smaller numbers of degrees of freedom, the tests of effects had great power, because the underlying trends were quite linear. A major advantage of the individual regression approach, in addition to estimation of model parameters for each subject, is that differences between groups in both mean and variance of parameter estimates are obvious, as was true for Cases III and IV. Such differences between groups affect the validity of tests of significance, yet are not apparent from the results of ANOVA or group regression analyses.

2. Probe-Trial Data

The second type of analysis performed on the sets of simulated data involved data from simulated probe trials. The probe-trial analyses computed after the ANOVAs were of satisfactory power—all of the 16 tests in which a difference was expected reached conventional levels of significance. However, the ANOVA approach is, in general, exploratory and not oriented toward testing parameters of a model. As such, probe-trial values were simply compared to those of the last habituation trial, rather than to some value predicted from a model of the preceding responses.

In contrast, both types of regression approaches assume that the general linear model is a model of the temporal course of response change. Because of this, probe-trial values may be compared to an expected probe-trial score predicted for each subject from the parameters of the regression model. Group regression analyses led to probe-trial results of power at least equal to those from ANOVA: all of the 16 comparisons in the above-sixteenth-trial and below-sixteenth-trial conditions were significant. The tests of significance of probe-trial scores after group regression analyses cannot be reduced below the group level. There is, therefore, no possibility of determining the representativeness of group trends for individual subjects.

The individual regression approach resulted in regression-parameter estimates for each subject, and these estimates were used to generate a predicted probe-trial score. Tests of significance of the difference between simulated and predicted probe values showed adequate power because a majority of tests in the above-sixteenth-trial and below-sixteenth-trial conditions revealed differences significant beyond the .05 level.

B. Real Data

Real data were analyzed to investigate the characteristics of the different statistical procedures when there was not only random error but possible significant influences affecting a restricted number of individual subjects that would not be present in the simulated sets of data because of the manner in which the random error term was generated. There were only minor differences among the results of the three general methods used:

the group regression analysis resulted in significant differences in three instances in which the other two methods did not.

These three instances—trial main effect for full song and female in view, and trial × group interaction for full song—may each be attributed to the same cause, the greater power of group regression analysis to identify linear trends in data. The group regression approach is more powerful than the ANOVA with trends that are basically linear, because group regression analysis tests each trend against its associated degrees of freedom, and ANOVA lumps all trends—some perhaps significant and others quite nonsignificant—into overall tests of significance. For example, consider trial main effect on the full song. The significant linear trial effect, tested directly with one degree of freedom in the group regression approach, explains approximately 26% of the variance attributable to trials. When the linear trend is combined with the eight additional, nonsignificant trial trends, as is done in testing the trial main effect with ANOVA, the overall test with nine degrees of freedom is nonsignificant, in spite of the fact that a rather larger proportion of variance is associated with the trial effect from the ANOVA (.022 for group regression and .084 for ANOVA).

In general, these analyses led to the conclusion that there was a significant increment in full song, a significant decrement in partial song, and no changes in the time the females were in view. When the individual regression analyses were examined carefully, however, interesting systematic differences appeared. Although none of the differences found with full song appeared to be of any real significance by group analyses, the individual analysis suggests that there were meaningful patterns embedded in the data: those birds that showed a significant response decrement all had an intercept significantly above zero, and most of those that showed a significant response increment did not have an intercept significantly above zero.

The above pattern of results suggests that there might be three types of birds with different behavioral patterns to the playback of song: one type does not respond initially and becomes more and more active, another type responds initially and drops off, while most (16 of 20) respond initially and continue to respond at the same level. The fact that most subjects respond at a constant level suggests that sensitization effects could be of primary importance as the mechanism regulating the levels of this behavior within any given experimental session (see Chapter 2).

The results for partial song were the same for all general analyses. Overall analysis of individual regression equations indicated that, although the response decrement was significant, only 7 birds had a significant response decrement, none showed a significant increment, and 13 did not change significantly (and only 2 of these showed a positive change). It could be argued that for this behavior, sensitization effects are of minor significance and that they do not override habituation effects.

There seemed to be no meaningful change in the time the female was in view based on the general methods of analysis. But analysis of individual regression equations suggested that there was a relationship between intercept level and change in slope: all birds with a significant response decrement were significantly above zero intercept, and those with a significant response increment were not significantly above zero. Again, there seems to be some relationship between those who show a significant decrement or increment and intercept level.

The importance of considering patterning of the individual differences can be seen also when the probe trials are considered. If one is to speak of spontaneous recovery or of dishabituation, then subjects should have met some behavioral criterion for habituation. Consider full song, for example: although all methods but the group regression indicated that there was a significant increase in response level on Trial 11, 4 of 20 subjects had a decrease on Trial 11, and these 4 were the only ones that had a significantly positive slope across the first 10 trials. The processes regulating the behavior of these four could be quite different from those regulating the behavior of the others. A systematic examination of the background variables for these four subjects could well be of considerable heuristic interest and lead to a further understanding of the underlying processes regulating behavior in situations similar to that used here.

IX. Recommendations

A. Group-Level Analysis

A consideration of the results based on the simulated and the real data led us to two conclusions. First, it has been amply demonstrated that the general linear model is a satisfactory model of most behavioral processes (Petrinovich, 1981; Wiggins, 1973). As mentioned earlier, nonlinear trends can be represented by a simple generalization from the linear model (Cohen & Cohen, 1975). Therefore, the use of the general linear model seems entirely appropriate in most instances.

When one's results meet the assumptions underlying the repeated measures ANOVA—notably, that the within group variances are equal across trials—all three methods of analysis (ANOVA, group regression, and individual regression) provide roughly equivalent tests of significance. The tests of significance from the individual regression approach are associated with fewer degrees of freedom, which may limit the power of the tests. But it should be noted that these latter tests are more appropriate than those from the ANOVA and group regression approaches, because each consists of a test of a given trend using individual differences in only that trend as an error term. Furthermore, because the individual regression approach identifies a great deal more of the total variance, the associated tests of significance have greater explanatory, in addition to statistical, power.

On the other hand, when one's data fail to meet the assumptions of the repeated measures ANOVA, as with Cases III and IV of simulated data, the individual regression analysis yields the more valid F ratios, as well as providing more explicit information pertaining to the possible invalidity of the tests of significance. Therefore, it appears that the individual regression model should be preferred when approaching real data for which the underlying parameters are not known and for which it not clear that one can meet the assumptions of the ANOVA.

B. Individual-Level Analysis

The individual regression analysis provides estimates of model parameters for each subject. This analysis permits one to move from the testing of a general model to an examination of individual differences. This examination is protected from the dangers of subjective qualitative analysis by an establishment of confidence levels for each parameter estimate for each subject.

The ability to examine the pattern of individual regressions in this way can be of paramount importance when attempting to understand the processes regulating behavior change. If one is interested in the process of dishabituation, for example, the subjects must have demonstrated a significant response decrement as a function of trials. It is possible to perform group analyses of all subjects treated alike, and find that group effects are large enough to swamp effects of the subjects that *did* habituate. We suggest that it is more valuable to identify different types of subjects and to study the effects of various experimental treatments on only those subjects who meet the behavioral requirement for the theoretical issues at hand. In addition, classifying individuals into response types should make it possible to identify systematic effects that abridge any general nomothetic laws that exist, or help cast a family of idiographic laws (see Section IX).

C. Probe Trials

The analysis of the simulated probe-trial data indicated that ANOVA-based results have adequate power. But it is possible to question the appropriateness of the model of reality involved in the use of ANOVA: the model does not take advantage of the preceding pattern of data, but utilizes only the last segment of the data to establish predicted response levels. The regression approaches are based on a temporal model. The individual regression approach had adequate, though rather lower, power than did the group regression with the simulated data. But, if there are different laws regulating the behavior of different subgroups of subjects, the individual regression approach will permit one to move beyond the mere statement of a p value that characterizes the assemblage of subjects to a representation of the separate laws regulating the behavior of the different subjects.

X. Approaches to Theory Construction

Egon Brunswik (1952) contrasted the nature of and methods involved in the nomothetic and idiographic ideal in scientific theory construction. The nomothetic ideal concentrates on the discovery of general laws that hold for groups of individuals. Individual differences are treated as part of the error variance when considering the effect of experimental treatments. The idiographic ideal is concerned with understanding behavior at the level of the individual case, and individual differences provide the basic data base. Brunswik suggested that we might best strive for an idiono-mothetic model—to understand the laws that govern the individual case—and argued that the optimum method would be idiographic–statistical. All statistical tests should be applied to each subject's behavior. The closest realization of this approach has been attained by Hammond (see Hammond & Wascoe, 1980) in his theory of social judgment. Those interested in pursuing idiographic–statistical procedures in more depth should consult Hammond's extensive writings.

The model developed in this chapter supports the research ideals suggested by Brunswik and Hammond and, through the embedded heuristic power of the model, permits the development of theoretical principles from obtained data rather than imposing them on the data at the outset.

Several philosophers of science have expressed concerns regarding the appropriateness of the standard methodological principles enshrined by many scientists. These concerns have led to the development of what Lakatos (1970) called a "sophisticated methodological falsificationism [p. 122]" that demands "that one should try to look at things from different points of view, to put forward new theories which anticipate novel facts, and to reject theories which have been superseded by more powerful ones [p. 53]."

The emphasis in this chapter has been to illustrate the advantages of such methodologies and to argue their appropriateness to the study of habituation. This methodological approach enhances the conceptual richness of our scientific conceptions: it focuses concern on the context of discovery rather than on the operations of justification. The major problem in the development of behavioral theory has not been with the controlled experimental testing of alternate theories: psychologists excel at the design and analysis of complex experiments. The problem has been in the discovery of the variables that should be included in our attempts to understand behavior.

We should adopt a set of rules that do not inhibit the development of alternative hypotheses against which facts can be evaluated. Brunswik's (1952, 1956) ideas of representative design and probabilistic functionalism provide the basic conceptual framework, and the use of the methods outlined here and in Petrinovich (1979, 1981) equip us with a set of methodological rules adequate to the context of discovery. If the outcomes of such research programs are cross-validated on independent samples and if critical variables are employed using representative designs, then one might move more quickly toward a theoretically productive science. This science will be theoretically progressive "if each new theory has some excess empirical content over its predecessor, that is, if it predicts some novel, hitherto unexpected fact [Lakatos, 1970, p. 118]."

Such a progressive science will place its emphasis on effect size rather than on significance tests, on theoretically predicted function forms rather than on rejecting the null hypothesis (see Meehl, 1978). In short, the preferable theory is one

> which tells us more; that is to say, the theory which contains the greater amount of empirical information or content; which is logically stronger; which has the greater explanatory and predictive power; and which can therefore be more severely tested by comparing predicted facts with observations. In short, we prefer an interesting, daring, and highly informative theory to a trivial one [Popper, 1963, p. 217].

References

Brunswik, E. The conceptual framework of psychology. In *International encyclopedia of unified science* (Vol. 1). Chicago: University of Chicago Press, 1952.

Brunswik, E. *Perception and the representative design of psychological experiments.* Berkeley: University of California Press, 1956.

Cohen, J. & Cohen, P. *Applied multiple regression/correlation analysis for the behavioral sciences.* Hillsdale, N.J.: Lawrence Erlbaum Associates, 1975.

Estes, W. K. The problem of inference from curves based on group data. *Psychological Bulletin,* 1956, *53,* 134–140.

Hale, G. A. On use of ANOVA in developmental research. *Child Development,* 1977, *48,* 1101–1106.

Hammond, K. R. Introduction to Brunswikian theory and methods. In K. R. Hammond & N. E. Wascoe (Eds.), *Realizations of Brunswik's representative design* (No. 3). 1980.

Hammond, K. R., & Wascoe, N. E. (Eds.). *Realizations of Brunswik's representative design* (No. 3). San Francisco: Jossey-Bass, 1980.

Hinde, R. A. Factors governing the changes in strength of a partially inborn response, as shown by the mobbing behaviour of the Chaffinch (*Fringilla coelebs*). I. The nature of the response and an examination of its course. *Proceedings of the Royal Society of London, Series B,* 1954(a), *142,* 306–331.

Hinde, R. A. Factors governing the changes in strength of a partially inborn response, as shown by the mobbing behaviour of the Chaffinch (*Fringilla coelebs*). II. The waning of the response. *Proceedings of the Royal Society of London, Series B,* 1954(b), *142,* 331–358.

Hinde, R. A. Factors governing the changes in strength of a partially inborn response, as shown by the mobbing behaviour of the Chaffinch (*Fringilla coelebs*). III. The interaction of short-term and long-term incremental and decremental effects. *Proceedings of the Royal Society of London, Series B,* 1961, *153,* 398–420.

Huynh, H., & Mandeville, G. K. Validity conditions in repeated measures designs. *Psychological Bulletin,* 1979, *86,* 964–973.

Kirk, R. E. *Experimental design: Procedures for the behavioral sciences.* Belmont, Calif.: Brooks-Cole, 1968.

Lakatos, I. Falsification and the methodology of scientific research programmes. In I. Lakatos & A. Musgrave (Eds.), *Criticism and the growth of knowledge.* London & New York: Cambridge University Press, 1970.

Meehl, P. E. Theoretical risks and tabular astrisks: Sir Karl, Sir Ronald, and the slow progress of soft psychology. *Journal of Consulting and Clinical Psychology,* 1978, *46,* 806–834.

Megela, A. L., & Teyler, T. J. Habituation and the human evoked potential. *Journal of Comparative and Physological Psychology,* 1979, *93,* 1154–1170.

Patterson, T. L., & Petrinovich, L. Field studies of habituation. II. Effect of massed presentation. *Journal of Comparative and Physiological Psychology,* 1979, *93,* 351–359.

Peeke, H. V. S., & Peeke, S. Parental factors in the sensitisation and habituation of territorial aggression in the convict cichlid (*Cichlasoma nigrofasciatum*). *Journal of Comparative and Physiological Psychology,* 1982, in press.

Peeke, H. V. S., Wyers, E. J., & Herz, M. J. Waning of the aggressive response to male models in the three-spined stickleback (*Gasterosteus aculeatus* L.). *Animal Behaviour,* 1969, *17,* 224–228.

Petrinovich, L. Probabilistic functionalism: A conception of research method. *American Psychologist,* 1979, *34,* 373–390.

Petrinovich, L. A method for the study of development. In K. Immelmann, G. Barlow, L. Petrinovich, & M. Main (Eds.), *Behavioral development*. London & New York: Cambridge University Press, 1981. Pp. 90–136.

Petrinovich, L. Field studies of habituation. VI. Dishabituation. *Journal of Comparative and Physiological Psychology*, in press.

Petrinovich, L., & Hardyck, C. Error rates for multiple comparison methods: Some evidence concerning the frequency of erroneous conclusions. *Psychological Bulletin*, 1969, *71*, 43–54.

Petrinovich, L., & Patterson, T. L. Field studies of habituation. I. Effect of reproductive condition, number of trials, and different delay intervals on responses of the White-crowned Sparrow. *Journal of Comparative and Physiological Psychology*, 1979, *93*, 337–350.

Popper, K. R. *Conjectures and refutations: The growth of scientific knowledge*. New York: Harper & Row, 1963.

Siegel, S. *Nonparametric statistics for the behavioral sciences*. New York: McGraw-Hill, 1956.

Thompson, R. F., Groves, P. M., Teyler, T. J., & Roemer, R. H. A dual-process theory of habituation: Theory and behavior. In H. V. S. Peeke & M. J. Herz (Eds.), *Habituation* (Vol. 1). New York: Academic Press, 1973.

Wiggins, J. S. *Personality and prediction: Principles of personality assessment*. Reading, Mass.: Addison-Wessley, 1973.

Winer, B. J. *Statistical principles in experimental design* (2nd ed.). New York: McGraw-Hill, 1971.

Wonnacott, T. H., & Wonnacott, R.-J. *Regression: A second course in statistics*. New York: Wiley, 1981.

PART II

Basic Processes

This second section contains four chapters ranging from the basic neurobiological, model-system approach to investigations of the role habituation may play in changes in human evoked responses. All of these chapters focus on physiological mechanisms, sometimes in tissue preparations, but all focus on explanations of the phenomena of sensitization and habituation as they occur in intact organisms. Hence, the chapters are not only appropriate to, but critical for, our understanding of habituation, sensitization, and behavior.

Chapter 6 by Thomas Carew is an elegant description of the research at Columbia on the neurobiological basis of learning in invertebrates. The research with *Aplysia* described in this chapter includes analyses of sensitization and habituation at the synaptic, biophysical, and neurochemical levels. The extension of the work with *Aplysia* to the study of the basis for associative as well as nonassociative learning processes promises to provide understanding of the possible similarities and the differences between the two classes of learning.

In Chapter 7, Teyler, Chiaia, DiScenna, and Roemer present data on habituation of evoked electrical activity in tissue samples taken from discrete mammalian brain areas. They find that some, but not all, areas have the intrinsic ability to show habituation or sensitization to repeated stimulation. The dentate gyrus of the hippocampus is alone among the areas studied that displays all of the traditional criteria of habituation. The experiments reviewed in this chapter represent a novel approach to understanding the function of discrete areas of the brain in the vastly more complicated mammalian brain and contrasts the approaches in the preceding chapter.

Chapter 8 by Michael Davis and Sandra File demonstrates another approach to understanding the neural mechanisms underlying habituation and senitization: the use of pharmacological interventions. They argue persuasively that pharmacological methods enjoy some distinct advantages over traditional lesion and ablation methods. They illustrate their approach through a discussion of research using two neurotransmitters, serotonin and norepinephrine, on the modulation of the startle response. As a third approach to understanding the mechanisms involved in facilitation and inhibition of response, it compliments the preceding two chapters.

Chapter 9 asks, in its title, Do human evoked potentials habituate? Roemer, Shagass, and Tyler conclude that it is not clear that an unequivocal positive answer can be given. They state that almost all of the existing literature can be interpreted in terms of neural refractory processes and that this interpolation is more compelling than one in terms of habituation. They point out, however, that there are several studies that seem to fulfill most of the traditional criteria of habituation. The final caution offered by the authors is that convincing demonstrations of dishabituation and sensitization must be presented before discarding the possibility that observed decremental processes are the result of recovery cycle phenomena.

CHAPTER 6

An Introduction to Cellular Approaches Used in the Analysis of Habituation and Sensitization in *Aplysia*

Thomas J. Carew

Department of Psychology
Yale University
New Haven, Connecticut

I. Introduction

In recent years significant progress has been made in the analysis of the neural mechanisms of behavior by a combination of traditional ethological and psychological approaches with new approaches from cellular biology, including modern neurophysiological, morphological, and biochemical techniques. In addition to new technical approaches to the neurobiology of behavior, a number of simplified preparations have been developed that have also proven advantageous. For example, because of their relatively simple nervous systems, several higher invertebrate animals—such as the leech, various arthropods, and several opisthobranch molluscs—have proven to be quite useful for relating nerve cells to behavior (Kupfer-

The author's contribution to the work reported in this chapter was supported by a fellowship from the National Institute of Mental Health (5KO2MH0081).

HABITUATION, SENSITIZATION,
AND BEHAVIOR

mann, Carew, & Kandel, 1974; Kupfermann & Kandel, 1969; Nicholls & Purves, 1970; Willows, 1968; Zucker, 1972). Among the invertebrates, the marine mollusc *Aplysia* has been one of the most extensively analyzed. Most of the behaviors of *Aplysia* have been studied at least to some degree on a cellular level (for review, see Kandel, 1976, 1979), and several of these behaviors have been shown capable of different forms of learning, which range in complexity from nonassociative to associative and in time course from short term to long term. In addition, a number of different electrophysiological and biochemical techniques have been brought to bear on the analysis of learning and memory in *Aplysia*. Thus this preparation, in addition to providing an excellent system for examining the cellular basis of behavior, is also useful as a system to illustrate the rationale and application of a number of cell-biological approaches to the study of behavior and learning.

This chapter therefore has two aims. One is to provide a review of recent studies of habituation and sensitization in *Aplysia*. These studies have utilized combined behavioral, neurophysiological, and biochemical approaches in the analysis of these two simple forms of nonassociative learning. The second goal of this chapter is to provide readers who might lack familiarity with some of the current methodology in neurobiology with a simple introduction to the rationale of these approaches as they have been applied to the study of learning and memory in *Aplysia*. The level of this introduction is intentionally nontechnical and intuitive. Several excellent sources can provide the interested reader with a more detailed and comprehensive treatment of these cellular biological approaches (Castellucci & Kandel, 1976a; Cooper, Bloom, & Roth, 1970; Greengard, 1978; Kandel, 1976; Kandel & Schwartz, 1981; Katz, 1966; Kuffler & Nicholls, 1976; Stevens, 1966).

My overall approach in this chapter is reductionistic. Thus I first describe some of the behavioral approaches used in studying habituation and sensitization in *Aplysia*, both in their short-term and in their long-term form. Next, I discuss some of the cellular approaches, focusing on three progressively more fundamental levels of analysis. The first level is a synaptic analysis, beginning at the level of complex synaptic potentials and then moving to a more fundamental level of monosynaptic potentials, which permits a quantal analysis of synaptic transmission at the synapses that mediate habituation and sensitization. The second level is a biophysical analysis of the ionic currents modulated during habituation and sensitization, and the third level is a biochemical analysis aimed at specifying the molecular events underlying habituation and sensitization. In the final section, I return to a behavioral level and briefly describe recent studies of associative learning in *Aplysia*, which may permit an investigation of the relationship between simple forms of nonassociative and associative learning at several levels of analysis.

II. Behavioral Approaches

In this part of the chapter I briefly review past behavioral studies of habituation and sensitization in *Aplysia* as a background for the neurophysiological and biochemical approaches which I discuss in later sections. More detailed reviews of these behavioral studies have been published previously (Carew & Kandel, 1974; Castellucci & Kandel, 1976a; Kandel, 1976).

A. Short-Term Habituation and Sensitization

Aplysia, like other opisthobranch molluscs, has a mantle cavity on its dorsal surface that houses a delicate respiratory organ, the gill. The gill lies under a protective sheet of skin, the mantle shelf, which terminates at the rear of the cavity in a fleshy, funnel-shaped spout, the siphon (Fig. 1a). A light tactile stimulus to the siphon elicits a brisk defensive withdrawal reflex of all the mantle organs: the gill, siphon, and mantle shelf (Fig. 1b). If the same stimulus is delivered repeatedly, however, the reflex readily habituates (Fig. 1c; see also Pinsker, Kupfermann, Castellucci, & Kandel, 1970). The amplitude of the reflex response can be restored in two ways: (1) by simply withholding the stimulus, allowing recovery to occur and (2) by delivering a strong sensitizing stimulus to another site on the body, such as the head region or the tail, which produces dishabituation (Pinsker *et al.,* 1970; see also Fig. 1d). Dishabituation of the gill-withdrawal reflex in *Aplysia* is a special case of a more general facilitatory process, sensitization. This was shown by Carew, Castellucci, and Kandel (1971) who found that habituation of the gill-withdrawal reflex by stimulating one pathway, the siphon, did not generalize to another non-stimulated pathway, the purple gland. Thus, they could examine the effects of a sensitizing stimulus both on habituated and nonhabituated responses in the same animal. They found that the same strong or novel stimulus that produced facilitation in the previously habituated pathway (dishabituation) also produced facilitation in the nonhabituated pathway (sensitization). Thus, dishabituation in *Aplysia* is not caused by the removal of habituation but rather is the result of a second superimposed facilitatory process, sensitization. The idea that habituation and dishabituation are independent processes was first suggested by Sharpless and Jasper (1956)

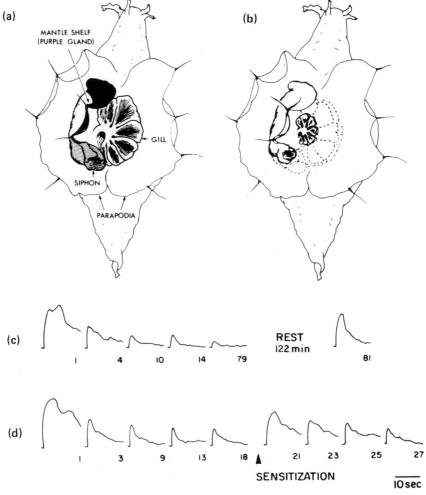

Fig. 1. (a, b) Defensive withdrawal reflex of *Aplysia* (dorsal view of an intact animal). (a) Parapodia retracted to reveal the mantle organs (gill, siphon, and mantle shelf) in their relaxed position. The shaded areas are the primary receptive fields for the reflex. (b) Comparison of the position of the mantle organs at rest (dashed lines) and at the peak of withdrawal. Note that both the siphon and the gill withdraw in response to siphon stimulation. From Kupfermann & Kandel (1969). Copyright 1969 American Association for the Advancement of Science. (c and d) Photocell records of gill withdrawal from two habituation sessions in a single animal. (c) Decrement of the response with repeated stimulation (stimulus number indicated beneath each trace) and almost full recovery after 122 minutes rest (ISI = 3 minutes; total = 80 stimuli). (d) Rehabituation of the same response. A strong sensitizing stimulus (arrow) to the neck produces dishabituation (sensitization) of the response (ISI = 1 minute; total = 20 stimuli). From Pinsker Kupfermann, Castellucci, & Kandel (1970). Copyright 1970 American Association for the Advancement of Science.

and subsequently was shown to be the case by Spencer, Thompson, and Neilson in the flexion reflex of the cat (1966). Habituation and sensitization produced in a single training session are relatively short lived in *Aplysia,* lasting at most several hours. But, one characteristic feature of learning in higher animals is that it is often long lasting. Thus, it was of interest to see whether habituation and sensitization in *Aplysia* might also be prolonged.

B. Long-Term Habituation and Sensitization

1. Long-Term Habituation

To examine whether habituation of the defensive withdrawal reflex in *Aplysia* could be produced in a long-term form, Carew, Pinsker, and Kandel (1972) studied the effects of repeating habituation training sessions across several days. In these studies the siphon-withdrawal component of the reflex was used because, unlike the gill-withdrawal component, it can be measured in the completely unrestrained, freely moving animal, permitting studies that can last several weeks. A single habituation training session consisting of ten trials (with an intertrial interval of 30 seconds) produced typical response decrement. Repeating these training sessions at one per day for 4 days, however, produced a progressive build up of habituation within each session (Fig. 2a). Retention of habituation was tested 1 day, 1 week, and 3 weeks after training. Control groups that had received no repeated habituation training were tested at the same time as experimental groups, and in all tests experimental and control animals were randomly mixed to ensure a blind testing procedure. Both experimental and control groups showed within-session habituation on each test day. Experimental animals, however, showed significantly greater habituation than controls 1 day, 1 week, and 3 weeks after training. Moreover, an intragroup analysis showed that the experimental group exhibited significantly less habituation in the 3-week test compared to their own scores in the 1-day test, but they still exhibited significantly more habituation than they did on the first day of training. Thus, although there was clear recovery, there was still significant retention of habituation 3 weeks after training.

The preceding experiments were carried out on the siphon-withdrawal component of the defensive withdrawal reflex. In a second series of experiments Carew *et al.* (1972) showed that the gill-withdrawal component also shows long-term habituation (Fig. 2c,d). This was established by first giving animals siphon habituation training as already described, and then measuring gill withdrawal (in response to siphon stimulation) in restrained

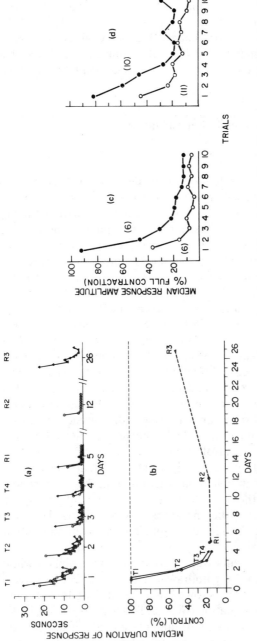

Fig. 2. Long-term habituation of siphon and gill withdrawal. (a, b) Siphon withdrawal. (a) Buildup of habituation during 4 days of training (T_1–T_4) and retention at 1 day (R_1), 1 week (R_2), and 3 weeks (R_3) after training [●, Experiment 1 ($n = 19$); ▲, Experiment 2 ($n = 14$)]. (b) Time course of habituation. Habituation within each session is expressed as a single score, the sum of 10 trials. Retention at 1 day (R_1), 1 week (R_2), and 3 weeks (R_3) is compared to control [Day 1) habituation (upper dashed line]. (c and d) Gill withdrawal: comparison of experimental (○) and control (●) habituation of gill withdrawal at 1 day (c) and 1 week (d) after long-term siphon habituation training (see text). The number of animals contributing to each curve is indicated in parentheses. From Carew, Pinsker, & Kandel (1972). Copyright 1972 American Association for the Advancement of Science.

animals 1 day and 1 week after training. Experimental animals exhibited significantly greater habituation of gill withdrawal than untrained controls 1 day and 1 week after training, showing that siphon training produces long-term habituation not only of the siphon-withdrawal component but also of the gill-withdrawal component of the reflex.

A final interesting finding that emerged from these studies was that, as often occurs in higher forms of vertebrate learning (Kientzle, 1946; Kimble & Shatel, 1952), distributed training was more effective in producing long-term habituation than was massed training. Two experimental groups were given either spaced training (4 days of training, 10 trials per day) or massed training (40 trials in a single day). Both groups, as well as an untrained control group, were tested 1 day and 1 week after training. The spaced-training group showed significantly greater habituation than the massed-training group in both retention tests. Thus, habituation training sessions distributed over days (or even over hours, as we will discuss later) is much more effective than is massed training in producing long-term habituation.

2. Long-Term Sensitization

Habituation can be considered as one of the most elementary forms of learning, because it is not usually thought to have an associative component (see, however, Kimmel, 1973) and involves activity in a single neural pathway. The results already discussed show that this rudimentary type of learning can exist in a relatively long-term form in *Aplysia*. *Aplysia* also exhibits another simple form of learning, sensitization (Carew *et al.*, 1971; Pinsker *et al.*, 1970), which is somewhat more complex than habituation because it involves the facilitation, by activity in one pathway, of a response produced by stimulation of another pathway. It thus was of interest to see whether sensitization of the gill-withdrawal reflex might also be produced in a long-term form in *Aplysia*. To examine this issue Pinsker, Hening, Carew, and Kandel (1973) gave a group of experimental animals 4 days of sensitization training (an electric shock was delivered to the neck of each animal four times per day), and a control group received no shock. Retention of sensitization of the siphon withdrawal component of the reflex was measured 1 day, 1 week, and 3 weeks after training. Experimental animals exhibited significantly greater siphon withdrawal than controls in both 1-day and 1-week tests. There was no significant difference between experimental and control groups in the 3-week test, but an intragroup analysis comparing the sensitization group to its own pretraining scores revealed significant sensitization in the 3-week test. Thus, although the effects of sensitization training are clearly diminished, animals can still exhibit a significant change in reflex responsiveness 3 weeks after sensitization training.

In summary, the defensive-withdrawal reflex shows habituation and sensitization, and in each case these simple forms of learning can exist in a short-term form, lasting hours, and a long-term form, lasting several weeks. Since the life span of *Aplysia* is thought to be only 1 year (Kriegstein, Castellucci, & Kandel, 1974; MacGinitie & MacGinitie, 1968), the duration of long-term memory for habituation and sensitization constitutes a significant fraction of the animal's total lifetime. This fact alone suggests that these simple behavioral modifications are likely to have important adaptive significance. But what specific adaptive value might these long-term changes have for *Aplysia*? Some clues can be gotten by taking a closer look at long-term habituation, which has been studied more extensively than long-term sensitization.

The conversion from short- to long-term habituation seems to depend on two factors: (1) repeated occurrence of training sessions and (2) distributed training sessions. These two elements seem to be provided by the natural environment of *Aplysia*. Carew and Kupfermann (1974), found that *Aplysia* in its natural habitat is exposed to a variety of tactile environments ranging from calm, protected bays to turbulent channels and tide pools. Animals that live in the calm environments show brisk withdrawal reflexes that habituate with a time course comparable to previous laboratory studies. But animals in turbulent environments show significantly reduced reflexes that habituate significantly faster than the calm-water animals (Fig. 3). There are two parallels between the tactile experiences of turbulent-environment animals in the natural environment and the long-term habituated animals in our controlled laboratory studies. First, both groups of animals received repeated trials: in turbulent environments, *Aplysia* are exposed to hours of recurrent strong surges of seawater and tactile contact both with seaweeds and other marine animals. Second, both groups received a form of distributed training: in the natural environment, animals are exposed to tidal changes which can radically alter their stimulus environment for several hours per day, in some cases leaving them completely out of the water for several hours (Kupfermann & Carew, 1974). Thus turbulent-environment animals are exposed to periods of repeated stimulation separated by periods of relative calm, which has proven to be an effective stimulus pattern for producing long-term habituation in the laboratory. In our laboratory studies it was initially surprising that so few mild tactile stimuli (10 per day for 4 days) could produce such long-lasting behavioral effects. In light of the field studies, however, it is possible that the propensity for *Aplysia* to show long-term habituation may reflect an adaptation to an environment where repeated

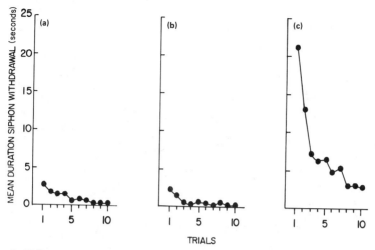

Fig. 3. Habituation in different natural environments. Habituation of siphon withdrawal was compared for animals living in (a) a turbulent environment [Scripps Institution of Oceanography (La Jolla, California) and Solana Beach (California)] in which they were exposed to air (*n* = 13); (b) a turbulent environment [Mission Bay Channel (San Diego, California)] in which they were never exposed to air (*n* = 10); and (c) a calm environment (Three Sisters, Mexico) in which they were never exposed to air (*n* = 11). From Carew & Kupfermann (1974).

and distributed exposure to innocuous tactile stimuli is an everyday occurrence.

III. Cellular Approaches

One of the primary advantages of a simple systems approach is that it permits a multilevel analysis of questions of behavioral relevance. Moreover, as one applies progressively more reductionistic analyses to these issues, answers obtained at one level give rise to a family of new questions at the next level. This process can be nicely illustrated in the analysis of habituation and sensitization of the defensive withdrawal reflex in *Aplysia*. A major advantage of the withdrawal reflex of *Aplysia* for a neural analysis of behavior is that it can be examined in a number of different simplified preparations that offer distinct technical advantages for cellular studies. For example, one can record intracellularly from identified neurons in the central nervous system of relatively intact animals to establish the role of those neurons in the reflex (Fig. 4a). The preparation can be further simplified to an isolated reflex system by surgi-

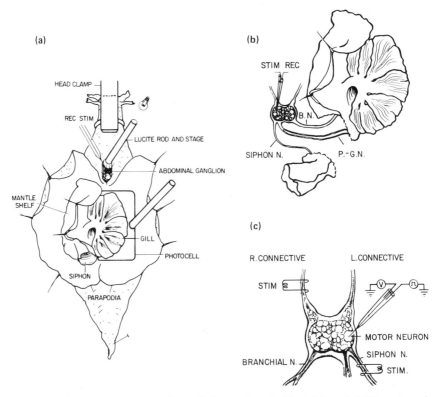

Fig. 4. Three preparations used in cellular studies of gill withdrawal. (a) Top view of the semiintact preparation. The abdominal ganglion was externalized through a small slit made in the skin above the ganglion. The Lucite rod and stage acted as a light guide, so that a strong light directed at the top of the rod transilluminated the ganglion, permitting intracellular recording from identified neurons. From Kupfermann, Castellucci, Pinsker, & Kandel (1970). (b) Diagram of the isolated reflex test system: the gill, siphon, and mantle shelf are left attached to the ganglion by their respective peripheral nerves. (c) Further simplified test system: the isolated abdominal ganglion. The siphon or branchial nerves are stimulated electrically, and the responses of one of the motor neurons (L7, usually) is recorded intracellularly. From Castellucci, Pinsker, Kupfermann, & Kandel (1970). Copyright 1970 American Association for the Advancement of Science.

cally removing the mantle organs, keeping them fully operational by leaving them attached to the central nervous system (the abdominal ganglion) by their peripheral nerves (Fig. 4b).

Finally, because unique neurons known to contribute to the reflex can be identified in the central nervous system, detailed electrophysiological, biophysical, and biochemical studies can be carried out in the completely

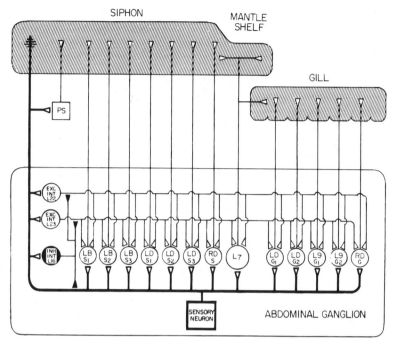

Fig. 5. Schematic diagram of neural circuit controlling the defensive withdrawal reflex. ▲, Inhibition; △, excitation. Sensory input from the siphon is mediated directly to
motor neurons (sensory neuron represents a class of sensory cells) and indirectly by
interneurons. Both motor neurons and interneurons are identified cells. From Kupfermann, Carew, & Kandel (1974); Kupfermann & Kandel (1969). PS, Represents a group of
perpiheral siphon motor neurons (Bailey, Castellucci, Koester, & Kandel, 1979.)

isolated abdominal ganglion (Fig. 4c). Using these different preparations
it was found that the defensive withdrawal reflex of *Aplysia* is quite simple, being controlled by a relatively small number of nerve cells. The basic
neural circuit consists of identified primary mechano–afferent neurons
that synapse directly onto gill and siphon motor neurons, as well as onto
interneurons, some of which have been identified. Each component of
this circuit has been studied in considerable detail [Bailey, Castellucci,
Koester, & Kandel (1979); Byrne, Castellucci, & Kandel (1978); Carew,
Pinsker, Rubinson, & Kandel (1974); Castellucci, Pinsker, Kupfermann,
& Kandel (1970); Hawkins, (1981a); Kupfermann *et al.*, (1974); for review,
see Kandel, (1976)], which has yielded the neural circuit for the reflex
shown in Fig. 5.

Having the behavioral observations just described on the one hand, and the neural circuit for the behavior on the other, a number of questions could now be analyzed at progressively more fundamental levels. First, where in the neural circuit do the critical changes that produce habituation and sensitization occur, and what class of mechanisms do they involve? The answer to these questions came from a *synaptic analysis* showing that a critical site was the synaptic connections made by the sensory cells onto their follower cells, the interneurons and motor neurons, and that the mechanism involved a depression of transmitter release from these synapses during habituation and a facilitation of transmitter release during sensitization. These findings raised questions at the next level of analysis: What are the cellular mechanisms underlying the depression and facilitation of transmitter release? A special form of synaptic analysis, a *quantal analysis,* provided the answer to this question. Synaptic depression and facilitation are produced by a presynaptic mechanism: a reduction or increase, respectively, in the number of transmitter quanta released from the sensory neuron terminals when an action potential invades them.

The next level of analysis involved investigating why fewer or more transmitter quanta are released during habituation and sensitization. Answers to these questions came from a *biophysical analysis* of the ionic currents that flow in the sensory neuron as a result of the action potential. These studies suggest that synaptic depression and facilitation are produced by modulation of the calcium current during the action potential in the sensory neuron: reduction of this calcium current produces less release of transmitter, and enhancement of this current produces greater release of transmitter. These observations in turn gave rise to another family of questions concerning the molecular events responsible for the modulation of transmitter release in the sensory neurons. Answers to some of these questions have come from a *biochemical analysis* of habituation and sensitization. These studies have thus far primarily focused on sensitization and indicate that the presynaptic facilitation underlying sensitization is caused by serotonin- (or a closely related amine) mediated increase in a "second messenger," cyclic AMP (adenosine $3',5'$-monophosphate) in the sensory neurons. Through a series of biochemical steps, this increase in intracellular cyclic AMP gives rise to greater transmitter release from the sensory neuron terminals.

This brief overview illustrates that progress in understanding simple instances of learning and memory can be made by combining a variety of cellular-biological approaches. In this part of the chapter I discuss each type of analysis, emphasizing first its basic rationale, and second, its application to the study of habituation and sensitization in *Aplysia*.

A. Synaptic Analysis

1. Short-Term Habituation and Sensitization

Two types of synaptic connections occur between nerve cells: electrical and chemical. Electrical synapses are capable of some forms of short-lasting plasticity [see, for example, Carew & Kandel (1976); Kater (1974); Spira & Bennett (1972)], but chemical synapses are by far the more modifiable [for review, see Eccles (1964); Kandel & Spencer, (1968)]. Although the capability for plasticity at chemical synapses has long been known, it is only recently that synaptic plasticity has been linked to behavioral plasticity. To accomplish this requires preparations in which synaptic activity related to the behavioral change can be measured with intracellular electrodes at the same time that the behavioral plasticity is being exhibited. The basic rationale for such an approach is that, by systematically monitoring different cellular elements and the synaptic interactions between them in a neural circuit for a behavior, while the behavior is being modified, one can home in on sites in the circuit where critical changes occur and exclude a number of possible mechanisms that might account for the behavioral plasticity. For example, two possible mechanisms for the behavioral decrement seen during habituation are sensory adaptation and motor fatigue. On a behavioral level these must be ruled out for the behavioral change to be considered an instance of habituation [see, for example, Thompson & Spencer (1966)]. These possibilities can be ruled out on a cellular level by (1) monitoring with intracellular electrodes the activity of the sensory neurons, showing that it does not decrement during repeated stimulation of the skin (Fig. 6a,b) and (2) repeatedly driving the motor neurons (by injection of depolarizing intracellular current pulses) at rates that would produce habituation if repeated tactile stimulation were delivered, and showing that the motor response also does not decrement (Fig. 6c,d). Because the sensory and motor responses were stable at rates at which the behavior shows decrement, this implied that the critical changes underlying habituation were occurring elsewhere in the neural circuit.

By recording intracellularly from gill motor neurons, Kupfermann, Castellucci, Pinsker, and Kandel (1970) and Castellucci *et al.* (1970) found that the synaptic input onto the motor cells, produced either by stimulation of the siphon skin or by electrical stimulation of the afferent nerve from the siphon, dramatically decreased during habituation and increased during dishabituation. This synaptic input consisted of a complex excitatory postsynaptic potential (EPSP) that in turn had two components: (1) a *monosynaptic* component—the direct input from the sensory neurons,

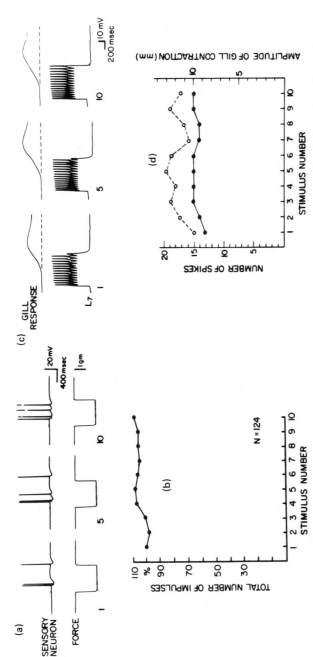

Fig. 6. Analysis of contribution of sensory adaptation and motor fatigue to habituation. (a, b) Stability of mechanoafferent discharges. (a) Intracellularly recorded discharges from a mechanoreceptor neuron (sensory neuron) to a 800-msec punctate stimulus (force) delivered to the siphon skin. The first, fifth, and tenth responses are shown (ISI = 30 seconds; n = 124). (b) Graph of mechanoreceptor stability: 100% corresponds to a mean discharge of 3.8 impulses, which was the response to the first stimulus (n = number of sessions). There is no decrement to repeated stimulation. From Byrne, Castellucci, & Kandel (1978). (c and d) Stability of gill contractions produced by identified motor neuron L7. (c) Sample records of contractions and the gill (upper trace, photocell record) produced by repeated intracellular depolarization of L7 (bottom traces). The first, fifth, and tenth responses are shown. (d) Graph of the number of spikes in each stimulus (●) and the amplitude of each contraction (○). There is no decrement with repeated stimulation (ISI = 30 seconds). From Carew, Pinsker, Rubinson, & Kandel (1974).

and (2) a *polysynaptic* component—the input from interneurons that were activated by the sensory neurons (see Fig. 5). As we shall see in later sections, analyzing the monosynaptic component of the reflex provides a very powerful system for investigating several detailed questions concerning the cellular mechanisms of habituation and sensitization; but important insights were gained initially by analyzing the complex EPSP.

a. Analysis of the Complex EPSP. Because the synapses onto the motor cells had been identified as possible sites of the changes underlying the behavioral plasticity, an important question to answer was, Is the reduction of the complex EPSP during habituation and the increase of the EPSP during dishabituation caused by presynaptic or postsynaptic mechanisms? Although these questions cannot be definitively answered by analyzing the complex EPSP, first steps toward an answer can be made at this level of analysis. For example, there are two main classes of possible postsynaptic mechanisms for synaptic decrement and facilitation: (1) a change in the electrical properties of the postsynaptic neuron; for example, an alteration of its input resistance (which I define below) and (2) a change in receptor sensitivity. The second possibility cannot be analyzed at the level of the complex EPSP, but the first possibility can. In discussing the electrical properties of a neuron it is important to understand why a change in input resistance in the postsynaptic neuron could produce a concomitant change in the complex EPSP. It follows from Ohm's law that the size of an EPSP (E) is the product of two factors: (1) the synaptic current (I_{syn}) that flows across the postsynaptic neuron's membrane multiplied by (2) the resistance across which that current flows (the input resistance of the neuron or R_{input} [for review, see Ginsborg (1967); Kandel, (1976)]. Thus,

$$E_{EPSP} = I_{syn}R_{input}.$$

Thus, if the synaptic current does not change but the input resistance decreases, the EPSP will decrease. The input resistance could decrease, for example, by an *increase* in the permeability of the postsynaptic cell to one or more species of ion. One measures the input resistance of neuron by passing a known amount of current into the cell (usually hyperpolarizing current is used to avoid firing the neuron) and measuring the voltage the current produces—this voltage deflection is called an *electrotonic potential*. During habituation and dishabituation, the input resistance of the motor neuron measured in this fashion does not change (Fig. 7), suggesting the possibility that the synaptic current is changing instead. A change in synaptic current could be produced by either a pre- or postsynaptic mechanism. One powerful means of distinguishing between these

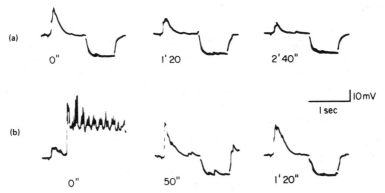

Fig. 7. EPSP decrement and heterosynaptic facilitation in the absence of input resistance change in the soma of motor neuron L7. (a) Decrement of the complex EPSP in L7. The siphon nerve was stimulated every 10 seconds and the EPSP recorded. A constant-current hyperpolarizing electrical pulse was applied through another intracellular electrode, and the resulting hyperpolarizing electrotonic potential was recorded concomitantly with the synaptic activity. During EPSP decrement, there was no significant change in soma input resistance in L7 as indicated by the relative constancy of the electrotonic potential (0″ is the first stimulus). (b) The heterosynaptic stimulation (left connective: 6 per seconds for 6 seconds at 0″) produced facilitation of the decremented EPSP, and the facilitation was also not accompanied by a change in soma input resistance. From Carew, Castellucci, & Kandel (1971).

possibilities is a quantal analysis that we will discuss in Section III,A,3. But with the kind of experiment illustrated in Fig. 7 we can rule out gross changes in the electrical properties of the postsynaptic neurons as a prime factor in producing alterations in the synaptic potential.

A second example of insights that can be gained from an analysis of the complex EPSP concerns the relationship between dishabituation and sensitization. We have mentioned that Carew *et al.* (1971) found that the same strong stimulus to the neck that produced facilitation of an habituated behavioral response (dishabituation) also produced facilitation of a nonhabituated response (sensitization). In parallel cellular studies, Carew *et al.* (1971) found that decrement of the complex EPSP produced by repeatedly stimulating one neural pathway (from the siphon) did not generalize to another nonstimulated neural pathway (from the purple gland). Thus the effects of a single strong input could be assessed on both decremented and nondecremented EPSPs (Fig. 8). They found that electrical stimulation of the nerves from the neck that carry the facilitating input in the intact animal (the pleuro-abdominal connectives) enhanced not only the decremented EPSP but also the nondecremented one (Fig. 8c,d). Taken together with the behavioral results, these data show that dishabituation of the gill-withdrawal reflex is a special case of sensitization.

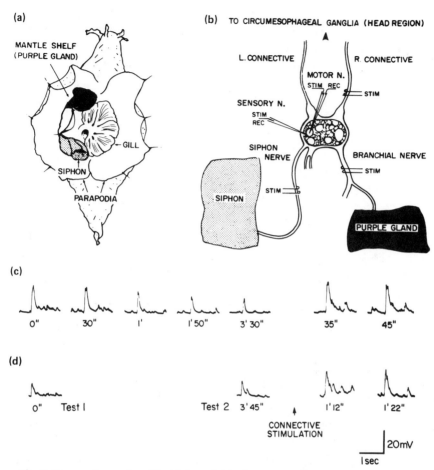

Fig. 8. Two pathways for gill withdrawal. (a) The anterior portion of the mantle shelf and its edge, the purple gland, are shown in solid black. This receptive field is referred to in the text as the *purple gland*. A second receptive field is the *siphon* shown as a stippled region. (b) Diagram showing innervation of the siphon and purple gland by their respective nerves, the siphon nerve and the branchial nerve. For cellular studies, activation of each pathway was accomplished by electrical stimulation of the appropriate nerve. Stimulation of either the left or right connective provided a pathway for heterosynaptic facilitation. (c, d) Facilitation of both decremented and nondecremented EPSPs following a train of stimuli to the connectives (ISI = 10 seconds). A single test stimulus [Test 1 (d)] was delivered to the branchial nerve and produced an EPSP in L7. Repetitive stimuli (c) were then applied to the siphon nerve to produce EPSP decrement. After a second test (d) to the branchial nerve (Test 2) revealed that no generalization of decrement had occurred from the siphon nerve EPSP to the branchial nerve EPSP, a train of stimuli was delivered to the left connective (6 per second for 6 seconds). Subsequent stimulation of the siphon nerve (c) and then the branchial nerve (d) revealed facilitation of both decremented and nondecremented EPSPs. From Carew, Castellucci, & Kandel (1971).

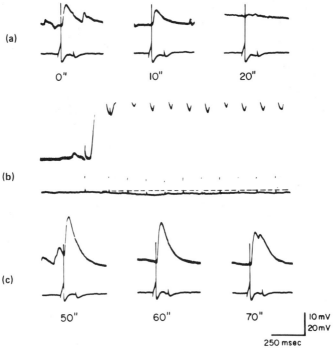

Fig. 9. Decrement and facilitation of an elementary, monosynaptic EPSP in the gill motor neuron L7. The intracellular stimulation of the sensory neuron (lower trace of each pair) was repeated every 10 seconds (ISI). After three stimuli (a), heterosynaptic stimulation was applied to the left connective (7 per second for 5.5 seconds). In (b) the heterosynaptic stimulus to the left connective is illustrated. Rather than firing the sensory neuron, the heterosynaptic stimulus (note stimulus artifacts in sensory neuron trace) caused a sustained hyperpolarization of the sensory neuron. After the heterosynaptic stimulation, the EPSP produced by the sensory neuron in L7 was facilitated for several minutes (c). All indicated times are referred to the first stimulus (0"). From Carew, Castellucci, & Kandel (1971).

b. Analysis of the Monosynaptic EPSP. Studies of the complex EPSPs onto motor neurons have thus provided important information concerning mechanisms of habituation and sensitization. To move the analysis further, however, required studying the monosynaptic connections between the sensory neurons and the motor cells. Castellucci *et al.* (1970) found that the EPSP produced in the motor neuron by intracellular stimulation of a single sensory neuron showed profound depression when elicited repeatedly, and, following a strong sensitizing stimulus, it showed a dramatic increase in amplitude (Fig. 9). Thus the same set of monosynaptic connections could be made functionally less effective by activation of the sensory neurons themselves (this is called homosynaptic depression), or could be made more effective by activation of a second sensitizing pathway [called heterosynaptic facilitation; see Kandel & Tauc (1965)]. Subsequent studies showed that the complex EPSP already described is caused largely by the summation of individual monosynaptic connections from the sensory cells to the motor neurons (Byrne *et al.,* 1978). These results, taken together, showed that the monosynaptic connections between the sensory neurons and their follower cells (both interneurons and motor neurons) are a critical site underlying short-term habituation and sensitization of the gill-withdrawal reflex. Because this reflex also shows long-term habituation, it was of interest to determine whether these same synapses might be involved in the long-term process as well.

2. Long-Term Habituation and Sensitization

The first clue that long-term habituation might share a common locus in the nervous system with short-term habituation came from studies on the complex EPSP carried out by Carew and Kandel (1973). They developed a shortened behavioral training procedure that could produce long-term habituation in a single day (Fig. 10a,b). Four training sessions (10 trials each) separated by 1.5 hours produced habituation that lasted longer than 1 week. They then used an analog of this training procedure to study long-term synaptic decrement in the isolated abdominal ganglion (see Fig. 4c). They recorded the complex EPSP in the motor neuron L7 produced by electrical stimulation of the afferent nerve from the siphon. They found that repeated stimulation produced synaptic depression of the EPSP that built up progressively across training sessions and was still significantly depressed 24 hours later, unlike an EPSP from a nonstimulated control pathway (Fig. 10c,d).

A direct analysis of the role of the sensory-to-motor monosynaptic connections in long-term habituation was carried out by Castellucci, Carew, and Kandel (1978). They gave intact animals long-term habituation training and then examined the sensory-to-motor connections in isolated abdominal ganglia either 1 day, 1 week, or more than 3 weeks after training, comparing these connections to those from untrained control animals. The most striking effect of habituation training was that most of the monosynaptic connections in trained animals were no longer detectable. The data were thus expressed as the number of detectable monosynaptic connections observed in each ganglion (Fig. 11). Control animals showed a mean of 89% connections (not every sensory cell connects directly to the motor neuron). By contrast, habituated animals showed significantly fewer detectable connections compared to controls in all

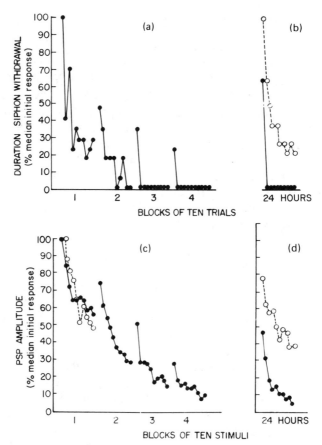

Fig. 10. Comparison of long-term behavioral response decrement and EPSP decrement. Acquisition (a) and retention (b) of long-term habituation of siphon withdrawal following four training sessions separated by 1.5 hours (interblock interval = 1.5 hours; intertrial interval = 30 seconds). All scores are expressed as a percentage of the median of each group's initial response (Block 1, Trial 1). The median duration of the initial response was 17 seconds for the experimentals (●) and 19 seconds for the controls (○). (c and d) Acquisition (c) and retention (d) of EPSP decrement. The EPSP amplitudes from both experimental (●) and control (○) nerves (n = 10) are expressed as a percentage of the initial amplitude. In acquisition, six experiments were run with the siphon nerve as experimental and four experiments with the branchial nerve as experimental. In Block 1, 10 stimuli were first applied to the experimental nerve and then to the control nerve, and produced comparable EPSP decrement in L7 from both nerves, indicating lack of EPSP generalization. Repeated blocks of stimuli to the experimental nerve produced progressive buildup of EPSP decrement. A single test to the control nerve produced an EPSP that was recovered to 84.5% control, indicating that deterioration cannot account for experimental EPSP decrement. In retention, the cell was reimpaled 24 hours later and repolarized to the membrane potential maintained for acquisition. The ordinate in retention was redrawn to indicate that, even though the repolarization can be closely approximated, it cannot be considered to be exact. In the retention test, stimulation of the experimental nerve produced significantly greater EPSP decrement than stimulation of the control nerve. From Carew & Kandel (1973). Copyright 1973 American Association for the Advancement of Science.

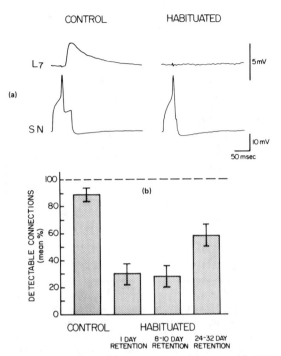

Fig. 11. Detectable and nondetectable connections. (a) Detectable EPSP from a control abdominal ganglion and a nondetectable EPSP from an experimental animal that received long-term habituation training and whose synaptic connections were examined 24 hours after the last training session. The sensory neuron (SN) was depolarized intracellularly to trigger a single action potential and to evoke a monosynaptic EPSP in the gill motor neuron L7. (b) Summary of the experiments illustrated in (a) in which the ratio of the number of detectable EPSPs over the total number of connections sampled was determined in control animals ($n = 10$; 58 cells) and in habituated animals 1 day ($n = 20$; 109 cells), 8–10 days ($n = 6$; 43 cells), and 24–32 days ($n = 5$; 30 cells) after their last training session. Each animal contributed one ratio, and the graph indicates the mean percentage (± standard error) of detectable connections. From Castellucci, Carew, & Kandel (1978). Copyright 1978 American Association for the Advancement of Science.

three retention tests. Animals tested 1 day and 1 week after training showed only 30 and 24% respectively, and after three weeks only 58% of the sensory cells showed detectable connections. A nondetectable connection can mean one of two things: either (1) the EPSP is really there but too small to detect (with our recording system we can resolve potentials greater than 50 μV), or (2) the synapse is so depressed that no transmitter is released with an action potential. Functionally these two possibilities are very similar, because an EPSP of less than 50 μV in amplitude will in most cases be of little consequence to the motor neuron.

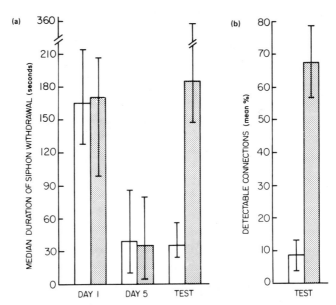

Fig. 12. Sensitization of long-term habituated animals and restoration of synaptic transmission in long-term depressed synapses. (a) Behavioral scores of control (open bars; $n = 11$) and experimental animals (shaded bars; $n = 12$) on Days 1 and 5 of habituation training and after a single sensitizing stimulus to the experimental animals (sum of Trials 1–10). Both groups of animals exhibited significant habituation on Day 5 compared to Day 1. After the sensitizing stimulus to the experimental animals, they exhibited significant dishabituation, whereas the long-term habituation of the control animals was unchanged. Data are expressed as medians plus or minus interquartile ranges. (b) Summary of 20 experiments in which the number of detectable EPSPs was determined in control (long-term habituated) animals ($n = 10$; 55 connections sampled) and in long-term habituated animals that were sensitized ($n = 10$; 54 connections sampled). Data were expressed as the ratio of the number of detectable EPSPs to the total number of connections sampled. Each animal contributed a single ratio. Sampling was obtained 1–2 hours after the experimental animals were given shocks. A blind procedure was used throughout the cellular experiments. Control and experimental animals were treated in exactly parallel fashion. Data are shown as the mean percentage (± SEM) of detectable connections. From Carew, Castellucci, & Kandel (1979). Copyright 1979 American Association for the Advancement of Science.

These data show that long-term habituation training produces a profound depression in synaptic transmission at the same synapses involved in short-term habituation. Normally, this depression takes longer than 3 weeks to recover (Fig. 11b). Because short-term depression at these synapses can be rapidly counteracted by a sensitizing stimulus (Castellucci *et al.*, 1970), this raised the question of whether long-term depression at these synapses could also be counteracted.

To study this question Carew, Castellucci, and Kandel (1979) first carried out a behavioral study to examine the effects of sensitization on long-term habituated animals. They found that a single sensitizing stimulus (an electric shock to the neck) significantly elevated the reflex response of long-term habituated animals, when compared to other long-term controls that received no sensitization (Fig. 12a). They then examined whether the long-lasting synaptic depression produced by long-term training (Fig. 11) could also be counteracted by a sensitizing stimulus. As in the studies already described, long-term habituation training produced a dramatic reduction in the incidence of detectable sensory-to-motor connections (only 9%; Fig. 12b). Animals receiving identical behavioral training, however, with the addition of a single sensitizing stimulus following habituation training, showed a significant restoration of synaptic transmission— 68% connections (Fig. 12b). Thus the profound synaptic depression produced by long-term habituation can be rapidly restored by a single sensitizing stimulus. This observation is interesting from both a functional and a theoretical perspective. Functionally it indicates that sensitization provides a behavioral mechanism whereby changing environmental demands can quite rapidly override the long-term depression of reflex responsiveness produced by habituation. Theoretically the observation is also interesting because it sets limits on the possible cellular mechanisms of long-term habituation, making especially unlikely possibilities such as the complete depletion of transmitter or radical structural alteration of the synapses (such as a physical disconnection), because it is unlikely that these possibilities would be rapidly reversible.

Thus far in this chapter we have seen that short-term and long-term habituation share both a common locus in the nervous system (the sensory neuron connections to their follower cells) and aspects of a common mechanism (synaptic depression). Further insights into the mechanisms underlying the synaptic depression can be gained by examining synaptic transmission at a more fundamental level of investigation by means of a quantal analysis.

3. Application of a Quantal Analysis to the Study of Short-Term Habituation and Sensitization

In earlier sections we reviewed the evidence indicating that habituation is produced by a reduction in the amplitude of the synaptic potential from the sensory neurons to their follower cells and that sensitization is caused by facilitation of that same synaptic potential. We have seen that such alterations of EPSP amplitude (e.g., depression of the EPSP) could be caused by presynaptic factors such as reduced transmitter release or postsynaptic factors such as a decline in receptor sensitivity. A quantal analysis can aid in distinguishing between these alternatives. I first give the basic rationale of a quantal analysis and then describe its application to the issues at hand.

An understanding of the rationale underlying a quantal analysis requires understanding the *quantal hypothesis* (for review, see Katz, 1966, 1969), which states that, when an action potential arrives at a presynaptic terminal, transmitter stored in vesicles in the terminal is released from that terminal in multimolecular packets called quanta (each quantum reflects the total content of one vesicle, which contains several thousand molecules of neurotransmitter). Each synaptic potential recorded in a postsynaptic neuron is actually composed of many quanta. The amplitude of the synaptic potential then will be determined by two factors: (1) the amplitude of the potential caused by a single quantum (this is called the *unit potential* and is signified by q) and (2) the number of quanta (signified by m) released by an action potential. Thus the average amplitude of an EPSP ($\bar{E}$) will be given by the equation

$$\bar{E} = m\bar{q}.$$

Because we can readily calculate $\bar{E}$ (the average of the amplitudes of a series of evoked synaptic potentials), by estimating either q or m we can easily determine the value of the other. A quantal analysis (del Castillo & Katz, 1954) provides us with a means of determining either the quantal number m or the size of the unit potential q.

The goal in using a quantal analysis in studying habituation and sensitization is to distinguish between pre- and postsynaptic factors that may contribute to changes in the amplitude of the monosynaptic EPSP. Let us first consider the case for habituation, which is accompanied by a decrease in the amplitude of the average evoked EPSP ($\bar{E}$). By considering our simple equation, a decrease in $\bar{E}$ could be produced either by a decrease in m, or by a decrease in $\bar{q}$ (or both). What are the mechanistic implications of each of these possibilities? If m decreases during the synaptic decrement, and $\bar{q}$ remains unchanged, this would suggest a *presynaptic mechanism*—fewer transmitter quanta are being released with each presynaptic action potential, and the postsynaptic receptor sensitivity (as estimated by $\bar{q}$) remains constant. If, on the other hand, $\bar{q}$ declined while m stayed constant, the interpretation is more complicated. A reduction in $\bar{q}$ could indicate either a postsynaptic change (the unit potential is smaller because the postsynaptic membrane is less sensitive), or it could indicate a presynaptic change (each presynaptic vesicle could be incompletely filled with transmitter). Thus outcomes in which $\bar{q}$ changes provide an ambiguous answer, but those in which m (and not $\bar{q}$) changes provide a clear answer.

There are two reliable ways to estimate m or $\bar{q}$. The first is called a *histogram method*, in which (at low levels of release using high-Mg^{2+}, low-Ca^{2+} solutions (Castellucci & Kandel, 1974), frequency histograms of EPSP amplitudes are generated for many consecutive responses, and the mean voltage value for the smallest postsynaptic potential measured following a presynaptic action potential is assumed to be $\bar{q}$ (the unit peak). Subsequent peaks of the histograms should be integral multiples of the first peak, because the first peak ($\bar{q}$) is the basic building block from which the other peaks are constructed. Thus, this method gives a direct estimate of $\bar{q}$, the first peak of the histogram. The second method is called a *failure analysis*, which assumes that release at these synapses can be approximated by a Poisson distribution (Castellucci & Kandel, 1974; Kandel, Brunelli, Byrne, & Castellucci, 1976). At low levels of release, sometimes no transmitter is released following an action potential, and thus no potential is recorded. This is called a failure. Using a property of the Poisson distribution, one can obtain an estimate of m by examining the ratio of failures to the total number of trials (del Castillo & Katz, 1954). The equation that gives us an estimate of the quantal content m is

$$m = \ln\left(\frac{\text{total number of trials}}{\text{number of failures}}\right).$$

Using both of these methods, Castellucci and Kandel (1974) performed a quantal analysis during synaptic decrement at the sensory-to-motor synapse. They found that with repeated stimulation, the value of $\bar{q}$ remained constant, but the value of m decreased by more than 50% (Fig. 13a). There is a third, less-direct way to estimate the value of m: using the *coefficient of variation* (CV) method. A property of the Poisson distribution is that the variance is equal to the mean, which in turn is equal to m. Thus the coefficient of variation (standard deviation/mean) is equal to $\sqrt{m}/m$. Solving for m we arrive at

$$m = \frac{1}{(CV)^2}.$$

Using this method, Castellucci and Kandel (1974) found the same trend as in the preceding methods (see Fig. 13a): with repeated stimulation, m decreased but $\bar{q}$ remained the same. In the subsequent study of facilitation at these same synapses (produced by stimulation of the pleuro-abdominal connectives), Castellucci and Kandel (1976b) found that, again, the value of $\bar{q}$ was unchanged during facilitation, but the value of m paralleled that

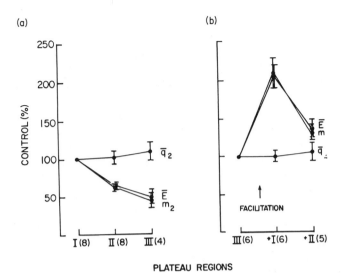

Fig. 13. A quantal analysis of synaptic depression and synaptic facilitation underlying habituation and sensitization. The data are based on estimates of m and $\bar{q}$, values derived by the failure method (see text for details). (a) Synaptic depression: data from eight experiments were normalized in relation to the region (I) where failures were first observed. During successive regions (II and III) the estimated values of $\bar{q}$ did not change significantly, but the average EPSP amplitude $\bar{E}$ and estimates of $\bar{m}$ decreased by 50% (ISI = 10 seconds). (b) Synaptic facilitation: data from six experiments were normalized in relation to the last region preceding the facilitating stimulus (III). During the successive region (+I), the estimates of $\bar{q}$ did not change significantly, but the average EPSP amplitude $\bar{E}$ and the quantal content m increased by 100%. Number in parentheses after each region indicates number of preparations. From Castellucci & Kandel (1976). Copyright 1976 American Association for the Advancement of Science.

of $\bar{E}$ and more than doubled (Fig. 13b). These data show that both habituation and sensitization of the gill-withdrawal reflex in *Aplysia* are *presynaptic processes*, involving a decrease or increase, respectively, in the number of transmitter quanta released with each action potential in the sensory neurons.

These results immediately raise additional questions. Why does repeated activity of the sensory neuron itself cause progressively less transmitter to be released, and why does activity in another (sensitizing) pathway produce presynaptic facilitation in those same terminals? Answers to these questions involve an analysis of the different ionic currents that flow in the sensory neuron in response to the action potential, in both the depressed and facilitated states.

B. Biophysical Analysis

One major goal of a biophysical analysis is to study current flow in neurons. Current flow is produced in nerve cells by charged molecules, ions, flowing either into or out of the neuron through channels in the membrane. Of particular interest for our purposes are the currents that flow in the presynaptic terminals during the action potential, because one of these currents, the calcium (Ca^{2+}) current, is directly responsible for the release of transmitter [Katz & Miledi, 1967; for review, see Katz (1969)], and we have already seen that it is transmitter release that is modulated during habituation and sensitization (Castellucci & Kandel, 1974, 1976b). To accurately measure these currents, a device called a *voltage clamp* is used. In the next two sections I will discuss the basic rationale underlying the voltage clamp and then describe its application to the analysis of habituation and sensitization in *Aplysia*.

The basic problem that the voltage clamp was designed to solve was to provide a means of determining the ionic conductances across a nerve cell's membrane by measuring the *current* that flows across the membrane. But many of the currents that one would like to measure in a neuron will vary as a function of the membrane potential—more current will flow at one membrane voltage than at another (this is called a *voltage-dependent conductance*). But, current flow itself will cause the membrane potential to change, and thus a feedback cycle is created. The sodium (Na^+) conductance during the action potential provides a good example: changing the membrane potential (depolarization) will cause Na^+ channels to open, and a Na^+ current will flow through them. This current flow will cause the membrane to depolarize further, opening more Na^+ channels, which gives rise to more Na^+ current, and so on. To study the Na^+ current at any particular membrane potential, the feedback cycle must be broken—and that is the function of a voltage clamp. Its design is actually quite simple—with special electronics it allows the experimenter to (1) move the membrane potential to a particular (command) level and (2) hold (clamp) the potential at that level by pumping as much current into or out of the cell as is necessary to maintain the membrane potential at the desired level. Thus the amount of current that the clamp must provide will be exactly equal to and opposite the current flowing through the nerve cell membrane. And therefore by measuring the clamp current we also measure the current flowing across the cell membrane at that command potential.

Another important point to appreciate is that, when one uses a voltage clamp to measure current flow in a nerve cell, the current measured is actually not a single current but a composite or *net current* that results from several different species of ions flowing at the same time through their respective channels. Ionic currents that flow *inward* (typically, Na^+ and Ca^{2+}) depolarize the neuron, and ionic currents that flow *outward* [typically, potassium (K^+)] hyperpolarize the neuron [the reason for this is beyond the scope of this chapter; for a detailed discussion, see Koester (1981)]. Measuring the net current alone can tell us neither the species of ion that is flowing nor the magnitude of a particular ionic current. Thus, if 10 nA of outward current and 30 nA of inward current flow at the same time, we will measure 20 nA of net inward current. But we would measure exactly the same net inward current with a 15-nA outward current and a 35-nA inward current. Moreover, if one performs an experimental manipulation (e.g., adds a drug) and observes an increase in the net inward current, this could be caused either by an actual increase in the inward current or by a *decrease* in the opposing outward current, or both. The way one determines which particular currents are flowing is by blocking one current at a time (by ion substitution or pharmacological agents) and examining the effects on the net current. In so doing one can reconstruct the contributions of each individual current to the net current [for review, see Hodgkin (1964)].

The ionic currents of interest to us occur in the synaptic terminals of the sensory neurons. These currents are responsible for the release of transmitter. Ideally, one would voltage clamp the synaptic terminals, but, in *Aplysia* this is not technically possible. The next best alternative is to voltage clamp the soma of the neuron and measure the currents in the cell body. This technique is imperfect because the soma is too far away from the terminals to permit the precise measurement of synaptic currents flowing at the synapse. But, in *Aplysia* this problem can at least partially be overcome because the soma membrane of *Aplysia* nerve cells contains many channels (e.g., Ca^{2+} and K^+ channels) whose properties are similar to channels in the synaptic membranes (Geduldig & Junge, 1968; Klein & Kandel, 1980; Stinnakre & Tauc, 1973). It has long been known that calcium channels are critically involved in transmitter release at the synapse [Katz & Miledi, 1967; for review, see Katz (1969)], and Klein and Kandel (1978) have shown that changes in the calcium current recorded in sensory neuron cell bodies are paralleled by changes in transmitter release from the sensory neuron terminals. Thus the calcium current in the soma provides an estimate of the calcium current in the terminals.

1. Short-Term Habituation

To analyze the ionic events occurring during habituation, Klein, Shapiro, and Kandel (1980) first used a non-voltage clamp technique that

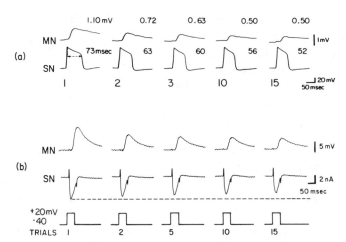

Fig. 14. Change in Ca^{2+} current during the homosynaptic depression that accompanies habituation. (a) Correlation between sensory neuron (SN) action potential–duration (dashed line in Trial 1; action potential–duration in MS shown above each action potential) in seawater containing 100 mM TEA and monosynaptic EPSP in the motor neuron (MN) with repeated stimulation (amplitude in millivolts shown above each EPSP). Action potentials fired at 0.1 Hz. (b) With sodium current blocked and a large amount of the potassium currents blocked, presynaptic voltage-clamp pulses (bottom trace) elicit EPSPs (top trace, MN) that undergo depression with repetition of the depolarizing command. The decrease in EPSP is paralleled by a decrease in the inward current (middle trace, SN). In the middle current trace, downward deflections indicate inward current. The dashed line shows the amplitude of the Trial 1 current. From Klein, Shapiro, & Kandel (1980).

allowed them to measure qualitative changes in the Ca^{2+} current. They measured the Ca^{2+} contribution to the action potential in the sensory neuron while simultaneously recording the monosynaptic EPSP from the sensory neuron onto a gill motor neuron. Usually the Ca^{2+} current during the action potential is quite small and is masked by a much larger (outward) K^+ current that is responsible for the repolarizing phase of the action potential. But this K^+ current can be blocked by the drug TEA (tetraethylammonium), which prolongs the duration of the action potential and permits the direct estimation of the calcium current. Klein *et al.* (1980) found that repeated stimulation of the sensory neuron at rates that produce habituation produced a progressive decrease in the amplitude of the EPSP together with a paralleled decrease in the Ca^{2+} current during the action potential, which is reflected by a narrowing of the action potential (Fig. 14a). They next voltage clamped the sensory cell and blocked both Na^+ and K^+ channels to permit direct measurement of the Ca^{2+} current. Then, to simulate the action potential, they injected repeated depolarizing command pulses in the soma (which produced the release of transmitter from the terminals, as measured by the synaptic potential in the postsynaptic motor neuron) and found that, as the EPSP declined, the Ca^{2+} current progressively declined in the sensory cell (Fig. 14b). These results suggest therefore that habituation involves a direct inactivation of the Ca^{2+} current in the sensory cell.

2. Short-Term Sensitization

Using techniques similar to those I have described, Klein and Kandel (1978, 1980) have examined the ionic events underlying sensitization. The presynaptic facilitation of transmitter release underlying sensitization can be produced by stimulation of the connectives, which carry the input from the neck and tail regions. In the following section, we see that presynaptic facilitation can also be produced either by application of the neurotransmitter serotonin or by causing an increase in cyclic AMP in the sensory neuron. Klein and Kandel (1978) found that all of these manipulations also increased the Ca^{2+} contribution to the action potential as reflected by a broadening of the action potential (Fig. 15a–d). When they voltage clamped the sensory neuron during facilitation they found that the net inward current increased (Fig. 15e), which was consistent with the idea that the (inward) Ca^{2+} current was increasing. But, this increase in the inward current was produced by a *reduction* in an opposing (outward) K^+ current. The result of the decrease in the K^+ current is that the action potential is prolonged (and thus produces more depolarization of the synaptic terminals), which in turn increases the inward Ca^{2+} current during the action potential, and leads to an increase in the release of transmitter.

These results show that both habituation and sensitization are the result of the modulation of a calcium current in the sensory cell. During habituation, the modulation appears to be directly on the calcium channel, and during sensitization the modulation is indirect, involving an increase in the inward calcium current as the result of increased polarization resulting from depression of an outward potassium current. An important insight from these studies is that simple forms of learning can be accomplished by modulating the preexisting properties of the nerve cell. No new connections were made, and no new currents were induced in the sensory cells by the simple learning experiences of habituation or sensitization. Rather, a preexisting and fundamental property of the neuron, the calcium-dependent release of neurotransmitter, is modulated by the learning experience. Having established that the modulation of a specific ionic current is involved in both habituation and sensitization, a more fundamental question concerns the molecular events that produce this modulation within the synaptic terminal.

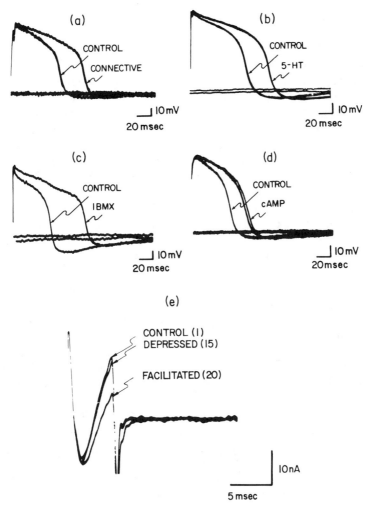

Fig. 15. Change in the Ca^{2+} current during the presynaptic facilitation which accompanies sensitization. (a–d) Increase in the duration of the sensory-neuron action potential (in seawater containing 100 m*M* TEA) after (a) stimulation of the connective (the pathway from the head and tail that mediates sensitization; (b) application of 0.2 m*M* serotonin (5 HT); (c) application of 0.1 m*M* IBMX, a phosphodiesterase inhibitor that blocks the breakdown of cAMP; and (d) intracellular injection of cAMP (from Klein & Kandel, 1978). (e) Superimposition of three current traces taken from a voltage-clamped sensory neuron (1) in response to an initial depolarizing command, (2) after 15 repeated commands (to simulate habituation), and (3) after connective stimulation to produce sensitization. There is no significant change in the (outward) currents during simulated habituation (Traces 1 and 15), but there is a significant reduction of the outward current and increase in the net inward current (inward current is downward) during sensitization. From Klein & Kandel (1980).

C. Biochemical Analysis

In applying biochemical approaches to the study of simple forms of learning in *Aplysia,* most progress has thus far been made in the analysis of short-term sensitization. The first step in this analysis was to identify the neurotransmitter that mediates presynaptic facilitation of transmitter release from the sensory neurons. There is now good evidence that the transmitter responsible for presynaptic facilitation is either the biogenic amine serotonin or a closely related transmitter substance. For example, Brunelli, Castellucci, and Kandel (1976) found (1) that application of serotonin (but not other amines such as octopamine or dopamine) to the bathing solution surrounding the abdominal ganglion enhanced synaptic transmission between the sensory cells and motor cells and (2) that the normally occurring facilitation of transmission produced by stimulation of the connectives could be blocked by the serotonin antagonist cinanserin. Moreover, Klein and Kandel (1980) found that serotonin enhances the Ca^{2+} current in the sensory neuron, thereby facilitating transmitter release. Finally, Hawkins, Castellucci, and Kandel (1981) have identified interneurons in the abdominal ganglion that produce presynaptic facilitation in the sensory neurons, and these interneurons have both the physiological and morphological features of serotonergic nerve cells (Bailey, Hawkins, Chen, & Kandel, 1981; Hawkins *et al.,* 1981). Thus, serotonin is strongly implicated as the transmitter responsible for sensitization.

If serotonin is the facilitating transmitter, how does it produce presynaptic facilitation in the sensory neurons? The first clue came from studies by Cedar and Schwartz (1972), who found that incubation of the abdominal ganglion in serotonin produced a rapid and dramatic increase in endogenous levels of cyclic adenosine monophosphate (cyclic AMP or cAMP). Moreover, Cedar, Kandel, and Schwartz (1972) found that stimulation of the connectives, which is known to produce presynaptic facilitation in the sensory cells, also produced an increase in cAMP in the ganglion. Finally, Brunelli *et al.* (1976) found that either exposing the ganglion to a membrane-permeable analog of cAMP or injecting cAMP into the cell body of a sensory neuron enhanced synaptic transmission. These data taken collectively suggest that serotonin mediates presynaptic facilitation by increasing cAMP in the terminals of the sensory neurons. But how might cAMP produce facilitation?

1. Mode of Action of Cyclic Adenosine Monophosphate

Because cyclic adenosine monophosphate (cAMP) is strongly implicated in sensitization, it is important to have a basic understanding of what this remarkable molecule does. Since its discovery in 1957 (Rall, Sutherland, & Berthet, 1957; Sutherland & Rall, 1957), cyclic AMP has been shown to be involved in numerous biological functions (for review, see Robison, Butcher, & Sutherland, 1971), and because of its mode of action it has been called a "second messenger" (Sutherland, Øye, & Butcher, 1965). A classic example of this mode of action can be seen in the way cyclic AMP is involved in the regulation of glycogen metabolism. The hormone epinephrine (the "first messenger") reaches liver cells through the blood and increases the activity of an enzyme (adenylate cyclase) in the liver cell membrane, which in turn increases the conversion of ATP to cAMP inside the liver cell. The increased intracellular cAMP acts as a second messenger, initiating the chain of events by which glycogen is broken down into glucose. The way cAMP produces its effects in most cells is to activate a class of enzymes called protein kinases (Kuo & Greengard, 1969; for review, see Greengard, 1978). Protein kinases are enzymes that catalyze the chemical reaction involved in the addition of phosphate groups to proteins, a process called protein phosphorylation. The phosphorylation of a protein can, in turn, dramatically alter its biological activity. The cyclic AMP-dependent protein kinase is a molecule composed of two subunits: (1) a *regulatory* subunit and (2) a *catalytic* subunit. When the kinase is in its inactive form, the regulatory subunits are attached to the catalytic subunits. Cyclic AMP activates the kinase by binding the regulatory subunits, disconnecting them from the catalytic subunits, thereby allowing the kinase to phosphorylate a protein substrate—that is, put one or more phosphates on it. With this brief background on the mode of action of cAMP we can now examine how this second messenger might mediate sensitization.

2. Role of Cyclic Adenosine Monophosphate in Sensitization

Based on their own neurohysiological and biophysical studies and the previous work by Brunelli *et al.* (1976), Klein and Kandel (1980) proposed a detailed molecular model for sensitization. The steps in this model are

1. Serotonin or a related transmitter is released from facilitator interneurons that synapse on the presynaptic terminals of the sensory neurons; then
2. Serotonin increases adenylate cyclase activity in the sensory neuron terminals, producing
3. An increase in intracellular cAMP concentration in the terminals, which
4. Increases cAMP-dependent protein kinase activity, which in turn

238   Thomas J. Carew

5. Phosphorylates a membrane protein (the K^+ channel or a protein associated with it)
6. Phosphorylation of the membrane protein causes a decrease in K^+ conductance (this K^+ current normally contributes to repolarization the action potential). Thus the action potential is prolonged, which
7. Allows more Ca^{2+} to enter the terminal with each action potential (because of an increased Ca^{2+} current), which produces
8. An enhanced release of transmitter from the sensory neuron terminals

The value of this model is twofold: first, it takes into account all the existing facts on presynaptic facilitation in *Aplysia* and integrates those facts with known biochemical processes; and second, it provides a number of specific predictions and testable hypotheses. For example, if the model is correct, one should be able to bypass Steps 1 and 2 and produce enhanced synaptic transmission by increasing the concentration of cAMP inside the sensory cell. Brunelli *et al.* (1976) showed that direct injection of cAMP (but not a number of control substances, including the

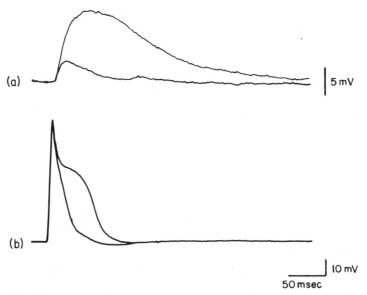

Fig. 16. Enhancement of transmitter release by injection of the catalytic subunit. Superimposed recordings of the action potentials in the sensory cell (b) and the monosynaptic EPSPs in the follower neuron (a) before and after injection of the catalytic subunit. After intracellular injection of the enzyme into the sensory cell, the duration of both the sensory cell action potential and its transmitter release were increased (top recording, cAMP-dependent protein kinase catalytic subunit; bottom recording, control).

breakdown product of cAMP, 5'-AMP) into the sensory neuron, produced facilitation of transmitter release. More recently, Castellucci, Kandel, Schwartz, Wilson, Nairn, and Greengard (1980) showed that they could bypass even more steps and simulate the effect that cAMP normally has on the protein kinase (binding to the regulatory subunit, thus freeing-up the catalytic subunit), by directly injecting the cAMP-dependent protein kinase into the sensory neuron (Fig. 16). This simulated both the action of the natural transmitter (produced by connective stimulation) and of serotonin by (1) increasing the Ca^{2+} current in the action potential, (2) decreasing a K^+ conductance in the sensory cell, and (3) enhancing transmitter release from the sensory neuron terminals. Finally, Castellucci, Schwartz, Kandel, Nairn, and Greengard (1981) have shown that intracellular injection into the sensory neuron of a molecule that inhibits the activity of the protein kinase [the Walsh inhibitor (Walsh, Ashby, Gonzalez, Calkins, Fischer, & Krebs, 1971)] can prevent the development of facilitation by serotonin. Thus this model provides an excellent framework to probe further the molecular events underlying sensitization. For example, efforts are underway to demonstrate enhanced protein phosphorylation within a single sensory neuron during facilitation and to characterize the proteins that are phosphorylated (Bernier, Eppler, Kandel, Saitoh, & Schwartz, personal communication).

IV. Relationship between Simple Forms of Nonassociative and Associative Learning

The work reviewed thus far shows that insights into the cellular mechanisms underlying elementary forms of learning can be gained by combining a variety of cellular-biological approaches. A question of major interest is whether these same strategies and approaches can be brought to bear on the analysis of other more complex forms of learning. It would be especially advantageous if the same reflex system in which nonassociative learning (habituation and sensitization) has been analyzed also was capable of a simple form of associative learning. To explore this possibility Carew, Walters, and Kandel (1981b) examined whether the gill- and siphon-withdrawal reflex in *Aplysia* could be classically conditioned. A light tactile stimulus to the siphon served as the conditioned stimulus (CS); an aversive electric shock to the tail served as the unconditioned stimulus (US). Tail shock was used as the US in these studies because of a recent observation that the tail of *Aplysia* provides a powerful input pathway for gill and siphon withdrawal (Carew, Walters, & Kandel, 1981a).

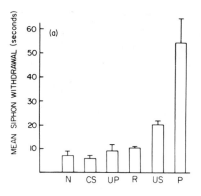
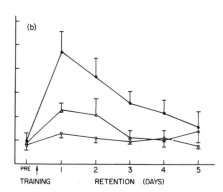

Fig. 17. Classical conditioning of the defensive withdrawal reflex. (a) Conditioned siphon withdrawal. Six groups of animals were trained: paired (P; $n = 9$), unpaired (UP; $n = 9$), random (R; $n = 8$), US alone (US; $n = 8$), CS alone (CS; $n = 9$), and naive (N; $n = 9$); retention was measured with the CS alone 24 hours later. Paired animals show significantly elevated scores compared to all other groups (see text for details). (b) Retention of conditioning. After pretraining (PRE), three groups were given 30 trials of paired (●; $n = 8$), unpaired (○; $n = 9$), or US-alone (△; $n = 8$) training (indicated by arrow) and were then tested with the CS alone once every 24 hours.

Six groups of animals were studied: (1) a *paired* group received the CS, immediately followed by the US; (2) an *unpaired* group received the CS and US specifically unpaired; (3) a *random* group received the CS in a random relationship to the US; (4) a *US-alone* group received only the US; (5) a *CS-alone* group received only the CS; and (6) a *naive* group received no training. All groups received 31 training trials with an intertrial interval of 5 minutes. The performance of all groups, as measured by the duration of siphon withdrawals in response to the CS alone, was assessed 24 hours after training (Fig. 17a). The paired group showed dramatically longer siphon withdrawals than all other groups, indicating a significant associative effect. In addition, the US-alone group showed significant sensitization, exhibiting longer siphon withdrawals than both the unpaired and random groups, which in turn were significantly elevated compared to groups that had no exposure to the US (the CS-alone and naive groups). In other experiments, we have found that the associative effect is rapidly acquired (within 15 trials) and can last for several days (Fig. 17b).

An interesting feature of the learning exhibited by *Aplysia* (Fig. 17a) is that, similar to vertebrates where certain "control" procedures actually produce different types of associative learning (Rescorla, 1967), different "control" forms of training in *Aplysia* are not ineffective (that is, produce *no* learning) but rather, they produce different forms of nonassociative learning. Thus our data are consistent with the following interpretation: (1) the CS alone and untrained groups show the lowest responses because they are not sensitized at all (having never experienced the US), and in the case of the CS alone, they may be partially habituated to the CS; (2) the random and unpaired groups are also partially habituated by exposure to the CS but are in addition sensitized by exposure to the US; thus their responses are intermediate between the CS-alone and untrained groups on the one hand, and the US-alone group on the other; (3) the US-alone group showed responses that are significantly higher than those of all the former groups, because it has had no habituation resulting from CS exposure; thus this group exhibits "pure" sensitization; (4) the paired group exhibits the greatest facilitation of all, because the US—when paired with the CS—adds to its efficacy in a nonlinear and temporally specific way. This interpretation, although consistent with all our observations, is admittedly speculative. But it has two merits: first, it provides a unifying explanation utilizing simple forms of nonassociative learning known to exist in this reflex. Second, it provides several testable hypotheses concerning the relationship between habituation, sensitization, and classical conditioning.

Our results show that the same reflex in which habituation and sensitization have been extensively analyzed also exhibits a simple form of classical conditioning. Thus it will be possible to study the relationship between simple forms of nonassociative and associative learning on the behavioral level and on several different cellular levels. Of particular interest is the relationship between sensitization and classical conditioning. Sensitization resembles classical conditioning in that it involves the enhancement of one set of responses by activity in another pathway; it differs from classical conditioning, however, in that there is no temporal requirement for activity in the two pathways. Because of these similarities, sensitization has been thought to constitute an elementary building block from which classical conditioning might be constructed (Kandel & Spencer, 1968; Razran, 1971; Wells, 1968). But the exact relationship between these forms of learning can only be resolved completely by analyzing and comparing their cellular mechanisms.

A comparison of these different types of learning on a cellular level will ultimately require an understanding of the neural circuit not only of the gill- and siphon-withdrawal reflex, but also of the neural pathways involved in the associative learning. As a step in this direction, it has been shown that (1) sensory neurons that mediate the US are located in another region of the central nervous system, the pleural ganglia (Walters, Carew, & Kandel, 1981); and (2) the US, in addition to activating gill and siphon motor neurons (Carew *et al.*, 1981a) also powerfully activates the identi-

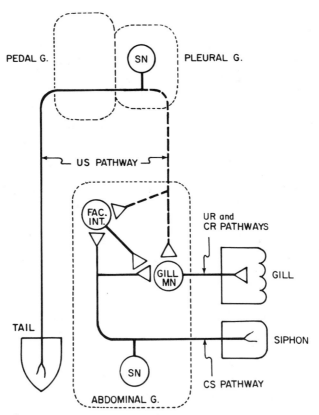

Fig. 18. Schematic wiring diagram of the neural circuits involved in conditioned gill and siphon withdrawal. Neural elements have previously been identified in the primary afferent pathways (SN, sensory neuron) for the conditioned and unconditioned stimuli (CS and US pathways) as well as in pathways that mediate the conditioned and unconditioned responses (CR and UR pathways; see text). In addition, the US pathway connects to identified facilitatory interneurons (FAC) and gill motor neurons (GILL MN) by means of one or more as-yet-unidentified interneurons (thick dashed lines). Anatomically distinct regions of the central nervous system [pedal, pleural, and abdominal ganglia (G.)] are indicated by thin dashed lines.

fied facilitatory interneurons that produce presynaptic facilitation in the sensory-to-motor synapses of the gill-withdrawal reflex (Hawkins, 1981b). Thus neurons have been identified in pathways for the CS, the US, and both the unconditioned and conditioned response (Fig. 18). These findings will greatly facilitate the search for neurons causally related to the conditioned response, which will be important not only for studying the cellular mechanisms of a simple form of associative learning, but also for comparing associative and nonassociative learning on a mechanistic level.

V. Summary and Perspectives

In this chapter I have tried to illustrate the rationale and application of a number of different cell-biological techniques to the analysis of habituation and sensitization in *Aplysia*. Using progressively more fundamental levels of analysis, these simple forms of learning have proven amenable to behavioral, cellular–physiological, biophysical, and biochemical investigation. With these combined approaches it has been possible to specify in some detail the cellular events that occur during habituation and sensitization. Both behavioral processes are produced by a modulation in the efficacy of synaptic transmission at an identified set of synapses between sensory cells and follower neurons. Both processes have been shown to be presynaptic, involving either direct or indirect modulation of calcium currents in the synaptic terminals of the sensory neurons. Finally, it has been possible to specify some of the molecular events underlying sensitization, events that involve a serotonin-mediated, cyclic AMP–dependent facilitation of transmitter release.

It should be emphasized that, although principles have emerged from the work described in this chapter concerning the cellular basis of habituation and sensitization in the defensive withdrawal reflex of *Aplysia,* this constitutes only a single instance of such an analysis in a single animal. Because habituation and sensitization constitute perhaps the most ubiquitous forms of behavioral plasticity in the animal kingdom (see, e.g., Peeke & Herz, 1973a, 1973b), it is quite likely that other cellular mechanisms have evolved to mediate these processes in other animals. It is in fact of great interest to analyze the cellular mechanisms mediating habituation and sensitization in other animals, for this permits a comparison of those aspects of cellular plasticity that are conserved across species and those that are not.

Although considerable progress has been made in the analysis of short-term habituation and sensitization in *Aplysia,* much less is known about the long-term forms of these processes. For example, we do not yet know the mechanism for long-term habituation. But we do have several important clues based on our understanding of short-term habituation: (1) both short- and long-term habituation result from synaptic depression; (2) both short- and long-term habituation share a common locus in the nervous system (the sensory-to-motor synapse), and short-term habituation at that synapse is caused by a presynaptic mechanism; and (3) both short-term

and long-term habituation can be overriden by sensitization, a process
known to occur by means of presynaptic facilitation. Thus there is cir-
cumstantial evidence to suggest that long-term habituation may also involve a presynaptic mechanism. A definitive answer to this question,
however, will require a quantal analysis of long-term depressed synapses.
The mechanisms underlying long-term sensitization also remain to be
explored. By applying a combination of the approaches described in this
chapter, it will be important to determine whether long-term sensitization
involves a prolonged facilitation of synaptic transmission and if so,
whether this process is mediated by cyclic AMP. Finally, by comparing
the mechanisms of these short- and long-term behavioral changes in synaptic, biophysical, and molecular terms, it may be possible to gain some
insight into the relationship between elementary forms of short-term and
long-term memory, at least in this simple behavioral system.

In this chapter I have restricted my review to a multileveled analysis of
habituation and sensitization carried out in *Aplysia*. But it should be
emphasized that considerable progress has also been made in several
other invertebrate animals [for review, see Horn & Hinde (1970); Peeke &
Herz (1973a, 1973b)]. For example, studies in the crayfish (Kennedy,
Selverston, & Remler, 1969; Krasne, 1969; Zucker, 1972) and in the cockroach (Callec, Guillet, Pichon, & Boistel, 1971) suggest that mechanisms
similar to those in *Aplysia* may be involved in habituation in these animals. Moreover, in addition to nonassociative learning, several invertebrates that hold promise for a cellular analysis have been shown capable
of associative learning (Crow & Alkon, 1978; Gelperin, 1975; Mptitsos &
Collins, 1975; Sahley, Gelperin, & Rudy, 1981; Walters, Carew, & Kandel,
1979), and in each of these instances correlates of the learning have been
observed in central neurons (Carew *et al.*, 1981a; Change & Gelperin,
1980; Crow & Alkon, 1980; Davis & Gillette, 1978). Thus the future for a
cellular analysis of nonassociative and associative learning in invertebrates is quite bright. It will be especially interesting, as parallel progress
is made in a number of these animals, to compare the relationship among
different forms of learning on a cellular level to determine whether some
aspects of synaptic plasticity are common to all learning or whether different forms of learning may require novel cellular mechanisms.

Acknowledgments

I am indebted to several friends and colleagues for their helpful criticism of early drafts of
this manuscript: Drs. V. Castellucci, W. Frost, E. Kandel, J. Koester, and I. Kupfermann. I
also thank K. Hilten and L. Katz for help in preparing the figures and H. Ayers for typing the
manuscript.

References

Bailey, C. H., Castellucci, V. F., Koester, J., & Kandel, E. R. Cellular studies of peripheral neurons in siphon skin of *Aplysia californica. Journal of Neurophysiology*, 1979, *42*, 530–557.

Bailey, C. H., Hawkins, R., Chen, M., & Kandel, E. R. Interneurons involved in mediation and modulation of the gill-withdrawal reflex in *Aplysia*. IV. The morphological basis of presynaptic facilitation. *Journal of Neurophysiology*, 1981, *45*, 340–360.

Brunnelli, M., Castellucci, V. F., & Kandel, E. R. Synaptic facilitation and behavioral sensitization in *Aplysia:* Possible role of serotonin and cyclic AMP. *Science*, 1976, *194*, 1178–1181.

Byrne, J., Castellucci, V. F., & Kandel, E. R. Contribution of individual mechanoreceptor sensory neurons to defensive gill-withdrawal reflex in *Aplysia. Journal of Neurophysiology*, 1978, *41*, 418–431.

Callec, J. J., Guillet, J. C., Pichon, Y., & Boistel, J. Further studies on synaptic transmission in insects. II. Relations between sensory information and its synaptic integration at the level of a single giant axon in the cockroach. *Journal of Experimental Biology*, 1971, *55*, 123–149.

Carew, T. J., Castellucci, V. F., & Kandel, E. R. An analysis of dishabituation and sensitization of the gill-withdrawal reflex in *Aplysia. International Journal of Neuroscience*, 1971, *2*, 79–98.

Carew, T. J., Castellucci, V. F., & Kandel, E. R. Sensitization in *Aplysia:* Rapid restoration of transmission in synapses inactivated by long-term habituation. *Science*, 1979, *205*, 417–419.

Carew, T. J., & Kandel, E. R. A cellular analysis of acquisition and retention of long-term habituation in *Aplysia. Science*, 1973, *182*, 1158–1160.

Carew, T. J., & Kandel, E. R. Synaptic analysis of the interrelationships between behavioral modifications in *Aplysia*. In M. V. L. Bennett (Ed.), *Transmission and neuronal interaction*. New York: Raven Press, 1974.

Carew, T. J., & Kandel, E. R. Two functional effects of decreased conductance EPSPs: Synaptic augmentation and increased electrical coupling. *Science*, 1976, *192*, 150–153.

Carew, T. J., & Kupfermann, I. The influence of different natural environments on habituation in *Aplysia californica. Behavioral Biology*, 1974, *12*, 339–345.

Carew, T. J., Pinsker, H. M., & Kandel, E. R. Long-term habituation of a defensive withdrawal reflex in *Aplysia. Science*, 1972, *175*, 451–454.

Carew, T. J., Pinsker, H., Rubinson, K., & Kandel, E. R. Physiological and biochemical properties of neuromuscular transmission between identified motoneurons and gill muscle in *Aplysia. Journal of Neurophysiology*, 1974, *37*, 1020–1040.

Carew, T. J., Walters, E. T., & Kandel, E. R. Associative learning in *Aplysia:* Cellular correlates supporting a conditioned fear hypothesis. *Science*, 1981, *211*, 501–504. (a)

Carew, T. J., Walters, W. T., & Kandel, E. R. Classical conditioning in a simple withdrawal reflex in *Aplysia. Journal of Neuroscience*, 1981, *1*, 1426–1437. (b)

Castellucci, V. F., Carew, T. J., & Kandel, E. R. Cellular analysis of long-term habituation of the gill-withdrawal reflex of *Aplysia californica. Science*, 1978, *202*, 1306–1308.

Castellucci, V. F., & Kandel, E. R. A quantal analysis of the synaptic depression underlying habituation of the gill-withdrawal reflex in *Aplysia. Proceedings of the National Academy of Sciences of the United States of America*, 1974, *71*, 5004–5008.

Castellucci, V. F., & Kandel, E. R. An invertebrate system for the cellular study of habituation and sensitization. In T. J. Tighe & R. N. Leaton (Eds.), *Habituation: Perspectives from child development, animal behavior and neurophysiology.* Hillsdale, N.J.: Lawrence Erlbaum Associates, 1976.

Castellucci, V. F., & Kandel, E. R. Presynaptic facilitation as a mechanism for behavioral sensitization in *Aplysia. Science,* 1976, *194,* 1176–1178.

Castellucci, V. F., Kandel, E. R., Schwartz, J. H., Wilson, F. D., Nairn, A. C., & Greengard, P. Intracellular injection of the catalytic subunit of cyclic AMP-dependent protein kinase simulates facilitation of transmitter release underlying behavioral sensitization in *Aplysia. Proceedings of the National Academy of Sciences of the United States of America,* 1980, *77,* 7492–7496.

Castellucci, V., Pinsker, H., Kupfermann, I., & Kandel, E. R. Neuronal mechanisms of habituation and dishabituation of the gill-withdrawal reflex in *Aplysia. Science,* 1970, *167,* 1745–1748.

Castellucci, V. F., Schwartz, J. H., Kandel, E. R., Nairn, A., & Greengard, P. Protein inhibitor of the cyclic AMP-dependent protein kinase can block the onset of, as well as reverse the electrophysiological correlates of sensitization of the gill-withdrawal in *Aplysia. Society for Neuroscience Abstracts,* 1981, *7,* 836.

Cedar, H., & Schwartz, J. H. Cyclic adenosine monophosphate in the nervous system of *Aplysia californica.* I. Increased synthesis in response to synaptic stimulation. *Journal of General Physiology,* 1972, *60,* 558–569.

Cedar, H., & Schwartz, J. H. Cyclic adenosine monophosphate in the nervous system of *Aplysia californica.* II. Effect of serotonin and dopamine. *Journal of General Physiology,* 1972, *60,* 570–587.

Chang, J. J., & Gelperin, A. Rapid taste aversion learning by an isolated molluscan central nervous system. *Proceedings of the National Academy of Sciences of the United States of America,* 1980, *77,* 6204–6206.

Cooper, J. R., Bloom, F. E., & Roth, R. H. *The biochemical basis of neuropharmacology.* London & New York: Oxford University Press, 1970.

Crow, T. J., & Alkon, D. L. Retention of an associative behavioral change in *Hermissenda. Science,* 1978, *201,* 1239–1241.

Crow, T. J., & Alkon, D. L. Associative behavioral modification in *Hermissenda:* Cellular correlates. *Science,* 1980, *209,* 412–414.

Davis, W. J., & Gillette, R. Neural correlate of behavioral plasticity in command neurons of *Pleurobranchaea. Science,* 1978, *199,* 801–804.

del Castillo, J., & Katz, B. Quantal components of the end-plate potential. *Journal of Physiology (London),* 1954, *124,* 560–573.

Eccles, J. C. *The physiology of synapses.* New York: Springer, Verlag, 1964.

Geduldig, D., & Junge, D. Sodium and calcium components of action potentials in the *Aplysia* giant neurone. *Journal of Physiology (London),* 1968, *199,* 347–365.

Gelperin, A. Rapid food-aversion learning by a terrestrial mollusk. *Science,* 1975, *189,* 567–570.

Ginsborg, B. L. Ion movements in junctional transmission. *Pharmacological Reviews,* 1967, *19,* 289–316.

Greengard, P. *Cyclic nucleotides, phosphorylated proteins, and neuronal function.* New York: Raven Press, 1978.

Hawkins, R. D. Interneurons involved in mediation and modulation of the gill-withdrawal reflex in *Aplysia.* III. Identified facilitating neurons increase the Ca^{++} current in sensory neurons. *Journal of Neurophysiology,* 1981, *45,* 327–329. (a)

Hawkins, R. D. Identified facilitating neurons are excited by cutaneous stimuli used in sensitization and classical conditioning of *Aplysia. Society for Neuroscience Abstracts,* 1981, p. 354. (b)

Hawkins, R. D., Castellucci, V. F., & Kandel, E. R. Interneurons involve in mediation and modulation of the gill-withdrawal reflex in *Aplysia*. II. Identified neurons produce heterosynaptic facilitation contributing to behavioral sensitization. *Journal of Neurophysiology*, 1981, *45*, 315–326.

Hodgkin, A. L. *The conductions of the nervous impulse*. Liverpool: Liverpool University Press, 1964.

Horn, G., & Hinde, R. N. *Short-term changes in neural activity and behavior*. London & New York: Cambridge University Press, 1970.

Kandel, E. R. *Cellular basis of behavior: An introduction to behavioral neurobiology*. San Francisco: Freeman, 1976.

Kandel, E. R. *Behavioral biology of aplysia*. San Francisco: Freeman, 1979.

Kandel, E. R., Brunelli, M., Byrne, J., & Castellucci, V. A common presynaptic locus for the synaptic changes underlying short-term habituation and sensitization of the gill-withdrawal reflex in *Aplysia*. *Cold Spring Harbor Symposia on Quantitative Biology*, 1976, *40*, 465–482.

Kandel, E. R., & Schwartz, J. H. Molecular biology of learning: Modulation of transmitter release. *Science*, 1981, *218*, 433–443.

Kandel, E. R., & Spencer, W. A. Cellular neurophysiological approaches in the study of learning. *Physiological Reviews*, 1968, *48*, 65–134.

Kandel, E. R., Tauc, L. Heterosynaptic facilitation in neurones of the abdominal ganglion of *Aplysia depilans*. *Journal of Physiology (London)*, 1965, *181*, 1–27.

Kater, S. B. Feeding in *Helisoma trivolis:* The morphological and physiological basis of a fixed action pattern. *American Zoologist*, 1974, *14*, 1017–1036.

Katz, B. *Nerve, muscle and synapse*. New York: McGraw Hill, 1966.

Katz, B. *The release of neural transmitter substances*. Springfield, Ill. Thomas, 1969.

Katz, B., & Miledi, R. A study of synaptic transmission in the absence of nerve impulses. *Journal of Physiology (London)*, 1967, *192*, 407–436.

Kennedy, D., Selverston, A. I., & Remler, M. P. Analysis of restricted neural networks. *Science*, 1969, *164*, 1488–1496.

Kientzle, M. J. Properties of learning curves under varied distributions of practice. *Journal of Experimental Psychology*, 1946, *36*, 187–211.

Kimble, G., & Shatel, R. B. The relationship between two kinds of inhibition and the amount of practice. *Journal of Experimental Psychology*, 1952, *44*, 355–359.

Kimmel, H. D. Habituation, habituability and conditioning. In H. V. S. Peeke & M. J. Herz (Eds.), *Habituation* (Vol. 1). New York: Academic Press, 1973. Pp. 219–238.

Klein, M., & Kandel, E. R. Presynaptic modulation of voltage-dependent Ca^{++} current: Mechanism for behavioral sensitization in *Aplysia californica*. *Proceedings of the National Academy of Sciences of the United States of America*, 1978, *75*, 3512–3516.

Klein, M., & Kandel, E. R. Mechanism of calcium current modulation underlying presynaptic facilitation and behavioral sensitization in *Aplysia*. *Proceedings of the National Academy of Sciences of the United States of America*, 1980, *77*, 6912–6916.

Klein, M., Shapiro, E., & Kandel, E. R. Synaptic plasticity and the modulation of the calcium current. *Journal of Experimental Biology*, 1980, *89*, 117–157.

Koester, J. Active conductances underlying the action *potential*. In E. R. Kandel & J. H. Schwartz (Eds.), *Principles of neural science*. New York: Elsevier/North-Holland, 1981. Pp. 53–62.

Krasne, F. B. Excitation and habituation of the crayfish escape reflex: The depolarizing response in lateral giant fibers of the isolated abdomen. *Journal of Experimental Biology*, 1969, *50*, 29–46.

Kriegstein, A. R., Castellucci, V. F., & Kandel, E. R. Metamorphosis of *Aplysia californica* in laboratory culture. *Proceedings of the National Academy of Sciences of the United States of America*, 1974, *71*, 3654–3658.

Kuffler, S. W., & Nicholls, J. G. *From neuron to brain*. Sunderland, Mass.: Sinauer Assoc., 1976.

Kuo, J. F., & Greengard, P. Cyclic nucleotide dependent protein kinases. IV. Widespread occurrence of adenosine 3′,5′-monophosphate-dependent protein kinase in various tissues and phyla of the animal kingdom. *Proceedings of the National Academy of Sciences of the United States of America*, 1969, *64*, 1349–1355.

Kupfermann, I., & Carew, T. J. Behavior patterns of *Aplysia californica* in its natural environment. *Behavioral Biology*, 1974, *12*, 317–337.

Kupfermann, I., Carew, T. J., & Kandel, E. R. Local, reflex, and central commands controlling gill and siphon movements in *Aplysia*. *Journal of Neurophysiology*, 1974, *37*, 996–1019.

Kupfermann, I., Castellucci, V., Pinsker, H., & Kandel, E. R. Neuronal correlates of habituation and dishabituation of the gill-withdrawal reflex in *Aplysia*. *Science*, 1970, *167*, 1743–1745.

Kupfermann, I., & Kandel, E. R. Neuronal controls of a behavioral response mediated by the abdominal ganglion of *Aplysia*. *Science*, 1969, *164*, 847–850.

MacGinitie, G. E., & MacGinitie, N. *Natural history of marine animals* (2nd ed.). New York: McGraw Hill, 1968.

Mpitsos, G. J., & Collins, S. D. Learning: Rapid aversion conditioning in the gastropod mollusk *Pleurobranchaea*. *Science*, 1975, *188*, 954–957.

Nicholls, J. G., & Purves, D. Monosynaptic chemical and electrical connexions between sensory and motor cells in the central nervous system of the leech. *Journal of Physiology*, 1970, *209*, 647–667.

Peeke, H. V. S., & Herz, M. J. (Eds.). *Habituation* (Vol. 1). New York: Academic Press, 1973. (a)

Peeke, H. V. S., & Herz, M. J. (Eds.). *Habituation* (Vol. 2). New York: Academic Press, 1973. (b)

Pinsker, H., Hening, W., Carew, T., & Kandel, E. R. Long-term sensitization of a defensive withdrawal reflex in *Aplysia*. *Science*, 1973, *182*, 1039–1042.

Pinsker, H., Kupfermann, I., Castellucci, V., & Kandel, E. Habituation and dishabituation of the gill-withdrawal reflex in *Aplysia*. *Science*, 1970, *167*, 1740–1742.

Rall, T. W., Sutherland, E. W., & Berthet, J. The relationship of epinephrine and glucagon to liver phosphorylase. IV. Effect of epinephrine and glucagon on the reactivation of phosphorylase in liver homogenates. *Journal of Biological Chemistry*, 1957, *224*, 463–475.

Razran, G. *Mind in evolution: An East–West synthesis of learned behavior and cognition*. Boston: Houghton Mifflin, 1971.

Rescorla, R. A. Pavlovian conditioning and its proper control procedures. *Psychological Reviews*, 1967, *74*, 71–80.

Robison, G. A., Butcher, R. W., & Sutherland, E. W. *Cyclic AMP*. New York: Academic Press, 1971.

Sahley, C. L., Gelperin, A., & Rudy, J. W. One-trial associative learning in a terrestrial mollusc. *Proceedings of the National Academy of Sciences of the United States of America*, 1981, *78*, 640–642.

Sharpless, S., & Jasper, H. Habituation of the arousal reaction. *Brain*, 1956, *79*, 655–680.

Spencer, W. A., Thompson, R. F., & Neilson, D. R., Jr. Response decrement of the flexion reflex in the acute spinal cat and transient restoration by strong stimuli. *Journal of Neurophysiology*, 1966, *29*, 221–239.

Spira, M., & Bennett, M. V. L. Synaptic control of electrotonic coupling between neurons. *Brain Research,* 1972, *37,* 294–300.

Stevens, C. F. *Neurophysiology: A primer.* New York: Wiley, 1966.

Stinnakre, J., & Tauc, L. Calcium influx in active *Aplysia* neurones detected by injected acquorin. *Nature (London) New Biology,* 1973, *242,* 113–115.

Sutherland, E. W., Øye, I., & Butcher, R. W. The action of epinephrine and the role of the adenyl cyclase system in hormone action. *Recent Progress in Hormone Research,* 1965, *21,* 623–646.

Sutherland, E. W., & Rall, T. W. The properties of an adenine ribonucleotide produced with cellular particles, ATP, Mg^{++}, and epinephrine or glucagon. *Journal of the American Chemical Society,* 1957, *79,* 3608.

Thompson, R. F., & Spencer, W. A. Habituation: A model phenomenon for the study of neuronal substrates of behavior. *Psychological Reviews,* 1966, *173,* 16–43.

Walsh, D. A., Ashby, C. D., Gonzalez, C., Calkins, D., Fischer, E. H., & Krebs, E. G. Purification and characterization of a protein inhibitor of adenosine 3',5'-monophosphate-dependent protein kinase. *Journal of Biological Chemistry,* 1971, *246,* 1977–1985.

Walters, E. T., Carew, T. J., & Kandel, E. R. Classical conditioning in *Aplysia californica. Proceedings of the National Academy of Sciences of the United States of America,* 1979, *76,* 6675–6679.

Walters, E. T., Carew, T. J., & Kandel, E. R. Associative learning in *Aplysia:* Evidence for conditioned fear in an invertebrate. *Science,* 1981, *211,* 504–506.

Wells, M. F. Sensitization and the evolution of associative learning. In J. Salanki (Ed.), *Symposium of neurobiology of invertebrates.* New York: Plenum, 1968. Pp. 391–411.

Willows, A. O. D. Behavioral acts elicited by stimulation of single identifiable nerve cells. In F. D. Carlson (Ed.), *Physiological and biochemical aspects of nervous integration.* Englewood Cliffs, N.J.: Prentice-Hall, 1968. Pp. 217–243.

Zucker, R. S. Crayfish escape behavior and central synapses. II. Physiological mechanisms underlying behavioral habituation. *Journal of Neurophysiology,* 1972, *35,* 621–637.

CHAPTER 7

Habituation of Central Nervous System Evoked Potentials: Intrinsic Habituation Examined in Neocortex, Allocortex, and Mesencephalon

T. J. Teyler
N. Chiaia
P. DiScenna

Neurobiology Program
Northeastern Ohio Universities College of Medicine
Rootstown, Ohio

R. A. Roemer

Health Sciences Center
Temple University
Philadelphia, Pennsylvania

I. Introduction

The study of habituation and sensitization at the neuronal level has provided insights into the ontogenetic and phylogenetic distribution of the phenomenon (Horn & Hinde, 1970; Peeke & Herz, 1973a, 1973b; Teyler, 1978; Tighe & Leaton, 1976). Of specific interest to neurobiologists is the

Supported in part by research grants (to T.J.T.) from the NSF and the NIH.

HABITUATION, SENSITIZATION,
AND BEHAVIOR

localization of regions that show habituation and sensitization within the brain. Knowledge of which structures display habituation–sensitization is important in understanding the role of habituation–sensitization in brain function and ultimately in understanding the neural mechanisms governing the phenomenon.

The study of the neural distribution of habituation–sensitization is made difficult by uncertainties about whether the response decrement recorded at some location is occurring there or has occurred elsewhere and is merely being reproduced at the recording site (Teyler & Alger, 1976). This potential problem becomes more serious the farther from the periphery one samples activity, culminating in responses recorded from the cerebral cortex. For example, studies of neuronal habituation–sensitization have indicated that cortical responses to peripheral stimuli do decrement with repeated stimulus presentations (these decrements, however, may or may not represent habituation; see Roemer et al., Chapter 9). Peripheral stimuli, ranging from simple, nonpatterned sensory stimulation (Callaway, 1973; Westenberg & Weinberger, 1976) to the relatively more complicated stimulation provided by linguistic and cognitive stimuli (Megela & Teyler, 1979), do indeed display a response decrement that displays some, if not all, of the parametric features of habituation–sensitization (Thompson & Spencer, 1966).

These results, however, must not be interpreted as evidence that the phenomena of habituation–sensitization have a cortical locus. It could be, for instance, that the actual response decrement occurs in subcortical structures and that the cortical response faithfully reproduces the decremented signal it receives. Alternately, the intrinsic properties of the cortex may support habituation–sensitization at the cellular level.

Much of the work on the neural aspects of habituation–sensitization suggests that different anatomical structures are responsible for different aspects of the response. In the cat spinal cord, Thompson and colleagues (Groves & Thompson, 1970) reported that different interneurons are concerned with habituating responses (type-H cells) and sensitizing responses (type-S cells). The sum of these two processes is imposed upon the alpha motoneuron for behavioral output. In *Aplysia*, Kandel and colleagues (Klein & Kandel, 1978) provided strong evidence that the cellular locus of habituation and sensitization are different and that different neurochemical systems are involved in the two facets of the behavioral response. In both cases, this anatomical dichotomy was not revealed by measuring the activity of the final output stage, motoneuron or gill, but was provided by a finer analysis of the neural elements in the system. These findings point out that the analysis of habituation–sensitization must be taken to the tissue and cellular level to begin dissecting the dynamics of the neural systems involved. In keeping with its postulated role in filtering out repetitive, nonmeaningful information from higher processing (Glass & Singer, 1972; Thompson & Glanzman, 1976), one might suppose that habituation occurs at relatively peripheral loci in the nervous system. Such a role would free cortical circuitry from this task and would allow it to specialize in other, presumably more sophisticated forms of information processing. Similarly, one might expect that sensitization could be mediated by a noncortical anatomical system as postulated in the dual-process theory (Groves & Thompson, 1970). With these considerations in mind, we examined the distribution of central nervous system (CNS) habituation–sensitization at the tissue–cellular level.

To accurately assess the tissue–cellular capability of a brain structure to exhibit habituation–sensitization one must be sure that the response dynamics observed at the recording site are not the result of extrinsic driving, neuromodulation, or any other extrinsic influence. This can be done (with difficulty) in intact preparations, but we chose the brain-slice techniques for these studies. The many advantages of the brain slice have been considered elsewhere (Andersen, 1981; Lynch & Schubert, 1980; Teyler, 1980). For the present purpose the brain slice's freedom from extrinsic influences is its most compelling feature.

To catalog the ability of every brain loci to demonstrate habituation–sensitization would require more than the authors' lifetimes combined and a chapter much longer than the present one. Even if such an undertaking were possible, it might not necessarily be the best use of one's time. Ultimately, we wish to understand the role of habituation–sensitization in brain function and behavior and to learn of the neural mechanisms underlying this variety of response plasticity. A catalog of plastic regions of the brain would help to achieve this goal. Therefore, we decided to examine several anatomically and embryologically distinct brain regions to see to what degree they displayed habituation–sensitization according to standard parametric criteria (Groves & Thompson, 1970). The regions chosen were the rat neocortex (as represented by cortical slices obtained primarily from dorsomedial parietal and occipital lobes), the rat allocortex (as represented by hippocampal slices), and the teleost mesencephalon (as represented by the goldfish optic-tectal explant.

II. The Experimental Preparations

In all experiments reported here, isolated and surgically reduced portions of the CNS have been employed. The hippocampal slice preparation is well known (Lynch & Schubert, 1980; Skrede & Westgaard, 1971;

Teyler, 1980). The neocortical slice preparation and the goldfish optic-tectal explant, however, are relatively new preparations and require a more complete description. Because many of the features of the hippo-campal slice preparation are carried over into the two other preparations, we briefly describe the hippocampal slice preparation and then use this as a basis for the two newer preparations.

A. The Hippocampal Slice: Allocortex

Hippocampal slices are prepared by slicing the grossly dissected hippo-campus along the plane of the transverse lamellae (Skrede & Westgaard, 1971). Such an approach preserves the intrinsic anatomy of the functional lamellae of the hippocampus and dentate gyrus. Contained within the hippocampal slice is a trisynaptic circuit that has major origins in the entorhinal cortex and medial septal nucleus. Fibers from cells in the en-torhinal cortex (which generally is not retained in the hippocampal slice) form the perforant path that project to the molecular layer of the dentate gyrus granule cells. These synaptic contacts, like the others in the main circuit, are *en passage* excitatory monosynaptic connections that are thought to be glutaminergic. Stimulation of the perforant path fibers gives rise to an evoked discharge in a population of dentate granule cells. Be-cause of the geometry of the hippocampal formation, with its tightly packed layer of cell bodies and homogeneously oriented dendritic pro-cesses, it is possible to obtain extracellular measures of the population postsynaptic potential (PSP) and population spike. Field-potential record-ings of these population responses are well understood (Andersen, Bliss, & Skrede, 1970) and are commonly used to obtain a reflection of the technically more difficult intracellular recordings. Figure 1 shows a dia-grammatic representation of a hippocampal slice with recording and stim-ulating electrodes in the dentate granule cells and perforant path, respec-tively. A second pair of electrodes are located in the CA1 region of the hippocampus.

Dentate granule-cell axons, known as mossy fibers, project to the CA3 area of the hippocampus where they form monosynaptic, excitatory con-tacts with the apical dendrites of the CA3 pyramidal cells. The CA3 cells, in turn, project to the CA1 region within the slice, and to the septum and contralateral hippocampus. The latter targets are, of course, not present in the hippocampal slice preparation. The CA3 axons projecting to the CA1 area are known as the Schaffer collaterals. The contact is, again, monosynpatic, *en passage*, and excitatory. The axons of the CA1 area project to the subiculum, the septum, and other extraslice targets. This,

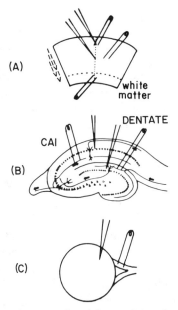

Fig. 1. The three preparations employed for studying the intrinsic tissue–cellular habituating and sensitizing properties of CNS structures. Each preparation represents an attempt to isolate a region of brain from influence by the other structures to which it is connected and from other, more general, neuromodulatory influences. In all, eight regions were examined to determine the degree to which each conformed to the theoretical predictions of Groves and Thompson's (1970) parametric description of habituation. (A) Neocortex. The cortical slice. White matter → Layer IV, white matter → Layer II, Layer II → Layer IV, Layer IV → Layer IV. (B) Allocortex. The hippocampal slice. Schaffer collaterals → CA1, perforant path → dentate, mossy fiber → CA3. (C) Midbrain. The goldfish optic-tectum explant. Optic nerve → optic tectum.

then, is the trisynaptic pathway of the hippocampal slice. Also present in the hippocampal slice are inhibitory neurons in each of the hippocampal-formation subfields. These γ-aminobutyric acid– (GABA) releasing interneurons are recurrent to the principal cells of the dentate gyrus and hippocampus [see Swanson, Teyler, & Thompson (1982) for a more detailed review of hippocampal anatomy]. Not preserved in a hippocampal slice are numerous and little-understood associational fiber systems that travel roughly normal to the lamellar plane.

B. The Cortical Slice: Neocortex

The physiology of the *in vitro* cortical slice of rat has been described in some detail (Shaw & Teyler, 1982). In brief, the dorsomedial aspects of the occipital and parietal lobes, including Area 17, are extirpated and sliced coronally. Slices so prepared display population responses similar to those seen *in vivo*. That is, on stimulation of the white matter, evoked responses are detected in various layers of the radially oriented cortical module. These responses display polarity inversions and have waveform patterns like those seen in intact preparations. In addition, stimulation of other regions in the cortical slice gives rise to other identifiable responses.

It should be emphasized that we were unable to selectively stimulate afferents in these experiments. For example, in stimulating the white matter and recording in superficial cortical layers, we record both the postsynaptic activity evoked by afferent stimulation as well as antidromic activity elicited by the concurrent stimulation of pyramidal cell efferents. Such antidromic activation is relatively easy to discriminate in the field potential by its latency, waveshape, and frequency-following characteristics. But, the subsequent synaptic events caused by antidromic collateral activation of postsynaptic elements are much more difficult to discriminate. Given the heterogeneity of organization of the cortex, it is apparent that the activation of antidromic collaterals is a potential impediment to interpretation of evoked waveforms from the cortical slice. We are engaged in experiments to isolate the components of the evoked population response.

In the cortical slice, which can be seen in Fig. 1 "lying on its side," we can also record the Layer-II response to white-matter stimulation and the Layer-IV response to lateral stimulation within Layer IV. Thus, with the recording and stimulating configurations described, we can activate the major modular inputs to the cortex from thalamus, homotopic cortex (callosal fibers), and ipsilateral association fibers by stimulating the white matter. We have also found that the intramodular pathway from Layer II to Layer IV elicits a large and consistent postsynaptic response when stimulating Layer II and recording from Layer IV. This pathway is presumably involved in the intrinsic processing of information at the modular or columnar level.

The one extramodular input, intrinsic to the cortex, that we have studied in this experiment is the response recorded in Layer-IV-to-Layer-IV stimulation. Given our orientation in slicing the cortex, this is a medial–lateral plane *in situ*. The results obtained with this electrode configuration suggest to us that these responses may be largely inhibitory influences imposed on the target module by neighboring modules, analogous to a center-surround inhibition as seen in retina and geniculate. These responses were markedly affected by bicuculline, a drug with known antagonistic effects on GABAminergic transmission.

These four intrinsic pathways were examined for the parameters of habituation in this experiment. From previous physiological experiments, we have determined that the white-matter-to-Layer-IV response is mono-synaptic (Shaw & Teyler, 1982). The necessary experiments to define the nature of the other intracortical pathways have not yet been performed. On the basis of incomplete knowledge it appears that each intracortical pathway displays both mono- and polysynaptic components. Their exact nature awaits further study.

C. The Goldfish Optic-Tectum Explant: Mesencephalon

The mesencephalic structure examined for the properties of habituation and sensitization was the goldfish optic tectum. We have devised methods of maintaining the goldfish tectum *in vitro* and have described its baseline physiology (Teyler, Lewis, & Shashoua, 1981) and its ability to demon-strate long-term potentiation (Lewis, Teyler, & Shashoua, 1981; Swanson *et al.*, 1982). The teleost optic tectum is a complex laminated structure shaped as a 400-μm-thick hemisphere floating above the ventricular space. Functionally, this structure receives a powerful sensory input from the optic nerves. It has been the subject of much research dealing with reinnervation following optic nerve crush (Yoon, 1975). Important sen-sory input is also provided the tectum from somatosensory and lateral-line sensory systems (Vanegas, Laufer, & Amat, 1974). The anatomical organization is reminiscent of cortical tissue with which it can be con-trasted in terms of its embryological origins and its connectivity. In the fish, the tectum plays a very important role in visual information process-ing and sensory integration.

The teleost optic tectum is prepared for *in vitro* examination by cutting the tectum's connectives to the retina, dorsal tegmentum, and contralat-eral tectum. A tectum, thus freed, is handled much the same as a brain slice. The important difference is that the tissue itself is not sliced. The connectives are severed, but the tectum is placed in the tissue chamber intact.

Our previous studies have shown that the tectal explant displays nor-mal physiological responses to stimulation of the optic nerves. Concur-rent biochemical studies determined that both RNA and protein synthesis are actively maintained *in vitro*. In experiments on the tectal explant, stimulating electrodes were inserted into the optic nerve stump remaining on the explanted tectum. A recording electrode measured the evoked monosynaptic field response of neurons in the *stratum fibrosum et gri-seum superficiale*. Such an electrode configuration permits the simultaneous recording of the afferent fiber volley, the monosynaptic response, and a longer latency, more variable, polysynaptic response. In this experiment we analyzed in detail only the monosynaptic response. We did note, however, that the amplitude and latency of the afferent volley was not altered by our procedures, indicating that the responses observed were not caused by alterations in fiber sensitivity. Figure 1 shows a diagrammatic representation of the goldfish optic-tectum explant preparation.

III. Tissue Preparation

A. Hippocampus

The results of the hippocampal habituation experiment have been published, and a more complete description of the methods and results can be found there (Teyler & Alger, 1976). A detailed accounting of the hippocampal slice preparation can be obtained in Teyler (1980).

Reported here are the results of experiments performed on 45 hippocampal slices obtained from 22 adult Sprague–Dawley or Lashley rats. Following rapid cervical dislocation, the hippocampus was dissected free and 400-μm-thick slices were cut on a tissue-sectioning machine [Stoelting Co.; Duffy & Teyler (1975)] in the plane of the functional hippocampal lamellae. The slices were transferred to a tissue chamber where they were maintained on a nylon net at the interface of 36°C medium (Earles BSS) saturated with warmed, humid gas (95:5%, $O_2:CO_2$). Slices were prepared in about 5 minutes, and the experiments were begun after a 30- to 60-minute period of equilibration.

Recording and stimulating electrodes were placed in the dentate gyrus, Area CA3 and Area CA1. Stimulating electrodes were 400-μm-diameter concentric bipolar electrodes placed in the perforant path, mossy fiber system, and Schaffer collaterals, respectively. Population recordings were made with electrolytically sharpened, insulated, stainless steel insect pins with a 10-to-15-μm exposed tip. In each case the monosynaptic afferents to the target cells were stimulated. Recordings were taken from the cell-body layer and the dendritic synaptic layer. It was discovered that only the response of the dentate granule cells displayed habituation (Alger & Teyler, 1976); data from the other regions, therefore, will not be reproduced here. Areas CA3 and CA1 failed to display a response decrement to repetitive stimulation of their afferents in the range of intensities and frequencies found effective for the dentate gyrus. In the dentate gyrus, response decrements were observed at frequencies ranging from $\frac{1}{10}$ to 1 per second and at various intensities, as will be discussed in the next section of this chapter. Details of the algorithm used to measure the population excitatory postsynaptic potentials (EPSPs) and population spikes are found in Teyler and Alger (1976) and Alger and Teyler (1976).

B. Neocortex

Ten cortical slices were prepared from adult Long–Evans rats. Animals were anesthetized by hypothermia, which also slows cortical metabolism, decreasing oxygen requirements during tissue preparation. Following anesthesia the dorsal surface of the brain was exposed and the dorsal parieto-occipital cortex removed by sharpened spatula. The cortex was coronally sectioned on a tissue-sectioning machine at 400-μm thickness. Experiments began 1 hour after placing the slices in the same tissue chamber used for hippocampal slice studies. Cortical slices were maintained in the same medium and atmosphere as hippocampal slices. The cortical slices, however, were maintained at 34–35°C and were supplied with a higher rate of O_2–CO_2 flow.

Concentric bipolar stimulating electrodes (400-μm diameter) were placed in the white matter, in Layer II, and laterally in Layer IV. Micropipette recording electrodes (1–3 Mohms, 2 M NaCl) were positioned in Layers IV and II, as indicated in Fig. 1. The typical response to stimulation consisted of a short-latency fiber volley or antidromic activation, followed by a presumptive monosynaptic response. A slower wave is often seen following the monosynaptic response (see Fig. 2a). This response is much more variable in amplitude and latency and may represent polysynaptic activation of the target population. In all cases, only the presumed monosynaptic response was analyzed. Response magnitude was measured in the same manner as used for hippocampal population activity (Alger & Teyler, 1976).

C. Tectum

Data from 24 tecta supplied by 18 Comet goldfish weighing between 2.5 and 4.5 grams were included in this experiment. Details of the surgical preparation of the goldfish tectum can be found in Teyler *et al.* (1981). The isolated tecta were placed in a standard hippocampal tissue chamber. The tecta were incubated in Tyrodes media, diluted 2 : 1 with distilled water or with a similar incubation media. The tectal explants were exposed to a 99 : 1%, O_2 : CO_2 atmosphere and were maintained at 21°C.

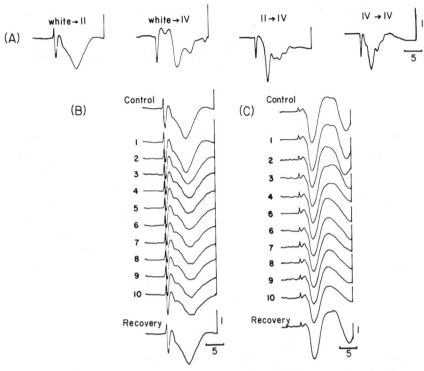

Fig. 2. (A) Examples of the waveforms recorded from the four intracortical pathways studied (neocortex). Responses are single field potentials to afferent stimulation. (B, C) Examples of response decrements to repeated afferent stimulation in the white-matter-to-layer-II recordings in the neocortical slice preparation (B) and in the optic-nerve (stimulation)-to-goldfish-optic-tectum (recording)-explant preparation (C). Both responses quickly declined about 30% to repeated stimulation and recovered within about 30 seconds.

Bipolar tungsten electrodes (tip spacing: 400–700 μm) were placed into the optic nerve stump. The tectal surface was mapped for the location giving the largest response. The recording electrode, a micropipette (1–3 Mohms, 2 *M* NaCl), was lowered 100 μm into the tectum at the point of maximal-evoked response amplitude. The magnitude of the response was measured from baseline to peak negativity.

IV. Experimental Design

In this series of experiments on three different experimental preparations, each with its own characteristics, we attempted to employ a uni-

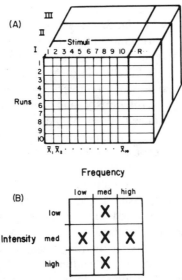

Fig. 3. (A) Five of the nine parameters of habituation were tested with a block experimental design. A block consisted of 10 runs; each run consisted of 10 stimulus presentations. Within a block, all 100 stimuli were presented at the same intensity and frequency. Between runs, a single stimulus was introduced at various times to test for spontaneous recovery. Average block values for Stimuli 1 $(\bar{x}_1)$, 2 $(\bar{x}_2)$, and so on, were computed across runs. (B) By combining five blocks, the parameters of the effects of intensity and frequency could be tested.

form experimental design. We were not completely successful, in that differences in response dynamics between the preparations mitigated against applying absolutely identical treatments to all. Given this, we attempted to apply the same relative treatments to all tissues. For example, the absolute frequencies of stimulation varied between $\frac{1}{10}$ and 1 per second for the dentate gyrus, whereas frequencies between $\frac{1}{2}$ and 2 per second were used for the cortical-slice and tectal explant. In each case, three frequencies were employed with the following approximate relationship within the three frequencies selected: $\frac{1}{2}x$, x, and $2x$.

The basic experimental design is shown in Figure 3a. In most instances a block design was used to examine the habituating properties of the tissue. A block consisted of ten runs. Each run was ten stimulus presentations at a particular intensity and frequency. All of the 100 stimuli within a block were presented at the same intensity and frequency. A fixed period of time elapsed between succeeding runs, generally 30 or 60 seconds, as was determined by the time required for spontaneous recovery between runs. Generally, three or more replications of each block were done.

Responses to the first, second, etc., stimuli were averaged across the runs of a block ($\bar{x}_1$, $\bar{x}_2$, etc. in Fig. 3a). Averaging was done to control for variability in the evoked response from moment to moment.

During the time between runs, single stimuli were presented at one of the following times: 5, 10, 20, 30, 40, or 50 seconds. This allowed us to chart the course of spontaneous recovery over time by constructing a composite recovery curve (obviously, one cannot probe recovery continuously on each trial, because to do so would keep the response at or near the habituated level). Results were normalized by expressing the response as a percentage of the response to the first stimulus. Exceptions to this procedure were noted when they occurred.

Figure 3b depicts how the effects of stimulus frequency and intensity were examined. For each tissue, three frequencies were chosen—on the basis of pilot experiments—as lying within the range of responsivity of the particular tissue. For the cortical slice and tectum the frequencies were $\frac{1}{2}$, 1, and 2 per second. For the hippocampus, the frequencies were $\frac{1}{10}$, $\frac{1}{5}$, and 1 per second. Stimulus intensities were selected for each individual preparation by first determining an input–output relationship. An input–output relationship or curve expresses response magnitude as a function of stimulus intensity. Once the input–output curve was determined, we selected stimulus intensities corresponding to a fixed percentage of the response magnitude for each preparation. Thus the absolute stimulus intensities varied for each preparation, but the relative magnitudes were identical. This manipulation controls for variability in tissue excitability and electrode placement among preparations.

For the cortical slice and the tectal explant, the stimulus intensities selected for the low, medium, and high values were 25, 50, and 75% of the input–output ranges, respectively. For the hippocampal slice, the same respective values were 20, 60, and 100%. Not all combinations were tested (Fig. 3b). Essentially, three stimulus frequencies were tested at one stimulus intensity, and three stimulus intensities were tested at one stimulus frequency. Because five blocks are contained within this design, each replication contained 5×100 stimuli plus recovery stimulations.

Completion of the five-block design provides data relevant to 5 of the 9 parameters of Thompson and Spencer (1966). They are (1) the time course of habituation, (2) spontaneous recovery, (3) habituation of habituation, (4) the effect of stimulus frequency, and (5) the effect of stimulus intensity. Habituation theory (Thompson & Spencer, 1966), and, in particular, the dual-process theory (Groves & Thompson, 1970) predicts the nature of the response to each of these parameters. The predictions are as follows. *Parameter (1)*, the time course of habituation: repeated stimulus presentations result in a progressive response decrement that is a negative exponential function of the number of stimulus presentations. *Parameter*

(*2*), spontaneous recovery: the response recovers fully over time if the stimulus is withheld. *Parameter* (*3*), habituation of habituation: given repeated series of habituating stimuli and spontaneous recovery, the habituation becomes progressively more rapid and/or pronounced. *Parameter* (*4*), the effect of stimulus frequency: with other factors constant, the higher the stimulus frequency the more rapid and/or pronounced the habituation. *Parameter* (*5*), the effect of stimulus intensity: with other factors constant, the weaker the stimulus the more rapid and/or pronounced the habituation (Teyler & Alger, 1976).

The remaining parameters are not contained within the five-block design and were investigated separately using medium values of stimulus frequency and intensity. *Parameter* (*6*), below zero habituation: prediction—additional habituation training given after asymptotic habituation results in slower recovery. This parameter was tested by presenting 10 or 40 repetitive stimuli and testing for partial recovery at fixed intervals. Habituation theory would predict delayed recovery following the presentation of 40 stimuli. *Parameter* (*7*), stimulus generalization, was not tested in these preparations for three reasons. The first reason relates to theoretical difficulties in applying to nervous tissue a concept from behavioral studies. Stimulus generalization, as generally used, refers to variations in stimulus positions along a continuum of pitch, brightness, loudness, and so forth. In a monosynaptic system, the only stimulus variations possible deal with intensity and frequency, already covered in Parameters (4) and (5). The alternative might be to activate another neural system projecting to the same population of neurons. The difficulty here and the second reason for not doing so, is in assuring that the second set of afferents is theoretically analogous to the kinds of stimulus variations along a continuum seen in behavioral stimulus generalization. The third reason for not investigating stimulus generalization dealt with the difficulty in reliably locating a second set or subset of afferents in some preparations.

Parameters (8) and (9) deal with sensitization and habituation of sensitization. Habituation theory predicts that the presentation of a more intense or different stimulus imbedded in a series of habituating stimuli results in a full or partial recovery (dishabituation) of the habituated response. Repeated presentations of the sensitizing stimulus will result in a progressive decrement of the sensitized response. See Chapter 9 by Roemer *et al.* (this volume) for an extensive consideration of dishabituation. These parameters were tested by interpolating a high-frequency (200 per second for 100 msec) train of stimuli between two habituation stimuli after response asymptote was reached. The response to the following habituation stimuli was examined for a recovery of the original response.

In dealing with heretofore-unexamined tissue for the presence of habituation–sensitization, we were particularly sensitive to the major alternate outcome. That outcome was that the tissue under study does not display the properties of habituation–sensitization. What, then, are the criteria for reaching such a conclusion? We have chosen the parametric criteria of Thompson and Spencer (1976), but does this mean that the tissue response must conform to *all* of the defined parameters? What about response patterns that fit most, but not all, of the tested criteria? Are they to be considered to fail to demonstrate habituation, or is it necessary to propose the existence of alternate forms of habituation–sensitization?

Clearly, this is an important distinction that focused our attention on the ability of the various parameters to discriminate habituation from other varieties of response decrement, particularly fatigue or fatigue-like processes. By fatigue or fatigue-like processes we refer to response decrements caused by neurotransmitter unavailability, receptor blockade, and the like. With this in mind one would predict exact parallels between habituation and fatigue for Parameters (1), (2), (4), and (6). Parameter (3) may hold if the fatigue process has a nonlinear, prolonged recovery. Parameter (7) is inapplicable. This leaves Parameters (5), (8), and (9) as critical. Under fatigue, one would expect a direct, not inverse, relationship to stimulus intensity, although even in habituating systems relative measures of habituation may not display this relationship (Farel, Glanzman & Thompson, 1973). Sensitization, then, remains a critical test for distinguishing a central fatigue or fatigue-like state from habituation. Although here too one is cautioned to consider that in a monosynaptic system a sensitizing stimulus in the form of an interpolated high-frequency stimulus train may be functionally equivalent to increasing, for a brief time, stimulus frequency. We return to these considerations later.

V. Results: Intrinsic Habituation in the Central Nervous System

The results of experiments on each brain structure are presented in terms of the parametric criteria of habituation–sensitization as outlined by Thompson and Spencer (1966). Because Parameter (7), stimulus generalization, was not tested, it will not be included in the results.

A. Allocortical Habituation: The Hippocampal Slice

1. Time Course of Habituation

Figure 4 presents the results of a 1-per-second stimulation on the dentate population EPSP and population spike. The left-hand portion of Fig.

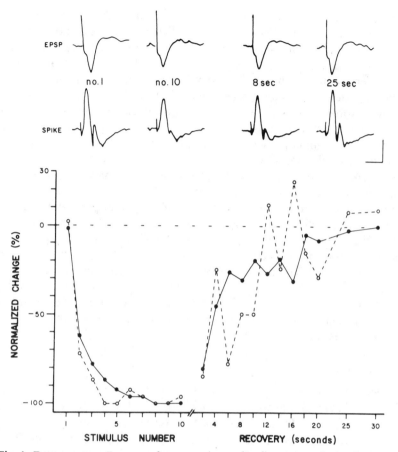

Fig. 4. Dentate gyrus. Response decrement (normalized) to repeated stimulation and spontaneous recovery following termination of the repetitive stimulation. Both the relative population EPSP (●) and population spike magnitude (○) decremented and recovered similarly. Single waveforms are shown above. From Teyler & Alger (1976).

4 plots the negative exponential decline in response amplitude to ten repetitive stimuli. Responses are normalized to allow a comparison of the dynamics of the population EPSP and spike data. The normalization procedure expresses the responses as a percentage of the maximal habituation obtained for each measure. As Fig. 4 shows, the population EPSP and population-spike measures are very similar.

The absolute magnitude of the response decrement is quite different for the two response measures, even though the normalized functions are similar. The absolute magnitude of the EPSP decrement—measured at asymptote—is about 70%, expressed as a percentage of prestimulus-control response level. That is, the response magnitude decrements to about 70% of control levels. The comparable value for the population spike is a decrement to 45% of control. These data indicate a significant nonlinearity in the coupling between the population EPSP and the population spike, an observation that holds for the relative changes seen on these two measures during long-term potentiation as well (Swanson *et al.*, 1982).

The responses decrement to asymptotic values very quickly, within 4-to-6 stimulus presentations. These values are quite rapid compared to the number of stimulus presentations required to reach asymptote in other systems. In behavioral systems, for example, hundreds of stimulus presentations may be required before asymptote is achieved (Hinde, 1970; Thompson, Groves, Teyler & Roemer, 1973). In studies of human sensory-evoked potential habituation, 50–100 stimulus presentations typically are required to demonstrate asymptotic response levels (Callaway, 1973; Naatanen, 1975). Similarly, the cat hindlimb flexion response habituates to asymptote after more than 50–100 stimulus presentations (Groves, Lee, & Thompson, 1969). Data more comparable to that obtained from dentate gyrus is generated from the ventral-root response to dorsal-root stimulation in the isolated frog spinal cord (Farel *et al.*, 1973). In this system, response asymptote is typically achieved after 4-to-8 stimulus presentations.

2. Spontaneous Recovery

Spontaneous recovery in the dentate gyrus occurs within 30 seconds (Fig. 4). Again, the normalized range-corrected data for the population EPSP and population spike indicate no differences in rates of spontaneous recovery for these two response measures. A composite recovery function was obtained by pooling the recovery data from each stimulus run. Clearly, spontaneous recovery occurs rapidly in this system, as might be predicted from the rapidity of the response decrement to repeated stimulation.

3. Habituation of Habituation

The dentate granule cell-population response [not shown here; see Teyler & Alger (1976)] displays habituation of habituation. Five runs (each consisting of 10 stimuli) of 1-per-second stimulation were presented, with 30 seconds between runs. Both the slope and the asymptotic level of habituation became increasingly negative across runs. The slope of the population EPSP and spike habituation curves, as determined in the responses to the first four stimuli of Runs 1, 3, and 5, are as follows: EPSP, -8.1, -8.4, and -10.5; spike, -12.9, -18.8, and -22.3. A similar trend

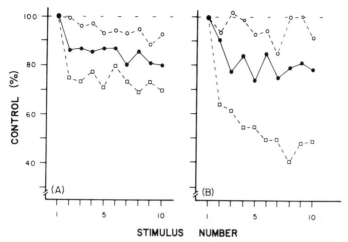

Fig. 5. Dentate gyrus. The effect of stimulus frequency on the dentate population EPSP (A) and spike (B) to repeated stimulation. As predicted by habituation theory, there was a direct relationship between stimulus frequency (O, $\frac{1}{10}$; ●, $\frac{1}{5}$; □, 1) and the magnitude of the response decrement. From Teyler & Alger (1976).

was seen for the average response amplitudes achieved over Stimuli 6–10. Asymptotic amplitude (percentage of control response) declined; that is, habituation became more pronounced across Runs 1, 3, and 5. The values were: EPSP, 72, 67.8, and 67.8%; spike, 40, 24.8, and 27.6%. The data also suggest that the habituation of habituation function approximated a negatively accelerating exponential function. These data are consistent with the predictions of habituation theory.

4. Effect of Frequency

Figure 5 presents population EPSP and spike responses as a function of repetitive stimulation at low ($\frac{1}{10}$ per second), medium ($\frac{1}{5}$ per second), and high (1 per second) frequencies. The number of stimuli presented was 10 in each case. Data are mean values from four replications and are expressed as a percentage of the response to the initial stimulus. The degree of response decrement is directly related to stimulus frequency for both the population EPSP and the population-spike data. Thus this data are consistent with the theoretical predictions of habituation theory.

It should be noted that the application of stimulus frequencies higher than 8 per second to this tissue will result in a response facilitation known as frequency potentiation (Alger & Teyler, 1976). Furthermore, repeated application of frequencies of 15 per second for 10 seconds or the single application of a higher frequency train (100 per second for 1 second) will

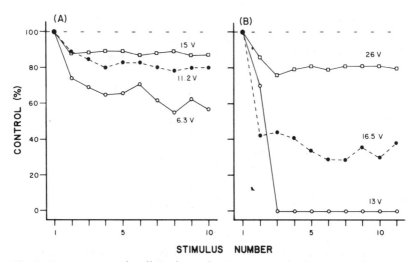

Fig. 6. Dentate gyrus. The effect of stimulus intensity on the dentate population EPSP (A) and spike response (B) to repeated stimulation. An inverse relationship was seen between stimulus intensity and the magnitude of the response decrement, as predicted by habituation theory. Intensity: 100%, □; 60%, ●; 20% ○. From Teyler & Alger (1976).

often lead to the development of long-term potentiation (LTP) (Alger & Teyler, 1976; Douglas & Goddard, 1975). There are also short-term consequences of stimulation at these higher frequencies. Posttetanic potentiation (PTP) can be observed immediately after the cessation of the stimulus train (Harris & Teyler, 1983); a heterosynaptic depression is often observed after 33-per-second stimulation (Alger, Megela & Teyler, 1978). Thus, the dentate gyrus displays quite a range of responses to stimuli differing in frequency. At low frequency, driving habituation ensues; at moderate frequencies, LTP, PTP, and, often, heterosynaptic depression are observed. But at high-frequency stimulation, LTP is more pronounced, PTP is still present, and heterosynaptic depression is no longer seen. These phenomena are each represented variously on a frequency continuum, and it follows that interactions among them are probable.

5. Effect of Intensity

Typical data relating to the effect of stimulus intensity on dentate response magnitude are shown in Fig. 6. We have seen that relative stimulus intensity was adopted to equate for differences in input–output functions for different slices. Relative stimulus intensities tested were 20, 60, and 100% of the input–output function.

The results for both the population EPSP and population spike indicate that the weaker the stimulus, the greater the response decrement. Thus the data conform to the prediction of habituation theory that an inverse relationship exists between stimulus intensity and degree of habituation. Most experiments yielded results similar to the preceding, but some exhibited an enhanced response to the highest (100%) stimulus intensity. Because, as we will see later, the dentate gyrus exhibits an enhanced response in a sensitization paradigm, it is supposed that this represents a sensitization response to a strong stimulus.

6. Below-Zero Habituation

Below-zero habituation [not shown here; see Teyler & Alger (1976)] was observed for the population spike response. The magnitude of spontaneous recovery, measured 30 seconds after the termination of 10 1-per-second stimuli, was found to be 97% of the control levels. That is, it had almost completely recovered. An equivalent measure taken 30 seconds after the termination of 40 1-per-second stimuli was only 67%. This indicates that the presentation of additional habituating stimuli after achieving asymptote had the predicted effect of delaying spontaneous recovery. Stated another way, the 10-stimulus train had completely recovered by 60 seconds, whereas after the 40-stimulus train the response had not completely recovered by 240 seconds.

7. Stimulus Generalization (not tested)

8. Sensitization

A brief high-frequency stimulus train was used as a sensitizing stimulus and was delivered in place of the tenth habituation stimulus. The magnitude of a sensitized response to the eleventh stimulus is postulated to be a function of the stimulus parameters of the sensitizing stimulus. In this experiment the sensitized response recovered to about 90% of control (from a habituated level of 50%). The results and a missing stimulus control experiment are discussed in more detail in Teyler and Alger (1976).

9. Habituation of Sensitization

To test this parameter we presented a continuous habituating stimulus at 1 per second. In place of every tenth stimulus the high-frequency train was given. As predicted by habituation theory, the magnitude of the sensitized response habituated over sensitization trials. The sensitized response recovered to about 92% of control after the first sensitization stimulus. The sensitized response recovered to only 81% of control after the fifth sensitization stimulus.

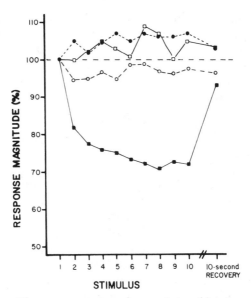

Fig. 7. Neocortex. The average response characteristics of four intracortical pathways to identical repeated stimulation. Only the white-matter-to-Layer-II response showed a response decrement. The decremented response spontaneously recovered to control levels in less than 30 seconds. (Layer IV to Layer IV, ●; Layer II to IV, □; white matter to Layer IV, ○; white matter to Layer II, ■).

We conclude that the perforant path to dentate gyrus pathway displays the properties of habituation–sensitization.

B. Neocortical Habituation: The Cortical Slice

Four separate intracortical pathways were tested for habituation. In each case a 50%-intensity 1-per-second train of 10 stimuli, followed by a single recovery stimulation at 10 seconds after the end of the train, was applied. Figure 7 shows average results of this experiment. Only the white-matter-to-Layer-II response displayed a response decrement (see, also, Fig. 2B). The other three pathways, white matter to Layer IV, Layer II to Layer IV, and Layer IV to Layer IV, all failed to exhibit a response decrement. Instead, their response levels varied within 8% of control levels. Additional experiments indicated that this failure to decrement was not related to the physical characteristics of the stimuli employed, because stimuli of different relative intensities and different frequencies also failed to elicit a response decrement. This result is quite interesting in relation to cortical processing of extrinsic inputs as opposed to intracortical processing of information, as we discuss later. Because only the white-matter-to-Layer-II response displayed response decrements, the other pathways were not further analyzed for the properties of habituation.

1. Time Course of Habituation

The average white-matter-to-Layer-II response (Fig. 7) displays an approximation of a negatively accelerating function. Response decrement appears to reach asymptote around the eighth stimulus presentation. The magnitude of the response at 50% intensity and 1-per-second frequency at asymptote is about 72% of control levels. The exact nature of the postsynaptic population response is unknown, but it probably represents summed slow potentials with some contribution from summed population spikes (Shaw & Teyler, 1982). Because of the heterogeneous cytoarchitecture of cortical tissue, it is not possible to unambiguously identify waveform origins—as can be done with hippocampus. The relative magnitude of the decrement is comparable to that seen in the hippocampal population EPSP and may support the contention that the waveform reflects summed slow potentials from a population of postsynaptic elements.

The magnitude and, particularly, the time course are comparable to dentate gyrus habituation. The time course of habituation is thus considerably quicker than the cortical evoked response seen in intact preparations to peripheral stimulation (Callaway, 1973). This implies that the dynamics of the cortically recorded response decrement over stimulus presentations in the intact animal is not an intrinsic property of the cortical processing module.

2. Spontaneous Recovery

Spontaneous recovery occurs quite rapidly, reaching 92% of control within 10 seconds (Fig. 7). Complete recovery is seen within 30 seconds.

3. Habituation of Habituation (not tested)

4. Effect of Frequency

The effect of stimulus frequency on cortical-relative habituation is seen in Fig. 8B. Stimulus frequencies of $\frac{1}{2}$ (low), 1 (med), and 2 per second (high) were examined in the white-matter-to-Layer-II response. Ten stimuli were presented in each case. Habituation theory predicts a direct relationship between stimulus frequency and the degree of habituation achieved. The asymptotic level of habituation (Fig. 8) increases with increasing stimulus frequencies. Similarly, the slope of the initial phase of

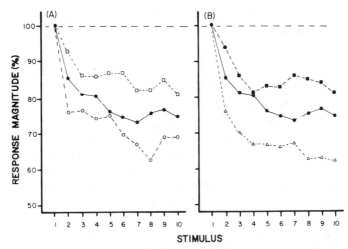

Fig. 8. Neocortex. The average white-matter-to-Layer-II response to (A) repeated stimuli of the three intensities (low intensity, ○; medium intensity, ●; high intensity, □) and (B) repeated stimuli of three frequencies (low frequency, ■; medium frequency, ●; high frequency, △). Both patterns of responding were as predicted by habituation theory.

the habituation function increases. Therefore, we conclude that this parameter is satisfied by this intracortical pathway.

In contrast to the hippocampus, we have not been successful in producing long-term potentiation through the use of high frequency tetanic stimulation in this or any other intrinsic cortical pathway. This is somewhat surprising, because a recent report (Lee, 1982) describes a long-lasting potentiation from white matter to Layer IV in rat cortical slices prepared and treated in a manner similar to our procedures. In our hands, however, we have been unable to demonstrate, to our own satisfaction, an enduring increase in synaptic efficacy as a result of the high-frequency stimulation that is greater than the response variability measured over an equivalent length of time. Our attempts to produce long-term potentiation in this tissue have assumed that treatment parameters found effective in producing long-term potentiation in the hippocampus will also be effective in cortical pathways. This assumption, however, may be incorrect.

5. Effect of Intensity

Figure 8A describes the intrinsic cortical response to three stimulus intensities, each defined as a percentage of the input–output function range. Examined were 1-per-second stimuli of low (25%), medium (50%), and high (75%) intensity. The asymptotic response decrement for the low-intensity stimulus was about 70% of control, the medium intensity stimulus produced a response of about 76% of control, and the high-intensity stimulus resulted in a response of about 84% of control levels. Thus there exists an inverse relationship between stimulus intensity and response decrement, as predicted by habituation theory.

6. Below-Zero Habituation (not tested)

7. Stimulus Generalization (not tested)

8. Sensitization

A high-frequency (200 Hz, 100 msec) stimulus was interpolated between the seventh and eighth stimulus presentation in a 1-per-second habituation run of 50% intensity. The asymptotic response magnitude prior to the sensitizing stimulus was 73% of control. The response to Stimulus 8 was a further reduction in response magnitude, to 54% of control, rather than the sensitized response predicted by habituation theory. Thus, instead of observing a dishabituated or sensitized response, the magnitude of the population response declined further. The decline recovered to the previous asymptotic level by Stimulus 10. Average values for Trials seven through ten were: Trial 7, 72%; Trial 8, 54%; Trial 9, 60%; Trial 10, 72%.

That this result was not a function of the physical properties of the sensitizing stimulus was confirmed in experiments wherein different stimulus frequencies, train durations, and stimulus intensities were employed. In no case did the response exhibit sensitization, rather a further response decrement was seen in virtually all cases. Because on these results we conclude that the cortical pathway from white matter to Layer II does not display the parameter of sensitization.

9. Habituation of Sensitization

Because we did not see a sensitization response, this parameter could not be tested.

Based on our results, we conclude that only one of the four intracortical pathways displays habituation. This pathway, white matter to Layer II, however, fails to exhibit sensitization.

C. Mesencephalic Habituation: The Tectal Explant

The goldfish tectal explant was tested to determine if the parameters of habituation–sensitization were represented in the field response to optic-nerve-stump stimulation.

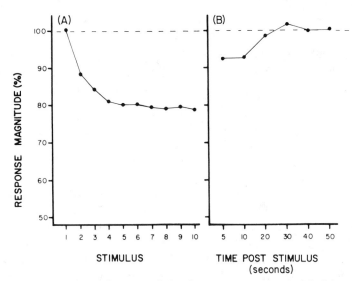

Fig. 9. Tectum. Response decrement (A) and spontaneous recovery (B) of the goldfish optic-tectum response to repeated optic-nerve stimulation. The magnitude, time course, and recovery parameters were similar to those observed in the dentate gyrus and in the neocortex.

1. Time Course

Figure 9A shows that the tectal response decrements to about 80% of control levels within five stimulus presentations at 1 per second. These values are comparable to those seen in the hippocampal and intracortical responses, both in terms of magnitude and time course (see, also, Fig. 2B).

2. Spontaneous Recovery

Tectal response recovery (Fig. 9B) is complete in less than 30 seconds. This rapid spontaneous recovery is, again, comparable to that seen in the other CNS monosynaptic systems and raises the possibility that these values are paradigmatic of habituating central synapses.

3. Habituation of Habituation

Habituation of habituation was examined in a series of 10 presentations of 10 1-per-second stimuli of 50% intensity. Successive 10-stimulus runs were separated by 60 seconds. The average response to the 10 stimuli in each run is plotted in Fig. 10A. The filled circles show that the predictions of habituation theory (x symbol) are not obtained. Rather than the negatively accelerating function predicted, the obtained response, in fact,

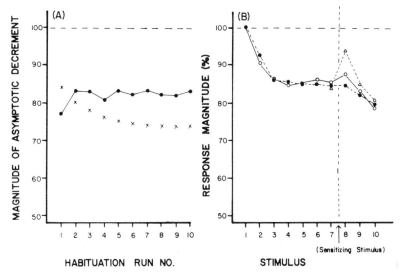

Fig. 10. Tectum. (A) The theoretical predictions of the habituation-of-habituation parameter (x symbols) were not obtained. Instead, the asymptotic level of the response decrement increased as a function of runs. (B) The tectal response to a sensitizing stimulus was either no recovery toward control levels or a small recovery, followed by a decline in response magnitude beyond the asymptotic level. The results of the tectal experiments suggest that those synapses do not demonstrate habituation (Experiment 1, O; Experiment 2, ●; positive data, Experiment 1, △).

shows less habituation as a function of runs. Such a result might be seen if a sensitizing response were simultaneously present. Because these stimulus parameters do not elicit a sensitized response, however, we do not feel that these data reflect the operation of this parameter. In fact, we establish in this chapter that sensitization is poorly represented, if present at all, in the isolated tectum. Therefore, we conclude that the parameter of habituation of habituation is not met in this mesencephalic tissue.

4. Effect of Frequency

Habituation theory predicts a direct relationship between stimulus frequency and magnitude of response decrement. This predicted relationship was observed, as is shown in Fig. 11B. The lowest frequency stimulus ($\frac{1}{2}$ per second; 50% intensity) elicited the smallest response decrement, whereas the highest frequency stimulus employed (2 per second; 50% intensity) elicited the greatest response decrement, averaging about 70% of control.

Interestingly, the response to the 2-per-second stimulus appears to not asymptote by the fourth stimulus presentation, whereas both the $\frac{1}{2}$- and

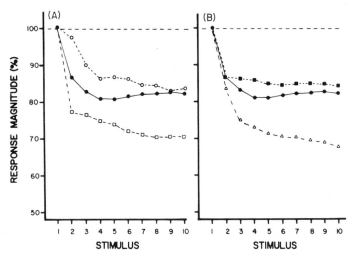

Fig. 11. Tectum. The effect of stimulus intensity (low intensity, ○; medium intensity, ●; high intensity, □) (A) and frequency (low frequency, ■; medium frequency, ●; high frequency, △) (B) on the magnitude of the tectal response to repeated stimulation. Both parameters were directly related to decreases in response magnitude, whereas habituation theory predicts an inverse relationship for stimulus intensity.

1-per-second stimulus rates do reach asymptote. The reason for this is not known.

5. Effect of Intensity

Habituation theory predicts an inverse relationship between stimulus intensity and response decrement. In the tectum, this parameter was tested presenting 1-per-second stimuli at low (25%), medium (50%), or high (75%) intensity with respect to the input–output function. In Fig. 10A, the obtained average response curves show that instead of an inverse relationship, we obtained a direct relationship between stimulus intensity and response decrement. The highest intensity stimulus produced the largest response decrement, averaging about 72% of control levels. This response, like that to the high-frequency stimulus, does not asymptote during the 10-stimulus run. On the basis of these data we conclude that the optic tectum response does not meet this parameter of habituation.

6. Below-Zero Habituation

Habituation stimuli were delivered at 50% intensity at 1 per second for either 10 or 40 stimulus presentations. Ten seconds after the last stimulus, a single recovery stimulus was presented to test for the magnitude of spontaneous recovery. After 10 habituation stimuli the 10-second recovery value was 94% of control, whereas the 10-second recovery value following 40 stimulus presentations was 84%. This result is consistent with the predictions of habituation theory wherein additional habituation stimuli given beyond response asymptote results in slower recovery.

7. Stimulus Generalization (not tested)

8. Sensitization

This parameter was tested by interpolating a high-frequency train (100 Hz; 100 msec) between the seventh and eighth habituating stimuli. Sensitization would be reflected in a larger response to the eighth stimulus, which would again decline back to the previously habituated level. The results of the experiment (Fig. 11B), however, show that something else happened. The sensitization stimulus failed to elicit much of a sensitization response in two replications (five tecta per replication).

Because the effect of a sensitizing stimulus is a function of the physical properties of the sensitizing stimulus, we used other sensitizing stimuli (different frequencies, higher intensity) with essentially the same results. Individual preparation analyses of the data from Experiment 1 indicated that some preparations displayed an augmented response following the introduction of the sensitizing stimulus. These data are plotted as "positive data." Why only some preparations should display this response is unknown. Another unexpected aspect of the responses following the sensitization stimulus is the reduced response magnitude to Stimuli 9 and 10. These responses are below the asymptotic level of the decremented response. Had such a drop in response magnitude occurred immediately following the sensitizing stimulus it would have suggested the operation of a fatigue-like process. Here, however, the response decline is maximal 2.5 seconds after the introduction of the sensitizing stimulus. Yet in 60 seconds, the interval between successive runs, the response returned to baseline levels. Based on these results we conclude that the tectum does not meet the sensitization parameter as defined heretofore.

9. Habituation of Sensitization

In the absence of a reliable sensitization response it could not be determined if this parameter holds for the tectum.

In summary, the tectum displays a response decrement comparable in time course and magnitude to other CNS monosynaptic responses. The decremented response spontaneously recovers, and the response conforms to the stimulus-frequency parameter and shows the below-zero effect. Significantly, however, the tectal response does not display habituation of habituation (the reverse obtains), an inverse function of intensity (again, the reverse obtains), or sensitization. Given these failures to conform to the predictions of habituation theory we conclude that the optic tectum response decrement studied here does not represent habituation as classically defined.

VI. Discussion

We have observed that habituation–sensitization are by no means equally represented throughout the brain. When tested using the criteria of Thompson and Spencer (1966), we find that only the dentate gyrus of the hippocampal formation conforms to all of the tested parameters. Two other allocortical monosynaptic junctions (Hippocampal Areas CA3 and CA1) did not display a response decrement. Indeed, quite to the contrary, they displayed a long-term increase in response magnitude (Alger & Teyler, 1976). Such long-term potentiation can also be seen in the dentate gyrus with appropriate treatment (Alger & Teyler, 1976).

We examined four intrinsic neocortical pathways, two representing extracortical inputs into the cortical module and two representing intramodular pathways. Only one of the pathways (the Layer-II response to white-matter stimulation) displayed a significant decrement to repeated afferent stimulation. The time course of the decrement and spontaneous recovery have the appearance of habituation as seen in the dentate gyrus. Given further examination, however, it became evident that not every parameter could be met by this pathway. In particular, this intracortical pathway failed to demonstrate sensitization.

In contrast to the systems already described, both of which show habituation and one of which shows sensitization as well, is the response of the tectum to repeated stimulation. This mesencephalic structure displayed a response that declined with repeated stimulation, recovered spontaneously, had a direct relationship with stimulus frequency, and demonstrated below-zero habituation. These results are consistent with the predictions of habituation theory. But none of the other parameters were confirmed. For example, the tectum demonstrated an inverse habituation-of-habituation function. That is, the degree of habituation, expressed as a percentage of control, achieved on successive runs actually increased over runs. Such a result might occur if a sensitizing process were simultaneously brought into play, yet no sensitization was observed when tested. The tectal response also displayed an inverse function with respect to stimulus intensity, in that the response magnitude was a direct function of stimulus intensity. Such a result is consistent with a fatigue-like process. These tectal results clearly indicate that the tectum does not conform to the predictions of habituation theory. We are left with the question of what, then, these tectal response characteristics mean.

Before considering the implications of these results, we would be wise to reflect on the necessity of exhaustive examination of a structure or tissue before hypothesizing about its functional role. The tectal response, for instance, would have been classified as demonstrating habituation if only parameters (1) and (2), decline and recovery had been tested. Such "false positives" can, of course, be very misleading. A review of the literature concerning electrophysiological measures of habituation indicates that most studies have been conducted with little apparent awareness or concern over demonstrating that the phenomenon fit the parametric definition of habituation. No one disputes that many central synapses are capable of showing a response decrement over repeated stimulus presentations. But to assert that response decrement and habituation are equivalent is to misrepresent an important distinction well established in the scientific literature (Hinde, 1970; Thompson & Spencer, 1966). This, coupled with the possibility that the decrement observed at the end of an electrode is, in fact, occurring elsewhere and is merely being reproduced there, makes many of the previously established demonstrations of central habituation suspect. We assert that statements regarding the locus of habituation and thus, statements about its utility to brain processes, can only be made (1) at the tissue level and (2) in reference to the parametric definition of habituation.

What can be said with respect to the unequal distribution of habituation–sensitization we have observed? Clearly, it follows that habituating synapses are not ubiquitous. Rather, in this rather unsystematic and biased sample of eight synapses (three in allocortex, four in neocortex, one in mesencephalon), only two adequately demonstrate habituation. Why not all the others? Presumably, habituating synapses are incorporated into the brain only where they are required to perform some specific function. What might that function be? Again, if we knew more about the distribution of habituating synapses in other brain regions, we could better infer a functional role. Lacking such detailed knowledge for the entire CNS, we shall try to suggest a functional role based on the limited data at hand. The dentate gyrus receives a major input from the entorhinal cortex. The entorhinal cortex, in turn, receives input from widespread regions of the brain. Thus the dentate is a major gateway from the cortex and rest of the brain into the hippocampus (Swanson *et al.*, 1982).

Given this, we suggest that the role of the short-term plastic alterations—habituation and sensitization—limit input into the hippocampus.

Thus habituation–sensitization acts as a novelty filter. To the extent that hippocampal long-term potentiation is related to memory storage or retrieval processes (Swanson *et al.*, 1982), the function of dentate habituation–sensitization might be to protect the hippocampal circuits from being overloaded with LTP to biologically insignificant information. Such a mechanism must be capable of being overridden by an alteration in environmental input, a provision provided for by the sensitizing properties of this synapse.

It should be recalled that LTP is also seen at the dentate synapse. This does not necessarily indicate that LTP and habituation are operating together. Pilot experiments, for instance, have indicated that *relative* habituation is the same before and after a 200% increase in baseline responsiveness produced by LTP. Thus the input filter is operative regardless of the presence or absence of a semipermanent alteration of the input pathway. The functional importance of a novelty input filter gains importance if the hippocampal formation processes several inputs associatively. Some evidence that associational plastic processing occurs has been provided by Goddard and Riives (1981). Given this, the ability to automatically scale the inputs to an associational system by their biological relevance becomes terribly important.

The only cortical region showing habituation (but not sensitization) receives afferent input primarily from nonspecific thalamic nuclei (Herkenham, 1979). Cortical regions receiving primarily specific thalamic projections (Layers III and IV) fail to show habituation. This suggests that the function of habituation in this tissue is not directly related to the receipt of sensory information from specific thalamic nuclei. To the extent that the Layer-IV response represents specific thalamic inputs, we conclude that the response decrements observed in intact preparations to peripheral stimulation are the result of extracortical processes. This conclusion is qualified by our imprecise knowledge of a functional properties of thalamo–cortical systems. For example, it is known that the nonspecific thalamic input is rather diffuse (Herkenham, 1979), and it is possible that specific thalamic afferents also project up into Cortical Layer II (Herkenham, 1980). Thus, it is quite possible that nonspecific and specific projections influence the same population of neural elements in Layer II. These statements are predicated on the assumption that the mechanism of habituation and sensitization is homosynaptic and probably involves presynaptic components, as has been demonstrated in *Aplysia* (Klein & Kandel, 1978). If this does not hold for central habituating synapses, then the origin and identity of the afferents becomes less important, and the nature of the postsynaptic element(s) becomes more important.

The nature of the response decrement in the white-matter-to-Layer-II response is quite difficult to ascertain. We have tentatively concluded that the response fits the parametric definition of habituation. But based on the origins of the thalamic projection to this area, another possibility should be considered. The classical conception of nonspecific thalamocortical systems is related to an arousal or biasing function (Jasper, 1958). According to the dual-process theory of habituation (Groves & Thompson, 1970) and as seen in the functional separation of interneuron populations in the spinal grey into type-H and type-S cells, we might expect to see a functional division of habituating (termed the S–R pathway by Thompson and colleagues) and sensitizing components (termed the state system) in the brain. The most likely location for the habituating component is somewhere in the direct polysynaptic circuit from receptor to neocortex. We have demonstrated that the final, thalamocortical link does not habituate. A likely candidate for the sensitizing component lies in the reticular core of the brain, including the nonspecific thalamic nuclei (Jasper, 1958).

If the Layer-II response represents the sensitization component of the dual-process theory, its decrement over stimulations is in accord with the theoretical predictions [Parameter (9)] of habituation theory. The failure of this pathway to demonstrate sensitization, although not considered in habituation theory, appears consistent. What, for instance, would constitute an appropriate sensitizing stimulus for the sensitization response? We employed a high-frequency train as a sentizing stimulus. If sensitization obeys the habituation parameters, we would expect an interpolated high-frequency train to further depress the response magnitude as predicted by Parameter (4). The sensitization component should respond to an interpolated stimulus with a further response decline because all such manipulations effectively increase the stimulus frequency briefly. This was the result we obtained. Such a result ought normally to accompany the delivery of an interpolated sensitizing stimulus onto a habituation–sensitizing system, but is usually not observed because of the overriding effect of the sensitization response.

A strong argument against this hypothesis is offered in the nature of the sensitization response to repeated stimulation. The dual-process theory infers that the sensitization component has a higher stimulus threshold and that its response to repeated stimulus presentations increases *above baseline* for a period of time (Thompson *et al.,* 1973). Clearly, the response observed here does nothing of the sort, although one could argue that the response might exceed baseline levels at higher stimulus intensities.

A better interpretation of these data is that this pathway, regardless of the precise origin of the fibers (which we do not know directly in any case), demonstrates habituation *but not sensitization*. The two parameters critical for sensitization—(8) and (9)—were not met in this tissue. The dual-process theory, as stated before, predicts the anatomical independence of the habituating and sensitizing components. Thus, at the level of the cortex, habituation and sensitization are mediated by different systems, only the habituation portion of which survives the slice procedure. The sensitization component may be intrinsic to the cortical slice, but inaccessible because of technical limitations or may be an extrinsic neuromodulatory influence no longer present.

Whatever the correct interpretation, we see in this preparation a further example of the functional and anatomical independence of habituation and sensitization. Interestingly, just as in the spinal grey, there is, probably, convergence upon the final common path. In this case, the final common elements are the projection pyramidal neurons located in the deeper layers of the cortex. Thus we believe these results further substantiate the dual-process theory of habituation–sensitization.

The functional role of the decrementing process intrinsic to cortex must await further clarification of its precise role. Several observations, however, may be made at this point. It is clear that response decrements occur in cortical-evoked responses (Roemer *et al.*, Chapter 9, this volume). If the decrements to sensory stimuli are occurring at or near the periphery, as opposed to intracortically, could the Layer-II response represent habituation of information less related to sensory experience and more closely related to cognitive processing? It has been shown that response decrements occur specifically to cognitive stimuli (Megela & Teyler, 1979). Cognitive information can be influenced by arousal systems prior to its processing and identification as cognitive information, but such information must also be processed by intrinsic or associational cortical systems. Therefore, the Layer-II response may represent a form of intrinsic cortical habituation of locally processed material.

We have shown that the white-matter-to-Layer-IV response, the presumed specific thalamic projection to neocortex, does not habituate. We suggest, therefore, the necessity for looking elsewhere in the system for the plastic link. Conceptually, no more than one habituating link is needed in a multisynaptic pathway. We have demonstrated that the plastic link is not intrinsic to the cortex. This is not to say that the cortex is not involved. Cortical feedback or feedforward loops to thalamic, cortical, or limbic structures may be necessary to effect a response decrement to peripheral stimuli. Wherever found, the plastic link(s) must be able to account for the large discrepancy between the rate of monosynaptic habituation as measured in the cortex and dentate gyrus, wherein asymptote is achieved in 4–6 stimulus presentations, as contrasted with the 50–100 stimulus presentations required in intact preparations recording cortical-evoked potentials to peripheral stimulation.

The response characteristics of the optic tectum indicate that the response decrement seen there does not conform to the parametric features of habituation–sensitization on several counts. The possibility exists that the response characteristics seen in this tissue represent a fatigue-like response. This is entirely possible, but it is known that the retinotectal projection responds equally well to the frequencies employed in this study (Teyler *et al.*, 1981).

The parameters of habituation are not met, but the tissue response to repeated stimulation definitely decrements. Whether habituation or not, this response decrement must be considered with respect to tectal neurobiology, and the consequences of a reduction in postsynaptic activation must be understood in relation to tectal function. In goldfish and frog retinotectal systems, it is known that extrinsic influences are critically important in attentive behavior (Ingle, 1975). The anatomy of fish and frog retinas provides many plastic functions not possessed by more complex organisms. Thus habituating cells located in the retina project upon tectal neurons (Lettvin, Maturana, McCulloch, & Pitts, 1961). Similarly, tectal activity is modulated to tonic inhibitory influences from the thalamus (Ingle, 1975). It thus appears that, deprived of essential components of the system, any order in the tectal response to visual stimulation has been disrupted. Clearly then, the tectum is different than the other systems studied, wherein they had the intrinsic capacity to respond in a habituating or sensitizing manner. Whether or not this is a general feature of mesencephalic structures is unknown.

Of the CNS synapses examined only a minority displayed habituating–sensitizing responses. Our tentative hypothesis is that habituating synapses will be found at the entry gates into brain circuits that serve a particular function. Such a hypothesis is an extension of earlier theoretical views of the function of habituation and is consistent with the results obtained here. Only further examination of other CNS synapses will tell if our hypothesis of the role of habituation is correct.

References

Alger, B. E., Megela, A. L., & Teyler, T. J. Transient heterosynaptic depression in the hippocampal slice. *Brain Research Bulletin*, 1978, *3*, 181–184.

Alger, B. E., & Teyler, T. J. Long-term and short-term plasticity in the CA1, CA3 and dentate gyrus regions of the rat hippocampal slice. *Brain Research*, 1976, *110*, 463–480.

Andersen, P. Brain slices—A neurobiological tool of increasing usefulness. *Trends in Neuroscience*, 1981, *4*, 53–56.

Andersen, P., Bliss, T. V. P., & Skrede, K. K. Unit analysis of hippocampal population spikes. *Experimental Brain Research*, 1970, *13*, 208–221.

Callaway, E. Habituation of averaged evoked potentials in man. In H. V. S. Peeke & M. J. Herz (Eds.), *Habituation* (Vol. 2). New York: Academic Press, 1973. Pp. 153–174.

Douglas, R. M., & Goddard, G. Long-term potentiation of the perforant path–granule cell synapse in the rat hippocampus. *Brain Research,* 1975, *86,* 205–215.

Duffy, C., & Teyler, T. J. A simple tissue slicer. *Physiology and Behavior,* 1975, *14,* 525–526.

Farel, P. B., Glanzman, D. L., & Thompson, R. F. Habituation of a monosynaptic response in the vertebrate central nervous system. *Journal of Neurophysiology,* 1973, *36,* 1117–1130.

Glass, D. C., & Singer, J. F. *Urban stress.* New York: Academic Press, 1972.

Goddard, G. V., & Riives, M. Inhibitory modulation of LTP in the hippocampal dentate area of awake rats. *Neuroscience Abstracts,* 1981, *7,* Abstract no. 250.18. P. 773.

Groves, P. M., Lee, D., & Thompson, R. F. Effects of stimulus frequency and intensity on habituation and sensitization in acute spinal cat. *Physiology and Behavior,* 1969, *4,* 383–388.

Groves, P. M., & Thompson, R. F. Habituation: A dual-process theory. *Psychological Review,* 1970, *77,* 419–450.

Harris, K. M., & Teyler, T. J. Developmental onset of long-term potentiation in area CA1 of the rat hippocampus. *Journal of Physiology,* 1983, in press.

Herkenham, M. The afferent and efferent connections of the ventromedial thalamic nucleus in the rat. *Journal of Comparative Neurology,* 1979, *183,* 487–517.

Herkenham, M. Laminar organization of thalamic projections to the rat neocortex. *Science,* 1980, *207,* 532–535.

Hinde, R. A. Behavioral habituation. In G. Horn & R. A. Hinde (Eds.), *Short-term changes in neural activity and behavior.* London & New York: Cambridge University Press, 1970. Pp. 3–40.

Horn, G., & Hinde, R. A. (Eds.). *Short-term changes in neural activity and behaviour.* London & New York: Cambridge University Press, 1970.

Ingle, D. The frog's visual system as a model for the study of selective attention. In. D. J. Ingle & H. M. Shein (Eds.), *Model systems in biological psychiatry.* Cambridge, Mass.: MIT University Press, 1975. Pp. 113–131.

Jasper, H. H. Recent advances in our understanding of ascending activities of the reticular system. In H. H. Jasper (Ed.), *Reticular formation of the brain.* Boston: Little, Brown, 1958. Pp. 319–331.

Klein, M., & Kandel, E. R. Presynaptic modulation of voltage-dependent Ca^{2+} current: Mechanism for behavioral sensitization in *Aplysia californica. Proceedings of the National Academy of Sciences of the United States of America,* 1978, *75,* 3512–3516.

Lee, K. S. Sustained enhancement of evoked potentials following brief, high-frequency stimulation of cerebral cortex *in vitro. Brain Research,* 1982, *239,* 617–623.

Lettvin, J. Y., Maturana, H. R., Pitts, W. H., & McCulloch, W. S. Two remarks on the visual system of the frog. In W. A. Rosenblith (Ed.), *Sensory communication.* Cambridge, Mass.: MIT University Press, 1961. Pp. 757–776.

Lewis, D., Teyler, T., & Shashoua, V. Development of long-term potentiation in the *in vitro* goldfish optic tectum. *Neuroscience Abstracts,* 1981, *7,* Abstract no. 23.12. P. 66.

Lynch, G., & Schubert, P. The use of *in vitro* brain slices for multidisciplinary studies of synaptic function. *Annual Review of Neuroscience,* 1980, *3,* 1–22.

Megela, A. L., & Teyler, T. J. Habituation and the human evoked potential. *Journal of Comparative and Physiological Psychology,* 1979, *93,* 1154–1170.

Naatanen, A. Selective attention and evoked potentials in humans—A critical review. *Biological Psychology,* 1975, *2,* 237–307.

Peeke, H. V. S., & Herz, M. J. (Eds.). *Habituation* (Vol. 1). New York: Academic Press, 1973. (a)

Peeke, H. V. S., & Herz, M. J. (Eds.). *Habituation*. (Vol. 2). New York; Academic Press, 1973. (b)

Shaw, C., & Teyler, T. J. The neural circuitry of the neocortex examined in the *in vitro* brain slice preparation. *Brain Research*, 1982, *247*, 35–47.

Skrede, K. K., & Westgaard, R. H. The transverse hippocampal slice: A well-defined cortical structure maintained *in vitro*. *Brain Research*, 1971, *35*, 589–593.

Swanson, L. W., Teyler, T. J., & Thompson, R. F. Hippocampal long-term potentiation: Mechanisms and implications for memory. *Neurosciences Research Program Bulletin*, 1982, *20* (4).

Teyler, T. J. (Ed.). *Brain and learning*. Stamford, Conn.: Greylock Publishers, 1978.

Teyler, T. J. The brain slice preparation: Hippocampus. *Brain Research Bulletin*, 1980, *5*, 391–403.

Teyler, T. J., & Alger, B. E. Monosynaptic habituation in the vertebrate forebrain: The dentate gyrus examined *in vitro*. *Brain Research*, 1976, *115*, 413–425.

Teyler, T. J., Lewis, D., & Shashoua, V. E. Neurophysiological and biochemical properties of the goldfish optic tectum maintained *in vitro*. *Brain Research Bulletin*, 1981, *7*, 45–56.

Thompson, R. F., & Glanzman, D. L. Neural and behavioral mechanisms of habituation and sensitization. In T. J. Tighe & R. N. Leaton (Eds.), *Habituation: Perspectives from child development, animal behavior, and neurophysiology*. Hillsdale, N.J.: Lawrence Erlbaum Associates, 1976. Pp. 49–93.

Thompson, R. F., Groves, P., Teyler, T. J., & Roemer, R. A. A dual process theory of habituation: Theory and behavior. In H. V. S. Peeke & M. J. Herz (Eds.), *Habituation* (Vol. 1). New York: Academic Press, 1973. Pp. 239–269.

Thompson, R. F., & Spencer, W. A. Habituation: A model phenomenon for the study of neuronal substrates of behavior. *Psychological Review*, 1966, *73*, 16–43.

Tighe, T. J., & Leaton, R. N. (Eds.). *Habituation: Perspectives from child development, animal behavior, and neurophysiology*. Hillsdale, N.J.: Lawrence Erlbaum Associates, 1976.

Vanegas, H., Laufer, M., & Amat, J. The optic tectum of a periform teleost. I. General configuration and cytoarchitecture. *Journal of Comparative Neurology*, 1974, *154*, 43–60.

Westenberg, I. S., & Weinberger, N. M. Evoked potential decrements in auditory cortex. II. Critical test for habituation. *Electroencephalography and Clinical Neurophysiology*, 1976, *40*, 356–369.

Yoon, M. G. Topographic polarity of the optic tectum studied by reimplantation of tectal tissue in the adult goldfish. *Cold Spring Harbor Symposia on Quantitative Biology*, 1975, *40*, 503–519.

CHAPTER 8

Intrinsic and Extrinsic Mechanisms of Habituation and Sensitization: Implications for the Design and Analysis of Experiments

Michael Davis

Department of Psychiatry
Yale University
New Haven, Connecticut

Sandra E. File

Department of Pharmacology
School of Pharmacy
University of London
London, England

I. Introduction

The history of the study and analysis of habituation is punctuated by a small number of highly influential reviews or theories. In 1943 Harris

This work was supported by National Science Foundation Grants GB-23685; BNS-75-01470, BNS-78-17421, by National Institute of Mental Health Grants MH-25642, MH-18949, MH-07114, by Research Scientist Development Award MH-00004 to M. Davis, by travel grants from the Royal Society and the Wellcome Trust (1979) to S. File, and by the State of Connecticut.

HABITUATION, SENSITIZATION,
AND BEHAVIOR

published the first comprehensive review of the literature on habituation. With noteworthy thoroughness, Harris found examples of habituation at all levels of the phylogenetic scale. The indelible impression was that habituation was "ubiquitous," a word that has been used to describe habituation ever since. The major contribution of Harris's review was to establish habituation as a fundamental property of living organisms. Interestingly, however, Harris did not attempt to try to explain habituation with any unified theory. Indeed, he firmly and perhaps prophectically stated that

> It will be obvious when once we have reviewed the fact of habituation from Protista to man, that no "mechanism" of habituation will be found. There are quite probably several mechanisms; we know, at least, that habituatory phenomena can be observed throughout so extreme a range of organisms and under such widely varied experimental conditions that any single explanatory principle would have to be too general to be satisfactory [1943, p. 388; italics added].

Probably because of this belief, Harris only broached some possible mechanisms that might underly habituation without critically assessing their relative contributions. Thus he simply acknowledged that refractory-like decrements might be involved in habituation but simultaneously asserted that a phenomenon less akin to fatigue and more akin to learning must also operate.

In 1960 a completely new approach to the study of habituation emerged. Unknown to most of the western world, active and highly creative research on habituation had been conducted in the Soviet Union. Much of this research was brought together by E. N. Sokolov in an article entitled "Neuronal models and the orienting reflex" (Sokolov, 1960). Based on a series of imaginative studies of habituation of the orienting reflex in humans, Sokolov proposed the first comprehensive theory of habituation. Sokolov's theory stated that during repetitive stimulus presentation, the brain—specifically, the cortex—formed a model of the stimulus. During subsequent stimulus presentations, incoming stimuli were compared with the model. If the incoming stimulus matched the model, responding was inhibited; if not, an orienting response occurred.

Sokolov's ideas were rapidly adopted by investigators of human habituation, but his cognitively oriented theory seemed somewhat irrelevant to those researchers examining habituation in animals that lacked a cortex and especially to those investigators working with animals lacking a brain altogether. Although one could envision comparator-like processes in simple neural circuits, the language of Sokolov's theory seemed inappropriate for the analysis of habituation in animals lower than man. In short, the theory simply could not be used by a substantial segment of investigators interested in habituation.

In 1966, Thompson and Spencer published a major review article on habituation that appealed to researchers interested in habituation in all animals including humans. Working with the flexion reflex in the spinal cat (i.e., a preparation in which the brain could not participate), Spencer, Thompson, and Neilson (1966a, 1966b, 1966c) showed that the spinal cord could mediate habituation in ways that looked very similar to those displayed by the intact organism. Thompson and Spencer (1966) then organized the existing habituation literature into nine parameters that would operationally define habituation. Habituation was said to occur if an organism responded to repetitive stimulation in conformance with these criteria. Thus Thompson and Spencer gave habituation a structure for the first time. It was now possible to categorize a multitude of data derived from the analysis of diverse stimulus response (S–R) systems in different organisms, compartmentalized according to whether or not they fulfilled the various criteria. In fact, following Thompson and Spencer's review, numerous studies appeared that used the nine criteria to see if a particular S–R system in a particular organism actually did show all the features of habituation.

Beyond giving structure to the literature, however, Thompson and Spencer's review had a more profound impact on the field. In particular, the fact that a single set of objective criteria could now describe habituation in many response systems across various species led to the general belief that habituation was mediated by a single, fundamental mechanism inherent to all organisms. Hence the Thompson and Spencer review encouraged researchers from a variety of disciplines to investigate "the mechanism" of habituation, in terms of their own expertise. Pharmacologists sought to determine which drugs would improve or retard habituation and which neurotransmitter system mediated habituation. Physiological psychologists tested how lesions of various parts of the central nervous system affected habituation. Physiologists investigated synaptic changes that might accompany habituation.

Thompson and Spencer's ideas also appealed to investigators who were less interested in habituation per se. That is, if habituation were a fundamental property of living organisms, deficits in habituation would be expected to have profound consequences on more complex behavior and, consequently, some investigators put certain questions to test. Do schizophrenics have major deficits in attention because of their inability to habituate to irrelevant sensory stimulation (cf. Depue and Fowles, 1973)? Is it possible that hallucinogens alter perception by impairing habituation (Bradley and Key, 1958)? Do hyperactive children have deficits in habituation, a deficit which might be analyzed in animal models (Shaywitz, Gordon, Klopper, and Zelterman, 1977)? Do habituation rates in infants predict intelligence later in life (Furby, 1974)? Thus, explicit measurement

of habituation might provide a sensitive diagnostic tool for exploring deficits in complex behavioral patterns. Some believed that if the mechanism
of habituation were known, it would be possible to restore normal habituation and thereby improve, or actually cure, abnormal behavior (e.g.,
Gruzelier, 1978).

But there was not universal agreement about whether the parametric
features outlined by Thompson and Spencer fitted all the literature. Hinde
(1970) enumerated many exceptions, especially from the ethological literature in which repetitive stimulation made responses increase instead of
decrease. Smooth habituation functions were rarely seen, even in
grouped data. Davis and Wagner (1968) pointed out that conclusions regarding habituation depended on the exact way habituation experiments
were conducted. Thus different paradigms resulted in habituation that
could be either directly or inversely related to the stimulus intensity,
rather than inversely related, as stated in one of Thompson and Spencer's
parametric characteristics. In addition, Davis and Wagner (1969) demonstrated that habituation could be more pronounced to a stimulus intensity
that the animal had never heard before than to a stimulus intensity it had
heard many times. These results posed special difficulties for a complex
brain comparator theory as well as for a simple, single-process theory
such as decreased transmitter release.

Another issue raised by the Thompson and Spencer review was the
phenomenon of dishabituation, whereby the introduction of a second
stimulus, following repetition of the first, led to a reinstatement of the
original response. In fact, dishabituation had long been regarded as the
primary evidence that habituation could not be explained by effector fatigue, because the effector could still function when activated by another
stimulus. Moreover, the term itself—*dis*habituation—implied that intro-
ducing another stimulus actually disrupted or reversed the *process* of
habituation.

Although this opinion generally prevailed, Humphrey (1933) and, later,
Sharpless and Jasper (1956) had explicitly suggested that dishabituation
might be separate and independent from habituation. In fact, Humphrey
had shown very nicely in the turtle that a stimulus that caused dishabituation following repetitive presentation of a habituating stimulus increased
initial responsivitity in turtles that had never been exposed to the habituating stimulus. Based on their own experimental evidence in the spinal
cat, Spencer *et al.* (1966a, 1966b, 1966c) and Thompson and Spencer
(1966) adopted a similar view, namely, that habituation and dishabituation
were separate and independent processes. Moreover, they suggested that
dishabituation could more profitably be viewed as a kind of sensitization
because it represented an excitatory effect that was simply superimposed
over a second habituation process.

In 1970, Groves and Thompson outlined a two-process theory of response plasticity that they called a "dual process theory of habituation" (Groves and Thompson, 1970). In brief, the theory proposed that stimulus exposure activates both a decremental (habituation) and an incremental (sensitization) process. The two processes were said to be independent and subserved by different underlying neural substrates. Importantly, however, behavioral output at any point in time represented the net influence of the two opposing processes. Thus the new idea also suggested by Davis and Wagner (1969), was that the eliciting stimulus *itself* could simultaneously activate two processes that had opposite effects on behavior. Groves and Thompson (1970) realized the significance of this idea and argued persuasively that two processes were required to account for existing data. Moreover, they provided important new data to suggest that different neural systems mediated the two phenomena.

The Groves and Thompson review had an immediate effect on the field. "Bumpy" habituation curves were no longer embarrassing or suspect. Numerous examples of initial response increments followed by response decrement appeared, confirming what Groves and Thompson had spotted in the earlier literature. By assuming that intense stimuli produce more sensitization than weak stimuli, some of the confusing effects of stimulus intensity on habituation curves could be understood. By assuming that shorter interstimulus intervals produced more sensitization, some confusing interval effects were also accommodated.

In addition to accounting for a great amount of data, the two-factor theory had important implications for the analysis of mechanisms of habituation. Thus a diminished response decrement caused by a drug, or lesion, or particular psychiatric state could result from reduced habituation or increased sensitization or both. Assuming that different neural mechanisms mediate habituation and sensitization, it is clear that the understanding of the behavioral deficit associated with these manipulations requires an analysis of the relative contributions of habituation and sensitization in producing the chance in response output being measured. Such an analysis must preceed any claim that a given treatment has altered the neural system subserving habituation or sensitization.

Although the Groves and Thompson theory could accomodate more data than any of its predecessors, it still was not entirely satisfactory. The theory had difficulty explaining some of the more complex but intuitively reasonable experimental results gathered from studies of habituation in humans. For example, the theory had trouble explaining the "missing stimulus effect" (Sokolov, 1960), whereby the orienting response was restored when a stimulus was omitted at some point within a series of repetitive stimulus presentations. Experiments in which a number out of sequence (e.g., 1, 2, 3, 4, 6) elicited a return of orienting (Unger, 1964) were also difficult to explain. Another difficult empirical result was the demonstration that the acoustic startle reflex could be directly related to the interstimulus interval used during testing; yet at the same time, inversely related to the interstimulus interval used in a previous training session (Davis, 1970a, 1970b). Thus another parametric feature of habituation listed by Thompson and Spencer and adopted by Groves and Thompson was shown to be dependend on how habituation was defined and measured. Moreover, these data suggested that two decremental processes might exist; a short-term refractory-like effect, dependent on the time since the presentation of an immediately previous stimulus, and another longer-term effect, which was more pronounced following distributed-versus-massed presentation.

To account for some of these results as well as some new ones (Wagner, 1976; Wagner & Pfautz, 1978) Wagner (1976) proposed a new theory of habituation. In essence, the theory said that habituation can be mediated both by a short-term refractory-like process and by a conditioning process, whereby background cues of the experimental situation become conditioned to the eliciting stimulus so as to inhibit response output. Hence both nonassociative and associative processes are used to account for habituation. But like other cognitively oriented theories, this one has also been difficult to assilimilate for those working with relatively simple systems. Thus the theory seems to use a more complex process (classical conditioning) to account for a simpler one (habituation). Although it includes two types of habituation processes, it is vague regarding how much data should be accounted for by each; but it seems to stress the importance of the associative one. But the most definitive work on habituation to date has provided strong evidence that much of habituation can be explained by nonassociative changes. This is best exemplified by the work of Kandel and his associates (Kandel, 1978). These investigators recognized the potential of studying habituation in an organism with an accessible and relatively simple nervous system. In an elegant series of experiments over the years, Kandel and colleagues have shown that habituation in the invertebrate *Aplysia* is best accounted for by a progressive decrease in transmitter release at the synapse between the sensory and inter- or motor neurons. Even relatively long-term decreases in responsivity stretching across days or weeks apparently involve a kind of long-term decrease in transmitter release (Castellucci, Carew, & Kandel, 1978). Farel and Thompson (1976) have come to essentially the same conclusion using the isolated spinal cord of the frog to study habituation. Hence in those rare preparations in which detailed physiological studies can be carried out to lead to interpretable results, the mechanism of habituation has proved to be similar in both invertebrate and vertebrates, quite like Thompson and Spencer might have predicted.

In summary, theories of habituation can be broadly classified into those that involve changes within the reflex pathways themselves (Groves & Thompson, 1970; Kandel, 1978; Sharpless, 1964; Thompson & Spencer, 1966; Wagner, 1976) versus those that involve some active process that develops in strength during stimulus repetition so as to suppress response output (Carlton, 1968; Hernandez-Peon, 1960; Konorski, 1967; Sokolov, 1963a, 1963b; Stein, 1966; Wagner, 1976). In general, investigators who work with relatively simple organisms adhere to the first, but those who work with complex organisms adhere to the second. It is equally likely, however, that complex organisms have many ways to mediate habituation and that several mechanisms of habituation may operate even when a simple stimulus is repeated. One of the purposes of our review will be to discuss how various results from different types of experimental paradigms can be used to draw conclusions about whether observed changes result from an alteration in habituation or an alteration in other systems that modulate response output. Indeed, we contend that a fuller appreciation of the fact that multiple habituation mechanisms can exist is critical for interpreting and designing experiments to study response change during stimulus repetition and that some better framework is needed to view these ideas.

In this chapter we describe a framework that can be used to view various ways in which neuronal plasticity can bring about response change during stimulus repetition, and we propose strategies for investigating the pharmacology of these mechanisms. Figure 1 outlines our framework, initially with regard to the startle response. A simple reflex pattern is shown from the eliciting stimulus [e.g., a loud tone (S_e)] to the response being measured [startle (R_1)]. Habituation or sensitization could occur in the S–R pathway. In this case the neuronal mechanism of habituation might involve a decrease in transmitter release (Farel & Thompson, 1976; Kandel, 1978) intrinsic to the pathway being stimulated. This could be considered an example of *intrinsic habituation*. Also influencing the response level is a modulatory system. Impulses from this system cannot themselves elicit startle, but they could reduce or enhance the response level (the latter case is illustrated). Hence the effects of the modulatory system cannot be manifested unless the response is elicited by some effective stimulus. The term *modulation* has been deliberately chosen to emphasize the different role this system has from that of the response-eliciting circuit. Modulatory (M) systems could be tonically active or their influence could be initiated by certain stimuli, including the eliciting stimulus itself. Conditioned changes in the modulatory system are also possible and are shown by the input C.

Hence another class of mechanisms that could mediate response decrement would be ones that involved these modulatory systems. Habituation

CONDITIONED
STIMULI

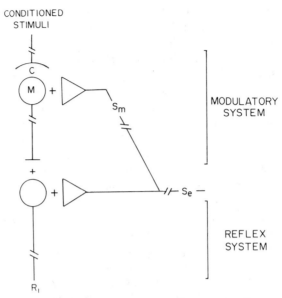

Fig. 1. Schematic representation of some potential interactions between a reflex pathway and modulatory system that are required to explain response change during repeated stimulus presentations. The eliciting stimulus (S_e) represents the sensory side of a reflex (R_l) arc. The same stimulus (then called S_m) may also activate some modulatory system that itself does not elicit the reflex but facilitates the reflex when activated by other eliciting stimuli. Conditioned activation of the modulatory system can also occur at C. Breaks in the line indicate an indefinite number of synapses between connections.

might be produced by a progressive activation of a modulatory system that was inhibitory to startle or a progressive decrease in another modulatory system that normally enhanced startle. In either case a neuronal circuit outside the actual startle S_e–R_l circuit would be involved, so that these types of habituation could be classified as *extrinsic habituation*.

Although the general classification of intrinsic-versus-extrinsic processes of habituation was proposed some time ago (Groves & Thompson, 1970), its effect on the field has not yet been fully realized. Moreover, when working with a complex animal it would seem impossible to analyze response changes in terms of these various mechanisms. Yet to deny that many different mechanisms might be operating would be an unrealistic oversimplification. On the other hand, if the neural circuit in a complex animal underlying a particular behavioral response were known, then it should be possible to begin to analyze where habituation and sensitization occur and to determine the transmitters involved in reflex modulation. The next section describes our attempts to separate neuronal sites that show response decrement from those that show response increment during repetitive elicitation of the acoustic startle reflex in the rat. Once this separation has been made, the next section distinguishes between various ways in which response change could occur. Finally, implications for pharmacological strategies of studying response change during stimulus repetition are explored.

II. Response Decrement and Response Increment of Acoustic Startle

The acoustic-startle reflex has proven to be a sensitive behavior with which to study the effects of repetitive stimulus presentation. Acoustic startle shows response decrement during stimulus repetition and fulfills all of the Thompson and Spencer (1966) criteria of "habituation." Under certain circumstances, however, repetitive elicitation of acoustic startle can lead to an actual increase in startle or an increase followed by a decrease. To explain such changes in startle, it has been suggested that repetition of an eliciting stimulus engages both decremental as well as incremental processes that interact in determining response output (Davis & Wagner, 1969; Groves & Thompson, 1970). Although emphasis is usually placed on the idea that both effects result from the presentation of the eliciting stimulus, it is possible that other factors in the experimental situation can alter response output so as to interact with the consequence of repeated presentation of some eliciting stimulus. For example, repetitive elicitation of acoustic startle in the presence of high levels of background noise can lead to a progressive response increment, whereas repetitive elicitation of acoustic startle at low noise levels leads to response decrement (Davis, 1974). These data suggested that exposure to background noise itself might increase startle in the absence of repetitive presentation of a startle-eliciting stimulus.

To test this, rats were placed in a cage specially designed to measure startle amplitude and then presented with a single startle-eliciting tone at various times after being exposed to a continuous level of 80 db background noise. Figure 2 shows that startle showed a progressive and marked increase the longer the period of exposure to background noise. Other experiments indicated that this effect was directly related to the intensity of the intervening noise.

This observation suggested, therefore, that exposure to background noise could be used as an independent method to enhance startle to see how it would interact with the consequences of repetitive presentation of

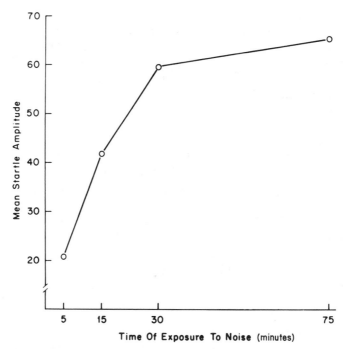

Fig. 2. Mean-amplitude startle response to a single tone presentation at various times after placing the rats in the chamber. From Davis (1974).

a startle-eliciting stimulus. For example, Fig. 2 shows that the excitatory noise effect grew rapidly over the first 30 minutes, but then remained relatively constant thereafter. Because of this, one would expect rather different response-change curves if startle-eliciting stimuli were initiated after brief-versus-prolonged exposure to background noise.

To test this, rats were placed in the startle test cages and then presented with startle-eliciting tones after either 5- or 30-minute exposure to background noise. Figure 3 shows that very different curves did emerge. Rats exposed for 5 minutes showed an initially low level of startle that then gradually increased over the first 30 minutes but decreased thereafter. In contrast, rats exposed for 30 minutes to background noise showed an initially high level of startle that decreased rapidly thereafter. Viewing Figs. 2 and 3 together, the following conclusions seem permissable. Repetitive presentation of startle-eliciting tones leads to response decrements, but continuous exposure to background noise leads to response increment. These two opposing influences interact to determine response output at any point in time.

Over the first half hour, noise-produced facilitation overcomes the dec-

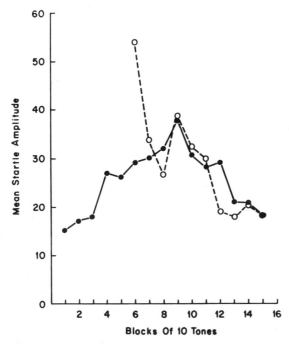

Fig. 3. Mean amplitude of the startle response over blocks of 10 tones when tones were initiated either 5 minutes (●) or 30 minutes (○) after placing the rats in the chamber. From Davis (1974).

remental effects produced by the tones, leading to a net increase in startle. After facilitation has reached its maximum, decremental effects begin to "show through," and startle amplitude declines. In contrast, when rats are first presented with tones after 30-minutes exposure to noise, startle amplitudes are initially high, because noise-produced facilitation has reached its maximum. Response decrement to tones then proceeds, and because noise-produced facilitation remains fairly constant, the net result is a decrease in startle. The acoustic-startle reflex provides a means, therefore, to study response increment and response decrement somewhat independently.

A. The Primary Acoustic-Startle Circuit

Another advantage of using acoustic startle is that it has a relatively simple neural circuit. In the rat, the latency of acoustic startle is 8 msec recorded electromyographically in the hindleg (Ison, McAdam, & Hammond, 1973), indicating that a only few synapses are involved in mediating startle. Figure 4 shows the structures and pathways thought to be involved in the rat acoustic startle response. This is based on a combination of methods using lesions, electrical stimulation, evoked potential recordings, and retrograde anatomical tracing techniques and has been described in detail elsewhere (Davis, Gendelman, Tishler, & Gendelman, 1982).

1. Ventral Cochlear Nucleus

The posteroventral cochlear nucleus (VCN) appears to be the first central synapse in the primary acoustic-startle circuit. Bilateral lesions of the VCN abolish acoustic startle. Lesions of the dorsal nucleus, however, fail to abolish startle. In conscious rats, bilateral, single-pulse stimulation (1-msec pulse width, 25–100 μA) of the VCN elicits startle-like responses with latency of 7.0–7.5 msec. In fact, this response looks so much like acoustic startle that it is difficult to discriminate the two visually.

2. Ventral and Intermediate Acoustic Stria

Fibers from the VCN course medially and ventrally to form the intermediate and ventral acoustic stria (VAS). Lesions of the VAS abolish or markedly attenuate startle. But lesions of the dorsal acoustic stria, which carry fibers from the dorsal cochlear nucleus, do not alter startle.

3. Dorsal and Ventral Nuclei of the Lateral Lemniscus

The second synapse in the primary acoustic startle circuit seems to be in the dorsal and ventral nuclei of the lateral lemniscus (DLL, VLL), which are known to receive direct projections from the ventral cochlear nuclei. Bilateral lesions of these nuclei abolish acoustic startle. Moreover, both ipsilateral and contralateral nuclei are involved, because lesions of both sides are required to abolish startle in animals in which clicks are presented to just one ear. Finally, electrical stimulation of these nuclei elicits discrete startle-like responses with an average latency of about 6.0 msec. Stimulation of the dorsal nucleus elicits exclusively ipsilateral leg movements, whereas stimulation of the ventral nuclei elicits bilateral leg movements.

4. Nucleus Reticularis Pontis Caudalis

The next synapse is probably located in a ventromedial region of the nucleus reticularis pontis caudalis (RPC). Previous ablation work had

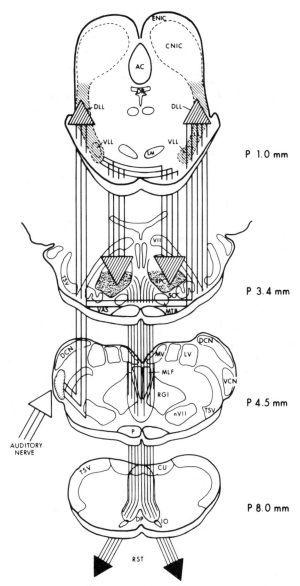

Fig. 4. Schematic diagram of a primary acoustic-startle circuit. AC, Aqueduct; DCN, dorsal cochlear nucleus; VCN, ventral cochlear nucleus; CNIC, central nucleus of the inferior colliculus; CU, cuneate nucleus; DP, decussation of pyramids; ENIC, external nucleus of the inferior colliculus; IO, inferior olive; LL, lateral lemniscus; DLL, dorsal nucleus of the lateral lemniscus; VLL, ventral nucleus of the lateral lemniscus; LM, medial lemniscus; MLF, medial longitudinal fasciculus; MTB, medial nucleus of the trapezoid body; NVII, nucleus of the seventh nerve; SO, superior olive; P, pyramids; DR, dorsal raphe nucleus; RGI, nucleus reticularis giganticocellularis; RPC, nucleus reticularis pontis caudalis; RST, reticulo spinal tract; TSV, spinal tract of the fifth nerve; VAS, ventral acoustic stria; VII, seventh nerve; LV, lateral vestibular nucleus; MV, medial vestibular nucleus. From Davis, Gendelman, Tischler, & Gendelman (1982). Copyright 1982, Society for Neuroscience.

pointed to the importance of this area for acoustic startle (Groves, Wilson, & Boyle, 1974; Hammond, 1973; Leitner, Powers, & Hoffman, 1980; Szabo & Hazafi, 1965). We find that bilateral lesions of this area abolish acoustic startle both acutely and chronically. Electrical stimulation of points within the RPC elicits startle-like responses with an average latency of about 5 msec. In contrast, lesions localized to dorsal or rostral areas of the RPC, or lesions of the caudally adjacent nucleus reticularis giganticocellularis (RGI) fail to abolish startle. Furthermore, electrical stimulation of these areas with reasonably low currents does not elicit startle responses. Thus cell bodies in the RPC may be involved in relaying auditory information down to the spinal cord. However, more recent evidence in our laboratory suggests that there may be direct connections between the VLL and the spinal cord. Hence it is possible that the effects of ablation and electrical stimulation of the RPC involves fibers of passage, rather than cell bodies alone.

5. Reticulospinal Tract

Cell bodies in the RPC send their axons to all levels of the spinal cord through the reticulospinal tract. This tract courses through the medial longitudinal fasciculus (MLF) on the midline and then bifurcates to form the ventral funiculi in the spinal cord. Midline lesions of the MLF abolish acoustic startle, provided the lesions have a great enough dorsal–ventral extent. Electrical stimulation on the midline through the MLF elicits leg movements with a latency of about 4.0–4.5 msec.

6. Lower Motor Neurons in the Spinal Cord

Fibers from the reticulospinal tract project to all levels of the spinal cord, forming connections to spinal motoneurons. Direct and indirect synapses onto motoneurons through an interneuron in the cord are possible. It has not been determined if interneurons in the cord are involved in acoustic startle.

B. Plasticity of Electrically Elicited "Startle"

We have described how repetitive presentation of startle-eliciting stimuli during continuous exposure to low levels of background noise produces progressive response decrement, whereas stimuli presented during exposure to high background noise produce response increments. It is conceivable that these two opposing influences alter transmission at different points along the acoustic startle circuit. If so, then repetitive elicita-

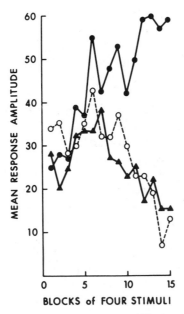

Fig. 5. Mean amplitude response over successive blocks of four stimuli (2-minute periods) when "startle" was elicited acoustically (▲) or electrically from either the cochlear nucleus (VCN; ○) or the nucleus reticularis pontis (RPC; ●; $n = 8$ in each group). From Davis, Parisi, Gendelman, Tischler, & Kehne (1982).

tion of electrically elicited "startle" at different points along the circuit might be used to separate the two processes.

To test this, rats were prepared with bilateral monopolar electrodes implanted in either the VCN or the RPC, using standard stereotaxic techniques. One week later they were placed in cages in which startle response amplitudes could be recorded. One minute later, they were given single pulses (1 msec, 25–100 μA to each electrode) bilaterally in either the VCN or the RPC every 30 seconds (Davis, Parisi, Gendelman, Tischler, & Kehne, 1982). A total of 60 stimuli were applied during the 30-minute test session. Throughout testing, a constant level of 80-db background noise was maintained. Another group of unimplanted rats was tested identically except that startle was elicited by 60 50-msec, 110-db tones, spaced 30 seconds apart. Figure 5 shows that "startle" elicited acoustically or electrically through the VCN showed an initial increase in amplitude followed by a gradual decrease toward the end of the session. In marked contrast, "startle" elicited through the RPC showed a progressive increase across the session, with no subsequent decline.

The data clearly show that under these conditions "startle" behaves quite differently when elicited electrically through the VCN or RPC. The results with acoustic startle or VCN stimulation are consistent with the results described earlier. If one assumes that the net decrease in startle toward the end of the session resulted because decremental changes overcame incremental ones, the data indicate that response decrement must occur at the cochlear nucleus or somewhere "downstream" (i.e., peripheral changes in the ear or changes in the auditory nerve could not account for this progressive decrease in startle).

The next question was whether the progressive response increment in the RPC animals was caused by repetitive stimulation through the RPC, or instead by continued exposure to the background noise. For example, if the response increments shown in Fig. 5 resulted from continuous exposure to background noise, then 30-minutes exposure to noise itself would be sufficient to enhance response amplitude to a high level in all three groups, with no need for concomitant elicitation of the startle reflex.

To test this, rats were prepared with electrodes implanted in the VCN or RPC. Another group of rats were set aside for acoustic testing. One week later each rat was placed in a startle test cage and 1 minute later given two electrical stimulations or two tones separated by 30 seconds to establish a preexposure baseline. All rats were then exposed to 80-db noise for 30 minutes followed by 60 electrical or acoustic stimuli, one stimulus every 30 seconds. The 80-db noise level was maintained throughout testing. Figure 6 shows that all three groups had similar response levels at the beginning of the session. Following 30-minutes exposure to background noise, all three groups showed a marked and essentially equivalent increase in amplitude when "startle" elicitation finally began, indicating that exposure to noise by itself was sufficient to produce response increments with no need for concomitant reflex elicitation. Thereafter, both the acoustic- and VCN-stimulated groups showed a decrease in "startle" amplitude. The RPC rats showed no decrease in "startle" over the comparable test period.

Taken together, the results indicate that background noise may influence response amplitude by an action in the RPC or parts of the startle circuit beyond the RPC because the enhancement by noise was similar in magnitude whether "startle" was elicited through the RPC or VCN. This effect seems to involve modulation instead of sensitization, because it occurred in the absence of reflex elicitation. On the other hand, stimulus repetition under these conditions may produce response decrement only in parts of circuit before the RPC because this occurred during repetitive stimulation through the VCN but not the RPC. Moreover, the decremental process before the RPC must be quite effective, because it can over-

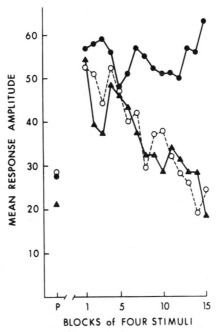

Fig. 6. Mean-amplitude response over two initial stimuli and then over successive blocks of four stimuli (2-minute periods) that began 30 minutes later when "startle" was elicited acoustically (▲) or electrically from either the cochlear nucleus (VCN; ○) or the nucleus reticularis pontis caudalis (RPC; ●; $n = 8$ in each group). From Davis, Parisi, Gendelman, Tischler, & Kehne (1982).

come a progressive enhancement of responses in the RPC or beyond. These data represent the first instance in which different anatomical loci within a complex vertebrate have been implicated in the processes underlying progressive response decrement and increment.

We have seen that it is not possible to determine from these behavioral results what neuronal mechanisms might mediate the response decrements observed when startle is elicited acoustically or electrically through the VCN. The data do indicate, however, that a good place to begin to look for the mechanisms would be in parts of the circuit before the RPC, and more information will be available once we record single units at various points along the startle pathway. On the other hand, the data do suggest that response increments involve a modulatory system that alters transmission in the RPC or "downstream" in the spinal cord. Hence the next section will describe our attempts to determine what neurotransmitters might be involved in spinal modulation of acoustic startle.

C. Spinal Neurochemical Modulation of
   Acoustic Startle

Our data indicate that facilitatory modulation of the startle response occurs in the RPC or spinal cord. Subsequent studies in which startle was elicited repetitively in the reticulospinal tract, beyond the RPC, also found response increments, suggesting an alteration of transmission in the spinal cord. The next step was to determine what neurotransmitters in the spinal cord might alter acoustic startle and whether these neurotransmitters might be involved in the facilitatory modulation produced by high background noise.

Considerable evidence indicates that the neurotransmitters serotonin (5-HT) and norepinephrine (NE) increase spinal reflexes when tested in acutely spinal rats (cf. Davis, 1980). To determine if these compounds would alter acoustic startle by an action in the spinal cord, rats were implanted with chronic indwelling catheters in the spinal subarachnoid space at the level of the lumbar enlargement (e.g., Davis, Astrachan, Gendelman, & Gendelman, 1980). After implantation, rats were given startle-eliciting tones before and after infusion of 5-HT, NE, or their agonists into the spinal cord (intrathecal administration). Yaksh and Rudy (1976) have shown that small amounts of substances infused in this way remain localized in the spinal cord, with only trace amounts in the brain when measured from 4 to 60 minutes later. We and others have confirmed this (Brautigam, Flosbach, & Herken, 1980; Davis & Astrachan, 1981).

Figure 7 summarizes data gathered from more than 200 rats in this way. Infusion of 5-HT increases acoustic startle. This effect is potentiated by intraperitoneal (ip) injection of pargyline, a drug that decreases 5-HT catabolism, and is blocked by ip administration of the 5-HT antagonist cinanserin. Startle is also increased by intrathecal administration of the 5-HT agonist 5-methoxy-N,N-dimethyltryptamine (5-MeODMT). This effect can be blocked by ip pretreatment with the 5-HT antagonist cyproheptadine, but not the NE antagonist WB-4101 or the dopamine (DA) antagonist haloperidol. All these data indicate that 5-HT plays an excitatory role in modulating startle in the spinal cord, consistent with a large literature showing that 5-HT facilitates spinal reflexes. Moreover, control infusions of 5-HT or 5-MeODMT intraventricularly do not increase startle but actually depress startle (Commissaris & Davis, 1982; Davis, Astrachan, & Kass, 1980).

Norepinephrine also seems to play an excitatory role in modulating startle in the spinal cord. Intrathecal NE itself increases startle. This effect seems to be mediated by activation of an α_1-adrenergic receptor,

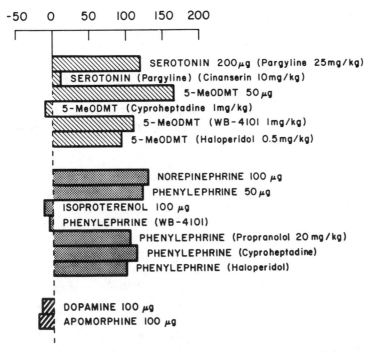

Fig. 7. Summary of the effects of various compounds on acoustic startle (expressed as mean percentage change in startle amplitude) when given directly into the subarachnoid space of the spinal cord (intrathecal administration). Other drugs given intraperitoneally to enhance or block the effects of intrathecal compounds are enclosed in parentheses. Data from Astrachan and Davis (1981), Davis, Astrachan, and Kass (1980), and Davis, Astrachan, Gendelman, and Gendelman (1980).

because it is mimicked by the α_1-adrenergic agonist phenylephrine, but not the β-adrenergic agonist isoproterenol. Moreover, the excitatory effect of phenylephrine is blocked by the α_1-adrenergic antagonist WB-4101 but not the β-antagonist propranolol, the 5-HT antagonist cyproheptadine, nor the dopamine (DA) antagonist haloperidol (Astrachan & Davis, 1981).

On the other hand, dopamine does not seem to play a role in modulating startle in the spinal cord. Neither intrathecal administration of dopamine itself nor the dopamine agonist apomorphine affects acoustic startle over a wide dose range. On the other hand, apomorphine markedly increases startle when given intraventricularly (R. L. Commissaris & M. Davis, unpublished).

D. Effects of Serotonin and Norepinephrine Antagonists on the Modulation Activated by Background Noise

Our data show that both 5-HT and NE increase startle when given intrathecally. The spinal cord is known to contain high levels of these biogenic amines. The response increment observed with stimulation through the RPC or MLF during exposure to high background noise must involve some incremental process that acts in the spinal cord. Given the excitatory effects demonstrated for 5-HT and NE in the spinal cord, it seemed reasonable to ask whether either of these transmitters might be involved in mediating response enhancement observed during stimulation of the RPC.

To test whether 5-HT or NE are involved in the excitatory effects of background noise, rats were prepared with electrodes implanted in the RPC. During testing a few initial stimuli were given to establish a baseline. A constant 80-db noise was then turned on, and a total of 64 pulses were given once every 30 seconds. At various times before the session different groups of rats were injected with either p-chlorophenylalanine (PCPA; a 5-HT synthesis inhibitor), cyproheptadine (a 5-HT antagonist), or WB-4101 [an α_1-adrenergic antagonist; Davis (1981)].

Under these conditions of a constant high level of background noise, repetitive elicitation of "startle" through the RPC again resulted in a marked increase in "startle" amplitude across the session. This increase was not attenuated either by PCPA or cyproheptadine using doses and treatment intervals known to block the effects of 5-HT in other situations. In contrast, the increase was completely blocked by the α_1-adrenergic antagonist WB-4101. Taken together, the data suggest that the enhanced responses under these conditions involve a release of NE rather than 5-HT. Thus this type of startle sensitization differs from sensitization in the invertebrate *Aplysia,* where response increments result from a modulatory system that uses 5-HT as its facilitatory transmitter (e.g., Kandel, 1978). More recent data suggest that 5-HT and NE may act synergistically to mediate sensitization of startle to background noise.

III. Modulatory Pathways

On the basis of the data described above, the following conclusions seem permissible with reference to the framework illustrated in Fig.1. The modulatory system might involve NE containing cell bodies that project down into the spinal cord. Activation of this system by background noise may release NE and thereby facilitate acoustic startle at the spinal level, as NE does when given intrathecally. To test this hypothesis, NE antagonists could be given systemically or intrathecally to see if they would decrease the response enhancement when "startle" is elicited either electrically through the RPC or acoustically.

Repetitive elicitation of "startle" through the VCN produces response decrement, whereas repetitive stimulation through the RPC does not. But transmission can be modulated in the spinal cord by intrathecal administration of drugs. An important implication of these concepts is that drugs given systemically might alter transmission, primarily in the spinal cord, by interacting with spinal modulatory systems. Because we are assuming that no habituation occurs in the cord under these conditions of testing, such a drug effect could be ascribed to a change in modulation rather than an interaction with the process of habituation.

A. Pharmacological Modulation

This line of reasoning would predict that intrathecal administration of a drug that enhances spinal NE should increase overall acoustic-startle levels by modulating the reflex in the spinal cord, but should not alter the course of response decrement, because this is mediated by supraspinal parts of the startle pathway. That is to say, if there is no decremental process in the spinal cord in the first place, enhancement of response output cannot result from blocking a decremental process. To test this, rats were implanted with intrathecal catheters and 2 days later infused either with saline or d-amphetamine, which releases NE and blocks reuptake. One minute later the rats were placed in the test cages and 30 minutes later presented with 90 tones at a 20-second intertone interval. Consistent with expectation, the left panel of Fig. 8 shows that d-amphetamine enhanced acoustic startle throughout the test session. Because the drug was injected intrathecally, we can reasonably assume that enhancement of startle resulted from an action on some spinal modulatory system and not because it blocked processes involved in startle decrement.

It should be emphasized, however, that some investigators have concluded that because a drug elevates response levels after systemic administration, it does so by blocking habituation. Similar conclusions have been made when a lesion or even a particular psychiatric state is associated with elevated response levels. In some cases, however, these conclusions may be the result of artifacts associated with procedures used for analysis of the treatment effect. For example, to handle the problem of a shift in baseline after a drug or a lesion, some investigators express their

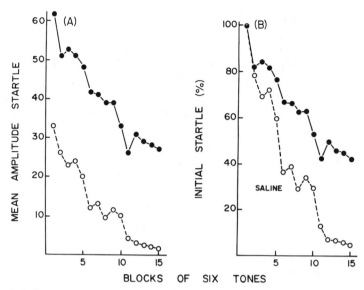

Fig. 8. (A) Mean amplitude startle responses elicited by tones presented every 20 seconds after intrathecal administration of 400 μg of d-amphetamine sulfate or saline (n = 10 in each group). (B) The same data expressed in percentage terms, where each data point has been divided by the first score and then multiplied by 100. ○, Saline; ●, amphetamine.

data as a percentage decrement relative to the initial score (e.g., Capps & Stockwell, 1968; Williams, Hamilton, & Carlton, 1974). This has even been done when different stimulus treatments are used that invariably alter initial amplitudes, such as comparing the effects of stimulus intensity on rate of habituation (e.g., Lukowiak & Peretz, 1980; Thompson & Spencer, 1966). Application of this technique for the analysis of the effects of intrathecal d-amphetamine is illustrated in Fig. 8B. Clearly, the drug reduces the slope of the decrement percentage curve, but this can be entirely accounted for by calling the first response 100% in both conditions and then using this formula to compute all subsequent numbers. But, it is impossible to determine from percentage statistics alone what the treatment actually did to overall response levels. If one's theory of response change used absolute rather than percentage figures, then the sole inclusion of percentage figures would obscure valuable empirical information. Hence, we would strongly recommend the inclusion of absolute response levels in any investigation that reports percentage figures.

In other cases, investigators have reported only the number of trials to reach some criterion of nonresponsiveness to determine the effect of a drug on habituation (e.g., Key, 1961). Because more trials would be required to reach criterion, the results in the left panel of Fig. 8A could again be used to conclude that amphetamine slowed habituation. But given the fact that the drug seemed to elevate only overall response levels and that intrathecal administration of a drug could not attenuate habituation in a system (the spinal cord) that shows no habituation under these conditions, the data indicate that these techniques of analysis are not justified under all conditions. Indeed, these techniques of analysis may lead to erroneous conclusions concerning the way different treatments alter response change during stimulus repetition.

B. Conditioned Facilitatory Modulation

In 1951, Brown, Kalish, and Farber demonstrated that the amplitude of acoustic startle could be increased by presenting the eliciting stimulus in the presence of a cue [conditioned stimulus (CS)] previously paired with a shock [unconditioned stimulus (US)]. This effect has been replicated a number of times and has been termed "the potentiated startle effect" (cf. Davis, 1980). In our framework, potentiated startle would represent a kind of "conditioned facilitatory modulation," whereby the CS activates the same modulatory system normally activated by the US. If the transmitters involved in conditioned modulation are different than those that mediate transmission along the startle pathway, then it should be possible to find drugs that would decrease potentiated startle but have no effect on acoustic startle itself. In fact, we have found that drugs such as diazepam and morphine can decrease potentiated startle without altering baseline startle levels (Davis, 1979a, 1979b).

C. Conditioned Inhibitory Modulation

We have proposed that pairing stimulus presentations with activation of a modulatory system can lead to a conditioned activation of that system. Potentiated startle is an example of a conditioned excitatory modulation. Our framework allows for the possibility of a conditioned inhibitory modulation. Figure 1 shows a special case where the eliciting stimulus also engages a modulatory system. If the modulatory system is excitatory, this would lead to an enhancement of the elicited startle response. This is the idea suggested by Groves and Thompson (1970), whereby the startle stimulus also engages some other mechanism that enhances responsivitity. If the modulatory system is inhibitory then the eliciting stimulus would also reduce startle amplitude. The nature of the stimulus is likely to determine whether facilitatory or inhibitory modulators are engaged. Groves and

Thompson (1970) suggested that more intense stimuli would be likely to engage the former.

Wagner (1976) has proposed that a conditioning process underlies response decrement in a variety of "habituation" experiments. In this theory, background environmental cues serve as the stimuli that become conditioned stimuli. These cues then act to reinstate a representation of the eliciting stimulus and thereby reduce responsivitity to that stimulus. From Wagner's theory it follows that habituation training in the presence of one set of environmental cues should not be well retained when testing occurs with a different set of cues. To test this with startle, the following experiment was done. In one group of rats the environmental conditions were the presence of a light (200-W bulb 1.2 m from the cages), 80-db steady white noise, and sandpaper on the floor of the startle test cage. For the other group, environmental conditions were no light; an 80-db, 10-kHz steady tone; and a grid floor. These conditions prevailed throughout the 15-minute preperiod and the training session. During the training sessions both groups of rats received 100 presentations of the startle stimulus, which in this case was the tap produced by dropping a 5-gram weight onto a steel plate from a distance of 3 cm every 15 seconds. This stimulus was used because exploratory work indicated it produced startle amplitudes comparable to those produced by loud tones but also resulted in substantial between-session habituation, which frequently is difficult to produce with very loud tones. These training session were given on each of three successive days.

The following day, half of the rats in each group were assigned to the same set of background cues that they had received during training; the other half of each group was switched to the opposite set of cues. All rats received a 15-minute preperiod and then a test session of stimulus presentations at intervals of 15 seconds.

Figure 9 shows the mean startle amplitude on the test and training days for rats trained and tested under the same background cues and those trained and tested under different cues. Retention of habituation was slightly better for the group that had the same cues in training and testing, but this effect was of only borderline significance ($p < .10$). Hence there was a great deal of retention (e.g., Day 1 versus Day 4) that was not affected by changing the environment.

These data suggest that although background cues may act as CSs for conditioned diminution of startle responses, this mechanism probably accounts for only a small amount of long-term response decrement in startle. Moreover, it is unlikely that we simply chose the wrong set of parameters to vary in the background, because we have also found only small effects of using a background order (amyl acetate) as a potential

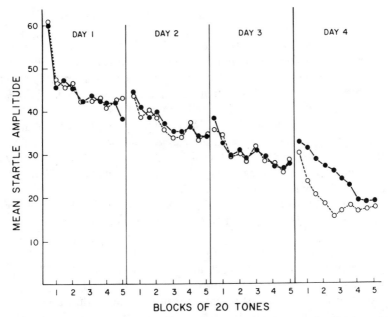

Fig. 9. Mean startle amplitude over successive blocks of 20 startle-eliciting stimuli during training (Days 1–3) and test (Day 4) days for groups trained and tested in the presence of the same background cues (O) and for those trained and tested in the presence of different cues (●; *n* = 20 in each group).

stimulus to mediate conditioned habituation. In an extensive series of experiments, Marlin and Miller (1981) were also unable to demonstrate conditioning of startle decrements to background cues. These negative results may not be entirely surprising, because the background cues are present for much of the time without the eliciting stimulus so that the pairing does not represent that most favorable for conditioning.

The role of background cues as conditioned stimuli mediating long-term decrement of orienting has also been explored. Because orienting results in the interruption of ongoing activity it is possible to measure orientation by the interruption of licking (File & Russell, 1972). Conditioning processes might be especially important in this paradigm, because it shows substantial retention over long intervals and can be produced even by presenting only one stimulus a day (File, 1973). If background cues were mediating this long-term response change, then prior exposure to these cues in the absence of tones should retard conditioning, because operationally this would be similar to latent inhibition (e.g., Lubow, 1973). But exposure to the background cues of the test chamber for several days did not alter subsequent response change to tone presentations when they were later presented at a rate of one per day (File, 1973).

Another prediction from Wagner's theory is "extinction of habituation," whereby exposing animals to the background cues during some retention interval should disrupt or retard retention (Wagner, 1976). In an early experiment, a test of essentially this same idea was carried out (File, 1969). When the animals no longer oriented to the tone stimulus (i.e., when tone presentations no longer interrupted licking) they were divided into three groups that differed in their experience with the test environment during a 2-day retention interval. All groups continued to get only 20 minutes access to water each day. One group remained in their home cages for the 2 days and there had access to water for 20 minutes. Another group received 20-minute sessions in the test box with the water bottle available, but no tones were presented. Because no tones were given to this group and they had exposure to the environment and hence the opportunity to extinguish, this group should have showed the worst retention. The third group received 20-minute sessions in the test chamber; water was available and the tones were presented. Hence this group should have showed the best retention, simply because they received two extra days of training. On the next day, all three groups were tested identically to see how a tone would affect their licking. No significant differences occurred among the groups in their response to the tone, measured by interruption of licking (File, 1969). Leaton (1974) has also been unable to show conditioning to background cues in a similar paradigm. Thus, even though long-term decrements of the orienting reflex could be mediated by background cues activating some inhibitory modulatory systems, experiments designed to test this idea have not confirmed this hypothesis. These data, coupled with the data on acoustic startle reported herein and other experiments in the literature, do not confirm, therefore, Wagner's (1976) theory of "habituation" as a conditioned process.

IV. Summary Analysis of Response Change during Stimulus Repetition

In conclusion, we discuss some implications of the idea of multiple mechanisms of habituation and sensitization as they relate to the design and interpretation of experiments dealing with response change during stimulus repetition.

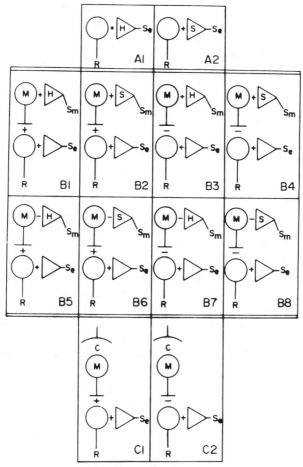

Fig. 10. (A1–A2) Reflex systems that can either habituate (A1) or sensitize (A2). (B1–B8) All possible combinations in which modulatory systems are either activated or inhibited by pathways that either habituate or sensitize where the modulatory system either facilitates or inhibits reflex behavior. (C1–C2) Conditioned facilitory (C1) or conditioned inhibitory modulation (C2).

A. Response Change within Reflex Pathways

1. Intrinsic Habituation

Figure 10,A1 illustrates a reflex pathway that can undergo intrinsic habituation. We have seen that the term *intrinsic habituation* is being reserved to describe mechanisms within the reflex pathway itself,

whereby repeated activation at some synapse leads to a decrease in transmission at that synapse. In *Aplysia,* the mechanism of intrinsic habituation involves a decrease in the amount of transmitter released per impulse
(cf. Kandel, 1978). Other types of intrinsic mechanisms might involve a
change in postsynaptic receptor sensitivity or changes within a second
messenger system within the postsynaptic neurons, although these have
not yet been identified. The important point is that the mechanism is
intrinsic to the synapse under study and not the result of some extrinsic
influence that regulates transmitter release (e.g., presynaptic inhibition),
because this would involve a modulatory system.

As Horn (1970) has pointed out, an intrinsic mechanism of habituation
can account for many of the phenomena within the "habituation" literature:

1. Response decrement to stimulus repetition will occur.
2. Recovery of responsiveness over time will occur when synaptic
transmission is restored to normal.
3. If one assumes that a relatively long time is required for transmission
to be fully restored to normal, then successive series of stimulus-repeti-
tion sessions might lead to faster and faster rates of response decrement
over time, as if "habituation" were retained over time.
4. Response decrement would be more rapid with shorter interstimulus
intervals, because these would favor the development of synaptic depression (e.g., if synthesis could not keep up with release).
5. Below-zero "habituation," measured as a delay in response recovery following a series of additional stimuli presentations (that no longer
elicit the measured response), could also occur, because synaptic depression could continue to increase with stimulus repetition even though the
amount of transmitter released was no longer sufficient to elicit the measured response. Depending on the sensitivity of the measurement system,
this could be very easy (low sensitivity) or rather difficult (high sensitivity) to demonstrate.
6. Stimulus specificity, measured by a reinstatement of the response
when a different stimulus is presented (sometimes misleadingly called
"dishabituation") would occur if a different stimulus pathway (not shown
in Fig. 1) could elicit the same response, but did not share all the synapses
used by the habituating stimulus. Operationally, this would be the procedure to determine if the response decrement obtained could be explained
by response fatigue.
7. Stimulus generalization, whereby repetition of one stimulus leads to
a decrease in response to a second stimulus, would occur when different
stimulus pathways (i.e., two Se pathways) shared some habituating syn-

apses. The greater the sharing, the greater the generalization. Hence, intrinsic mechanisms of habituation could account for many parametric features that have been described to occur during repetitive stimulus presentations. Indeed, this is the most parsimonious way to handle a great deal of data in the literature.

If intrinsic habituation were responsible for producing response decrement, then a lesion could not alter habituation without also obliterating the response being measured. Hence, if one sets out to determine if a lesion will prevent habituation, one is implicitly assuming that extrinsic rather than intrinsic habituation is the underlying mechanism. Studies showing that lesions of many areas fail to alter response decrement might be used, therefore, to suggest that the mechanism of habituation is intrinsic rather than extrinsic. For example, no studies have consistently found that lesions in many different areas prevent within-session startle habituation (Capps & Stockwell, 1968; Coover & Levine, 1972; Davis & Sheard, 1974; Fox, 1979; Geyer, Puerto, Menkes, Segal, & Mandell, 1976; Groves et al., 1974; Jordan & Leaton, 1982; Miller & Treft, 1979; Yunger & Harvey, 1973).

An interesting exception to this idea comes from the work in the crayfish (cf. Krasne, 1978). Here, habituation seems to involve an intrinsic mechanism between sensory afferents and lateral, giant command neurons. But the presynaptic terminal of the sensory afferents can be inhibited by activation of other, nonlateral command neurons. When presynaptic inhibition occurs, habituation is retarded. In this case, therefore, a lesion of some distant structure could presumably alter intrinsic habituation, but notice that the prediction would be one where a lesion improved habituation.

Intrinsic mechanisms of habituation would also have implications for the types of drugs chosen to alter response decrement. For example, suppose that the excitatory transmitter in Fig. 10,A1 were acetylcholine acting on a muscarinic postsynaptic receptor, and that habituation resulted from a progressive decrease in the amount of ACh released per impulse. One would expect that the drug scopolamine would actually accelerate response decrement, because it would block postsynaptic receptors and hence decrease ACh transmission, similar to that produced by intrinsic habituation. Similar effects would be expected from drugs that decreased ACh synthesis or decreased release. When dealing with intrinsic habituation, therefore, the predictions are exactly opposite to the predominant idea within the literature that ACh antagonists should *prevent* response decrement (Carlton, 1968). At a more molecular level, however, it is likely that a different class of drugs would have to be found actually to alter the process responsible for intrinsic habituation. Thus drugs that interact more directly with the regulation of potassium and calcium channels might have to be employed because these are the changes that seem to account for intrinsic habituation (e.g., Kandel, 1978). Moreover, such drugs should only work when applied locally to the circuit under study but not when applied to sites distant from the reflex pathway. In fact, the enterprise of trying to block intrinsic habituation pharmacologically will have a low probability of success until a firmer understanding of the processes underlying intracellular alteration in synaptic transmission is available. An interesting variant on this idea, however, is the suggestion by Glanzman and Schmidt (1981) that drugs that facilitate presynaptic inhibition should actually *retard* habituation, given the data of Krasne (1978). Note again how different this idea is from the one in which a build up of presynaptic inhibition would be expected to improve habituation (e.g., MacDonald & Pearson, 1979) in the case where the mechanism of habituation is assumed to be extrinsic.

It is particularly interesting in this regard that no drug tested thus far has blocked within-session response decrement of acoustic startle (cf. Davis, 1980). If response decrement in this case is caused by intrinsic habituation within the startle pathway, the lack of drug effects on the rate of response decrement would be consistent with this idea.

2. Intrinsic Sensitization

Figure 10,A2 illustrates a reflex pathway that can undergo intrinsic sensitization. In this case, intrinsic sensitization is being reserved for some intrinsic synaptic mechanism that leads to an increase in transmission at a particular synapse during stimulus repetition (e.g., posttetanic potentiation). In general, little evidence supports such a process at rates of stimulus repetition typically used within the literature. Nonetheless, one could envision some intrinsic mechanisms that might lead to an increase in the amount of transmitter per impulse or an increase in postsynaptic receptor sensitivity. For example, corelease of a peptide with some excitatory transmitter would perhaps enhance the degree to which subsequent release of that transmitter would excite the postsynaptic neuron. If the effects of the initial stimulus were submaximal, and the second stimulus had occurred within the time period of enhanced postsynaptic receptor sensitivity, sensitization would occur. Again, the important point is that the term *intrinsic sensitization* is being reserved for the logical possibility that local synaptic mechanisms within reflex pathways could mediate response increment.

Given this definition, it would again be illogical to lesion some part of the nervous system in an attempt to block intrinsic sensitization unless that lesion were placed directly in the reflex pathway, a procedure that would make further study impossible. Similarly, it would be illogical to ask whether electrical stimulation of parts of the nervous system distant to the reflex pathway would block intrinsic sensitization. Finally, the choice of drugs that might be expected to alter this type of sensitization would depend on the actual mechanism under study. Thus a peptide antagonist might block the development of intrinsic sensitization if co-release of peptides enhanced postsynaptic receptor sensitivity. Moreover, this same effect would have to occur with local application of the drugs at the point in the reflex pathway where sensitization occurs. But local application of drugs at a site outside the reflex pathway could not logically alter this type of sensitization.

B. Response Change Involving Modulatory Pathways: Extrinsic Habituation and Sensitization

Changes in the reflex pathway alone cannot account for "dishabituation," whereby presentation of another stimulus leads to an increase in response that has decremented during stimulus repetition (cf. Thompson & Spencer, 1966). Changes in the reflex pathways alone also could not account for the finding that presentation of a strong stimulus prior to a sequence of eliciting stimuli can increase initial levels of responsivitity (e.g., Humphrey, 1933). To account for these phenomena a modulatory system must be assumed that can influence the magnitude of the measured response but does not itself elicit the response. Response modulation can have a net facilitatory or inhibitory effect that we will assume does not show any plasticity. But there are three ways inputs to the modulatory system could show plasticity—namely, through intrinsic habituation, intrinsic sensitization, or classical conditioning.

Figure 10,B1–B8 shows the eight possible combinations whereby stimuli can excite or inhibit modulatory systems that are either excitatory or inhibitory to the measured response through inputs that can either show habituation or sensitization. It should be emphasized that this is not to imply an eight-factor of response change that we wish to adopt, but simply to illustrate the logical possibilities—some of which have implicitly been assumed in other theories of "habituation" and "sensitization." For example, it is frequently assumed that response decrement occurs because of a progressive enhancement in some brain area that serves to inhibit the measured response (e.g., Fig. 10,B4; see page 313). Hidden within this assumption, however, is the idea that a progressive increase in inhibition must ultimately involve an increase in neural transmission at some point. One way this could occur would be by intrinsic sensitization at some point within the pathway S_m in Fig. 10,B4. Indeed, we would not dispute that this is a possible mechanism. But in this case one would have to conclude that habituation was ultimately caused by sensitization. In contrast to intrinsic habituation, therefore, this process must be considerably more complex. Indeed, it is curious that habituation is constantly stated as being the ''simplest form of learning'' and hence should serve as a good startling point for the understanding of more complex forms of learning. This might be true for intrinsic habituation, but the development of extrinsic habituation seems no simpler than more traditional measures of learning such as classical conditioning. In fact, habituation might even be more complicated, because the response decrement being measured could be mediated both by intrinsic and extrinsic mechanisms that would be differentially sensitive to drugs, lesions, and the like. In any case, one has to be very clear about these possibilities when setting out to study ''habituation.''

Figure 10,B2 is of special interest, because this is the situation suggested by Groves and Thompson (1970) and used as their definition of sensitization. In this case, the eliciting stimulus itself engages some excitatory modulatory system that then increases subsequent responsivity to that stimulus. Activation of excitatory modulation in a system extrinsic to the reflex pathway is also the mechanism of sensitization discovered in the *Aplysia*. In this case the modulation affects the presynaptic terminals of sensory or interneurons that synapse onto motoneurons (Kandel, 1978). The important point for this discussion is that this particular mechanism represents only one way among several whereby an external stimulus could produce response increments. Thus turning off a tonically inhibitory modulatory influence (Fig. 10,B7, or B8) would be just as effective in increasing response output. In fact, we have found that the glycine antagonist strychnine causes a dramatic increase in acoustic startle at subconvulsant doses (Kehne, Gallager, & Davis, 1981). This suggests that glycine exerts a pronounced tonic inhibition of acoustic startle. Thus, stimuli that increase startle could do so by inhibiting glycine's effect on startle.

It should now be obvious how easy it would be for a drug or a lesion to affect overall response levels without actually affecting processes responsible for habituation. Thus if habituation was intrinsic in a pathway tonically inhibited by some modulatory system (Fig. 10,B3, B4, B7, B8), then drugs that decreased release or synthesis inhibitors or postsynaptic antagonists would elevate overall response levels but do nothing to the rate of habituation. In many cases this would be easy to interpret, because the drug would simply cause a parallel shift in the curve but not alter the rate of response decrement (e.g., Fig. 8). But, under conditions where a ceiling effect might operate, or when the scale of measurement was not necessarily linear, changes in overall response levels might be associated with changes in the slope of habituation curves.

It may also be appreciated that similar reasoning can be applied when habituation involves extrinsic mechanisms. Thus, if habituation involved a progressive build up of inhibitory modulation (e.g., Fig. 10,B4), one could block this with a drug that interfered with the inhibitory transmitter. Other modulatory influences, however, could also exert effects on the reflex pathway under study, which themselves were not involved in mediating habituation. Drugs that altered these modulators could alter overall response levels, again without interfering with the process actually responsible for habituation. Considerable caution has to be used, therefore, before implicating a neurotransmitter system in the process of habituation, based on the effects of a drug on the course of response decrement. On the other hand, pharmacological experiments are very useful in determining transmitters involved simply in modulating reflex output.

Finally, we suggest that modulatory systems could be activated by various conditioned inputs as shown in Fig. 10,C1–C2. A conditioned input is simply a special case of an input that initially was ineffective in activating a modulatory system, but then became effective as a result of pairings with an activation of that same system. Ultimately, classical conditioning might simply involve a long-term sensitization (i.e., an intrinsic enhancement of synaptic transmission) of some input to the modulatory system along a pathway that was initially ineffective in activating the modulatory system.

The net effect of a modulatory system on some measured response could be either facilitatory or inhibitory, depending on the nature of the transmitter at point M. Hence, conditioned activation of the modulatory system will either enhance or depress the measured response depending on the modulatory system to which it has been conditioned. Several testable predictions arise from this type of reasoning. Pairing of some neutral stimulus (e.g., a CS) with activation of a modulatory system by some other stimulus (e.g., a US) should eventually allow the initially neutral stimulus to activate the modulatory system. Drugs that block the ability of the modulatory system to alter response output should also block the ability of the CS to alter response output. The anatomical location in which the US is known to alter response output should be the same location where a CS ultimately alters the measured response. Thus local application of drugs at this site should determine the neuromodulator involved. Antagonists of this neuromodulator should decrease both conditioned and unconditioned effects. By working "backward" in this way, it should be possible to determine where the conditioning actually changes response transmission, and eventually how this change is brought about at a cellular level.

Acknowledgments

Our sincere thanks are extended to Keith Berg, Jim Cassella, Randy Commissaris, John Kehne, and John Mollon for their many helpful comments on versions of this chapter.

References

Astrachan, D. I., & Davis, M. Spinal modulation of the acoustic startle response: The role of norepinephrine, serotonin, and dopamine. *Brain Research,* 1981, *206,* 223–228.

Bradley, P. B., & Key, B. J. The effect of drugs on arousal responses produced by electrical stimulation of the reticular formation of the brain. *Electroencephalography and Clinical Neurophysiology,* 1958, *10,* 97–110.

Brautigam, M., Flosbach, C. W., & Herken, H. Depression of reserpine-induced muscular rigidity in rats after administration of lisuride into the spinal subarachnoid space. *Naunyn-Schmiedeberg's Archives of Pharmacology,* 1980, *315,* 177–180.

Brown, J. S., Kalish, I. I., & Farber, I. E. Conditioned fear as revealed by magnitude of startle response to an auditory stimulus. *Journal of Experimental Psychology,* 1951, *41,* 317–327.

Capps, M. J., & Stockwell, C. W. Lesions in the midbrain reticular formation and the startle response in rats. *Physiology and Behavior,* 1968, *3,* 661–665.

Carlton, P. L. Brain acetylcholine and habituation. *Progress in Brain Research,* 1968, *28,* 48–60.

Castelluci, V. F., Carew, T. J., & Kandel, E. R. Cellular analysis of long-term habituation of the gill-withdrawal reflex of *Aplysia californica. Science,* 1978, *202,* 1306–1308.

Commissaris, R. L., & Davis, M. Opposite effects of *N,N*-dimethyltryptamine (DMT) and 5-methoxy-*N,N*-dimethyltryptamine (5-MeODMT) on acoustic startle: Spinal vs. brain site of action. *Neuroscience and Biobehavioral Reviews,* 1982, *6,* 515–520.

Coover, G. D., & Levine, S. Auditory startle responses of hippocampectomized rats. *Physiology and Behavior,* 1972, *9,* 75–78.

Davis, M. Effects of interstimulus interval length and variability on startle response habituation in the rat. *Journal of Comparative and Physiological Psychology,* 1970, *72,* 177–192. (a)

Davis, M. Interstimulus interval and startle response habituation with a "control" for total time during training. *Psychonomic Science,* 1970, *20,* 39–41. (b)

Davis, M. Sensitization of the rat startle response by noise. *Journal of Comparative and Physiological Psychology,* 1974, *87,* 571–581.

Davis, M. Morphine and naloxone: Effects on conditioned fear as measured with the potentiated startle paradigm. *European Journal of Pharmacology,* 1979, *54,* 341–347. (a)

Davis, M. Diazepam and flurazepam: Effects on conditioned fear as measured with the potentiated startle paradigm. *Psychopharmacology,* 1979, *62,* 1–7. (b)

Davis, M. Neurochemical modulation of sensory-motor reactivity: Acoustic and tactile startle reflexes. *Neuroscience Biobehavioral Reviews,* 1980, *4,* 241–263.

Davis, M. Habituation and sensitization of a startle-like response elicited by electrical stimulation at different points in the acoustic startle circuit. *Advances in Physiological Sciences,* 1981, *16,* 67–78.

Davis, M., & Astrachan, D. I. Spinal modulation of acoustic startle: Opposite effects of clonidine and *d*-amphetamine. *Psychopharmacology,* 1981, *75,* 219–225.

Davis, M., Astrachan, D. I., Gendelman, P. M. & Gendelman, D. S. 5-Methoxy-*N,N*-dimethyltryptamine: Spinal cord and brainstem mediation of excitatory effects on acoustic startle. *Psychopharmacology,* 1980, *70,* 123–130.

Davis, M., Astrachan, D. I. and Kass, E. Excitatory and inhibitory effects of serotonin on sensorimotor reactivity measured with acoustic startle. *Science,* 1980, *209,* 521–523.

Davis, M., Gendelman, D. S., Tischler, M. D., & Gendelman, P. M. A primary acoustic startle circuit: Lesion and stimulation studies. *Journal of Neuroscience,* 1982, *2,* 791–805.

Davis, M., Parisi, T., Gendelman, D. S., Tischler, M. D., & Kehne, J. H. Habituation and sensitization of 'startle' responses elicited electrically from the brainstem. *Science,* 1982, *218,* 688–690.

Davis, M., & Sheard, M. H. Habituation and sensitization of the rat startle response: Effects of raphe lesions. *Physiology and Behavior,* 1974, *12,* 425–431.

Davis, M., & Wagner, A. R. Startle responsiveness following habituation to different intensities of tone. *Psychonomic Science,* 1968, *12,* 337–338.

Davis, M., & Wagner, A. R. Habituation of the startle response under a incremental sequence of stimulus intensities. *Journal of Comparative and Physiological Psychology,* 1969, *67,* 486–492.

Depue, A., & Fowles, D. C. Electrodermal activity as an index of arousal in schizophrenics. *Psychological Bulletin,* 1973, *79,* 233–238.

Farel, P. B., & Thompson, R. F. Habituation of a monosynaptic response in frog spinal cord: Evidence for a presynaptic mechanism. *Journal of Neurophysiology,* 1976, *39,* 661–666.

File, S. E. *Habituation—a parametric study of the behavioural phenomenon.* Unpublished doctoral thesis, London University, 1969.

File, S. E., & Russell, I. S. Specificity and savings of behavioural habituation over a series of intra- and inter-modal stimuli. *Quarterly Journal of Experimental Psychology,* 1972, *24,* 465–473.

File, S. E. Inter-stimulus interval and the rate of behavioural habituation. *Q. J. Exp. Psychol. 25,* 360–367.

Fox, J. E. Habituation and prestimulus inhibition of the auditory startle reflex in decerebrate rats. *Physiology and Behavior,* 1979, *23,* 291–298.

Furby, L. Attentional habituation and mental retardation. A theoretical interpretation of MA + IQ differences in problem solving. *Human Development,* 1974, *17,* 118–138.

Geyer, M. A., Puerto, A., Menkes, D. B., Segal, D. S., & Mandell, A. J. Behavioral studies following lesions of the mesolimbic and mesostriatal serotonergic pathways. *Brain Research,* 1976, *106,* 257–270.

Glanzman, D. C., & Schmidt, E. C. Ethyl alcohol inhibits habituation of the nictitating membrane reflex response in the intact frog. *Physiological Psychology,* 1981, *9,* 117–125.

Groves, P. M., & Thompson, R. F. Habituation: A dual process theory. *Psychological Review,* 1970, *77,* 419–450.

Groves, P. M., Wilson, C. J., & Boyle, R. D. Brain stem pathways, cortical modulation and habituation of the acoustic startle response. *Behavioral Biology*, 1974, *10*, 391–418.

Gruzelier, J. H. Propranolol acts to modulate autonomic orienting and habituation processes in schizophrenia. In E. Roberts & P. Amacher (Eds.), *Propranolol and schizophrenia*. New York: Alan R. Liss, Inc., 1978. Pp. 99–118.

Hammond, G. R. Lesions of pontine and medullary reticular formation and prestimulus inhibition of the acoustic startle reaction in rats. *Physiology and Behavior*, 1973, *10*, 239–243.

Harris, J. D. Habituatory response decrement in the intact organism. *Psychological Bulletin*, 1943, *40*, 385–422.

Hernández-Peón, R. Neurophysiological correlates of habituation and other manifestations of plastic inhibition (internal inhibition). *Electroencephalography and Clinical Neurophysiology*, 1960, *13*, 101–114.

Hinde, R. A. Behavioural habituation. In G. Horn & R. A. Hinde (Eds.), *Short term changes in neural activity and behavior*. London & New York: Cambridge University Press, 1970. Pp. 3–40.

Horn, G. Changes in neuronal activity and their relationship to behavior. In G. Horn & R. A. Hinde (Eds.), *Short term changes in neuronal activity and behavior*. London & New York: Cambridge University Press, 1970. Pp. 567–606.

Humphrey, G. *The nature of learning:* New York: Harcourt, Brace & Co., 1933.

Ison, J. R., McAdam, D. W., & Hammond, G. R. Latency and amplitude changes in acoustic startle reflex of the rat produced by variation in auditory prestimulation. *Physiology and Behavior*, 1973, *10*, 1035–1039.

Jordan, W. P., & Leaton, R. N. Startle habituation in rats after lesions in the brachium of the inferior colliculus. *Physiology and Behavior*, 1982, *28*, 253–258.

Kandel, E. R. *A cell-biological approach to learning*. Bethesda, Maryland: Grass Lecture Monograph, 1978.

Kehne, J. H., Gallager, D. W., & Davis, M. Strychnine: Brainstem and spinal mediation of excitatory effect on acoustic startle. *European Journal of Pharmacology*, 1981, *76*, 177–186.

Key, B. J. Effects of chlorpromazine and lysergic acid diethylamide on the rate of habituation of the arousal response. *Nature (London)*, 1961, *190*, 275–277.

Konorski, J. *Integrative activity of the brain: An interdisciplinary approach*. Chicago: University of Chicago Press, 1967.

Krasne, F. B. Extrinsic control of intrinsic neuronal plasticity: An hypothesis from work on simple systems. *Brain Research*, 1978, *140*, 197–216.

Leaton, R. N. Long-term retention of the habituation of lick suppression in rats. *Journal of Comparative and Physiological Psychology*, 1974, *6*, 1157–1164.

Leitner, D. S., Powers, A. S., & Hoffman, H. S. The neural substrate of the startle response. *Physiology and Behavior*, 1980, *25*, 291–297.

Lubow, R. E. Latent inhibition. *Psychological Bulletin*, 1973, *79*, 398–407.

Lukowiak, K., & Peretz, B. Control of gill reflex habituation and the rate of EPSP decrement of L7 by a common source in the CNS of *Aplysia*. *Journal of Neurochemistry*, 1980, *11*, 425–434.

MacDonald, J. F., & Pearson, J. A. Some observations on habituation of the flexor reflex in the cat: The influence of strychnine, bicuculline, spinal transection and decerebration. *Journal of Neurobiology*, 1979, *10*, 67–78.

Marlin, N. A., & Miller, R. R. Associations to contextual stimuli as a determinant of long-term habituation. *Journal of Experimental Psychology, Animal Behavior Processes*, 1981, *7*, 313–333.

Miller, S. W., & Treft, R. L. Habituation of the acoustic startle response following lesion of the medial septal nucleus. *Physiology and Behavior*, 1979, *23*, 645–648.

Sharpless, S. K. Reorganization of function in the nervous system—Use and disuse. *Annual Review of Physiology*, 1964, *26*, 357–388.

Sharpless, S. K., & Jasper, H. H. Habituation of the arousal reaction. *Brain*, 1956, *79*, 655–680.

Shaywitz, B. A., Gordon, J. W., Klopper, J. H., & Zelterman, D. A. The effect of 6-hydroxydopamine on habituation of activity in the developing rat pup. *Pharmacology, Biochemistry and Behavior*, 1977, *6*, 391–396.

Sokolov, E. N. Neuronal models and the orienting reflex. In M. A. B. Brazier, (Ed.), *The central nervous system and behavior*. New York: Josiah Macy Foundation, 1960. Pp. 187–276.

Sokolov, E. N. Higher nervous functions: The orienting reflex. *Annual Review of Physiology*, 1963, *25*, 545–580. (a)

Sokolov, E. N. *Perception and the conditioned reflex*. Oxford: Pergamon, 1963. (b)

Spencer, W. A., Thompson, R. F., & Neilson, D. R. Response decrement of the flexion reflex in the acute spinal cat and transient restoration by strong stimuli. *Journal of Neurophysiology*, 1966, *29*, 221–239. (a)

Spencer, W. A., Thompson, R. F., & Neilson, D. R. Alterations in responsiveness of ascending and reflex pathways activated by iterated cutaneous afferent volleys. *Journal of Neurophysiology*, 1966, *29*, 240–252. (b)

Spencer, W. A., Thompson, R. F., & Neilson, D. R. Decrement of ventral root tonus and intracellularly recorded PSPs produced by iterated cutaneous afferent volleys. *Journal of Neurophysiology*, 1966, *29*, 253–274. (c)

Stein, L. Habituation and stimulus novelty: A model based on classical conditioning. *Psychological Review*, 1966, *73*, 352–356.

Szabo, I., & Hazafi, K. Elicitability of the acoustic startle reaction after brain stem lesions. *Acta Physiologica Academiae Scientiarum Hungaricae*, 1965, *27*, 155–165.

Thompson, R. F., & Spencer, W. A. Habituation: A model phenomenon for the study of neural substrates of behavior. *Psychological Review*, 1966, *73*, 16–43.

Unger, S. M. Habituation of the vasoconstriction orienting reaction. *Journal of Experimental Psychology*, 1964, *67*, 11–18.

Wagner, A. R. Priming in STM: An information processing mechanism for self-generated or retrieval-generated depression. In T. J. Tighe & R. N. Leaton (Eds.), *Habituation: Perspectives from child development, animal behavior, and neurophysiology*. Hillsdale, N.J.: Lawrence Erlbaum Associates, 1976. Pp. 95–128.

Wagner, A. R., & Pfautz, P. L. A bowed serial position function in habituation of sequential stimuli. *Animal Learning and Behavior*, 1978, *6*, 395–400.

Williams, J. H., Hamilton, L. W., & Carlton, P. L. Pharmacological and anatomical dissociation of two types of habituation. *Journal of Comparative Physiology and Psychology*, 1974, *87*, 724–732.

Yaksh, T. L., & Rudy, T. A. Chronic catheterization of the spinal subarachnoid space. *Physiology and Behavior*, 1976, *17*, 1031–1036.

Yunger, L. M., & Harvey, J. A. Effect of lesions in the medial forebrain bundle on three measures of pain sensitivity and noise-elicited startle. *Journal of Comparative and Physiological Psychology*, 1973, *83*, 197–183.

CHAPTER 9

Do Human Evoked Potentials Habituate?

Richard A. Roemer
Charles Shagass

Health Sciences Center
Temple University
Philadelphia, Pennsylvania

Timothy J. Teyler

Neurobiology Program
Northeastern Ohio Universities College of Medicine
Rootstown, Ohio

I. Introduction

Response decrements with repeated stimulation were noted soon after human evoked potential (EP) recording became feasible; often these decrements have been taken to reflect habituation. But when "habituation" only denotes a decrement in the amplitude of an EP peak or component, the observed phenomenon may not be caused by a process of habituation as parametrically defined by Thompson and Spencer (1966). Response decrement can result simply from refractoriness in the recovery cycle. Without testing for each of the Thompson and Spencer criteria, one cannot attribute response decrement to either habituation or to refractoriness. Consequently, it is incumbent upon investigators to distinguish between response decrements caused by habituation and those that indicate refractoriness. And because various EP components reflect different

Supported in part by USPHS grant MH 12507.

HABITUATION, SENSITIZATION,
AND BEHAVIOR

brain activities, an EP recorded at a specific interstimulus interval (ISI) may yield decrements which, in some components, are caused by refractory processes, and, in other components, result from habituation. The purpose of this chapter is to evaluate the habituation interpretation of EP decrement.

It should be recognized that EPs cannot readily be equated with the effector activities used in most studies that demonstrate response habituation. Investigations of gill withdrawal, eye blink, flexor reflex, electrodermal responses, startle response, and so forth all measure some type of effector activity. The neural activity that mediates these responses also may be considered part of effector processes. But, scalp-recorded EPs are not, by and large, mediators of effector activation but of hypothetical intermediate processes: sensory encoding, stimulus evaluation, and so forth.

Indeed, M. Davis and Heninger (1972), demonstrated a dissociation between human eye-blink and EP vertex-wave responses to repeated stimuli. Although the eye-blink response showed clear response decrement, the vertex response did not; the intermediate processes reflected in the vertex wave were "decoupled" from the effector activation represented by eye blink. This finding is consistent with evidence that certain types of intermediate processes do not meet all parameters that have been used to define habituation operationally (Teyler *et al.*, Chapter 7, this volume). The human EP studies reviewed here have also, so far, not provided convincing demonstrations that EPs manifest all parameters of habituation.

II. Human Evoked Potentials

It may be appropriate to present some general information about the nature of human EPs before considering EPs and habituation. A punctate stimulus, such as an abrupt sound or a flash of light, evokes a characteristic sequence of fluctuations in brain electrical activity that can be visualized in recordings from the human scalp by means of averaging. These characteristic fluctuations are taken as EP components; they are described by their polarity and usual peak latency in accordance with the nomenclature recommended by the Committee on Publication Criteria (Donchin, Callaway, Cooper, Desmedt, Goff, Hillyard, & Sutton, 1977). The prefixes A, S, and V denote modality of stimulation if confusion might occur. Thus, SP30 would indicate a positive peak at 30 msec following somatosensory stimuli, and AN115 would denote a negative potential at about 115 msec after an auditory stimulus.

The vertex wave is a negative–positive inflection occurring between 100 and 200 msec poststimulus (AN115–P180, VN110–P180, SN130–P180) and is of maximal amplitude at the vertex. It has been the EP phenomenon most actively investigated in terms of habituation and recovery cycles. A number of other EP components are also of potential interest in the context of habituation studies. In somatosensory evoked potentials (SEPs), these include P15, N20, P30, P45, N60, P100, and P300. In the auditory domain, P50 and P300 may justify investigation. Also of interest are VEP N75, P90, and P300. These components are illustrated in Fig. 1. Note that the EPs were recorded with linked ear reference; alternate references produce EPs of somewhat different configuration.

One must regard inferences about "vertex waves" with some caution. Conclusions based upon EP amplitude changes during the 100- to 200-msec period must be evaluated with regard to specific lead locations (Goff, Allison, & Vaughan, 1978; Lehtonen, 1973; Vaughan, Ritter, & Simson, 1980). Emerging evidence indicates that modality-specific activity, recorded over primary sensory regions, occurs at the same time as the vertex waves, and that these waves appear to reflect different neural activity.

A. Origins of Human Evoked Potentials

Desmedt and Debecker (1979) make a strong argument for taking into account neurophysiological data in the interpretation of EPs: "disregard for available neurophysiological data could eventually allow the ERP field to drift into a rarefied and unrealistic context that would become reminiscent of the black box approach of psychologists [Desmedt & Debecker, 1979, p. 648]." This is compatible with our interest in relating neural substrates, psychological constructs, and human EP studies. Consequently, this section reviews the neuroanatomical origins of human EPs. Following dipole theory, an EP component is inferred to be generated in the brain region, where a phase reversal is noted. In the absence of phase reversals, the locus of the largest amplitude of the component is considered relevant but not definitive.

Much of the data reviewed here come from direct cortical recordings obtained during neurosurgery; they must be interpreted with consideration for the likelihood that the subjects did not have "normal" brains. The most common reason for the surgery was intractable epileptic sei-

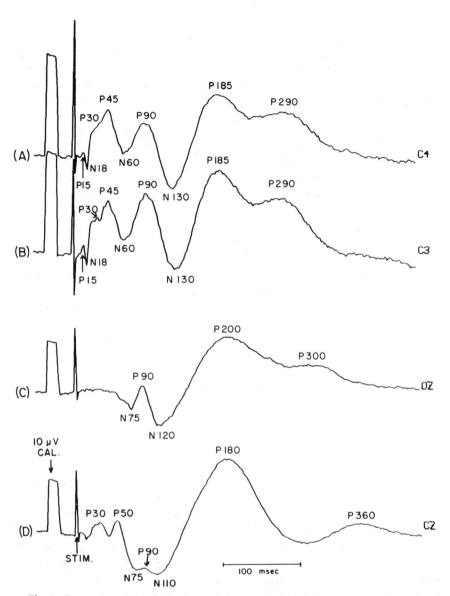

Fig. 1. Group mean EPs of 25 subjects from specified leads (band pass, 0.15–500 Hz; linked ear reference). (A) Left median nerve. (B) Right median nerve. (C) Visual pattern flash. (D) Auditory click. Some of the component peaks noted are discussed more extensively in text.

zures. As electrode placements were predicated upon diagnostic goals, occipital regions were rarely explored. The paucity of direct brain records from the human occipital region contributes to the lack of knowledge about precise cortical and subcortical EP generators in the visual system. And because EP testing was performed subject to the time constraints of the operating theatre, data are less extensive than one might desire from a scientific perspective.

In general, scalp records are less complex and "fine grained" than those obtained directly from cortical and subcortical regions. But, there is sufficient correspondence between the two kinds of recordings to impart confidence in the scalp EPs as a kind of "veiled window into the central nervous system (CNS)"; outlines are visible, but the images may not be sharp.

Some of the EP components considered in this section have not been examined in habituation investigations. As more is learned about their origins and functional relationships, including interactions with psychological variables, these components will be increasingly studied. There is much evidence that scalp-recorded EPs can provide direct measures of signal and information processing in the intact human. They offer an important means for distinguishing between brain correlates of such hypothetical constructs as "efferent modulation of afferent transmission," stimulus set, and response set. An important feature is that events primarily related to sensory processing (exogenous potentials) and those related to cognitive processing (endogenous potentials) can be recorded during the same trial (Donchin, Ritter, & McCallum, 1978).

B. Components of Somatosensory Evoked Potentials

Allison, Goff, Williamson, and VanGilder (1980) review evidence concerning the localization of the anatomical sources of P15, N20, and P30. They suggest that P15 is the scalp recording of a combination of lemniscal inflow to the venteroposterolateral nucleus of the thalamus (VPL), synaptic events in VPL, and the subsequent thalamocortical volley. That P15 at the scalp is a far-field potential is indicated by the fact that it is not usually seen with a frontal scalp reference (Desmedt & Brunko, 1980). The N20–P30 complex appears to be generated in the posterior bank of the central sulcus (Allison *et al.,* 1980; Broughton, 1967; Papakostopoulos & Crow, 1980). Another early SEP component, P25, appears to be generated in the crown of the postcentral gyrus (Allison *et al.,* 1980; Goff *et al.,* 1978). This event is very localized; scalp electrodes 2 to 3 cm distant tend not to pick it up.

Apparently, P45 is generated postcentrally; following stimulation of the forearm skin contralateral and, to a smaller degree, ipsilateral responses are recorded postcentrally (Desmedt & Brunko, 1980). Direct cortical recordings reveal a potential that may correspond to P45; it is best recorded postcentrally in some patients, but precentrally in others (Allison et al., 1980). But, neither Papakostopoulos and Crow (1980) or Goff, Williamson, VanGilder, Allison, and Fisher (1980) reveal ipsilateral responses to median nerve stimuli in direct cortical recordings during the first 50 msec poststimulus. This indicates that the ipsilateral response seen in scalp records is probably volume conducted.

Apparently, N60—directly recorded from posterior precentral gyrus—is proprioceptive (Goff et al., 1980; Papakosotopolous & Crow, 1980).

As usually recorded, P100 appears to be a compound potential generated partly extracranially and partly by brain; the myogenic potential is more anteriorly distributed, but a neurogenic potential of the same polarity is more posteriorly distributed. The neurogenic P100 component may reflect, at the scalp, the early positive positive portion of the directly recorded cortical event called the somatic late potential (SLP) (Goff et al., 1980). The SLP is positive between 80 and 100 msec; however, it is also negative between 150 and 200 msec, meaning that it overlaps the two SEP peaks that follow P100. The somatosensory vertex potential (N140–P200) appears to contain at least two major neurogenic components. In direct cortical recordings, the negative portion of the SLP is of opposite polarity to the scalp-recorded P200. Goff et al. (1980) presented a strong argument that the SLP and somatosensory vertex potential represent different neural activity. Of particular relevance is the observation that SN140 and SP200 invert from cortical surface to depth as well as across the rolandic sulcus. Velasco, Velasco, and Olvera (1980) presented direct subcortical records which may be interpreted to indicate enhancement of a P200-like event but no subcortical N140-like event. This suggests that the SN140–SP200 vertex potential is not a unitary phenomenon. Supporting this view is the evidence that the negative and positive phases of the auditorially evoked potential (AEP) vertex potential may be differentially altered by behavioral tasks (Hillyard, Hink, Schwent, & Picton, 1973; Wilkinson & Morlock, 1967; Wood, Goff, & Day, 1971). The generators of P300 will be considered together with AEP and visually evoked potential (VEP) P300.

C. Components of Auditorially and Visually Evoked Potentials

AP25 and AP50 are seen in scalp recordings and also from the lateral temporal surface of the cortex (Celesia, Broughton, Rasmussen, &

Branch, 1968; Goff *et al.*, 1978; Ruhm, Walker, & Flanigin, 1967). Allison, Lyons, Fisher, and Conte (1977) concluded that neither AP25 or AP50 are the primary response of auditory cortex, because they are suppressed by barbiturate; and depth electrodes passing near to Heschl's gyrus revealed no phase reversals. Scalp records of Vaughan and Ritter (1970), suggest a phase reversal of AP50 at an electrode located, as demonstrated by carotid angiography, below the Sylvian fissure. Thus, scalp and direct cortical recordings indicate that AP25 and AP50 are generated in the temporal region. Vaughan *et al.* (1980) presented topographic maps of scalp-recorded AN100 and AP200 that are concordant with generators lying in a superior temporal plane above the AP50 locus and close to the Sylvian fissure. Although a primary event has not been identified, it appears that the major auditory components arise in or near the upper portion of the temporal lobe.

VEP components are more difficult to evaluate than SEP and AEP events. This is because VEPs are systematically altered by a number of experimental variables, including stimulus intensity (which alters latencies), frequency, hue, and location of stimuli in the visual field. Many of these effects may be retinal in origin. Particularly relevant to this discussion is the fact that the three most widely used visual stimuli, unpatterned flash, patterned flash and pattern reversal, produce quite different EPs. Generators for the pattern reversal response will not be considered here because few, if any, observations pertinent to habituation have been made.

With unpatterned and with patterned flash, P90 appears to be generated in the region of the striate cortex (Corletto, Gentilomo, Rosadini, Rossi, & Zattoni, 1967; Goff *et al.*, 1978; Jeffreys & Axford, 1972a). Examination of Fig. 19 in Goff *et al.* (1978) indicates that the largest amplitude of P90 is found rather deep in the occipital lobe and not directly in cortical laminae of Area 17. The component VN110 appears to be generated in the extrastriate cortex (Brodmann Area 18) (Corletto *et al.*, 1967; Jeffreys & Axford, 1972b). Again, Goff et al.'s (1978) Fig. 19 reveals N110 at both the surface and depth of the cortex. The P200 component appears to phase-reverse between the cortical surface and the depth lead where P90 is maximal, suggesting a cortical locus for P200 in the striate region.

D. P300

A family of "endogenous" EPs, which are not "stimulus bound," occur after about 100 msec poststimulus: N200, P300, P3a, P3b, contingent negative variation (CNV), postimperative negative variation (PINV), and so on. Generally, N200, P300, and others of these later-occurring potentials vary substantially and systematically as a function of psychological variables and the types of tasks cued by the stimulus. These events have been reviewed by Galambos and Hillyard (1981). We consider only those reports bearing on the origins of P300. We will not consider N200, because it is best visualized by subtraction of EP waves and is not easily demonstrated in a habituation paradigm.

Snyder, Hillyard, and Galambos (1980) evaluated scalp topographies of P300 to visual, auditory, or somatic stimulation and reported no relevant differences among the three modalities. The response to visual stimuli was of greater amplitude and longer latency than those to auditory or somatic stimulation. They concluded that the data suggest a common neural-generating system for P300 to all three modalities of stimulation. The idea of common neural generators for P300 is compatible with a number of observations. Desmedt and Debecker (1979), drew the inference that P300 may result from a transient reduction of cortical DC negativity, which is under mesencephalic reticular-system control. Such mediation would be reflected by P300-like potentials recorded throughout the cortex and subcortex. Indeed, both Wood, Allison, Goff, Williamson, and Spencer (1980) and Velasco et al. (1980) present direct cortical and subcortical records of P300-like activity broadly distributed throughout the subcortex. That the subcortical distributions seem highly similar for auditory- and median-nerve stimulation is in accord with the evidence that P300 is independent of stimulus modality. An early onset of P300-like activity is noted in records from probes located midway between surface and depth, with increasing latencies at both the scalp and at deeper locations (Wood et al., 1980). Particularly relevant to Desmedt and Debecker's inference is the report of Velasco et al. (1980). They described P300-like components in a widespread region of the thalamus, including the centromedian nucleus and the thalamic reticular formation; this is quite compatible with known pathways from the reticular formation to the frontal cortex. It appears that P300 is independent of modality and has substantial subcortical mediation. The extent to which single or multiple generators are involved remains to be determined.

III. Methodological Problems

Five methodological issues relevant to EP recording during habituation paradigms will be considered:

1. Amplifier characteristics and sampling rates
2. Electrode linkages

3. Control of biological artifacts
4. Selection of paradigms to test for response dishabituation
5. Control of extraneous stimuli in the environment

Frequently, insufficient attention is paid to these issues, thus rendering interpretation of results difficult.

Digital sample rates should be at least 2.5 times the high-frequency cutoff. Too low a high-frequency cutoff may produce both amplitude attenuation and a phase shift that may be interpreted, erroneously, as a shift in onset latency. Desmedt, Brunko, Debecker, and Carmeliet (1974) demonstrated significant distortion in the first 40 msec of SEP with high-frequency cutoffs below 100 Hz. They demonstrated that, to adequately record the early SEP components, the high-frequency cutoff should extend to 2 kHz. Later components (after about 70 msec) are adequately resolved with more restricted upper-frequency limits and correspondingly slower sample rates. In general, narrow band passes make for smooth and pretty records, but distort the amplitude and latency of potentials occurring before 50 to 100 msec, depending on the stimulus modality.

Two kinds of electrode linkages, bipolar and unipolar, are generally employed. Bipolar recordings involve linkages between two electrodes on the scalp and are so named because both electrodes are liable to record potential differences on the surface of the head. Unipolar recordings involve a linkage between an electrode on the scalp and a reference electrode, usually on the lobe of one ear or both ears linked together. This reference electrode is presumably electrically indifferent, being assumed to be relatively insensitive to potential changes within the head. The idea of the unipolar method is to simplify interpretation of the EP by recording only those potential changes presumed to occur under or near the electrode on the scalp.

With the bipolar method, at any one point in time, the recording reflects the difference in potentials picked up by the two electrodes. Thus the choice of the vertex lead (Cz) as an "indifferent" reference actually produces a bipolar record whose EP interpretation is ambiguous. For example, misleading SEP profiles are produced when bilateral EP distributions are tested by using the vertex as reference, because Cz is not inactive even during the first 20 msec poststimulus (Desmedt & Brunko, 1980). For most SEP and AEP applications, earlobe or linked ear references appear to be adequate. In cases where phase reversals of AEP components over the temporal region are being sought, a nose reference is preferred (Vaughan & Ritter, 1970). The use of a frontal reference produces larger amplitude VEPs. In our multimodality topographic studies we use a linked ear reference to record SEP, AEP, and VEP (Roemer,

Shagass, Straumanis, & Amadeo, 1978; Shagass, Roemer, Straumanis, & Amadeo, 1978).

Many bioelectric potentials recorded from the scalp originate from structures other than the brain. Major sources of extracranial artifacts in EPs include (1) electrooculographic (EOG) potentials from corneoretinal and orbital generators; (2) electromyographic (EMG) potentials of scalp muscles; and (3) cardiac activity producing mechanical pulse waves and scalp pickup of the electrocardiogram (EKG).

To minimize EOG contamination of EPs by eye blinks or eye movement, it is useful to monitor the EOG with two pairs of electrodes, one pair above and below the eye for blink and the other pair at the outer canthi of the eyes for movement. If only one monitor channel is available, a good compromise is to record between a lead above and one at the outer canthus of one eye. During the averaging process, if the EOG exceeds a predefined threshold, the scalp records associated with that record may be discarded or entered into the second average. If they are retained, there will be two sets of averages for each block of trials, one with less and one with more EOG contamination; but the two sets of averages may contain differing numbers of sweeps. With a number of leads and with adequate computer facilities, it is possible to estimate the voltage drop between the EOG lead and any scalp lead during a "calibration" trial, and to use this gradient estimate to subtract the estimated EOG contribution from the scalp EP recordings. A further approach is to perform factor analyses of EP measurements across the leads. This procedure isolates the EOG factor, which can then be excluded from data analysis; we have employed this method in recent studies.

Reduction of temporalis EMG may be accomplished by various relaxation maneuvers, such as having the subject hold a gauze-wrapped tongue depressor gently between the teeth. Artifact resulting from EKG is best avoided by maintaining interelectrode impedances less than 5 kΩ and securing the electrodes firmly with collodion or the use of a recording cap or "casque" (Shagass, 1972).

Attention to these sources of artifact is particularly relevant to EP studies of habituation, because one is usually employing a small number of stimuli for each successive average, and electrical potentials associated with eye blinks occur during the same time period as the EP vertex potentials. The small number of sweeps per average is germane, because the signal-to-noise ratio improves as the square root of the number of sweeps. If the noise level is increased because of uncontrolled EMG or EKG influences, then the reliability of the recorded EP is compromised by the reduction in signal-to-noise ratio.

Dishabituation has been difficult to demonstrate in human EP studies.

It is possible that dishabituation and habituation of dishabituation are obscured by the response-averaging necessary to extract the EP from the background electroencephalograph (EEG). Typically, the dishabituating stimulus is presented in a predictable position in a stimulus train. When this is done repetitively to enable EP averaging, habituation of dishabituation probably attenuates the EP associated with the dishabituation test.

Extraneous stimuli may dishabituate a subject independently from the paradigm in use. A major difficulty in human studies is that extraneous stimuli may be internally produced; in other words, cognitive state changes or postural changes. Any alteration in the ambient stimuli may substantially confound the habituating paradigm. Attention must be given to subject comfort and control of, at least, external extraneous stimuli.

IV. Recovery Cycles of Evoked-Potential Components

When one stimulus is followed after an interval by a second stimulus, the magnitude of the response to the second (test) is altered. An EP recovery cycle can be determined by presenting pairs of stimulu at varying ISIs and plotting the ratio of the first and second EP amplitudes as a function of ISI. That is, a recovery function, or cycle, is revealed by plotting the relative test amplitude against the ISIs. The size of the second EP relative to the first is considered to indicate the extent to which the central nervous system has recovered its capacity to respond. This is seen as a way to estimate the size of the neuronal pool available for responding.

It is well known that, with ISIs of less than 300–400 msec, EP amplitudes may increment rather than decrement (Butler, 1968, 1973). In fact, one of the authors has worked extensively with SEP response increments seen with ISIs of 10–20 msec (Shagass, Overton, & Straumanis, 1974). The effects seen with very short ISIs (<500 msec) are not considered in this chapter. Thus, brief-latency EPs such as seen in the auditory brainstem potentials are not considered, because the ISIs used are usually less than 100 msec. Instead, discussion will concentrate on 500-msec to 10-second ISIs.

Callaway (1973) argued that, in general, recovery cycles and EP habituation studies could be lumped together. This was based on the conclusion that habituation could be "considered a recovery cycle phenomenon [produced] when the refraction period is related to loss of novelty subsequent to stimulus repetition, i.e., the similarity between stimuli is remembered [p. 166]." Although one may choose to consider recovery and habituation to be similar, they do not appear to be the same phenomenon from a theoretical point of view. At minimum, habituation may be a particular subset of the more general physiological property of recovery or relative refractory periods. But to attribute an EP response decrement to habituation requires meeting a set of criteria different than refractory periods.

At ISIs greater than 500 msec, one would predict from recovery-cycle theories response decrements that are independent of stimulus intensity, and no dishabituation to novel stimuli. One would predict the opposite results from habituation theory. Ritter, Vaughan, and Costa (1968) reported no dishabituation of the auditory vertex response with a 2-second ISI. As we shall see, they actually were evaluating the EP response to the dishabituating stimulus (generalization) rather than dishabituation. Megela and Teyler (1979) demonstrated complete dishabituation of VP300 and AP300 with a 1-second ISI, which suggests that habituation processes were involved.

For our purposes, we consider refractory periods and habituation processes to be different, interacting, and testable. In a later section, we consider predictions based upon Thompson and Spencer's (1966) model of habituation, which may help to disentangle the two processes. In this section we summarize data that can be interpreted as recovery phenomenon. Note should be taken that the recovery function observations considered here have likely been confounded with habituation processes, particularly at longer ISIs, although definitive confirmation is lacking. When an EP component yields no decrement in amplitude following repeated stimulation, then neither recovery nor habituation processes are operating.

ISI is one of the major determinants of the amplitude of an EP. Each component of a sensory EP has its own recovery function. Changes in ISIs have been used to dissect out different EP components by observing the differences in their relative recovery periods (Hillyard, Picton, & Regan, 1978). This section summarizes the duration of refractory periods for the several EP components that have been of interest in habituation studies In general, durations of refractory periods tend to increase with increasing latencies of EP components. But P300 is an exception; reports indicate that P300 recovery is shorter than that of the vertex waves (Megela & Teyler, 1979. Woods, Courchesne, Hillyard, & Galambos, 1980).

Allison (1962), employing a different method of naming peaks, determined recovery functions for the major somatosensory peaks occurring prior to P300. Table 1 presents a summary of the maximum duration of the refractory period for each of those SEP components employing two median-nerve shocks. Some of these measures were taken peak-to-peak between consecutive negative–positive peaks. Others, indicated by only

TABLE 1

Maximum Duration of Relative Refractory Periods of Selected Evoked-Potential Peaks

Peak	Recovery period	Reference
Somatosensory		
N20/P25	200–500 msec	Allison (1962), Shagass & Schwartz (1964)
P30	1 second	Allison (1962); Shagass & Schwartz (1964)
P45	Probably comparable to P30	
N60/P90	1–3 seconds	Allison (1962)
N140/P200	3–4 seconds	Allison (1962)
	10 seconds	Gjerdingen & Tomsic (1970)
Auditory		
P50	2–3 seconds	Callaway (1973); Hillyard, Picton, & Regan (1978)
N115/P200	3–6 seconds	H. Davis, Mast, Yoshie, & Zerlin, (1966); Roth, Krainz, Ford, Tinkleberg, Rothbart, & Kopell (1976)
	10 seconds	Gjerdingen & Tomsic (1970)
P300	1 second	Megela & Teyler, (1979); Wood, Allison, Goff, Williamson, & Spencer (1980)
Visual (unpatterned flash)		
N75	1 second	Lehtonen (1973)[a]
P100	1 second	Lehtonen (1973)[a]
N75/P100	100–200 msec	Schwartz & Shagass (1964)
N120	3 seconds	Lehtonen (1973)[a]
P200	3 seconds	Lehtonen (1973)[a]
N120/P200	10 seconds	Gjerdingen & Tomsic (1970)[b]
P200/N280	>1 second	Megela & Teyler (1979)
P300	1 second	Megela & Teyler (1979)

[a] Occipital lead.
[b] Vertex lead.

one polarity and time, were taken from prestimulus baseline. For this discussion, maximum duration of a refractory effect is defined as the ISI at which the EP amplitude to the test stimulus is of the same magnitude as to the conditioning stimulus (100%).

Turning to rate effects on the auditory EP, H. Davis, Mast, Yoshie, and Zerlin (1966) presented recovery curves for the vertex potential. They indicated the reduction of vertex wave amplitude extends to ISIs of about

6 seconds. Several other investigators have presented material also bearing on the AEP recovery time for the components of interest. Table 1 also summarizes these data and similar data for the visual EP.

Bess and Ruhm (1972) also present data indicating at least a 3-second recovery period for the N115–P200–N250 "component."

The VEP vertex response is more sensitive to increasing rates of stimulation than is a similar latency response at the occiput (Lehtonen, 1973). But, Lehtonen did not record from the vertex (CZ) but from the more lateral C4 lead.

From these data it is quite clear that ISIs of 1 or 2 seconds will present stimuli during the relative refractory portion of most EP later components (after about 75–100 msec poststimulus). It appears that ISIs in the range of 3 to 10 seconds provide the best opportunity to evaluate habituation processes with minimum confounding by refractory-period effects.

V. Operational Definition of Habituation: Which Parameters Differentiate Habituation and Recovery?

In 1966, Thompson and Spencer enumerated nine parametric characteristics or properties common to all habituating physiological systems.

We examine this set of parameters to reveal several ways that EP component decrements in amplitude (and latency) may distinguish habituation processes and refractory processes. Table 2 summarizes EP habituation studies bearing on these parameters.

This summary suggests that EP components may demonstrate properties of habituation. But the next section reexamines these data to determine the extent to which results can be accounted for by relative refractory period phenomena or by habituation.

1. *Response decrement following a negative exponential curve with repeated stimulation.* Both processes predict similar response decrements. The slope of the curve may be greater with refractory cycles than with habituation. Fruhstorfer, Soveri, and Jarvilehto (1970) directly tested the "negative exponential course" in the context of a habituation paradigm. They found that the EP decrement curve did not fit the hypothesized course.

2. *Spontaneous recovery to prestimulus levels when stimulation is withheld.* Spontaneous recovery is predicted by both processes and fails to differentiate the two.

TABLE 2

Human Evoked-Potential Studies of Habituation

Source	Component
1. Response decrement to repeated stimuli	
Schwent, Hillyard, & Galambos (1976)	Auditory N1
Ohman & Lader (1972)	Auditory N1/P2
Wastell & Kleinman (1980)	Visual N1/P2
Megela & Teyler (1979)	Auditory N1/P2, P2/N2, P300; visual P300
Fruhstorfer (1971)	Auditory and somatic N1 and P2
M. Davis & Heninger (1972)	Auditory N1/P2, P2/N2
Picton, Hillyard, & Galambos (1976)	Auditory N1/P2, P2/N2
2. Spontaneous recovery[a]	
3. Repeated series of habituation training leading to more rapid response decrement	
Megela & Teyler (1979)	Auditory and visual (see Property 4)
Ohman & Lader (1972)	Visual
4. Direct relation between ISI and response decrement	
H. Davis, Mast, Yoshie, & Zerlin (1966)	Auditory N1/P2
M. Davis & Heninger (1972)	Auditory N1/P2, P2/N2
Bess & Ruhm (1972)	Auditory
Roth, Krainz, Ford, Tinkleberg, Rothbart, & Kopell (1976)	Auditory N1 and P2
Allison (1962)	Somatosensory
Lehtonen (1973)	Visual N1/P2
Gjerdingen & Tomsic (1970)	Auditory, visual, and tactile N1/P2
5. Relative response decrement inversely related to stimulus intensity; absolute degree of response decrement directly related to stimulus intensity[b]	
6. Below-zero effects[c]	
7. Generalization to similar stimuli; less generalization to different stimuli	
Intramodal generalization	
Picton, Hillyard, & Galambos (1976)	Auditory
Megela & Teyler (1979)	Auditory and visual
Butler (1968)	Auditory
Intermodal generalization	
Fruhstorfer (1971)	Auditory to somatic and somatic to auditory
8. Dishabituation	
Megela & Teyler (1979)	See Property 9
9. Habituation of dishabituation	Not demonstrated

[a] All studies noted in Properties 1 and 2 indicate spontaneous recovery. Megela and Teyler (1979) directly tested for the effect.

[b] Absolute degree of response decrement was supported; relative response decrement was not (Megela & Teyler, 1979).

[c] Below-zero effects on response decrement have not been tested with EP habituation.

3. *With repeated series of habituation training and spontaneous recovery, the response decrement is more rapid.* This parameter should clearly differentiate between recovery and habituation processes. It is not immediately apparent how refractory processes could contribute to more rapid response decrement over repeated habituation trials. But the only report that directly tested this yielded inconsistent results. Megela and Teyler (1979) noted, "These data showed that response magnitudes tended to show more rapid decreases to the habituated level with more habituation series [p. 1162]." Ohman and Lader (1972) demonstrated greater EP decrements with repeated series of stimulation. But their data did not test for changes in the rate at which the EPs decremented (within repeated trains), only for the change in mean amplitude between trains. In this study, they averaged EPs for each train of 10 stimuli; the EP amplitudes were smaller from train to train. It appears that the support for this parameter of EP habituation is not conclusive.

4. *A direct relation between stimulus repetition rates and the rate and magnitude of response decrement.* This is predicted by both processes.

5. *Inverse relation between stimulus intensity and the rate and magnitude of response decrement.* This parameter was modified by Groves and Thompson (1970) and provides a potentially powerful tool to differentiate rate effects and habituation processes. Stimulus intensity is now considered to have only a weak effect on the degree of habituation (Megela & Teyler, 1979; Thompson, Groves, Teyler, & Roemer, 1973) but a direct effect on the degree of sensitization. Recovery cycles predict response decrements independent of stimulus intensity, habituation does not. At low intensities Groves and Thompson predict response decrement, but at high intensities the model predicts response increments. Thus, with high-intensity stimuli and with increasing ISIs (>400 msec), one should be able to distinguish rate effects from the dual-process effects of habituation and sensitization. For ISIs greater than $\frac{1}{2}$ second, a recovery or refractory model predicts EP response decrements at all intensities of stimulation. Conversely, the dual-process model predicts response decrement at low intensities and increment at higher intensities independent of ISI. Therefore, identification of ISIs that result in response increments (or no change from prehabituation levels) with high-intensity stimuli would imply that simple refractory functions were not predominant. Then one would be justified in using lower intensities of stimulation to examine the EP decrements associated with habituation proper.

Property 5, as modified by Groves and Thompson, is weakly supported by the data of Megela and Teyler. There is, apparently, no human EP study which evaluates the effects of ISI and intensity on the EP amplitude over a sufficiently wide range of intervals (to at least 10 seconds) to tease apart recovery and sensitization. Roth, Krainz, Ford, Tinkleberg, Rothbart, and Kopell (1976) do so with a narrow range of ISIs from 0.75 to 3 seconds and report the effects on the vertex responses to loud [85 db sound pressure level (SPL)] or soft (65 db) tones. They did not compare the extent of response decrement at 3-second ISI with that of 10 seconds. Again, we find no data to help to differentiate the two processes.

6. *Below-zero effects: slower recovery of response after habituation training beyond asymptotic response decrement.* This parameter has not been tested in human EP studies. Demonstration of such effects would favor habituation as opposed to refractory periods.

7. *Generalization: given a train of stimuli and a test stimulus, the magnitude of difference between the last training response and the response to the test stimulus is directly related to the magnitude of difference between the two stimuli.* With generalization, a test stimulus is presented that differs from the habituating stimuli. Presentation of this novel stimulus produces a response (generalization) and may return the magnitude of the response following the next training stimulus to or toward its prehabituation level (dishabituation). A generalization stimulus of different frequency or intensity should produce different amounts of generalization depending on its relation to the habituation stimulus.

It may be relevant to note that this procedure is rather similar to those that produce P300 and other endogenous potentials. That is, a "rare" stimulus is intermingled with a frequent stimulus (the "odd ball" paradigm). The extent endogenous potentials may actually reflect a habituation process is undetermined.

To return to generalization per se, the amount of EP generalization should be a function of the degree of overlap of the neural elements activated by the two stimuli. Butler (1968) and Picton, Hillyard, and Galambos (1976) presented evidence of generalization to a broad range of tones. Changing stimulus frequency or intensity would activate new neural units or cease activation of old ones. The extent to which the neural units activated by a generalization stimulus were also activated by the habituating stimulus would be reflected in the vertex response generalization gradient. Consequently, generalization gradients would be predicted to intramodal tests but not intermodal tests. These are precisely the results, already summarized, that provide support for the idea of modality-specific vertex responses. As this is predicted by both habituation and refractory effects, generalization tests shed no light on our problem. Basically, generalization provides no method to disentangle habituation and refractory periods, because generalization is predicted by both models.

8. *Dishabituation: recovery of the previously habituated response after the presentation of a test stimulus whose properties differ from the habituating stimuli.* This parameter is a powerful tool to differentiate habituation and refractory effects. Dishabituation is demonstrated following presentation of a dishabituating stimulus that results in recovery of a habituated response. With refractory periods, the amplitude of the first response after the dishabituating stimulus should not increase. Conversely, habituation per se would be associated with an increase in such response amplitudes. As noted, some studies show a generalization effect without demonstrating dishabituation.

Several authors have reported attempts to demonstrate dishabituation (Fruhstorfer, 1971; Picton *et al.,* 1976; Ritter *et al.,* 1968; Salamy & McKean, 1977) in human EPs. Ritter *et al.* (1968) concluded their EP decrements were the result of refractory periods. Salamy and McKean (1977) and Fruhstorfer (1971) confused the dishabituating stimulus with demonstration of dishabituation. All three reports described EP responses to the dishabituating stimulus as if they were testing dishabituation. Actually, they were testing generalization (Property 7). Generalization is measured by the response to a test (dishabituating) stimulus; dishabituation is measured by the response to the first stimulus (habituating stimulus) that follows the test stimulus. Thus the generalization or test stimulus is a dishabituating stimulus, but dishabituation is demonstrated at resumption of the habituation train. Salamy and McKean changed stimulus intensity or ISI and reported the EP alteration with the new stimulus as dishabituation. The correct test for dishabituation is to evaluate EP characteristics to the resumption of habituation training subsequent to a dishabituating stimulus. Fruhstorfer (1971) employed a click training stimulus and a somatic generalizing stimulus and vice versa. This was an intermodality test for generalization; one would not expect to observe cross-modality refractory effects at the level of the CNS activity reflected in vertex EPs.

It seems pertinent to draw attention to the method used by Megela and Teyler to test for EP dishabituation. The dishabituating stimulus, which they correctly call generalization, was presented randomly at 1 of 4 positions during an 11 stimulus train. This manipulation appeared to yield dishabituation of the EP measures used. But ISI of the training stimuli was 1 second; the interval between the training stimulus preceding and the one following the generalization stimulus was 2 seconds. Because the training ISI was 1 second, the apparent dishabituation may have been caused by decreased refractory effects related to the change in ISI from 1 to 2 seconds. In fact, the amount of dishabituation reported is of the same magnitude as that predicted simply by changing ISIs from 1 to 2 seconds.

To demonstrate dishabituation, the training stimuli should not be discontinued when presenting the dishabituating (generalization) stimulus. The dishabituating stimulus may be presented asynchronously $\frac{1}{2}$ or 1 second prior to one of the training stimuli. There is a logical dilemma here. With intramodality tests for dishabituation, rate effects and habituation processes appear always to be confounded. Apparently, only intermodal dishabituation tests may separate the two. The intermodal dishabituating stimulus could be presented coincident with the habituating stimulus; dishabituation would be evaluated at the next habituating stimulus.

9. *Habituation of dishabituation: less recovery of the response decrement upon repeated presentations of the test stimuli.* There are no human EP reports of habituation of dishabituation. This is not surprising given the tenuous nature of dishabituation in human EP studies.

VI. Conclusion

The term "habituation" tends to be used in at least two ways in the evoked-potential (EP) literature. One way is in terms of the operationally defined properties already discussed. The second way is as a psychological hypothetical construct. Such constructs usually carry a number of excess meanings that do not further our understanding of the CNS mechanisms that may underly the electrical phenomena. Neither use satisfactorily accounts for the EP data reviewed.

We conclude that few, if any, human EP studies clearly differentiate habituation and refractory (or recovery) aspects of EPs. In the absence of convincing evidence that habituation accounts for EP response decrements, simplicity requires that these decrements be attributed to refractory periods. The two critical tests of habituation include dishabituation and sensitization. Convincing demonstrations of sensitization and dishabituation are lacking in human EP studies. Before an interpretation of response decrement in human EPs is interpreted as habituation, the possibility that decrements may reflect recovery cycle phenomenon as outlined here must be ruled out.

Acknowledgments

We thank Donald Overton, Craig Cegavske, R. Mac Turner, and Richard Josiassen for their comments.

References

Allison, T. Recovery functions of somatosensory evoked responses in man. *Electroencephalography and Clinical Neurophysiology*, 1962, *14*, 331–343.

Allison, T., Goff, W. R., Williamson, P. D., & VanGilder, J. C. On the neural origin of early components of the human somatosensory evoked potential. In J. E. Desmedt (Ed.), *Clinical uses of cerebral, brainstem and spinal somatosensory evoked potentials.* Basel: Karger, 1980. Pp. 51–68.

Bess, J. C., & Ruhm, H. B. Recovery cycle of the acoustically evoked potential. *Journal of Speech and Hearing Research*, 1972, *15*, 507–517.

Broughton, R. J. Discussion. Average evoked potentials. *NASA [Special Publication] SP*, 1967, *NASA SP-191*, 79–84.

Butler, R. A. Effect of changes in stimulus frequency and intensity of habituation of the human vertex potential. *Journal of the Acoustical Society of America*, 1968, *44*, 945–950.

Butler, R. A. The cumulative effects of different stimulus repetition rates on the auditory evoked response in man. *Electroencephalography and Clinical Neurophysiology*, 1973, *35*, 337–346.

Callaway, E. Habituation of averaged evoked potentials in man. In H. V. S. Peeke & M. J. Herz (Eds.), *Habituation* (Vol. 2). New York: Academic Press, 1973. Pp. 153–171.

Celesia, G. G., Broughton, R. J., Rasmussen, T., & Branch, C. Auditory evoked responses from the exposed human cortex. *Electroencephalography and Clinical Neurophysiology*, 1968, *24*, 458–466.

Corletto, C. J., Gentilomo, A., Rosadini, G., Rossi, G. F., & Zattoni, J. Visual evoked potentials as recorded from the scalp and from the visual cortex before and after surgical removal of the occipital pole in man. *Electroencephalography and Clinical Neurophysiology*, 1967, *22*, 378–380.

Davis, H., Mast, T., Yoshie, N., & Zerlin, S. The slow response of the human cortex to auditory stimuli recovery process. *Electroencephalography and Clinical Neurophysiology*, 1966, *21*, 105–113.

Davis, M., & Heniger, G. R. Comparison of response plasticity between the eyeblink and vertex potential in humans. *Electroencephalography and Clinical Neurophysiology*, 1972, *33*, 283–293.

Desmedt, J. E., & Brunko, E. Functional organization of far-field and cortical components of somatosensory evoked potentials in normal adults. In J. E. Desmedt (Ed.), *Clinical uses of cerebral, brainstem and spinal somatosensory evoked potentials.* Basel: Karger, 1980. Pp. 27–50.

Desmedt, J. E., Brunko, J., Debecker, J., & Carmeliet, J. The system bandpass required to avoid distortion of early components when averaging somatosensory evoked potentials. *Electroencephalography and Clinical Neurophysiology*, 1974, *37*, 407–410.

Desmedt, J. E., & Debecker, J. Waveform and neural mechanism of the decision P350 elicited without pre-stimulus CNV or readiness potential in random sequences of near-threshold auditory clicks and finger stimuli. *Electroencephalography and Clinical Neurophysiology*, 1979, *47*, 648–670.

Donchin, E., Callaway, E., Cooper, R., Desmedt, J. E., Goff, W. R., Hillyard, S. A., & Sutton, S. Publication criteria for studies of evoked potentials in man: Report of a components of the ERP. In E. Callaway, P. Tueting, & S. Koslow (Eds.), *Event-related*

Donchin, E., Ritter, W., & McCallum, W. C. Cognitive psychophysiology: The endogenous components of the ERP. In E. Callaway, P. Tueting, & S. Koslow (Eds.), *Event-related brain potentials in man.* New York: Academic Press, 1978. Pp. 349–412.

Fruhstorfer, H. Habituation and dishabituation of the human vertex response. *Electroencephalography and Clinical Neurophysiology*, 1971, *30*, 306–312.

Fruhstorfer, H., Soveri, P., & Jarvilehto, T. Short-term habituation of the auditory evoked response in man. *Electroencephalography and Clinical Neurophysiology*, 1970, *28*, 153–161.

Galambos, R., & Hillyard, S. A. (Eds.) Electrophysiological approaches to human cognitive processing. *Neurosciences Research Program Bulletin*, 1981, *20*(2).

Gjerdigen, D., & Tomsic, R. Recovery functions of human cortical potentials evoked by tones, shocks, vibrations and flashes. *Psychonomic Science*, 1970, *19*, 228–229.

Goff, W. R., Allison, T., Lyons, W., Fisher, T. C., & Conte, R. Origins of short latency auditory evoked potentials in man. In J. E. Desmedt (Ed.), *Auditory evoked potentials in man: Psychopharmacology correlates of evoked potentials*. Basel: Karger, 1977. Pp. 30–44.

Goff, W. R., Allison, T., & Vaughan, H. G. The functional neuroanatomy of event-related potentials. In E. Callaway, P. Tueting, & S. Koslow (Eds.), *Event-related brain potentials in man*. New York: Academic Press, 1978. Pp. 1–80.

Goff, W. R., Williamson, P. D., VanGilder, J. C., Allison, T., & Fisher, T. C. Neural origins of long latency evoked potentials recorded from the depth and from the cortical surface to the brain in man. In J. E. Desmedt (Ed.), *Clinical uses of cerebral, brainstem and spinal somatosensory evoked potentials*. Basel: Karger, 1980. Pp. 126–145.

Groves, P. M., & Thompson, R. F. Habituation: A dual-process theory. *Psychological Review*, 1970, *77*, 419–450.

Hillyard, S. A., Hink, R. F., Schwent, V. L., & Picton, T. W. Electrical signs of selective attention in the human brain. *Science*, 1973, *182*, 177–180.

Hillyard, S. A., Picton, T. W., & Regan, D. Sensation, Perception and Attention: Analysis using ERPs. In E. Callaway, P. Tueting, & S. Koslow (Eds.), *Event-related brain potentials in man*. New York: Academic Press, 1978. Pp. 223–322.

Jeffreys, D. A., & Axford, J. G. Source locations of pattern-specific components of human visual evoked potentials. I. Component of striate cortical origin. *Experimental Brain Research*, 1972, *16*, 1–21. (a)

Jeffreys, D. A., & Axford, J. G. Source locations of pattern-specific components of human visual evoked potentials. II. Component of extrastriate cortical origin. *Experimental Brain Research*, 1972, *16*, 22–40. (b)

Lehtonen, J. B. Functional differentiation between late components of visual evoked potentials recorded at occiput and vertex: Effect of stimulus interval and contour. *Electroencephalography and Clinical Neurophysiology*, 1973, *35*, 75–82.

Megela, A. L., & Teyler, T. J. Habituation and the human evoked potential. *Journal of Comparative and Physiological Psychology*, 1979, *93*, 1154–1170.

Ohman, A., & Lader, M. Selective attention and "habituation" of the auditory averaged evoked response in humans. *Physiology and Behavior*, 1972, *8*, 79–85.

Papakostopoulos, D., & Crow, H. J. Direct recording of the somatosensory evoked potential from the cerebral cortex of man and the difference between precentral and postcentral potentials. In J. E. Desmedt (Ed.), *Clinical uses of cerebral, brainstem and spinal somatosensory evoked potentials*. Basel: Karger, 1980. Pp. 15–26.

Picton, T. W., Hillyard, S. A., & Galambos, R. Habituation and attention in the auditory system. In W. D. Keidel & W. D. Neff (Eds.), *Handbook of sensory physiology* (Vol. 5). Berlin: Springer-Verlag, 1976. Pp. 343–389.

Ritter, W., Vaughan, H. G., & Costa, L. D. Orienting and habituation to auditory stimuli: A study of short term changes in average evoked responses. *Electroencephalography and Clinical Neurophysiology*, 1968, *25*, 550–556.

Roemer, R. A., Shagass, C., Straumanis, J. J., & Amadeo, M. Pattern evoked potential measurements suggesting lateralized hemispheric dysfunction in chronic schizophrenics. *Biological Psychiatry, 1978, 13*, 185–202.

Roth, W. T., Krainz, P. L., Ford, J. M., Tinkleberg, J. R., Rothbart, R. M., & Kopell, B. S. Parameters of temporal recovery of the human auditory evoked potential. *Electroencephalography and Clinical Neurophysiology, 1976, 40*, 623–632.

Ruhm, H., Walker, E., & Flanigin, H. Acoustically-evoked potentials in man: Mediation of early components. *Laryngoscope, 1967, 77*, 806–822.

Salamy, A., & McKean, C. M. Habituation and dishabituation of cortical and brainstem evoked potentials. *International Journal of Neuroscience, 1977, 7*, 175–182.

Schwartz, M., & Shagass, C. Recovery functions of human somatosensory and visual evoked potential. *Annals of the New York Academy of Sciences, 1964, 112*, 510–525.

Schwent, V. L., Hillyard, S. A., & Galambos, R. Selective attention and the auditory vertex potential. I. Effects of stimulus delivery rate. *Electroencephalography and Clinical Neurophysiology, 1976, 40*, 604–614.

Shagass, C. Electrical activity of the brain. In N. Greenfield & R. Sternbach (Eds.), *Handbook of psychophysiology*. New York: Holt, Rinehardt, & Winston, 1972. Pp. 263–328.

Shagass, C., Overton, D. A., & Straumanis, J. J. Evoked potential studies in schizophrenia. In H. Mitsuda & T. Fukuda (Eds.), *Biological mechanisms of schizophrenia and schizophrenia-like psychoses*. Tokyo: Igaku-Shoin, Ltd., 1974. Pp. 214–234.

Shagass, C., Roemer, R. A., Straumanis, J. J., & Amadeo, M. Evoked potential correlates of psychosis. *Biological Psychiatry, 1978, 13*, 163–184.

Shagass, C., & Schwartz, M. Evoked potential studies in psychiatric patients. *Annals of the New York Academy of Sciences, 1964, 112*, 526–542.

Snyder, E., Hillyard, S. A., & Galambos, R. Similarities and differences among the P3 waves to detected signals in three modalities. *Psychophysiology, 1980, 17*, 112–122.

Thompson, R. F., Groves, P. M., Teyler, T. J., & Roemer, R. A. A dual-process theory of habituation: Theory and behavior. In H. V. S. Peeke & M. J. Herz (Eds.), *Habituation* (Vol. 1). New York: Academic Press, 1973. Pp. 239–271.

Thompson, R. F., & Spencer, W. A. Habituation: A model phenomenon for the study of neuroal substrates of behavior. *Psychological Review, 1966, 173*, 16–43.

Vaughan, H. G., & Ritter, W. The sources of auditory evoked responses prerecorded from the human scalp. *Electroencephalography and Clinical Neurophysiology, 1970, 28*, 360–367.

Vaughan, H. G., Ritter, W., & Simson, R. Topographic analysis of auditory event-related potentials. *Progress in Brain Research, 1980, 54*, 279–285.

Velasco, M., Velasco, F., & Olvera, A. Effect of task relevance and selective attention on components of cortical and subcortical evoked potentials in man. *Electroencephalography and Clinical Neurophysiology, 1980, 48*, 377–386.

Wastell, D. G., & Kleinman, D. Fast habituation of the late components of the visual evoked potential in man. *Physiology and Behavior, 1980, 25*, 93–97.

Wilkinson, R. T., & Morlock, H. C. Auditory evoked response and reaction time. *Electroencephalography and Clinical Neurophysiology, 1967, 23*, 50–66.

Wood, C. C., Allison, T., Goff, W. R., Williamson, P. D., & Spencer, D. D. On the neural origin of P300 in man. *Progress in Brain Research, 1980, 54*, 51–56.

Wood, C. C., Goff, W. R., & Day, R. S. Auditory evoked potentials during speech perception. *Science, 1971, 173*, 1248–1251.

Woods, D. L., Courchesne, E., Hillyard, S. A., & Galambos, R. Split-second recovery of the P3 component in multiple decision tasks. *Progress in Brain Research, 1980, 54*, 322–330.

PART III

Functional Processes

In this third group of chapters the functional and evolutionary aspects of habituation and sensitization are discussed. Chapter 10, by Michael Shalter, reviews studies conducted in both laboratory and field aimed at elucidating the role habituation might play in the relationship between predator and prey. Placing the studies in the perspective of current conceptions of predator and prey behavior leads Shalter to conclude that habituation does influence many aspects of the behavior of both but that discrepancies between laboratory and field observations should provide a cautionary note. Shalter's careful placing of the studies in their biological context serves well to provide a model for future work.

In Chapter 11, Harman Peeke reviews the literature on habituation and sensitization as it is related to current views of territory and territorial defense. The case is presented that the basis for the "dear enemy" phenomenon may be habituation, as E. O. Wilson suggested in *Sociobiology*. Peeke further suggests that, in its broadest interpretation and extensions, the multiprocess theories derived from Richard Thompson's original work may provide a foundation for an understanding of the mechanisms underlying territorial behavior. Two of these extensions appear in this volume. In Part I, Petrinovich provides a "molar reductionist" approach based on his field work with birds. In Part II, Carew provides a clear description of the molecular approach initially championed by the Kandel group.

Chapter 12 is an analysis of the evolutionary basis of habituation placed within a context of response likelihood. Using concepts from game theory and evolutionarily stable strategies, Michel Treisman presents an intricate and extensive analysis of aggression and conflict. Treisman uses these strategies to develop conceptions regarding the role habituation might play in his theoretical matrix.

CHAPTER 10

Predator–Prey Behavior and Habituation

Michael D. Shalter

Clinical Research and Development
Wyeth Laboratories
Radnor, Pennsylvania

I. Introduction

The role of habituation has been emphasized in relation to avoidance and fright behaviors because it is in this connection that habituation first appears in phylogeny; and it is here that its importance seems greatest and most obvious (Thorpe, 1956). In this chapter, I consider the extents and circumstances in which these behaviors habituate in both nature and the laboratory. No attempt will be made to discuss the evolutionary theory or physiological aspects of habituation. Instead, attention will be focused on (1) the role habituation plays in predator recognition, (2) the variables, particularly spatial, that confer specificity on habituation, (3) the extent habituation influences the form and function of alarm calls, and (4) the role of habituation in the development of prey capture.

I discuss habituation of prey under the separate rubrics of natural observation and laboratory experimentation because there have been certain

HABITUATION, SENSITIZATION,
AND BEHAVIOR

discrepancies between the results obtained from the two sources. These inconsistencies have cast doubt on the general applicability of conclusions drawn from experiments with captive animals (Curio, 1975). As I hope will become evident, more systematic and biologically realistic studies should clear up some of the current confusion.

Before discussing habituation in the context of predation, a few remarks concerning the importance of predation pressure on form and behavior seem appropriate. In the struggle to come by food but not become food, natural selection can be expected to increase the efficiency of a predator in locating and consuming prey. Conversely, it can generally be expected to favor a prey that manages to avoid such a fate. These two selection forces act in concert, but at opposite poles: as prey evolve characteristics that enhance their ability to escape being preyed upon, predators evolve more effective means of preying upon them. In this evolutionary game of "one-upsmanship," it is commonly assumed that the prey are usually but one short jump ahead of the predators.

Many of the more striking anatomical and behavioral characteristics of animals are adaptations resulting from selection pressures related to predation. The postures and cryptic coloration of certain insects and ground-nesting birds, the form and flight of falcons, the eyespots of a variety of moths and fishes, and the stripes of tigers and zebras are examples of innumerable adaptations that provide either enhanced protection from predators or armament to obtain prey.

Predation, whether by or on the species, is only one of many selection pressures. In some cases it is extremely important, such as in the tropical Clay-colored Robin (*Turdus grayi*), where it appears to play an even more instrumental role than food availability in determining the timing of the reproductive period (Morton, 1971). In other species, the importance of predation in the evolution of behavior is secondary to that of other selection pressures. In addition, the relative importance of different pressures may change as the species evolves. Bertram (1975), for example, suggested that the advantages of communal hunting were probably the major pressures in tending to make lions evolve into social animals; the relative importance of those initial advantages may now, however, be less than that of more recent benefits of their social organization, the foremost being cooperative reproduction. On the other hand, cooperative surveillance of predators is believed by many investigators to be a major advantage of participation in social groups (e.g., Crook,, 1965; Treherne & Foster, 1980). Social and solitary modes of existence potentially bestow certain advantages on individual predators and prey [for a discussion, see Morse (1970), Milinski and Curio (1975), Hoogland and Sherman (1976), Bertram (1978), and Shaw (1978)].

II. Habituation to Predators in Nature

Unlike the slowly evolving behavioral machinery and organization already mentioned that result from the trials and successes of generations of interacting predators and prey, habituation develops through a one-on-one interaction between an individual and its environment. For the purposes of this chapter, habituation is the waning of response as a result of repeated or continuous stimulation that neither results from altered properties of sensory receptors or effectors nor is followed by any kind of reinforcement. As Humphrey (1930) pointed out some time ago, habituation—or something very much like it—occurs in animals of all evolutionary levels.

A. A Prototype

Despite the ubiquitousness of habituation among the phyla, one example in particular is often cited in elementary texts on animal behavior (e.g., Immelmann, 1976; Tinbergen, 1965). It is the antipredator crouching response of gallinaceous birds to the sight of flying objects.

Without having been taught to do so, newly hatched chicks crouch or perform other defensive behaviors in response to a wide variety of stimuli appearing overhead. After a few uneventful experiences with flying sparrows and falling leaves, their crouching response to such innocuous stimuli wanes. Thereafter, it is elicited only by unfamiliar flying objects such as goshawks, for example.

The fact that the chick has no way of knowing that a hawk is dangerous (never having experienced an attack by one) gives the crouch the appearance of an innate response. Experiments with various-shaped models led some investigators (e.g., Green, Green, & Carr, 1968; Lorenz, 1939; Tinbergen, 1948) to conclude that the chick has an inborn ability to differentiate between short-necked raptors and long-necked harmless birds. Failure to replicate certain results cited by Tinbergen (see Hirsch, Lindley, & Tolman, 1955; McNiven, 1960; Melzack, 1961) provided fuel for the inflammatory nature–nuture controversy. Actually, as Schleidt (1961) cleverly demonstrated with turkeys (*Meleagris gallopavo*), the poult merely learns what objects are not dangerous and, as it grows older, confines its crouching to all others until they, too, are shown on the basis of familiarity to post no threat. Familiarity breeds neglect, rarity engenders reaction. Since birds of prey are far rarer than nonpredatory species or inanimate objects wafting by, the selective advantage of learning not to crouch at the drop of every leaf is obvious.

B. Predator Recognition

The cues by which prey actually go about recognizing predators have
been the subject of numerous investigations (Altmann, 1956; Curio, 1969,
1975; Dill, 1973; Ewert & Traud, 1979; Gallup, Nash, & Ellison, 1971;
Hinde, 1954; Hurley & Hartline, 1974; Jones, 1980; Mueller & Parker,
1980; Nice & ter Pelkwyk, 1941; Schleidt, 1961; Shalter, 1974). These and
other studies [e.g., moth reactions to ultrasonic stimuli rather than to
specific bat sounds (Fenton & Fullard, 1981)] suggest that prey recognize
a few key stimulus characteristics of *classes* of predators.

Tinbergen (1948) stated that "any bird, or even a cardboard dummy,
that has a short neck releases an escape response independently of the
shape of the wings, tail, etc. and of color [p. 536]." Schleidt (1961), on the
other hand, emphasized that turkeys respond to aerial stimuli primarily on
the basis of (1) relative speed and apparent size of the stimulus object and
(2) differential habituation. Grubb (1977), however, observed that coots
(*Fulica americana*) gave significantly more alarm reactions to Bald Eagles, which are well-known predators of waterfowl (Brown & Amandon,
1968), than to fish-eating Ospreys. The coots' discrimination between
these two raptorial predators suggests that they and probably many other
prey species know more about flying predators than just their ratio of
neck to body lengths, apparent size, frequency of appearance, or relative
speed (also see White & Weeden, 1966). Curio (1975) has established in
the Pied Flycatcher, for example, the existence of at least two enemy-
specific "channels" (releasing mechanisms) tuned to different predator
types—owls and shrikes, respectively—and based on innate recognition
of sign stimuli such as the dark eye stripe of the shrike and two frontal
eyes of owls. Interaction of sign stimuli or *Gestalt* perception, as opposed
to their additivity, seems to be a salient feature of the underlying releasing
mechanism in that it safeguards against confusing harmless birds possessing one of the predator's sign stimuli. For a discussion of the usefulness of
the concept of the innate releasing mechanism, see Curio (1975, pp. 98–
107).

Mueller & Parker (1980) have shown that the variance in the heart rate
of naive Mallard ducklings (*Anas platyrhynchos*) is greater in response to
a silhouette of a hawk than that of a goose. Although many aspects of the
problem require further investigation, Mueller and Parker's results constitute evidence for the ability of Mallards to discriminate between configu-
rational stimuli without prior, specific experience. They contended that
the more irregular heart rate in response to the hawk model than to the
goose model is correlated with the duckling's fear, basing their argument
on the rationale that it is obviously adaptive for a duckling to recognize a

hawk on the first encounter since it could be the last. Their contention would be supported by a demonstration of adaptive behavioral responses that are correlated with cardiac response. Such correlations have yet to be demonstrated.

As Thorpe (1944) pointed out, most animals are subject to an array of predator species, and specific recognition of each one is usually out of the question. The general rule appears to be that young prey possess a disposition to respond to a wide variety of stimuli, and, through the process of habituation, they narrow the array. I would expect any exceptions to this rule to involve prey with a very limited number of predators.

1. Aggressive Mimicry

In the process of predator recognition, cases of mistaken identity occur—often as a result of the sudden appearance of an innocuous stimulus object that the prey confuses with a predator. Less commonly, the prey commits the mistake because the predator, to minimize its detection until after it comes within striking distance, has evolved a disguise of its true identity.

This disguise tactic has become known as "aggressive mimicry," reports of which are for the most part observational. As such, they should be taken as little more than a starting point for a more penetrating analysis, especially of the role habituation plays in the process.

One species, the uncommon Zone-tailed Hawk (*Buteo albonotatus*) differs from related hawks and closely resembles the common Turkey Vulture (*Cathartes aura*) in color, shape, and manner of soaring. A foraging *B. albonotatus* often glides with vultures and, on occasion, has been observed to dive at prey from such an assemblage. Willis (1963, 1966) suggested that the Zone-tailed Hawk may be an aggressive mimic that resembles the vulture in order to get close to prey, which in this case may have habituated to the repeated overflights of the inoffensive scavengers.

Other examples of aggressive mimicry that have been suggested include robberflies (*Mallophora bomboides*), which are mimics of and predators of bumblebees (*Bombus americanorum;* Brower, Brower, Van, & Westcott, 1960). In this case and in similar cases among insects and spiders it is uncertain, however, whether the mimicry is aggressive or protective, or both. The South American fish *Monocirrhus polycanthus,* which resembles a floating leaf in the current, glides close to smaller fish and devours them (Cott, 1957). This example appears to bridge the gap between aggressive mimicry and commonplace resemblance to the background.

As Wickler (1968) pointed out, both concealment and mimicry—other than, strictly, the Muellerian type—involve deception of the signal re-

Fig. 1. Hunting Hausa bowmen of northern Nigeria disguised with Ground Hornbill headdress. (Insert) A Ground Hornbill. From E. Curio (1976). Courtesy of the author and Springer-Verlag.

ceiver. This is no doubt true, but concealment and mimicry nevertheless create different demands on the signal emitter, and, as such, a distinction between the two tactics seems useful if the research concentrates on the behavior of the predator rather than on that of the prey (Curio, 1976).

Several other suspected cases of aggressive mimicry are discussed by Curio in his extensive review of the ethology of predation. Some of the more interesting ones are those of man, who is apparently the only aggressive mimic among mammals. The biblical metaphor of the "wolf in sheep's clothing" applies not to wolves but to man himself, or an occasional insect such as the larva of the green lacewing, *Chrysopa slossonae* (Eisner, Hicks, Eisner, & Robson, 1978). Hausa bowmen of northern Nigeria, for instance, hunt disguised with hornbill (*Bucorvus abyssinicus*) headdress (Fig. 1). Such stalking technique is known from cave drawings to be thousands of years old. The animals hunted by the Hausa are thoroughly habituated to the common and harmless hornbill and can be approached by disguised hunters to within arrow range. Similarly, North American plains Indians dressed in buffalo skins to approach bison, and Australian aborigines don kangaroo hides when hunting, enhancing their disguise by mimicking the kangaroo's normal browsing, locomotory, and comfort behaviors.

2. Mistaking the Innocuous

More commonplace cases of mistaken identity on the part of prey involve confusing a harmless object or animal with a predator and not, as with aggressive mimicry, the other way around. Heinroth, for example, observed that swifts and storks returning to Berlin from their winter quarters elicit strong flight reactions from fowl and cranes [citation in Schleidt (1961); for other reports, see Gibb (1960); Hinde (1952); R. C. Miller (1921); Morley (1953); Morse, (1970)]. The common denominator in these cases seems to be the sudden appearance of the stimulus object that is mistaken for a predator.

Flocks of titmice (*Parus* spp.) in eastern North America, for example, invariably respond with alarm reactions to Mourning Doves (*Zenaida macroura*) flying rapidly through the forest. This long-tailed dove superficially resembles a principal predator on small birds, the Sharp-shinned Hawk (*Accipiter striatus*). The tits' reaction, however, is probably triggered by the sudden appearance of the dove, rather than by a particular shape (Morse, 1970). Even in areas devoid of avian predators and in winter, when alarm reactions cut deeply into valuable foraging time, the titmice continue to react to doves and other innocuous flying objects. Failure of the tits to habituate to doves under such circumstances is not surprising, however, in view of startle and position effects (see Section III,A).

3. Recognizing Nonhunting Predators

Not only do prey learn to recognize predators and nonpredators, but certain prey give every indication that they are able to distinguish between hunting and nonhunting predators (see Curio, 1963). For example, so long as lions remain in view they seldom evoke evasive responses from grazing ungulates that have learned that "a visible lion is a safe lion [Schaller, 1972b, p. 19]." Individual prey, such as Thomson's gazelle, learn the habits of each type of predator as well as the degree of danger it represents, and they adjust their flight distance accordingly [see Rowe-Rowe (1974) for variables affecting flight distance within a species]. For instance, they invariably ignore jackals but warily view a lion or leopard from at least 30 m away. The gazelle's flight distance to cheetah, which sprint fast but not far, is about 100 m (M. D. Shalter, personal observations), whereas hunting dogs, capable of speeds nearly 40 km per hour over several kilometers, are avoided as soon as the pack moves into view (Schaller, 1972b).

According to Schaller, many newborn animals lack such knowledge and display no fear of predators. He once observed, for example, a lost wildebeest calf "trustingly plod behind two male lions for over a kilometer, drawn by its innate tendency to follow something, anything [1972b, p. 19]."

It has been suggested that small birds are able to distinguish, like any good falconer, between a hungry raptor and one that is not inclined to hunt. Hamerström (1957), for example, observed that a Red-tailed Hawk elicited more mobbing from songbirds when it was hungry than when it was well fed (also see Markgren, 1960; Tinbergen, 1957).

C. Habituation to Hunting Predators

Thorpe (1956) pointed out that the inability to learn to stop reacting to repeatedly appearing harmless stimuli would "make life impossible [p. 243)." One can, I think, reverse the emphasis and state that the inability to keep reacting (or at least keeping vigilant) to a predator, unless it is unlikely to attack, would make life very short! There are only two examples I am aware of where prey give the appearance of habituating to hunting predators in natural situations.

The predaceous bug *Nabis* sp. performs a unique behavior that enables it to prey upon caterpillars. At first, the bug probes the larva only with a foreleg. These initial contacts elicit violent defensive movements of the larva's thorax that cause the bug to withdraw its leg. Repeated probing gradually causes these defensive movements to subside to the point where the bug can keep its foot in contact with the prey's body. The bug then positions its proboscis directly beside the foot and inserts it into the larva as the foot is withdrawn (Arnold, 1971). It would appear that the caterpillar's defense breaks down through habituation to the repeated mechanical stimulation by the bug. In the absence of experimental evidence, however, it is impossible to rule out fatigue or sensory adaptation as the cause for the larva's response waning.

The second example of alleged habituation to hunting predators involves the aggressive responses of terns (*Sterna* spp.) and gulls (*Larus* spp.). Buckley and Buckley (1972) suggested that Royal Terns (*S. maxima*) have become habituated to the continuing presence of Laughing Gulls (*L. atricilla*), the chief cause of tern egg mortality, with which they are associated throughout the year. All antipredator responses are directed exclusively toward occasional egg robbers such as other gulls and crows. The detrimental effects of this apparent habituation for Royal Terns might be mitigated by the fact that the gulls cease to prey on them as soon as the chicks hatch. This is not the case, however, with larger Black-headed Gulls that continue to prey on larid chicks if the opportunity arises (Kruuk, 1964).

Similarly, McNicholl (1973) observed that Arctic Terns (*Sterna paradisaea*) that nested in colonies on whose borders no avian predators nested attacked Herring Gulls (*Larus argentatus*) and Parasitic Jaegers (*Stercorarius parasiticus*) whenever they approached the terns' nests. Members of one tern colony on whose periphery two pairs of Herring Gulls nested never attacked the gulls.

Rydén (1970) reported that Common Terns' aggressive reactions to a pair of Herring Gulls nesting nearby did not diminish in intensity over an 11-day observation period. He suggested several possible explanations to account for this, including (1) reinforcement of the terns' attack responses each time the gulls left their nest and the colony and (2) the disruption of the constancy of the stimulus situation by the arrival of the gulls from different directions (see Section III,A). Rydén's observations began when the young terns were beginning to hatch, and the parents' aggressiveness probably increased continuously throughout the observation period. Because no corresponding increase in the terns' aggressiveness toward the gulls was observed, habituation might have occurred.

1. Responses to Predators during Nesting

A decrease in the prey's flight distance (see Hediger, 1964) or an increase in the prey's threshold to flee in response to an attack by a predator nesting in the area would appear at times to have positive selective value. For example, some habituation to predators might ensure adequate care of the young (see Shalter, 1979). Continual disturbance by predators has been known to cause prolonged parental neglect by prey for their young (e.g., Austin, 1951; J. T. Emlen, Jr., Miller, Evans, & Thompson, 1966; Hatch, 1970). Curio (1975) reported that the incessant mobbing by Pied Flycatchers (*Ficedula hypoleuca*) at nearby nesting Redbacked Shrikes (*Lanius collurio*) suppressed brood care to the extent that, in one case, the flycatchers' eggs chilled and, in another case, the brood starved to death (but see Section II,C,1,*a*). As McNicholl (1973) suggested, a balance between antipredator aggression and habituation, depending on the local situation, would seem to ensure minimal loss of eggs or young. This balance could, of course, be modified by such factors as the effectiveness of the particular predator species in a particular area.

The relaxation of response to predators nesting near prey would be all the more facilitated if the predator tended to feed away from the immediate vicinity. The two pairs of nonattacked Herring Gulls cited by McNicholl did in fact invariably feed away from their nests.

a. Burgfriede. In Germany in the Middle Ages, there was a rule that squabbles and vendettas would cease during the time the feuding parties took refuge in the *Burg* (fortress) or fortified town. This voluntary renunciation of animosity and cessation of hostilities among neighbors confined to close quarters became known as *Burgfriede*.

Predators and prey, for one reason or another, occasionally find themselves nesting neighbors. In such situations, there is a potential advantage for the predator to maintain a "low profile." At the same time, there is a potential for the prey to habituate to the frequent comings and goings of the resident predator.

Kruuk (1964) observed that Black-headed Gulls (*Larus ridibundus*) attacked avian predators that nested away from the colony more readily than those that nested on the periphery. In the tundra, falcons (*Falco peregrinus, F. rusticolis*) share nesting areas with various ducks (Cade, 1960; Fischer, 1973; Uspenski, 1957); *Branta ruficollis* nests almost exclusively near Peregrine Falcons, sometimes as close as 1.5 m from the falcon's nest. Larger falcons and eagles (e.g., *Aquila chrysaetos*) have been observed to nest near breeding crows, gulls, and herons (Dementjew & Gortschakowkaya, 1945; Feiler, 1961; Fischer, 1973). Hagen (1947) noted that the closer thrushes (*Turdus pilarus*) nested to breeding Merlin Falcons (*Falco columbarius aesalon*), the greater their reproductive success, because thrushes whose nests were farther away suffered nest predation by crows. The African falcon *Polihierax semitorquatus* and weaverbirds (*Philetairus socius*) nest in the same area. Meinertzhagen (1959) and MacLean (1970, 1973) observed that the weaverbirds provisioned their young without disturbance from the falcons. Schnurre (1934, 1935) found that many pairs of woodpeckers (*Dryocopus martius*) and doves (*Columba oenas*) successfully reared young in the area of nesting goshawks (*Accipiter gentilis*).

Other observations indicate that the area around a raptor's nest does not provide inviolate sanctuary to neighbors. Great Horned Owls (*Bubo bubo*), for example, have been seen to prey mainly upon neighboring Laughing and Herring Gulls (Schnurre, 1941), and Schnell (1958) observed a female capture several ducklings (*Anas platyrhynchos*) within 60 m of her nest.

The only experiments, to my knowledge, designed to investigate the matter of *Burgfriede* between predators and prey in the area of the former's nest are those of Wyrwoll (1977). He offered live domestic pigeons (*Columba livia*) to wild pairs of nesting goshawks. The pigeons were tethered on the ground at distances ranging from 25 to 200 m from the goshawk's nest. Wyrwoll found that females spurned pigeons offered during the incubation period. During the nest-building and posthatching phases, however, females preferred pigeons less than 75 m from the nest. Males, which preyed upon the pigeons during the entire study period, made the majority of captures between 100 and 150 m from the nest, although they occasionally took pigeons as close as 25 m from the nest.

There was a tendency for males to hunt farther from the nest during the posthatching phase (up to 200 m). Both sexes carried their quarry farther from the nest before they plucked it.

It is uncertain to what extent the goshawks were "enticed" to prey upon pigeons as close as 25 m from the nest. The fact that the pigeons were tethered might have caused them to move about in a manner resembling a wounded or incapacitated bird and, as such, represented an easy catch. Pimlott, Shannon, and Kolenosky (1969), for example, found that wolves in winter predominantly kill fawns and older age classes of White-tailed Deer (also see Schaller, 1972a). A close parallel to wolf predation upon sick prey (Mech, 1970) has been observed in various raptors (Fischer, 1970; Tamisier, 1970; Ullrich, 1971). Man-trained falcons (*Falco peregrinus, F. rusticolus*) were seen by Eutermoser (1961) to select debilitated carrion crows, when "thrown" at them, significantly more often than did a human hunter (40% versus 21%; also see Kenward, 1978). The evolution of the "broken wing" distraction display of birds, whereby the bird mimics a sick or lame animal, supports the hypothesis that many vertebrate predators prefer to prey upon disabled individuals.

It is also possible that Wyrwoll's goshawks were attracted to the tethered pigeons because the latter were conspicuous or odd (for a discussion, see Curio, 1976; Krebs, 1973; Milinski, 1977a, 1977b; Mueller, 1968). Wyrwoll's study does not contradict the hypothesis that nesting predators tend to avoid hunting in the immediate vicinity. He suggested, however, that if they do so it is not because of any *Burgfriede*, but the result of changes in the behavior of the potential prey—notably, increased wariness and vigilance. Additional studies employing trained falcons are almost certain to provide answers to currently unresolved questions.

b. Vigilance of Prey. Wyrwoll (1977) observed that starlings (*Sturnus vulgaris*) nesting 30–50 m from a goshawk's nest never flew beneath it, although, according to him, it would have been "convenient" for them to have done so. They also were never seen to incur an attack from the goshawks. Wood Pigeons (*Columba palumbus*) nesting 100 m away tended to perch high in the canopy, from which vantage point they kept the hawks under frequent surveillance. In addition, they tended to follow the male goshawk from a safe distance when he flew in the vicinity. In this regard, it is noteworthy that Buturlin (in Cade, 1960) observed that ducks nesting near Peregrine Falcons usually walked to their nests. If they flew to them, they were often attacked.

Schnurre (1935) noted that a goshawk refrained from hunting birds that nested near it but attacked nonresidents that came into the area. He suggested that the reason for this difference was that residents were more aware of the threat (i.e., were more attentive). These observations, albeit anecdotal, lend support to the idea that predators do not avoid hunting in the area of their nests because of *Burgfriede* (see Bruell & Stuelcken, 1939; Glutz von Blotzheim, Bauer, & Bezel, 1971) but because they have little chance of capturing an alert prey (Rudebeck, 1950, 1951; Shalter & Schleidt, 1977).

Available evidence would seem to indicate that prey do not habituate *fully* to the presence of a nearby resident predator. They may cease to react overtly with fright or mobbing behavior (but see Section II,C,1 for an example of brood starvation), but they remain attentive to the predator's actions while tolerating its presence for one reason or another (costs of renesting, protection against other predators, etc.). As Thorpe (1956) pointed out, habituation of fear responses to a predator is a result of a change in the organization of behavior in which "emotional disruption is replaced by nonemotional orienting responses [p. 161]." This notion of vigilance on the part of prey is supported by the findings of Melzack (1961) who showed that Mallard ducks continued to orient toward hawk and goose models after they had ceased to evoke any overt fear responses. The ducks' orienting responses were still evident after more than 2000 presentations of the models.

The behavioral observation that high-arousal fright responses habituate, whereas orienting responses persist, is supported by the results of Russell (1967) and Sharpless and Jasper (1956). The latter found that the EEG arousal reaction can habituate after as few as 20–30 presentations of a novel stimulus. But the orienting response, reflected by evoked cortical potentials, requires thousands of stimulus presentations before habituation occurs.

From the foregoing, it seems clear that a prey cannot simply ignore a predator unless the predator is unlikely to attack (see Section II,B,3). Flight responses need not occur, but surveillance and wariness would seem to be highly adaptive. On the other hand, no animal can remain constantly alert or avoid all precarious situations. Indeed, where the predator poses no immediate threat, overt antipredator responses would be maladaptive insofar as they would interrupt foraging, reproduction, and other necessary activities.

D. Influence of Predation Pressure on Antipredator Behavior

There are several indications that the influence of aerial predation on flocks of woodland songbirds in certain areas of the United States, including that of the tits mentioned in Section II,B,2, is lower now than in the past (Morse, 1970). Morse suggested that the apparent discrepancy between the presence of a well-developed alarm system and low levels of predation may be the result, in part, of this decrease in the density of predators. The relatively low degree of response to alarm calls by some passerines in Louisiana might represent the action of selective forces moving toward a new equilibrium.

Morse further suggested that, like many songbirds, large game such as deer, whose traditional predators (wolves and mountain lion) have been exterminated in vast areas of their former range, retain innate defensive behaviors that are maladaptive to their current situation. The fact that deer still possess a sophisticated antipredator behavior system (Hirth & McCullough, 1977) suggests either that (1) predation pressure from other sources (e.g., man and dogs) is sufficient to maintain it, (2) that strong selection pressures in the past have produced a relatively immutable genome (Morse, 1980), or (3) both. Some evidence for the resistance of antipredator behavior to change was provided by Curio (1969), who found that the Galapagos finch *Geospiza difficilis acutirostris* of Tower and Wenman Islands responds to models of raptors despite the fact that no aerial predators inhabit the island. The Tower finch does respond, however, less strongly than other Galapagos finches who inhabit islands with resident aerial predators, which indicates the tendency for antipredator behavior to be selected against in the absence of predators. Further evidence of the adaptiveness of response to decreased predation pressure is the fact that Darwin's finches—without individual experience—do not avoid mammalian predators, which are absent from the native Galapagos fauna.

Conversely, titmice under considerable predation pressure in Wytham Woods, Oxford, England distinguish predators from inappropriate stimuli more effectively than do their congeners in eastern North America (Morse, 1980). The frequent presence of sparrowhawks in Wytham Woods may have resulted in a time-saving response of the tits (Morse, 1973). Sparrowhawks often fly over a flock before launching an attack from a lower altitude. Flock members generally remain under cover longer following the initial flyover than after an actual attack. Like most avian predators, sparrowhawks seldom attack twice in quick succession, no doubt because of their general inability to capture an alerted prey (Rudebeck, 1950). This minimizing of costs associated with pursuing and capturing prey accords well with predictions of available predator–prey models (e.g., J. M. Emlen, 1968; MacArthur & Pianka, 1968; Pulliam, 1974). The tits of Wytham Woods appear to have made the most of this consequence by minimizing the amount of time in antipredator activities (Morse, 1980).

III. Habituation Experiments

Overt antipredator responses habituate far more readily in the laboratory setting than in the wild (Lorenz, 1939; Morse, 1980; Nice & ter
Pelkwyk, 1941; Shalter, 1975; White & Weeden, 1966). Hinde (1954), for
example, observed a considerable decrement in the mobbing response of
captive Chaffinches after just one presentation of a predator model. Even
when the presence of a live owl in the aviary was reinforced by an indubi-
tably unpleasant stimulus—the Chaffinch being held against the owl while
small feathers were plucked out—habituation, nonetheless, proceeded
rapidly (also see Melzack, Penick, & Beckett, 1959; Martin & Melvin,
1964; Melvin & Cloar, 1969). This discrepancy prompted Hinde (1954) to
inquire about what reinforcement exists in the natural environment that
prevents habituation to a predator. One possibility Hinde suggested is
that the reinforcement, in the case of the mobbing response of Chaffinches, is not an attack by the owl but the disappearance of the owl as it
flies away (which did not occur in his experiments), like the mailman is
"chased away" so successfully by the resident dog. In Martin and
Melvin's study the hawk did disappear after the response had been elicited, yet habituation occurred nonetheless. I, too, observed habituation in
my laboratory studies with galliforms (Shalter, 1974), despite the disappearance of a live roadside hawk following its brief presentation.

Martin and Melvin proposed that, in the case of fear responses of quail
(*Colinus virginianus*), the reinforcement may be inherent in some phase
of attack by the predator (also see Paulson, 1973). Admittedly, this hypothesis has not been systematically tested in the natural setting. In the
laboratory, Chaffinches habituated to a live owl that caused them to flee
and occasionally supplanted them (Hinde, 1954). For at least some species of prey, the relatively high percentage of successful attacks by a
predator would seem to preclude this sort of reinforcement for the prey:
large-mouth bass on other fish, 94%; Osprey on fish, 80–96%; puma on
deer and elk, 82%; hyena on wildebeest calves, 32% [see Curio (1976, p.
194) for other success rates].

Spatial Specificity of Habituation

An alternate hypothesis to account for the differential rate of habituation observed in the laboratory and in the wild was suggested by Schleidt
(1961)—namely, the failure of most laboratory experiments to provide for
adequate stimulus specificity of the predator by changing its location of
presentation or direction of repeated flyovers. The desire to obtain readily

reproducible quantitative data often results in the subject being maintained in an environment far more depauperate than the natural one, and stimuli relevant to the behavior under study are either lacking or presented in a perfunctory, excessive, or otherwise biologically unrealistic fashion.

Of all the properties of a stimulus, it is the spatial properties that have received the least consideration in habituation studies. The spatial relationship between the stimulus and the respondent has only rarely been studied, as, for example, by Eikmanns (1955) and Hale and Almquist (1960). The latter investigators reported that stud bulls, which had ceased to respond sexually to a stationary cow, displayed renewed sexual behavior when the cow was repositioned as little as 1 m from her former position.

Similarly, Falls (1969) found that male White-throated Sparrows (*Zonotrichia albicolis*) responded more to the recorded song of a strange male than to that of a neighboring male, so long as both songs were broadcast at the territorial boundary adjacent to the neighbor whose song was employed. At the opposite boundary, however, the resident's response to the neighbor's song was similar to that evoked by the stranger's song. In other words, when the neighbor was located in the "wrong place," it was treated as a stranger. This finding can be viewed in terms of renewed responsiveness to the stimulus at the new location after habituation to it had occurred at the original site (see Petrinovich & Patterson, 1981; Petrinovich & Peeke, 1973; Schleidt, 1973). Peeke and Veno (1973) similarly showed that habituation of the aggressive responses of territorial sticklebacks (*Gasterosteus aculeatus*) is highly specific to the location of a stimulus fish and that the response is made on the basis of individual recognition. Curio (1963) reported that ducks and geese, which had habituated to dogs at one shore of a lake, proved not to be habituated to them at the opposite shore. A more recent example of position-specific habituation has been reported for territorial scent-marking in ring-tailed lemurs (*Lemur catta;* Mertl, 1977).

With certain of these observations in mind, I wanted to determine in the laboratory whether the spatial relationship of a predator *vis-à-vis* the prey or the inanimate environment might account for the relative lack of habituation to recurring predators in the wild.

As experimental animals I used laboratory-reared domestic and Burmese red jungle fowl (*Gallus* sp.), and as the "predator" I employed a 15-cm-diameter black sphere. The predator was presented by motor-driven monofilament lines at two positions within an audiometric room [see Shalter (1975) for details].

A simple change in the position from which the predator appeared

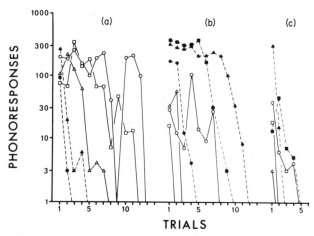

Fig. 2. Total phonoresponses (bucks and squawks) form six domestic fowl, as evoked by a visual stimulus (black sphere) presented from two locations. Subjects represented by solid symbols received the stimulus–location sequence ground–overhead–ground in Series I (a), II (b), and III (c), respectively. Open symbols represent responses of subjects that received the location sequence overhead–ground–overhead. One subject did not emit phonoresponses in Series I, and another subject did not respond vocally in Series III. From Shalter (1975). Copyright 1975 by the American Psychological Association. Reprinted by permission of the publisher.

(overhead or ground) resulted in renewed responsiveness of the birds (Fig. 2). The significantly greater response to the predator in the overhead position may reflect an aspect of temporal novelty in conjunction with some stimulus generalization. The majority of stimuli impinging on the birds throughout their ontogeny emanated from the horizontal (conspecific, feed, etc.).

Since appropriate responses to communication signals providing information about the presence of a predator are just as vital to the prey's survival as appropriate responses to the predator itself, I tested the effect of changing locations on the response to warning calls as well. [Employing the functional label "alarm" or "warning" call is a convenient and perfectly useful procedure, so long as it is kept in mind that the signal so labeled may function in other than just the context of predation (Morton & Shalter, 1977; W. J. Smith, 1968).] In the rich vocal repertoire of the domestic fowl, described by Baümer (1962) and Konishi (1963), there are several so-called "warning" calls emitted by a bird when it sights a potential predator.

Jungle fowl (Fig. 3) displayed renewed phonoresponsiveness to warning calls when they were broadcast at a new location (Loudspeaker C,

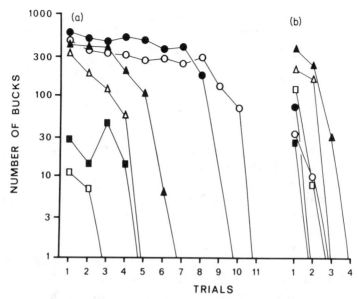

Fig. 3. Total number of bucks emitted in response to a warning-call stimulus by six Burmese red jungle fowl (open and closed symbols) in all trials of Series I [(a); Loudspeaker A or B] and Series III [(b); Loudspeaker C]. There were no phonoresponses to the stimulus in Series II. From Shalter (1975). Copyright 1975 by the American Psychological Association. Reprinted by permission of the publisher.

Series III) after habituation to them had occurred in the original position (Loudspeaker A or B, Series I). Because there were no responses to the playbacks in Series II (different loudspeaker in the same location as in Series I), it can be inferred that the birds did not distinguish minor differences in frequency response between Loudspeakers A and B. Half the birds received the loudspeaker sequence A–B–C and the other half sequence B–A–C [see Shalter (1975) for details].

It is noteworthy that even after the visual and acoustic stimuli had ceased to elicit phonoresponses in these experiments, the birds invariably exhibited general arousal and frequent orientation toward the source where the predator or warning calls had just been presented. This underlines the importance of avoiding statements such as "The birds habituated to the predator." What habituates is a specific type of response, in this case phonoresponse (see Section II,C,1,*b*).

The importance of the spatial context on overt responses to a predator or to alarm calls demonstrated in these short-term habituation tests appears adaptive, because in nature it is unlikely that two attacks will come from the same location or direction (also see Curio, 1975, p. 44). A change in the spatial context, however, would reflect a new and possibly lethal situation to which, within limits, the prey should continue to be responsive. This finding of spatial specificity may have pragmatic implications for those who are attempting to rid airfields of birds by broadcasting alarm or distress calls from fixed loudspeakers (see Busnel & Giban, 1965).

1. Spatial Oddity of Prey

The demonstration that habituation results, in part, from a position effect—together with the findings of Schleidt (1961), who showed the importance of temporal rarity of a predator in eliciting a prey's response—suggests that the relative lack of habituation to predators in nature is the result of their combined temporal and spatial novelty vis-à-vis the prey or inanimate environment. Reinforcement need not enter the picture at all.

It is well known that, in many species, individual prey that stray from their group are subject to increased predation (Hobson, 1968; Schaller, 1972a). Whether this is caused ultimately by movement oddity on the part of the prey (Neill, 1970) or spatial oddity (Mueller, 1968), or other factors has not been systematically investigated. It is possible that the predator is attracted to the "odd man out" because of past unrewarding efforts to capture a member of a group, either through the "confusion effect" (Welty, 1934) of scattering group members or diminished access.

A prey's separation from the group may be mitigated somewhat by increased wariness. Wood Pigeons and Ostriches (Struthio camelus), for example, look up more frequently when alone than when in the flock (Bertram, 1980; Jennings & Evans, 1979; Lazarus, 1979a, 1979b; Murton, 1971; J. N. M. Smith, 1977). Similarly, solitary cervids display greater flight tendency than individuals in the herd (Altmann, 1958; Tilson, 1980).

The role, if any, the predator's habituation (or something akin to it) to more frequently encountered and less-vulnerable group members plays in concentrating its attention on spatially odd prey remains to be investigated (see Section V).

2. Mobbing Responses of Free-Ranging Prey

To determine to what extent free-ranging prey react to repeated appearances of a predator—depending on the spatial context—I chose to examine the mobbing response of Pied Flycatchers (Ficedula hypoleuca), because there is considerable information available about the general response (Curio, 1959, 1975). The calling rate was selected as the best and most readily quantifiable measure of the mobbing reaction. [See Shalter (1978a) for a short review of quantifiable mobbing studies and Curio (1978) for a discussion of the adaptive significance of mobbing.]

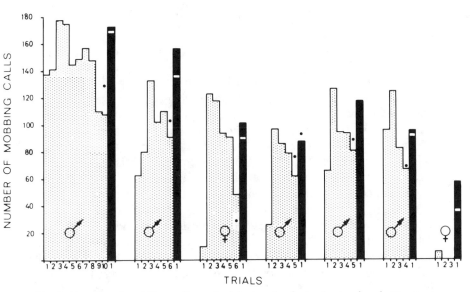

Fig. 4. Number of mobbing calls evoked during the first minute of each 15-minute trial in response to the predator model from the more vociferous member of seven pairs of Pied Flycatchers. Large black dots or white bars refer to the number of calls emitted during the fifth minute of both the last trial with the model at the original position (shaded bars) and the first trial at the new position (black bars). From Shalter (1978b).

Seven pairs of breeding flycatchers were repeatedly shown a life-like stuffed specimen of a pygmy owl (*Glaucidium passerinum*) from a specific location (1.5–2 m from the nest) until the mobbing-call response had waned [see Shalter (1978b) for details]. The flycatchers displayed renewed mobbing of the owl when its position was changed (but equidistant to the nest; Fig. 4). Their renewed response suggests that the perceptual processes of predator recognition (see Section II,B), if occurring repeatedly, entail a subtle evaluation of the spatial context and not merely the inherent characteristics of the predator alone. Over and above cues emanating from the predator, there appears to be a finely tuned perception of the entire environmental situation far more subtle than is generally assumed (see Thorpe, 1956, p. 72). The renewal of escape responses of silver angelfish (*Pterophyllum eimeki*), depending on a change in the "predator's" (shadow stimulus) location, points to general lack of spatial generalization of predators among vertebrate prey (Eikmanns, 1955; Schleidt, Shalter, & Carawan, 1983) and possibly many invertebrates as well (Wolda, 1961).

a. Priming and Labile Properties of Predators. A surprisingly high proportion (42%) of the Pied Flycatchers I tested failed to mob the stuffed owl (5 of 12 pairs) when it was placed near their nests. Curio (1975, also personal communication) presented the *identical* model in *identical* fashion to 73 flycatchers in the breeding seasons of 1961 through 1965. Moreover, one of his study sites was the same as mine. Yet of those 73 birds only 6 (8%) failed to mob the dummy upon its initial presentation.

The pygmy owl has been extinct in the study area for decades, if not centuries. Less is known, however, about changes in the populations of other pygmy owls that inhabit the flycatcher's winter quarters in central West Africa (Stresemann & Portenko, 1960). Although it seems unlikely, the only explanation to account for the difference in the incidence of mobbing observed since 1963 is that the number of owls encountered by flycatchers in their winter quarters has diminished significantly. An influence of experience with live predators on mobbing reactions of prey has been reported by Owings and Coss (1977). They observed that ground squirrels (*Spermophilus beecheyi*) from rattlesnake-adapted populations mobbed snakes less intensely than did rattlesnake-nonadapted squirrels. They suggested that the presence of venomous snakes increases the risk to the mobber, thereby favoring an adaptive attenuation in mobbing intensity.

To determine whether the range of effective stimuli eliciting mobbing could be extended in the five pairs of "nonmobbing" flycatchers, I briefly exposed to each pair a live pygmy owl that resembled the ineffective dummy in all static owl traits. [For a discussion of how elicitation of response involves changes in the range of effective stimuli, see Curio (1969); Eibl-Eibesfeldt (1958); Hinde (1970); Roth & Luthardt (1980).] The live owl evoked immediate and vigorous mobbing from both members of the five pairs. Moreover, all birds immediately mobbed the stuffed owl when it was presented again 24 hours later. The birds' responses to the dummy were somewhat less intense than those directed at the live owl. It might be argued that habituation caused the slightly weaker mobbing response during the second presentation of the dummy, as compared with the response evoked by the live owl 24 hours earlier (see Hinde, 1954). A more likely explanation for the weaker reaction to the dummy is that it lacked the enhancing labile property of erratic and subtle movement. In any event, the results demonstrate that the basis of mobbing is more complex than generally believed, particularly the priming role of experience with live predators and the effect of their labile properties [see Shalter (1978d) for details].

3. Effects of Domestication on Antipredator Responses

In addition to experiential influences on responsiveness such as those seen in Pied Flycatchers, there is evidence that certain domesticated

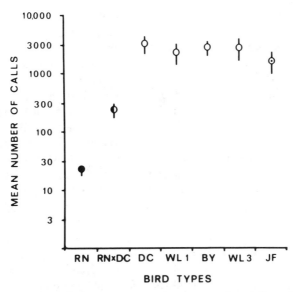

Fig. 5. Mean number of phonoresponses of seven experimentally naive bird types evoked by a predator model. The vertical bars represent one standard deviation ($n = 35$; 5 birds of each type). RN, Ring-necked Pheasant (*Phasianus colchicus*); RN × DC, pheasant × dark cornish hybrids; DC, dark cornish chickens; WL 1, white leghorn chickens tested at 12 months of age; BY, chickens of mixed breed reared in an outdoor barnyard; WL 3, white leghorn chickens tested at 15 months of age; JF, Burmese red jungle fowl.

animals have different thresholds of fear than do their wild counterparts (Darwin, 1874; Price, 1972; Schaller & Emlen, 1962; R. H. Smith, 1972). Tinbergen (1957) cited domestication as a possible factor to account for the discrepancy between his observations of the antipredator responses of wild gallinaceous birds and those of Hirsch *et al.* (1955), who employed white leghorn chickens.

The studies of Collias, Collias, and Saichuae (1964) and Kruijt (1964) revealed an overall similarity in social organization between wild and domestic fowl. The alarm communication systems of wild and domestic forms are also quite similar (Shalter, 1974). We have seen that the phonoresponses of red jungle fowl and a domesticated breed were quantitatively similar (see Figs. 2 and 3). Further evidence of similarity can be seen in Fig. 5, which depicts the number of alarm vocalizations elicited from seven groups of birds during the first presentation of a predator model [see Shalter (1974) for details]. The only statistically significant differences were between pheasants and chicken × pheasant hybrids and between the hybrids and the domestic and wild fowl. Despite demonstrated differences among breeds of domestic fowl (Potter, 1949), all three breeds used in my experiments responded to the predator model or warning calls in a fashion both qualitatively and quantitatively similar to that of their wild counterpart (also see D. B. Miller, 1977).

It is interesting in this regard that habituation of fear responses to stimuli such as sudden loud noises did not differ between two stocks of domestic fowl ("docile" and "flighty") studied by Murphy and Duncan (1977, 1978), whereas distinct differences were found in their responses toward human beings. The docile stock showed significantly more habituation of withdrawal, but this withdrawal reaction could be increased by preventing habituation to humans early in the birds' ontogeny. W. M. Schleidt (personal communication) noted that the only striking difference between domesticated and wild turkeys was that the former learned to step carefully over long garden hoses, but the latter continued to fly over them.

Similarity in antipredator behavior between wild and domestic fowl might be the result of continued, although different, predator selection (e.g., dogs instead of foxes) or because of a relatively resistant behavior against which no direct artificial selection has been concentrated. Whatever the reason, the findings indicate that a demonstration of behavioral differences between wild and domestic animals is essential to any strong argument for restraint in the use of domestic animals in behavioral studies. They certainly contradict general statements such as "domesticated animals do not respond to various types of threatening situations in the laboratory as do wild animals of the same or related species [Dubos, 1965, p. 109]."

IV. Habituation and Acoustic Alarm Communication

No single aspect of antipredator behavior has engendered more theories and produced fewer facts than that of the evolution and function of alarm calls in birds and mammals (see Sherman, 1977). [For reviews of the literature on this extensive subject, consult W. J. Smith (1977), Harvey and Greenwood (1978), and Klump and Shalter (in press).] No attempt will be made here to examine more than a few aspects of alarm communication germane to the topic of habituation.

A. *Seeet* and Mobbing Calls

One type of alarm vocalization emitted by many songbirds and certain small mammals has physical characteristics that allegedly render it diffi-

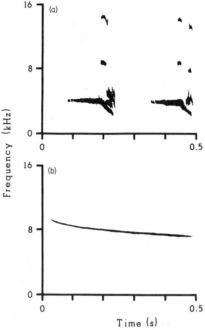

Fig. 6. Sound spectrograms (Kay Electric Company Sonagraph 7029A) of the playback stimuli presented to goshawks and pygmy owls. (a) Two of the mobbing calls (wide band). (b) The *seeet* call (narrow band). From Shalter (1978c).

cult for a predator to localize (Marler, 1955). This so-called *seeet* or "aerial predator" call is a relatively pure tone that lacks transients (abrupt onset and end) and consists of a narrow frequency band within the range 6–9 kHz (Fig. 6). These characteristics are assumed to afford avian predators a minimum binaural comparison of differences in phase, intensity, and arrival time at the two ears useful in locating a sound source. The *seeet* call is, in fact, located by man only with difficulty (Shalter & Schleidt, 1977). But the findings of Schwartzkopff (1962), Brosset and Chappuis (1968), Konishi (1973), and Coles, Lewis, Hill, Hutchings, and Gower (in press) indicate that sound localization for man may not be at all the same for other animals. In the only tests of the "nonlocalizability" hypothesis, Barn Owls (*Tyto alba*), pygmy owls (*Glaucidium* spp.), and goshawks localized the allegedly nonlocalizable (Shalter, 1978c; Shalter & Schleidt, 1977). Not only did the goshawks localize the *seeet* calls, they habituated to them more rapidly than they did to mobbing calls. To account for this differential habituation rate, it is necessary to understand something about both the structure and function of the two call types.

If *seeet* alarm calls are located accurately by relevant predators (as appears to be the case), how then to explain the frequent convergence upon the *seeet*-call structure? The answer derives, in part, I think from Darwin's "antithesis" principle (1872), which postulates that structurally distinct signals will minimize the possibility of communication errors and thereby increase the fitness of the sender [that communication may benefit the receiver is incidental, see Dawkins & Krebs (1978)]. The *seeet* and mobbing calls of most songbirds are, in fact, nearly antithetical both structurally and functionally. The *seeet* call, which lacks transients and is a pure tone, is associated with fright or escape responses. Mobbing calls, on the other hand, that have transients and broad frequency bands readily attract other songbirds that then confront or harass a predator. The *seeet* call may have been selected to contrast maximally with the structure of the mobbing call, which provides maximum cues for localization. If so, intra- and interspecific selection (mixed-species mobbing) could account for the convergence of the *seeet*-call's structure.

Recent studies by Rydén (1978a, 1978b, 1980) have shown that the aversive reactions of Great Tit (*Parus major*) nestlings to *seeet* calls could be reversed by manipulating the birds' auditory environment. He suggested that the *seeet* call owes its aversive effect to the fact that it contrasts sharply with the nestlings' normal auditory milieu (sounds of low-to-middle frequencies), including the begging call, which is associated with approach.

Rooke and Knight (1977) have challenged the nonlocalizability hypothesis on theoretical grounds, stating that the *seeet* call "provides interaural cues that would allow most birds and mammals to locate its source [p. 196]." The idea that pure tones can be accurately localized has been supported by Isley and Gysel (1975), who demonstrated that the red fox (*Vulpes vulpes*) can easily locate pure tones from 0.9 to 14 kHz (also see Boudreau, 1968).

I want to emphasize, however, that I do not disagree with the notion that the *seeet* call may be somewhat more difficult than a mobbing call for a predator to localize. It probably is and possibly by reason of its structural antithesis to the mobbing call, whose physical structure appears to have been selected to provide maximum cues for its localization. What I disagree with is the hypothesis that the *seeet*-call form has evolved to avoid giving orientational cues to predators.

Both *seeet* and mobbing calls are occasionally emitted in other than the context of predation; for example, in intraspecific aggression or flock cohesion, respectively (N. G. Smith, 1975; E. S. Morton, personal communication). In general, the common motivational denominator for the signaller in those situations seems to be the same as those associated with avoiding or mobbing a predator, namely, flight–fright and attraction, respectively. Clearly there is a dearth of understanding of the various circumstances in which *seeet* and mobbing calls are employed and the motivational state of the caller (Morton, 1977). The heuristic value of the antithesis principle may lie in drawing attention to both the motivational and functional aspects of both call types.

In addition to evidence indicating the ability of those raptors tested to locate the source of a *seeet* call to within several degrees of arc, there is another argument against the nonlocalizability hypothesis. The assumption of that hypothesis is that the predator utilizes auditory signals in prey capture. To my knowledge, there is no evidence that diurnal raptors use acoustic cues in locating prey. For goshawks and other falcons that sight prey while hunting on the wing, the sheer velocity at which they are moving would seem to render auditory localization improbable. For other predators whose hunting strategy is to perch and wait to spring upon unwary prey (e.g., pygmy owl; Scherzinger, 1970), acoustic alarm signals could, in theory, be of use in locating prey. But in fact this, too, seems unlikely (see Rudebeck, 1950), as should become apparent.

In the Barn Owls, pygmy owls, and goshawks we tested, the *seeet* call, although it was accurately located, elicited fewer responses than did mobbing calls (Shalter, 1978c; Shalter & Schleidt, 1977). This suggests that, rather than being difficult to localize, there is either something in the quality of the *seeet* call or the manner it is processed by the predator that elicits less responsiveness than do transient sounds with broad frequencies. This is altogether consistent with the concept of Lorenz and Tinbergen (1938) that a stimulus can have eliciting as well as orienting properties. Along the same lines, Brosset and Chappuis (1968, p. 389) reported that different bird calls elicited varying levels of predatory response from mammalian carnivores, an effect they attributed to a cortical filtering mechanism.

Smythe (1970), in proposing his "pursuit-invitation" hypothesis, suggested that prey animals may actually gain an advantage from advertising their whereabouts to predators by inducing futile attacks while they are still outside the prey's flight distance (also see Zahavi, in Dawkins, 1976). Actually, I think the term "pursuit inhibition" is more accurate (see Coblentz, 1980), because the predator normally gives up hunting when an alarm signal is given (Rudebeck, 1950, 1951; Schaller, 1975; Yahner, 1980). Mobbing calls, in some ways, appear to be at least as conspicuous as the white "flash patterns" of cursorial mammals cited by Smythe to support his hypothesis. The *seeet* call, on the other hand, which elicits considerably less responsiveness from diurnal raptors, might do so because of those predators' inability to capture prey already aware of their presence. Rudebeck observed, for example, that "in most cases, the predatory bird does not even make any attempt to attack, simply because it was discovered in time [1950, p. 74]." Selection for decreased responsiveness to such calls might be counter strategy to minimize futile energy expenditure in attacking or otherwise responding to a wary seeet caller. This relatively low responsiveness to narrow-band frequencies might be the result of an auditory filtering mechanism in the Barn Owl, for whom wide-band sounds (e.g., noise of mice scurrying through the leaf litter) are more relevant for prey capture.

On the other hand, for diurnal raptors such as goshawks the differential responsiveness to *seeet* and mobbing calls might be the result of conditioning. One observation (Shalter, 1978c) is at least consistent with the notion of negative reinforcement: the goshawk that showed the lowest response to the *seeet* playbacks (9 of 10 trials; Table 1) was the only bird captured from the wild as an experienced hunter. As such, she must have experienced many more unrewarding encounters with *seeet*-calling birds than any of the other hawks tested. That experience, coupled with stimulus generalization of *seeet* calls, might account for her low level of response. So might a number of other factors, I hasten to add. Clearly, ontogenetic studies of a predator's responsiveness to alarm calls are needed.

Unlike responses to the *seeet* calls, the relative lack of habituation of the goshawks' orienting responses to mobbing call playbacks (Table 1) might have been the result of their having associated those signals with similar sounds encountered during the annual falconing season, when they were often harassed by mobbing songbirds. Their frequent display of stress behaviors (talon flexion, stretching, etc.) concurrent with broadcast of the mobbing calls is consistent with the notion that the hawks were "bothered" by that sound. No stress reactions were observed in any of the hawks during the *seeet*-call playbacks.

Experiential differences of individual goshawks probably account for some of the observed interindividual variation in responsiveness. Shalter, Fentress, and Young (1977), for example, demonstrated that the responses of sibling wolf pups to acoustic stimuli were greatly influenced by differences in both past and present contexts (also see Leger, Owings, & Boal, 1979; Robinson, 1980).

Dawkins (1976) pointed out that it has become a "kind of sport" to dream up explanations to account for the evolution of alarm calls. He discounts altruism other than that possibly associated with kin selection and gives several "selfish" functions, which involve influencing the behavior of other prey to the advantage of the signaller (also see Harvey & Greenwood, 1978). None of these explanations precludes an additional

TABLE 1

Responses of Goshawks and Pygmy Owls to Playbacks of *Seeet* (S) and Mobbing (M) Calls[a]

Bird																				
	Trials																			
	1		2		3		4		5		6		7		8		9		10	
	S	M	S	M	S	M	S	M	S	M	S	M	S	M	S	M	S	M	S	M
Goshawk 1	+	+	+	+	+	+	+	+	+	+	+	+	+	+	+	+	0	+	+	+
Goshawk 2	0	+	0	+	0	+	((+))	+	0	+	0	+	0	+	0	+	0	+	0	+
Goshawk 3	+	+	+	+	+	+	+	+	+	+	+	+	+	+	+	+	+	+	0	+
Goshawk 4	+	+	+	+	+	+	+	+	+	+	+	+	+	+	(+)	+	+	+	(+)	+
Goshawk 5	+	+	+	+	+	+	+	+	((+))	+	0	+	0	+	0	+	0	+	0	0
Goshawk 6	+	+	+	+	+	+	+	+	+	+	+	+	+	(+)	((+))	0	0	(+)	0	+
Pygmy owl 1 (*Geospiza brasilianum*)	+	+	+	+	+	+	+	+	+	+	+	+	+	(+)	((+))	+	0	(+)	+	+
Pygmy owl 2 (*G. perlatum*)	+	+	0	+	+	+	(+)	+	+	+	+	+	(+)	+	((+))	+	((+))	+	+	0

[a] Ten successive trials. 0, "No response" to that playback; +, positive response with a latency to respond of <2 seconds; (+), positive response with a latency to respond of 2–5 seconds; ((+)), positive response with a latency of 5–10 seconds. A head movement toward the activated speaker was counted a "positive response," and away from the activated speaker a "negative response," when performed after a new stimulus was presented but before it had terminated. When no head movements occurred during a stimulus presentation, it was classified as "no response." Note that there were no errors or "negative responses."

influence of the calls on the predator as well. To date, all functional hypotheses have been based on the assumption that the "pioneer" alarm callers—those whose calls were not quite "perfect" (i.e., localizable for predators)—drew the predator's attention and subsequent attack. In so doing, many of the pioneer callers died, selfishly or otherwise. Considering the lack of evidence that diurnal predators in the past utilized sound in locating prey any more than they do at present—in conjunction with what would seem to be a positive selective value for a predator not to waste time or energy in responding to an alert alarm caller—the antithesis hypothesis could account for the evolution of the structural peculiarities of both *seeet* and mobbing calls.

I have gone into some detail regarding the differential responsiveness of predators to *seeet* and mobbing calls in order to exemplify a basic consideration occasionally omitted in habituation studies. That is that phylogenetic adaptations and predispositions not only influence the nature of the response to a stimulus but, as modified by experience, the waning of that response as well. Barn Owls and goshawks fail to show much responsiveness to *seeet* alarm calls and rapidly habituate to them. Only an understanding of their different natural histories can provide insight into the biological significance of their low responsiveness or rapid response waning. In the case of Barn Owls, the *seeet* stimulus may not be at all relevant in predation, whereas for goshawks it may represent a situation in which the chance of successful prey capture is slim and energy is best conserved. For the purpose of this discussion, it is irrelevant whether or not this interpretation happens to be true or not. What is relevant, in general, is that an understanding of the species' behavior in natural conditions can suggest appropriate biological questions to investigate in field and laboratory experiments.

B. Minimizing Habituation to Alarm Calls among Prey

The preceding discussion dealt with the relative unresponsiveness of certain predators to alarm calls of their prey. I now discuss briefly a subject that has received even less attention—namely, adaptations to minimize habituation to alarm signals between prey.

The Carolina Wren (*Thryothorus ludovicianus*) forms permanent pair bonds and defends a territory throughout the year. In the vocal repertoire of this species, there is a signal termed the *chirt,* which is structurally variable and is emitted in a temporally variable fashion (Morton & Shalter, 1977). We elicited *chirt*s from one or both members of wren pairs by

TABLE 2

Characteristics of Wren *Chirts* Emitted When Hawk Was Still or Moving Its Head[a]

Chirt characteristics (means)	Hawk still	Hawk moving head
—	1–5 *chirt* bouts	Continuous *chirts*
Number of *chirts* per bout in 60 seconds		
1-*chirt* bouts	5.83 ± 5.06 SD[b]	—
2-*chirt* bouts	22.64 ± 11.31	—
3-*chirt* bouts	15.36 ± 14.19	—
4-*chirt* bouts	3.73 ± 5.06	—
5-*chirt* bouts	2.09 ± 5.97	—
Repetition rate (*chirts*/second)	1.44 ± 1.26	7.30 ± 3.39
Frequency range (kHz)	1.65–2.55	2.02–3.01

[a] Data obtained 1–30 minutes after hawk was introduced.
[b] SD, Standard deviations.

presenting them with a tethered live hawk. The results of field and labora-tory experiments suggest two aspects of the chirt system that appear to be unique in avian communication: (1) *chirts* vary in amplitude, frequency, and inter*chirt* interval that correlate with small movements and orienta-tion of the predator, and (2) the female member of a pair is far more vocal than the male.

The initial vocal response to the hawk was a sustained bout of evenly spaced *chirts* lasting from 10 to 60 seconds. Thereafter, the chirts were emitted in bouts of one to five calls. When the hawk moved its head and, in particular, when it oriented toward the wrens, the *chirts* (1) increased in repetition rate, (2) became more evenly spaced in time, and (3) increased in amplitude and frequency (Table 2). When the female emitted variable numbers of *chirts* in bouts, the male was seen to feed, preen, or explore the surroundings, paying little attention to the predator. When the hawk moved, the female's *chirts* changed, as I have described, and the male oriented toward the predator and performed rapid bobbing motions. Dif-ferences in the pattern of calling thus determined whether or not the male would respond with alertness. The female's continuous calling provided him with the information that she was remaining alert. These and other observations (see Morton & Shalter, 1977) suggest that the Carolina Wren *chirt* system is a vocal form of predator surveillance. The "message" (sensu W. J. Smith, 1968, 1977) of *chirts*, which incidentally are also used intraspecifically during territory formation, for example, may be one of "alert" and "escape" (see Morton, 1977).

To understand why female wrens perform the function of predator surveillance, it is necessary to consider the social and ecological constraints on the species. Foraging behavior of the wrens involves entering cavities and rummaging through leaf litter, habits that drastically reduce the forager's ability to detect a predator. Then, too, a male wren is able to hold a territory alone, whereas a female cannot. We believe that the female's role in predator surveillance has evolved to permit the male increased foraging time, even in the presence of a predator, and to enable him to allot more energy to defense of the territory (e.g., singing), without which the female would not survive. By protecting the male, even at the expense of not obtaining food for herself, the female is protecting her own territorial integrity and increasing her reproductive success.

We suggest that the antipredator function of the female's *chirt*s has favored their being emitted in variable sequences in order to maintain the male's attention. By altering the temporal pattern of the calls, the male's habituation to them is minimized, thus ensuring his rapid response when they change to indicate changes in the predator's behavior. The graded *chirt* signals of the Carolina Wren may represent an evolutionary convergence toward a primate-like communication system because of similarities in their social organization as well as associated antipredator strategies. Comparative and ontogenetic studies should shed light on the extent to which variation in alarm-signal transmission may function to maintain responsiveness.

Repetition is one way of varying an alarm signal. One usually thinks of repetition as a basis for habituation, but within limits it is informative and can augment responses. For example, a 30-second playback of warning calls elicited many more poststimulus responses from fowl than did bouts that were only 10 seconds long (Shalter, 1974). Similarly, Beer (1973) discovered that repetition of a signal was a crucial feature in eliciting alarm responses from captive Laughing Gull chicks.

C. Effect of Context on Habituation to Alarm Calls

There is some evidence that free-ranging songbirds habituate to species-specific alarm calls. Zucchi (1979a, 1979b) played back mobbing calls to pairs of breeding Chaffinches. He found that, although the birds' phonoresponses to the playbacks gradually diminished over days, the decrement was not continual. Concomitant contextual occurrences, such as the hatching of the young or the appearance of a predator, could reverse the waning of response. The reversal in both instances is highly adaptive. Zucchi's findings suggest that the Chaffinches' habituation was the result of the unnatural nonreinforcing situation, namely the repeated occurrence of mobbing calls in the absence of the very thing that normally elicits them—a predator.

Effects of reproductive stage on the prey's responsiveness, similar to those observed by Zucchi, have been shown for distress calls (Stefanski & Falls, 1972), human interloper (Andersson, Wiklund, & Rundgren, 1980; Barash, 1975; Grieg-Smith, 1980), predator models (Biermann & Robertson, 1981; M. J. Smith & Graves, 1978), and alarm calls (Shalter, 1979).

In my study, playback stimuli were broadcast to each of 16 pairs of breeding Blue Tits (*Parus caeruleus*) with nestlings ranging in age from 2 to 13 days. Six 5-minute stimuli were employed: (a) human whistle of the opening to Beethoven's Fifth Symphony (control), (b) mixed-species mobbing chorus, (c) blackbird (*Turdus merula*) *seeet* calls, (d) Blue Tit *seeet* calls, (e) Stimuli (b) and (c) combined, and (f) Stimuli (b) and (d) combined. Eight pairs of Blue Tits were presented with random sequences of four stimuli: (a), (b), (c), and (e). The other eight pairs received sequences of Stimuli (a), (b), (d), and (f).

A loudspeaker was hidden near each nest while the parents were off foraging. Each stimulus in the sequence was then broadcast at approximately 5-minute intervals and upon the return of a parent to the nest.

To determine the reactions of Blue Tits away from their own nest and young, the mobbing chorus, followed by one of the seeet or combined stimuli, was played at the nests of six pairs of breeding Coal Tits and Pied Flycatchers with Blue Tit neighbors (see Shalter, 1979, for details).

The responses of only the first resident Blue Tit arriving at each of the 16 nests are depicted in Fig. 7a, because the mates of these first arrivals, which invariably arrived at the scene a bit later, might have been influenced by their partners' behavior and not by the playback stimuli alone.

Responses of the first arrivals varied greatly with the type of stimulus presented. The control [Stimulus (a)], although novel and similar to the other stimuli in terms of sound-level pressure and duration, lacked the requisite features to elicit antipredator behavior of any kind. The mobbing-chorus playback evoked immediate mobbing calls from all 16 birds, but neither flight-to-cover nor "freezing." The two combined stimuli elicited initial flight-to-cover or freezing from 5 birds and immediate mobbing from the other 11. Both *seeet* stimuli caused initial freezing or fleeing from 14 of the 16 Blue Tits, but these behaviors were quickly followed by mobbing reactions. Regardless of the type of initial response, each of the first arrivals interspersed subsequent mobbing with provisioning of the young. Those first arrivals that immediately mobbed upon broadcast of the *seeet* calls had the oldest nestlings, and those that fled or froze in response to the combined stimuli had the youngest. In response to all but

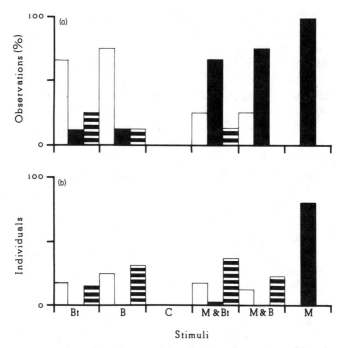

Fig. 7. Responses of resident Blue Tits (a) and nonresident species (b) to the six play-back stimuli. Bt, Blue Tit *seeet* alarm call; B, blackbird *seeet*; Ç, human whistle control; M & Bt, mixed-mobbing chorus plus Blue Tit *seeets*; M & B, mixed-mobbing chorus plus blackbird *seeets*; M, mixed-mobbing chorus; □, freeze; ■, mob; ▬, flee. From Shalter (1979).

the control stimulus, the mates of the first arrivals immediately mobbed upon returning to the nest area, and both parents in 13 of the 16 pairs shared provisioning duties. There was no apparent habituation of the mobbing response of any resident Blue Tit throughout the playback sequence.

With respect to nonresident birds (i.e., those other than the 16 pairs of Blue Tits), there was virtually no mobbing response to other than the mobbing-chorus stimulus, which attracted approach and mobbing from 78 birds (Fig. 7b). Many of those birds had eggs or nestlings of their own within earshot of the broadcasts. Approximately half of the nonresidents ceased to emit mobbing calls before completion of the 5-minute mobbing-chorus playback, although the majority of them remained in the vicinity of the loudspeaker throughout the broadcast. Responses to the *seeet* and combined stimuli were from birds already present in the resident Blue Tits' territories at the time of playback. Those stimuli invariably evoked immediate flight out of the area or departure after initial freezing.

The responses of nonresident Blue Tits ($n = 9$) at the nests of Coal Tits and flycatchers resembled those of other nonresidents. At least 6 of those blue tits from adjacent territories had young of their own. The resident Coal Tits and flycatchers, on the other hand, reacted to the playbacks in a fashion similar to that of the Blue Tits in their own nest areas.

These differences in response of residents and nonresidents can most likely be attributed to differences in parental investment (Trivers, 1972). The tendency of resident Blue Tits with older nestlings to mob immediately in response to *seeet* alarm calls, rather than to flee or freeze, is consistent with this interpretation. Although prior investment, in itself, does not commit an individual to future investment (see Dawkins, 1976), it seems possible that past investment, whose duration influences in part the probability of successful renesting, could be assessed by a parent to determine the appropriate amount of present investment—in this case, the degree of risk taken by the parent in the face of potential danger signaled by a *seeet* call.

These results indicate that antipredator responses to mobbing and alarm calls are greatly influenced not only by the reproductive stage but by whether or not the animal is near its own young or at least within its own territory. One study (Patterson, Petrinovich, & James, 1980) further demonstrated that the pattern and level of antipredator responses in White-crowned Sparrows (*Zonotrichia albicollis*) is influenced by (1) whether or not the stimulus represents a relevant predator at the particular stage of the breeding cycle, and (2) the changing reproductive value of the offspring (see Milinski, 1978).

V. Habituation of Predators' Fear of Prey

As mentioned in the beginning of this chapter, a young galliform chick exhibits fright responses to novel stimuli. In part through the process of habituation, commonplace innocuous stimuli gradually cease to elicit such responses. This fear of novelty (see Bronson, 1968) is not limited to situations in which a prey confronts a potential predator. Many young predators display some degree of fear when confronting potential prey. After initial orientation and approach by the predator, defensive actions of the prey usually dictate the predator's subsequent behavior. If the prey is completely novel to the predator, it might evoke an initial flight response. If the prey is recognized as slightly dangerous, the predator may show ambivalence—approaching and withdrawing. In cases where the predator is somewhat familiar with the prey and where the prey is small and fleeing, the predator generally attacks (Eisenberg & Leyhausen, 1972). The young predator's initial fear probably is an adaptation to the possibility that a live prey might inflict injury in the process of defending itself.

Captive young Tawny Owls appear to overcome their fear of the prey's movements by repeated encounters with live prey (Meyer-Holzapfel & Raeber, 1976). Similarly, golden hamsters permitted to feed on freshly killed insect prey enhanced their chances of subsequently capturing live prey. Moreover, their latency to capture live prey decreased with repeated testing (Polsky, 1978a, 1978b).

These few available studies suggest that habituation plays a role in the development of efficient prey capture. The predator has to learn, from among a wide array of potential prey, those that are edible. This process is probably not merely a matter of learning by trial and error as is generally assumed; in addition to positive association, habituation also plays its negative role, resulting in neglect of objects and situations that fail to provide a satisfactory sensation or any advantage (see Thorpe, 1956). The degree to which habituation influences the predator's behavior vis-à-vis a potential meal has not received the attention it should. One reason for this may be the deep-rooted notion that predators are "big and bad" animals that sit somewhere on the summit of a food pyramid. In fact, most predators occupy far less lofty positions and are themselves preyed upon, particularly young predators. Habituation of fright responses for them, although probably not so obvious or important for survival as that of perennial prey (i.e., animals having many predators), would appear nonetheless to be an important factor in the development of efficient prey capture. Peeke and Peeke (1972), for example, showed that the predatory responses of goldfish (Carassius auratus) and paradise fish (Macropodus opercularis) habituated to prey (brine shrimp) confined in clear plastic tubes. Reinstatement of the biting response could be achieved by either reinforcement (permitting the fish to chase and consume the prey) or the passage of time (>10 days). It could not be achieved by presenting a novel stimulus, nutritive stimuli, or a recovery period shorter than 10 days. The predator's learning (by habituation) to inhibit responses to prey appears, in this case, to be relatively long term. Such learning could serve as the basis for the discrimination needed in the formation of a "search image" by enabling the predator to ignore unobtainable or inappropriate prey.

References

Altmann, S. A. Avian mobbing behavior and predator recognition. *Condor*, 1956, *58*, 241–253.

Altmann, M. The flight distance in free-ranging big game. *Journal of Wildlife Management*, 1958, *22*, 207–209.

Andersson, M., Wiklund, C. G., & Rundgren, H. Parental defense of offspring: A model and an example. *Animal Behaviour*, 1980, *28*, 536–542.

Arnold, J. W. Feeding behaviour of a predaceous bug (Hemiptera: Nabidae). *Canadian Journal of Zoology*, 1971, *49*, 131–132.

Austin, O. L. Group adherence in the Common Tern. *Bird-Banding*, 1951, *22*, 1–15.

Baümer, E. Lebensart des Haushuhns, dritter Teil—Über seine Laute und allgemeine Ergänzungen. *Zeitschrift für Tierpsychologie*, 1962, *19*, 394–416.

Barash, D. Evolutionary aspects of parental behavior: Distraction behavior of the alpine accentor. *Wilson Bulletin*, 1975, *87*, 367–373.

Beer, C. G. A view of birds. *Minnesota Symposium on Child Psychology*, 1973, *7*, 47–86.

Bertram, B. C. R. Social factors influencing reproduction in wild lions. *Journal of Zoology*, 1975, *177*, 463–482.

Bertram, B. C. R. Living in groups: Predators and prey. In J. R. Krebs & N. B. Davies (Eds.), *Behavioral ecology—An evolutionary approach.* Sunderland, Mass.: Sinauer Associates, 1978. Pp. 64–96.

Bertram, B. C. R. Vigilance and group size in Ostriches. *Animal Behaviour*, 1980, *28*, 278–286.

Biermann, G. C., & Robertson, R. J. An increase in parental investment during the breeding season. *Animal Behaviour*, 1981, *29*, 487–489.

Boudreau. G. W. Alarm sounds and responses of birds and their application in controlling problem species. *Living Bird*, 1968, *7*, 27–46.

Bronson, G. W. The fear of novelty. *Psychological Bulletin*, 1968, *69*(5), 350–358.

Brosset, A., & Chappuis, C. Effets de la prédation sur l'evolution des cris des jeunes oiseaux. I. *La Terre et La Vie*, 1968, *4*, 373–389.

Brower, L. P., Brower, J., Van, Z., & Westcott, P. W. Experimental studies of mimicry. *American Naturalist*, 1960, *94*, 343–355.

Brown, L., & Amandon, D. *Eagles, hawks and falcons of the world* (Vol. 1). New York: McGraw-Hill, 1968.

Bruell, H., & Stuelcken, K. Zur Brutbiologie von Habicht und Sperber. *Zeitschrift für Jagdtkunde*, 1939, *1*, 109–130.

Buckley, F. G., & Buckley, P. A. The breeding ecology of Royal Terns *Sterna* (*Thalasseus*) *maxima maxima. Ibis*, 1972, *114*, 344–359.

Busnel, R.-G., & Giban, J. (Eds.). *Colloque: Le probleme des oiseaux sur les aerodromes.* Paris: I.N.R.A., 1965.

Cade, T. J. Ecology of the peregrine and gyrfalcon populations in Alaska. *University of California, Berkeley, Publications in Zoology*, 1960, *63*, 151–290.

Coblentz, B. E. On the improbability of pursuit invitation signals in mammals. *American Naturalist*, 1980, *115*, 438–447.

Coles, R. B., Lewis, D. B., Hill, K. G., Hutchings, M. E., & Gower, D. M. Directional hearing in the Japanese Quail (*Coturnix c. japonica*). II. Cochlear physiology. *Journal of Experimental Biology*, in press.

Collias, N. E., Collias, E. C., & Saichuae, P. A field study of the red jungle fowl (*Gallus gallus*) in southeast Asia and India. *American Zoologist*, 1964, *4*, Abstract 22.

Cott, H. B. *Adaptive coloration in animals*. London: Methuen, 1957.

Crook, J. H. The adaptive significance of avian social organization. *Symposia of the Zoological Society of London*, 1965, *14*, 181–218.

Curio, E. Verhaltensstudien am Trauerschnäpper. *Zeitschrift für Tierpsychologie, Beiheft*, 1959, *3*(1), 1–118.

Curio, E. Probleme des Feinderkennens bei Vögeln. *Proceedings of the 13th International Ornithological Congress*, 1963, 206–239.

Curio, E. Funktionsweise und Stammegeschichte des Flugfeinderkennens einiger Darwinfinken (Geospizinae). *Zeitschrift für Tierpsychologie*, 1969, *26*, 394–487.

Curio, E. The functional organization of anti-predator behaviour in the Pied Flycatcher: A study of avian visual perception. *Animal Behaviour*, 1975, *23*, 1–115.

Curio, E. *The ethology of predation* (Vol. 7). Berlin: Springer-Verlag, 1976.

Curio, E. The adaptive significance of avian mobbing. I. Teleonomic hypotheses and predictions. *Zeitschrift für Tierpsychologie*, 1978, *48*, 175–183.

Darwin, C. *The expressions of the emotions in man and animals*. London: John Murray, 1872.

Darwin, C. *The descent of man* (2nd ed.). Chicago: Rand-McNally, 1874.

Dawkins, R. *The selfish gene*. London & New York: Oxford University Press, 1976.

Dawkins, R., & Krebs, J. R. Animal signals: Information or manipulation? In J. R. Krebs & N. B. Davies (Eds.), *Behavioral ecology. An evolutionary approach*. Sunderland, Mass: Sinauer Associates, 1978. Pp. 282–309.

Dementjew, G. P., & Gortschakowskaya, N. N. On the biology of the Norwegian Gyrfalcon. *Ibis*, 1945, *87*, 559–565.

Dill, L. M. An avoidance learning submodel for a general predation model. *Oecologia*, 1973, *13*, 291–312.

Dubos, R. *Man adapting*. New Haven, Conn.: Yale University Press, 1965.

Eibl-Eibesfeldt, I. *Putorius putorius* (L.). *Beutefang I (Toeten von Wanderratten)*. Göttingen: Institut Wissenschaftlicher Film, 1958.

Eikmanns, K.-H. Verhaltensphysiologische Untersuchungen über den Beutefang der Erdkröte. *Zeitschrift für Tierpsychologie*, 1955, *12*, 229–253.

Eisenberg, J., & Leyhausen, P. The phylogenesis of predatory behavior in mammals. *Zeitschrift für Tierpsychologie*, 1972, *30*, 59–93.

Eisner, T., Hicks, K., Eisner, M., & Robson, D. S. "Wolf-in-sheep's clothing" strategy of a predaceous insect larva. *Science*, 1978, *199*, 790–794.

Emlen, J. M. Optimal choice in animals. *American Naturalist*, 1968, *102*, 385–389.

Emlen, J. T., Jr., Miller, D. E., Evans, R. M., & Thompson, D. H. Predator-induced parental neglect in a Ring-billed Gull colony. *Auk*, 1966, *83*, 677–679.

Eutermoser, A. Schlagen Beizfalken bevorzugt kranke Krähen? *Vogelwelt*, 1961, *82*, 101–104.

Ewert, J.-P., & Traud, R. Releasing stimuli for antipredator behaviour in the common toad *Bufo bufo* (L.). *Behaviour*, 1979, *68*(1/2), 170–180.

Falls, J. B. Functions of territorial song in the White-throated Sparrow. In R. A. Hinde (Ed.), *Bird vocalizations. Their relation to current problems in biology and psychology*. London & New York: Cambridge University Press, 1969. Pp. 207–232.

Feiler, M. Der Wanderfalk (*Falco peregrinus*) als Brutvogel in den drei brandenburgischen Bezirken. *Maerkblatt Heimat*, 1961, *6*, 421–424.

Fenton, M. B., & Fullard, J. H. Moth hearing and the feeding strategies of bats. *American Scientist*, 1981, *69*(3), 266–275.

Fischer, W. *Die Seeadler*. Wittenberg-Lutherstadt: Ziemsen, 1970.

Fischer, W. *Der Wanderfalk*. Wittenberg-Lutherstadt: Ziemsen, 1973.

Gallup, G. G., Jr., Nash, R. F., & Ellison, A. L., Jr. Tonic immobility as a reaction to predation: Artificial eyes as a fear stimulus for chickens. *Psychonometric Science*, 1971, *23*, 79–80.

Gibb, J. A. Populations of tits and goldcrests and their food supply in pine plantations. *Ibis*, 1960, *102*, 163–168.

Glutz von Blotzheim, U. N., Bauer, K. M., & Bezel, E. *Handbuch der Vögel Mitteleuropas* (Vol. 4). Frankfurt: Akademische Verlag, 1971.

Green, M., Green, R., & Carr, W. J. The hawk–goose phenomenon: A replication and an extension. *Psychonometric Science*, 1968, *4*, 185–186.

Grieg-Smith, P. W. Parental investment in nest defense by stonechats (*Saxicola torquata*). *Animal Behaviour*, 1980, *28*, 604–619.

Grubb, T. C. Discrimination of aerial predators by American Coots in nature. *Animal Behaviour*, 1977, *25*(4), 1065–1066.

Hagen, Y. Does the Merlin sometimes play a role as a protector of Fieldfare colonies on the fjells? *Var Fagelvarld*, 1947, *6*, 137–141.

Hale, E. B., & Almquist, J. O. Relation of sexual behavior to germ cell output in farm animals. *Journal of Dairy Science*, 1960, *43*, 145–169.

Hamerström, F. The influence of a hawk's appetite on mobbing. *Condor*, 1957, *59*, 192–194.

Harvey, P. H., & Greenwood, P. J. Antipredator defense strategies: Some evolutionary problems. In J. R. Krebs & N. B. Davies (Eds.), *Behavioural ecology: An evolutionary approach*. Sunderland, Mass.: Sinauer Associates, 1978. Pp. 129–151.

Hatch, J. J. Predation and piracy by gulls at a ternery in Maine. *Auk*, 1970, *87*, 244–254.

Hediger, H. *Wild animals in captivity*. New York: Dover, 1964.

Hinde, R. A. The behaviour of the Great Tit (*Parus major*) and some other related species. *Behaviour, Supplement*, 1952, *2*, 1–201.

Hinde, R. A. Factors governing the changes in strength of a partially inborn response, as shown by the mobbing behaviour of the Chaffinch (*Fringilla coelebs*). II. The waning of the response. *Proceedings of the Royal Society of London, Series B*, 1954, *142*, 331–358.

Hinde, R. A. *Animal behaviour: A synthesis of ethology and comparative psychology* (2nd ed.). New York: McGraw-Hill, 1970.

Hirsch, J., Lindley, R. H., & Tolman, E. C. An experimental test of an alleged innate sign stimulus. *Journal of Comparative Physiological Psychology*, 1955, *48*, 278–280.

Hirth, D. H., & McCullough, D. R. Evolution of alarm signals in ungulates with special reference to white-tailed deer. *American Naturalist*, 1977, *111*(977), 31–42.

Hobson, E. S. Predatory behavior of some shore fishes in the Gulf of California. *Research Report—United States Fish and Wildlife Service*, 1968, *73*, 1–92.

Hoogland, J. L., & Sherman, P. W. Advantages and disadvantages of Bank Swallow (*Riparia riparia*) coloniality. *Ecological Monographs*, 1976, *46*, 33–58.

Humphrey, G. Le Chatelier's rule and the problem of habituation and dehabituation in *Helix albolabris*. *Psychologische Forschung*, 1930, *13*, 113–127.

Hurley, A. C., & Hartline, P. H. Escape responses in the damselfish *Chromis cyanea* (Pisces: Pomacentridae): A quantitative study. *Animal Behaviour*, 1974, *22*, 430–437.

Immelmann, K. *Einführung in die Verhaltensforschung*. Berlin: Parey, 1976.

Isley, T. E., & Gysel, L. W. Sound localization in the red fox. *Journal of Mammalogy*, 1975, *56*, 397–404.

Jennings, T., & Evans, S. M. Influence of position in the flock and flock size on vigilance in the starling, *Sturnis vulgaris*. *Animal Behaviour*, 1979, *28*, 634–635.

Jones, R. B. Reactions of male domestic chicks to two-dimensional eye-like shapes. *Animal Behaviour*, 1980, *28*, 212–218.

Kenward, R. E. Hawks and doves: Factors affecting success and selection in goshawk attacks on Wood Pigeons. *Journal of Animal Ecology*, 1978, *47*(2), 449–460.

Klump, G., & Shalter, M. D. Acoustic behaviour of birds and mammals in the predator context. *Zeitschrift für Tierpsychologie* (in press).

Konishi, M. The role of auditory feedback in the vocal behavior of the domestic fowl. *Zeitschrift für Tierpsychologie*, 1963, *20*, 349–367.

Konishi, M. Locatable and nonlocatable acoustic signals for Barn Owls. *American Naturalist*, 1973, *107*, 775–785.

Krebs, J. R. Behavioral aspects of predation. In P. P. G. Bateson & P. H. Klopfer (eds.), *Perspectives in ethology*. New York: Plenum, 1973. Pp. 73–111.

Kruijt, J. P. Ontogeny of social behavior in Burmese red jungle-fowl (*Gallus gallus spadiceus*). *Behaviour, Supplement*, 1964, *12*.

Kruuk, H. Predation and antipredator behaviour of the Black-headed Gull (*Larus ridibundus*). *Behaviour, Supplement*, 1964, *11*.

Lazarus, J. Flock size and behavior in captive Red-billed Weaverbirds (*Quelea quelea*): Implications for social facilitation and the functions of flocking. *Behaviour*, 1979, *71*(1/2), 127–145. (a)

Lazarus, J. The early warning function of flocking in birds: An experimental study with captive weaver birds (*Quelea quelea*). *Animal Behaviour*, 1979, *27*(3), 855–865. (b)

Leger, D. W., Owings, D. H., & Boal, L. M. Contextual information and differential responses to alarm whistles in California ground squirrels. *Zeitschrift für Tierpsychologie*, 1979, *49*(2), 142–155.

Lorenz, K. Vergleichende verhaltensforschung. *Zoologische Anzeiger*, 1939, *12*, 69–102.

Lorenz, K., & Tinbergen, N. Taxis und Instinkthandlung in der Eirollbewegung der Graugans. *Zeitschrift für Tierpsychologie*, 1938, *2*, 1–29.

MacArthur, R. H., & Pianka, E. R. On optimal use of a patchy environment. *American Naturalist*, 1968, *102*, 385–389.

MacLean, G. L. The Pygmy Falcon (*Polihierax semitorquatus*). *Koedoe*, 1970, *13*, 1–21.

MacLean, G. L. The sociable weaver. Part 4. Predators, parasites, and symbionts. *Ostrich*, 1973, *44*, 241–253.

Markgren, M. Fugitive reactions in avian behavior. *Acta Vertebratica*, 1960, *2*(1).

Marler, P. Characteristics of some animal cells. *Nature (London)*, 1955, *176*, 6–8.

Martin, R. C., & Melvin, K. B. Fear responses of Bobwhite Quail (*Colinus virginianus*) to a model and a live Red-tailed Hawk (*Buteo jamaicensis*). *Psychologische Forschung*, 1964, *27*, 323–336.

McNicholl, M. K. Habituation of aggressive responses to avian predators by terns. *Auk*, 1973, *90*, 902–904.

McNiven, M. A. "Social-releaser mechanisms" in birds—A controlled replication of Tinbergen's study. *Psychological Record*, 1960, *10*, 259–265.

Mech, D. L. *The wolf: The ecology and behavior of an endangered species*. Garden City, N.Y.: Natural History Press, 1970.

Meinertzhagen, C. R. *Pirates and predators*. Edinburgh: Oliver & Boyd, 1959.

Melvin, K. B., & Cloar, F. T. Habituation of responses of quail (*Colinus virginianus*) to a hawk (*Buteo swainsoni*): Measurement through an "innate suppression" technique. *Animal Behaviour*, 1969, *17*, 468–473.

Melzack, R. On the survival of Mallard ducks after "habituation" to the hawk-shaped figure. *Behaviour*, 1961, *17*, 9–16.

Melzack, R., Penick, E., & Beckett, A. The problem of "innate fear" of the hawk shape: An experimental study with Mallard ducks. *Journal of Comparative and Physiological Psychology*, 1959, *52*, 694–698.

Mertl, A. S. Habituation to territorial scent marks in the field by *Lemur catta*. *Behavioral Biology*, 1977, *21*(4), 500–507.

Meyer-Holzapfel, M., & Raeber, H. The ontogeny of the prey-catching behavior of the Tawny Owl (*Strix aluco aluco* L.): Observations and experiments. *Behaviour*, 1976, *57*(1/2), 1–50.

Milinski, M. Experiments on the selection by predators against spatial oddity of their prey. *Zeitschrift für Tierpsychologie*, 1977, *43*, 311–325. (a)

Milinski, M. Do all members of a swarm suffer the same predation? *Zeitschrift für Tierpsychologie*, 1977, *45*, 373–388. (b)

Milinski, M. Kin selection and reproductive value. *Zeitschrift für Tierpsychologie*, 1978, *47*, 328–329.

Milinski, M., & Curio, E. Untersuchungen zur Selektion durch Raüber gegen Vereinzelung der Beute. *Zeitschrift für Tierpsychologie*, 1975, *37*, 400–402.

Miller, D. B. Social displays of Mallard ducks (*Anas platyrhynchos*): Effects of domestication. *Journal of Comparative and Physiological Psychology*, 1977, *91*(2), 221–232.

Miller, R. C. The flock behavior of the Coast Bush-Tit. *Condor*, 1921, *23*, 121–127.

Morley, A. Field observations on the biology of the Marsh Tit. *British Birds*, 1953, *46*, 233–238; 273–287; 332–346.

Morse, D. H. Ecological aspects of some mixed-species foraging flocks of birds. *Ecological Monographs*, 1970, *40*, 119–168.

Morse, D. H., Interactions between tit flocks and sparrowhawks, *Accipiter nisus*. *Ibis*, 1973, *115*, 591–593.

Morse, D. H. *Behavioral mechanisms in ecology*. Cambridge, Mass.: Harvard University Press, 1980.

Morton, E. S. Nest predation affecting the breeding season of the Clay-colored Robin, a tropical songbird. *Science*, 1971, *171*, 920–921.

Morton, E. S. On the occurrence and significance of motivation–structural rules in some bird and mammal sounds. *American Naturalist*, 1977, *111*, 855–869.

Morton, E. S., & Shalter, M. D. Vocal response to predators in pair-bonded Carolina Wrens. *Condor*, 1977, *79*(2), 222–227.

Mueller, H. C. Prey selection: Oddity or conspicuousness? *Nature* (*London*), 1968, *217*, 92.

Mueller, H. C., & Parker, P. G. Naive ducklings show different cardiac response to hawk than to goose models. *Behaviour*, 1980, *74*(1/2), 101–113.

Murphy, L. B., & Duncan, I. J. H. Attempts to modify the responses of domestic fowl towards human beings. I. The association of human contact with a food reward. *Applied Animal Ethology*, 1977, *3*, 321–334.

Murphy, L. B., & Duncan, I. J. H. Attempts to modify the response of domestic fowl towards human beings. II. The effects of early experience. *Applied Animal Ethology*, 1978, *4*, 5–12.

Murton, R. K. The significance of a specific search image in the feeding behaviour of the Wood Pigeon. *Behaviour*, 1971, *40*, 10–42.

Neill, S. R. A study of antipredator adaptation in fish with special reference to silvery camouflage and schooling. Doctoral dissertation, Oxford University, 1970.

Nice, M., & ter Pelkwyk, J. Enemy recognition by the Song Sparrow. *Auk*, 1941, *58*, 195–214.

Owings, D. H., & Coss, R. G. Snake mobbing in California ground squirrels: Adaptive variation and ontogeny. *Behaviour*, 1977, *62*(1/2), 50–69.

Patterson, T. L., Petrinovich, L., & James, D. K. Reproductive value and appropriateness of response to predators by White-crowned Sparrows. *Behavioral Ecology and Sociobiology*, 1980, *7*, 227–231.

Paulson, D. R. Predator polymorphism and apostatic selection. *Evolution*, 1973, *27*, 269–277.

Peeke, H. V. S., & Peeke, S. C. Habituation, reinstatement and recovery of predatory responses in two species of teleosts, *Carassius auratus* and *Macropodus opercularis*. *Animal Behaviour*, 1972, *20*, 268–273.

Peeke, H. V. S., & Veno, A. Stimulus specificity of habituated aggression in the stickleback (*Gasterosteus aculeatus*). *Behavioral Biology*, 1973, *8*, 427–432.

Petrinovich, L., & Patterson, T. L. Field studies of habituation. IV. Sensitization as a function of the distribution and novelty of song playback to White-crowned Sparrows. *Journal of Comparative and Physiological Psychology*, 1981, *95*(5), 805–812.

Petrinovich, L., & Peeke, H. V. S. Habituation to territorial song in the White-throated Sparrow. *Behavioral Biology*, 1973, *8*, 743–748.

Pimlott, D. H., Shannon, J. A., & Kolenosky, G. B. The ecology of the timber wolf. *Research Branch of the Department of Wildlife*, 1969, No. 87.

Polsky, R. H. Influence of eating dead prey on subsequent capture of live prey in golden hamsters. *Physiological Behavior*, 1978, *20*(6), 677–680. (a)

Polsky, R. H. The ontogeny of predatory behavior in the golden hamster (*Mesocricetus a. auratus*). IV. Effects of prolonged exposure, size of prey and selective breeding. *Behaviour*, 1978, *65*(1/2), 27–42. (b)

Potter, J. Dominance relations between different breeds of domestic hens. *Physiological Zoology*, 1949, *22*, 261–280.

Price, E. O. Novelty-induced self-food deprivation in wild and semi-domestic deermice (*Peromyscus maniculatus bairdii*). *Behaviour*, 1972, *41*, 91–104.

Pulliam, H. R. On the theory of optimal diets. *American Naturalist*, 1974, *108*, 59–75.

Robinson, S. R. Antipredator behaviour and predator recognition in Belding's ground squirrels. *Animal Behaviour*, 1980, *28*, 840–852.

Rooke, I. J., & Knight, T. A. Alarm calls of honeyeaters with reference to locating sources of sound. *Emu*, 1977, *77*, 193–198.

Roth, G., & Luthardt, G. The role of early sensory experience in the prey-catching responses of *Salamandra salamandra* to stationary prey. *Zeitschrift für Tierpsychologie*, 1980, *52*(2), 141–148.

Rowe-Rowe, D. T. Flight behaviour and flight distances of blesbok. *Zeitschrift für Tierpsychologie*, 1974, *34*, 208–211.

Rudebeck, G. The choice of prey and modes of hunting of predatory birds with special reference to their selective effect. I. *Oikos*, 1950, *2*, 65–88.

Rudebeck, G. The choice of prey and modes of hunting of predatory birds with special reference to their selective effect. II. *Oikos*, 1951, *3*, 218–231.

Russell, E. M. Changes in the behaviour of *Lebistes reticulatus* upon a repeated shadow stimulus. *Animal Behaviour*, 1967, *15*, 574–585.

Rydén, O. On the behaviour in an alarm-evoking constant stimulus situation in a "natural environment." Observations on a pair of Herring Gulls (*Larus argentatus*) and Common Terns (*Sterna hirundo*) breeding on the same islet. *Journal für Ornithologie*, 1970, *111*(1), 48–53.

Rydén, O. Differential responsiveness of Great Tit nestlings, *Parus major*, to natural auditory stimuli. *Zeitschrift für Tierpsychologie*, 1978, *47*, 236–253. (a)

Rydén, O. The significance of antecedent auditory experiences on later reactions to the "seeet" alarm call in Great Tit nestlings (*Parus major*). *Zeitschrift für Tierpsychologie*, 1978, *47*, 396–409. (b)

Rydén, O. Heart rate response in Great Tit nestlings (*Parus major*) to an alarm call. *Journal of Comparative and Physiological Psychology*, 1980, *94*(3), 426–435.

Schaller, G. B. *The Serengeti lion.* Chicago: University of Chicago Press, 1972. (a)

Schaller, G. B. *Serengeti. A kingdom of predators.* New York: Alfred A. Knopf, 1972. (b)

Schaller, G. B. *Golden shadows, flying hooves.* Chicago: University of Chicago Press, 1975.

Schaller, G. B., & Emlen, J. T. The ontogeny of avoidance behavior in some precocial birds. *Animal Behaviour,* 1962, *10,* 370–381.

Scherzinger, W. Zum Aktionssystem des Sperlingskauzes (*Glaucidium passerinum*). *Zoologica,* 1970, *118,* 1–120.

Schleidt, W. M. Reaktionen von Truthühnern auf fliegende Raubvögel und versuche zur Analyse ihrer AAM's. *Zeitschrift für Tierpsychologie,* 1961, *18,* 534–560.

Schleidt, W. M. Tonic communication: Continual effects of discrete signs in animal communications systems. *Journal of Theoretical Biology,* 1973, *42,* 359–386.

Schleidt, W. M., Shalter, M. D., & Carawan, T. The effect of spatial context on habituation to predators. *Zeitschrift für Tierpsychologie,* 1983, *61,* 67–70.

Schnell, J. H. Nesting behavior and food habits of goshawks in the Sierra Nevada of California. *Condor,* 1958, *60,* 377–403.

Schnurre, O. Zwei Habichtsbruten in gegensätzlichen Landschaftsformen. *Mitteilungen von Verein Sächsischer Ornithologen,* 1934, *4,* 99–109.

Schnurre, O. Ein Beitrag zur Frage der Reviergrenzen und Siedlungsdichte beim Habicht. *Mitteilungen des Vereins Sächsischer Ornithologen,* 1935, *4,* 221–225.

Schnurre, O. Der Uhu als Mitbewohner einer Kormorankolonie, nebst brutbiologischen Beobachtungen an anderen Vogelarten. *Mitteilungen des Vereins Sächsischer Ornithologen,* 1941, *17,* 121–131.

Schwartzkopff, J. Die akustische Lokalisation bei Tieren. *Ergebnisse der Biologie,* 1962, *25,* 136–176.

Shalter, M. D. A semiotic analysis of acoustic alarm communication in gallinaceous birds. Doctoral dissertation, University of Maryland, 1974.

Shalter, M. D. Lack of spatial generalization in habituation tests of fowl. *Journal of Comparative and Physiological Psychology,* 1975, *89*(3), 258–262.

Shalter, M. D. Studies of mobbing behaviour abound. *Journal für Ornithologie,* 1978, *119,* 462–463. (a)

Shalter, M. D. Effect of spatial context of the mobbing response of Pied Flycatchers to a predator model. *Animal Behaviour,* 1978, *26,* 1219–1221. (b)

Shalter, M. D. Localization of passerine *seeet* and mobbing calls by goshawks and pygmy owls. *Zeitschrift für Tierpsychologie,* 1978, *46,* 260–267. (c)

Shalter, M. D. Mobbing in the Pied Flycatcher. Effects of experiencing a live owl on responses to a stuffed facsimile. *Zeitschrift für Tierpsychologie,* 1978, *47,* 173–179. (d)

Shalter, M. D. Responses of nesting passerines to alarm calls. *Ibis,* 1979, *121,* 362–368.

Shalter, M. D., Fentress, J. C., & Young, G. W. Determinants of response of wolf pups to auditory signals. *Behaviour,* 1977, *60,* 98–114.

Shalter, M. D., & Schleidt, W. M. The ability of Barn Owls, *Tyto alba,* to discriminate and localize avian alarm calls. *Ibis,* 1977, *119,* 22–27.

Sharpless, S., & Jasper, H. Habituation of the arousal reaction. *Brain,* 1956, *79,* 655–680.

Shaw, E. Schooling fishes. *American Scientist,* 1978, *66,* 166–175.

Sherman, P. W. Nepotism and the evolution of alarm calls. *Science,* 1977, *197,* 1246–1253.

Smith, J. N. M. Feeding rates, search paths, and surveillance for predators in Great-tailed Grackle flocks. *Canadian Journal of Zoology,* 1977, *55*(6), 891–898.

Smith, M. J., & Graves, H. B. Some factors influencing mobbing behavior in Barn Swallows. *Behavioral Biology,* 1978, *23*(3), 355–372.

Smith, N. G. "*Spshing* noise": Biological significance of its attraction and nonattraction in birds. *Proceedings of the National Academy of Sciences of the United States of America*, 1975, *72*(4), 1411–1414.

Smith, R. H. Wildness and domestication in *Mus musculus:* A behavioral analysis. *Journal of Comparative and Physiological Psychology*, 1972, *79*(1), 22–29.

Smith, W. J. Message-meaning analysis. In T. A. Sebeok (Ed.), *Animal communication*. Bloomington: Indiana University Press, 1968. Pp. 44–60.

Smith, W. J. *The behavior of communicating: An ethological approach*. Cambridge, Mass.: Harvard University Press, 1977.

Smythe, N. On the existence of "pursuit invitation" signals in mammals. *American Naturalist*, 1970, *104*, 491–494.

Stefanski, R. A., & Falls, J. B. A study of distress calls of Song, Swamp, and White-throated Sparrows (Aves: Fringillidae). I. Interspecific responses and functions. *Canadian Journal of Zoology*, 1972, *50*(12), 1501–1512.

Stresemann, E., & Portenko, L. A. (Eds.). *Atlas der Verbreitung paläarktischer Vögel* (1 Lief.). Berlin: Akademie-Verlag, 1960.

Tamisier, A. Signification du gregarisme diurne et de l'alimentation nocturne des Sarcelles d'Hiver *Anas crecca crecca*. *La Terre et La Vie*, 1970, *4*, 511–562.

Thorpe, W. H. Some problems of animal learning. *Proceedings of the Linnean Society of London*, 1944, *156*, 70–83.

Thorpe, W. H. *Learning and instinct in animals*. Cambridge, Mass.: Harvard University Press, 1956.

Tilson, R. Klipspringer (*Oreotragus oreotragus*) social structure and predator avoidance in a desert canyon. *Madoqua*, 1980, *11*(4), 303–314.

Tinbergen, N. Social releasers and the experimental method required for their study. *Wilson Bulletin*, 1948, *60*(1), 6–52.

Tinbergen, N. On antipredator responses in certain birds—A reply. *Journal of Comparative and Physiological Psychology*, 1957, *50*, 412–414.

Tinbergen, N. *Animal behavior*. New York: Time, 1965.

Treherne, J. E., & Foster, W. A. The effects of group size on predator avoidance in a marine insect. *Animal Behaviour*, 1980, *28*, 1119–1122.

Trivers, R. L. Parental investment and sexual selection. In B. Campbell (Ed.), *Sexual selection and the descent of man*. Chicago: Aldine, 1972. Pp. 136–179.

Ullrich, B. Untersuchungen zur Ethologie und Oekologie des Rotkopfwürgers (*Lamius senator*) in Südwestdeutschland im Vergleich zu Raubwürgern (*L. excubitor*), Schwartzstirnwürger (*L. minor*) und Neuntöter (*L. collurio*). *Vogelwarte*, 1971, *26*, 1–77.

Uspenski, S. M. Zur Biologie des Wanderfalken auf der Nowaja Semlja. *Deutsche Falkenorden*, 1957, 16–17.

Welty, J. C. Experiments in group behavior of fishes. *Physiological Zoology*, 1934, *7*, 85–128.

White, C. M., & Weeden, R. B. Hunting methods of Gyrfalcons and behavior of their prey (ptarmigan). *Condor*, 1966, *68*, 517–519.

Wickler, W. *Mimicry in plants and animals*. London: World University Library, 1968.

Willis, E. O. Is the Zone-tailed Hawk a mimic of the Turkey Vulture? *Condor*, 1963, *65*, 313–317.

Willis, E. O. A prey capture by the Zone-tailed Hawk. *Condor*, 1966, *68*, 104–105.

Wolda, H. Response decrement in the prey-catching activity of *Notonecta glauca* L. (Hemiptera). *Archives Neerlandaises de Zoologie*, 1961, *14*, 61–89.

Wyrwoll, T. Die Jagdbereitschaft des Habichts (*Accipter gentilis*) in Beziehung zum Horstort. *Journal für Ornithologie*, 1977, *118*(1), 21–34.

Yahner, R. H. Barking in a primitive ungulate, *Muntiacus reevesi:* Function and adaptiveness. *American Naturalist,* 1980, *116,* 157–177.

Zucchi, H. Gewöhnung an Signale der innerartlichen Kommunikation beim Buchfinken, *Fringilla coelebs,* unter Freiland- und Laborbedingungen. Doctoral dissertation, Phillips-Universität, Marburg/Lahn, 1979. (a)

Zucchi, H. Do free-living songbirds habituate to species-specific alarm calls? *Experientia,* 1979, *35,* 758. (b)

CHAPTER 11

Habituation and the Maintenance of Territorial Boundaries

Harman V. S. Peeke

Department of Psychiatry
University of California
San Francisco, California

I. Introduction

The hypothesis entertained in this chapter is that habituation, viewed as an active inhibition of response to a constant or repeated stimulus, is a major process involved in the reduction of aggressive interactions between territorial neighbors. The observation that, during the initial stages

HABITUATION, SENSITIZATION,
AND BEHAVIOR

of territorial establishment, there are frequent and often intense aggressive interactions that subside with time and experience to less-frequent and lower-intensity interactions between (usually) conspecifics support the habituation hypothesis.

To explore the evidence for the habituation hypothesis I review, briefly, the concept of territoriality, the definition of territoriality as used in this chapter, and the characteristics of a mechanism to explain the maintenance of the territorial boundaries must have. Next, the nature of interspecific aggression and the characteristics of habituation in species that are predominately territorial are discussed. Finally, a synthesis is attempted that integrates what is known about habituation and territorial behavior to evaluate the thesis that habituation plays a major role in the maintenance of territorial boundaries.

II. Fish and Birds

The concept of territoriality arose and continues to be developed primarily from observations and experimental studies of bird and fish behavior. Territoriality is definitely not confined to these two taxa, but it is within these two unrelated groups of animals that the major work has been done. In comparing lekking behavior in birds and fish, Loiselle and Barlow (1978) referred to similarities between teleost fish and birds, particularly in behavior (see Marshall, 1960). They commented that such apparent similarities are clearly the result of convergent evolution, and that analysis of similarities may reveal some basic principles of the behavioral biology of these species. Loiselle and Barlow were concerned with lekking behavior, but similar principles will be used in this chapter to develop a theory employing one mechanism for the maintenance of territorial integrity.

III. Territoriality

The concept of territoriality in modern scientific literature stems from Howard's *Territory in Bird Life* (1920). Although two earlier references are often quoted (Altrum, 1868, and Moffot, 1903, cited in van den Assem, 1967), Howard's work marks the beginning of an extensive literature, particularly in relationship to spacing in birds. The vastness of the literature is reflected in Nice's (1941) review of the literature, which contains almost 400 references, and Hinde's (1956) with nearly 200.

Definitions of territory and territoriality abound. Noble's (1939) definition ("any defended area") is perhaps the most often cited, and is accepted by van den Assem (1967) in his classic study of territoriality in three-spined stickleback. The strength of Noble's definition is it's simplicity and flexibility, but some authors have refined the definition to include what is defended and against what it is defended. A detailed definition is put forth by Meral (1973) in his extensive but, unfortunately, unpublished study of the functions of territory in cichlids. Meral's definition combines the spatial and ecological levels with the behavioral: "Territoriality is the aggressive exclusion of at least conspecifics from a limited area, the territory, containing a resource. The territorial animals, through behavior or physical appearance, inform other animals that the resource will be defended [p. 5]." This definition covers virtually all bases, but is cumbersome.

A quite different definitional approach has been suggested by Davies (1978): "I . . . recognize a territory whenever individual animals or groups are spaced out more than would be expected from a random occupation of suitable habitats [p. 317]." This is basically a statistical definition lacking any hint of mechanism. Because this chapter concentrates on proximate causes, a definition containing some mention of mechanism is desirable. I adopt Brown's (1975) definition, "A territory is a fixed area from which intruders are excluded by some combination of advertisement (e.g., scent, song), threat, and attack [p. 61]." This definition serves well insofar as it highlights the fixed area, the rejection of intruders and specifies how they are rejected (in terms of threat and attack).

Essentially, then, a territory is a relatively fixed geographic area that is actively defended. Territories do not always have common boundaries with other territories, but with even minimal density they do. It has been demonstrated that, with heavy utilization of space by territory holders, the shape of territories will become polygons (polyhedron if the three-dimensional character of territories is considered). An example of such a territorial structure is mapped in Fig. 1. These territories in the Willow Warbler (May, 1949) share common boundaries, and the density is such that some of the territories are polygons. As has been predicted by Grant (1968) and demonstrated clearly by Barlow (1974), in a uniform medium the maximal density of territorial animals will result in hexagonal territories. Figure 2 shows the territories of an African cichlid fish (*Tilapia mossambica*). These fish excavate nests and spit the sandy material in the direction of (at) their neighbor thus creating "sandy parapets that are conspicuous territorial boundaries [Barlow, 1974, p. 876]." As Fig. 2 shows, many of the territories are hexagonal, many are pentagonal, and some have less definite shapes.

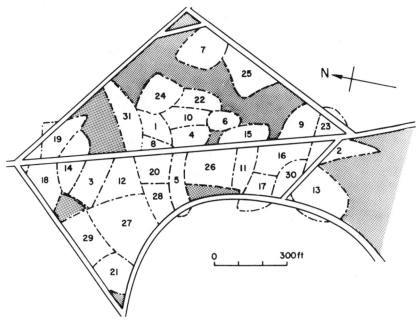

Fig. 1. Map of the territories of a group of willow warblers in birch woodlands, Englefied Green, England. Shaded areas were not occupied. After May (1949).

IV. Establishment and Defense of Territory

During the initial establishment of a territory, overt aggression in the form of physical contact (biting, pecking, etc.) seems to be the rule. This gives way shortly to more ritualized forms of aggressive interaction such as signalling and threats, by body posture, singing, or chemical communication. Actual attacks on conspecifics are usually restricted to unfamiliar animals or those that intrude into the established territory. This behavioral sketch was provided for warblers by Morse (1976) and for other bird species by Klomp (1972; cited in Morse, 1980). In fish such a description was presented by Baerends and Baerends-van Roon (1950) for cichlids and by van den Assem and van der Molen (1969) for the three-spined stickleback. The question raised in the current chapter, restated from these observations, is, What kind of behavioral mechanism(s) might account for (1) high initial aggression that changes to less frequent, more distant aggressive communication while (2) at the same time maintaining a readiness to attack either a novel protagonist or one that violates the established territorial boundaries? Such a mechanism also should be (3) long lasting (at least long enough to cover a breeding cycle in cases where territoriality is concerned with protecting a breeding area). The observation that a territorial neighbor appears rarely to be a threat has been labeled as "the Dear Enemy Phenomenon" (see Wilson, 1975, pp. 273–274). Wilson went on to propose habituation as one of the mechanisms involved in the phenomenon, a proposition discussed previously by several authors, including Peeke and Peeke (1973).

V. Waning of Conspecific Aggression: Minimal Definitional Requirements for Habituation

A distinction must be made between definitions and listings of the parametric characteristics of habituation. A thoughtful treatment of both has been provided by Thompson and Spencer (1966) in a paper that must be viewed as a major progenitor of modern research on habituation.

Fig. 2. Top-view photograph of the territories of male *Tilapia mossambica*. The boundaries of the territories, the rims of the nest pits, form the pattern of polygons. The breeding fish are the black shapes, the gray shapes are the females, juveniles, and nonbreeding males. From Barlow (1974).

Observations of fish and bird behavior from field and laboratory replicas of field conditions reveal a diminution in frequency of aggressive behaviors after the first stages of territorial establishment. Such a decrease in response may reflect any of several decremental phenomena, habituation being only one of them. Therefore, there are numerous definitions of habituation—as there are for territoriality—and these differ primarily in their specificity. The core of most definitions has to do with a decrement in *response* as a result of repeated stimulation. This is the basis for both Humphrey's (1933) and Harris's (1943) definitions. A more detailed definition has been provided by Thorpe in his 1956 edition of *Learning and Instinct in Animals* and in a slightly different one in the 1962 revision of the same work. The definition to be used here is a modification of Thorpe's: "Habituation . . . can . . . be defined as the relatively permanent waning of a response as a result of repeated stimulation which is not followed by any kind of reinforcement [1962, p. 61]." To this definition I have added *or constant* following "repeated" to cover all of the many studies that have used constant or long durations of individual exposures of stimuli. Further, "waning of response" tends to suggest that the inhibition is exerted on a response mechanism rather than at a central level. Addition of the term *readiness* after "response" would indicate that a central process has been altered as a function of the experience that is independent of the motor response but is measured as a change in motor behavior. This argument is similar to the "learning" versus "performance" distinction in associative learning. Such a distinction is necessary for a definition of habituation, because there are several clear indications of the independence of habituation from performance of a motor response. Studies have been published that indicate that the presentation of incremental stimulus intensities, each below the threshold of response, result in later response inhibition (Applewhite, Gardner, & Lapan, 1969; Davis & Wagner, 1969) as well as one report of response prevention producing a similar decrement (Peeke & Veno, 1976).

The definition becomes, then, *Habituation is the relatively permanent waning of response readiness as a result of repeated or constant stimulation*. The last phrase, "which is not followed by any kind of reinforcement," is deleted insofar as reinforcement itself is frequently defined in terms of response change, hence its inclusion in the definition of habituation would either be circular or redundant.

Repeated or constant stimulation can alter response readiness through mechanisms other than habituation—primarily by fatigue or sensory adaptation. Presenting a new stimulus after waning has taken place reinstates the response and provides a sufficient demonstration that the waning is relatively stimulus-specific and not the result either of adaptation or effector fatigue. Most definitions include a statement ruling out adaptation and fatigue as a corollary to the main definition, and that is adopted here also. The complete definition used in this chapter is, *Habituation is the relatively permanent waning of a response readiness as a result of repeated or constant stimulation; the response decrement is specific to the original stimulus, and it can be reinstated by another, equally strong, stimulus.*

VI. Habituation of Aggression in Fish

Studies of waning of aggressive responses in fish and the relationship of such diminution was discussed briefly by Lorenz (1964), who was primarily concerned with the mechanisms whereby cichlid pairs (male and female) were able to maintain readiness to chase intruders from their territory but not to aggress against each other. Lorenz posited two mechanisms, and the first was concurrent sexual motivation. Indeed, it has been shown that sex and aggression are mutually inhibitory in the convict cichlid (Cole, Figler, Parente, & Peeke, 1980). The second mechanism was habituation to the mate. This, Lorenz (1964) correctly pointed out, requires recognition of the personal characteristics of the mate. Lorenz postulated that such habituation is the prerequisite for the origin of personal bonds. Such personal recognition is considered crucial for the inhibition of hostility between mates by Baerends and Baerends-van Roon (1950).

Laboratory studies of the habituation of conspecific aggression in fish prior to 1972 have been reviewed in detail elsewhere (Peeke & Peeke, 1973). A brief review of those studies will be presented followed by a discussion of more recent work.

A. Early Work with an Inadequate Model: The Siamese Fighting Fish

Researchers in animal behavior with an interest in aggression in fish, particularly psychologists, have a penchant for studying the Siamese fighting fish (*Betta splendens*). This animal, native to the swamps and waterways of Southeast Asia, has been domesticated and bred for colorful plumage and a willingness to fight in small containers. Such fights are a "sport" in that area of the world, and sums of money are waged on the outcomes of such contests. Unfortunately, it is this strain, subjected as it has been to generations of artificial selection, that predominate in the research with this species. The original stock has neither the plumage nor bright colors of the domesticated stock, nor is it as aggressive (Smith, 1945, cited in Goldstein, 1975). But, easy availability (*Betta* is available in any aquarium store), ease of maintenance, and willingness to fight seem to have outweighed, for some researchers, the biological disadvantages of this species.

The first paper perporting to demonstrate waning of aggression in *Betta* was published by Baenninger (1966). In that study, the diminished visual contact with a mirror image or a conspecific over a continuous 32-hour period was interpreted as waning of the response. This study, while the first of a series of *Betta* habituation studies by various authors, could just as easily be interpreted as a learned avoidance. Clayton and Hinde (1968) studied habituation of several discrete responses in *Betta* exposed to their own mirror image. This study, and others, has been criticized by Peeke and Peeke (1970) for the use of the mirror-image stimulus, because Simpson (1968)—in his careful, descriptive monograph—showed that the normal fighting postures of *Betta* contain segments of frontal display by one fish to a lateral display of his antagonist. These postures cannot be attained when fighting one's own image. Figler (1972) studied the relationship between the strength of an eliciting stimulus and rate of habituation in a well-controlled study. Habituation was clearly demonstrated, and the rate of waning was positively correlated with the original elicitation strength of this stimulus.

These studies used either very small aquaria, studied fish shortly after they had been placed in the experimental aquaria, or did both. Peeke and Peeke (1970) studied bettas housed in large aquaria to which they had been adapted for 10 days. The stimulus used to elicit aggression was a conspecific male confined to a glass tube that was intruded into the aquarium. Whether presented in a "massed" or "distributed" fashion, the responses to the intruded male habituated. The long, 10-day adaption period was used in the hopes that possession of an aquarium for that length of time would entice the resident *Betta* to adopt it in its entirety for a territory. This was predicated on the belief that *Betta* is a territorial fish, as stated by Forselius (1957). But, other research has tended to erode the belief in *Betta* territoriality (Goldstein, 1975; Klein, Figler, & Peeke, 1976). This and subsequent research has frequently found decreasing levels of aggression to be a function of experience with conspecifics (e.g., Cain, Anderson, Stein, & Jessen, 1980; Goldstein, 1975), but such "habituation" is considered a "secondary mechanism for the control of aggression—a kind of war of attrition whereby the least persistent animal eventually conceded [Bronstein, 1981, p. 446]." Most of these papers, and several others by Cain and collaborators (e.g., Cain, Anderson, Stein, & Jessen, 1980; Cain, Jessen, & Flanagan, 1980; Cain, Flanagan, & Jessen, in press), are concerned more with a model of dominance behavior than one centered on the maintenance of territorial boundaries.

A report by Chantrey (1978) provides important data on habituation and suggests there is an incremental process in *Betta* aggression as well. This paper has some theoretical importance and is mentioned later. In general, work with *Betta* has demonstrated habituation to be a phenomenon commonly found in the laboratory. The importance of this research contributes little to the central theme of this chapter—the maintenance of territorial integrity—insofar as the species is not clearly territorial in nature. And if it is the behavior of the artifically selected domestic *Betta* used in all of the cited studies is unlikely to accurately reflect that of the wild members of this species.

B. Habituation in Two Territorial Genera: Sticklebacks and Cichlids

Two species that are clearly territorial in the wild and which can easily be studied in the laboratory have been the focus for most of the work on fish aggression and habituation. The convict cichlid (*Cichlasoma nigrofasciatum*) pair is territorial in the laboratory; or if housed in single-sex groups, either sex will become territorial. In nature they are territorial as a pair, with the female usually selecting the site and being joined thereafter by a male. Cichlid territoriality has been described in some detail in Baerends and Baerends van-Roon (1950), and territoriality specifically in *C. nigrofasciatum* has been described in great detail in the aforementioned unpublished dissertation by Meral (1973). The other species with which much work has been done is the three-spined stickleback (*Gasterosteus aculeatus*). The male stickleback is a solitary territorial animal. Description of its territorial behavior abound. Earlier work by van Iersel (1958) was elaborated upon in a detailed monograph by van den Assem (1967). An excellent secondary source is Wootton (1976).

The work done with the two species is often parallel or complementary, so the two will be discussed together. It must be borne in mind that the two species are very different in that the convict cichlid is territorial in bonded pairs, and it's distribution is limited to fresh water in central America. The three-spined stickleback is singly (male) territorial, is often anadromous (i.e., migrates between salt and fresh waters), but can live and reproduce in brackish or fresh water, and is distributed throughout

much of the coastal areas of north America, Europe, and Asia. Behavior-
ally, we are emphasizing the fact that they both show territoriality and
aggressiveness.

There are a number of observations of fish behavior in the field that
have been or could be interpreted as evidence for an habituation-like
mechanism involved in territorial maintenance. But virtually all of the
research on fish aggression and habituation has been done in the laboratory. The reasons for this are probably several, but prominent among
them is the presumed ease of creating a laboratory analog of the natural
situation. Such ease may be more illusory than real, but it is supported by
observations that large tanks, pools, and "stream replicas" indoors and
outdoors, seem to support natural behavior, and these behaviors seem not
to become distorted in any significant way when smaller lab tanks are
used.

This well may be the case, but for some species, particularly the three-
spined stickleback, not enough field work has been published to make the
assertion with certainty, although an encouraging start with results based
on field observation of sticklebacks has been presented by Wootton
(1972). Examples of detailed work done in environments intermediate
between field and aquaria environments is the research on territoriality in
the stickleback by van den Assem (1967) and Jenni (1972; Jenni, van
Iersel, & van den Assem, 1969), and the demonstrations of hexagonal
territories in the cichlid *Tilapia mossambica* (Barlow, 1974). The work
with cichlids is based on firmer field observations than the work with the
stickleback. The difficulties in generalizing from field behavior to laboratory may represent a problem in limiting conclusions based on laboratory
research of fish territoriality or territoriality in general. The work that has
been done, however, has led to an understanding of the role that habituation might play in the establishment and maintenance of territorial integrity.

1. Demonstrations of Habituation

Reports abound describing waning of conspecific aggression in both the
convict cichlid and the three-spined stickleback. The first important paper
was a report by van den Assem and van der Molen (1969), which described the waning of aggressive behavior between neighboring stickleback confined in laboratory aquaria. Some of the pairs were separated
from each other by glass partitions, and some were not. They demonstrated that aggressive motivation was lowered after mutual interaction
between neighbors, as tested by one of the territorial fish's response to an
entirely different male stimulus fish. They did not test habituation be-

tween neighbors directly, and this has been cited as evidence against the stimulus-specific nature of such waning (Wootton, 1976, p. 182). Without any data to the contrary, it might well be that the waning of response to the territorial neighbor was much more profound and that the reactivity to the novel stimulus male might represent a motivation-, but not a stimulus-, specific factor in the waning. Motivation as well as stimulus-specific effects have been experimentally demonstrated for this species (Peeke, 1983a, 1983b; Peeke & Peeke, 1983). One of the most important aspects of the van den Assem and van der Molen study was that they were able to demonstrate the waning effect when the territorial neighbors were separated by a glass partition and when they were allowed free access to each other. Thus the waning was not an artifact produced by physical separation. A similar effect was recently demonstrated between unrestrained territorial pairs of convict cichlids where waning of aggression was demonstrated with no physical restraint between combatants (Peeke & Peeke, 1983).

There have been two additional reports of waning of conspecific aggression. The first demonstrated waning of the aggressive responses of a male stickleback that varied in the amount of red coloration on the ventral anterior surface of wooden models (Peeke, Wyers & Herz, 1969). Red on the ventral anterior portion of the male stickleback has long been regarded as the crucial "releaser" for aggressive responses in the three-spined stickleback (Tinbergen, 1951). But, Peeke et al. (1969) were unable to support that contention, and other work tends to question that assumption (see Muckenstrum, 1967, 1968, cited in Wootton, 1976, p. 174). Peeke et al. (1969) demonstrated that responses to all models waned over 12 days of daily 2-minute presentation. In the earlier studies the proper controls for stimulus specificity were not included, and interpreting the results as caused by habituation, as I have defined it, is inappropriate.

Peeke (1969) presented territorial sticklebacks with a live conspecific confined to a clear glass tube or, in another group, a model of a male stickleback, for 15 minutes per day over 10 days. Responses to both stimuli waned and could be interpreted as habituation because there was a test for stimulus specificity at the end of the experiment and the decrement lasted between daily sessions. These two demonstrations would appear to eliminate fatigue or sensory adaptation as valid interpretations.

In a study designed to observe the habituation of neighboring territorial convict cichlid males to one another, it was demonstrated that mutual inhibition of response occurred relatively rapidly—within a few hours (Peeke, Herz, & Gallagher, 1971). This study also compared behavior following brief, frequent encounters between antagonists and a group allowed continuous exposure to one another. In terms of accumulated mutual exposure time, the group with constant exposure "habituated" more rapidly, a finding that was interpreted to be analogous to Hull's (1943) conception of conditioned and unconditioned inhibition (further similarities between modern habituation theory and Hullian concepts is discussed by Petrinovich, Chapter 2, this volume). The response did not completely recover when the fish were tested 21 days after the last stimulus. It was found that when using artificially delineated territories and permitting fighting only through a glass divider, mutual habituation did occur with great reliability, as indicated by measures of threat or attack.

A later study (Gallagher, Herz, & Peeke, 1972) made it clear that social isolation of the territorial males was not a factor in the fighting except in the initial willingness to fight (i.e., overcoming timidity). The data clearly demonstrated that the time course of the waning of threat behavior preceded the attainment of the asymptote and then declined in the frequency of violent attack (in the form of bites at the opponent).

This demonstration of the sequencing of behaviors from threat to attack led to another study in which the main purpose was to demonstrate that a drug well known to increase aggression (ethanol) did so by disrupting the normal sequence of the aggressive behaviors—in other words, threat preceding attack (Peeke, Peeke, Avis, & Ellman, 1975). But more important to the development of the concepts developed in this chapter was the demonstration that the habituated responses were completely reinstated by substituting a new stimulus fish; a demonstration of stimulus specificity that is crucial, many believe, to any interpretation of waning as "habituation." As important as stimulus specificity is for definitional considerations, it is crucial to the thesis that habituation is responsible for lowered aggression between territorial neighbors. If the behavior is stimulus-specific, then a new stimulus should reinstate the response to that stimulus. A wandering conspecific would represent an infrequent intruder in the territory and would be just such a stimulus. It should elicit immediate aggression, even though the territorial resident is hypoaggressive toward his neighbors.

2. Stimulus Specificity of Habituation

Using the three-spined stickleback as the subject species, the issue of stimulus specificity was investigated in some detail (Peeke & Veno, 1973). A male stickleback confined in a clear glass tube was introduced into the territory of a resident male, a method used by Peeke (1969). It was demonstrated that habituation was stimulus-specific both in regard to the individual fish used as the intruding stimulus and to where in the territory the fish was presented. When the stimulus male was presented on the left side of the experimental aquarium, all the territorial male habituated to

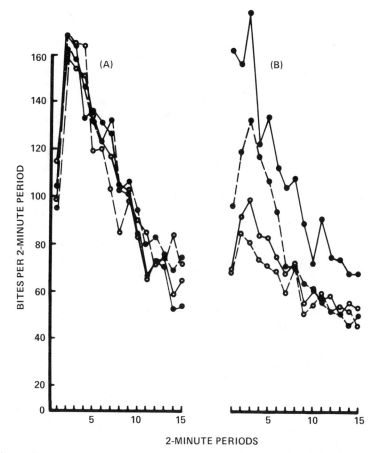

Fig. 3. Stimulus specificity of habituation of the biting response of the three-spined stickleback. (A) Session 1. Responding during the initial training session for all fish tested. (B) Session 2. The amount of responding seen in the same fish during the second session, depending on the familiarity of the stimulus presented—whether the same fish in the same place or a different place (SF,SP or SF,DP) or a different fish in the same place or a different place (DF,SP or DF,DP). The last group resulted in the greatest response during the second session. After Peeke and Veno (1973).

the intruder. When the same male stimulus was reintroduced in the same spot after a short period of removal, there was complete retention of the habituation. If, at reintroduction, the same male was presented on the opposite side of the aquarium, some recovery of response was seen. If, at reintroduction, a different stimulus male was presented in the same place as before, more recovery was found. Finally, if both the stimulus male and the place of presentation were changed, complete recovery was demonstrated (Fig. 3). Stimulus specificity of response to potential territorial rivals has both individual- and geographic-specific aspects; a fact noted previously in studies of the territorial responses of birds (e.g., Falls, 1969; see Falls, 1978, for an overview).

3. Retention and Recovery of Habituation

The issue of retention of the inhibition of the response tendency was already discussed briefly in relation to the study by Gallagher *et al.* (1972). Convict cichlids showed some recovery of response after 21 days. A study with stickleback, using basically the same methodology as in the previously described studies, demonstrated that habituation showed no recovery after 3–5 days, but showed moderate recovery after 14 days (Peeke, Figler, & Blankenship, 1979). Thus, with both the cichlid and the stickleback, there is long-term retention of the effects. In both cases the time is long enough for the fish to mate, spawn, and raise a clutch. Both studies, however, were conducted in somewhat restricted laboratory environments, making it possible that what was really being studied was permanence of an engram without use. How retention might fare in a complicated field environment with constant interactions between the subject fish and many neighbors, as well as frequent wandering novel intruders, is not known.

4. Field Observations of Habituation in Fish

Although most of the research I have reviewed comes from restricted laboratory situations, there are some field data that support the thesis being developed. It seems clear that lowered aggression between neighbors is the result of habituation which, because of the stimulus-specific nature of the process, leaves an animal hypoaggressive to its neighbors and ready to react and attack a novel intruder. Thresher (1976) in a careful and detailed field study of the aggressive and territorial behavior of the three-spot damselfish (*Eupomacentrus planifrons*) provides considerable data to support the contention that habituation is a mechanism responsible for the stability of the territorial social system.

VII. Habituation of Aggression in Birds

Paralleling the descriptions of lower aggression after the initial stages of territorial establishment in fish, are field observations of bird behavior by Klomp (1972) and Morse (1976). Whereas the research with fish concentrated on laboratory experiments, there are, to my knowledge, no parallel studies with birds. There are, however, a number of field experiments on habituation in birds, many of the more recent of which are quite extensive and detailed.

With fish, the eliciting stimulus for territorial aggression and defense is the physical presence of a conspecific or some visual representation of an antagonist such as a model or mirror image. But the studies with birds characteristically use auditory stimuli. Bird song has been demonstrated to be a mechanism used for territorial defense. Krebs (1977) demonstrated that if a Great Tit (*Parus major*) holding a territory was removed, the space would be usurped within 10 hours. If, however, the recorded song of the removed territorial resident were played in the territory, the space would remain inviolate for 20–30 daylight hours. According to Morse (1980), the Goransson, Hogstedt, Karlsson, Kallander, and Ulfstrand (1974) paper reported that a similar procedure prevented a new Thrush Nightingale (*Luscinia luscinia*) from occupying vacant territory for as long as a breeding season. The proposition that habituation might play a role in the maintenance of territorial boundaries in birds was first suggested by Falls (1969), and evidence that the strength of response of the territory holder changes to different neighbors' and strangers' vocalizations seems to date from a paper by Beer (1970).

A. Initial Evidence of Response Waning to Song Playback

Studies of the change in response of territorial birds to repeated playing of the songs of conspecifics predominate in the literature. Verner and Milligan (1971) studied the responses of territorial White-crowned Sparrows (*Zonotrichia leucophrys*) to song playback. This sparrow is the subject species for the preponderance of studies on habituation and playback, partly because a good deal is known about their natural history, partly because their song and it's development has been studied extensively (e.g., Marler, 1971; Petrinovich & Baptista, in press; Baptista & Petrinovich, in press), and because they are so readily available in the field. The White-crowned Sparrow occupies, in the bird-habituation literature, an place analogous to the one held by three-spined stickleback in the fish literature. Verner and Milligan's paper purports to demonstrate habituation of responses of territorial White-crowned Sparrows to repeated playbacks of the song of a conspecific. But the paper is not well documented and adds little to our understanding of the process, because it lacked virtually all of the control conditions necessary to demonstrate that the waning is really habituation.

In the first study of a series of papers by Petrinovich and collaborators (Petrinovich & Peeke, 1973), clear evidence for waning of three components of the territorial behavior of resident White-crowned Sparrows was found as a result of playing an unfamiliar song of the resident's dialect. A speaker was placed within the territorial boundaries of the resident and eight series of 10 songs with a 1-minute break and then 10 more songs were played using the normal intersong interval of the White-crowned Sparrow (11 seconds). As with all of Petrinovich's field experiments, a very complete catalog of responses was recorded. In this initial study, the number of flights by the resident male, the number of songs, and the intersong interval was reported. It was found that the number of flights per minute at first increased and then habituated, as did the number of songs. The average intersong interval was initially shortened, a normal sign of heightened territorial advertisement, then lengthened nearly to the normal interval (11 seconds). Following a 70-minute silent period, there was slight recovery, but rehabituation was rapid. Waning, then, was demonstrated, and the interpretation as habituation is strengthened by the inclusion, with some of the birds, of a novel stimulus of the same song dialect at the end of the experiment. This resulted in a reinstatement of the initial response level; stimulus specificity was clearly demonstrated. An important aspect of this study was the demonstration of an initial increase in response followed by habituation. This increase is termed "sensitization" and is an important aspect of modern dual-process habituation theory as originally formulated by Thompson and colleagues (Groves & Thompson, 1970; Thompson, Groves, Teyler, & Roemer, 1973) and since extended and modified by numerous workers (see Petrinovich, Chapter 2, this volume, for one approach). This theory and its applicability as an explanatory nexus and as a heuristic agent will be discussed later in this chapter.

B. Habituation to Song Playback: Parametric Field Studies

Following the Petrinovich and Peeke (1973) paper, Petrinovich published a series of six reports dealing with habituation of territorial behaviors during playback. All of these reports used some variation of the basic methodology I have already described. Following a paper describing differences in the reactivity and patterning of territorial behavior as a function of where in the breeding cycle the birds were [eggs, nestlings, fledglings; Petrinovich, Patterson, & Peeke (1976)], Petrinovich and Patterson (1979) demonstrated clear evidence for habituation of many of the basic response patterns used by White-crowned Sparrows during territorial behavior. Stimulus specificity was found when there was a recovery of response to the playback of a novel conspecific song. Recovery was found for most of the responses. Hence, evidence for habituation was demonstrated, and the habituation differed for different response measures as a function of reproductive condition. In the second report of the series (Patterson & Petrinovich, 1979), the effect of massing the stimulus presentations was assessed. Little direct effect of the manipulation was found in this study, but it did demonstrate long-term retention effects. Persistence occurred for at least 7 days and for as long as 13 days between first experience and a subsequent test. Hence in the first three studies, habituation of territorial behavior was demonstrated, as was stimulus specificity and long-term retention. Thus, the three criteria of a mechanism that might be responsible for the maintenance of the "dear enemy" phenomenon have been demonstrated: initial aggression that changes to less frequent aggressive communication (habituation), while maintaining a readiness to respond to a novel protagonist (or protagonist's song; stimulus specificity), and long-term retention.

VIII. Response Variability and Contemporary Habituation Theory: The Interaction of Incremental and Decremental Processes

The evidence I have marshalled for the role that habituation might play in the maintenance of territorial boundaries is clearly oversimplistic. Animals do not show a simple decrease in aggressive behaviors from initial confrontation to stable territoriality. The change is not the simple monotonic function that is commonly ascribed to "habituation." Indeed, bouts of intense fighting and threatening erupt at various times during "stable" periods of territorial occupation. Furthermore, responses change as an apparent function of states or transitions within the reproductive cycle of the territory holders. Sometimes, initial aggression is hard or impossible to observe, although territoriality later appears typical, and finally, a territorial resident is occasionally displaced by another. It is in attempts to explain this behavioral variability within the overall context of behavioral changes that result in stable territorial boundaries that field and laboratory observations can be coupled with hypotheses derived from contemporary habituation theory to lead to new predictions that can be confirmed or refuted in laboratory and field.

The theory I am concerned with is that put forth originally by Richard Thompson, colleagues, and students. Based on studies of the hind-limb flexion response of the acute spinal-cat preparation, Thompson and co-workers were able to identify two types of interneurons that responded to repeated stimulation (Groves & Thompson, 1970, 1973; Thompson & Glanzman, 1976). One of these, labeled Type H, appears to be the substrate for a purely decremental response to the repeated stimulation. A second, Type S, seems to underlie an increase in response. The purely decremental process is called habituation, the incremental, sensitization. The general principles demonstrated in this neurobiological preparation have been extrapolated to the behavior of intact, behaving organisms (see Thompson *et al.*, 1973). The extrapolation follows the general lines that, for a given constant or repetitive stimulus (1) there is one process, habituation, that represents an inferred decremental process in the S–R pathway where the S–R pathway is defined as a direct route through the central nervous system from stimulus to response. (2) There is a second process, sensitization, that results in an initial increment in response followed by a decremental one. Sensitization occurs by a state system considered akin to arousal, activation, or a tendency to respond.

The response change shown in the behavior of an organism to constant or repetitive stimulation is a function of the summation of the two processes. From these assumptions one would predict a response function that shows an initial increase in response, followed by a decrease. This prediction has been borne out in many studies of intact organisms, particularly when care was exercised to provide small enough data bins for the points on the graphs to reflect the early, transient increase in response. Thompson clearly demonstrated this response pattern in a number of studies that were already in the literature, including several from our laboratory, when the data were replotted in smaller response-time bins (Thompson *et al.*, 1973). A typical example of the response pattern predicted by this theory can be found in Fig. 3. Stimulus-specific, short-term, incremental, and decremental effects have also been demonstrated in a study with the ubiquitous Siamese fighting fish (Chantrey, 1978), as well as the aforementioned demonstrations in Thompson *et al.* of the function in convict cichlids and the three-spined stickleback.

IX. State Change and Sensitization

Concentrations on factors that might modulate the arousal ("state") system and affect sensitization, Peeke, Avis, and Peeke (1980) used the convict cichlid and varied water temperature, distance from the nest, and the size of the stimulus fish. They found that greater response increases occurred in cooler water as opposed to warmer, with a close antagonist as opposed to a more distant one, and with a larger antagonist as opposed to a smaller one. In this study three measures of aggression were observed: display (threat) frequency, display duration, and the frequency of bites at the stimulus fish.

In all three experiments the level of aggression elicited from the resident fish was affected by the operations used. More aggression resulted from higher aquarium temperatures than from cooler ones, from near intruders than from distant ones, and from large intruders than from small ones. These results complement findings with other species of fish using the same variables.

The point, however, was not to replicate previous findings. These methods of manipulating the level of aggression (motivational "state") were used to evaluate the effects of varying levels of "state" on sensitization and habituation to test the empirical generality of the Groves and Thompson model to explain the behavior of intact organisms. The methods for varying motivational state were selected to affect the animals by different substrates to test the hypothesis that changes in sensitization and habituation would result from changes in motivational state. In other words, it was assumed that water temperature would affect the internal state of the organism by a different substrate than would size of antagonist or distance from territory center.

All three methods of varying "state" yielded the most sensitization in the condition that produced the greatest amount of aggression. This is consistent with the Groves and Thompson model. But it is also clear that the three response measures changed in a different fashion to the various methods of varying state or aggression level. Both display and biting were most frequent in the "high-motivation" condition and lowest in the "low-motivation" condition, but the same cannot be said of average display duration. When size of intruder was varied, the higher-motivational condition elicited the longest displays, whereas the high-motivation condition elicited the shortest displays.

When temperature was varied, frequency display yielded results consistent with Groves and Thompson's model. But the response topographies (the interrelationships between responses) were very different in the three experiments.

X. State Change, Sensitization, and the Reproductive Cycle

Another approach to the issue of state changes on the habituation and sensitization of territorial aggression was to investigate the effects of the reproductive stage of the territory holder, whether in the field or laboratory. Petrinovich, Patterson, and Peeke (1976) demonstrated that the response pattern both of the male and the female White-crowned Sparrow differed depending on the stage of the reproductive cycle (i.e., whether the pair had eggs, nestlings, or fledglings). This paper was followed by one demonstrating that there was differential habituation and sensitization of component responses during the differing stages (Petrinovich & Patterson, 1979). Thus there was a differential "sensitizing" or "state" effect produced appropriate to each response stage. For example, there were many more *chinks*—which serve as warning calls for the young—when the young had fledged and almost none when there were eggs or nestlings. During the fledgling stage the females also flew about more, which is understandable because the warnings to the young must cover a larger area because of the mobility of the young. These are examples, and the reader is referred to the original paper (Petrinovich & Patterson, 1979) for the full effect of the changes in response texture documented in a detailed inventory of responses and their changes as a function of response condition. In yet another paper, Petrinovich and Patterson (1980) discovered a state variable that accounted for most of the response variance using this paradigm. The state factor seemed to influence the male White-crowned Sparrow and was revealed when the males were classified as high or low responders (an analysis of previous work using the same methods supported the same conclusions). The "state" was defined as a striking difference in the number of songs emitted by the male of the pair but affected the overall level and pattern of behavior of the male. The data indicated that a state change in one member of the dyad affects both the rate of response decrease and response increase in both. The basis for the dichotomy is not understood.

A somewhat parallel finding in convict cichlids has been reported by Peeke and Peeke (1983). This study investigated the role changes from stage to stage in the parental cycle of convict cichlid pairs might have on the processes of habituation and sensitization. An initial observation was made on seven pairs of cichlids: two pairs, each holding a territory in an aquaria. The pairs were free to interact, observations were made once per day, and the frequency of attacks and the place of attack were recorded. Aggressive interactions waned over the 12 days of the experiment for all seven pairs, but there was also a great deal of variability. This variability was correlated with changes in parental stage for one or the other pair. For example, if one pair laid eggs, they became more aggressive; if a pair had their eggs hatch, they became even more aggressive. It was also demonstrated that the stage transitions resulted in expanded territorial boundaries for the pair going through the transition.

A second experiment followed pairs through the whole parental cycle, sampling brief, aggressive interchanges when a conspecific was intruded into the territory for a very brief period. The briefness of the once-per-day exposure assured that habituation would not play a role in response to the intruder and that the level of aggression measured would reflect "state" or a readiness to respond—that is, the measure would sample the initial sensitization. At each stage of transition, there was an increase in aggression that stayed somewhat stable over the several days of that stage and then increased at the transition to the next stage. The changes were most pronounced at the transitions from having no spawn to having eggs, and from having a larvae to having free swimming fry. In both of these cases, the pair had a potential food source to protect from predation. In the latter case, the fry become very mobile and hence difficult to protect. It is clear from these observations that there are parental factors that contribute to a "state" effect that we label, within the current context, as sensitization.

In a third experiment, pairs were allowed to progress into the parental cycle in visual isolation from one another. When the pairs satisfied the requirements of being at different stages in the cycle (e.g., one pair with no spawn, another with fry, one with eggs, and another with larvae, etc.) they were allowed visual access to each other. The pair at the most advanced stage in their cycle were initially more aggressive, but in all cases there was significant habituation of the behaviors. The conclusion from this last experiment is that progress through the parental cycle confers an increase in aggressive readiness (an increased "state" effect) on the pair with young, and that this increasing readiness makes sense when considered in terms of parental investment and increasing needs for defense of the young as they become both larger (a better food source for predators) and more mobile (more difficult to defend).

The findings from this laboratory study support conclusions from field work by Myrberg and Thresher (1974), who showed aggression and territoriality in reef fish, where they refer to the "common observance that intensity of interspecific territoriality increases tremendously in Damselfishes which are guarding eggs [p. 94]." Added to the work by Petrinovich already described, the picture becomes clearer that variance in response can be, and probably is, affected by changes in reproductive status of the animal or pair. Such a change is here viewed as affecting the process of sensitization.

Thus the dual-process theory of habituation proposed initially by Groves and Thompson (1970) has been extended to include several sources of incremental input other than simple arousal from the target stimulus (i.e., the stimulus to which the organism is orienting or behaving). I suggest that the sources of response increment can be roughly classified as (1) those that are stimulus-specific (specific to the stimulus that is the target of the behavior—e.g., a bird's call or a threatening conspecific); (2) those that may be motivation-specific (specific to the motivational complex being elicited—e.g., territorial defense, but not incremental to other behavioral categories—e.g., predation); and (3) those that are caused by general arousal.

Behavioral response to any situation becomes a matter, then, of the interaction of sources of sensitization specific to the target stimulus and those that are extra-target. Target-stimulus sensitization may be stimulus-specific, motivation-specific, generally arousing, or all three. Extratarget sources of sensitization (water temperature, hormone levels, diurnal cycles, etc.) can have all of the above characteristics except stimulus specificity, because it is defined in terms of the response to the target stimulus. Habituation, the proposed decremental process, has been assumed to be, and has been defined as, stimulus-specific; but there are general decremental effects such as fatigue and adaptation. One of the goals of developing such a taxonomy of incremental and decremental effects is to lead to predictions regarding effects of nontarget stimuli on specific behaviors. The experiments cited in this section are directed at that goal. It is clear that the basic nature of response to a constant or repeated stimulus (the interaction of incremental and decremental effects) provides a useful basis for expansion and development of behavior theory.

XI. Motivational Specificity, General Arousal, and Sensitization: The Redirection of Behavior

Another aspect of the interaction of target and nontarget stimuli on the incremental (and decremental) processes can be studied by observing changes in behavior to a target stimulus and the effect those changes may have on response to other similar and dissimilar stimuli in the environment. Two studies on this aspect have recently been completed. In the first, territorial male stickleback were habituated to an intruded conspecific in a glass tube, and both the fish's response to a neighbor and the changes in the response to the intruder were monitored (Peeke, 1982). There was an increase in aggression directed at the neighbor to which the resident had formerly been habituated, and this aggression covaried with the decrease in response to the intruder. This was termed "redirected aggression," and was interpreted as evidence for motivation-specific sensitization. But the possibility that there was a general arousal factor could not be eliminated.

In a second study, a similar method was used (Peeke, 1983). Territorial stickleback males were maintained in individual aquaria with an adjacent compartment containing either another male stickleback, a gravid female, or a nongravid female neighbor. This provides a social context to study the habituation and sensitization of aggression elicited by a conspecific male intruder into the subject's territory.

Typical sensitization–habituation curves, such as illustrated in Fig. 3, were found for all fish regardless of the kind of neighbor. But behavior redirected as a result of the sensitization produced by stimulation from the intruded male differed between conditions. The group with a male neighbor showed increased aggression toward the neighbor, the group with a gravid female neighbor showed courtship, and the group with the nongravid female showed neither. A third behavior, nest building, showed no difference between conditions, thus providing little evidence for a simple explanation in terms of general arousal in that all behaviors were equally influenced by sensitization. For example, the motivational taxon was changed to predation feeding when the behavior was elicited by presenting live brine shrimp in the clear glass tube. In this experiment, aggression did not change during habituation, but the waning predation was redirected to another food-securing behavior, "picking at the substrate."

The results of these two experiments provide evidence that sensitization has energizing effects on responses specific to both the precise stimulus being presented and to other responses that appear to belong to the same motivational taxon. In addition, behavior seems to be sensitized in response to stimuli in the environment other than those to which the initial response is associated; in other words, sexual responses are sensitized when aggression is elicited and a courtship-eliciting stimulus is nearby. But all behaviors are not equally sensitized, and evidence for a general arousal factor, one that should influence all behaviors more or less equally, is elusive.

XII. Response-Independent Habituation

One observation (or nonobservation) somewhat disconcerting for the proposition that habituation may be a primary mechanism for maintaining territorial integrity was that, sometimes, in large laboratory analogs of the natural situation, all of the aspects of habituation such as stimulus specificity and lowered aggression between neighbors was observable, but either the initial aggression that had presumably habituated occurred without notice or there was little or no initial aggression. It has previously been demonstrated with other animals that responding was not necessary for habituation to take place. Davis and Wagner (1969) presented an incremental series of stimuli (sounds) to rats, each one at a level too low to elicit a startle response. Another group, habituated in the normal manner, demonstrated that a nonincremental series that used the same level of auditory stimuli did initially elicit the response. At the end of the experiment, both groups were receiving the same level of stimulation, and both were no longer responding. Applewhite *et al.* (1969) studied the contraction response of the protozoan *Spirostonmum* and demonstrated a similar phenomenon, as did Curio (1969) in a study of bird predatory behavior.

Response-independent habituation was demonstrated in the stickleback by the simple expedient of presenting the intruding conspecific in a clear glass tube behind a glass partition separating the stimulus from the territorial resident by a distance great enough not to elicit biting, but at which it could be easily observed by the resident (Peeke & Veno, 1976). When the clear glass partition was removed, the resident attacked at a low rate, equivalent to that of a group that had undergone normal habituation training when a tube-confined conspecific was presented without the partition. A group presented with the glass partition and an empty tube showed no hesitancy in attacking a tube with a conspecific after the glass partition was removed. This demonstrates that it is possible for an animal to habituate to another without actual physical interaction. As mentioned in Section I, this is similar to the learning-without-response paradigm that forced changes in associative learning theory in the 1950s.

XIV. Summary and Conclusions

The "dear enemy" phenomenon, whereby territorial neighbors maintain boundaries without the constant aggression that might be predicted when two conspecifics reside close to each other and compete for common resources, may be accomplished through a basic form of learning called "habituation." This was suggested by Wilson (1975), and this chapter has attempts to marshal the evidence to support such an interpretation of the phenomena.

Territorial fish and birds do inhibit their aggression to neighbors after an initial period of fighting. There is ample evidence that this hypoaggressive state does not extend to wandering intruders or neighbors that violate boundaries. This is accomplished by the stimulus-specific nature of the waning, both in terms of individual recognition and geographic specificity. This waning, with the demonstration of stimulus specificity, is appropriately termed *habituation;* it is long lasting and extends at least over a single breeding cycle—and probably for a whole season. Changes in aggression—increases, particularly—seem to accompany internal state changes produced both by external factors such as temperature change and internal ones such as changes in parental cycle. Observation of these changes appears to be consistent with functional interpretations of increased readiness for aggression in the defense of young in the sociobiological tradition of Wilson (1975) and Trivers (1972).

As changes in motivational state clearly interact with the waning of response, prediction of behavior becomes more complicated. Fortunately, a theory of habituation, the dual-process formulations of Thompson, provide a basis to understand and predict changes in the complicated texture of behavioral change in freely moving, intact animals. On the other hand, behavior in the field provides a rich source of observations that must be explained and that may produce inductive modifications of the theory. This method of theory building does not provide the clear, easily falsifiable predictions that theories such as those proposed in this volume by Treisman (Chapter 12), Petrinovich (Chapter 2), and Whitlow and Wagner (Chapter 4) do. But through the close interaction of observation and change in theory, a formulation may be produced that is closely tied to functional aspects of territorial behavior.

References

Altrum, B. *Der Vogel und sein Leben.* Wilhelm Riemann Verlag: Menster, 1968.

Applewhite, B. P., Gardner, F. T., & Lapan, E. Physiology of habituation learning in a protozoan. *Transactions of the New York Academy of Sciences,* 1969, *31,* 842–849.

Baenninger, R. Waning of aggressive motivation in *Betta splendens. Psychonomic Science,* 1966, *4,* 241–242.

Baerends, G. P., & Baerends-van Roon, J. M. An introduction to the study of the ethology of cichlid fishes. *Behaviour, Supplement,* 1950, *1,* 1–242.

Baptiste, L. F., & Petrinovich, L. Social interaction, sensitive phases and the song template hypothesis in the White-crowned Sparrow. *Animal Behaviour* (in press).

Barlow, G. W. Hexagonal territories. *Animal Behaviour,* 1974, *22,* 876–878.

Beer, C. G. Individual recognition of voice in the social behavior of birds. *Advances in the Study of Behavior,* 1970, *3,* 27–74.

Bronstein, P. M. Commitments to aggression and nest sites in male *Betta splendens. Journal of Comparative and Physiological Psychology,* 1981, *95,* 436–449.

Brown, J. L. *The evolution of behavior.* New York: Norton, 1975.

Cain, N. W., Anderson, R., Stein, L., & Jessen, C. Effects of prior social experience on agonistic responding in Siamese fighting fish (*Betta splendens*). *Animal Learning and Behavior,* 1980, *8,* 497–501.

Cain, N. W., Flanagan, M., & Jessen, C. Social and environmental factors in the agonistic behavior of community-housed male Siamese fighting fish (*Betta splendens*). *Journal of Comparative and Physiological Psychology*, 1983, in press.

Cain, N. W., Jessen, C., & Flanagan, M. Social responsiveness and physical space as determinants of agonistic behavior in *Betta splendens*. *Animal Learning and Behavior*, 1980, *8*, 502–504.

Chantrey, D. F. Short-term changes in responsiveness to models in *Betta splendens*. *Animal Learning and Behavior*, 1978, *6*(4), 469–471.

Clayton, F. L., & Hinde, R. A. Habituation and recovery of aggressive display in *Betta splendens*. *Behaviour*, 1968, *30*, 96–106.

Cole, H., Figler, M. H., Parente, F. J., & Peeke, H. V. S. The relationship between sex and aggression in the convict cichlid (*Cichlasoma nigrofasciatum*): The role of the dyad composition. *Behaviour*, 1980, *75*, 1–21.

Curio, E. Funktionsweise und Stammesgeschichte des Flugfeinderkennens einiger Darwin-finken (Geospizinae). *Zeitschrift für Tierpsychologie*, 1969, *26*, 394–487.

Davies, N. B. Ecological questions about territorial behavior. In: J. R. Krebs & N. B. Davies (Eds.), *Behavioral ecology*. Oxford: Blackwell, 1978. Pp. 317–350.

Davis, M., & Wagner, A. R. Habituation of startle response under incremental sequence of stimulus intensities. *Journal of Comparative and Physiological Psychology*, 1969, *67*, 486–492.

Falls, J. B. Functions of territorial song in the White-throated Sparrow. In R. A. Hinde (Ed.), *Bird vocalizations*. London & New York: Cambridge University Press, 1969. Pp. 207–232.

Falls, J. B. Bird song and territorial behaviour. *Advances in the Study of Communication and Affect*, 1978, *4*, 61–89.

Figler, M. The relation between eliciting stimulus strength and habituation of the threat display in male Siamese fighting fish, *Betta splendens*. *Behaviour*, 1972, *42*, 63–96.

Forselius, S. Studies of anabantid fishes. *Zoologiska Bidrag fran Uppsala*, 1957, *32*, 93–98.

Gallagher, J. E., Herz, M. J., & Peeke, H. V. S. Habituation of aggression: The effects of visual social stimuli on behavior between adjacently territorial convict cichlids (*Cichlasoma nigrofasciatum*). *Behavioral Biology*, 1972, *7*, 359–368.

Goldstein, S. R. Observations of the establishment of a stable community of adult male and female Siamese fighting fish (*Betta splendens*). *Animal Behaviour*, 1975, *23*, 179–185.

Goransson, G., Hogstedt, G., Karlsson, J., Kallander, H., & Ulfstrand, S. Sangens foll for revirhallandet hos naktergal *Luscinia luscinia* nagra experiment med play-back-teknik. *Var Fagelvarld*, 1974, *33*, 201–209.

Grant, P. R. Polyhedral territories of animals. *American Naturalist*, 1968, *102*, 75–80.

Groves, P. M., & Thompson, R. F. Habituation: A dual-process theory. *Psychological Review*, 1970, *77*, 419–450.

Groves, P. M., & Thompson, R. F. Dual-process theory of habituation: Neural mechanisms. In H. V. S. Peeke & M. J. Herz (Eds.), *Habituation* (Vol. 2). New York: Academic Press, 1973.

Harris, J. D. Habituatory response decrement in the intact organism. *Psychological Bulletin*, 1943, *40*, 385–422.

Hinde, R. A. The biological significance of the territories of birds. *Ibis*, 1956, *98*, 340–369.

Howard, E. *Territory in bird life*. London: John Murray, 1920.

Hull, C. L. *The principles of behavior*, New York: Appleton-Century-Crofts, 1943.

Humphrey, G. *The nature of learning*. London: Kegan, Paul, Trench & Trubner, 1933.

Jenni, D. A. Effects of conspecifics and vegetation on nest site selection in *Gasterosteus aculeatus* L. *Behavior*, 1972, *42*, 97–118.

Jenni, D. A., van Iersel, J. J. A., & van den Assem, J. Effects of preexperimental conditions on nest site selection and aggression in *Gasterosteus aculeatus* L. *Behaviour*, 1969, *35*, 61–76.

Klein, R. M., Figler, M. H., & Peeke, H. V. S. Modification of consummatory (attack) behavior resulting from prior habituation of appetitive (threat) components of the agonistic sequence in male *Betta splendens* (Pisces, Belontiidae). *Behaviour*, 1976, *58*, 1–25.

Klomp, H. Regulation of the size of bird populations by means of territorial behavior. *Netherlands Journal of Zoology*, 1972, *22*, 456–488.

Krebs, J. R. The significance of song repertoires: The Beau Geste hypothesis. *Animal Behaviour*, 1977, *25*, 475–478.

Loiselle, P. V., & Barlow, G. W. Do fish lek like birds? In E. S. Reese & F. J. Lighter (Eds.), *Contrasts in behavior.* New York: Wiley, 1978. Pp. 31–76.

Lorenz, K. Z. Ritualized fighting. In J. D. Carthy & F. J. Ebling (Eds.), *The natural history of aggression.* New York: Academic Press, 1964. Pp. 39–50.

Marler, P. A comparative approach to vocal learning: Song development in White-crowned Sparrows. *Journal of Comparative Psychology*, 1970, *71*(2), 1–25. (Monograph)

Marshall, A. J. Reproduction in male bony fishes. *Symposia of the Zoological Society of London*, 1960, *1*, 137–151.

May, D. J. Studies on a community of Willow-Warblers. *Ibis*, 1949, *91*, 24–54.

Meral, G. H. The adaptive significance of territoriality in New World Cichlidae. Unpublished doctoral dissertation, University of California, Berkeley, 1973.

Moffat, C. B. The spring rivalry of birds. Some views on the limit to multiplication. *Irish Naturalist*, 1903, *12*, 152–166.

Morse, D. H. Hostile encounters among Spruce-Wood Warblers (*Dendroica Parulidae*). *Animal Behaviour*, 1976, *24*, 764–771.

Morse, D. H. *Behavioral mechanisms in ecology.* Cambridge, Mass.: Harvard University Press, 1980.

Myrberg, A. A., Jr., & Thresher, R. E. Interspecific aggression and its relevance to the concept of territoriality in reef fish. *American Zoologist*, 1974, *14*, 81–96.

Nice, M. M. The role of territory in bird life. *American Midland Naturalist*, 1941, *26*, 441–487.

Noble, G. K. Dominance in the life of birds. *Auk*, 1939, *56*, 263–273.

Patterson, T. L., & Petrinovich, L. Field studies of habituation. II. The effect of massed stimulus presentation. *Journal of Comparative and Physiological Psychology*, 1979, *93*, 351–359.

Peeke, H. V. S. Habituation of conspecific aggression in the three-spined Stickleback (*Gasterosteus aculeatus*). *Behaviour*, 1969, *36*, 232–245.

Peeke, H. V. S. Stimulus- and motivation-specific sensitization and redirection of aggression on the three-spined stickleback (*Gasterosteus aculeatus*). *Journal of Comparative Physiological Psychology*, 1982, *96*(5), 816–822.

Peeke, H. V. S. Habituation, sensitization and redirection of aggression and feeding behavior in the three-spined stickleback (*Gasterosteus aculeatus*). *Journal of Comparative Psychology*, 1983, *1*, 43–51.

Peeke, H. V. S. Avis, H. H., & Peeke, S. C. Motivational variables and the sensitization and habituation of aggression in the convict cichlid (*Cichlasoma nigrofasciatum*). *Zeitschrift für Tierpsychologie*, 1980, *51*, 363–379.

Peeke, H. V. S., Figler, M. H., & Blankenship, N. Retention and recovery of habituated territorial aggressive behaviour in the three-spined stickleback (*Gasterosteus aculeatus* L.). *Behaviour*, 1979, *69*, 171–182.

Peeke, H. V. S., Herz, M. J., & Gallagher, J. E. Changes in aggressive interaction in

420										Harman V. S. Peeke

adjacently territorial convict cichlids (*Cichlasoma nigrofasciatus*): A study of habituation. *Behaviour*, 1971, *40*, 43–54.

Peeke, H. V. S., & Peeke, S. C. Habituation of aggressive responses in the Siamese fighting fish (*Betta splendens*). *Behaviour*, 1970, *36*, 232–245.

Peeke, H. V. S., & Peeke, S. C. Habituation in fish with special reference to intraspecific aggressive behavior. In H. V. S. Peeke & M. J. Herz (Eds.), *Habituation* (Vol. 1). New York: Academic Press, 1973. Pp. 59–85.

Peeke, H. V. S., & Peeke, S. C. Parental factors in the sensitization and habituation of territorial aggression in the convict cichlid (*Cichlasoma nigrofasciatum*). *Journal of Comparative and Physiological Psychology*, 1982, *6*, 955–966.

Peeke, H. V. S., Peeke, S. C., Avis, H. H., & Ellman, G. L. Alcohol, habituation and the patterning of aggressive responses in a cichlid fish. *Pharmacology, Biochemistry and Behavior*, 1975, *3*, 1031–1036.

Peeke, H. V. S., & Veno, A. Stimulus specificity of habituated aggression in three-spined sticklebacks (*Gasterosteus aculeatus*). *Behavioral Biology*, 1973, *8*, 427–431.

Peeke, H. V. S., & Veno, A. Response independent habituation of territorial aggression in the three-spined stickleback (*Gasterosteus aculeatus*). *Zeitschrift für Tierpsychologie*, 1976, *40*, 53–58.

Peeke, H. V. S., Wyers, E. J., & Herz, M. J. Waning of the aggressive response to male models in the three-spined stickleback (*Gasterosteus aculeatus*). *Animal Behaviour*, 1969, *17*, 224–228.

Petrinovich, L., and Baptiste, L. F. Song dialects, mate selection and breeding success in the White-crowned Sparrow. *Animal Behaviour* (in press).

Petrinovich, L., & Patterson, T. L. Field studies of habituation. I. Effect of reproductive condition, number of trials, and different delay intervals on responses of the White-crowned Sparrow, *Journal of Comparative and Physiological Psychology*, 1979, *93*, 337–350.

Petrinovich, L., & Patterson, T. L. Field studies of habituation. III. Playback contingent on the response of the White-crowned Sparrow. *Animal Behaviour*, 1980, *28*, 742–751.

Petrinovich, L., Patterson, T., & Peeke, H. V. S. Reproductive condition and the response of White-crowned Sparrows (*Zonotrichia leucophyrs nuttalli*) to song. *Science*, 1976, *191*, 206–207.

Petrinovich, L., & Peeke, H. V. S. Habituation of territorial song in the White-crowned Sparrow (*Zonotrichia leucophrys*). *Behavioral Biology*, 1973, *8*, 742–748.

Simpson, M. J. A. The display of the Siamese fighting fish (*Betta splendens*). *Animal Behavior Monograph*, 1968, *1*, 1–73.

Smith, H. M. The fresh water fishes of Siam or Thailand. *Smithsonian Institution United States National Museum, Bulletin*, 1945, *188*.

Thompson, R. F., Groves, P. M. Teyler, T. J., & Roemer, R. H. A dual-process theory of habituation: Theory and behavior. In H. V. S. Peeke & M. J. Herz (Eds.), *Habituation* (Vol. 1). New York: Academic Press, 1973.

Thompson, R. F., & Spencer, W. A. Habituation: A model phenomenon for the study of neuronal substrates of behavior. *Psychological Review*, 1966, *43*, 258–281.

Thompson, R. F., & Glanzman, D. L. Neural and behavioral mechanisms of habituation and sensitization. In T. J. Tighe & R. N. Leaton (Eds.), *Habituation; perspectives from child development, animal behavior and neurophysiology*. New York: Lawrence Erlbaum, 1976. Pp. 82–117.

Thorpe, W. H. *Learning and instinct in animals* (1st ed.). London: Methuen, 1956.

Thorpe, W. H. *Learning and instinct in animals* (Rev. ed.). London: Methuen, 1962.

Thresher, R. E. Field analysis of the territoriality of the threespot damselfish (*Eupomacentrus planifrons*) (Pomacentridae). *Copeia*, 1976, 266–276.

Tinbergen, N. *The study of instinct*. London & New York: Oxford University Press, 1951.

Trivers, R. L. Parental investment and sexual selection. In B. G. Campbell (Ed.), *Sexual selection and the descent of man, 1871–1891*. Chicago: Aldine, 1972. Pp. 136–179.

van den Assem, J. Territory in the three-spined stickleback (*Gasterosteus aculeatus* L.), an experimental study in intraspecific competition. *Behaviour Supplement*, 1967, *16*, 1–164.

van den Assem, J., & van der Molen, J. Waning of the aggressive response in the three-spined stickleback upon constant exposure to a conspecific. I. A preliminary analysis of the phenomenon. *Behaviour*, 1969, *34*, 286–324.

van Iersel, J. A. A. Some aspects of territorial behaviour of the male three-spined stickleback. *Archives Neerlandaises de Zoologie*, 1958, *13*, Supplement 1, 383–400.

Verner, J., & Milligan, M. M. Responses of male White-crowned Sparrows to playback of recorded songs. *Condor*, 1971, *73*, 56–64.

Wilson, E. O. *Sociobiology: The new synthesis*. Cambridge, Mass.: Harvard University Press, 1975.

Wootton, R. J. Measures of aggression of parental three-spined sticklebacks. *Behaviour*, 1971, *40*, 228–261.

Wootton, R. J. The behaviour of the male three-spined stickleback in a natural situation: A quantitative description. *Behaviour*, 1972, *41*, 232–241.

Wootton, R. J. *The biology of the sticklebacks*. New York: Academic Press, 1976.

CHAPTER 12

Evolutionary Determination of Response Likelihood and Habituation

Michel Treisman

Department of Experimental Psychology
University of Oxford
Oxford, England

I. Introduction

It is a central feature of behavior, even in the simplest organisms, that what animals do is not solely determined by the stimuli that may be present. We do not blink continually, eat continually, or talk continually, even though we may be in environments in which we blink, eat, or talk sometimes. Of course, we know that we normally blink only so often as is necessary to keep the cornea moist and clean, that eating is related to our need for nutrients, and that talking is governed by social constraints. Such arguments refer to a principle of good design, and the accepted basis for this is natural selection, the claim that behavior is adapted to further survival.

Even though food is available, an animal may not eat all the time. To explain this on an evolutionary basis we note that when an animal has

This work was done while in receipt of support from the Medical Research Council of Great Britain.

423

HABITUATION, SENSITIZATION,
AND BEHAVIOR

eaten a sufficient amount, it may not be to its advantage to continue eating. If it eats too little it will be deficient in nutrients. If too much, it incurs the cost of disposing of a burden of unusable energy, or diverts itself from more profitable alternative activities. Animals so constructed that they ceased eating at just the right point were, in the past, most successful in surviving and reproducing, and it is their descendants, replicating their genetic structure, we see about us today.

Evolutionary theory offers general explanations of the ability of animals to schedule many behaviors. In any particular case, two questions arise—evolutionary and physiological. First, what features of the real world, what environmental constraints, make the pattern of behavior we see the best for the animal? Second, what anatomical and physiological devices match the aptitudes of the animal to the requirements of its evolutionary situation? In this chapter we are concerned with the evolutionary question.

For feeding we have some idea of the answers to both questions. The animal's energy and nutrient balances change over time. This produces consequential changes in an internal state, "drive," which regulates eating. But if we look at behavior such as intraspecific conflict, the answers are much less clear. If two animals are opposed in a standard conflict, why will the one sometimes attack, sometimes refrain from attacking the other? What is the evolutionary sense of this variability? If the probability of attack is less than unity, why does it have the value it has? This is the problem of the occurrence of fixed levels of behavior or response likelihoods in the absence of determination by internal cycles. A further complication is the variation in such probabilities that may accompany recurrence of the situation, the problem of habituation. We commence by examining the evolutionary determination of fixed levels of aggression.

II. The Problem of Aggression

Why is aggression between members of the same species so restrained? If a contestant is powerful it might seem he should attack with sufficient force to win what he wants. If opponents are equivalent in age and sex and in competition for a prize each needs it might appear that the one that most ruthlessly pursues his advantage can only benefit from doing so; and there should be no limit to the violence he may employ to get his way. But adaptations which reduce the damage done by conflict within a species are ubiquitous. Why do rattlesnakes not bite one another? A snake that departed from the innate prohibition would both shorten and win its battle, and the representation of its genes in the next generation should increase. But Hamilton (1971) noted, "Usually . . . as soon as it becomes obvious which combatant is likely to win, and thus just when serious wounding might be expected to occur, the fight stops [p. 59]."

Wilson (1975) asked, "Why do animals prefer pacifism and bluff to escalated fighting?" and responded, "The answer is probably that for each species, depending on the details of its life cycle, its food preferences, and its courtship rituals, there exists some optimal level of aggressiveness above which individual fitness is lowered [p. 247]." Wilson listed two constraints that might restrict aggressiveness. The first is kin selection (Hamilton, 1964a, 1964b; Maynard Smith, 1964): a gene leading to the infliction of damage on related animals—who are more likely to possess that gene than the population at large—will tend to reduce its own representation in the gene pool. This may be important, but it is not a universal explanation: restraint may be shown between unrelated animals. The second is that "an aggressor spends time in aggression that could be invested in courtship, nest building, and the feeding and rearing of young [p. 248]." This is an economic argument but it is not obviously cogent. Aggression may not be an alternative, but a means to success in reproduction, and less time may be invested and more profit gained if combat is ended quickly by a death blow than if restraint leads to its inconclusive prolongation.

Another cause for restraint might be that "we have to live together." This would be a version of Trivers's (1971) explanation for altruism, which requires that the cost of his kindness to the altruist must be outweighed by future benefits he will receive from reciprocal altruistic acts. This explanation requires that altruists should perform altruistic acts when the cost to the altruist is less than the benefit to the recipient (where cost and benefit are defined in terms of eventual reproduction), and the relation is reciprocal over time. But this can hardly apply to aggressive conflicts. If an animal's restraint makes it less likely that it will gain a present good, but increases the probability that it will win the same reward on a future occasion—when its opponent will be similarly restrained—then the cost to it now is not below but equal to the benefit to its opponent. And the cost is not outweighed by a future gain, because the rewards—on average—are the same, and an immediate benefit is of more value than one delayed, which it may not survive to enjoy.

There is a special problem for any evolutionary explanation of restraint in the frequency and magnitude of aggression. A characteristic such as the possession of tusks that facilitate digging for food affects only the animal that possesses it, making it more likely to survive and produce viable offspring containing the same genes. But aggression is social behavior involving interactions with other members of the species. The acts of each contestant in a fight may affect production of offspring by both. And the contestants may be in some respects genetically similar, in others genetically different. Fortunately, previous work has laid a basis for evolutionary accounts of such behavior by bringing together concepts from genetics and decision theory (Hamilton, 1971; Maynard Smith, 1974, 1982).

In the simplest genetic model, inheritance of a social characteristic is controlled by a single gene, that is, by the alleles at a single locus. Then selection of the genetically determined action depends on whether it increases or decreases the proportion of the responsible allele in the gene pool of the species, whether it does this by affecting the reproduction of the actor or that of his opponent. Here we do not define "fitness" in terms of the viable offspring produced by the actor, but relate it to changes in the representation of the responsible allele in the gene pool of the succeeding generation.

But if we consider two dogs with one bone, how do we relate their problem to a model of gene selection? A major contribution to advancing this question was made when Hamilton (1971) introduced, and Maynard Smith (1974) developed, the application of game theory to such problems. Gaining the bone offers the advantage of an increase in the probability of survival, but fighting for it incurs a cost through loss of energy and physical damage. These outcomes can be assigned utilities in terms of their effects on the future representation of the allele in the gene pool. If we arrange these utilities in a payoff matrix and relate them to a set of strategies, we have the groundwork of a game-theory analysis.

Game theory deals with the analysis of a player's choices between alternative strategies. But natural selection is not the product of an agent making decisions. What the term refers to is the net effect of large numbers of encounters between contestants of varying phenotypes and histories, competing for bones of various sizes and suffering minor or major injuries when they execute the actions they find in their behavioral repertoires. We simplify our account of this process by considering only randomly chosen contestants of similar abilities whose behavior is not modified by prior experience of one another, assigning the same payoff matrix for each occurrence of the game, which is played once only by the same opponents, and defining a fixed and limited set of behavioral strategies that the players may employ.

The link between the game-theory account and the problem of selection is the link between phenotype and genotype. In relation to the game, each characteristic behavior open to an animal is a strategy. From the genetic point of view, it is the phenotype corresponding to a given genetic constitution. The distinction between player and strategy becomes the connection between a genotype and its expression. The loss or gain to a strategy is calculated as the change in fitness of the corresponding allele. The total payoffs resulting from actions determined by a given genotype and accruing to that genotype determine its representation in the next generation. Then the game constitutes a model of selection, and its solution tells us how evolution will proceed. It is a highly simplified model of the complexities and variations of the real world. But if it works, it may provide a starting point for the analysis of those complexities.

But the game is a non-zero-sum game with no standard solution. The problem this poses was solved when Maynard Smith (1974) introduced the concept of an evolutionarily stable strategy (ESS). In the next section I describe a simple model for intraspecific aggression and define the ESS for it. I then look at the implications of this model for the frequency of attacks in aggressive encounters.

III. Evolutionary Stability of the Probability of Attack

Maynard Smith and colleagues have developed theoretical treatments of a number of cases of intraspecific aggression (Maynard Smith, 1974, 1978; Maynard Smith & Parker, 1976; Maynard Smith & Price, 1973); this section is largely based on their work. In it I review a simple model that represents conflict as a two-person, two-strategy game.

We consider two members of a species who are competing for a prize of some value to each of them, and who are capable of inflicting damage on each other. The outcomes of the conflict have values and costs in terms of their effects on reproduction. The contestants come at random from the population as a whole; there is no special degree of genetic relationship between them; they are equivalent in age, sex, and apparent strength; have no prior experience of one another; and there is no asymmetric condition, such as prior possession of a territory by one of them, that might bias the result (Maynard Smith & Parker, 1976). For simplicity, it is often assumed that the species is parthenogenetic and haploid. But treatments dealing with sexual diploid species and conflicts between kin have been developed (Grafen, 1979; Treisman, 1977, 1981).

The term *strategy* sometimes applies to the different actions a contestant may choose between and sometimes to the principle he applies in making this choice. Where confusion might arise, I use strategy for the latter, and refer to the former as policies, gambits, or behaviors constituting the support of the general strategy. There are two main ways in which the game and the genetic constitution of the population may be linked. If the alternative gambits are e_1 and e_2, representing different degrees of aggression, it may be that e_1 is the policy that animals of one haploid genotype always follow, and e_2 the policy characteristic of a second genotype. The population contains these two genotypes alone, and the probability that a randomly chosen contestant will choose e_1 is the frequency of genotype e_1 in the population, p_E. We describe the population in this case as heterogeneous, and the population strategy corresponds to the mixture of the two genotypes it contains, that is, the genetic polymorphism.

Alternatively, the population consists of animals of a single genotype characterized by a probability p_E of choosing e_1 in a contest. This is the homogeneous case, and the probability p_E defines the population strategy. Both assumptions lead to the same results for unrelated animals, but not necessarily for kin (Grafen, 1979; Treisman, 1981).

The problem is now, What relations may exist, under natural selection, between the values and costs governing the contest and the probability that a contestant will select the more aggressive gambit (e_1)? The answer depends on a powerful concept introduced by Maynard Smith (1974). He defined the solution to the game as a strategy that is stable in a special sense: an evolutionarily stable strategy is one that is stable and that will be preserved by natural selection, because any alternative strategy that may be played against it has a lower expected utility (fitness). If a population of the wild (original) type plays the evolutionarily stable strategy, and it is invaded by a mutant playing an alternative strategy then, by definition, the expected return for the latter (which is its fitness) will be less, and it will be selected against.

A two-person, two-strategy conflict may be represented in general by the non-zero sum matrix

		F	p_F	$1 - p_F$	
	E		f_1	f_2	(M1)
p_E		e_1	a,a	b,c	
$1 - p_E$		e_2	c,b	d,d	

This gives the payoffs to two contestants E and F (defined by their strategies). In each cell the payoff on the left goes to E, on the right to F. Contestant E may choose between two policies e_1 and e_2, and F has two corresponding choices (e_1 and f_1 represent the same gambit, as do e_2 and f_2). These may be referred to as "attack" and "display," respectively, when the matrix is used to model aggression.) If the two contestants choose the pair of strategies (e_1, f_1), then E will receive the payoff a and F the payoff a. If the policies chosen are e_1 and f_2, then E receives b and F receives c. If E selects e_1 with probability p_E and e_2 with probability $(1 - p_E)$ his strategy may be represented as $E = (p_E, 1 - p_E)$. If $0 < p_E < 1$, either e_1 or e_2 may be chosen, and E is referred to as a mixed strategy. But if only one policy, say e_1, is in the support of E (i.e., $p_E = 1$), then E is a pure strategy.

The expected return (increase in fitness) to animals that play strategy E against F is given by

$$E(E,F) = p_E E(e_1, F) + (1 - p_E)E(e_2, F), \tag{1}$$

where $E(e_1, F)$ is the expected return when the policy e_1 is played by E against F. This is given by

$$E(e_1, F) = p_F a + (1 - p_F)b, \tag{2}$$

and $E(e_2, F)$ is defined similarly.

In a homogeneous population of mixed strategists, two randomly chosen opponents will both have the same genetic constitution, and so we may replace both E and F by the common strategy $I = (p_I, 1 - p_I)$. (We also refer to the two gambits as i_1 and i_2.) If I is stable, it is an evolutionarily stable strategy if the fitness of type I is greater than that of any mutant J playing the strategy $J = (p_J, 1 - p_J)$, $p_J \neq p_I$ that may invade the population. That is, the expected return for I, played against such a mixed population, must always be greater than that for J:

$$E(I, I + J) > E(J, I + J). \tag{3}$$

Here "$I + J$" is used as an abbreviatioin for $wI + (1 - w)J$, that is, to represent a population containing Type I in some proportion w, and Type J in the proportion $(1 - w)$. Maynard Smith (1974) gave two conditions for an ESS, both of which can be derived from Eq. (3). The first is

Condition 1

$$E(I,I) > E(J,I). \tag{4}$$

The return to Strategy I, played against itself, must be greater than that to any other strategy that may be played against it. If this does not hold, then

Condition 2

$$\text{If} \quad E(I,I) = E(J,I), \quad \text{then} \quad E(I,J) > E(J,J). \tag{5}$$

If both strategies do equally well when played against I, then I must have the advantage when both are played against J.

To find the value of p_I defining the evolutionarily stable strategy for the payoffs in Matrix (M1), we commence by identifying a stable attack probability. Consider a homogeneous population, all of whose members play Strategy I. If either gambit may sometimes be chosen, then stability requires

$$E(i_1,I) = E(i_2,I), \tag{6}$$

(Bishop and Cannings, 1978) which we may write as $p_1'a + (1 - p_1')b = p_1'c + (1 - p_1')d$, which has the solution

$$p_1' = \frac{d - b}{a - b - c + d}. \tag{7}$$

If p_1' is greater than 1 (or <0), then i_1 always has the advantage over i_2 (or the reverse) and selection will increase p_1 to its maximum (or the reverse). If $0 < p_1' < 1$, the two policies are equally advantageous when we define $p_1 = p_1'$. It can be shown that p_1 will be stable provided

$$A_0 = a - b - c + d < 0, \tag{8}$$

and it is then also evolutionarily stable against challenge by any mutant.[1]

From Eq. (7) the value of p_1 determining the ESS is

$$p_1 = \text{intermed}(0,p_1',1), \tag{9}$$

where intermed(x,y,z) is to be read "x, y, or z, whichever lies between the other two." This constrains the solution to lie in the unit interval.

Matrix (M1) can model any interaction between two randomly chosen conspecifics that might be governed by a payoff matrix. For example, it provides a basis for a model of altruism (Treisman, 1982). A special case that provides a useful model of conflict is known as Hawks and Doves (Maynard Smith & Parker, 1976; Maynard Smith & Price, 1973) and is represented by the fitness increment matrix

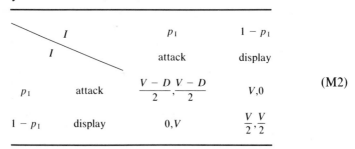

(M2)

[1] Suppose that at a given time the strategy is determined by $p_j \neq p_1$. Then $E(j_1,J) \gtrless E(j_2,J)$ if $p_j \gtrless p_1$. Thus selection must move p_j toward p_1, so that p_1 is stable. If I is a pure strategy (e.g., $p_1 = 1$) and p_j is any alternative, then $E(I,I) > E(J,I)$, which meets Condition 1. If p_1 lies within the open unit interval then $E(I,I) = E(J,I)$ and $E(I,J) - E(J,J) = -A_0(p_1 - p_j)^2 > 0$, which satisfies the second condition for an ESS provided $A_0 < 0$.

There are two gambits: (a) display: if opponent attacks, retreat; (b) attack and continue attacking until either the opponent retreats or one is oneself injured. If both animals attack, one wins the prize V and the other suffers damage $-D$ (the payoffs shown are expected values; $V > 0$ and $D > 0$). If one attacks and the second merely displays, V goes to the former and the latter retires uninjured. If both display, neither is hurt and the prize goes to either with equal probability. Then each expects $V/2$. This assumes that if both contestants attack or both display, each has an equal chance of gaining the prize. Note that "attack" and "display" are used below in a technical sense to refer to the more aggressive and less aggressive of two strategies adopted by a species. The actual form of the behavior will depend on the species.

The expected return for I becomes

$$E(I,I) = \frac{V}{2} - \frac{p_{\mathrm{I}}^2 D}{2}, \tag{10}$$

and if J is played against I,

$$E(J,I) = \frac{(1 - p_{\mathrm{I}} + p_{\mathrm{J}})V}{2} - \frac{p_{\mathrm{I}} p_{\mathrm{J}} D}{2}. \tag{11}$$

Equation (9) reduces to

$$p_{\mathrm{I}} = \min(V/D, 1), \tag{12}$$

where "$\min(x,y)$" is to be read "x or y, whichever is the less."

This concludes the argument, so far as frequency of attack is concerned. If animals have the choice between the more aggressive policy, attack, or the less aggressive, display, and we analyze the effects of their encounters on the expected replication of the alleles determining their choices, we find there may be selection for constraints on attack, depending on the values and costs involved. If the damage that can be inflicted is minor ($D \leq V$) members of this homogeneous population will always attack. [Equation (12) will also apply to a heterogeneous population.] If a mutant J does not always attack, then $E(J,I) < E(I,I)$, which accords with Condition 1. Thus we should expect that puppies, who can do each other little harm, would attack freely and without restraint. But as their teeth grow longer, their forbearance will increase. When $D > V$, the probability of attack falls below unity. In this model, its frequency directly reflects the relative importance of the gain that can be won and the damage that can be suffered.

Note that the expected return to a population stable at the ESS is not the best possible. From Eq. (10), that would be achieved when $p_{\mathrm{I}} = 0$: a population playing this strategy would receive $E(I,I) = V/2$. But these animals would be displaced by any mutants with $p_J > 0$, who would receive $E(J,I) = (1 + p_J)V/2$ when playing against them.

For a homogeneous population of mixed strategists, Eq. (12) defines the evolutionarily stable strategy. For a heterogeneous population of pure strategists (each animal plays only one gambit), the equation is best described as defining a stable genetic polymorphism (Maynard Smith, 1982).

IV. Evolutionary Control of the Magnitude of Damage

We now have a theory of the stability of frequencies of attack (Maynard Smith, 1974) that tells us that members of a population may be selected to attack less frequently than the maximum possible, even when individuals forgo advantages thereby. Because the cost of a death is high, rattlesnakes will wrestle with but not strike each other; D high gives V/D low. This leads us to a second question. The level of aggression is determined by two parameters V and D. The value of the prize is set by the outside world, but why should the damage inflicted (D) have one value rather than another? Many species have powerful armaments yet employ specialized styles of combat against their own kind far less destructive than are available to them. Why should this be?

Maynard Smith's (1974) theory took V and D as fixed parameters and examined selection for p_I. We can extend this approach to the problem of magnitude of aggression by considering a population containing more than one genetic strain, each characterized by the magnitude of the damage D its members typically inflict (Treisman, 1977). In this model V is again constant and we examine selection between these strains. Selection acts to modify the strategy pursued by each strain (its frequency of attack) and the proportion of that strain in the population. We will see that for each strain the strategy undergoing positive selection will depend not only on V and on its own and its opponents' values of D, but also on the proportion of each genotype in the population. If, when the different types are present at given levels, the strategies favored by selection do not produce equal expected returns for each genotype, the less favored will decrease. Changes in their relative proportions in the population may require that their strategies change, too. This process will continue until a stable balance is reached in which each strain, employing its optimal strategy, receives the same return, and no invader does better. The nature of this balance determines the expected value of the damage inflicted.

This analysis is presented in more detail later, although derivations available in Treisman (1977) are not repeated. We start by examining the conditions for an ESS more deeply. If the wild type I exists in the population in the proportion w, and type J in the proportion $(1 - w)$, then we may write the general condition for I to be an ESS [Eq. (3)] as

$$E(I, I + J) = wE(I,I) + (1 - w)E(I,J) > E(J, I + J)$$

$$= wE(J,I) + (1 - w)E(J,J) \qquad (13)$$

or

$$E(I,I) - E(J,I) > \frac{(1 - w)}{w} [E(J,J) - E(I,J)].$$

If we define the advantage of strategy I over strategy J, when each is played against I, as $A(I:J,I) = E(I,I) - E(J,I)$, we can write the general condition just given as

$$A(I:J,I) > \frac{(1 - w)}{w} A(J:I,J). \qquad (14)$$

It can be shown that the values of p_I that satisfy Condition 1 [which requires $A(I:J,I) > 0$] and Condition 2 [for which $A(I:J,I) = 0$] are independent of w, $0 < w < 1$, for the two-by-two game (Treisman, 1984a). But a third case is possible, in which although $A(I:J,I)$ is negative it is still greater than the right-hand side of Eq. (14). What does this mean for selection?

When Eq. (14) holds, selection for I will proceed and w increase. If the advantage terms are both negative, this implies that $wA(I:J,I)$ will become smaller and $(1 - w)A(J:I,J)$ larger, until eventually they are equal. Selection for I beyond this point will reverse the direction of the inequality, so that J becomes the favored type. So there is now an equilibrium between the two strains at a value w_e such that

$$w_e A(I:J,I) = (1 - w_e)A(J:I,J). \qquad (15)$$

If $0 < w_e < 1$, we have a stable balance between two types characterized by the attack probabilities p_I and p_J (neither of which, of course, is itself the ESS). So we may describe the population as a whole as being in an evolutionary stable state $S = (p_S, 1 - p_S)$, with $p_S = w_e p_I + (1 - w_e)p_J$. If we solve for w_e and substitute in the expression for p_S, we obtain $p_S = V/D$. So it may seem that we have merely rediscovered what we knew already: that an evolutionarily stable population can be constituted by a mixture of different types provided that, overall, Eq. (12) holds.

But Eq. 15 has implications that go beyond this. Consider two strains that differ not only in attack probability but also in a second characteristic, the damage they inflict when they attack. Let type I occur in the proportion w, inflict damage D_I, and attack with probability p_I; and let type K occur in the proportion $(1 - w)$, attack with probability p_K, and inflict damage $D_K > D_I$. Type K is the "strong" type and I the "weak" in terms of the damage they can do, but they are not recognizably different: a contestant cannot predict the outcome of a fight simply by looking at his opponent, and so he must employ a single strategy against all comers. But if two contestants attack each other, the one that fights more fiercely always wins; so that for a contest between a randomly chosen member of each type, the payoff matrix becomes

		K	p_K	$1 - p_K$
	I		attack	display
p_I	attack		$-D_K, V$	$V, 0$
$1 - p_I$	display		$0, V$	$\dfrac{V}{2}, \dfrac{V}{2}$

(M3)

When two contestants are both of type I (or K) the payoffs are given by Matrix (M2) with D_I (or D_K) substituted for D.

If w, D_I, and D_K are fixed, we can find the stable attack probability for members of a given type, say K, by comparing the expected return for an attack with the expected return for a display when these are played against opponents chosen at random from the mixed population. If attack does better than display, whatever the value of p_K, there must be selection for attack and p_K will rise to $p_K = 1$. If attack does better than display below an intermediate value of p_K, and worse above, then this intermediate value will define a stable mixed strategy. Similarly, a stable strategy can be found for type I, and the two strategies are not necesarily the same.

The description of these strategies as "stable" must be qualified. The equations defining p_I and p_K are functions of w (Treisman, 1977), thus we can be sure they will be stable under selection only if w does not change. (To avoid confusion, I shall use the term "stable$_w$" to refer to stability of p_I or p_K contingent on the value of w remaining fixed.) But even if selection ensures that each type plays its stable$_w$ strategy, the expected returns $E(I, I + K)$ and $E(K, I + K)$ may be different, and if the return to one type is greater than to the other, the former will increase in the population. Thus if $E(I, I + K) < E(K, I + K)$, w will decrease and the values of the stable$_w$ strategies may change in consequence.

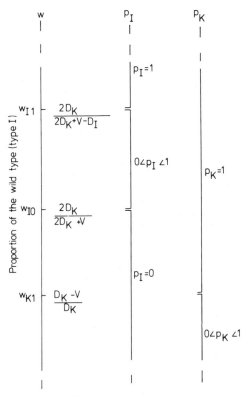

Fig. 1. The changeover points (in terms of w, the proportion of the population which consists of the wild type I) at which the stable $_w$ value of p_I changes from 1 to $p_I < 1$, or from an intermediate value to 0, and at which p_K changes from 1 to an intermediate value.

Figure 1 illustrates the relations between the stable $_w$ attack probabilities p_I and p_K for given values of V, D_I, and D_K, as w varies. We see that $p_I = 1$ for $w \geq w_{I1}$, and p_I falls below this point. Similarly, $p_K = 1$ for $w \geq w_{K1}$ and falls below this point. Whether the changeover points lie within the unit interval (and so correspond to achievable proportions) depends on the parameters. Thus if $D_I > V$ then $w_{I1} > 1$, and p_I can never reach 1.

For a given set of parameters a comparison between $E(I, I + K)$ and $E(K, I + K)$ will show the direction of selection between the two types. We shall use this to examine the effect of variation in the magnitude of damage. Consider first $0 < D_I < D_K \leq V$. This case is simple—whatever the value of w, type K always receives a greater return than type I, and so I will disappear; the more destructive type outbreeds the type that inflicts less damage. If a new type L now appears, such that $D_K < D_L \leq V$, then

K will be displaced by L, and this process may continue until the population is uniformly of a type that attacks with such vigor that $D = V$.

Equation (12) showed that the evolutionarily stable probability of attack would be the lesser of V/D and 1. We can now add that a population with $D < V$ and $P_I = 1$ will not be stable so long as it is possible for D to be greater. Young animals at play are free to show a high level of attack ($p_I = 1$); their immaturity sets a low upper limit to their destructiveness. But this limit will rise as they mature.

The state $D = V$ is not necessarily final. Suppose we have a homogeneous population I characterized by D_I, and it is invaded by type K, with $D_K > V$ and $D_K > D_I$. Then it can be shown that $E(K, I + K)$ is greater than $E(I, I + K)$ for all values of $w > w_{K1}$. Thus the proportion of the original type I will decrease, and the mutant K will increase until w falls at least to w_{K1}. At this point $p_K = 1$ and $p_I = 0$.

The proportion w_{K1} is given by the same expression as w_e [see Eq. (15)]; if there is an equilibrium this will be it. At this point the population consists of the proportion $w_{K1} = (D_K - V)/D_K$ of type I, and $(1 - w_{K1}) = V/D_K$ of type K. The probability of attack for the population as a whole, as it might be recorded by an observer who cannot distinguish between the types, will be $p_S = w_e p_I + (1 - w_e) p_K = V/D_K$; we now have a heterogeneous population of attackers and nonattackers, exactly in the proportions required by Eq. (12). The population mix, however, is not necessarily stable at this point.

The reason is as follows. Equation (15) applies when p_I and p_J are constant. In the present case this holds for p_I, which is always zero when w is near w_{K1}. If p_K retained the value 1 even when w dips below w_{k1}, then $w_{k1} = w_e$ would indeed be an equilibrium point and the proportion of the strong type would be maintained at V/D_K. But p_K is not constant, it is stable$_w$; if w falls to any value $w' < w_{K1}$, selection will immediately ensue for a corresponding reduced value of p_K, $p_K' < 1$, and this stable$_w$ intermediate value p_K' is so defined that the level of attack shown by the population as a whole will be $p_S = (1 - w') p_K' = V/D_K$. Thus w can drift down to any value less than w_{K1} and p_K' will adjust itself accordingly. There is no selective pressure forcing w to take one value in this range rather than another.

In short, when a type that inflicts damage greater than the value of the prize invades a weaker population, it will not wholly displace animals of the weaker type; but it will suppress the expression of their more restrained level of damage. When K first appears, the stable$_w$ value of p_K is 1, and the proportion of K will increase until they represent at least V/D_K of the whole. This sets a lower limit to their presence in the population, but their proportion can drift higher provided p_K simultaneously drops to the corresponding lower stable $_w$ value. Once the proportion of the strong type equals or exceeds V/D_K, selection does not maintain w constant and it does not maintain a fixed value of p_K, but it does require that $(1 - w')p'_K = V/D_K$.

We have now seen that if D is originally less than V and if it is possible for mutations to produce greater values of D, then selection will increase D until it is greater than V. To examine this further, consider a population with three strains I, J, and K, with $D_I < D_J < D_K$. If $D_K < V$ then selection will proceed against I and J until they are wholly displaced. If $D_K > V$ then selection will cause both p_I and p_J to decrease to 0 (at this point there is no longer any phenotypic difference between I and J, and thus no further differential selection between them), and the proportion of type K will increase at least to V/D_K. It may drift above this point, with p_K decreasing in correspondence so as to keep the probability of attack for the population as a whole at V/D_K.

Thus in the end we have a population divided phenotypically into two types. A strong type prepared to attack when involved in a conflict and to inflict damage $-D_K$, and a residue of animals that never attack. But the latter may contain unexpressed variance for the magnitude of damage.

This state will always be unstable if it is possible for a yet more destructive mutant to appear. If one does, it will eventually replace the previously strongest animals, now of intermediate strength, or reduce their possibility of attack to zero, reestablishing a phenotypically bimodal population.

These processes do not define a unique upper value for D for a given population, but the maximum value of D is not wholly indeterminate. Two factors will influence the magnitude of the damage that is normally inflicted in a given species, and these factors result in very different values of D in different species. The first is the range of options offered by the species' behavioral repertoire. For example, rattlesnakes in conflict may have little choice except either to wrestle, fairly harmlessly, or to strike and kill (Eibl-Eibesfeldt, 1961). Second, if D_K is very large, then V/D_K will be very small. But if selection maintains a given type at a very low level, random variation about this level can readily reduce it to zero. The population will then revert to the highest level of damage latent in those animals that phenotypically did not attack before, and it will remain in this state unless mutations succeed in reintroducing type K and raising its proportion to its former, vulnerably low, level.

We see that evolutionary game theory not only defines the frequency with which members of an evolutionarily stable population will choose to attack, it also throws light on the magnitude of the damage that may be inflicted. This is not defined uniquely, but in most cases D is likely to be greater than V. If V is small, D is unlikely to be very much greater; only if the prize is very high, such as a unique mating opportunity, is D likely to rise to the level of serious injury or death.

It is tempting to apply the possibility revealed by this analysis—that a population may contain two phenotypic types—to the occurrence of violence in humans. The most that can be said is that the figures do not reject it. For example, Johnson (1972) noted that most crimes of violence are committed by recidivists. In a study of 10,000 boys in Philadelphia, 6% of the boys accounted for 53% of all personal attacks. But in view of the enormous potential effects of social, domestic, economic, and other environmental factors on human behavior, it is not possible to say what interpretation should be given to such observations.

We have assumed that the weak and strong types are indistinguishable as such. If we consider types that are recognizably different, it can be shown that selection will proceed against the weak until they are wholly eliminated, unless they evolve an appearance of strength (Treisman, 1977). Thus selection will tend actively to produce the population of indistinguishable animals that the theory initially assumed.

V. Some Applications of the Theory

Evolutionary game theory provides a very simplified model of phenomena that can be very complex, but it may serve as an initial account of real behavior in some cases. No extended review will be attempted, but it may be of interest to consider a few applications of the theory.

If members of a species belong to two genetic strains manifestly differing in strength, then the weaker should either disappear or acquire characteristics—such as deceptive displays—that simulate strength. This prediction is supported by the ubiquity of features that make the actor's appearance more impressive. Manes, the erection of hair, postures that increase apparent body size—all of which may be poorly correlated with effectiveness—help to obscure real differences and favor the appearance of equivalence between opponents. If, however, a weaker strain persists in the population although it remains recognizably different, we should expect it to possess an additional strategy that gives it a countervailing advantage. One such example is provided by the sugarcane beetle (*Podischnus agenor*), which has two male forms, major (large, with substantial horns) and minor (small, with minimal horns); the former are the better fighters. But the latter have an alternative strategy: their proportion in the population is maintained because beetles of the minor form emerge from the soil earlier in the season and disperse over a wider area (Eberhard, 1980). This allows them successfully to preempt prizes before a major opponent can come on the scene. In the bearded weevil (*Rhinostomus barbirostris*), in which the male guards his mate, minor forms follow a strategy of avoiding contests with the large males. Instead, they use their small size to help them sneak past a guard to mate surreptitiously without being noticed (Eberhard, 1980). They have added a gambit, deceit, in which they are superior.

Another interesting prediction is that populations may consist of two forms having different behavioral potentialities: a proportion equipped to inflict serious damage and that will sometimes do so, and a residue that restrict themselves to the minor gambit. Evidence that this distinction may be realized in animal behavior is provided by studies of agonistic behavior in the White-crowned Sparrow (Petrinovich & Patterson, 1980). These authors repeatedly played the song of an unfamiliar male within the territories of mated pairs of White-crowned Sparrows when the female was brooding eggs, and recorded their responses. They found that the resident males fell into two types: one that sang (an aggressive response) a great deal and one that responded hardly at all. There were other behavioral differences as well. For example, males that sang a lot also approached the loudspeaker more often and for longer periods. The classification into two groups of different pugnacity is supported by data from other experiments.

Although singing and approach are not themselves attack, they provide evidence of preparedness to mount an attack if the intruder precipitates this. Thus the finding of bimodality supports the model.

The theory I have presented also suggests that the proportion of highly destructive encounters that may occur in natural populations will be low. Wilson (1975) has observed, on murder in animals, "The annals of lethal violence among vertebrate species are beginning to lengthen . . . murder is far more common and hence "normal" in many vertebrate species than in man [p. 246]." However, the following statement, "I have been impressed by how often such behavior becomes apparent only when the observation time devoted to a species passes the thousand-hour mark [Wilson, 1975, p. 246]" suggests that, in view of the number of contests that must surely be seen in a thousand hours of observation, extreme violence is inflicted by relatively few animals—or only infrequently,— which accords with the present model. Such observations do not suggest that it represents an extreme—often approached, sometimes reached—of a continuum of violence.

VI. Reencounters: An Evolutionary Basis
for Dominance

We have seen that evolutionary constraints may limit the magnitude and frequency of aggression (choice of the major gambit) between two unfamiliar conspecifics. These constraints arise because agonistic encounters are a recurring part of the social life of a species, and therefore the behavior of animals of a given type in such conflicts makes recurring contributions to the fitness of their type. But in species with any continuing social life, contests between unfamiliar opponents are likely to be less common than encounters between animals known to one another and that may have clashed before; the degree of aggression seen in the former case is usually greater than in the latter. Within a social group, this reduction in overt aggression may be partly determined by the development of dominance relations. With animals that do not form social groups but maintain contiguous territories, we may see a reduction in aggression between neighbors. Can the theory of evolutionarily stable strategies be extended to these cases?

We start by considering two animals, both of type I, that have faced each other in an initial bout (contest$_0$) in which both attacked. I shall refer to the two randomly chosen contestants as A and B, and describe any contest in which both opponents choose to play attack as a duel. The payoff matrix (M2) applies to the initial contest. Before examining subsequent bouts, we need to look again at the assumptions embodied in that matrix.

Because the opponents are randomly chosen, their strengths will each come from the same distribution, but they are unlikely to be identical. We may assume identical strengths are sufficiently rare to be ignored. To predict the outcome of the initial bout we need to know the probability that B is stronger than A. Because the contestants are randomly assorted the best initial estimate will be

$$P[S(B) > S(A)] = 0.5,$$

where $S(A)$ is the strength of A and $S(B)$ the strength of B. The stronger animal is more likely to win if both attack. We may define the conditional probability of a win by B in a duel, if it is stronger, as

$$P[\text{win by } B \mid S(B) > S(A)] = m, \quad 0.50 < m \leq 1. \quad (16)$$

Then the probability that B is the victor in contest$_0$ if a duel is fought may be defined as

$$q_0 = mP[S(B) > S(A)] + (1 - m)P[S(A) > S(B)] = 0.5, \quad (17)$$

from which it follows that the expected return to A if both attack is $(1 - q_0)V - q_0D = (V - D)/2$, as given in Matrix (M2).

We now turn to the first repeat encounter, contest$_1$. Contests of this class differ from the initial bout in that the contestants are not now unfamiliar. They have met each other before, and that first encounter provided information that must affect the expected returns when they meet again. Let us assume that in contest$_0$, when both animals chose to attack, B won. Then Bayes's theorem tells us that

$$P[S(B) > S(A)|\text{win by } B] = \frac{mP[S(B) > S(A)]}{mP[S(B) > S(A)] + (1 - m)P[S(A) > S(B)]}$$

$$= m. \tag{18}$$

From this we can derive the probability that B will win if a duel is fought in the second contest:

$$q_1 = mP[S(B) > S(A)|\text{win by } B] + (1 - m)P[S(A) > S(B)|\text{win by } B]$$

$$= m^2 + (1 - m)^2 = 0.5 + 2(m - 0.5)^2 > 0.5. \tag{19}$$

Therefore, the payoff matrix that will apply to contest$_1$ is

		p_B	$1 - p_B$
B		attack	display
A			
p_A	attack	$-q_1D + (1 - q_1)V, -(1 - q_1)D + q_1V$	$V, 0$
$1 - p_A$	display	$0, V$	$\frac{V}{2}, \frac{V}{2}$

(M4)

Both A and B are members of type I, and of those members of type I that become involved in contests in which duels are fought, half will end up as loser in the first duel ("A") and half as winner ("B"). In contest$_0$ both played the strategy $I = (p_I, 1 - p_I)$. But now the payoff matrix is asymmetrical, because $q_1 \neq 0.5$, and the ESS for contest$_1$ may require that the players in the two roles vary their behavior accordingly; that is, p_A, the probability that A will attack, may differ from p_B. Asymmetrical contests have been studied by Maynard Smith and Parker (1976), and it has been shown that if the opponents can perceive the asymmetry with at least partial accuracy, such contests must have pure strategy ESSs (Selten, 1980). The present case is now analyzed along similar lines.

Let us describe the strategy for contest$_1$ as $I_1 = (p_A, p_B)$. (In this asymmetric case, the notation now gives the attack probability for each opponent.) If this is an ESS it must resist replacement by any mutant $J_1 = (p_X, p_Y)$ that may appear in the population (where the distribution of strength over members of J_1 is the same as for I_1, X corresponds to A, and Y to B). When mutants first appear, the proportion of type I will be w, a little less than 1, and the proportion of type J_1 will be $1 - w$, a near-zero quantity. If I_1 is the ESS, Eq. (3) must hold. We can express this in the form (dropping the subscripts)

$$wE(I,I) + (1 - w)E(I,J) > wE(J,I) + (1 - w)E(J,J), \qquad (20)$$

which, in the present case, becomes

$$w[0.5E(A,B) + 0.5E(B,A)] + (1 - w)[0.5E(A,Y) + 0.5E(B,X)]$$

$$> w[0.5E(X,B) + 0.5E(Y,A)] + (1 - w)[0.5E(X,Y) + 0.5E(Y,X)],$$

$$\frac{w}{2}[V - p_A p_B D] + \frac{1 - w}{2}\left\{V\left[1 + \frac{p_A + p_B}{2} - \frac{p_X + p_Y}{2}\right.\right.$$

$$\left. + (p_B p_X - p_A p_Y)(q_1 - 0.5)\right] - D[p_B p_X(1 - q_1) + q_1 p_A p_Y]\Big\}$$

$$> \frac{w}{2}\left\{V\left[1 - \frac{p_A + p_B}{2} + \frac{p_X + p_Y}{2} + (p_A p_Y - p_B p_X)(q_1 - 0.5)\right]\right.$$

$$\left. - D[p_A p_Y(1 - q_1) + q_1 p_B p_X]\right\} + \frac{1 - w}{2}(V - p_X p_Y D),$$

or

$$\frac{1}{2}\left\{(p_B p_X - p_A p_Y)[q_1 D + (q_1 - 0.5)V] - D[w p_A + (1 - w)p_X]\right.$$

$$\times (p_B - p_Y) + \frac{V(p_A - p_X)}{2} + \frac{V(p_B - p_Y)}{2}\right\} > 0. \qquad (21)$$

If there is a strategy I_1 such that Eq. (20) holds for any competing J_1, then I_1 will be an ESS. Once established it cannot be dislodged by a mutant strategy. We now consider the alternative possible ESSs. If we let our aspirant ESS be $I_1 = (0,1)$ (i.e. A always displays, B always attacks), and remember that $q_1 > 0.5$, $D > V$ (on the basis of the earlier discussion), and $1 - w$ (the proportion of the mutants when they first appear), will be very small, the left-hand side of Eq. (21) reduces to

$$\frac{1}{2}\left\{p_X[q_1(D + V) - V] + (1 - p_Y)\left[\frac{V}{2} - p_X(1 - w)D\right]\right\}, \qquad (22)$$

which will be greater than 0 for any $J_1 \neq I_1$. This establishes that $p_A = 0$, $p_B = 1$ constitutes an ESS.

It is possible for a game to have more than one ESS. In the present case it is easy to show that neither $p_A = p_B = 0$ nor $p_A = p_B = 1$ is an ESS. If, however, we let our candidate ESS by $I'_1 = (1,0)$ (i.e., the loser in the initial contest attacks, the winner displays), the left-hand side of Eq. (21) reduces to

$$\frac{1}{2}\left(p_Y\{[w + (1 - w)p_X - q_1]D - q_1 V\} + \frac{(1 - p_X)V}{2}\right) \qquad (23)$$

The mutant policy most likely to make this negative is $J'_1 = (0,1)$ (i.e., the ESS previously described). If we substitute J'_1 in the expression above, the condition for the expression to be positive is

$$(w - q_1)D > (q_1 - 0.5)V. \qquad (24)$$

Thus when the cost D is high and the relative superiority of B is low, I'_1 may constitute an ESS.

We see that the long-term effect of the biased biological lottery that constitutes evolution will be to establish the level of attack given by Eq. (12) for the initial encounter; but to require that in a second conflict between opponents who have duelled once (and subsequent contests: if the contestants no longer duel, the parameters remain unchanged), one animal always displays, the other always attacks. This establishes an evolutionary basis for a system of dominance relations in which one animal always has priority over another.

If the opponents do not both attack in the initial contest, then either this bout is disregarded and a later duel decides the issue; or the initial win, however achieved, is treated as an indicator of relative strength and determines a subsequent dominance relation.

A number of consequences follow when this model applies. The asymmetrical ESS I_1 arises because the payoff Matrix (M4) is asymmetrical. By extension, suppose that in a contest between A and B, B is the victor; and in a contest between B and C, C is the victor; then, to the extent that relative strength determines the result, it is more likely that C would win in a contest with A than the reverse. This establishes an asymmetrical payoff matrix for the initial bout between A and C, so that I_1 is the ESS for the first contest between them. Thus a hierarchical dominance relation can be based on an initial defeat of A by B, and A's observation of the defeat of B by C.

The ESS is not concerned with rewarding the stronger animal, but with rewarding the allele that determines that ESS. The ESS I_1 establishes that animal as dominant which wins the first contest, whether it triumphed by a real superiority in strength or by a lucky accident. The advantage of this ESS arises from the reduction in dueling which the stable strategy leads to. The expected return to a pure I_1 population is

$$E(I_1, I_1) = \frac{V}{2} - \frac{p_A p_B D}{2},\qquad(25)$$

which is maximal when $p_A = 0$ and also for $p_B = 0$, as in I_1'. However, I_1' is likely to be rare because the propensities that constitute the raw material of behavioral evolution are more likely to include a tendency to repeat a rewarded action (attack) than the reverse.

There is, of course, no genetically determined, visible difference between A and B; we have seen that if there were, selection would eliminate it. If a nongenetic factor makes it evident on the first encounter that one animal is stronger than the other (for example, an accidental injury to the opponent, a difference in maturity, possession of a vantage point) then the ESS I_1 should apply (Maynard Smith & Parker, 1976).

Because there is an advantage to playing I_1, markers that correctly indicate an individual's status and thus allow the initial stage of probing to be bypassed will be of value. Such indications are provided by the winter plumage of the Harris sparrow. In this bird dominance in winter is indicated by the amount of black on throat and crown, and this appears to contribute to avoiding serious fights (Rohwer, 1977).

The Bayesian probability q may enter the argument twice. It enters first as a parameter determining what direction selection should take. Game theory tells us what strategies will be favored by selection; it does not tell us how closely nor by what behavioral means a given species can approximate the favored strategy. The probability q may enter again at this second, behavioral, stage of the argument, when I_1 requires the animal to assign itself the role A or B. In one species it may choose a role immediately and finally, on the basis of the outcome of the initial contest. In another it may proceed by forming an estimate $\hat{q}$ of the probability that its opponent would win a duel. The way in which it reaches and employs this estimate may determine how closely or how soon it adheres to the requirements of the ESS. If animals of a given species underestimate the departure of q_1 from 0.5, or their estimates are limited by noise and in encounter i they require $|q_i - 0.5|$ to exceed a high criterion before a role is chosen, then they may update q_i through several contested encounters before they are fully committed to the evolutionarily stable strategy I_1. It will also take longer to obtain an adequate estimate of q_i if m, which reflects the differences in capacity between the contestants is low [see Eq. (16)].

The way the animals estimate $\hat{q}$ may determine the facility with which they switch from I to I_1. If estimation of $\hat{q}$ is immediate and sensitive, dominance will be quickly established. If $\hat{q}$ is revised in response to each win by a dominant animal, however that win occurred, then the dominance relation should be very stable. If $\hat{q}$ may be modified by evidence from other sources, such as observing that the dominant animal is injured, or its failure in a contest with a third opponent, this could result in a return to duelling or an immediate reversal of roles.

Establishment of I_1 may be slow if more than one duel is fought and wins alternate. Another factor that may retard adoption of I_1 is the presence of alleles for "cheating," that is for wrongly taking the role of B rather than A if it can be managed; this would favor treating evidence for an asymmetry in q conservatively.

Once B has established his dominance over A, a change may occur in the way he conducts an attack. He must continue to choose attack and cannot substitute display: $J = (0,0)$ is not an ESS. But his attacks may be abortive because they reliably encounter submission. As long as it remains evident that B is prepared to carry through an attack, any reduction in the investment he makes in demonstrating this will be a gain. Thus, as the growth in q_i establishes an increasing predisposition to expect B to attack and win, his demonstration of preparedness can be ritualized and minimized; raised eyebrows can substitute for flailing fists.

Support for this prediction is provided by the behavior of *Betta splendens* as reported by Cain, Anderson, Stein, and Jessen (1980). Fish were paired with an opponent until dominance was established. Before this occurred both fish in a pair attacked equally often. After dominance was determined, the subordinate fish no longer attacked and rarely displayed. Once the opponent had submitted, the dominant fish rarely attacked, but it continued to emit threat displays at the same rate as before. In this case, the passivity of the subordinate fish may correspond to "display" in the game hawks and doves, but the maintained threat displays of the dominant fish can be considered as demonstrations of his continuing preparedness to carry through an attack if necessary.

Some observations by Le Boeuf and Peterson (1969) demonstrate how effective dominance relations may be in suppressing attack. They observed elephant seals in the mating season. During this period the males compete for females. They do not occupy territories but establish a dominance hierarchy, those at the top monopolizing mating opportunities. In these observations 4% of the males inseminated 85% of the females. Males recognize each other individually and maintain a linear dominance hierarchy (with some triangular relations) by aggressive encounters. In more than 6000 such encounters the observers saw 90 duels—that is, clashes occurred in only 1.5% of contests. Because mating is the ultimate genetic prize, Eq. (12) would predict a very high probability of attack between randomly selected unfamiliar opponents.

It has been argued that the conduct of a conflict may be determined by an assessment of the opponent's ability to win, or "resource holding potential [Parker, 1974]" or that threat displays may provide useful information, or deceptive information, or no information about a contestant's intentions (Andersson, 1980; Caryl, 1979). It is likely that the role of threat displays is complex, and a game theory analysis of them is presented elsewhere (Treisman, 1984b). But an indicator whose significance cannot be obscured is the set of past outcomes. We saw that in a social species animals will be selected to estimate $\hat{q}$ and there will be a corresponding transition to a pattern of dominance that reduces the probability of duelling. As memory, in the form of the current estimates of $\hat{q}$, takes over the function of prescribing interpersonal relations, the "attacks" can be correspondingly simplified, but never wholly forgone, even if they are reduced to vestigial status symbols. When the present analysis holds, it is an evolutionary requirement that stimuli (a given opponent) that on the first or the first few occasions evoke attack should, on repeated exposure, cease to produce attack in one animal, and produce a reduced form in the other.

We may note that although the ESS for an initial encounter I does not maximize the return to the players [cf. Eq. (10), remembering that $p_i > 0$], the return when the dominance strategy I_1 (or I_1') is the ESS [Eq. (25) with $p_A = 0$ or $p_B = 0$] is the best that can be achieved.

VII. Territorial Defense

Possession of a territory may be essential for procreation, making the territory's defense of great moment to the species. The owner of a territory may be faced with two types of challenge: usurpation or encroachment. In the first a stranger with no territory of its own may invade and attempt to take over the territory. This can be analyzed as an example of hawks and doves with opponents having different roles, resident and intruder. In this asymmetric game, the ESS will be a pure strategy, usually resident wins (Maynard Smith & Parker, 1976; Maynard Smith, 1982; Selten, 1980). In the second case, which will be considered next, a neighbor, known to have his own territory, seeks to extend his boundary forward.

In encroachment the prize is the disputed border area. But the payoffs are not given by Matrix (M2) because the value of the area at risk is different for the two contestants. For the encroacher it is V—the benefit of an extension of his foraging area—reduced by the considerations that he may not necessarily obtain proportionately more food by foraging more widely, and he will have a larger border to defend. But its value to the resident is greater, let us say $V + \delta$, because a reduction in the size of a standard territory may do more harm to the resident than it confers benefit on the encroacher. The probability of attracting a mate and rearing young to maturity may suffer severely if the territory is too small. And success may encourage the encroacher to seek further annexations. The larger the disputed area, the greater the difference in its value δ to the two contestants may be. The payoff matrix is

Resident (A) \ Encroacher (B)	p_B attack	$1 - p_B$ display
p_A attack	$\dfrac{V + \delta - D}{2}, \dfrac{V - D}{2}$	$V + \delta, 0$
$1 - p_A$ display	$0, V$	$\dfrac{V + \delta}{2}, \dfrac{V}{2}$

(M5)

Members of the same type may play both roles. We apply Eq. (3), as before, to find the strategy I that is resistant to challenge by any mutant J. Entering the resident's and encroacher's attack probabilities in that order we have $I = (p_A, p_B)$ and $J = (p_X, p_Y)$. It can be shown that

$$E(I,I) = \frac{1}{2}\left[V - p_A p_B D + \frac{\delta}{2}(1 + p_A - p_B)\right], \qquad (26)$$

and

$$E(I,J) = \frac{1}{2}\left\{V - \frac{D}{2}(p_A p_Y + p_B p_X) + \frac{V}{2}(p_A + p_B - p_X - p_Y) + \frac{\delta}{2}(1 + p_A - p_Y)\right\}. \qquad (27)$$

Applying Eq. (20), the requirement for an ESS is

$$\frac{1}{2}\left[\frac{(V + \delta - p_Y D)(p_A - p_X)}{2} + \frac{(V - p_X D)(p_B - p_Y)}{2} - wD(p_A - p_X)(p_B - p_Y)\right] > 0. \qquad (28)$$

As the matrix is asymmetric, we may expect the ESS to require pure strategies (Selten, 1980). Assuming, as before, that $D > V$, and that w is close to 1 when J first appears, it can be shown that none of the strategies

$p_A = p_B = 0$, or $p_A = p_B = 1$, or $p_A = p_B = V/D$ is an ESS. But if we try $I = (1,0)$, the left-hand side of Eq. (28) becomes

$$\tfrac{1}{4}[(1 - p_X)(V + \delta) + p_Y(wD - V) + p_Y D(2p_X - 1)(1 - w)], \quad (29)$$

which is positive for any $J \neq I$. The expected return is $E(I, I) = (V + \delta)/2$.

This shows that when a border encroachment occurs, selection will favor a strategy in which the resident attacks, and the encroacher displays—even in the first encounter between them. These gambits may take the form of an advance by the resident and retreat by the encroacher. If this goes so far as to carry the battle into B's territory, this will reverse the payoff matrix; δ will change its position as A becomes the encroacher, threatening B as resident. Thus we may expect an oscillating, back-and-forth encounter at a boundary.

Strategies of this sort are familiar in territorial behavior. For example, Tinbergen (1951) noted, "Within its own territory, a male [three-spined stickleback] invariably attacks every other male. Outside its territory, the same male does not fight but flees [p. 114]." Oscillating advance and retreat may be seen at the boundary.

A second strategy, however, also meets the test for an ESS: $I' = (0,1)$—the resident displays, the encroacher attacks. If we substitute I' in Eq. (28), the left-hand side becomes

$$\tfrac{1}{4}[(1 - p_Y)V + p_X(D - V) - 2p_X(1 - p_Y)(1 - w)D - p_X\delta]. \quad (30)$$

For $J \neq I'$ this is positive provided δ is sufficiently small. If the alternative strategy is $J = (1,0)$ (i.e., I above), then Eq. (30) approximates $(D - \delta)/4$, which indicates that if I' is the ESS in force for δ small, it will retain an advantage over I as long as $\delta < D$. The expected return for a population playing I' is $E(I', I') = V/2$, which is less than $E(I, I)$; but it is Eq. (3), not the expected return to the type, that determines the direction of selection.

If I is the universal strategy it will not be displaced by I'. If I' is universal, it will not be displaced by I for δ small, but it will give way when δ is large enough. This tells us that two patterns of response to border encroachments may be seen. In the first, I determines an immediate response to the slightest infringement: if δ departs from 0 the resident will attack. We may describe this as an assertive strategy. The second pattern of response plays I' when the border infringement is minor and changes to I only when δ becomes large. The resident disregards or retreats before a small incursion; he attacks only if it is pressed deeper. We may describe this as a tolerant strategy.

There is an advantage to the tolerant approach which has not been made explicit in our treatment. When I is applied in all cases, error in recognizing whether or not a border encroachment has really occurred—which in nature may be uncertain when borders are fuzzy, and minor, unintentional, or temporary incursions occur—can result in unnecessary and costly conflicts, which the tolerant strategy avoids. Thus we might expect to see either pattern of response in a species in which individuals defend territories or other resources from their fellows.

We have considered the case in which the value to resident and encroacher of any disputed territory will differ. This will apply when the population is large and territory sizes are near their biological minima. But if numbers are low and territories more ample, a small incursion may bring into dispute an area or resources of equal value to both animals. If so, for reasons similar to those which applied in the discussion of dominance, a strategy will evolve in which one animal, say B, may safely choose to make such incursions into the territory of A, or may even annex the area of equal value to both; but A is less likely to risk similar invasions into B's territories. Thus large territories might have "common zones" between them, in which one animal dominates the other when they meet; or some animals might have extralarge territories and others be reduced to areas such that $\delta > 0$. In such a case, an invasion of A's small territory by B might bring $I (=1,0)$ into action; but A would be subordinate to B if he ventured into the latter's territory.

These arguments may have an application to the distinction between a home range and a territory. Coyote groups or individuals may have a home range where they hunt; this has a flexible, undefended boundary but may include a defined area, the territory, from which other coyotes are excluded and which is actively defended against them (Bekoff & Wells, 1980). If the range is large enough, there may be so little to gain by seeking to monopolize it that, for a clash with an occasional intruder, V/D [Eq. (12)] is negligible. Alternatively, if we define incursion as "attack," and failure to resist as "display," such behavior may embody a distinction between tolerable incursions (I') and those that are excessive and must evoke a vigorous reaction by the owner and flight by the intruder (I). Bekoff and Wells (1980) noted that the intensity with which an area is defended is related to the presence in it of large, clumped food resources (elk carrion, in their observations) that will increase V.

VIII. Probabilistic Information

Any organism capable of making differentiated responses faces the problem of obtaining sufficient information about its environment to make good choices. For a given species, some stimuli are unambiguous; they require no interpretation, only a response. The significance of others may need to be learned. For example, naive puppies will respond to the smell of meat, but not to the sight of it behind glass. Stimuli are important if they indicate a situation or provide information relevant to the animal's needs. We may call such stimuli *signals*. They may indicate the probability that food is present to an animal seeking prey, or suggest the presence of a predator to an animal wishing to avoid becoming prey. When the signal is seen, the animal faces a choice: to act on what information he has or to await fuller information.

The signal may indicate a threat so dire that it is best to flee at once. But in many cases it may be more economic to obtain further information. The responses the animal makes to such a signal may include components facilitating the gain of such information—sometimes known collectively as the "orienting reflex"—and responses appropriate to the situation that may be revealed by the signal. For example, if a bird hears what may be the song of an intruder in its territory it may fly to a vantage point, look in the direction of the signal, and countersing. If it hears a predator, it may watch and listen and also utter warning cries.

The signal may be confirmed by events: if an opponent approaches, the bird may attack; if a predator approaches, the bird may flee. But what should the bird do if the signal is repeated but the consequences suggested by the repeated signal do not manifest themselves? What behaviors will natural selection prefer in response to a sequence of signal repetitions? The animal observer is now playing a game against nature, and the answer will lie in considering the alternative gambits open to it, and finding the strategy that will maximize the expected return.

Consider an example. A signal S, say a rustling in the undergrowth, occurs. It indicates that there may be a predator. The listener I must choose a response. There is some probability that I will be attacked if a predator is present and was responsible for the signal. Even if the signal was caused in some other way, there is a baseline probability that a predator is present and may attack. But the signal has increased this probability, and in response to this signal the animal interrupts its activity and orients toward it. No danger emerges, but from time to time the signal recurs. What response should I make on each successive trial?

Let the initial probability that such a signal indicates the presence of a predator be $P_0(\text{pred}) = p$. Then the probability that the signal was produced by some other harmless cause Q is $P_0(Q) = 1 - p$. [The state of the world (Q) does not exclude the possibility that a predator is coincidentally present: this determines the baseline probability of an attack.] A predator may attack (A) or it may fail to attack ($\bar{A}$). There is some low probability that no attack will be made even if a predator produced the signal: $P(\bar{A}|S$ & pred$) = g$. If the signal was produced by a harmless cause, then a higher baseline probability of safety obtains: $P(\bar{A}|S$ & $Q) = h$, $g < h$.

Suppose that nothing happens after an initial signal, S_0. This absence of event is significant information about the possibility that danger lurks nearby and modifies this possibility in accordance with Bayes's theorem. If the signal recurs on Trial$_1$, given that no attack occurred on Trial$_0$, the probability that a predator is responsible becomes

$$P_1(\text{pred}|\bar{A}) = \frac{P(\bar{A}|S \;\&\; \text{pred})P_0(\text{pred})}{P(\bar{A}|S \;\&\; \text{pred})P_0(\text{pred}) + P(\bar{A}|S \;\&\; Q)P_0(Q)}$$

$$= \frac{gp}{gp + h(1 - p)},$$

and the probability that will apply on Trial$_n$ (assuming that "no attack" has occurred n times, on Trials 0 through $n - 1$) is

$$P_n(\text{pred}|n\bar{A}) = \frac{g^n p}{g^n p + h^n(1 - p)}. \tag{31}$$

Now the probability that the signal on Trial$_n$ will not be followed by an attack is

$$P_n(\bar{A}) = P(\bar{A}|S \;\&\; \text{pred})P_n(\text{pred}|n\bar{A}) + P(\bar{A}|S \;\&\; Q)[1 - P_n(\text{pred}|n\bar{A})]$$

$$= \frac{g^{n+1}p + h^{n+1}(1 - p)}{g^n p + h^n(1 - p)}. \tag{32}$$

As $g < h$, $p_n(\bar{A})$ will increase over a series of trials in which signal occurrences have no ill consequences. We suppose that on each trial, I may choose one of three gambits. The first is a strong orienting response Or_s that will require an extended attempt to locate any predator. This involves a major investment of effort, but if a predator is in fact present and attacks, the additional cost of successful flight is small. The second gambit is a weak orienting response Or_w, a more cursory inspection costing less effort but more likely to result in an expensive or difficult escape or even capture if a predator is present and attacks. The third alternative is that I may make no response $(\overline{Or})$; if the predator is present this can be very costly. The returns for these three gambits—given that an attack does or does not take place—are set out in the following matrix, with numerical quantities included for illustration.

	A	$\bar{A}$	
Or_s	$a = -6$	$b = -5$	(M6)
Or_w	$c = -12$	$d = -1$	
$\overline{Or}$	$e = -20$	$f = 0$	

Here, $a > c > e$, and $b < d < f$. The expected return for the strong orienting response on Trial$_n$ is then

$$E_n(Or_s) = a[1 - P_n(\bar{A})] + bP_n(\bar{A}),$$

and the returns for the other gambits are defined similarly. The strategy maximizing the return to I is to choose on each trial that response having the lowest expected cost. Because no type that follows a different strategy can do better, this defines an evolutionarily stable course for habituation. For the illustrative quantities in Matrix (M6) and the parameters given in the legend to Fig. 2, that figure shows the expected return for each gambit, for seven occurrences of a signal. An initial strong response is followed by several weak responses, and finally, response ceases.

This example illustrates the course of habituation that is prescribed by natural selection. It is determined by the decreasing probability that the signal reliably heralds a need for action as time passes, and the fact that the cost of the orienting response changes in opposite directions as a function of its magnitude, depending on whether or not an attack occurs. If the situation is such that the significance of the signal does not change over trials, an absence of habituation is required. Examples are the practically inexhaustible recurrence of retrieval of young mice by their parents in response to their supersonic call (Thorpe, 1963) or the contraction of the pupil in response to a flash of light.

In the preceding example three levels of response are assumed, but there could be a greater number or a continuous range of response. As any mechanism producing behavior is likely to be noisy to some extent, fluctuations of response between neighboring categories may occur.

We have examined the simplest situation, in which successive signals recur at more or less regular intervals. What if this succession is interrupted by a long gap, and the stimuli then resume? Before we can examine this, two types of signals must be distinguished.

A. Probabilistic Indicators

If I hear sounds such as an unseen animal may produce as it moves through the undergrowth, then it is likely that the successive crashes come from the same animal. But if the sounds stop and later similar sounds start again, they may be produced by the same or by a different animal; and the longer the intermission has been the less sure can I be that I am listening again to the identical individual, or even an animal of the same type. A signal of this type may correspond, with varying probability, to a number of different causes.

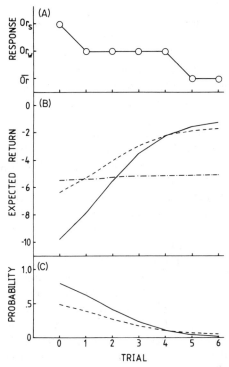

Fig. 2. The evolutionarily prescribed course of habituation for the parameters in Matrix (M6) is shown for an initial signal and six subsequent repetitions of the signal. The initial probability [Panel (C)] that the signal is caused by a predator is P_0 (pred) = p = .8; the probability that an attack will follow if the signal was caused by a predator is [1 − $P(\bar{A}|S$ & pred)] = 1 − g = .6; the baseline probability of an attack, if the signal was coincidental, is [1 − $P(\bar{A}|S$ & Q)] = 1 − h = .05. For successive occurrences of the signal not followed by an attack, the probability that a predator is producing the signals [Panel (C)] is shown decreasing toward zero [—, P_n (pred|$n\bar{A}$)], and the probability that an attack will occur on the current trial [− − −, $P_n(A)$] decreases toward the baseline level. The expected return [Panel (B)] is at first greatest for Or_s (—·—·); it is then overtaken by E_n (Or_w) (- - -), and finally by E_n ($\overline{Or}$) (—). The responses elicited are shown in Panel (A).

B. Deterministic Indicators

Some signals may be uniquely recognizable from one time to another and may be associated with an initiator possessing unchanging properties; but we may not know, to start with, what these properties are. An example is the facial features by which we recognize a person whom subsequent experience proves to be English-speaking and deaf.

The distinction between these two types of signals is not always hard and fast. It may also depend partly on the observer's perceptual capacities: if I cannot recognize individual faces, then the presence of a face becomes a probabilistic indicator. Applying this distinction to the problem of interruption in a series of signals, we consider probabilistic indicators first. If a sequence is interrupted, the relevance of the animal's initial experience of the indicator will decline as the interval continues. During the initial sequence the probability that, for example, the signal meant that a predator was present may have fallen to $P_n(\text{pred}|n\bar{A})$. But after an interval, this probability should rise to a value given by a weighted combination of this quantity and of the prior probability that a new signal may indicate a predator $P_0(\text{pred})$. Thus if the signals resume, some degree of spontaneous recovery should be shown, and this is a very familiar finding. It is made the more familiar because in the laboratory most experimental stimuli are likely to be probabilistic indicators; they are usually arbitrary, unfamiliar, or artificial in relation to the experience of the subject.

The situation is very different for deterministic indicators. The probability that falls during the initial series of exposures to the signal is the probability that the indissociable cause or initiator of that signal has certain properties, such as a disposition to attack, and an interruption in the sequence of trials will not decrease the relevance of the information that has been gained. Such an interruption should produce little or no spontaneous recovery. If a puppy has found that a possible food object is in fact a pebble, bland and nonnutritive, exploratory feeding responses should not recur each time it is reencountered. If a female's initial distrust of a male has died away during courtship, avoidance responses should not reemerge after each temporary separation.

An illustration of this distinction is provided by territorial defense. Territorial animals may attack strangers that appear in the vicinity, but show much greater tolerance for settled neighbors. This implies individual recognition of those neighbors, based on the discrimination of distinctive deterministic indicators. Mechanisms of habituation to familiar neighbors have been discussed by Peeke and Peeke (1973).

Habituation to neighbors would result from the absence of invasions or attacks over time. This has been studied by Petrinovich and Patterson (1979) and Patterson and Petrinovich (1979), who played the song of a male through a speaker located within the territorial boundaries of a pair of resident White-crowned Sparrows. The song was recorded from an individual of the local dialect group who was normally too distant to be heard by the resident pair. Habituation was recorded. This would be expected in the absence of personal intrusions or attacks by the experimental interloper, whose voice and characteristics must have become as clearly identifiable to the residents as those of any of their other neighbors. When habituation was interrupted, almost no spontaneous recovery occurred after intervals ranging from 60 minutes to 15 days. This is in accord with the present distinction, and supports our interpretation that patterns of habituation have been evolutionarily selected for efficient information-handling in relation to real-world demands.

IX. Conclusion

This chapter reviews the evolutionary determination of levels of behavior, of which habituation is one case. Evolutionary analysis allows us to anticipate the behaviors that should occur, but it does not say how a species will produce these behaviors. It is for the psychologist and physiologist to discover how the requirements imposed by natural selection have been met (Treisman, Chapter 3, this volume). If members of a given species do not show the evolutionarily prescribed strategies we expect, this should prod us to reexamine our analysis of the environment and the determinants of selection. If the behaviors *are* seen, we know that they are not accidental or arbitrary consequences of other developments. Rather, they are adaptations; and the mechanisms that produce them will be as simple or as complex as may have proved necessary to meet the requirements imposed by selection. If we know that habituation is a necessary feature of an information-handling device, we will not interpret it as an accidental consequence of inadequate resistance to fatigue at a synapse.

If the same organism faced with the same environment behaves differently on different occasions, then either we are wrong to think that it is the same organism or it is not the same environment. The evolutionary approach may help us discover implications of the demands of the environment or of the requirements for selection. At one extreme consider behavior such as feeding. It is customary to explain eating by a hunger cycle, determined by variation in the state of the organism consequent on physical and physiological laws: energy is acquired, utilized, and must be replenished.

But a more careful examination of the demands of the environment may raise questions for this analysis. In the world in which we evolved, food is acquired in at least two situations. The first requires a separate effort of search and acquisition for each item: for example, a series of hunts for separate small prey. Here, the effort expended must be related to the return: hunting should end when energy needs have been satisfied and when other needs deserve priority. Second, there is the windfall situation in which a large quantity of food, which may be perishable or subject to competition, becomes suddenly and unpredictably available: a fruit tree, a thicket of berries. To exploit this best, it would be advantageous to eat as much as possible, with little satiation. An adult can profit from both situations, a child mainly from the latter.

This consideration of the evolutionary environment suggests the possible existence of two drives or strategies for controlling feeding. The first would have a clear hunger and satiation cycle, be especially evident in adults, and be perhaps more strongly linked to savory tastes. The second would be opportunistic, relatively insatiable, most evident in children, linked to sweet and, perhaps, bitter tastes. This distinction is an evolutionary speculation, but it may possibly throw light on a number of features of eating, such as: the different behaviors and preferences of adults and children, the custom of following a savory main course with a sweet dessert (perhaps adding drive competition to satiation), and, perhaps, patterns of eating in the obese that appear to be more opportunistic and less committed to the expenditure of effort than in the lean and that have been described as determined more by external and less by internal cues (Schachter, 1968, 1974). Thus, consideration of the evolutionary background may suggest the possible causal role of an imbalance between different drive systems in some cases of obesity.

Aggression presents a different problem. It requires both an object of contention and an opponent. But animal A, faced with an unfamiliar opponent B, may attack or may fail to attack. What accounts for this variability? To say that the opponent is on one occasion more threatening or provocative than on another begs the question; we still do not know why such stimulus differences should determine which behavior is chosen. The evolutionary analysis shows that the state of the world, including not only the value of the prize and the possible costs of battle but also the selective consequences of the distribution of genotypes in the population, may require that behavior to be stochastic: the variation from one time to another may be a necessary randomness, whether this randomness is realized by exploiting trigger features of the opponent or in some other way.

If we consider change in performance over repeated trials, whether social interaction or the simplest response to a signal, we find that it is not the actual state of the world on a given trial that necessarily determines the performance shown, but it is the expected state of the world—given the information conveyed by previous trials, so far as the actor can extract it—that evolution seeks to match performance to. This may be a subtle determinant of behaviors ranging from dominance and territorial defense to habituation. Evolutionary analysis would be of value even if it did no more than replace hypotheses of random or accidental variation with selective explanations for the different features of habituation (or its absence) to such stimuli as a shadow (a probabilistic indicator), the light flash evoking a pupillary response (a deterministic indicator of unchanging significance for this reflex), the high-frequency cry eliciting retrieval of young mice, or the song of a rival in a bird's territory.

References

Andersson, M. Why are there so many threat displays? *Journal of Theoretical Biology,* 1980, *86,* 773–781.

Bekoff, M., & Wells, M. C. The social ecology of coyotes. *Scientific American,* 1980, *242*(4), 112–120.

Bishop, D. T., & Cannings, C. A generalised war of attrition. *Journal of Theoretical Biology,* 1978, *70,* 85–124.

Cain, N. W., Anderson, R., Stein, L., & Jessen, C. Effects of prior social experience on agonistic responding by Siamese fighting fish (*Betta splendens*). *Animal Learning and Behavior,* 1980, *8,* 491–496.

Caryl, P. G. Communication by agonistic displays: What can games theory contribute to ethology? *Behaviour,* 1979, *68,* 136–169.

Eberhard, W. G. Horned beetles. *Scientific American,* 1980, *242*(3), 124–131.

Eibl-Eibesfeldt, I. The fighting behavior of animals. *Scientific American,* 1961, *205,* 112–122.

Grafen, A. The hawk–dove game played between relatives. *Animal Behaviour,* 1979, *27,* 905–907.

Hamilton, W. D. The genetical evolution of social behavior. I. *Journal of Theoretical Biology,* 1964, *7,* 1–16. (a)

Hamilton, W. D. The genetical evolution of social behavior. II. *Journal of Theoretical Biology,* 1964, *7,* 17–51. (b)

Hamilton, W. D. Selection of selfish and altruistic behavior in some extreme models. Chapter 2. In J. F. Eisenberg & W. S. Dillon (Eds.), *Man and beast: Comparative social behavior.* Washington, D.C.: Smithsonian Institution Press, 1971. Pp. 57–91.

Hinde, R. A. Animal signals: ethological and games-theory approaches are not incompatible. *Animal Behaviour,* 1981, *29,* 535–542.

Johnson, R. N. *Aggression in man and animals.* Philadelphia: Saunders, 1972.

Le Boeuf, B. L., & Peterson, R. S. Social status and mating activity in elephant seals. *Science,* 1969, *163,* 91–93.

Maynard Smith, J. Group selection and kin selection. *Nature (London),* 1964, *201,* 1145–1147.

Maynard Smith, J. The theory of games and the evolution of animal conflicts. *Journal of Theoretical Biology,* 1974, *47,* 209–221.

Maynard Smith, J. The evolution of behavior. *Scientific American,* 1978, *239*(3), 136–145.

Maynard Smith, J. *Evolution and the theory of games,* Cambridge: Cambridge University Press, 1982.

Maynard Smith, J., & Parker, G. A. The logic of asymmetric contests. *Animal Behaviour,* 1976, *24,* 159–175.

Maynard Smith, J., & Price, G. R. The logic of animal conflict. *Nature (London)*, 1973, *246*, 15–18.

Parker, G. A. Assessment strategy and the evolution of fighting behaviour. *Journal of Theoretical Biology*, 1974, *47*, 223–243.

Patterson, T. L., & Petrinovich, L. Field studies of habituation. II. Effect of massed stimulus presentation. *Journal of Comparative and Physiological Psychology*, 1979, *93*, 351–359.

Peeke, H. V. S., & Peeke, S. C. Habituation in fish with special reference to intraspecific aggressive behavior. In H. V. S. Peeke & M. J. Herz (Eds.), *Habituation* (Vol. 1). New York: Academic Press, 1973. Pp. 59–83.

Petrinovich, L., & Patterson, T. L. Field studies of habituation. I. Effect of reproductive condition, number of trials, and different delay intervals on responses of the White-crowned Sparrow. *Journal of Comparative and Physiological Psychology*, 1979, *93*, 337–350.

Petrinovich, L., & Patterson, T. L. Field studies of habituation. III. Playback contingent on the response of the White-crowned Sparrow. *Animal Behaviour*, 1980, *28*, 742–751.

Rohwer, S. Status signalling in Harris sparrows: some experiments in deception. *Behaviour*, 1977, *61*, 107–129.

Schachter, S. Obesity and eating. *Science*, 1968, *161*, 751–756.

Schachter, S. *Obese humans and rats*. New York: Wiley, 1974.

Selten, R. A note on evolutionarily stable strategies in asymmetric animal conflicts. *Journal of Theoretical Biology*, 1980, *84*, 93–101.

Thorpe, W. H. *Learning and instinct in animals* (2nd ed.) London: Methuen, 1963.

Tinbergen, N. *The study of instinct*. London & New York: Oxford University Press (Clarendon), 1951.

Treisman, M. The evolutionary restriction of aggression within a species: A game theory analysis. *Journal of Mathematical Psychology*, 1977, *16*, 167–203.

Treisman, M. Evolutionary limits to the frequency of aggression between related or unrelated conspecifics in diploid species with simple Mendelian inheritance. *Journal of Theoretical Biology*, 1981, *93*, 97–124.

Treisman, M. Evolutionarily stable levels of altruism in haploid and diploid species. *Journal of Theoretical Biology*, 1982, *97*, 437–480.

Treisman, M. On the conditions for an evolutionarily stable strategy in the two-by-two game. 1984, manuscript in preparation. (a)

Treisman, M. Dominance and threat in intraspecific conflict: Two applications of evolutionary game theory. 1984, manuscript in preparation. (b)

Trivers, R. L. The evolution of reciprocal altruism. *Quarterly Review of Biology*, 1971, *46*, 35–57.

Wilson, E. O. *Sociobiology*, Cambridge, Mass.: Harvard University Press, 1975.

Index

E

F

Ficedula hypoleuca, 33, 366
Field experimentation, in behavior study,
    11–13
Flash patterns, of cursorial mammals, 373
Fowl, domestic, see Domestic fowl
Fright behavior, habituation in, 349
Fringilla coelebs, 22, 157
Frog, dummy prey habituation tests with,
    81–82
Fulica americana, 352

G

Galapagos finch, antipredator behavior of, 361
Galvanic skin response
    cross-modality adaptation of, 18–19
    early research on, 18–19
Game theory, aggression and, 426
Gasterosteus aculeatus, 23, 157, 363, 401
Geospiza difficilis acutiostris, 361
Gill-withdrawal reflex, in Aplysia, 209–216
Glaucidium passerinum, 367
Glycine, in acoustic-startle reflex, 318
Goldfish, predatory responses in, 382
Goldfish optic tectum explant
    habituation and sensitization studies in,
        257–258
    mesencephalic habituation and, 273
    tissue preparation for, 259
Goshawk
    preying of on pigeons, 358–359
    response to playbacks of seeet calls, 375
    seeet calls in, 370–371, 375
Ground Hornbill headdress mimicry, 354
Ground squirrels, mobbing behavior in, 368
Group-level analysis, 196–197
Group regression
    in repeated data measures analysis, 180–181
    in statistical analysis, 159
Group regression analysis, 170
Group regression line, in testing for
    dishabituation, generalization, and
    spontaneous recovery, 162–163
GSR, see Galvanic skin response
Gulls, aggressive responses of, 356

H

Habituation
    A1 and A2 states of, 110–113, 143, 148

versus adaptation, 19–20
in Aplysia, 205–244
in avoidance and fight behavior, 349
behavior selection and, 57
below-zero effects in, 269–341
calcium current modulation in, 234
in Chaffinch, 22
characteristic effects as definition of,
    105
characterization of, 34
classical conditioning and, 292
cognitive-oriented theories of, 292
concurrent stimulation and, 132–138
conditioned responses and, 19
coordinating effectors and, 58
coordinative system or decision mechanism
    in, 59
in convict cichlid, 23
crouching response in, 351
decay of, 24
defined, 4–5, 21–22, 51, 105, 338,
    398–399
of dishabituation, 343
dual-process theory of, see Dual-process
    theory
early research on, 18–19
ethology of, 21–24
evolutionary determination of, 423–457
extrinsic influences on, 148, 317–320
of habituation, 266–267, 274–275
of human evoked potentials, 325–343
intrinsic and extrinsic mechanisms of,
    287–320
in invertebrates and vertebrates, 292
ionic events during, 232–234
language, see Language habituation
long-term stimulus-specific, 33
long-term versus short-term, 37
main features of, 58
memory and, 103–149
memory-oriented approach to, 106
minimal definitional requirements of,
    397–399
molar behavior theories and, 104
and monotony threshold in birds, 22
of morphine analgesia, 128
neural distribution of, 252
neural models of, 58–59
at neuronal level, 251–252
nervous system locus for, 227
operational definition of, 338–343